MANAGING SUSTAINABILITY IN THE HOSPITALITY AND TOURISM INDUSTRY

Paradigms and Directions for the Future

T0330681

ADVANCES IN HOSPITALITY AND TOURISM BOOK SERIES

Editor-in-Chief:

Mahmood A. Khan, PhD

Professor, Department of Hospitality and Tourism Management, Pamplin College of Business, Virginia Polytechnic Institute and State University, Falls Church, Virginia

email: mahmood@vt.edu

BOOKS IN THE SERIES:

Food Safety: Researching the Hazard in Hazardous Foods
Editors: Barbara Almanza, PhD, RD, and Richard Ghiselli, PhD

Strategic Winery Tourism and Management: Building Competitive Winery Tourism and Winery Management Strategy
Editor: Kyuho Lee, PhD

Sustainability, Social Responsibility and Innovations in the Hospitality Industry
Editor: H. G. Parsa, PhD
Consulting Editor: Vivaja "Vi" Narapareddy, PhD
Associate Editors: SooCheong (Shawn) Jang, PhD, Marival Segarra-Oña, PhD, and Rachel J. C. Chen, PhD, CHE

Managing Sustainability in the Hospitality and Tourism Industry: Paradigms and Directions for the Future
Editor: Vinnie Jauhari, PhD

Management Science in Hospitality and Tourism: Theory, Practice, and Applications
Editors: Muzaffer Uysal, PhD, Zvi Schwartz, PhD, and Ercan Sirakaya-Turk, PhD

MANAGING SUSTAINABILITY IN THE HOSPITALITY AND TOURISM INDUSTRY

Paradigms and Directions for the Future

Edited by
Vinnie Jauhari, PhD

Apple Academic Press

TORONTO   NEW JERSEY

DEDICATED

Dedicated to my parents, in-laws, Sunil, Shaurya and Shallen

Apple Academic Press Inc. | Apple Academic Press Inc.
3333 Mistwell Crescent | 9 Spinnaker Way
Oakville, ON L6L 0A2 | Waretown, NJ 08758
Canada | USA

©2014 by Apple Academic Press, Inc.

First issued in paperback 2021

Exclusive worldwide distribution by CRC Press, a member of Taylor & Francis Group

No claim to original U.S. Government works

ISBN 13: 978-1-77463-299-4 (pbk)
ISBN 13: 978-1-926895-72-7 (hbk)

Library of Congress Control Number: 2014932556

Library and Archives Canada Cataloguing in Publication

Managing sustainability in the hospitality and tourism industry: paradigms and directions for the future/edited by Vinnie Jauhari, PhD.

Includes bibliographical references and index.
ISBN 978-1-926895-72-7 (bound)
1. Hospitality industry--Management. 2. Tourism--Management. 3. Sustainable development--Management. I. Jauhari, Vinnie, editor of compilation

TX907.M28 2014   338.4'791   C2014-900919-4

Apple Academic Press also publishes its books in a variety of electronic formats. Some content that appears in print may not be available in electronic format. For information about Apple Academic Press products, visit our website at **www.appleacademicpress.com** and the CRC Press website at **www.crcpress.com**

ABOUT THE EDITOR

Vinnie Jauhari, PhD

Vinnie Jauhari, PhD, is a Director at IIMT (Institute for International Management and Technology) (Oxford Brookes University), Gurgaon, in the National Capital Region (NCR Delhi), India. Dr. Jauhari was earlier Region Lead for HP Labs Open Innovation Office for India. She won the Innovator Award in the worldwide team in 2009. She also won the HP Empower grant for women during her tenure at HP Labs. She has over 17 years of experience in academics and the corporate world. She has authored nine books published from New York and Springer in Germany in the domain of services, hospitality, and technology. She has authored over 100 papers published in international and national journals of repute. She is the Founding Editor of the *Journal of Services Research* and the *Journal of Technology Management for Growing Economies*. She has been a guest editor of numerous international journals and has been a recipient of various awards for research contributions in international journals.

CONTENTS

LIST OF CONTRIBUTORS

Rumki Bandyopadhyay
Institute for International Management and Technology, Gurgaon, India;
E-mail: rumki.banerji@gmail.com

Kirti Dutta
Bharatiya Vidya Bhavan's Usha and Lakshmi Mittal Institute of Management, New Delhi, India;
E-mail: duttakirti@yahoo.co.in

Banafsheh M. Farahani
University of Science Malaysia - School of Housing, Building and Planning, Pulau Pinang, Malaysia;
E-mail: banafsheh.farahani@gmail.com

Vinnie Jauhari
Institute for International Management and Technology, Gurgaon, India;
E-mail: vinnie.jauhari@yahoo.com

Navdeep Kaur Kular
Institute for International Management and Technology, Gurgaon, India;
E-mail: novikular@rediffmail.com

Nastaran Laleh
MA student in Tourism Planning, Iran, Santai, Kembara & Pelancongan.

Willy Legrand
IUBH School of Business and Management, Muelheimerstrasse, Germany; E-mail: w.legrand@iubh.de

Moni Mishra
Lal Bahadur Shastri Institute of Management, Delhi, India; E-mail: moni.india@gmail.com

Parul Munjal
Ansal University, Sushant School of Art and Architecture, Gurgaon, India;
E-mail: Parul.g.munjal@gmail.com

Sandeep Munjal
Institute for International Management and Technology, Gurgaon, India;
E-mail: sandeep.munjal1973@gmail.com

S. K. Nandi
Institute for International Management and Technology, Gurgaon, India;
E-mail: sknandi2011@gmail.com

H. G. Parsa
Daniels College of Business, University of Denver, USA; E-mail: hparsa@du.edu

Bandana Rai
Institute for International Management and Technology, Gurgaon, India;
E-mail: vandyrai@rediffmail.com

Larissa Rheindorf
IUBH School of Business and Management, Germany

Meghna Rishi
Lal Bahadur Shastri Institute of Management, New Delhi, India; E-mail: meghna.14@gmail.com

Sanjay Sharma
Institute for International Management and Technology, Gurgaon, India; India;
E-mail: sanjayihm@yahoo.co.in

Anjana Singh
Institute for International Management and Technology, Gurgaon, India;
E-mail: singhanjana@gmail.com

Swati Singh
Bharatiya Vidya Bhavan's Usha and Lakshmi Mittal Institute of Management, New Delhi, India;
E-mail: swatiyadav8k@gmail.com

Philip Sloan
IUBH School of Business and Management, Muelheimerstrasse, Germany.

Gaurav Tripathi
Institute for International Management and Technology, Gurgaon, India;
E-mail: tripathi_gaurav@hotmail.com

Tanya Verma
Ansal University, Sushant School of Art & Architecture, Gurgaon;
E-mail: tanayaverma@ansaluniversity.edu.in

Clara Wagmann
IUBH School of Business and Management, Muelheimerstrasse, Germany

Parul Wasan
Apeejay Stya University, Sohna, Gurgaon, India; E-mail: parul.wasan@yahoo.co.in

PREFACE

Sustainability in the current context is no longer a necessity but a critical factor which deserves serious attention by industry, government and society. It is a precursor for a livable world where there is more equitable access to resources. Growth at the cost of environmental damage can have serious ramifications. This is clear from the natural calamities in the form of floods, landslides, droughts, shortages of water and power. The current pace of resource consumption is a tenable position and there is a need to relook at how new businesses can adopt a radically different approach to designing green buildings. Sustainability is an interdisciplinary concept that embeds aspects of environment, economic aspects as well as socio cultural aspects. The emerging economies can have a radically very different approach to building their cities and designing their buildings and transportation. Even existing businesses need to look at green elements, which can make their businesses more profitable and sustainable. Water, energy, other resources are all aspects which will dramatically impact how the world lives in the coming century. As the nonrenewable sources of energy decline, the rush for investing in renewable sources will increase. Businesses, countries and governments which invest in next generation technologies and create more aware citizens who would be better prepared to cope up with the future. The current generation would have to relook at its consumption habits so that our future generations can inherit a more livable world.

Tourism destinations have to consider how will they continue to attract consumers. The climate and ecosystem has to be harmonious and preserved. The water bodies, reefs, mountains, ice caps have to be preserved so that consumers continue to visit these places. Also there have to be sustainable livelihoods as well. There are questions, which need to be addressed. Can we learn from some of the global best practices? Can we take some steps, which would build sustainable tourism destinations? What could be the factors, which could contribute to sustainable tourism?

The consumers across the globe now care for green practices as they are witnessing the consequences of the environmental damage in the form of changing disease patterns, global warming, emissions and also difficulty in access to natural resources. There are a lot of challenges that have to be addressed to bring about a change in the mindset of consumers. Different consumers would be receptive to changes in the environment but these have to be matched with educating them of effects of engaging in green behavior. The marketers also have to figure out a way of creating awareness without taking away elements of consumer experience.

An insight into how much resources do luxury hotels consume is quite alarming. For example in Delhi, according to data published in The Hindustan Times* (2013), water consumption of approximately 15 million liters of water by 35 five star hotels in Delhi is enough to cater to 180,000 people or 36,000 households. The power consumption is about 1,000-kilo calories/sqm. The daily average consumption of energy by one five star hotel consumes power needs of 600 households. These 35 hotels generate about 10 million liters of sewage every day. This is equal to amount generated by a population of 4,50,000.

This does provide insights into how a change in practices adopted by hotels can lower resource consumption and waste generation.

This book, "Managing Sustainability in the Hospitality and Tourism Industry: Paradigms and Directions for The Future," provides insights into sustainability efforts which could be championed across various areas in a hotel. The book not only looks at aspect across various divisions in a hotel but also looks at aspects related with sustainable tourism. The book is divided into 14 chapters, which have been authored by various contributors who bring in global insights by blending in research from various international chains and their practices. Some indigenous practices have also been looked at which could be replicated by global chains.

The key themes, which have been covered in the book, are as follows:

Designing green hotels, which bring in perspectives from global examples such as Masdar City and some of the leading Indian brands such as ITC, Taj, Suzlon. There are insights from indigenous guidelines, which could lead to developing sustainable buildings.

The book covers aspects such as measures that could be taken across departments to minimize energy consumption. There is also a perspective from Germany on energy audits. There are best practices shared from some of the leading international brands.

---

*Singh, D. (2013) The Hindustan Times April 12, Stop Wasting, govt. tells 5-stars, pg. 1. Gurgaon edition.

The book also assesses technologies and equipment, which could contribute to sustainability. The book covers sustainable practices in designing restaurants, accommodation practices as well as looking at culinary practices, which could enable hotels to be more sustainable.

Sustainable tourism has also been covered. There are insights into what kind of role can be played by industry, city governments, heritage preservations bodies, industry and consumers. There are lots of global heritage sites, which need attention and need to be preserved so that they can continue to attract tourists.

There are also chapters, which discuss the role of consumers and how sustainability can be marketed to them. There are insights into how different elements of marketing mix can be looked at in light of sustainability. The books looks at how communication strategies could be formulated targeting the consumers. The challenges around targeting the consumers have also been discussed.

People are key stakeholders in an organization. The book also covers HR practices that could contribute to sustainability in the organizations.

This book

- provides a comprehensive framework for applying sustainability to different aspects of hospitality and tourism;
- analyzes different components of hospitality and tourism from a sustainability perspective;
- shares best practices across various components of hospitality and tourism from a sustainability perspective;
- introduces a range of technologies and practices that have application toward sustainability;
- provides a glossary of important terms;
- provides clear frameworks and actions that can be replicated.

I would like to acknowledge with gratitude the support that I have received from the contributing authors. Their rich insights and dialog with industry has enabled to bring in lot of unique insights into different aspects of sustainability. I am indebted to organizations that have supported in writing the various chapters and have been willing to share their data. We are also grateful to a lot of industry practitioners who have discussed their ideas with the authors. We would like to acknowledge the support received from my parent organization-IIMT. A deep gratitude to Dr. Ramesh Kapur, Chairman, Radisson Blu Plaza, Delhi and Varanasi and Mr. Amit Kapur, Director Business Development, Radisson Blu Plaza Delhi for their support and inspiration.

I would like to express my heartfelt thanks to Prof. Mahmood Khan for his inspiration and support for this work. I would like to acknowledge that without his support it would not have been possible to put this all together. Thanks for reposing faith in me! I would also like to acknowledge support from my colleagues Mr. Sandeep Munjal, Dr. N. H. Mullick, Dr. Durgmohan, and Manjit, who have helped and supported me and my work in numerous ways.

I would like to express my deepest gratitude to my parents, in-laws, my husband—Sunil, and our wonderful son, Shaurya, for having supported me all along. I would also like to thank my brother, Dr. Shallen Verma, for his encouragement and always being there for me. Without their patience, support and encouragement this work would never have been completed. My family has always been a great anchor and always had a great role in all my accomplishments. Their being with me is the greatest joy, which enables me to make a meaningful contribution.

— Vinnie Jauhari
Editor

INTRODUCTION

As the world becomes more complex, sustainability as a concept will gain more ground. Changing technologies, more affluence and widening digital divide, urban migration across economies, global climate changes and imbalance in resources will exude more demands on finite resources. The issues of water, energy, transport, housing, healthcare will become more pronounced in the coming decades.

In light of these changes, sustainability in the context of hospitality industry will assume more importance. Hospitality as an industry has an immense ability to contribute to economic growth of the world. It is estimated by UNWTO Tourism Highlights (2013) at several destinations tourism has been a key driver of socioeconomic growth, creation of jobs and infrastructure development. Despite occasional shocks, international tourist arrivals have shown a great increase from 528 million in 1995, to 1,035 million in 2012. International tourist arrivals worldwide will increase by 3.3% a year from 2010 to 2030 to reach 1.8 billion by 2030. The sector currently accounts for 5% of direct global GDP, 30% of the world's services exports and generates one in 12 jobs worldwide (UNWTO, 2013).

The WTO data (2012) highlights that international tourist arrivals (overnight visitors) worldwide exceeded the 1 billion mark for the first time ever in 2012, with 1,035 million tourists crossing borders, up from 995 million in 2011. Asia and the Pacific recorded the strongest growth with a 7% increase in arrivals, followed by Africa (+6%) and the Americas (+5%). International tourist arrivals in Europe, the most visited region in the world, were up by 3%. International tourism receipts reached US$ 1,075 billion worldwide in 2012, up from US$ 1,042 billion in 2011.

According to UNWTO long-term forecast for Tourism towards 2030,

- between 2010 and 2030, arrivals in emerging destinations (+4.4% a year) are expected to increase at double the pace of that in advanced economies (+2.2% a year).
- the market share of emerging economies increased from 30% in 1980 to 47% in 2012, and is expected to reach 57% by 2030, equivalent to over 1 billion international tourist arrivals.

Tourism is increasingly considered an engine for economic development (Gartner, 1996). Also, tourism is growing fastest in the developing world and accounted for 30% of international arrivals in 1998. This is of importance because it is in those regions where governments may not have the means—or the priorities—to regulate and enforce legislation for environmental protection as tourism develops.

Also it is important to note that hospitality industry is also a big consumer of energy and a large deployer of water and generator of waste as well. It is pertinent to look at different aspects of hospitality and tourism so that resource consumption can be optimized and also impacts on environment can be minimized. There has to be an understanding of issues across various divisions of hospitality and tourism sector. Hotels constitute an important segment of hospitality and tourism sector.

As cities get developed, the rate of urbanization is bound to increase. There will be migration of people from villages to urban areas specially in emerging economies. There are different aspects around urbanization, which need to be understood. Along with urbanization come in the challenges of managing infrastructure, energy, water, and impact on other resources. Sustainability of hospitality and tourism is also linked with efficient use of these resources.

It is estimated that in India, by 2030, the urban population would be close to 590 million people (Sankhe et al., 2010). The cities in such a scenario would generate 70% of the GDP and this would also impact how energy is sourced, generated and consumed. There would be an impact of development of habitats and offices, transportation and infrastructure requirements.

Tourism is considered one of the most highly climate-sensitive economic sectors (UNWTO, 2013 a). Many tourism destinations are dependent on climate as their principal attraction, sun-and-sea or winter sports holidays for example, or on environmental resources such as wildlife and biodiversity. A changing climate will have profound consequences on tourism flows and subsequently on the important contribution of tourism to poverty reduction and economic development, especially in developing countries. At the same time, tourism also contributes to global warming. It is estimated that tourism accounts for approximately 5% of global carbon emissions (UNWTO, 2013a). The same report also shares the breakup of carbon emissions as well. Of this 5%, 40% of emissions are contributed by air transport, 32% by car transport, 21% by accommodation, 4% by activities, and 3% by others (UNWTOUNEP Climate Change and Tourism, 2008).
WATER

Water is a scarce resource and with increased urbanization and wastages, it will even be a scarcer commodity. Jauhari and Wasan (2014) have discussed that lack of access to clean water and sanitation is a problem that affects large number of people. Ground water, which is a major source of fresh water, has an average renewal cycle of 1400 years (UNEP/GEMS, 1991). Water being a public good should be made available to all rather than a privilege of few on account of their paying capacity. Please see some insights into availability of water as shared in Exhibit 1.

Exhibit 1. The state of water availability in the world.
The statistics shared by UNWater.org (http://www.unwater.org/statistics_use.html) are as below:

Water use has been growing at more than twice the rate of population increase in the last century
(Source: Food and Agriculture Organization of the United Nations (FAO) and UN-Water).

How the world uses freshwater:
• about 70% for irrigation;
• about 20% for industry;
• about 10% for domestic use.
Source: World Water Assessment Program (WWAP).

A 70% of the blue water withdrawals at global level go to irrigation. Irrigated agriculture represents 20% of the total cultivated land but contributes 40% of the total food produced worldwide.
Source: FAO, 2012.

The world's population is growing by about 80 million people a year, implying increased freshwater demand of about 64 billion cubic meters a year. Competition for water exists at all levels and is forecast to increase with demands for water in almost all countries.
Source: WWDR, 2012.

Part of the current pressure on water resources comes from increasing demands for animal feed. Meat production requires 8–10 times more water than cereal production.
Source: WWDR, 2012

> Water withdrawals are predicted to increase by 50% by 2025 in developing countries, and 18% in developed countries.
> *Source*: Global Environment Outlook: environment for development (GEO-4).
>
> Over 1.4 billion people currently live in river basins where the use of water exceeds minimum recharge levels, leading to the desiccation of rivers and depletion of groundwater.
> *Source*: Human Development Report 2006.
>
> In 60% of European cities with more than 100,000 people, groundwater is being used at a faster rate than it can be replenished.
> Source: World Business Council For Sustainable Development (WBCSD)—See more at: http://www.unwater.org/statistics_use.html#sthash.fFgpFgL7.dpuf

The situation of fresh water and sanitation in India is alarming. Excess consumption puts a strain on the resources for the tourism industry specially hotels. The firms should build up scenarios for future growth and consequent resource needs. Depleting water table in most parts of India would be a grave concern in near future (Manaktola and Jauhari, 2007).

According to UN World Tourism Organization UN WTO (2013):

With over 1 billion people traveling the world every year, the tourism sector can play an educational role as a water-conscious sector. Though tourism only uses 1% of global water consumption, challenges remain for water use at destinations, since the sector often competes with other sectors for water. There is significant room for increasing efficiency and reducing cost of water consumption in hotels (water accounts for 10% of utility bills in many hotels, most of which pay for the water they consume twice, first in buying fresh water and by disposing of it as wastewater). Investing in green technology is economically beneficial, with profits from water sanitation and wastewater treatment having a return on investment (ROI) of one to three years.

ENERGY

Energy is another aspect, which needs lot of attention globally. It is one of the most critical resources, which is a lifeline for industry and human existence.

1.4 billion people have no access to reliable electricity. WWF (2011) remarks that while most of us take energy for granted as a basic right, a fifth of the world's population still has no access to reliable electricity—drastically reducing their chances of getting an education and earning a living. As energy prices increase, the world's poor will continue to be excluded. According to the International Energy Agency (IEA, 2009), production from known oil and gas reserves will fall by around 40–60% by 2030. Yet the developed world's thirst for energy is unabated, while demand is rocketing in emerging economies, such as China, India and Brazil. If everyone in the world used oil at the same rate as the average Saudi, Singaporean or U.S. resident, the world's proven oil reserves would be used up in less than 10 years[1].

According to Hotel Energy Solutions (2013), there are great opportunities for the hotel sector to save on operational costs by taking advantage of the potential of energy efficiency and renewable energies. About 40% of the energy used by hotels is electricity, and 60% comes from natural gas and oil fuels. Three-quarters of this energy is used for:

- Space heating;
- Hot water production;
- Air conditioning and ventilation;
- Lighting.

These are all uses where energy efficiency can be increased dramatically, and where renewable energies can also be easily harnessed by use of simple, proven technologies. Human quality of life and productivity relies on secure, affordable and sustainable energy. As economies expand and the world population continues to grow, energy demand is increasing worldwide. Currently, 80% of the world energy supply comes from fossil fuels (coal, petrol and natural gas), which emit greenhouse gases causing climate change and other negative environmental impacts. Fossil fuels are finite and nonrenewable, and their reserves are decreasing faster than new ones are being formed.

Energy consumption by hotels has a major environmental impact. Hotels are among the top five types of buildings in the service sector for energy consumption, below food, sales and health care facilities. Europe has the world's largest hotel stock with approximately 5.45 million hotel rooms—nearly half of the world's total.

---

[1]Per capita oil consumption in the U.S. and Canada is about 3 tons annually, in Saudi Arabia about 5 tons and in Singapore 10 tons. Proven oil reserves are estimated at about 205 billion tons in 2010 (BP, Statistical Review, 2010

The world is also increasingly deploying Internet to drive businesses and interact with consumers. There is a lot of R&D that is required to generate solutions to enhancing efficiency of networks and also using servers to manage these transactions more effectively.

On one hand, people have deployed Internet for productivity and connectivity, on the other hand, there needs to be a clear understanding of what it takes for Internet to function. According to data shared by Economic Times (2013, data centers consume energy equivalent to 30 nuclear power plants output. This would be equivalent to energy consumption of Russia. There are 3 million data centers worldwide. European data centers would consume 100 TWH of electricity by 2015. In 2012, there are 2.4 billion people who use Internet. Power consumed by data centers of Facebook is about 60 million watts while as Google data centers consume 300 million watts of power. 90% of electricity is wasted by data centers as online companies typically run their facilities at max capacity 24´7. Servers in data centers use a 6 to 12% of average power worldwide.

The 2013 Energy Efficiency Indicator (EEI) study, conducted by the Johnson Controls Institute for Building Efficiency, analyzes the energy efficiency technologies, practices and investments made by over 3000 executive decision-makers around the world (2013 Global Results Released: Energy Efficiency Indicator Survey, 2013).

Conducted annually since 2006, this year's respondents come from ten countries and a variety of commercial, industrial and institutional facilities (such as hospitals, schools, and government buildings).

Five key trends emerge from the 2013 Energy Efficiency Indicator survey are:

- Energy Management—there has been a global increase of 10% year over year in companies that are paying "a lot more attention" to energy efficiency.
- Motivations and Policy Priorities: Cost savings remain the number one driver for the sixth year of the EEI survey, but regional markets recognize other key drivers such as energy security, increased building asset value, and enhanced brand or public image. Policies that improve the economics of energy efficiency sought by all, but beyond incentives, regions see different policy opportunities in their unique markets.
- Lack of funding to pay for improvements remained the greatest barrier to pursuing more energy efficiency, but barriers differ by market, and technical capacity to evaluate performance remains a significant barrier.

- Among government energy efficiency policies, building decision-makers were most attracted to those aiming to reduce financial barriers to efficiency investments, but markets also saw building codes and appraisal standards as priority policies that could increase investment.
- Green tenant spaces and net zero energy buildings are emerging trends in building energy performance.

IMPACT ON OTHER RESOURCES

There is a need to look at how the new cities can be built. In India, 80% of it is yet to be built so there is a huge scope for bringing in planned development. A study was initiated by Janaagraha, a nonprofit organization based in Bangalore. It has been found that (Economic Times, 2013) Indian cities face numerous problems, most evident in the poor quality of roads, transport, air quality, clean water and power. In contrast to the global best practices, city corporations across India do not have adequate manpower, or a framework of systems, and processes for urban governance. These aspects will have a bearing on state of tourism. Some of the following issues need to be addressed:

- urban planning and design;
- urban capacities and resources;
- empowered and legitimate political representation;
- transparency, accountability and participation.

In light of the discussions on water, energy and emergence of urbanization, the concept of sustainability assumes lot of importance.

SUSTAINABILITY

The Brundtland Report established the concept of sustainability. The report defined the concept as development that meets the needs of the present without compromising the ability of future generations to meet their own needs. The report suggested that sustainability includes an obligation to future generations. The report suggests that sustainability includes an obligation to future generations. It is related with ethical use of resources and preserving and sharing between people (Bhushan and Jauhari, 2008). Creating enterprises at the cost of destroying others and environment is not sustainable (Bhushan and Jauhari, 2008). There will be costs that would be borne by future generations.

Hence there is a need to relook at how resources are sourced, consumed and recycled.

UNWTO (2013b) defines sustainable tourism as tourism that takes full account of its current and future economic, social and environmental impacts, addressing the needs of visitors, the industry, the environment and host communities." Thus sustainable tourism should take into account resources, respect the sociocultural authenticity of host communities and provide viable, long-term socioeconomic benefits to all.

WHY IS SUSTAINABILITY IMPORTANT?

Sustainability is important for number of reasons. Sustainability approach would enable companies to mitigate impact on environment, which is important to maintain equilibrium in the world. It is also important to reduce emissions and also minimize climate changes. It would enable to contribute meaningfully to the society as well as build up positive relationship with communities. Sustainability approach would also enable to build a unique competitive advantage for the firms. It would enable to create a stronger bond with employees and stakeholders as well. It enables optimizing the utilization of resources as well as reduces impact of operations on nearby areas.

Hotel Energy Solutions (2013):
"In a world looking for new models of economic growth and development, fighting climate change and adopting sustainable management practices is no longer an option, but a condition for survival and success..."

The "green" hotel business is a growing niche because not only do these establishments differentiate themselves from the similar non-green hotels, but they also fulfill a need in the market for less environmentally damaging hotels. According to Fitiadisa (2013) this is mainly realized with decreases in costs achieved by the reduction of resource consumption and decreases in expenses and expected future expenses. There are many other benefits realized from the introduction of more environmentally friendly practices such as reduced energy consumption, the avoidance of penalties enacted by environmental authorities, and accompanying improvements in customer trust and public image.

Manaktola and Jauhari (2007) remark that becoming a green hotel can be the foundation for a great marketing strategy, and the first step in marketing is providing consumers with what they want or need. A growing consumer base exists for green hotels, and marketing the green practices of a hotel can help to position it distinctly in the market place.

The environment is the major recipient of negative impacts created by the construction and operation of hotel and facilities. The success of tourism, as well as the hotel industry, largely depends on the availability of a clean environment. Roarty (1997, p. 248) discussed two others that should be added as factors exerting pressure for change: the increase in influence of the "green" investor including banks that want to limit exposure to environmental risk, and the "disproportionate influence on consumer behavior" of environmental pressure groups.

The sustainability also involves deploying innovations to achieve higher efficiency. The Global Innovation Index (WIPO, 2012), which measures innovation efficiency of 141 economies, is in 2012 based on two subindices the innovation input subindex (institutions, human capital and research, infrastructure, market sophistication and business sophistication) and the innovation output subindex (knowledge and technology outputs and creative outputs (Korez-Vide, 2013).

Nizic and Drpic (2013) quote Doxey (1975):

During the tourism development of a destination, local inhabitants experience the following four different stages (Doxey 1975, 98–195):

1. euphoria (in the initial development of a tourism phenomenon);
2. apathy (in its development, tourism becomes a part of life of the local community);
3. annoyance (it appears when tourism starts complicating everyday life of the local community—the problem of overpopulation, destruction of landscape particularities, summer crowds…);
4. antagonism (the anti-tourist behavior appears).

When destinations are being developed, there are different aspects which need to be considered to maintain the destination and ensure that it continues to benefits the communities, enhance economic growth and also preserve the resources. If the destinations are not preserved, then there would be reduction in number of visitors. The ice caps need to be preserved. The rivers must have flowing and clean water. The lakes have to be cleaned; the infrastructure must be able to meet with the growing population. Safety, security and well being of tourists are also concerns that have to be addressed.

There need to be partnerships between various stakeholders. The governance and legislative frameworks need to be looked at appropriately.

This book addresses many issues around sustainability of the hospitality and tourism industry.

ABOUT THE BOOK

This book looks at sustainability aspect not just from a singular perspective but looks at issues through entire life cycle of a product. Please *see* Figure 1 for details.

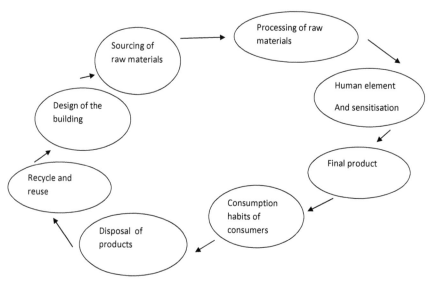

FIGURE 1   The life cycle of a product from its origin to consumption.

The Figure 1 gives an insight into how designing a building or a product involves complex decisions even before it is produced or a service is offered. A service or hospitality offering involves choosing a location of a hotel or a site, identifying supply chain, designing the room and other services, marketing to consumers, consumption of an experience and then there would be waste generation and consequently waste recycling. At each stage there would be certain decisions that would be required which would demonstrate sustainability or lack of it is the complete design of an experience.

Through this book, an effort has been made to embed sustainability at each stage of an experience. The edited book comprises of 14 chapters, which focus on various aspects of sustainability. A short summary of each chapter is indicated in the following sections:

Chapter One, *Designing Green Hotels* authored by Vinnie Jauhari and Tanaya Verma focuses on how green practices can be built in from design perspective. The indigenous designing approach from the perspective of GRIHA and LEED guidelines has been discussed. Inputs from hospitality firms such as ITC, Lemon Tree, Samode Safari Lodge, Banjaar Tola, architects and IHG have been taken. The chapter makes specific recommendations related with design elements both in terms of technologies as well as human component. The chapter also contains insights from Suzlon's green building in India as well as the newly emerging MASDAR city in UAE.

Chapter Two, *From Output to Input: The Road From Energy and Carbon Emissions to Principles of Sustainable Hotel Design* authored by Willy Legrand, Phillip Sloan, Clara Wagmann and Larissa Rhein Dorf analyze the importance of energy and CO_2 audits. The benefits, challenges and costs around such auditing processes have been discussed. The role of Free of Charge Self Administered Energy Audits has been discussed. The chapter has specific recommendations for the practitioners.

Chapter Three, authored by Navdeep Kular is titled, *Energy Conservation in Hotels—A Green Approach*. This chapter focuses on the need for energy conservation in the hotels and the measures that can be undertaken to achieve this. The resources deployed by the hotels and its impact on environment has been studied along with major green initiatives undertaken by the hotels. The chapter discusses major design and operation changes which can be initiated by the hotels in achieving a sustainable future. There are numerous examples from industry, which have been covered in this chapter.

Chapter Four, *Sustainable Technology in Hospitality Industry—Some Future Directions* authored by Parul Wasan focuses on the sustainable technologies that hotels could adopt. The chapter focuses on aspects such as cloud based platforms, mobile/hand held computing devices, social media, analytics, customized/personalized systems for guests, systems and process integration in hotels. Various technologies and their impacts have been discussed along with specific industry examples in this chapter.

Chapter Five, Marketing *Sustainability in The Hospitality and Tourism Industry*, authored by Meghna Rishi focuses on how marketing as a tool can be deployed to achieve sustainability in the context of hospitality industry. The chapter looks at marketing mix elements and demonstrated as to how each element could be channelized to contribute to sustainability. The chapter is embedded with many practical examples, which help in a better understanding of sustainability achieved through various elements. The chapter also discusses how consumers can be engaged on the concept of sustainability.

Chapter Six, *Destination Management and Sustainability*, authored by Kirti Dutta, Swati Singh, H. G. Parsa and Vinnie Jauhari focuses on how destination management and sustainability can be integrated together. The paper provides perspectives on how tourism can be more sustainable. It explores the four M's—management of resources, monetary aspects, manpower and marketing model by taking a holistic view of the ecosystem and draws constructs from UNEP and WTO's guide to policy makers. The chapter also explores consumers' feelings and draws their attitude towards participation in and evaluating tourist destinations employing these practices. Examples of Air New Zealand and Antarctica have been discussed in detail.

Chapter Seven, *SustainableTourism Destinations: Creation and Development* authored by Sandeep Munjal and Parul G. Munjal have focused on sustainable tourism destinations can be created and developed. It looks at various approaches by taking specific examples from international and Indian context across the developed and developing economies. The suggestions for the various stakeholders are also embodied in this chapter. Numerous cases such as Indeco Leisure Hotels, Tamilnadu, Shimla, Lugu Lake in China have been discussed along with numerous others such as Udaipur.

Chapter Eight, *Heritage communication and Sustainable Tourism* authored by Gaurav Tripathi and Sandeep Munjal focuses on the importance of communication and deploying sustainable measures at the Heritage sites in India. The focus is on how the tourists can play pivotal role in maintaining the heritage value of the tourists premise. The case study of City Palace museum Udaipur has been taken to elaborate on the importance of communication.

Chapter Nine, *Sustainable Culinary Practices* authored by Sanjay Sharma focuses on how the culinary practices adopted by production departments in the hotels could contribute to sustainability. Sharma discusses how the total life cycle concept must be initiated for every single activity that is undertaken. Right from sourcing of food, ingredients and portioning of food, the chapter looks at waste minimization and also alternate production techniques to build in sustainability. The chapter also explores the concept of eating responsibly.

Chapter Ten, *Sustainable Employee Practices* authored by Moni Mishra focuses on sustainable employee practices. The chapter assesses the significance of understanding and implementing issues of sustainability in organizations in various sectors of business. IT documents an empirical study of the process of developing sustainable employee practices. The chapter looks into organizations such as Williamson Magor and Hindustan Unilever and draws on sustainable HR practices.

Chapter Eleven, *Efficient Equipment—Sources for Sustainability* in the hotel Industry focuses on how sustainability goals can be accomplished by efficient deployment of equipment across various divisions in a hotel. Equipment that have been discussed are the power generators, air conditioning equipment, laundry and lighting systems, restaurant appliances among others. Some global best practices and case studies have been highlighted in this chapter.

Chapter Twelve, *Sustainable Restaurants* authored by Rumki Bandyopadhyay and Sandeep Munjal focus on how sustainable practices can be incorporated in restaurants. The study focuses on the case of Hauz khas village in Delhi. It also identifies deliverables of sustainable approaches of the five star hotels. Specific recommendations have been made for managing green restaurants.

Chapter Thirteen, *Conception of Sustainable Accommodation Practices in Hotels for Tomorrow* authored by Anjana Singh and Bandana Rai focus on how sustainability can be achieved in the Accommodation sector. The chapter has been authored by conducting an in-depth review of literature as well critical analysis of 3I's framework for accommodation practices.

Chapter Fourteen, *Tourism Policy: A Comparative Study of Malaysia and Turkey* authored by Nastaran Laleh and Banafshed M. Farjani focuses on Tourism policy and draws comparison between Malaysia and Turkey. It explores how the two countries have witnessed tourism growth but have followed a different path. There are lessons to be learned which other economies can emulate from experience of Malaysia and Turkey.

The book presents rich insights from a diverse range of hotel operations. It also has recommendations for various stakeholders such as governments, industry, consumers and civil society.

REFERENCES

Bhushan, S. and Jauhari, V. (2008) *From Chaos to Serenity, The Divine Perspective on Management*, Samskriti, New Delhi.

Doxey, G.V. (1975) A causation theory of visitor—resident irritants: Methodology and research inferences, in Proceedings of the Travel Research Association 6th annual Conference, San Diego California, Travel Research Association, pp. 98–195.

Economic Times (2013) The Power That Keeps You Up To Speed With the World, *The Economic Times New Delhi*, November 24, 2013, pg.1.

Economic Times (2013a) India's Best and Worst Cities, *The Economic Times*, New Delhi, pg.18.

Energy Efficiency Indicator Survey (2013) *Global Results Released: Energy Efficiency Indicator Survey, 2013*, Institute for Building Efficiency, Downloaded from http://www.institutebe. com/Energy-Efficiency-Indicator/2013-Energy-Efficiency-Indicator-Global-Results.aspx, Downloaded on December 20, 2013.

Fotiadisa, Anestis K.; Vassiliadisb, Chris A., and Rekleitisc, Panayotis D. (2013) Constraints and benefits of sustainable development: a case study based on the perceptions of small-hotel entrepreneurs in Greece, *Anatolia—An International Journal of Tourism and Hospitality Research*, *24(2)*, 144–161.

Hotel Energy Solutions (2013) http://hotelenergysolutions.net/en/content/energy-school, downloaded on Dec 20, 2013.

IEA (2009) *World Energy Outlook* (WEO), Paris.

Jauhari, Vinnie (2012) Strategic growth challenges for the Indian Hotel Industry, *Worldwide Hospitality and Tourism Themes*, Volume 4, Number 2.

Jauhari, Vinnie (2013) Urbanizationand Managing Energy: Opportunities and Challenges, *Journal of Technology Management for Growing Economies*, Vol. 4, No. 1.

Jauhari, Vinnie and Wasan, Parul (2014) *Humanizing Science and Technology: Some Case Studies*, Concept, New Delhi.

Korex Vide, Romana (2013) Enforcing sustainability principles in Tourism via creative development, *Journal of Tourism Challenges and Trends*, *6(1)*, 35–58.

Manaktola, Kamal and Jauhari, Vinnie (2007) Exploring consumer attitude and behavior towards green practices in the lodging industry in India, *International Journal of Contemporary Hospitality Management*, *19(5)*, 364–377.

Mcintire, G. et al. (1993) Sustainable Tourism Development: Guide for Local Planners, WTO, Madrid.

Nizic, M.; Kristinic and Drpic, D. (2013) Model for Sustainable Tourism Development in Croatia, *Tourism in Southern and Eastern Europe*, pp. 159–173.

Sanjeev, G. and Jauhari, Vinnie (2012) The Emerging Strategic and Financial Issues in the Indian Hospitality Industry, *Worldwide Hospitality and Tourism Themes*, Volume 4, Number 5.

Sankhe, S.; Vittal, I.; Dobbs, R.; Mohan, A.; Gulati, A.; Ablett, J.; Gupta, S.; Kim, A.; Paul, S.; Sanghvi, A.; and Sethy, G. (2010) *India's Urban Awakening: Building Inclusive Cities Sustaining Economic Growth*, McKinsey Global Institute, April.

UNWTO (2013) UNWTO Tourism in the Green Economy, downloaded on Dec 20, 2013. From http://dtxtq4w60xqpw.cloudfront.net/sites/all/files/docpdf/greeneconomy2.pdf

UNWTO (2013a) Tourism and Climate Change http://dtxtq4w60xqpw.cloudfront.net/sites/all/files/docpdf/climatechange.pdf Downloaded on Dec 2013.

UNWTO (2013b) Tourism and Sustainability http://dtxtq4w60xqpw.cloudfront.net/sites/all/files/docpdf/sustainability.pdf Downloaded on Dec. 20, 2013.

UNWTOUNEP (2008) Climate Change and Tourism, 2008.

World Tourism Organization UNWTO (2013) World Tourism Day on "Tourism and Water": greater efforts on water preservation needed, Sept 27, Downloaded from http://media.unwto.org/press-release/2013–09–27/world-tourism-day-tourism-and-water-greater-efforts-water-preservation-need on Dec 20, 2013.

WTO (2013) UNWTO World Tourism Highlights 2013 downloaded on Dec 20, 2013 from http://dtxtq4w60xqpw.cloudfront.net/sites/all/files/pdf/unwto_highlights13_en_lr_0.pdf

WWF (2011) The Energy Report 100% renewable energy by 2050, WWF, Switzerland.

CHAPTER 1

DESIGNING SUSTAINABLE HOTELS: TECHNICAL AND HUMAN ASPECTS

VINNIE JAUHARI and TANAYA VERMA

CONTENTS

ABSTRACT

One of the key sectors, which could influence lesser emissions, is the housing sector whether domestic or commercial. Designing green hotels could have a great impact on sustainable future. This chapter focuses on the design principals that govern the green buildings. The chapter also elaborates on the framework and guidelines, which influence the framework for sustainability. The chapter discusses some best practices in designing green buildings and green hotels in the context of India. The case of ITC Hotels in India, which houses the world's largest green building and the world's largest Green Hotel-Chola Sheraton in Chennai, is discussed. The chapter also focuses on efforts of Lemon Tree Hotels along with insights on Samode Safari Lodge and Banjaar Tola. A review of architectural practices by conducting interviews with architects has also been discussed here. Griha (Green Rating for Integrated Habitat Assessment) and LEED standards have also been discussed. The chapter also draws insights from practitioners on what are the challenges towards implementing green practices. Implications for government industry practitioners and consumers have also been discussed. The chapter also discusses examples of green practices adopted by Suzlon and at Masdar City, Dubao. The chapter also brings in perspectives from various stakeholders such as hotels, architects, engineers and designers. Recommendations and implications for future are also discussed at the end of the chapter.

1.1   GREEN BUILDING DESIGN

The progress of humanity is measured in inventions and how man has conquered the forces of nature. The mindless race to be in control of everything has resulted in a catastrophic imbalance of the ecosystem. Sustainability is a necessity for humanity to survive as a species. Practices and technologies that do not harm the basis of our existence need to be developed and put in use. Promoting the progress of mankind without depleting our world's recourses while safeguarding the evolution of future generation is one of the principal challenges today (Anon., n.d.)(Beyond-Sustainability. n.d). The very existence of our species is heavily dependent on fossil based energy, for its comfort and day-to-day services. The introduction of sustainable building design measures can make an important contribution to minimize the impact on our recourses. For example, the entire building sector (production, construction, use and demolition) accounts for 40% of total energy requirement. It is the single largest sector, which has the potential for achieving energy efficiency (ICAEN, 2004). The lifestyle changes and the demand for higher comfort by the end-users, manifested in rising energy demand through more electrical devices, especially air conditioning installation.

The recent interest in green building is part of a larger movement toward sustainability in our society and around the world. Hospitality is one industry, which is totally dependent on consumers, which in turn demands comfort resulting in high-energy consumption. The hospitality industry has many aspects, which are not in harmony with the principles of sustainability. Its dependence on magnificence of its design, hi-tech gadgetry, perfect comfort conditions in all weather conditions all of which result in total dependence on energy. Sustainability or green design concepts for hotel design are a complex concept having a multidisciplinary character.

"Its operationalization requires the effort of architects, builders, planners, and all other key stakeholders involved in the processes of designing, planning, construction and running the place. A key role is played by the end user, not only through his/her responsibility to use the building efficiently, but also through his/her demand for integration of sustainable building design aspects as additional quality element, thus influencing and orienting the future building sector" (Magaldi, 2004).

Building projects in general, including their design, construction, and operation, results in potentially significant energy and environmental impacts. Development frequently converts land from biologically diverse natural habitat to impervious hardscape with greatly reduced biodiversity (ASHRAE and US Green Building Council, 2011).

The green technology aim's for optimization of existing technology and improving production efficiency without increasing cost, limiting wastage of drinking water and other precious resources and monitoring the waste disposal procedure.

1.2   OBJECTIVE

This chapter provides insights from architectural and design perspective for developing green buildings. The chapter provides insights into ITC's orientation towards designing green buildings. ITC Hotels is the second largest hospitality firm in India. It is a business conglomerate which has presence in the hospitality domain in several different categories such as luxury, business and heritage hotels.

ITC Grand Chola at Chennai in India is the world's largest LEED Platinum green hotel. It is six hundred-room luxury hotel with over 100,000 square feet of banqueting and conventional facilities and ten restaurants. It is powered by 100 percent renewable energy.

ITC Hotels division is located Gurgaon in the world's first green building called the ITC Green Centre.

The Lemon Tree Hotel Company is India's fastest growing chain of upscale, midscale and economy hotels. This award winning Indian hotel chain was founded in September 2002 and currently owns and operates 24 hotels in 14 cities with 2,800 rooms and ~3,000 employees. This speedy growth has made the group the 3rd largest hotel chain in India by owned rooms, currently. By 2015–2016, the company will own and operate over 4000 rooms across most of the major cities in India including Ahmedabad, Aurangabad, Bengaluru, Chandigarh, Chennai, Ghaziabad, Gurgaon, Goa, Hyderabad, Indore, Jaipur, Muhamma (Kerala), Mumbai, New Delhi and Pune.

The group offers three brands to meet hotel needs of guests across all levels:

1.   Lemon Tree Premier Upscale Segment
2.   Lemon Tree HotelsMidscale Segment
3.   Red Fox Hotels Economy Segment

The chapter also provides insights into Samodh Safari lodge. Banjaar Tola, a brand owned by Taj is another case featuring in this chapter. The chapter explores the green orientation through discussing the above cases and provides design and architectural insights from Indian perspective that could influence global design practices.

1.3 APPROACH

An attempt has been made to seek insights from various hotel properties that deploy indigenous practices to designing green buildings. Interviews have been conducted with practitioners from organizations such as ITC, Lemon Tree, Samode Safari Lodge, Banjaar Tola. A review of architectural practices by conducting interviews with architects has also been discussed here. Griha (Green Rating for Integrated Habitat Assessment) and LEED standards have also been discussed.

The chapter also draws insights from practitioners on what are the challenges towards implementing green practices. Implications for government industry practitioners and consumers have also been discussed.

1.3.1 THE CASE OF SUSTAINABLE PRACTICES INITIATED BY ITC

1.3.1.1 BACKGROUND

ITC is one of India's foremost private sector companies and a diversified conglomerate with interests in fast moving consumer goods, hotels, paperboards and packaging, agri business and information technology. With a market capitalization of around US $42 billion and a turnover of over US $7 billion, ITC has been ranked as the world's 6th largest 'sustainable value creator' among consumer goods companies globally, according to a report by the Boston Consulting Group (BCG). It is the only company in the world to be carbon positive, water positive and solid waste recycling positive, with its businesses supporting over 5 million sustainable livelihoods. Recently, ITC Chairman Mr. Y. C. Deveshwar was ranked the 7th Best Performing CEO in the world by the *Harvard Business Review*.

1.3.2 SUSTAINABLE INITIATIVES BY ITC IN THE DOMAIN OF HOSPITALITY INDUSTRY

There are numerous initiatives undertaken by ITC in the domain of hospitality industry. These are enumerated in the section below:

1.3.3 APPROACH TOWARDS DEVELOPING GREEN BUILDINGS

The ITC Green Center in Gurgaon is the physical expression of the commitment to sustainability-ecological, social and economic. The building was awarded Platinum rating by the US Green Building Council-LEED. Some of the key features of the Platinum rated building is as follows:

1. Sustainable Site: The site has the following facilities:
   a. Alternative transportation: Parking, shower and changing facilities for bicyclists, pool cars and charging facilities
   b. Storm water management: Rainwater rechargeable pits to ensure zero discharge into municipal drainage
   c. Heat island effect: 80% underground parking. More than 75% of the terrace has been insulated and coated with albedo roof paint.
   d. Light pollution reduction: Minimum exterior lighting to limit night sky pollution
2. Water Efficiency:
   a. Water efficient landscaping: Native plants with high efficiency irrigation system and 100% recycled water for irrigation
   b. Innovative waste water technologies: Fluidized aerobic bioreactors sewage plant provided
   c. Water use reduction: Reduction in water usage over base case
3. Energy and Atmosphere:
   a. Energy: Exceeds ASHRAE 90.1 base case standards by 51%
   b. Envelope: External wall of 250 mm thickness. Autoclaved aerated concrete blocks, double glazed windows, 75 mm thick extruded polystyrene roof insulation
   c. HVAC: Chillers of COP 6.1 double skinned AHUs, VFDs, VAVs, Heat Recovery Wheel
   d. Hot Water: Solar thermal technology
   e. Ozone Depletion: All HVAC equipment are free from CFC/HCFC/Halons

4. Materials and Resources:
   - Storage and collection of recyclables: Separate storage bins provided at each floor for recyclable materials such as glass, paper, cardboard, glass, plastic and metals.
   - More than 10% of the building materials are refurbished/salvaged from other sites
   - Recycled content: Fly ash based cement, fly ash based AAC blocks, acoustic ceiling, glass, ceramic tiles, MDF cabinets etc.
   - Regional materials: More than 40% of the building materials are from within 500 miles of the project site
   - Rapidly renewable materials: such as medium density fiber board
   - Certified wood: New woods are certified under the Forest Stewardship Council US.
5. Indoor Environmental Quality:
   - Low emitting materials: Low VOC levels of adhesives/sealants used for carpets/composite woods/paints
6. Innovation and Design Process:
   - Green education: Educating visitors, construction workers, employees and consultants on sustainability

1.3.4 DEPLOYMENT OF TECHNOLOGY

Technology also plays a very important role in optimally using the resources. It becomes the empowering element.

In the last 20 years, it has dawned on the world community that resources are finite. The kind of lights that are used, from incandescent, to CFL, to LED lighting, has been a revolutionary change. Sensor-based lighting is another area where investments have been made. Using natural lighting and building in design elements where during the day natural lighting helps energy optimization. Also the designing of the furniture, staircases, lobbies in a manner that makes accessibility possible for differently enabled people also builds in sustainability aspect. The cooling technologies, equipment deployed in rooms, baths all promote sustainability.

ITC hotels has applied reflective paint on the roof top whereby 47% heat can be reflected from the roof top to the atmosphers to reduce energy consumption for A/C. Installation of energy efficient chillers can bring down the electricity consumption. Deploying of day light in the lobby and the whole building has health benefits and work productivity.

Water recycling, installing sewage treatment plants are all examples of initiatives which have been implemented.

1.3.5   INFLUENCING INDIVIDUAL ATTITUDES

ITC believes in the concept of individual corporate responsibility. An individual drives changes in thought patterns and behavior. The corporate thinking needs to be assimilated and reflected in behavior patterns of an individual.

Changing attitude of an individual is the biggest challenge. There are numerous ways through which ITC tries and influences individual attitudes of people.

1.3.5.1   FOOD WASTAGE

Food wastage is an aspect that ITC cares about. They launched an initiative called green banquets. In green banquets, natural lighting would be deployed. Also engagement with the guest is considered very important. Day lighting is used in banquets, which are built to have natural lighting. E-cards, and menus are created for the guests. The materials deployed are recycled.

With more deployment of lights, come in numerous aspects such as climate change, mining, transportation, and implicit and explicit deployment of resources. There is also a backdrop, which gets created in many events. The same is given away to Goonj, which is deployed for creating shelter for poor people. ITC has also influenced the government in influencing policies, which have now become laws.

1.3.5.2   CELEBRATION OF BIRTHDAYS

The concept of celebrating birthdays should not just be about cutting of the cake. It should be about planting saplings. How many saplings a child has planted? The concept of Individual social responsibility should be initiated. The domestic help training program could be initiated by school students. Each one, teach one-some of these aspects should be initiated. Rights and privileges for people working at home should also be taken up

1.3.5.3   COMMUNITY LUNCH SPACES

There are common areas where all categories of employees dine together. The same food is served to all. Also vegetarian food is served as it is considered as a sustainable option.

1.3.5.4   WORK LIFE BALANCE

In the interest of saving energy, employees confine themselves to fixed hours. The office is shut down at a particular time and people are encouraged to leave office in time so that energy is not used for few people staying back.

1.3.5.5   WORK RELATED ASPECTS

RESOURCE OPTIMIZATION

Food wastage is an aspect that ITC hotels works on; the hotels have developed an in-room menu with small portions to avoid waste.

The hotel chain launched an initiative called green banquets. In green banquets, natural lighting is deployed where feasible. Also co-engagement with the guests in sustainable development is important. Ecards are recommended for guest invitations. The event materials are recycled; for example vinyl backdrops are used in many events. The same is given away to an NGO, Goonj, which deploys the vinyl material for creating shelter for shelterless people.

CAFETERIA

In the cafeteria all categories of employees dine together. The same food is served to all.

WORK LIFE BALANCE

In the interest of work life balance, employees leave the ITC Green Centre on time. The office is shut at 5pm and people are encouraged to leave the office in time so that energy is not wasted for a few people.

WORK RELATED ASPECTS

People are encouraged to pool cars. Recycled water is used in toilets. Paper is used on both sides. Lamps are deployed in offices.

In the design of ITC green buildings, five basic principles are deployed:

1. Energy efficiency and atmosphere: Buildings have a huge impact on the design element. By design the energy consumption can be reduced by 51%.
2. Water consumption is also something to be looked at. The water balance account should be looked at. Water is poorly priced and abused.

In fact, it is grossly subsidized for rich people. There should not only be inflow meter but also an outflow meter to check how much water is wasted. Germany taxes only not inflow of water but also outflow of water as well. The recycled water should be deployed for horticulture, gardening etc.

3. Material consciousness: Use materials from a 500-mile radius. Gandhi's 2 km rule should be applicable.

4. Green material solvents should be deployed. Avoid materials with volatile organic compounds. Wood certification also needs to be looked at. A percentage of wood from certified sources only should be deployed. The wood should be certified from a forest stewardship council. Sustainability should be deployed selectively. Trees should be planted as compensatory afforestation

1.4 LEMON TREE HOTELS

Founded in 2002, Lemon Tree Hotels is the fastest growing hotel chain in India and the third largest (by owned rooms) currently. The group owns and operatesthree brands—Lemon Tree Premier, Lemon Tree and Red Fox Hotels in the upscale, midscale and economy segments, respectively. This award winning Indian hotel chain was founded in September 2002 and currently owns and operates 24 hotels in 14 cities aggregating 2800 rooms with over 3000 employees. This speedy growth has made the group the third largest hotel chain in India by owned rooms, currently. By 2015–16, the company will own and operate over 4000 rooms across most of the major cities in India including Ahmedabad, Aurangabad, Bengaluru,Chandigarh, Chennai, Ghaziabad, Gurgaon, Goa, Hyderabad, Indore, Jaipur, EastDelhi, Muhamma (Kerala), Mumbai, New Delhi and Pune. The group designs, builds, owns and operates all its hotels to ensure a consistent guest experience across all hotels.

The Lemon Tree Hotels have championed various sustainable efforts. Many of these are linked with design elements. However, one of the very outstanding effort is about deploying different abled people in the food service areas. They have been trained in sign language and have created a life for these people. The details of these initiatives are as under:

1.4.1 CARING FOR THE PLANET

1.4.1.1 CARING FOR THE ENVIRONMENT

- Lemon Tree's existing and upcoming hotels are designed and constructed to qualify for the L.E.E.D Gold Standard. Leadership in Energy and Environment Design (L.E.E.D) is the internationally recognized eco-friendly building certification standard awarded by the United States Green Building Council (USGBC) and the Indian Green Building Council (IGBC)to buildings designed for energy savings, efficient use of water, reduction of CO_2 emission and overall improvement in environmental quality.
- Planting of trees, shrubs on hotel premises.
- Universal design, for greater access for differently abled people.

1.4.1.2 ENERGY CONSERVATION

- Variable Refrigerant Volume (VRV) technology for air-conditioning.
- Heat Recovery Ventilators (HRV) with thermal enthalpy wheels: for heat recovery from washroom exhausts.
- Chilled water reset through building automation: to reduce power consumption required for cooling building.
- Heat pumps: for heat recovery, for heating domestic water.
- LED lighting and CFL Lighting: both consume far less energy than traditional lighting.
- Key Tag Energy Saver System: conserves energy in unoccupied rooms.
- Natural/day lighting: reduces power consumption dramatically.
- Double Glazed Vacuum Sealed Windows: conserves energy (bv ~5%) and reduces noise.
- Auto Time Management (for lighting, air-conditioning and ventilation fans)through timers and motion sensors: helps conserve energy.
- Energy-Efficient Hydro-Pneumatic System with Variable-frequency Drive (VFD)motors for water supply: ensures constant pressure and reduces load on pumps.
- LT Voltage Stabilizer: is energy saving and prevents damage to equipment due to sudden power fluctuations.
- Thermal Insulation: increases room comfort and conserves energy.
- Use of BEE certified equipment,for example,air-conditioner, refrigerator, fans, etc., reduces energy consumption.

- Solar Panel for hot water: alternative, renewable energy.
- Wind power: alternative, renewable energy. Being implemented in a phased manner at our hotels in Chennai followed by Aurangabad and Pune.

1.4.1.3   WATER CONSERVATION

- Sewage Treatment Plant (STP): recycles water used across the hotel. Approximately 30% of this recycled water is used in the garden and flush systems.
- Aerators/Flow Restrictors including Duel Flush System: maintains water force and yet reduces outflow, hence saving water.
- Rain Water Harvesting: protects and replenishes the ground water table.
- Auto Flush For Public Urinals: minimizes water wastage.
- Guest engagement program—water saving poster placed in all rooms that quantifies the saving of water each guest can do by not getting their linen changed daily—encourages them to do their small bit to save precious water when they are traveling.

1.4.1.4   GREEN FUELS AND GREEN MATERIALS

- Use of CNG instead of LPG: leads to reduction of pollution.
- Use of Green Building Material, for example:
  - Recycled Wood/Medium Density Fiberboard (MDF): saves trees.
  - Rubber Wood: environmentally friendly as it makes use of trees that have already served a useful function.
  - Particle Board: engineered wood manufactured from wood chips, sawmill shavings or saw dust.
- AAC blocks, that is, cement concrete blocks in flyash: offers several benefits including thermal efficiency, that is, reduces the heating and cooling load in buildings; resource efficiency gives it lower environmental impact in all phases of its life cycle; light weight increases chances of survival during seismic activity.

1.4.1.5   WASTE MANAGEMENT

- Sewage Treatment: prevents pollution.

1.4.1.6 NOISE POLLUTION MANAGEMENT

- Double Glazed Vacuum Sealed Windows: reduces external noise level below 50 decibels.
- Environmental Seals: prevents entry of noise and smoke (in case of fire) into the room.
- Noiseless Generators: acoustically insulated, the sound level is dampened to a minimal level.

1.4.1.7 OPERATIONAL PRACTICES

- Laundry Paper/Cloth bags instead of plastic: environmentally friendly.
- Recycled Garbage Bio-degradable Bags: environmentally friendly.
- Water Glasses inverted and placed on a cork surface: thereby doing away with plastic covers.
- Pencils not plastic pens.

1.4.1.8 FUTURE INITIATIVES

1.4.1.8.1 SHORT/MEDIUM TERM

- **Wind power** in Aurangabad and Pune.
- **Agro power,** that is, burn agricultural waste: agreement signed for Hyderabad.
- **Recycled water** for ac cooling tower (target replacement of fresh water by 15–20%).
- **Heat pump** for energy conservation (using ac plant's hot air for cooling). Done in DIAL.

1.4.1.8.2 LONG TERM

- **Solar photo–voltaic (PV)**system for lighting.
- **Extensive** use of **LED** light fittings (post cost reduction).
- **Geo thermal energy.**

The next part of the chapter draws insights from architecture and design point of view. Various examples are discussed and the insights are drawn from GRIHA and LEEDs guidelines as well.

1.5 VERNACULAR ARCHITECTURE

The term "vernacular architecture" stands for the art of constructing habitable dwellings and shelters, which is spontaneous, environment-oriented, and community-based (Amresh, 2013). It does not acknowledge a specific architect for its design and reflects the technology and culture of the indigenous society and environment. Vernacular architecture is the opposite of high traditional architecture, which belongs to the grand tradition (e.g., palace, fortress, villa, etc.) and requires special skills and expertise which an architect must have knowledge of and for which he enjoys a special position. The indigenous people employ their basic skills of understanding the climate, available environmental resources and developing indigenous construction techniques with the available recourse in their native homeland. No material is outsourced and any high tech equipment for construction is also not deployed. It is observed that vernacular construction is comfortable and also sustainable as it is constructed from locally available materials and in response to the climate of that region.

Vernacular Architecture is unique to its native place, and so keeps on transforming from region to region depending on the climate, culture and the available raw material of construction. It has the beauty of the expression of the natives' cultural beliefs, their traditions that are adorned on the walls and other elements of their dwelling. Many hospitality ventures are having their properties developed on the vernacular patterns, as their sites are located in such regions. Some examples are the Taj Safari Resort of Pashan Ghar, Banjara tola in Khana Madhya Pradesh, and Samode Safari lodge in Bandhavgarh India.

1.6 SAMODE SAFARI LODGE

Samode Hotels is an exclusive luxury hotel group in Rajasthan and Bandhavaghar. They have a range of Palaces, Bagh, Havelies, Safari Lodge and Heritage properties carefully restored to its original magnificence. The group is managed by Rawal Raghavendra Singh and Yadavendra Singh, decedents of the royal family of Samode (Figures 1–4).

The Samode Safari Lodge is located on the fringes of the Bandhavgarh Tiger Reserve, near the town of Umaria in Madhya Pradesh. The lodge occupies 11 acres of countryside and has a monsoon-fed stream that runs along the southern and eastern boundaries of the site.

One of the main considerations while designing the project was that while the lodge needed to provide guests a luxurious environment to relax and enjoy the wilderness, it had to also have a strong sense of place. It was important that the guest had a sense of being in a safari lodge in Bandhavgarh and not a generic luxury property that could be anywhere in the world.

FIGURE 1   Adaptation of the local vernacular architecture.
Source: Architect Pradeep Sachdeva.

FIGURE 2   The room overlooking the pool.
Source: Architect Pradeep Sachdeva.

FIGURE 3   Local house in the region.
Source: Architect Pradeep Sachdeva.

FIGURE 4   Local craft around the doorway.
Source: Architect Pradeep Sachdeva.

The architecture of the lodge therefore draws extensively from the building and craft traditions of the surrounding villages of Tala, Mardari, Gohdi and Ranchha. The architecture therefore responds to the local climate and environmental conditions. This also allowed the use of local villagers and craftsperson to construct the buildings.

The buildings incorporate traditional architecture features of the area such as the ornamental plasterwork around doorways, the tiled roofs, wooden columns and fencing.

Regional craft traditions have been incorporated extensively in the design. "Gond" wall paintings done by tribal artists, metal work from the surrounding region has been extensively used in the property along with local pottery as accents and to embellish spaces.

No trees were cut while building the project. The existing vegetation has been supplemented with hardy native trees, grasses and shrubs that enhance the natural landscape. Since the plant species have been selected based on their suitability of for the site, the need for intensive irrigation and maintenance is eliminated. The minimal irrigation requirements are met through the treated water generated by the Sewage Treatment Plant.

This project is a good example of how an architect does the balancing act of giving a design solution which is high on comfort, meeting all the clients requirement and also adapting the vernacular local cultural and construction methodology for its design and construction. The project is in total harmony with its surrounding, the material of construction, to the scale and proportion of its elements which are as per the traditional Gond Architecture. It results in providing the local crafts person an opportunity to showcase their traditional arts and craft in the Samode resorts.

1.6.1 SOCIAL RESPONSIBILITY

The Samode group promotes Sustainable and Progressive community by providing employment in numerous ways to the villagers. They encourage use of local produce in the kitchen, Local methods of construction and the use of locally available materials, Fabrics, Art and Crafts, décor used are created and crafted by local artisans and artists. The Samode Family, synonymous with the hotels, encourages education and assists with healthcare. They run schools, hospitals and veterinary clinics in the village. They build and help maintain temples to support the faith of the people. They bring in companies that sponsor education and healthcare.

1.7 BANJAAR TOLA

On the edge of the Banjaar River, peacefully overlooking Kanha National Park on the opposite bank, sits Banjaar Tola, a Taj Safari Lodge. Kanha is one of the best-maintained National Parks in India. These lodges were built with standards that maximize the positive impacts on the local environment with a minimum ecological footprint, while still providing the ultimate style and comfort (Taj Hotels, 2013)(Figure 5).

FIGURE 5   Tent overlooking the forest.
Source: Architect Sanjay Prakesh.

1.8 STRUCTURAL SYSTEM

All buildings have a very light footprint. They are raised structures supported at only a few points on the ground, allowing continuity to the natural under-growth and drainage. Being lightweight and temporary, this type of construction dramatically reduces the impact on the surroundings as compared to a regular building of say, concrete and brick. The main intention is to be as close to nature as possible. All efforts are done to minimize the carbon footprint (Figure 6).

FIGURE 6   Structural system of the tent.
Source: Architect Sanjay Prakesh.

A space enclosed only by canvas walls and roof can become uncomfortably hot in the summer and cold in the winter, and many top-class tented camps in the hospitality sector in India are cooled and heated by very large electrical systems. Instead, at Banjaar Tola, the use of double layers of canvas with insulation materials and air gaps has been an intrinsic part of this design. The insulated bamboo floor is heated with gas-heated water piped below and adds an extra touch of comfort in the winter. A fogging system cools the air between the two roof layers and cools the roof, reducing summer load. The ecofriendly air-conditioning system, taking up the residual load, uses a reversible cycle to efficiently deliver both cooling and heating. Though Kanha temperatures can vary from near zero to above 40°C, air-conditioning and heating energy demand are reduced by a factor of four by careful design. The electricity demand has been further reduced through energy-saving lights and gas based water heating (Figures 7 and 8).

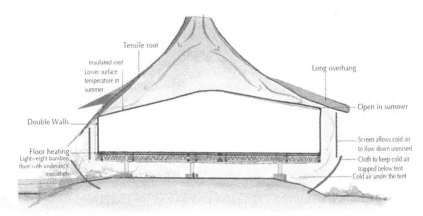

FIGURE 7   Movement of cool air in the tents.
Source: Architect Sanjay Prakesh.

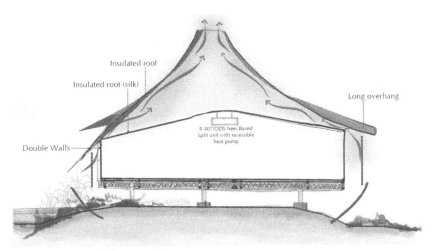

FIGURE 8   Hot air flow out of the tent.
Source: Architect Sanjay Prakesh.

Local materials like tiles, bamboo and local timber reduce dependence on imported resources. Apart from small quantities of canvas and steel, local materials and methods dominate the design approach. The service buildings, located near the roadside are derived from local village architecture.

Small but sensitive interventions in the natural landscape help conserve the land and its features. Soil erosion is being checked, indigenous species of trees are being introduced wherever necessary, water drainage by natural channels is being established, and waste disposal is monitored. Wastewater is treated by wetland systems before being used for irrigation or released into to the earth for recharge. A man-made natural lake, without artificial liners, will assist the collection of water in the second phase and become an innate part of the native landscape.

No wilderness project leaves the ecology untouched, albeit in ever so slight ways. This project seeks to maximize the positive impacts on the local environment with a minimum ecological footprint. It seeks to let nature repair itself, and replicate the spirit of stewardship with which such travel needs to be undertaken in these last preserves of our global bio-diversity.

1.9   GREEN BUILDING RATING SYSTEM IN INDIA

There are various green rating systems developed around the world, each has its own benefits and drawbacks. As there are various climatic regions world over the response to it in design is also wearied. There are currently two rating system being used in India which is LEED (Leadership in energy and environmental design) and the other one is GRIHA (Green Rating for Integrated Habitat Assessment).

1.9.1   LEED (LEADERSHIP IN ENERGY AND ENVIRONMENTAL DESIGN)

LEED is most widely used rating system in North America and was developed and managed by USGBC (US Green Building Council). Buildings are given rating of Platinum, Gold, and Silver or certified based on various benchmarks set by the rating system. In 2001, CII (Confederation of Indian industry) and a private manufacturer Godrej founded IGBC (Indian Green Building Council), India's version of LEED, which was based on the similar guidelines as US based LEED but with few changes with regards to Indian construction scenario. According to research conducted by IGBC on the executed projects in India, green buildings can be constructed with an incremental cost of 1–6% and there is no much-cost difference between normal buildings.

LEED-INDIA promotes a whole building approach to sustainability by recognizing performance in the following five key areas:

- Sustainable site development;
- Water savings;
- Energy Efficiency;
- Material selection; and
- Indoor environmental quality.

1.9.2 PATNI COMPUTER SYSTEMS, NOIDA

Patni was awarded the prestigious LEED Platinum (Leadership in Energy and Environmental Design) rating for its green IT-BPO center in Noida (Figure 9).

FIGURE 9   Patni computer system, noida.
Source: http://green.in.msn.com/cleantechnologies/article.aspx?cp-documentid=3350517&page=2.

1.9.3 GRIHA-GREEN RATING FOR INTEGRATED HABITAT ASSESSMENT

GRIHA is developed by TERI (The energy and recourse Institute) for the ministry of New and Renewable Energy, Government of India. This is the indigenous national rating system developed by the ministry to cover the climatic variation, architectural practices, indigenous construction techniques, and also revive the passive architecture practices. GRIHA rating system takes into account the provisions of the National Building Codes 2005, the energy conservation Building Codes 2007 developed by BEE (Bureau of Energy Efficiency) and other Indian Standards. GRIHA—the National Rating System will evaluate the environmental performance of a building holistically over its entire life cycle, thereby providing a definitive standard for what constitutes a 'green building.'

1.9.3.1 KEY HIGHLIGHTS OF GRIHA

- Sets out guidelines for design, construction and operation.
- Combination of qualitative and quantitative criteria.

- Sets performances benchmarks for key resources like, energy and water.
- Facilitates integration of traditional knowledge on architecture with present day technology.
- Integrates all relevant Indian codes and standards (e.g., National building code 2005, Energy Conservation Building Code 2007, IS codes).
- Is in complete alignment with government policies and programs (e.g., Environmental clearance by the MoEF).

1.9.4 SUZLON ONE EARTH

Suzlon One Earth is Suzlon group global headquarter based at Pune, India. The project has received provisional Five Star Rating under GRIHA green building rating system and also a LEED platinum certified building. It has the minimum ecological footprint and is in line with the company's motto of "Powering a Green Tomorrow." The amount of energy and water saving shows the high standard for energy and water management. The Suzlon one earth campus has provisions to minimize its environmental impact while giving a very contemporary feel to the building and spaces, thus breaking the misconception that green buildings are not esthetically pleasing and functional as any conventional building. Thus resulting in minimal impact on the environment.

FIGURE 10   Suzlon One Earth, Pune.
*Source:*http://www.architecturelive.in/project/193/suzlon-one-earth-Pune-Christopher-Charles-Benninger-Archi/?sid=2.

1.9.4.1   KEY SUSTAINABLE FEATURES

- Passive design strategies ensuring visual and thermal comfort).
- Majority of building facades face North, South, North-west and South-east enabling adequate day lighting and glare control.
- Glazing on the first and second floors has been shaded from direct solar radiation using louvers.
- Break out spaces have been created in the form of terraces and pavilions, which have been interspersed within building profile.
- The interior integrates the user needs and enhanced productivity with optimized day light harvesting.
- The landscape incorporates the principles of Xeriscape with efficient water management systems.
- Use of higher ration of native and naturalized plant species to sustain and enhance local ecology.
- High efficiency mechanical systems integrated with the efficient building envelope.
- All the workstations are equipped with task lighting, which is governed by motion sensors turning (Teri, 2013).

1.10   CONSIDERATION FOR SUSTAINABLE BUILDING DESIGN

Sustainability, in context of building and habitat design, has multidimensional effects, which can be summarized as below:

- Environmental sustainability.
- Social sustainability.
- Economic sustainability.

A sustainable building/habitat is one that is economically viable, environmentally benign, and socially acceptable (Figure 11).

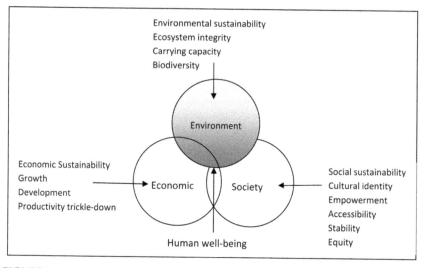

Environmental sustainability
Ecosystem integrity
Carrying capacity
Biodiversity

Environment

Economic Sustainability
Growth
Development
Productivity trickle-down

Economic   Society

Social sustainability
Cultural identity
Empowerment
Accessibility
Stability
Equity

Human well-being

FIGURE 11   Sustainable aspects of habitat design.

1.10.1 SITE SELECTION AND ANALYSIS

Sustainable site planning begins with the assessment of the building site. Analysis and assessment of the site characteristics—in terms of its capacity to provide natural resources, such as light, air, and water, and the extent to which the existing natural systems will be able to support the construction (Table 1).

TABLE 1   Site characteristics affecting the site and building design elements.

Site characteristics	Building design element	Site design element
Geographical latitude and microclimatic factors such as wind loads	Building a layout for solar orientation Location of windows, entrance, and loading docks Location of air inlets Architectural elevation Surface to volume ratios	Location of green and paved areas Selection of vegetation and integration with the native landscape Biodiversity Use of landscape elements such as buffer zones

TABLE 1 *(Continued)*

Site characteristics	Building design element	Site design element
Topography and adjacent landforms	Building proportions Wind loads Architectural elevations Drainage strategies	Gravity-fed sewer lines Land filling Naturaliste features for rain/storm water drainage Location of ground water detention ponds
Solar access	Building position for day lighting, photovoltaic's, and solar passive techniques Construction of walls Selection of building materials and finishes	Location of energy-efficient features such as solar ponds Placement of selective species of trees such as deciduous trees on the southside
Geologic and seismic data	Foundation type Structural specifications	Structural considerations for site landscaping, such as retaining walls, fixed seating's, etc.
Soil type, textures, and load-bearing capacity	Foundation design and location	Site-grading procedures that minimize erosion Plant selections as per soil type
Air movement patterns	Placement of wind towers Location of fenestration on the basis of pressure differentials, passive solar cooling design	Site layout of building structures to trap wind for ventilation
Neighboring or proposed future developments	Design flexibility for future extension	Location of utility and infrastructure for future extension

Source: Sustainable Building Design Manual, Site Planning, p. 19.

1.10.2 EFFICIENT WATER AND WASTE MANAGEMENT

The increased demand and limited resource availability make it essential to have an efficient water management system as well as strategies for efficient water reuse. Major water resources include surface water, groundwater, and precipitation.

Portable water is required for bathing, toilet flushing, drinking and cooking, washing and gardening. The water supply requirements for various building categories in India are given in Table 2.

TABLE 2   Water supply requirement (as recommended by the National building code).

S. No.	Category	Quantity (liters per head per day)
1.	Residences	
	<20,000 population	70–100
	20,000–100,000	100–150
	>100,000	150–200
2.	Hospitals	
	>100 beds	450
	<100 beds	340
3.	Hotels	180
4.	Offices	45
5.	Restaurants	70*
6.	Cinema, theaters, recreation centers	15*
7.	Schools	
	Day school	45
	Boarding school	135

Indicates water consumption per seat
Source: Bureau of Indian standards.

1.10.3 SOLID WASTE MANAGEMENT

Increasing urbanization and consequent rise in the generation of solid wastes in cities has made solid waste management an important area of concern. The environmental impacts associated with improper management along with an increased awareness on the resourceful potential of wastes has created an urgent need to develop systems for recovery of useful resource as well as safe disposal of wastes.

1.10.4 PASSIVE SOLAR DESIGN

The main objective of a climate-sensitive approach is to provide a high standard of comfort quality, which also results in energy saving with environmental benefits. 'Comfort' can be defined as the optimal thermal condition in which the least extra effort is required to maintain the human body's thermal balance. Factors that effect human comfort are broadly divided into two types.

1. Environmental factors
    - Air temperature
    - Temperature of surrounding surface
    - Relative humidity
    - Air velocity
2. Physiological factors
    - Clothing
    - Activities
    - Age
    - Gender

The above factors play an important role in deciding the building design. The building also has certain aspect, which play an important role in solar heat gain, which are as follows.

- Orientation-East and West receive the maximum solar radiation during summer. Southward orientation has radiation during the winters. It also affects the daylight factor.
- Surface type weather opaque, translucent or transparent, this greatly affects the interior environment greatly.
- Shading devices

1.10.5 BUILDING MATERIALS

Building industry has been dependent on a seemingly endless supply of high quality material, supplies, and energy resources. Rarely has this practice been judged with respect to the environmental impact of using these material; the environmental 'costs' that go into extracting, producing, manufacturing, transporting, installing, and recycling these materials. Architects and designers should take a judicious call while selecting material for projects keeping all the above aspects into mind.

1.10.6 BUILDING TECHNOLOGIES

The climatic and cultural diversity manifests itself in variety of basic materials and construction systems used, and in the manner each region has developed unique ways of using local building materials, such as stone, timber, bamboo, and soil (mud, adobe, and baked bricks). The material industry is fast developing newer and better performing material. The building technology also evolves to the challenges of sustainable practice.

1.10.7 ASHRAE AND US GREEN BUILDING COUNCIL GUIDELINES FOR HIGH PERFORMANCE GREEN BUILDINGS

ASHRAE and US Green Building Council have laid down 189.1–2011 guidelines for designing high performance green buildings. The guidelines cover aspects related with the following:

- Site selection
- Water Use Efficiency
- Energy Efficiency
- Indoor Environmental Quality (IEQ)
- The Building's Impact on the Atmosphere, Materials, and Resources
- Construction and Plans for Operation

1.11 MASDAR FUTURE CITY

Masdar City is a unique 7-squarekilometer (2.7-square mile) economic zone and business cluster in Abu Dhabi, the United Arab Emirates, powered by renewable energy, with the aspiration for carbon neutrality and zero waste. The first six building of the Masdar Institute campus—a clean-technology research and innovation hub-are now complete. No skyscrapers or cars will be allowed and the streets are designed for pedestrians. Boundary walls prevent urban sprawl and on the narrow streets, buildings are so closely aligned that they shade each other (Figure 12).

FIGURE 12   Futuristic view of Masdar City.
source: http://www.militaryphotos.net/forums/showthread.php?150475-masdar-solar-city

1.11.1   OPTIMALLY ORIENTED

The city and street grid are oriented on a south-east-north-west axis, thereby providing some shading at the street level throughout the day, minimizing thermal gain on building walls and facilitating the flow of cooling breezes through the city.

1.11.2   INTEGRATED

There are no separate zones for industry or culture. The university and traditional business elements are embedded in the heart of the community, as are entertainment and leisure facilities. Residents and commuters living and working here will find everything they need close at hand (Figure 13).

FIGURE 13   Interior view.
Source: http://www.bustler.net/index.php/article/masdar_plaza_oasis_of_the_future/.

1.11.3 LOW RISE, HIGH DENSITY

These two elements are central to a lower energy urban community for a variety of reasons, including lower energy use on transportation (both between and within buildings) and reduced heating/cooling loads. Vibrant urban Realm Public spaces are as important as the buildings in Masdar City, with a variety of tactics used to activate these spaces. As a result, the city is a place where streets and squares facilitate interaction and engagement with fellow residents, commuters and visitors.

1.11.4 PEDESTRIAN FRIENDLY

A pedestrian city on the pedestrian level of the street allows buildings to be closer together, thereby providing greater over-shading and a cooler street environment.

1.11.5 HIGH QUALITY OF LIFE

Masdar City is designed to provide the highest quality of life with the lowest environmental impact, in part to demonstrate that environmentally responsible living does not imply hardship.

1.11.6 CONVENIENT PUBLIC TRANSPORTATION

Whether through the network of electric buses, other clean-energy transport solutions and the PRT system being test piloted, or the Abu Dhabi light rail and metro systems, Masdar City is designed to be comfortably and easily reached and traversed by public transportation (Figure 14).

FIGURE 14 Electric car for public transport.
*source:*http://green.autoblog.com/2009/04/29/masdar-city-personal-rapid-transit-designer-talks-transport/.

1.11.7 DESIGN

The city's master planners, took inspiration from traditional Arabian city planning. Not only does this indigenous design incorporate numerous strategies to address the desert climate, but it also is characterized by relatively low overall energy consumption. That's because traditional Arabian cities are compact and densely populated. They are also socially diverse places where people live and work in the same environs, and feature lively and enjoyable public spaces.

1.11.8 ENVIRONMENTAL PYRAMID

As this simple pyramid shows, the biggest environmental gains come from the least financial investment: the city's orientation and form. This is equally true of the buildings. In the middle of the pyramid is building performance optimization, with tools such as responsive shading and maximizing the use of natural lighting and ventilation. At the top, where you have active controls such as heat recovery and photovoltaic's, you spend the most money with the lowest (relative) returns. Given this, designers concentrated on the lower two tiers of the pyramid first, thereby reducing a large amount of energy demand with little cost, and only then focused on the active controls because they are the most expensive. (Anon., n.d.)

Masdar City is an example of how the future cities of the world should transform into. The foresight of planning for a sustainable city with a horizon of 50 to 100 years ahead should be the aim of architects and planners. The dependence on fossil fuel has to be reduced and a shift to the perpetual resource energy has to be made. The sun is the infinite source of power, which is waiting to be trapped, similarly the wind, geothermal and the tidal energy all have immense potential for meeting our future energy demands.

1.12 RECOMMENDATIONS

There are several recommendations that can be drawn from the cases discussed in the chapter. The design of a building constitutes a very important aspect that could contribute to achieving sustainability. The sustainability element can be embedded considering a life cycle concept of a building. So even before it originates, the topography, geography, climate conditions and the socioeconomic surroundings can have a bearing on the design elements. There is a lot that can be learnt from interventions initiated at ITC, Lemon Tree, Samari Safari Lodge, LEED guidelines and GRIHA guidelines as well.

The recommendations from ITC Hotels sustainability efforts are as follows:

- The life cycle analysis should be initiated in building industry.
- Design to a large extent can influence large savings. The orientation of the building, building natural lighting, investments in water and energy conservation can make a huge impact. Technology can be a

great enabler and can help reduce wastage of various resources . There are several ways by which technology can be a game changer. Human element plays an important role in bringing together technology and practice.

- Education can play a great role here in bringing about a change. Sensitizing people about concern for the environment and its impact can have a great cascading effect on people. It is the little changes that can create a big impact.

- Implementing innovations: Changing office timings, which allows beating the traffic, is again a big contributor, saving lights. Switching off lights for entire office after 6 pm enables huge energy cost savings and also leaves a low carbon footprint.

- In India almost 1.5 billion square feet is under construction. TERI (The Energy and Resources Institute) and GRIHA (Green Rating for Integrated Habitat Assessment) have also millions of feet which are being created. Building in sustainable designs can greatly help in our mission towards sustainability.

- Sustainability will need to be embedded in the curriculum. We need to exploit the solar energy, also bringing down reliance on oil as a source of energy. Over $145 billion worth of oil is imported. In terms of agriculture, we need to care about soil security, agricultural security, and also ensure that land is more productive. The top soil is 10-12 inches, and also we will need to use drip technology.

- Roads for pedestrians, cycling, public transportation and deploying private cars are some of the aspects which could be initiated.

Some of the other recommendations emanating after discussion with other practitioners are as below:

- The building design is an important aspect in achieving energy savings. The solar and wind impact also affect the impact building design. The VRV systems and chiller systems need a proper understanding. The common misperception is that VRV systems are a better technology option. However, if the business context for hospitality industry is seen, industry has low profit margins and sensitive to economic cycles. When sustainability is sought as a goal, there are initial investments, which are required. To get good solution, consultants need to be engaged for a good engineering design and design cooling systems. Many investors in India do not see value in deploying good consultants. This is in contrast to the situation in the middle east where there is a willingness to deploy consultants. The VRV technology has done well in India as there has been a good PR around the same. The initial capital cost is low. With chiller design, consultants would be required. A proper system lasts for 23–30 years. For a longer time frame, the chiller system remains active and the coefficient of performance is also high. The operating costs are better as well. The VRV system has a life span of 10 to 12 years. Another instance is that air coolers on roofs sitting on high-density sites could contribute to acid rain. The owner focuses on cash flows and the immediate pricing. Also VRV technology deploys a refrigerant and has great impact on environment. The air throw on an individual is also higher. When deploying technology, the whole life cycle impact needs to be looked at. Embodied carbon value of a 20 or 30 years life cycle needs to be looked at. Consultants' fees should be seen as an investment. A detailed cost analysis should be done and also other by products should also be looked at.

- Another aspect contributing to sustainability that legislation needs to be proactive and also there could be incentives by way of taxes and disincentives for not engaging in green practices. In a hotel, energy consumed for running A/c's constitutes 40 to 60% of the bill and managing the same is absolutely essential. The design of the building, direction of the same, glazing, maintenance of chiller plants, cleaning condensers regularly, cycling when not in use, cleaning filters—all impact the energy consumption.

- The behavior element is also extremely important. Green thinking can be enhanced by a participatory approach. Green awareness should be created in the community. At IHG, there is an idea library. There is social website on intranet where initiatives are show and the same can be copied by other employees.

- A carrot and stick approach can be adopted for compliance and adopting green practices. Name and shame approach could also make a difference. In Asia, ego aspect plays an important role and most people would like to be associated with positive achievements. Tax penalties should be levied. Australia has been toying with an idea of carbon taxs. There is a political debate on deploying of mineral taxs, carbon taxs. Because of legislative and effective planning it has started affecting solutions adopted by people. People can't buy incandescent lamps and have increased tariff for power consumption. Households are curtailing energy consumption. People are motivated to produce energy and sell back to the grid at a higher price. Regulatory environment should be strong. The bottom up approach must be deployed. Wind energy has lot of potential.

- Globally well-established standards are there for design and India could follow these guidelines.
- In India, the technology does not really percolate below. Adaptation to green building requires investment. As the demand for green products increases, the costs will come down.
- For implementing sustainability, wind power and solar power needs to be deployed.
- In construction standards, we are way behind and not conducive to weather conditions. If proper steps are taken towards design, 46% of energy consumption can be reduced. A well-insulated house leads to a lower energy consumption.
- The building materials need to be relooked at. The bricks are not sustainable material as it traps the temperature. An alternate material such as reinforced concrete is a better option.
- Internationally, doing a LEED building or a green building can really be helpful. The concrete building creates a heat island effect. The standards tell you how to design but a guideline does not. There is an autonomy to break the rules in case of just the guidelines. Supervision and implementation of standards is poor in India.
  A key question to ask is about future budgeting—What is the life cycle of all equipment and what are their efficiencies? For example, one needs to look at cooling through chilled water. If the temperature of the chiller is reset and humidity levels are optimized, energy consumption can come down. If the humidity is maintained at 45–60% level and temperature set back by 1°C, electricity saving can emanate by 5–7%. A 27% of the cost of hotel is energy cost. Building in automation helps.
- Leverage experience of older professionals is helpful. Retirement age should also be extended to 65 years.
- Deployment of PV cells is also helpful. The return on investment in Canada of PV cells is 20 years. Subsidy helps to produce electricity through PV cells and feeder can be initiated into the grid during peak demand. People generate electricity and 3-tier plans are there—Plan for peak period, mid Peak and off peak period. Tariffs need to re looked at People who feed into grids can be given rebate on electricity.

Architecture plays an important role in how the building performs in its life cycle. Careful planning in terms of:

- Site selection.

- Orientation of the building to minimize the dependence on energy for achieving comfort conditions.
- Use of local materials for construction so as to reduce the cost of transport and the embodied energy of the materials.
- Integrating local building techniques and traditions.
- Installing energy efficient fixtures.
- Rain water harvesting.
- Shifting to renewable energy sources like solar.

The architect is the visionary and thinker who can envisage and plan the things in advance at the level of planning the projects, which will result in a sustainable future.

There is a lot of innovation possible in design. In every building the right from the sourcing of materials to disposal of products, all aspects must be considered. There are best practices, which have been evolved globally. Designing next generation cities and buildings involves a coordinated effort between various agencies. The government, industry, consumers, associations and civil society need to put in joint efforts to bring about a change. Unless, partnerships are involved and messages communicated to the stakeholder, change will not come in. It is not only corporate behavior but also individual attitude that needs to a radical reform. Different institutions can play a key role in ushering this change. School and higher education can play a key role in instituting sustainable values in the next generation. The current generation can go through a mind set change if there is a value that they derive from their efforts. Lessons from Canada on sharing of grids and tariffs can play a role in modulating the demand and supply.

ACKNOWLEDGMENTS

The authors deeply acknowledge the support received from the following professionals who spared their time to share their valuable insights for this work.

Mr. Niranjan Khatri, General Manager, ITC Hotels, Gurgaon, India.

Mr. Shailen Verma, Assistant Vice President-Engineering Services, Lemon Tree Hotels, The Lemon Tree Hotel Company, Aero City, Delhi, India.

Mr. Mahinda Gunewardena, Director Design and Engineering, India and Middle East, InterContinental Hotels Group, India

Mr. Pradeep Sachdeva, Pradeep Sachdeva Design Associates, Aya Nagar Village, New Delhi, India.

Mr. Sanjay Prakash, SHiFt: Studio for Habitat Futures, Hauz Khas Market, New Delhi, India.

KEYWORDS

- **green hotels**
- **GRIHA**
- **India**
- **ITC hotels**
- **LEED**
- **sustainable building design**

REFERENCES

Amresh, R. K., 2013. *Scribd.* [Online] Available at: http://www.scribd.com/doc/47390772/kerala [Accessed 12 January 2013].

Anon., 2004. *Sustainable Building Design Manual.* New Delhi: The Energy and Resources Institute.

Anon., n.d. *Beyond-Sustainablity.* [Online][Accessed 15 August 2013].

Anon., n.d. *Byond-Sustainablity.* [Online] Available at: http://www.beyond-sustainability.com/ [Accessed 22 August 2013].

Anon., n.d. *Masdar City.* [Online]

ASHRAE and US Green Building council (2011)*Standard for the Design of High Performance Green Buildings*, ASHRAE and US Green Building Council, Atlanta, USA. Available at: http://www.masdarconnect.com/userfiles/files/Exploring-Masdar-City-Site-Tour-Booklet.pdf [Accessed 1 May 2013].

Deveshwar, Y.C. 2010, Innovation for a sustainable future, The Economic Times, June 28. Featuring in Enduring Value, January 2013.

GRIHA, 2013. *Green Rating for Integrated Habitat Assessment.* [Online] Available at: http://www.grihaindia.org/index.php?option=com_content&view=article&id=87

ICAEN, 2004. *Sustainable Building: Design Manual, Vol. 1.* New Delhi: The Energy and Resoutce Institute.

Institute, T. E. A. R., 2009. *An Exploration of sustainability in the provision of basic urban services.*New Delhi: Batra Art Press.

ITC, 2013. About ITC, http://www.itcportal.com/about-itc/profile/index.aspx accessed on Dec 10, 2013.

Koenigsberger, 1973. *Manual of Tropical Housing and Building Design.* s.l.: Orient Longman.

Kumar, M. B. A. V., 2010. *Status of Green Building Sector in India,* New Delhi: s.n.

M. J. K. A. J., n.d. *Thematic space in Indian Architecture.* India: Research Press.

Magaldi, I. N. I., 2004. *Sustainable Building.* 1st ed. New Delhi: The Energy and Resources Institute.

Standards, B. O. I., 1987. *Handbook on functional Requirements of Building (other than Industrial Building).* New Delhi: Government of India.

Standards, B. O. I., 1989. *Indian Standard: Guide for Day Lighting of Building.* New Delhi: s.n.

Standards, B. O. I., 1996. *Indian Standard Code of Practice for Natural Ventilation of Residential Buildings.* New Delhi: s.n.

Taj Hotels, 2013. *Taj Hotels, Resorts and Palaces.* [Online] Available at: http://www.tajhotels. com/Luxury/Taj-Safaris/Banjaar-Tola-Kanha-National-Park/Overview.html[Accessed   18 September 2013].

Teri, 2013. *Sustainable Habitats: Balancing Traditional wisdom and Modern Architecture.* [Online]   Available   at: http://www.sustainable-buildings.org/index.php?option=com_ cstudy&task=details&sid=87 [Accessed 1 july 2013].

USGBC, 2008. LEED For Home Rating System.

Winther B.N. and Hestnes A.G., 1999. *Solar Versus Green: The Analysis of Norwegian Row House.* Norway: s.n.

For more details please long on to www.lemontreehotels.com.

CHAPTER 2

FROM OUTPUT TO INPUT: THE ROAD FROM ENERGY AND CARBON EMISSIONS TO PRINCIPLES OF SUSTAINABLE HOTEL DESIGN

WILLY LEGRAND, PHILIP SLOAN, CLARA WAGMANN, and LARISSA RHEINDORF

CONTENTS

ABSTRACT

In the light of steady increases in electricity, gas and oil prices, improving energy efficiency and gaining energy independence has become an important goal for many hoteliers in regards to investments for greater sustainability. This article examine energy auditing process is and the basic application of online energy audit tools available to hoteliers. The discussion evolves from the analysis of environmental emissions (e.g., carbon emissions measurement and mitigation) to the inputs (e.g., embodied energy in construction methods and choice of material). Particular attention is then given to the principles of sustainable hotel design, which is rooted to low-energy usage with examples of best practices. Recommendations are made regarding steps required by the hospitality industry in the transition to a low-carbon economy.

2.1 INTRODUCTION

While issues surrounding the management of waste produced or water con-sumed in hotels are important features of any environmental management program, greenhouse gas emissions (GHGs) in particular carbon dioxide (CO_2) emissions, which is one of the many GHGs along with methane and nitrous oxide, have taken the center stage in the mitigation of environmental impacts (Sloan, Legrand and Chen, 2012). The necessity of reducing CO_2 emissions "has come to occupy a prominent position in responsible-business agendas of most multinationals operating in the global economy" (Zientara and Bohdanowicz, 2010). Reasons for the increased interest in CO_2 emissions are many including the media frenzy over global warming (The New York Times, 2013) and the prospect of having to pay carbon taxes. National and regional governments have implemented or are considering various forms of ecological taxs. Heavy industry in the European Union is faced with a cap on the amount of carbon dioxide and nitrous oxide that can be emitted since a ruling in 2005 (European Commission, 2013). The cap-and-trade is known as the European Union Emission Trading Scheme. Similarly, the Regional Greenhouse Gas Initiative (RGGI) is a cap-and-trade system for CO_2 emis-sions for power plants and is implemented in nine member states located in the north east of the United States and eastern Canada (Regional Greenhouse Gas Initiative, n.d.). A similar system has been established in other parts of the United States such as the Western Climate Initiative (WCI) (Western Climate Initiative, n.d.). One of the most recent developments is a tax passed by the Australian government in late 2011 setting the price of roughly AUD$23 per ton of carbon tax (What is the Carbon Tax?, n.d.). The tax on selected fossil fuels consumed by major industrial emitters took effect as of July 2012 (What is the Carbon Tax?, n.d.). It is projected that CO_2 emissions will thus be cut by an "annual 160 million tons by 2020 while generating \$15.5 billion a year in receipts by 2015" (WorldWatch Institute 2010, 30). In the service industry, the recent partnership formed to develop Carbon Footprint Standards between the International Tourism Partnership (ITP), the World Travel and Tourism Council (WTTC) and large international hotel players is a clear imitative aimed to make carbon measurement in hospitality possible (International Tourism Partnership, n.d.).

The importance of measurement of energy usage and the resulting CO_2 emissions in the hospitality industry is well-established (e.g., Bohdanowicz, 2006; Gössling, 2009; Richins and Scarinci, 2009; Xuchao, Priyadarsini and Eang, 2010, Legrand et al., 2012). Heating, ventilation and air conditioning equipment, lighting fixtures, cooking equipment, hot water use and laundry services are a few of the key areas of energy consumption in hotels (Richins and Scarinci, 2009). Interestingly, the United States Environmental Protection Agency (EPA) has published calculations showing that a 10% reduction in energy consumption equals an increase of \$1.35 in average daily rate (ADR) for a full-service hotel and \$0.60 for a limited service property (EPA in Butler, 2008). Since it is estimated that a 30% energy saving can be the norm, ADRs could rise by \$4 and \$1.8, respectively (Butler, 2008) in addition to the cost savings incurred.

Beyond energy usage, the basic framework of carbon footprint management is geared towards calculating total carbon emissions in a given setting to calculate the amount of greenhouse gases produced in relation to certain activities, thus, helping to analyze an entity's level of energy efficiency (Minoli, 2010). It is important to realize that due to a resource intense utilization of energy, water, and consumables in hotel facilities, the environmental footprint of hotels is typically larger than those of buildings of similar size (Rada, 1996). This is partly explained by the fact that hospitality operations are made up of a diversity of small operations from restaurants and banqueting to housekeeping and spas. Each of those operations accounts for a rather small share of environmental pollution in terms of energy and water consumption, food waste and other resource wastage but it is the cumulative impact of each operation which makes hotel facilities among the largest energy users per square meters in the service industry. According to estimations, the average hotel releases between 160 and 200 kilograms (kg) of CO_2 per square meter of room floor area per year (Hotel Energy Solutions, 2011). Kilograms of CO_2

per guest per night are averaging between 8 kg CO_2 (Becken and Patterson, 2006) to 11 kg CO_2 (Schegg and Amstutz, 2004), to 18 kg CO_2 (Schächtele and Hertle, 2007) and up to 33 kg CO_2 in upscale hotels due to the multitude of services provided (Environmental Protection Agency, 2005). The emissions stemming from guest food consumption are not included in the above-mentioned figures. However, it is estimated that a non-vegetarian diet results in 8 kg of CO_2 per person per day without including the emissions involved in the food preparation itself (Kim and Neff 2009). These emissions represent only the output without any consideration of the embodied energy of the hotel buildings which varies greatly depending on the type of material chosen for both the construction and the furnishings contained in the hotel building. Embodied energy is the non-renewable energy consumed by all of the processes associated with the production of a building, from the acquisition if the raw material (e.g., mining) and processing of natural resources to manufacturing and transport to the site (Canadian Architect, n.d.). As such, embodied energy is the 'upstream' or 'front-end' component of the lifecycle environmental impact of a hotel.

Due to the aforementioned considerations numerous hoteliers are now modifying their business operations towards the principles of long-term business sustainability. One of the first steps in this process involves auditing current energy use and related emissions.

2.2 ENERGY AND CO_2 AUDITING

While sustainability in the hospitality industry is an applied approach to environmental, social and economic concerns, the environmental pillar has long been at the center-stage of activities (Sloan, Legrand and Chen, 2012). Environmental protection is often perceived in terms of degrees of energy consumption and related carbon emissions other areas are however equally important such as wastewater disposal or solid waste disposal. Continuous energy cost increases has led to improved energy efficiency, which has become the ultimate goal for many hoteliers in regards to investments for greater sustainability (Legrand et al., 2012). Before considering individual activities, which aim at mitigating both the use of energy and CO_2 emissions, proper auditing must first be conducted (Djassemi, 2012). Olson (2010) states that a clear tendency towards the measurement of different greenhouse gas emissions can be noted which is supported by the development of regulations in different countries. Various regulations such as Australia's National Greenhouse and Energy Reporting (NGER) Act of 2007 or the Global Warming Solutions Act, or "AB 32" legislation in California, USA, and policies such the European Union's (EU) 20–2020 goal which aims in reducing greenhouse gases (GHG) by 20% by 2020 compared to 1990 levels (European Commission, 2012) are all examples of mechanisms acting as a push factors for companies to take up auditing to report energy use and energy conservation performance. Voluntary auditing of GHGs and CO_2 in particular is a trend across all industries including the hospitality industry (Olson, 2010). Energy auditing is seen to play an important role in energy efficiency measures and energy management programs (Krarti, 2011; Thumann, et al., 2009).

2.2.1 TYPES OF ENERGY AUDITS

An energy audit is defined as a process evaluating a building's energy usage in addition to identifying opportunities to reduce energy consumption (Thumann, et al., 2009). In the case of a hotel the audit is completed through a systematic review of energy consuming activities (Sloan, Legrand and Chen, 2012). Three levels of energy audits are commonly used; (1) the walk-through audits (2) the standard audit, and (3) the computer simulation. The level one audit, the *walk-through audit* entails a tour of a property to visually inspect the systems, which are using energy (Thumann, et al., 2009). The walk-through audit also involves the analysis of energy bills resulting in an estimate of energy efficiency of the business and its processes. The level one audit is the easiest of the three levels but also produces the crudest results. The second level is the *standard audit* where energy uses and losses are quantified through a detailed analysis involving engineering calculations and economic analysis of recommended conservation measures (often in form of a Return on Investment analysis or ROI) (Thumann, et al., 2009). The third level audit, the *computer simulation*, analyzes energy use patterns and produces detailed information on energy use by function to assure that all possible risks are assessed and reliable estimates of performance are given (Thumann, et al., 2009). To keep the approach as organized as possible, the walk-through audit process is often split into three components being the (1) self explanation/pre-site work (2) the site visit, and (3) the post-site work.

2.2.2 INTERNAL AUDITING

The Institute of Internal Auditors (IIA) established guidelines for internal audits through its Standards for Professional Practice of Internal Auditing that offers advisory and practical guidance (Cascarino and Van Esch, 2007). The

2002 revised definition of internal auditing by the IIA defines it as "an independent, objective assurance and consulting activity designed to add value and improve an organization's operations (helping) an organization accomplish its objectives by bringing a systematic, disciplined approach to evaluate and improve the effectiveness of risk management, control, and governance processes (Cascarino and Van Esch, 2007). Contrary to external auditing where external auditors examine conditions common in the industry or local area (Shirvastava, 2003), internal auditing is a neutral and independent assessment within the company (Strich, 1996). The internal auditing process studies the practices and policies of the company giving special relevance to "the review of internal practices, the policy impact assessment and the management audit" (Shirvastava, 2003). The review of internal practices evaluates the direct impact of the organization's activities. In the case of an environmental audit, the energy efficiency of machines, recycling or disposal of waste or the impact of it's purchasing. Thereafter the policy impact assessment analyzes the impact of the firm in its role as motivator, regulator, educator, enforcer and enabler (Shirvastava, 2003). Finally, the organizational structures, job descriptions, patterns of their responsibility and communication are evaluated (Shirvastava, 2003). While internal audits generally aim to test and improve the company's efficiency and effectiveness, the exact scope of such an internal audit is decided by the management and can be focused strictly inwardly or be wide enough to include a review of the efficiency of the enterprise's resource utilization (Gupta, 2005).

2.2.3 SELF AUDITING

Self-audits, an abbreviation of self-administered or self conducted audits, are described as "a system for obtaining and verifying audit evidence, objectively examining the evidence against audit criteria, and incorporating the audit findings into business planning, for the purpose of continuous improvement" (Karapetrovic and Willborn, 1984). Self-administered audits are conducted and evaluated by the same person at the same location where it is commonly performed (Legrand, et al., 2012). Environmental self audits are less costly and more accurate than audits performed by regulators (Pfaff and Sanchirico, 2004) Self audits carry the following benefits for companies: increased awareness of the environmental impacts of the operation, operational activities requiring permits, waste minimization possibilities, leading to possible cost savings, efficiency and productivity enhancement, improved employee morale and public image (NHDES, 2004).

2.2.4 BENCHMARKING

Benchmarking can be understood as a tool incorporated by businesses to compare and evaluate their performance in relation to other organization with same practices or a similar portfolio and structure (Sloan et al., 2012). The primary objective of benchmarking is a continuous improvement of processes and performance and the establishment of more efficient operational standards (Bohdanowicz and Martinac, 2007). Benchmarking, similar to audits, can be separated into internal, measuring within an organization among the same or different departments and external, the comparison with other either competing (called competitive benchmarking), non-competing (best practice benchmarking) companies or with specific industries (sector benchmarking) (Bohdanowicz, Simanic and Martinac, 2005). While benchmarking provides a relative simple method to compare performance 'cautions must be practiced when averages are used as benchmark, since individual buildings with excessive energy intensity may significantly increase averages, especially when the sample is small. Medians are less sensitive to extremes, but like averages, information conveyed by such a benchmark is rather limited' (Xuchao, Priyadarsini and Eang, 2010). Despite the word of caution, environmental benchmarking has become an important and accepted management tool already incorporated in many businesses (Chan, 2012). Environmental Benchmarking is used to achieve a good understanding of the businesses' current energy use and to decide on the measures, which could or should be taken (Xuchao, Priyadarsini and Eang, 2010). Both the use of energy and the GHGs emissions are two very important sections with an environmental benchmarking in hotel organizations (Sloan, Legrand and Chen, 2012; Xuchao, Priyadarsini and Eang, 2010).

2.2.5 BENEFITS, CHALLENGES AND COSTS TO ENERGY AND CO_2 AUDITING

Environmental audits and specifically energy and CO_2 audits provide hospitality organizations with a clear understanding of current energy efficiency and an evaluation to what extent the set goals are met. Additionally, audits help managers to identify the areas in need of improvement. More extensive environmental audits which include the auditing of resources beyond energy such as water use, waste disposal or wastewater output can be beneficial because they enable organizations to detect deviations from environmental legislation and provide companies with the possibility to correct such deviations

(Emery and Watson, 2003). A formal audit enables a company in publishing and communicating its environmental performance (Emery and Watson, 2003). If sufficient importance is attached to the audit and its implementation is done extensively, it can help to vitalize and advance corporate environmental protection initiatives and can increase diffusion and enhancement of the environmental performance of the organization (Brümmer, 2000). Diffusion in this context means an increasing adherence of the entire organization to its Environmental Management System and a rising of environmental consciousness and engagement among all employees (Brümmer, 2000). Finally, according to the American Hotel and Lodging Association (2001), energy management and auditing of performance can lead to various benefits for an organization, such as:

- Reduced cost for electricity,
- Reduced costs for purchased fuel,
- Reduced costs for water,
- Reduced maintenance costs,
- Extended equipment lifetime,
- Improved employee morale,
- Improved awareness of operations,
- Positive environmental image for guests and community, and
- Positive contributions to reducing environmental impacts (American Hotel and Lodging Association, 2001).

Finally, financial investors are increasingly interested in including energy management in their analysis of an organization's market value (Tunnessen, 2004).

The most apparent disadvantage of energy and CO_2 auditing is that it requires time, effort and often incurs costs (Hoggart, 2001). According to the American Hotel and Lodging Association (2001), energy management and the consequent auditing of performance can lead to various challenges and costs for an organization, such as:

- Labor costs for historical and diagnostic energy audits,
- Labor costs to achieve initial activities,
- Labor and equipment costs for preventative maintenance,
- Equipment costs to achieve initial activities,
- Costs for auditing and training materials,
- Costs for in-house energy program marketing materials such as flyers, posters, guest room materials, staff buttons and stickers, and

• Incentive program costs to include materials and rewards (American Hotel and Lodging Association, 2001).

Although each hospitality organization must take into consideration the challenges and costs of implementing an energy management program and conducting energy audits, it is important to retain a return on investment approach to decision making. Continuous energy price increases can be offset against the benefits accrued through auditing Energy management and auditing may be best described by the adage "one needs to spend money to save money." Hospitality organizations are advised to devise a budget with predetermined funding and a quantification of expenses (American Hotel and Lodging Association, 2001). Additionally, small- and medium-sized hospitality organizations and hospitality entrepreneurs may be particularly interested in the use of Free-of charge Online Self-administered Energy Audit (FOSEA) tools that can assist in the challenges of energy auditing and reduce the costs.

2.3   FREE-OF CHARGE ONLINE SELF-ADMINISTERED ENERGY AUDIT (FOSEA)

The use of information technology can greatly contribute to overall reduction in environmental impacts of hoteliers. Self-help online tools support hoteliers in auditing their operations and lead to informed decision making. The basic concept behind FOSEA tools, besides being free of charge for the user, is for hotels to enter specific data into the online tool such as occupancy rates, energy usage, energy costs, resources used in maintaining the buildings and efforts already undertaken to reduce energy consumption and improve sustainability. Afterwards, the tools evaluate energy efficiency and the respective carbon footprint created by the hotel(s) (Legrand, et al., 2012). In addition, tips and recommendations for investment with estimated returns on investment are presented, helping managers and owners of hotel properties to achieve higher levels of energy efficiency (Legrand, et al., 2012). Online self-reporting software also serves as an industry-benchmarking tool. There are a plethora of FOSEA tools available to businesses to measure, benchmark and conduct self-audits of their buildings and operations. However, free FOSEA tools applicable to hospitality operations are in limited supply. Amongst the most prominent FOSEA tools available to hoteliers, with a particular focus on energy management are Hotel Energy Solutions E-Toolkit, Energie-Spar-programm, Hotel Power, Hotel Energy Check, Energy Star Portfolio Manager and GreenQuest (Legrand, et al., 2012).

2.3.1   FOSEA TOOLS APPLICABLE TO HOTELS

The six most dominant tools applicable to hotel energy auditing as identified by Legrand et al. (2012) are reviewed accordingly.

2.3.1.1   HOTEL ENERGY SOLUTIONS E-TOOLKIT

The Hotel Energy Solutions (HES) toolkit is the result of a partnership between the United Nations World Tourism Organization (UNWTO), the United Nations Environment Program (UNEP), the International Hotel and Restaurant Association (IH&RA), the French Agence de l'Environnement et de la Maîtrise de l'Énergie (Environment and Energy Management Agency or ADEME) and the European Renewable Energy Council (EREC) (HES, 2011). HES helps small and medium-sized hoteliers to measure, analyze and reduce energy consumption and CO_2 emissions in their operations (HES, 2011). The tool requires registration but is free of charge to all hoteliers (and non-hoteliers) and can be used in a multitude of geographical conditions (see http://www.hes-unwto.org).

2.3.1.2   ENERGIE-SPARPROGRAMM OF THE ENERGIEKAMPAGNE GASTGEWERBE

The Energiekampagne Gastgewerbe (energy campaign accommodation industry) is a project initiated by the Deutsche Hotel-und Gaststättenverband (DEHOGA), the German Hotel and Restaurant Association. The tool aims to help German hotels and restaurants improve all aspects of energy efficiency. The tool is free of charge to all DEHOGA members (see http://energiekampagne-gastgewerbe.de/) (DEHOGA, n.d.).

2.3.1.3   HOTEL POWER

Hotelpower is developed and managed by the Swiss hotel association Hotelleriesuisse and aims at the improvement of energy efficiency in the hotel and gastronomy sectors. Hotelpower is available without any registration and can be used for properties in different countries but of similar geographical factors (see http://www.hotelpower.ch/) (Hotelpower, n.d.).

2.3.1.4 HOTEL ENERGY CHECK

Hotel Energy Check is an initiative of Green Globe, a certification program for the travel and tourism sector, in cooperation with Avireal AG a facility management company headquartered in Switzerland. Hotel Energy Check calculates the hotel's saving potential and provides benchmarking and tips (see http://www.hotelenergycheck.ch) (Energy Check, 2004).

2.3.1.5 ENERGY STAR PORTFOLIO MANAGER

Energy Star is a program of the United States Environmental Protection Agency (EPA) and the United States Department of Energy, aiming at the reduction of energy usage and the increase in energy efficiency in private homes as well as large enterprises (Star, n.d.). Through the certification program, products and buildings in the United States are assessed according to energy efficiency. Energy Star offers a Portfolio Manager that is part of the FOSEA tool to assess energy and water consumption of buildings. The Portfolio Manager awards a performance score relative to similar properties, ranging from one to 100. For scores of 75 or above, a property is eligible for the EPA's Energy Star (see https://www.energystar.gov/istar/pmpam/) (Star, n.d.).

2.3.1.6 GREENQUEST

The FOSEA GreenQuest was instigated by EnergyCAP an energy management software retailer. It enables the user to track the usage and cost of electricity, water and fuel for a single building. Additionally, it tracks the buildings' carbon footprint and in correlation with Energy Star can benchmark the building against similar properties (See http://www.energycap.com/products/greenquest-features/energy-starbenchmarking) (GreenQuest, n.d.).

2.3.2 RECOMMENDED DATA PREPARATION FOR FOSEA TOOLS

The basic premise of each of these tools is to assist small and medium sized hotels, which may not have the necessary resources to pay a professional in-house audit team nor the financial means to hire an energy consultant to increase their use of energy efficiency (EE) and invest in renewable energy (RE) technologies. The outcome of a self-audit should be three-fold: (1) a reduction of costs (2) an increase in competitiveness and (3) a reduction of the industry's impact on climate change. The depth of data used or requested by the various FOSEA tools varies immensely. To provide a clear and reliable picture of a property's energy performance one can apply the adage 'the more data the better the output.' The choice of which tool is based on multiple factors such as geographical location, complexity or flexibility of the tool or desired support from a national hotel association. It is recommended that any tools available to hoteliers should incorporate eight major sections: (1) type of hotel; (2) occupancy figures; (3) staffing figures; (4) building features; (5) geographical location; (6) hotel size and types of facilities; (7) energy consumption and (8) energy efficiency activities implemented to date (see Table 1).

1. TYPE OF HOTEL

All information pertaining to the hotel type (resort, spa, city, etc.) as well as its classification must be included.

2. OCCUPANCY

Data on occupancy levels and the number of room nights sold must be included. Ideally there should be the possibility to differentiate between time periods in case the hotel is closed for long durations (e.g., due to seasonality).

3. HOTEL STAFF

The number of full time employees as well as the number of rooms and meals provided for staff should also be asked. (In a thorough energy audit even the distance traveled and method of transport used by the staff has to be taken into account, thus implementing some aspects relating to internalizing external costs).

4. FEATURES OF THE BUILDING

The building features play an important role in the calculation of its energy performance. Information on the year of construction or the year of the last major refurbishment must be requested. The type of building construction, whether it is detached or shares walls with adjacent buildings, is essential as well as the volume of the building (does it occupy the whole building or only part of the building, etc.) is relevant since the number of surface square meters determines how much heat is lost. Furthermore, the material and structure of the building (steel-concrete, wood, solid structure, etc.) as a whole and especially the structure and insulation of walls, roof, windows and doors should be taken into account since energy losses frequently occur. Finally window-glazing questions should be asked along with questions about draft proofing and sun shading devices.

5. GEOGRAPHICAL AREA

Outside temperature fluctuations need to be taken into account, the climate zone as well as the height above sea level and average outside temperatures.

6. HOTEL SIZE AND FACILITIES

The FOSEA tools should emphasize a correct reflection of the actual physical properties of the hotel and facilities. Total floor area of the hotel as well as the total percentage of floor area that is heated or cooled, floor area of guest rooms. Additionally, the number of levels of the buildings, the number of guest rooms, the number of guest beds and the total floor area of the conference facilities has to be included. Moreover the inclusion of the floor area of the spa facilities is essential because of its high-energy usage. It is important to declare the size of cooking facilities, restaurants, laundry, sauna/steam room, gym and swimming pool. Another important factor influencing energy consumption and efficiency of a hotel property is the presence and type of air conditioning and ventilation. Finally, data should be given to the FOSEA tool on the type and age of hotel water boilers and landscaping techniques used.

7. ENERGY CONSUMPTION

The FOSEA tool requires energy-consumed readings. The tools should (not all FOSEA tools do) offer the possibility to enter the energy usage from renewable sources to calculate CO_2 emission figures.

8. ENERGY EFFICIENCY

As a measure of what the hotel property is doing to increase its energy efficiency the calculation should take into account high efficiency electric appliances, key card systems, central regulation of room temperature and lighting used. Additionally the communication of efficiency measures to staff and guests is also an essential indicator of the energy performance and is evaluated by the FOSEA tools.

TABLE 1   Recommended data requirements for FOSEA tools.

Category	Criteria
1. Type of hotel	Type
	Classification
2. Occupancy	Occupancy percentage
	No. of room nights sold
	No. of meals served
3. Hotel staff	No. of full time staff equivalents
	No. of staff beds provided
4. Building features	Year of construction/last major refurbishment
	Type of building construction
	No. of detached buildings
	Occupation of building
	Building structure
	Structure of walls
	Insulation of walls
	Roof structure
	Insulation of roofs
	Windows
	Doors
5. Geographical area	Climate zone
	Meters above sea level
	Average temperature
6. Hotel size and facilities	Total floor area
	Total floor area of guest rooms

TABLE 1 *(Continued)*

Category	Criteria
	No. of stories
	No. of guest rooms
	No. of guest beds
	Total floor area of conference facilities
	Total floor area spa
	Types of packages offered
	Percentage of heated total floor area
	Availability of…
	…Laundry
	…Kitchen/restaurant
	…Freezers/coolers
	…Hotel lounge/bar
	…Sauna/steam room
	…Gym
	…Swimming pool
	…Air conditioning
	…Ventilation
	…Hot water boilers
	…Landscaping to reduce energy needs
7. Energy consumption	Electricity…
	…Used For
	…Amount consumed
	Other energy sources
	…Used For
	…Amount consumed
	Renewable energy sources…

TABLE 1   *(Continued)*

Category	Criteria
	…Used For
	…Amount consumed
8. Energy efficiency	High efficiency electric appliances
	Key card systems
	Central regulation of room temperature and lighting
	Staff and guest communication on efficiency measures

After the information is put into the system it generates individual reports on the energy performance and the carbon footprint of the hotel. The FOSEA tool recommends a preliminary set of energy technology solutions as well as an estimate of investment required and the return on investment.

The benchmarks used in those various FOSEA tools are based on energy data readings of different hotels obtained from literature reviews and analyzes based on those reviews. For example, in terms of energy consumption, the HES eToolkit determined a range for most hotels to be between 200 and 400 kilowatts per square meters per year ($kWh/m^2/yr$). The HES eToolkit has established, through a statistical meta-analysis, that the average energy use lies in a range between 305 and 330 $kWh/m^2/yr$ for hotels located in the European Union. Consequently, the benchmarks regarding hotel energy consumption were established as follows (HES, 2011):

<195 $kWh/m^2/yr$	Excellent
195–280 $kWh/m^2/yr$	Good
280–355 $kWh/m^2/yr$	Average
355–450 $kWh/m^2/yr$	Poor
> 450 $kWh/m^2/yr$	Very poor

FOSEA tools only serve as indicators of an establishment' energy status and should always be combined with professional audits. At this moment in time these tools cannot be viewed as an alternative to professional audits but rather as a preliminary indicator of the energy performance of a property.

Those FOSEA tools were largely developed for use by privately owned and operated hospitality properties, which may not have the resources to build their own computerized audit systems. However, many of the hospitality facilities around the world are small and independently owned and operated businesses. Collectively their resource consumptions and the overall environmental impact are relatively large (Alonso and Ogle, 2010; Tzschentke, Kirk and Lynch, 2008; Xuchao, Priyadarsini and Eang, 2010). On the other hand, international hotel chains have the potential, due to their global presence, to positively impact the entire hospitality industry. Independent facilities are especially dependent on the attitude of the managers, while chain affiliated properties are often requested to use sustainable practices and show environmental awareness by the corporate office and internal company policies (Bohdanowicz, 2005).

2.3.3   ENVIRONMENTAL MANAGEMENT IN CHAIN HOTELS

Corporate leadership is a main driver of environmental management programs (Scanlon, 2007). Due to the missing standards in the hospitality and tourism industry concerning environmental policies and the various possibilities in certification systems, leading hotel chains have developed their own environmental programs and policies (Butler, 2008; Zhang, Joglekar and Verma, 2012). Additionally, there seems to be a general agreement regarding the role chain affiliated hotels play in the development of environmental management initiatives and the responsibility those properties have to push the sustainability agenda on the entire hospitality industry (Claver-Cortés, Molina-Azorin, Pereira-Moliner and Lopez-Gamero, 2007; Butler, 2008; Bohdanowicz and Zientara, 2009; Bohdanowicz, Zientara and Novotna, 2011).

2.3.3.1   EXAMPLES OF CHAIN HOTELS ENVIRONMENTAL PROGRAM WITH FOCUS ON ENERGY MANAGEMENT

The hotel chains presented in Table 2 were selected based on their popularity among different researchers (Bohdanowicz, Simanic and Martinac, 2005; Euromonitor International, 2012; Grant, 2012; Zhang, Joglekar and Verma, 2012). Many hotel groups have implemented some form of Corporate Social Responsibility (CSR) programs aiming at the three pillars of sustainability. Special attention has been given to report on the hotel chain programs with a focus on environmental management and in particular on energy management (see Table 2).

TABLE 2   Hotel chain environmental programs (examples).

Hotel Company	Number of hotels	Name of environmental/CRS program and features	Name of internal tool and features (if available)
Accor (Accor, 2013)	3516 hotels worldwide with a diversified portfolio from budget to luxury brands	Accor's Planet 21 encourages customers to contribute to the hotels' actions and achievements with 7 pillars of health, nature, carbon, innovation, local, employment and dialogue with 21 commitments all hotels are expected to meet by 2015.	OPEN, environmental management tool is a self-developed tool through which hotels report: Number of actions they implemented from the Environment Charter Water and energy consumptions Results on the Plant for Planet project Quantity and cost of produced waste
Fairmont; (Fairmont Hotels and Resorts, 2013)	69 Hotels worldwide, luxury hotels and resorts	Fairmont's Green Partnership program, a comprehensive commitment to minimizing the organizations' impact on the planet. The focus is on improvements in waste management, sustainability, and energy and water conservation at all properties.	Energy and Carbon management program (20% reductions from 2006 to 2013) measured through audits and external consultant Best practices Collaboration with: Energy Star Program, Green Key Eco Rating Program
Hilton (Hilton International, 2013)	3900 hotels and resorts worldwide from budget to luxury hotels	Hilton's Light Stay is a proprietary sustainability measurement system is a brand standard across the portfolio of Hilton hotels and helps improve hotel performance and profitability while decreasing the company's overall impact. The goals from 2009–2013 are to reduce: energy consumption by 20% CO_2 emissions by 20% waste output by 20% water consumption by 20%	Hilton uses the ISO 14001 environmental management certification, as well as their own developed Environmental Management Systems (EMS) Light Stay analyzing performance across 200 operational practices in all hotels, with four steps: Measuring Reporting (using a third party verification system) Learning (using best practices) Improving

TABLE 2 *(Continued)*

Hotel Company	Number of hotels	Name of environmental/CRS program and features	Name of internal tool and features (if available)
Hyatt; (Hyatt International Corp., 2013)	492 Hotels and resorts worldwide from midscale to luxury full-service premises	Hyatt Thrive, a Corporate Social Responsibility program which is designed to help make communities places where associates are proud to work, where guests want to visit, neighbors want to live and owners want to invest. It includes four areas of focus: Environmental sustainability (Hyatt Earth) Economic development and investment Education and personal advancement Health and wellness	Hyatt EcoTrack, is a web-based tracking tool that gathers monthly data from the properties to help benchmarking the performance and drive improvements. Goals for reductions have been established to be achieved by 2015, compared to the 2006 baseline: 25% energy 20% water 25% greenhouse gases 25% waste sent to landfills Over 100 Hyatt hotels are certified by the external Green-Key Eco rating program
IHG (InterContinental Hotels Group, 2013)	Over 4500 hotels worldwide from budget to luxury properties	IHG has a Corporate Responsibility Program installed with is set to: Drive environmental sustainability Have a positive impact on the local community and drive economic opportunity Embed and strengthen Corporate Responsibility elements into the brands Engage stakeholders to champion and protect IHG's trusted reputation and deliver against public affairs policy.	Green Engage is a comprehensive online sustainability system. 1700 IHG hotels are enrolled in the program. A point-based metric system is used providing ongoing tracking reporting and analysis.

TABLE 2   *(Continued)*

Hotel Company	Number of hotels	Name of environmental/CRS program and features	Name of internal tool and features (if available)
NH (NH Hotels, 2013)	384 hotels worldwide with a hotel portfolio of mainly up-scale hotels	NH Hotels has a Corporate Social Responsibility program which focuses on: Employees Customers Suppliers Society Environment Shareholders The aims are to: Give all of the actions in the area of Corporate Social Responsibility a global and transversal quality. Globally promote the Social Action that the NH Hotels brand carries out as "Social Innovator." Make a commitment to Corporate Volunteering as a vehicle for social action and internal reputation. Have Sustainable innovation as a lever of brand differentiation and reputation strengthening. Reinforce responsible and sustainable NH communication with employees, customers and society in general.	The environmental management system used is certified by ISO 14001. Their Green Certification Project aims to install an EMS in all hotels. The overall goals from 2008–2012 were: A 20% reduction in energy consumption (–25% was reached) A 20% reduction in waste generation (–34% was reached) A 20% reduction in water consumption (–30% was reached) A 20% reduction in CO_2 (–44% was reached)

From the independent hotelier with FOSEA tools to the global corporate-driven environmental programs, there are numerous opportunities for hotels to measure, benchmark and consequently mitigate their energy usage and resulting CO_2 emissions. However, the *output* represents only one side of the medal in energy management. Many hotel businesses are now turning toward managing the *input*.

2.4   FROM OUTPUT TO INPUT

Custom-made and customizable locally sourced furniture, curved water fountain, natural anti-allergen fabrics and responsible, reusable, biodegradable amenities: the list of chic eco-design materials for the hospitality industry is already long, yet still largely unexplored by many industry players. The hospitality industry has made tremendous progress over the past decade in managing its output: waste is reduced, reused and recycled; water is conserved and recycled; energy use is tracked and diminished, carbon dioxide emissions are mitigated. Managing the output is the now the accepted if not expected norm (Legrand et al., 2012). Differentiation today takes place in the input stage. In other words, the choice of material, construction methods and furniture greatly affects the long-term environmental impact, well being of guest and employees alike and the financial bottom-line.

2.4.1 RESOURCE USE IN INPUTS

Sustainability in terms of building material is a relative term. Construction items built with sustainable material such as bricks, soft wood flooring and ceramic tiles often travel long distances from the point of production to the building site incurring a substantial carbon footprint in the process. Long gone are the days where only material that could be carried by a horse and cart or on a boat would be used for buildings.

Many essential, but non-renewable, materials are now in short supply. This translates into using less of these materials by building more simply, with more local, plentiful and renewable materials and with less waste. Choices of materials and construction methods can significantly change the amount of energy embodied in the structure of a building. Embodied energy is the energy consumed by all of the processes associated with the production of a building, from the mining and processing of natural resources to manufacturing, transport and product delivery (Canadian Architect, n.d.). Embodied energy content varies enormously between products and materials. Usually, the energy units used to calculate embodied energy of material are megajoules per kilograms of product. It is also possible to calculate kilograms of carbon dioxide (CO_2) per kilogram of product (although this highly depends on the type of energy used to manufacture the product (oil, wind, nuclear, etc.). In other words, one hotel window measuring 1.20 ′ 1.20 meter, double glazed with an aluminum frame would represent embodied energy of roughly 5,470 megajoules per window or 279 kilogram of CO_2, the same window with a polyvinyl chloride (PVC) frame would translate in approximately 120 kilograms of CO_2, while a timber frame would range anywhere between 12 and 25 kilograms of CO_2 (GreenSpec, n.d.). A single window multiplied by hundreds, and suddenly the carbon footprint of inputs of a property is enormous. Of course, one must remember the concept of durability of building material. And embodied energy does not include the operation and disposal of the building material. This would be considered in a life cycle approach. Embodied energy is one way to look at the 'upstream' or 'front-end' component of resources used in the hospitality industry. The full circle of inputs and outputs form the lifecycle impact of a hotel. Measuring the embodied energy of a material, component or whole building is complex let alone the life-cycle assessment of a hotel.

2.4.2   FROM INPUTS TO ECO-DESIGN

Many hospitality travelers demand more from hospitality facilities for their money. Relentlessly, they seek experiences that cater to their needs and wants. In addition, the modern guest wishes for earth-conscious experiences without scarifying ambiance and comfort. Innovations in technologies have allowed for energy efficiency and resource conservation across hotel properties. Today much of the innovations are taking place at the planning and designing of a hotel facility. This process has become known as eco-design but also as green design, or sustainable design.

The goal of eco-design is to find architectural and design solutions that guarantee the well being and coexistence of society, the environment, as well as profitability. Not only does eco-design attempt to reduce negative effects on humans and on the environment, it also attempts to create greater resource efficiency than found in conventionally constructed buildings. Efficiency means that these buildings save costs in terms of energy and water, while providing at least the same ambient quality. Additionally, the social impacts such as health, safety, comfort, productivity or quality of life are equally important in eco-design.

2.4.3   PRINCIPLES OF ECO-DESIGN

There are seven principles to eco-design of buildings (Sloan, Legrand and Chen, 2012):

1. Local Vegetation Cover

Trees, especially when fully grown, are valuable in terms of biodiversity, whole ecosystems rely on them. They are like sponges absorbing rain water and releasing it slowly into the environment in drier times. They are also natural mitigators of CO_2 like all vegetation in the process of photosynthesis, converting it into energy with the help of the sun. It makes sense to preserve them on site and adapt the construction design in consequence. This point becomes increasingly important for locations of natural beauty, rich in biodiversity or un-touched forested terrains that are very often preferred for the development of resorts.

2. Energy and Resources Independence

Most hotel buildings still rely on fossil fuel based heating in cooler climates. There are now options to build construction projects that are completely off-grid and rely on a combination of renewable energy sources such as solar, wind and geothermal. With a good design, it is easy to produce more energy than a building actually needs. The same independence concept applies to other resources. Some hotels and restaurants are starting to explore the idea of producing part of their food supplies on site or nearby the structures. Vertical farming and eliminating the reliance on external sources is key for the buildings of the future.

3. Sun Effect

A fundamental principle of passive solar design is that the warming effects of the sun's rays should be maximized in the winter and minimized in the summer. This can be achieved in three ways: (a) glazing (b) orientation, and (c) thermal mass.

(a) Controlled glazing is the vital component of environmental design. Although glass allows 90% or more of the energy in the sun's rays to pass through, it is a very poor insulator. Double-glazing is the norm now but still only has the insulating power of a single layer of bricks. Glass has to be used with caution, having enough glass to benefit from the free heat of the sun and let in plenty of daylight, but not so much that the house overheats during sunny days and freezes at night. There are two keys to this problem (b) orientation and (c) thermal mass.

(b) Correct orientation of the building is crucial for determining the amount of sun it receives, because the direction and height of the sun in high northern latitudes and low southern latitudes changes dramatically throughout the year. Only surfaces facing south receive sun all year round. For this reason, solar panels and windows that will capture solar warming in winter should face as close to south as possible. Surfaces facing north are in the shade all year round. For this reason solar design concentrates insulation and minimizes glazing on this side of a building. The winter sun is low, the summer sun is high. Vertical South facing windows work best for maximizing solar heating in the winter as they capture the low winter sun. The high summer sun makes it easy to design shading for vertical windows. Only a small overhang is needed to completely shade vertical south facing windows in summer.

(c) Internal heat is known as thermal mass. Buildings with a high thermal mass take a long time to heat up but also take a long time to cool down. As a result, they have a very steady internal temperature. Buildings with a low thermal mass are very responsive to changes in internal temperature—they heat up very quickly but they also cool down quickly. They are often subject to wide variables in internal temperature. Brick, concrete and stone have a high thermal mass capacity and are the main contributors to the thermal mass of a building. Air has a very low thermal capacity, it warms up fast but cannot stay warm for long. Only when the walls and floors in a building have warmed up will the air stay warm. Sustainable buildings are designed to have a high thermal mass for several reasons:
- To hold over daytime solar gain for nighttime heating.
- To keep houses cool during the day in summer.
- To increase the efficiency of the central heating system.

A small boiler working at maximum efficiency will slowly and steadily raise the temperature of a building with high thermal mass before turning itself off for a long period. Buildings with a low thermal mass tend to have much wider fluctuations in temperature, and the boiler is constantly switching on and off to compensate. The positioning of exterior wall insulation can affect the thermal capacity of a house significantly.

4. Natural Lighting

Maximizing natural light not only saves light but also creates a better working and relaxing internal environment. The best way to achieve this is once again through good design that takes into account aspects such as building orientation, open concept and the type of material used. Whatever can be done to naturally brighten indoor spaces will reduce the need for artificial lights at a later stage.

5. Stack Effect

In warm climates, it is very important during the design stage to plan for maximizing the use of natural airflow and cooling. This can be achieved in a range of ways, starting from the orientation of buildings and how they are conceived to amplify and capture air breezes. There are also passive techniques to capture wind and create airflows within buildings through the stack or chimney effect.

Air expands and rises when it warms, in a process is called convection. In this way, heat moves around rooms and entire buildings. Ventilation with fresh air is vital and convection plays a leading role. Hot air rises and escapes through small gaps in the building fabric at the top of the house. Escaping warm air draws in new cold air through similar gaps at the bottom of the house, this is called the stack effect, or sometimes the chimney effect because it is the same process that draws smoke up a chimney. Badly controlled, the stack effect can produce unwanted cold drafts. However, when carefully controlled, it can produce a low and effective level of natural ventilation. The stack effect is by far the most effective way of keeping a building ventilated in summer. Over the past ten years, sustainable architecture has paid increasing attention to generating the stack effect to create natural ventilation, especially in large buildings like hotels. Excessive use of air conditioning (which is a major source of energy usage in warm countries) is the less desirable alternative and often due to poor cooling efficiency design. Natural ventilation gained from the stack effect is an alternative to mechanical ventilation with several benefits: low running cost, zero energy consumption and low maintenance.

6. Construction Materials

There are now a number of alternatives to conventional concrete, including modified cement that contains a high percentage of recycled material (e.g., fly ash from incineration plants), materials from more sustainable sources (e.g., bamboo, hemp, and soft woods from well managed plantations) or raw materials from natural sources such as clay (e.g., adobe or mud bricks). Moreover, certain construction techniques can significantly reduce the use of structural steel (e.g., Ferro-cement and composite wooden beams) and the amount of material used (e.g., geodesic designs like domes and partial underground structures). Sustainable design is about integrating a much greater proportion of reused materials in new construction projects (e.g., demolition site rubble, even old automobile tires have many uses in sustainable construction).

7. Embodied Energy

The principle of embodied energy divides new ecobuildings into two distinct groups. The first group of ecobuildings, which now account for those hotels built along the principles of sustainable architecture, aims at low energy consumption with the most efficient available technology, such as solar water heating panels and photovoltaic panels that produce electricity. Such buildings have a high-embodied energy, which they try to justify with large savings in their energy consumption, or even by becoming a producer of surplus energy that they can supply to others. The other group of ecobuildings such as some ecolodges aims to achieve the lowest possible embodied energy by using salvaged building material or simple local materials (straw bales, compacted earth bricks, wood-fiber boards, sheep wool, wood frames with wattle and daub). Such buildings usually have higher annual energy consumption and are less durable, but often have a lower overall environmental impact over the course of their lifespan.

2.4.4   EMBODIED ENERGY IN EXISTING HOTEL PROPERTIES

Renovating an existing building will always use less energy than building a new hotel. However, in comparison to using new buildings it can sometimes be more challenging to use redesign techniques and technology when renovating. Especially when the building has evolved over time, there are often restrictions due to historic status, making an environmentally friendly approach more complicated to implement. There are always some technologies available that can be used to improve the environmental performance of old buildings. These include:

- Use local raw building material; where possible uses of local raw building material, such as, local stone or wood from environmentally managed forest.
- Avoid materials that have the highest embodied energy; such as laminated beams, chipboard and hardboard that are bonded with formaldehyde especially materials coming from far away that embody transport generated energy costs.
- Use salvaged materials. Using salvaged materials obtained locally from demolition sites or salvage yards effectively cuts down on embodied energy loss other than energy used in transport.

2.4.5   ECO-DESIGN IN PRACTICE

While the above-mentioned principles are applied in the planning stage of entire buildings, principles of eco-design equally apply to individual components to be found in a guestroom: furniture, fabrics, amenities, flooring. Here is a selection of examples demonstrating some aspects of eco-design linked to the seven principles.

For Example, Energy And Resources Independence

Plus-Energy Concept at the Romantik Hotel Muottas Muragl, Samedan, Switzerland

Photovoltaic panels generate solar power for heating both space and water with the excess production stored in the thermal loop field in the ground and drawn on when required by a heat pump and resulting in carbon neutrality in output.

Zero-Energy balance at the Boutique Hotel Stadthalle, Vienna, Austria

Energy independence is feasible within an urban agglomeration via the use of multisources of energy production such as photovoltaic panels, geothermal heat pumps and urban wind turbines (in planning)

For example, Local vegetation cover, sun effect, stack effect and natural lighting

Wood hermitage at the Urnatur, Ö deshög, Sweden

Small and simple handcrafted cottages, tree houses, with fireplace are located within a forest environment. The vegetation cover here is the main attraction.

The Tree Houses at Chewton Glen Hotel and Spa, New Forest, Hampshire, United Kingdom

An example of a five-star property embedded in a natural forest setting with floor to ceiling glass providing panoramic forest views and flooding suites with light. The rooms are naturally shaded by the tree leafs during the warm summer months and warmed up by the winter sun once the leafs have fallen from the trees.

For example, Construction materials and embodied energy

Local construction material at the Ard Nahoo, Dromahair, Co. Leitrim, Ireland

Each cabin is build using Irish timber for the frame, hemp for the insulation, cedar covering for the walls, heated with wood pellet and finished with natural paints. There is a minimal use of concrete and with absence of petro-chemicals components.

2.4.6   ECO-DESIGN FOR HUMANITY AND THE ENVIRONMENT

Design for humanity and the environment is concerned with providing harmony for all parts of the global ecosystem, including mankind, the flora and the fauna. This humanitarian principle is founded on the belief that mankind should respect his neighbors and the planet. It is deeply rooted in the need to preserve the ecosystems that allow human survival. Building construction must be limited to improving human life within the carrying capacity of resources and ecosystems. Sustainable architecture is about providing built environments in hospitality operations that provide guests with comfort and provide workers with optimal conditions for productivity.

2.5   CONCLUSION

The transition to a low-carbon economy can only take place once all stakeholders realize the importance of cooperation in mitigating emissions. In other words, it is about governments' long-term approach to innovation and green growth, it is also about business current energy management practices and about individual behavior towards consumption and use of resources. While the momentum is picking up in terms of energy efficiency in businesses (as reported by the OECD, 2010), there is still great potential for improvement in both energy efficiency measures and use of renewable energy in the hospitality industry. This article pointed out that one of the first actions to be undertaken by hotels is the measurement and disclosure of carbon emissions. This helps companies assess the impacts of their activities and the costs related to the use of resources and mitigation of those impacts.

On the road to mitigation, the use of free-of-charge online self administered energy audit tools (FOSEA) can help hotel companies to understand their current use of energy and overall emissions. This particularly applies to small and medium-sized (SMEs) hospitality operations, which often do not have energy measurement and auditing proprietary systems. FOSEA tools have been created to allow SMEs to engage in sustainable practices by measuring performance without an initial cost. Most FOSEA tools offer basic values in providing sufficient, easy to understand information for SME managers who are at the beginning of their sustainable initiatives. Following a clear understanding of the energy use and consequent carbon dioxide emissions, hoteliers can then take actions to reduce emissions. Chain hotels on the other hand pay an important role in the development in the hospitality industry and have, generally speaking better financial means to implement sustainable practices. Many hotel chains have implemented their own environmental management program or corporate social responsibility initiatives and have additionally developed their own measurement and audit tools to track sustainability performance. Hoteliers have the responsibility to protect the environment and increase sustainable activities, independent from the hotel size, age or financial means (Oderwald, 2008). However, once a hotelier decides to either refurbish or renovate a property or alternatively to build a new facility, then considerations should be made in terms of choice of construction material (embodied energy) and alternative design practices (passive solar design/eco-design). This represents the 'input' stage of the life-cycle approach to the management of facilities. Considerations at the input stages will directly affect the output (in terms of emissions or waste) from the operations. While numerous hoteliers have implemented some principles of eco-design and given considerations to material used in construction, these are few and far in between. In the context of sustainable development, hospitality ventures must strive to create optimum relationships between people and their environments. Sustainable development in hospitality equates to operations, which should have absolute minimal impact on the local, regional, and global environments.

KEYWORDS

- **carbon emissions**
- **energy audits**
- **green hotels**
- **life cycle assessment**
- **online energy auditing**
- **sustainable design principles**
- **sustainable hotel design**

REFERENCES

Accor. Accor Sustainable Development, [Online] **2013**, http://accor.com/en/sustainable-development.html (accessed April 4th, 2013).

Alonso, A.D.; Ogle, A. Tourism and hospitality small and medium enterprises and environmental sustainability. Management Research Review. **2010**, *33(8)*, 818–826.

American Hotel and Lodging Association. Energy Management and Conservation Guide. Washington, DC: American Hotel and Lodging Educational Foundation. 2001.

Becken, S.; Patterson, M. Measuring National Carbon Dioxide Emissions from Tourism as a Key Step Towards Achieving Sustainable Tourism. Journal of Sustainable Tourism, **2006**, *14*, 323–338.

Bohdanowicz, P. Responsible resource management in hotels—attitudes, indicators, tools and strategies. Unpublished Doctoral Thesis, School of Industrial Engineering and Management, Stockholm, Sweden, 2006.

Bohdanowicz, P.; Martinac, I. Determinants and benchmarking of resource consumption in hotels—Case study of Hilton International and Scandic in Europe. Energy and Building, **2007**, *39*, 82–95.

Bohdanowicz, P.; Simanic, B.; Martinac, I. Sustainable hotels—environmental reporting according to green globe 21, green globes Canada/gem UK, IHEI benchmark hotel and Hilton environmental reporting. The 2005 World Sustainable Building Conference, **2005**, Tokyo, 27–29 September 2005.

Bohdanowicz, P.; Zientara, P. Hotel companies' contribution to improving the quality of life of local communities and the well-being of their employees. Tourism and Hospitality Research, **2009**, *9(2)*, 147–158.

Bohdanowicz, P.; Zientara, P.; Novotna, E. International hotel chains and environmental protection: an analysis of Hilton's we care! program (Europe, 2006–2008). Journal of Sustainable Tourism, **2011**, *19(7)*, 797–816.

Brümmer, E. Interne Auditierung als Instrument zur Weiterentwicklung von betrieblichem Umweltschutz und von Umweltmanagementsystemen; Peter Lang Internationaler Verlag der Wissenschaften: Pieterlen, 2000.

Butler, J. The Compelling "Hard Case" for "Green" Hotel Development. Cornell Hospitality Quarterly, **2008**, *49(3)*, 234–244.

Canadian Architect. Measures of sustainability. [Online] http://www.canadianarchitect.com/asf/perspectives_sustainibility/measures_of_sustainablity/measures_of_sustainablity_embodied.htm (accessed January 14, 2013).

Casal, P. Luxury Travel Goes Green. Euromonitor International, 2012.

Cascarino, R.; Van Esch, E. S. Internal Auditing: An Integrated Approach. Juta Academic: Lansdowne, SA, 2007.

Chan, W. Energy benchmarking in support of low carbon hotels: Developments, challenges, and approaches in China. International Journal of Hospitality Management, **2012**, *31*, 1130–1142.

Claver-Cortés, E.; Molina-Azorín, J.F.; Pereira-Moliner, J.; López-Gamero, M.D. Environmental Strategies and Their Impact on Hotel Performance. Journal of Sustainable Tourism, **2007**, *15(6)*, 663–679.

DEHOGA, Energie Monitoring und Benchmarking für Hotels und Gaststätten. [Online] http://energiekampagne-gastgewerbe.de/hotels-gaststaetten/energieverbrauchenergieeffizienz- (accessed March 03, 2013).

Djassemi, M. A computer-aided approach to material selection and environmental auditing. Journal of Manufacturing Technology Management, **2012**, *23(6)*, 706–716.

Emery, A.R.T.; Watson, M. Ecoauditing and environmental liability: an international perspective. Managerial Auditing Journal, **2003**, *18(8)*, 631–636.

Energy Check, H., 2004. Hotel Energy Check. [Online] http://www.hotelenergycheck.ch/Seiten/ToolEingabeHotel.aspx?language=EN (accessed March 03, 2013).

Environmental Protection Agency. CHP in the Hotel and Casino Market Sectors. [Online] **2005**, http://www.epa.gov/chp/documents/hotel_casino_analysis.pdf (accessed March 03, 2013).

Euromonitor International. Global Hotels: Innovating for Growth. Euromonitor International Report. 2012.

European Commission. The EU climate and energy package. [Online] **2012**, http://ec.europa.eu/clima/policies/package/index_en.htm (accessed September 10, 2013).

European Commission. The EU Emissions Trading System (EU ETS). [Online] **2013**, http://ec.europa.eu/clima/policies/ets/index_en.htm (accessed January 04, 2013).

Fairmont Hotels and Resorts, Green Partnership Program, [Online] **2013** http://www.fairmont.com/corporate-responsibility/environment (Accessed April 4th, 2013).

Gössling, S. Carbon neutral destinations: a conceptual analysis. Journal of Sustainable Tourism, **2009**, *17(1)*, 17–37.

Grant, M. Global Hotels Going Green. Euromonitor International, **2012.**

GreenQuest, GreenQuest Powered by EnergyCAP. [Online] http://www.energycap.com/products/greenquest-features/energy-starbenchmarking (accessed March 03, 2013).

GreenSpec. Embodied Energy [Online] http://www.greenspec.co.uk/embodied-energy.php (accessed September 30, 2013).

Gupta, K. Contemporary Auditing. 6th ed.; McGraw-Hill: New Delhi, 2005.

HES. Supports the adoption of energy efficiency and renewable energy technologies. [Online] **2011**, http//hes.e-benchmarking.org/ (accessed March 03, 2013).

Hilton International, Corporate Social Responsibility, [Online] **2013**, http://www.hiltonworldwide.com/corporate-responsibility/sustainably/ (accessed April 4th, 2013).

Hoggart, C. Environmental Auditing for the Non-Specialist, Chandos Publishing: Oxford. 2001.

Hotel Energy Solutions. Analysis on Energy use by European hotels: Online Survey and Desk Research, [Online] **2011**, http://hes.unwto.org/sites/all/files/docpdf/analysisonenergyusebyeuropeanhotelsonlinesurveyanddeskresearch2382011–1.pdf (accessed March 03, 2013).

Hotelpower, Hotelpower: Energie-Effizienz im Hotel. [Online] http://www.hotelpower.ch/ (accessed March 03, 2013).

Hyatt International Corp., Hyatt Thrive Program, [Online] **2013**, http://thrive.hyatt.com (accessed April 4th, 2013).

InterContinental Hotels Group. Corporate Responsibility Report [Online] 2013 http://www.ihgplc.com/index.asp?pageid=727 (accessed April 4th, 2013).

International Tourism Partnership. Major international hotel companies demonstrate leadership through new initiative to standardize the industry's carbon measures, [Online] http://www.tourismpartnership.org/media-center/23-major-international-hotel-companies-demonstrate-leadership-through-new-initiative-to-standardize-the-industrys-carbon-measures (accessed January 13, 2013).

Karapetrovic, S.; Willborn, W. Self Audit Process Performance. International Journal of Quality and Reliability Management, **1984**, 24–45.

Kim, B.; Neff, R. Measurement and Communication of greenhouse Gas Emissions from U.S. Food Consumption via Carbon Calculators. Ecological Economics, **2009**, 186–196.

Krarti, M. Energy Audit of Building System: An engineering approach. Taylor and Francis Group, LLC.: Boca Rato, FL, 2011.

Legrand, W.; Kirsche, K.; Sloan, P.; Simons-Kaufmann, C. Making 20–2020 happen: is the hospitality industry mitigating its environmental impacts? The barriers and motivators that German hoteliers have to invest in sustainable management strategies and technologies and their perceptions of online self help toolkits. In The Sustainable Tourism V, Pineda, F. D.; Brebbia, C. A. Eds.; Wessex Institute of Technology Press: Southampton, 2012; Vol. V; pp. 115–127.

Line, N. D.; Runyan, R.C. Hospitality marketing research: Recent trends and future directions. International Journal of Hospitality Management, **2012**, *31*, 477–488.

Minoli, D. Designing Green Networks with Reduced Carbon Footprints. Journal of Telecommunications Management, **2010**, *3/1*, 15–35.

NH Hoteles, CSR Management, [Online] 21013 http://corporate.nh-hoteles.es/en/corporate-responsibility-and-sustainability/csr-management (accessed April 4th, 2013).

NHDES, The Small Business Guide to Environmental Awareness: A Simplified Approach to Environmental Compliance. [Online] 2004, http://des.nh.gov/organization/commissioner/pip/forms/ard/documents/ard-04.3.pdf (accessed March 03, 2013).

Oderwald, M. Destination "Green" land—a Look at the Sustainable Effort of the Air Travel Industry. Hosteur, 2008, 17(1), 13–17.

OECD. Transition to a Low-carbon Economy: Public Goals and Corporate Practices. OECD Publishing. [Online] **2010**, http://dx.doi.org/10.1787/9789264090231-en (accessed November 24, 2013).

Olson, for example, Challenges and opportunities from greenhouse gas emissions reporting and independent auditing. Managerial Auditing Journal, **2010**, *25(9)*, 934–942.

Pfaff, A.; Sanchirico, C. W. Big field, small potatoes: An empirical assessment of EPA's self-audit policy. Journal of Policy Analysis and Management, **2004**, *23(3)*, 415–432.

Rada, J. Designing and building ecoefficient hotels. Green Hotelier Magazine, **1996**, *4*, 10–11.

Regional Greenhouse Gas Initiative. http://www.rggi.org/ (accessed January 04, 2013).

Richins, H.; Scarinci, J. Climate Change and Sustainable practices: A Case Study of the Resort Industry in Florida. *Tourismos:* An International Multidisciplinary Journal Of Tourism, **2009**, *4(2)*, 107–128.

Scanlon, N.L. An analysis and assessment of environmental operating practices in hotel and resort properties. Hospitality Management, **2007**, *26*, 711–723.

Schächtele, K.; Hertle, H. Die CO_2 Bilanz des Bürgers: Recherche für ein Internetbasiertes Tool zur Erstellung persönlicher CO_2 Bilanzen: Endbericht im Auftrag des Umweltbundesamtes. [Online] 2007, http://www.umweltdaten.de/publikationen/fpdf-l/3327.pdf (accessed June 05, 2013).

Schegg, R.; Amstutz, M. Erarbeitung von multiplizierbaren Maßnahmen zur Erhöhung der Energieeffizienz und zur Senkung der CO_2 Emissionen in der Schweizer Hotellerie: Bericht zur Projektphase 1. [Online] 2004, http://www.hotelpower.ch/sites/default/files/Energieeffizienz_und_CO$_2$Emissionen_in_Schweizer_Hotellerie_2003.pdf (accessed January 14, 2013).

Shrivastava, A. K. Environmental Auditing. A. P. H. Publishing Corporation: New Delhi, 2003.

Sloan, P.; Legrand, W.; Chen, J. S. Sustainability in the Hospitality Industry, Routledge: Oxford, 2012.

Star, Energy Star Portfolio Manager. http://www.energystar.gov (accessed March 03, 2013).

Strich, D. Auditierung als Kontrollinstrument für Geschäftsprozesse, Peter Lang Europäischer Verlag der Wissenschaft: Frankfurt A.M, 1996.

The New York Times. Global Warming and Climate Change. [Online] 2013, http://topics.nytimes.com/top/news/science/topics/globalwarming/index.html (accessed September 30, 2013).

Thumann, A.; Younger, W. J.; Niehus, T. Handbook of Energy Audits, 8th ed.; Fairmont Press: Lilburn, 2009.

Tunnessen, W. Closing the Energy Management Gap. Environmental Quality Management. **2004**, *14(1)*, 49–57.

Tzschentke, N.A.; Kirk, D.; Lynch, P.A. Going green: Decisional factors in small hospitality operations. International Journal of Hospitality Management, **2008**, *27*, 126–133.

Western Climate Initiative. http://www.westernclimateinitiative.org/ (accessed January 14, 2013).

What is the Carbon Tax? [Online] http://www.carbontax.net.au/category/what-is-the-carbon-tax/ (accessed January 14, 2013).

WorldWatch Institute. State of the World 2012: Moving Toward Sustainable Prosperity, Island Press: Washington, 2010.

Xuchao, W.; Priyadarsini, R.; Eang, L.S. Benchmarking energy use and greenhouse gas emissions in Singapore's hotel industry. Energy Policy, **2010**, *38*, 4520–4527.

Zhang, J.J.; Joglekar, N.R.; Verma, R. Exploring Resource Efficiency Benchmarks for Environmental Sustainability in Hotels. Cornell Hospitality Quarterly, **2012**, *53(3)*, 229–241.

Zientara, P.; Bohdanowicz, P. The hospitality sector. In Bridging Tourism Theory and Practice, Jafar, J.; Liping, C. A., Eds.; Emerald Group Publishing Limited: Oxford, 2010; p 92.

CHAPTER 3

ENERGY CONSERVATION IN HOTELS: A GREEN APPROACH

NAVDEEP KAUR KULAR

CONTENTS

ABSTRACT

This chapter explores the need for energy conservation in hotels and the measures that can be undertaken to achieve it. The resource usage by hotels and its impact on environment has been studied along with the green initiatives of the major hotel chains and small operators around the world. The twin approach of energy efficiency through optimal usage of resources and consumption of energy generated by renewable sources are prerequisites for sustainability in the hospitality industry. The changes in design and operations within the hotels will result in energy conservation leading to a sustainable future. The ways and means through which hotels can conserve energy, which would lead to lesser carbon dioxide emissions and global warming, nurture biodiversity and result in financial savings for the hotels.

3.1   INTRODUCTION

This chapter highlights the importance of hospitality and tourism industry, its growth in the last few years and future prospects. The large amount of energy usage and energy consumption pattern in hotels and the impact it has on environmental degradation has been studied. The guidelines to reduce this consumption have been proposed. The design of the hotel and its operational aspects has been dealt with in detail to propose the changes needed to conserve energy. The financial investments necessary to bring about the changes from the conventional approach towards the green approach have been assessed. The return on such financial investment and the associated payback period has been studied. The challenges encountered while implementing such moves have been discussed. Along with the economic viability of such changes, the positive role they would play in job creation, alleviation of the communities surrounding the property and nurturing biodiversity too, have been dealt with. The roles and motivations of various stakeholders to adopt green initiatives to save energy have been studied. It calls upon the policy makers to provide incentives to the hospitality and tourism industry to invest in the sustainability ventures, which would lead to long-term environment preservation. Case studies from across the world to illustrate the points mentioned above have been included in the relevant sections. In the end it proposes model through which the hotels can adopt a green approach.

The importance of the tourism industry can be gauged from the fact that more than 1 billion tourists have traveled the world in year 2012 and US$ 1.3 trillion was generated in export earnings. This sector accounts for one in 11 jobs and contributes 30% to the world's services exports (UNWTO, 2013). The world has become a global village. People travel more now for work and leisure as compared to the past decades. Tourism is one of the main sources of earning foreign exchange for the developing and least developed countries in the world (UNCTAD, 2010). Increase in the world's population is leading to depletion of the natural resources. The energy consumption in the world is nearly three times than what it was 40 years ago and coal, oil and natural gas are used to meet 80% of the energy needs (Accor Hotels, 2013). Their reserves are limited and take millions of years to replenish and the combustion of these resources pollutes the environment. The global CO_2 emissions are estimated to increase from 31.6 gigatons in 2011 to 37 gigatons in 2030 (UNEP, 2013). Tourism sector contributes 5% of the total gas emissions in the world. The burning of fossil fuels resulting in harmful emissions and climate change limits the business growth of this sector. This effect is particularly pronounced in the case of wildlife, beach and winter sports destinations. Most international hotels chains are aware of the environmental degradation and have set targets to reduce the GHG emissions. The target set by InterContinental Hotel group is reduction of CO_2 emissions by 25% by 2017, Marriott International by 20% and Hilton Worldwide by 20% in 2009–2014 (Zientara and Bohdanowicz, 2010). The promotion of renewable sources of energy has the potential to save 220–560 gigatons of carbon emissions worldwide from 2010 to 2050 (UNEP, 2013).

The tourism industry is being influenced by the four trends of globalization, urbanization, demographic changes and climatic changes. Tourists tend to consume greater resources than at home people, therefore, their impact needs to be studied to minimize the same. There is a growing trend towards ecotourism the growth rate of which is estimated to be six times that of the industry growth rate in general, which indicates the desire of the mankind to explore the realms of the nature. Many developing countries have potential for ecotourism due to their natural environment, cultural heritage and opportunities for adventure activities (UNEP, 2013). Sustainability of the current hotels and new ones has become a major issue for the policymakers, developers, hotel chains, technocrats and designers throughout the world. The recent natural calamities like hurricanes, floods, droughts and cloud bursts have brought the focus on prevention measures to stop the continuous degradation of the environment and on preservation of the ecosystem. Whether an existing hotel is refurbished or a new one is constructed, it requires natural materials and large amounts of energy for its operation. The green approach in the hotels is associated with overcoming the negative effects of energy and water usage, waste reduction, improving the indoor air quality, preserving the natural environment, bio-diversity, culture and heritage of the region.

The hotels design should be such that energy is conserved, energy efficient fixtures and equipment should be chosen and periodic maintenance of the same should be adhered to. In a survey of Dutch, Italian and German tourists 63% took account of the hotel's environment protection measures while deciding their accommodation. Robinot and Giannelloni (2010) in their study found that the environmental initiatives by the hotels contribute to the customers' satisfaction when they evaluate them favorably. The hospitality industry's response to these demands and meeting the ever-increasing guest expectations are critical for success. It should be the endeavor of the management to maintain a high level of performance on these initiatives. The challenge facing the current generation is to make their hotels green, that is, to introduce sustainability measures so that the needs of the future generations are not compromised.

Hotels vary in sizes and the facilities they provide depending upon their location for example whether they are located on an island, mountainous region, coastal area or city center. There is variation in the energy consumption pattern in each hotel based upon the services they provide. The location of the hotel determines whether the bulk of the energy is being consumed for heating or cooling and the requirements for de-humidification. Hotel operations are energy intensive as heating, cooling, refrigeration, ventilation, lighting, preparation of food and beverages, cleaning, recreational facilities, etc., all require energy equipment. Further the demand for energy in the hotels is directly proportional to the number of guests staying at the hotel. The market share of emerging economies is expected to increase from 47% to 57% in the next two decades. With international tourist arrivals projected to reach a 1.8 billion in 2030, tourism is bound to play an important role in the world economy (UNWTO, 2013). There is a growing trend among tourists to travel longer distance for shorter duration of time, which too leads to greater consumption of energy. The time-starved tourists try to accomplish and enjoy as many activities as possible in their short vacations. The greater health consciousness has led to increasing use of gymnasium facilities, swimming pools, spas, etc., located in the hotels, which are energy intensive facilities. So the demand for energy is going to increase with each passing year. Hence, there is need to assess the reduction in energy consumption by the hotels and the effectiveness of the measures they employ.

3.2   ENERGY CONSUMPTION PATTERN AND GUIDELINES

The energy consumed by the building sector is 2500 Mega tons of oil equivalent (Mtoe) and accounts for 40% of the total energy consumed in the world (International Energy Agency, 2008). In the US the energy cost on an average $2196 per room available in the hotels which constitutes 6% of the total operating cost (Energy Star, 2007). Hotels operate 24 hours a day offering various services and amenities to the guests. Tourists usually tend to consume more energy in hotels as compared to their homes mainly because they pay a flat rate for the room and use various facilities available in the hotel and indulge themselves while they are on a vacation (Warnken et al., 2004). Chan (2005) in his study of the hotels in Honk Kong found that more than half of the energy consumed was on heating, cooling and air conditioning and almost 20% each by electrical appliances and lighting and the rest by elevators and escalators. This study found that the occupancy level of the hotels and the number of days that cooling was required were the two significant variables on the basis of which the projections on the energy consumption of Honk Kong hotels was made for the next few years.

Hotels located in various parts of the world provide different types of services to the guests ranging from lodging to restaurants to banquet halls to business centers to spas to swimming pools to name a few. The kitchen and laundering facilities are located onsite. The vending machines, recreational rooms, lounges and retail facilities all consume energy. Energy usage and consumption varies from property to property. UNEP (2000) has linked the consumption to occupancy rates of the hotels and has prescribed energy consumption rate of 25KWh per guest in a day located in Europe.Heating, water heating, lighting and cooling require nearly three fourths of the total energy consumed in hotels (Energy Star, 2007). Cooling and lighting combined account for half of the energy consumption. The energy intensity in the various hotels varies according to the climate of the region in which it is located, the number of rooms and the amenities offered onsite. There are ample opportunities to do energy savings as hotels provide numerous services round the clock.

The hotels need to have a pleasing ambience to reflect luxury and comfort, so they have large open spaces. These spaces need to be cooled and heated as per the seasonal requirements of various climatic regions around the world. According to Deng and Burnett (2000), electricity consumption accounts for almost three-fourths of the energy consumed in hotels.

The heating, cooling, ventilation and air-conditioning of the atrium, lobbies, restaurants, recreational spaces and rooms are major energy consumption areas. Also the lighting in such spaces consumes energy. The light also emits heat, which is mitigated by cooling of the air. The decorative lights are required to show the opulence of the hotels. Efficiently operating the heating cooling and lighting system of the hotel can achieve substantial savings without making significant equipment investments. Sensors can be deployed to switch off the lights and air-conditioning of the unused spaces. By making some investment in the replacing the fluorescent bulbs with light emitting diode bulbs the energy consumption can be reduced. Key cards can be used to automatically switch off all the energy devices once the guest leaves the room. The thermal comfort plays an important part in the visitor's satisfaction level and since people have different preferences, having a responsive heating/cooling system is a must for any hotel property. The energy management system can be employed to preprogram the energy requirements of the guest and customize the setting for energy needs of the guest. This will serve the dual purpose of energy optimization as well as providing a higher level of service to the guest.

As compared to any office building or commercial building the restaurants in the hotels are high-energy consumption area. The lighting intensity is more as compared to the office buildings as these are used for décor also. Lighting costs are almost quarter of the energy costs in a hotel. The lighting audits and measures taken can cut the lighting cost by 50% or more and also reduce the cooling needs by 10 to 20% depending upon the facility (Energy Star, 2007). The air conditioning load is more as the normal temperature recommended for enjoying a meal is less than the one required for work. In addition to energy consumption for cooking in the kitchen, there are also large refrigeration units to stock the food items used for cooking. The larger the area of refrigeration and greater the amount of food stored in it, the greater would be the energy requirement to keep it at a requisite temperature. In addition to this since there is wide variety of cuisine being served in restaurants so for preparation the refrigeration unit's door is opened frequently and sometimes left open leading to energy loss. The way the food items are stocked for easy accessibility in the refrigeration units with the most frequently used ones nearer to the doors and least used ones at the back will save energy as well as time of the staff while cooking meals. Also training the staff to shut the door every time they open it and reinforcing such instructions would lead to lower the energy losses. The kitchen heat needs to be extracted and that too is an area of energy consumption. This heat can be used to warm up other areas. The cooking oil, which is used for frying is discarded after a certain number of hours of usage. This waste amount can be used to generate energy. So efficiency in operations of restaurant can yield considerable saving in energy consumption, which leads to monetary gains.

The need of the hour is to reduce the energy consumed through efficient devices and greater use of renewable sources of energy. The use of daylight to light the indoor spaces is the most practical measure (Heschong et al., 2002) and the advantages of using daylight on sustainability, efficiency and health (Leslie, 2002) have been highlighted by many researchers. Yildrim et al. (2012) have shown how the daylight should be limited during the peak sunlight hours to reduce the glare and directed indoors during limited daylight periods by using the "Moving Sunshade Double Layer System" roof system in the buildings.

Design of the building can have a huge impact on the energy consumed. Ecologically sustainable buildings can be built to be more energy efficient by taking the following measures into consideration.

- Reduction the heating/cooling losses through proper insulation and use of glazed windows. Infrared thermography can be used to detect the losses through constructional elements and repairs and refurbishments can be undertaken to improve energy efficiency.
- Using drapes to reduce the heating/cooling loss during winter/summer.
- Keeping the HVAC settings at the minimum in lobbies, offices and other areas when not in use.
- Booking the hotels rooms in such a way that only certain buildings have to be heated or cooled. The top floor rooms, the corner rooms, the ones facing the west in the summer and the ones facing the north in the winter are most energy intensive and therefore should be let out in the end.
- Utilization of solar energy to heat the building by having glass atrium.
- Use of solar concentrators for heating water.
- Reduction in heating/cooling losses through doors by having double door and reducing the size of the door.
- Using daylight wherever possible without glare, unwanted heat or uneven lighting. Daylight controls can be used to dim the electric lighting in response to the intensity of the light outside.
- In tropical climates, providing shade to the building by planting deciduous trees in the south-west direction.
- By having split curtains in the refrigeration areas of the restaurants to separate the lesser accessed areas from the rest.
- Kitchen refrigeration equipment using water-cooled refrigerants instead of air-cooled refrigerants.

- Placing refrigeration compressors away from the kitchen reduces the heat in the kitchen, which leads to better performance of freezers and refrigerators using less electricity.
- Using the kitchen heat to warm the dining areas of the restaurants.
- By having controls that automatically switch off or keep at a minimum the unused kitchen equipment.
- By using circulating fresh air for ventilation when the temperature outside is mild.
- By using the waste kitchen oil for energy generation.
- The induction hob uses energy only when the utensil is placed on it and thus consumes lesser energy as compared to the regular electric hob.
- By using the waste biomass for energy generation.
- By upgrading the lighting in the guest rooms, lobbies and hallways using light emitting diode bulbs for lighting.
- Key cards activated energy saving system, which automatically switches off the devices when the guest is not in the room.
- Using sensors to minimize the energy requirements of common areas of least usage by automatically switching off the lights of unoccupied spaces.
- Occupancy based guestrooms energy controls.
- Regular commissioning of the building to check that the systems are operating efficiently and as intended. Studies have shown that 100,000 square foot hotel can reduce 10 to 15% of its energy consumption leading to approximately saving of $20.000 per annum This can be achieved by resetting the controls of the HVAC system to reduce waste and at the same time maintain of even enhancing the comfort of the guests (Energy Star, 2007).
- Mitigating problems due to fluctuations in voltage, which cause issues in lighting and alarms through monitoring at regular intervals.
- Regular maintenance of the fire alarm and smoke detection system to increase the safety of the guests.
- Ensuring that the indoor air quality is maintained.
- Replacing old equipment with certified energy efficient equipment like Energy Label in the European Union, Top Runner program of Japan or US Energy Star. Modern air conditioning systems use less energy than the ones that are two decades old and the heat generated can be deployed for heating the water of swimming pools or for laundry.

The energy conservation initiatives should include installing the energy efficient devices and environmental management systems, shifting to renewable sources of energy (solar, wind and hydro power) and increasing the ecological awareness among staff and guests.

The Heat and Power Plant of Savoy Hotel

The Savoy Hotel in London with 268 bedrooms and suites managed by Fairmont Hotels and Resorts reopened in 2010 after it was retrofitted at an expense of pound 220 million. The hotel is now meeting 50% of its electricity demand through its combined heat and power plant. The investment of pound 2.7 million is expected to be paid back within five years. The refrigeration plant with a heat exchanger has been installed which reclaims the exhaust heat from the kitchen appliances and uses it to heat the water. The hotel is discharging its food waste and scraps to the biomass energy plant for generation of electricity. This exercise is saving pound 22,000 a year and carbon emissions by 11 tons are reduced.

Source: The Guardian, 2010; Green Hotelier, 2012.

More than 3300 hotels (over 710 million square feet area) have used the Environment Protection Agency's Energy Star rating and over 300 have earned the Energy Star. These hotels consume less than half the energy consumed by regular buildings and give out one third the carbon dioxide (The 2010 Travel and Market Research Handbook).

3.3   HOTEL DESIGN

For the design, construction and operation of buildings the accepted benchmark is Leadership in Energy and Environmental Design (LEED. This certification ensures that the building is environmentally responsible and has healthy interiors for its occupants.

According to the U.S. Green Building Council, the LEED certified hotels have the following performance attributes:

- Reduction in energy use of 15 to 40%
- Reduction in water use of 10 to 30%
- Reduction in waste to landfills of 50 to 90%

LEED Platinum Rating for ITC Grand Chola, India

Chennai's ITC Grand Chola (India), which opened in September 2012, is the largest LEED Platinum certified hotel (1.5 million sq. ft.) in the world. It is a 600 room hotel with 100,000 sq. ft. banquet and convention center, 30,000 sq. ft. ballroom, 10 food and beverage outlets. The parent company ITC Limitedhas a strong focus on environment protection. The green initiatives were introduced by the ITC Hotels in 1993 by the name 'Welcomenviron.' At present all the luxury hotels of the group are LEED platinum rated making it a greenest hotel chain in the world. The company measures its performance on economic, environmental and societal parameters. The sustained initiatives of the company have resulted in it being a Carbon positive, Water positive and Waste Recycling positive.

The ITC Grand Chola Chennai meets its 100% of its electrical energy demand through its 12.6 MW capacity wind power plant. The glazed windows, rooftop insulation material and the composite materials of the walls exceed the standards set by ASHRAE (www.ashrae.org) and ECBC (Energy Conservation Building Code). The indoor environment of the hotel is managed through a programmable heating, ventilation and air conditioning system to achieve 20% energy efficiency. The fresh air-handling units are operated by the integrated building management system and have CO_2 sensors to optimize the gust comfort level and at the same time saving energy. The hotel provides customized room climate through Digital Valet System. The hotel has installed energy efficient boilers, which consume lesser oxygen and have low fuel consumption. The solar concentrators provide a quarter of the hot water requirement. The mood lighting in the public areas is controlled through programmable lighting control. The refrigerants in the kitchen are water cooled instead of air cooled to save energy. The sensor based jet ventilation system in the basements instead of ducted one saves energy.

All of the rainwater is harvested. The sewage treatment plant recycles the effluent, which is used horticulture, cooling towers and toilet flushing. The excess water is given to outside parties for their horticulture needs. The installation of water efficient fixtures has reduced the water needs by 35%. The landscaping has been done by planting of low maintenance vegetation saves water. Drip irrigation and time based sensor valves are used to minimize the water wastage.

The employees undergo environment awareness training at the time of joining and it is reinforced every year thereafter. Hence ITC Hotels is a pioneer in the green movement in India.

Source: ITC Hotels, 2013; The Economic Times, 2012; Green Hotelier, 2102

3.4   FINANCIAL IMPLICATIONS

The hospitality industry is a competitive one with number of players competing with one another to take the share of the pie. It is not always possible to increase the room rate in this competitive scenario. The energy costs are only second to the labor costs for hotel's operating costs, so any effort at reducing these costs leads to improved margins. With the energy costs escalating each year it is imperative for hotels to look at means to reduce these. Sloan et al. (2009) have listed the best practices being followed for energy, water and waste management in the Estonian and German hotels in their study. Most of the hotels studied had achieved cost savings and increased market share through the deployment of the environment friendly technologies.

The U.S. Environmental Protection Agency estimates that 10% less consumption of energy is equal to increasing the tariff by $1.35 in hotels offering all amenities and $0.62 in an economy hotel (Energy Star, 2007).

Green Design and Operations of Hotels

The following were the benefits of green design and operation of hotels as expressed by the hotel owners in a survey by the *Lodging Hospitality.*

83% reduction in operational costs

80% less affect on nature

56% in hotel guest expectations

54% in capacity to distinguish

32% in resale ease

29% increased return on investment

22% increased occupancy

22% increased tariff

Source: Richard K. Miller and Associates (2010)

Financial savings derived from cost advantages is one of the most important factors that determines whether a hotel takes up green initiatives or not (Graci and Dodds, 2008). Investments in green initiatives are in the areas which are not traditionally the core competence of the hotels (Kasim, 2004); so the investment needs to be justifiable and economic benefits from the same should be visible at the start of the project to compute the payback period for the same.

Energy bills represent a significant cost of the hotel and any measure to reduce these would add to the hotel's bottom line. Hotels come in the top five commercial buildings as far as consumption of energy is concerned (UNWTO, 2013). After natural gas and fuel oil electricity is the most used resource. Hotels can reduce the energy costs by 20% without making any significant investment (O'Hanlon, 2005). This can be achieved by focusing on optimal use of available resources and avoiding wastage.

The four areas where higher capital investment is required are solar control film, sensors for air conditioners, key tag switches and energy efficient lighting (Chan, 2009). The sensors for air conditioners and key tag switches can lead to significant savings and have a payback period of less than three years (Carbon Trust, 2007). The compact fluorescent lamps (CFLs) and light emitting diodes (LEDs) consume 75 to 80% less energy, have a life span of ten to 20 five times that of traditional light bulbs (U.S. Department of Energy, 2012). The guestroom key card system with a price of $21 per system saved $0.3 per room assuming the main switch was left on by one third of the occupants while going out, gave a payback period of 70 days (Chan, 2009)

Cost benefit analysis needs to be done while upgrading and purchasing new energy equipment. If the operational time of devices such as lamps, motors, compressors and other equipment is reduced per day, then it increases the time period these would last thus delaying replacement. So the reduced annualized replacement cost for the equipment needs to be computed and should be added to the savings gained through lower operations costs. Similarly the reduced maintenance labor costs can be quantified to arrive at the total savings achieved.

Big Savings Through Retro-Commissioning

The 1000 room Los Angeles Airport Marriott conducted the retro-commissioning of its facility. The project was undertaken by the in house staff and engineers headed by a regional vice president of engineering with consultation from and outside expert. The cost of the project was $125 per room or 22 cents per square foot of the hotel area. The in-house team was able to develop the expertise, which could be employed at other units of the chain too. The project team proposed changes to the in house air-handling unit, the water-cooling plant and other units. The 17 measures proposed had an average cost of $7500 to implement and the payback period of this investment was less than a year. The changes to a single air-handling unit led to 30% of the savings. The hotel saved $153,000 annually by the implementation of the recommendations.

Source: Energy Star, 2007

Various hotel studies have found that occupied rooms in hotels remain vacant for more than 12 hours or more per day. If the energy management system of the hotel is able to keep the room ventilated and heating or cooling at minimum during the period the room is empty and switch on the heating, ventilation and air conditioning (HVAC) system an hour before the guest is expected back in the room then energy savings in the range of 35 to 45% can be achieved with a return on investment of 50 to 75% on such a system. Starwood Hotels and Resorts, Hilton and others chains are using such systems in their hotels.

3.5 CHALLENGES

Large hotels are apprehensive that by saving energy the level of service promised to their guests will be affected (Dalton et al., 2007). There is an increase in the energy consumption pattern of hotels as we move from one-star to four-star hotels. However, recent studies show that guests are willing to pay extra for the green accreditation of the property. Balanced environmental-economic outcomes can only be achieved through the management of operations and customers both (Zhang et al.2012). There is lack of industry wide standards (Unruh and Ettenson, 2010) and a result the major hotel companies have developed their own environment management systems to monitor and evaluate the impact of their operations on the environment (Hilton Worldwide, 2012; Intercontinental Hotels Group, 2013).

Hotels have to take into consideration their energy costs and the guest's willingness to support efficiency measures and arrive at a delicate balance between the two. Potential benefits and societal pressures green initiatives for need to be evaluated. Hotels will implement the green measures if they lead to cost savings, competitive advantage, higher customer satisfaction and retention, compliance with government regulations or lower operational risks (Graci and Dodds, 2008). There is widespread recognition of the fact that hotels need to be concerned about the environment(Bohdnowicz, 2005) Cespedes-Lorente et al., 2005) The green measures drive is influenced by potential benefits which would accrue as a result of such implementation (Cespedes-Lorente et al., 2005). Other researchers have also highlighted the importance of cost-benefits as a driver for environmental investments. There are differences in the expectations of consumers from various countries and regions regarding the sustainability measures being adopted by the hotels and their influence on customer satisfaction.

Robinot and Giannelloni (2010) have concluded that the French customers took the environment initiatives by hotels as "basic" which contributed negatively if they are unfavorably evaluated but did not have a significant positive effect when they were positively evaluated. Thus the researchers concluded that the French customers had a long way to go before they could be considered as truly "green consumers." The Indian consumers are conscious of environment friendly practices being followed by the hotels and do patronize the hotels adopting green practices without compromising on the service quality (Manaktola and Jauhari, 2007). The Indian consumers are reluctant to pay for these greening initiatives although such hotels do have a competitive advantage over similar offering.

Financial support for making changes for sustainability is being given by national and international institutions.

Hotels vary in size, type, level of luxury, construction material used and the electrical appliances used and so a uniform energy measure is difficult to employ. That is why there is lack of benchmarking in the industry for doing evaluation of the energy efficiency of the hotels (Warnken et al., 2005). Nonetheless the success of the measures can be assessed by having the comparable quality of the services and guest satisfaction with lower costs of energy (Hrs Borkovic et al., 2008). The monitoring, recording, documenting and analyzing the results of energy needs and consumption patterns would definitely lead to newer ideas to reduce, recycle and renew wherever possible.

The implementation of the building upgrades such as occupancy sensors, thermostat settings and any time clock setting should be done in such a way so that they do not provide any discomfort to the guests.

3.6 STAKEHOLDERS ENGAGEMENT

The technological innovation is happening at a fast pace and the market is flooded with new gadgets and equipment for energy saving each year. The decision to choose the fixtures and the equipment lies with the property owners who in most cases are non-technical personnel.

The technical experts can set the standards for efficient usage of all equipment in the hotels but the ultimate objective of reducing energy costs has to be achieved through the behavior of the guests who are going to use the facilities and the employees who are going to work there. So making these two key stakeholders aware of what it costs and how much of an environmental impact it has is of utmost importance. Communication is the starting point of successful implementation of the intended programs. Mere awareness is not sufficient these two groups need to be convinced about using less energy to reap any rewards in the real term. It is important to provide the hoteliers with important information concerning the energy conservation measures along with the policy measures adopted by the government.

Behavioral science is involved as far as motivating the guests to set the standard thermostat setting, minimize the heating/cooling loss through open windows and doors and switching off appliances not in use when they are in the room. The employees too need to be fully involved and engaged in all energy efficiency programs and projects so as to make them committed and have a sense of ownership towards the objective. Success in this arena requires motivational training to encourage active participation of employees and genuine empowerment, which ignites their competitive spirit. By generating awareness, better product standards and stringent regulations gradual progress towards energy efficiency can be made. There is technical sophistication, which interacts with the human dimension that makes this area complex one. The rewards for adopting sustainable practices are both financial and feel good ones.

Hotel Leela Palace's Energy Optimization Programs

India is one of the leading destinations for travel with the World Travel Organization estimating 25 million tourists in the year 2015. The Hotel Leela Palace is a five star luxury hotel owned and managed by the Hotel Leelaventure Ltd. a company renowned in the luxury five star segment in the hospitality sector. This group owns numerous hotels and resort properties. The Leela Palace Hotel in New Delhi is an impressive 16 story building located in the diplomatic enclave area of with 260 guest rooms and various restaurants offering Indian, Japanese, French and Italian cuisine. The hotel went in for the energy optimization program for improving the energy efficiency in the hotel without compromising the guest comfort with an intelligent building management system from Siemens. The fire alarms to video surveillance to HVAC control to electrical monitoring of the hotel premises were integrated in a single system to provide a unique experience to the guest as well as address the environmental concerns. The guests have complete control over their environment in the room with a touch of a button from mood lighting to temperature and curtain control. The system is reliable and flexible enough to cope up with the extreme temperature differences and humidity experienced in New Delhi and is simple to use and has brought down the energy consumption of the hotel by 10% in the first 12 months of its installation. The use of water in the hotel has come down by more than 40%. The hotel has received a LEED platinum rating from Indian Green Building Council.

Source: The Economic Times, 2012; Green Hotelier, 2012

Coming up with special schemes on Earth day, Water day, etc. would enhance the awareness level of the employees, guests and the surrounding communities. Training sessions by the staff for schools, institutes of the local areas would exhibit the endeavors of the company towards sustainability and would generate positive publicity. Exhibitions on sustainability programs can be jointly held with the local community organizations to make the movement widespread.

The purchase of inputs from local areas saves transportation costs and storage costs as same day delivery is possible. It also promotes the local industry leading to job creation and increase in goodwill of the property in the area. The guests get the opportunity to relish the delicacies of the local area and develop appreciation for the local crafts.

The attitude of the hotel owner or the manager impacts the sustainability initiatives in the hotel.

The legislative framework determines the steps that the businesses take to abide by the governing mechanisms, which provide subsidies or incentives and deter the bad practices by imposing penalties. The Greek legislative framework focuses on reducing the energy use without clarifying the guidelines for renewable energy technologies (Maleviti et al., 2012). Governments need to provide incentives businesses, which proactively take up the greening initiatives. These can be in the form of tax concessions or subsidies. On the purchase of equipment or technology subsidies can be provided for a limited time period to boost its absorption in the marketplace.

Policy makers need to set stringent standards for manufacture of energy equipment so that the inefficient equipment is progressively phased out. The additional cost to manufacture energy efficient gadget is small as compared to the benefits, which will accrue in terms of reduction in energy bills and emissions over the lifetime of a gadget.

Kleinrchert et al. (2012) have studied how the boutique hotels use the web and the social media to communicate with discerning ecoconscious consumers in the Bay Area of San Francisco, California and Istanbul in Turkey. The hotels in these two areas use the international standards for legitimizing their green practices. The end result depends upon how much the guests and the employees abide by the green guidelines and how much of resources reduction (setting the thermostat to 72 instead of 68) the business is able to do without lowering the customer satisfaction level.

It provides competitive advantage, builds brand loyalty, highlights the company corporate social responsibility initiatives, builds goodwill among the surrounding communities and also helps in job creation. It leads to higher levels of customer satisfaction and retention generating increased profitability, enhanced image, and increased ability to attract and retain people.

3.7 LARGE HOTEL CHAINS VERSUS SMALL OPERATORS

It is not that hotels around the world are not aware of the implications of continuing with the traditional methods of energy generation and consumption. There are serious efforts being made by the leading chains as well as some small operators to green their hotels.

Accor Group's Sustainable Development Through Planet 21

The Accor Group with 4,426 hotels and 531,714 rooms located in 92 countries is a major player in the global hotel market. It has presence in Europe, North and South America and the Asia-Pacific region. It caters to every customer segment with its Sofitel brand in the luxury segment and Pullman in upscale hotels. It is a world leader in the mid segment with brands like Novotel, Mercure, Grand Mercure, Adagio, MGallery and Thalassa. All seasons and Ibis brands cater to the economy lodging. Motel 6, Etap, hotelF1 and Studio 6 chains are targeted towards the budget segment. The group plans to expand its operations and have 700,000 rooms by 2015. The group has come up with several new programs for energy, water, waste and biodiversity conservation. In 2012, Accor's new sustainable development program named PLANET 21 has been launched with seven focus areas named Nature, Heath, Innovation, Carbon, Employment, Local and Dialogue on which assessment is made. Accor's results for the year 2012 showed that:

89% of its hotels use eco label products;

79% of the hotels recycle their waste;

39% of hotels participate in reforestation project;

6% of the hotels use renewable energy;

23% have eco-designed rooms;

68% purchase and promote locally sources products;

31% of all nonbudget hotels are ISO 140001 certified.

Accor has developed a system for doing technical analysis of various fixtures and equipment in its hotels and through employee training and action plans it has been able to reduce energy and water consumption of up to 25% in some of its hotels without any additional investment on installations.

Source: Accor Hotels, 2013

The large chain hotels are well aware of need for environment preservation and have the requisite resources to implement the green initiatives. The hotels chains undergo a learning process and successful practices are transferred across other hotels brands and locations. They have advantage of knowing what worked well and where and how. They can leverage this information across other individual units.

Sharing of Best Practices in Hilton Worldwide

The Hilton Worldwide, the multi brand hospitality company (Hilton, Hilton Garden Inn, Hampton Hill, Embassy Suites, Embassy Vacation Resort, Doubletree, Conrad, Home2Suites, Homewood Suites and Waldorf Astoria) in the world has made sustainability a brand standard. As quality, service and revenue, sustainability too is a critical performance measure used for the business. The company has a strategy for efficient use of energy and renewable energy; minimization of water usage, waste and carbon dioxide emission; sustainable hotel design, construction and operation and also on purchasing. Across its portfolio, it aims lower energy usage, carbon dioxide emission and waste generation by 20% each and water usage by 10% in the five-year period from 2009 to 2014. The sustainability performance is being improved on a continuous basis on its properties. The damage to the environment by any conference or meeting held at its hotels is evaluated. Through the active involvement and training tools the staff is motivated to participate in these initiatives. The company shares its best practices and complies with the local, national and international legislation. It also partners with its suppliers to improve the overall performance. It influences the use of land according to the environment and supports local initiatives. The achievements on the sustainability venture and communicated to the stakeholders. The results achieved against the set targets are published.

The performance of Hilton Worldwide in the year 2010 showed savings of 6.6% and 3.8% in energy and water usage respectively. There were savings of 7.8% and 19%, respectively in carbon emissions and waste generation as compared to the year 2008.

Source: HiltonWorldwide, 2012

The Starwood Hotels and Resorts committed to reduce the energy and water usage by 30% and 20%, respectively by 2020 as compared to that of 2008. Panasonic has partnered with Choice Hotels to develop low power consuming televisions, which have one fourth the energy cost when in off mode as compared to regular models.Choice Hotels International is a franchise organization with brands like Clarion, Quality Inn, Comfort Inn, Sleep Inn, Roadway Inn, Econo Lodge and Mainstay Suites. The multiplier effect of such initiatives can be gauged from the fact the savings obtained would be substantial when all of these hotel properties adopt the energy efficient device. Marriott

International has developed a comprehensive plan to lower itsoverall environ-ment footprint of 2.9 MT of CO_2 emissions. Its hotels worldwide have in the past decade installed fluorescent lights in place of more than four and a half million traditional light bulbs. It plans to have solar power in 40 hotels by 2017 (Zientara and Bohdanowicz, 2010). It is partnering with its main suppli-ers to offer greener products and to choose and design new hotels according to the Green Building Council's LEED standards.

Westin Convention Centre's Energy Efficiency Measures

Westin Convention Centre invested $120,000 for the installation of the keycard system at its property in Pittsburg. The keycard system activates the lighting and the HVAC system of the room as the guest enters and switches it off automatically all the power consuming devices as the card is removed on exit. In the first year after the installation of this system the energy consumption reduced by 10% and the investment made was recovered in just ten months period.

Source: Energy Star, 2007.

In the case of small operators their knowledge, attitude and the willingness to act play a determining role in whether the sustainability ventures are incor-porated in the management of the property or not. The stand-alone operators also do not have the projects to reflect upon and learn from and the financial resources too are constrained (Kleinrchert et al., 2012). The small operators also lack the access to capital to initiate green measures.

Small Operator's Big Savings

Leaf Lifestyle, a 1500 square feet wellness facility located in Santa Mon-ica, California offers personal training, massage services and nutrition consultancy. In 2010, it invested $750 on making minor improvements to its facility. The sauna was insulated to retain the heat for a longer duration. The traditional light bulbs were replaced by energy efficient lighting. The natural daylight was used by installing frost windows and taking off the blinds. This resulted in a reduction in the monthly electricity bill by 80% and led to $2400 saving per annum. The payback period in this case was less than four months.

Source: Goodman (2012)

The varied nature of the hotels and the facilities they provide onsite to the guests makes it difficult to devise a standard energy management systems for all types of hotels whether they are business hotels, part of an international chain or a small independent property.

Guests comfort and satisfaction should be in the forefront while making provision for any improvements. Thermal comfort has a huge bearing on the satisfaction level of the guest. So responsive heating, ventilation, air-conditioning and cooling system needs to be put in place to meet the guest's needs and at the same time being energy efficient. There should be sufficient but not excessive lighting in the corridors and staircases and exterior portions of the hotel to make the guest feel secure. Efficient light sources, occupancy controls and timers can achieve this objective. Indoor air quality should be monitored so that it is free of any molds and cleaning agent odors, so as to provide a healthy stay for the guest.

3.8   A GREEN APPROACH

The green approach (Figure 1) in hotels calls for efficient energy, water and waste management. The sourcing and hiring from the local areas would give impetus to the local industry. The efforts to mitigate the damage to natural environment—terrestrial as well as marine life, culture and heritage of the place would in the long run lead to sustainable tourism. The improvements in these spheres would lead to creation of more jobs direct as well indirect in this human resource intensive industry.

Hotels are income producing assets and the green initiatives if they help the company in achieving its financial strategic objectives, then they should be fully embraced and implemented (Jackson, 2010). It is important to improve the guest comfort, lower the operating costs, increase the life of the equipment and enhance the corporate image.

When tourists respect the local culture, preserve the heritage of the place they visit, buy meals and souvenirs made by local people and employ local guides for their trips then they boost the economy of the culture by providing avenues of jobs to the local people. The choice each tourist makes has a potential for making this world a more inclusive and sustainable place. Economic, social and environmental benefits can be derived by following the green approach by the hotels.

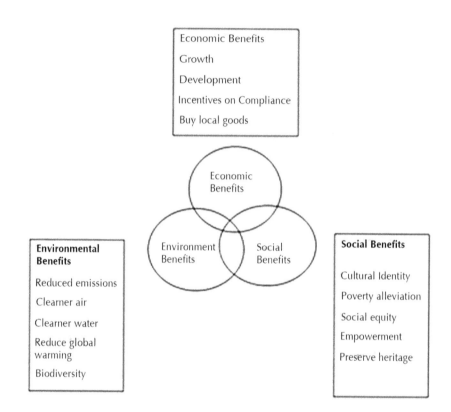

A Green Approach

FIGURE 1   A green approach.

The decision to choose the location to develop a new property, the building materials used and the operational decisions made are going to have an important impact on the world we live in today. The fact that hotel has a sustainable approach towards doing its business is fast becoming a differentiator with the environmentally conscious consumers in the competitive hospitality industry today.

As the hospitality and tourism industry is growing at a fast past pace and the fact that it consumes large amount of energy it becomes imperative for the hotel owners to adopt measures that would lead to a sustainable future. Whether it is a large hotel chain or a small operator the green initiatives are bound to be implemented sooner or later to differentiate the brand. The design of the hotel, use of renewable sources of energy, use of energy efficient fixtures and equipment, training staff to adopt energy efficient procedures and periodic maintenance of the installed equipment will go a long way in not only preserving the environment but also in the much needed financial savings. This chapter summarizes how the stakeholders can be made aware of and partners in this drive towards sustainability. The policymakers guidelines and encouragement towards sustainable use of resources would hasten the changes required. The case studies incorporated illustrate the ways and means through which various organizations are trying to make this world a better place to live in.

KEYWORDS

- energy conservation
- energy efficiency
- environment protection
- green hotels
- green tourism
- hospitality
- sustainability

REFERENCES

Accor Hotels (2013) 'Planet 21-Reinvent hotels-sustainable-Accor' (online) (cited 12 July2013). Available from <http://www.accor.com/en/sustainable-development/the-planet-21-program.html>.

Bohdanowicz, P. (2005) 'European hoteliers' environmental attitudes,'*Cornell Hotel and Restaurant Administration Quarterly*, 46:2, pp. 188–204.

Carbon Trust (2007) *Sector Review Hospitality: Saving Energy without Compromising Services*(CTV013), Carbon Trust, London.

Cespedes-Lorente, J., Burgos-Jimnez, J.D., and Alvarex-Gil, M.J. (2003) 'Stakeholders environmental influence: An empirical analysis in the Spanish hotel industry'*Scandivian Journal of Management*, 19:3, pp. 333–358.

Chan, W.W. (2005) 'Predicting and saving the consumption of electricity in subtropical hotels,'*International Journal of Contemporary Hospitality Management*, 17:3, pp. 228–237.

Chan, W.W (2009) 'Environmental measures for hotel's environmental management systems ISO 140001' *International Journal of Contemporary Hospitality Management*, 21:5, pp. 542–560.

Dalton, G. J., Lockington, D. A., Baldock, T. E. (2007) 'A survey of tourist operator attitudes to renewable energy supply in Queensland: Australia,'*Renewable Energy*, 32, pp. 567–586

Deng, S. M., and Burnett, J. (2000) 'A study of energy performance of hotel buildings in EN-ERGY STAR (2007) 'ENERGY STAR Building Upgrade Manual Chapter 12: Hotels and Motels' (online) (cited 9 June 2013). Available from <http://www.energystar.gov/buildings/sites/default/uploads/tools/EPA_BUM_CH12_HotelsMotels.pdf?5eca-3023>.

Goodman, M. (2012) 'EcoSpending'*Entrepreneur*, November, pp. 58–62.

Graci, S., and Dodds, R. (2008) 'Why go green? The business case for environmental commitment in the Canadian hotel industry'*Anatolia: An International Journal of Tourism and Hospitality Research,* 19: 2, pp. 251–270.

Green Hotelier (2012) 'Green Hotelier's Green Business Case Studies' (online) (cited 8 June 2013) Available from <http://www.greenhotelier.org/our-themes/new-builds-retro-fits/green-hoteliers-green-building-case-studies/>.

Green Hotelier (2012) 'LEED Platinum: ITC Grand Chola' (online) (cited 16 June 2013) Available from <http://www.greenhotelier.org/our-themes/new-builds-retro-fits/best-practice-itc-grand-chola/>.

Green Hotelier (2013) 'Siemens tells us about how luxury and integrated technology goes hand in hand' (online) (cited 8 June 2013) Available from<http://www.greenhotelier.org/our-themes/energy/siemens-tells-us-about-how-luxury-and-integrated-technology-go-hand-in-hand/>.

Heschong, L., Wright, R.L., and Okura, S. (2002), 'Daylighting impact on human performance in school'*Journal of illuminating Engineering Society*, 31:2, pp. 21–25.

Hilton Worldwide (2012) 'Positively influencing tomorrow' (online) (cited 15 June 2013) Available from <http://www.hiltonworldwide.com/corporate-responsibility/sustainably/>.

Hong Kong.'*Energy and Buildings,* 31:1, pp. 7–12.

Hotel Energy Solutions (2011) Analysis on Energy Use by European Hotels: Online Survey and Desk Research, Hotels Energy Solution project publication (online) (cited 26 July 2013) Available from <URL:http//hes.unto.org/sites/all/files/docpdf/analysisonenergy usebyeuro-peanhotelsonlinesurveyanddeskresearch2382011–1.pdf>.

Hrs Borkovic, Z., Kulisic, B., and Zidar, M.(2008), 'Energy Audit—Method for Energy Conservation in Hotels,'*Tourism and Hospitality Management*, 14: 2, pp. 349–358.

InterContinental Hotels Group (2013) Corporate Responsibility Report (online) (cited 25 July, 2013) Available from <http://www.ihgplc.com/index.asp?pageid=740&tools=glossary>.

International Energy Agency (2008) 'Energy Efficiency Requirements in Building Codes, Energy Efficiency Policies for New Buildings,' IEA Information Paper (online) (cited 23 June, 2013). Available from<http://www.iea.org/publications/freepublications/publication/Building_Codes.pdf>.

International Energy Agency (2013) '2012 Key World Energy Statistics' (online) (cited 17 June 2013). Available from <http://www.iea.org/publications/freepublications/publication/kwes.pdf

ITC Hotels (2013) 'Responsible Luxury' (online) (cited 16 June 2013) Available from <http://www.itchotels.in/itcgrandcholanew/responsibleluxury.html>.

Jackson, L.A. (2010) 'Toward a framework for the components of green lodging'*Journal of Retail and Leisure Property*, 9:3, pp. 211–230.

Kasim, A. (2004) 'Socio-environmentally responsible: Do tourists to Penang island Malaysia care?'*Journal of Hospitality and Leisure Marketing*, 11:4, 5–24.

Kleinrchert, D., Ergul, M., Johnson, C., and Uydaci, M. (2012) 'Boutique hotels: technology, social media and green practices,'*Journal of Hospitality and Tourism Technology*, 3, pp. 211–225.

Leslie, R.P.(2002), 'Capturing the daylight dividend in buildings: why and how?' *Building and Environment*, 38:2, pp. 381–5.

Maleviti, E. Mulugetta, Y., and Wehrmeyer, W (2012), 'Energy consumption and the attitude for the promotion of sustainability in buildings—the case of hotels'*International Journal of Energy Sector Management*, 2: 6, pp. 213–227.

Manaktola, K., and Jauhari, V. (2007) 'Exploring consumer attitude and behavior towards green practices in the lodging industry in India'*International Journal of Contemporary Hospitality-Management*, 19:5, pp. 364–377.

O'Hanlon, A. (2005) *Managing Energy: A Strategic Guide for Hotels (Sustainable Energy Ireland), Dublin, Ireland: Begley Hutton.*

Richard K. Miller and Associates (2010), *The 2010 Travel and Tourism Market Research Handbook.*

Robinot, E., and Giannelloni, J.L. (2010) 'Do hotels "green" attributes contribute to customer satisfaction?'*Journal of Services Marketing*, 24:2, pp. 157–169.

Sloan, P., Legrand, W., Tooman, H., and Fendt, J. (2009) 'Best Practices in Sustainability: German and Estonian Hotels' *Advances and Hospitality and Leisure*, 5, pp. 89–107.

The Economic Times (2012) 'ITC inaugurates Rs 1200 crore Grand Chola hotel in Chennai' (online) (cited 16 June 2013) Available from <http://articles.economictimes.indiatimes.com/2012–09–15/news/33862953_1_itc-grand-chola-chennai-airport-itc-group>.

The Economic Times (2012) 'Leela Palace hotel gets LEED platinum green building rating' (online) (cited 8 June 2013) Available from <http://articles.economictimes.indiatimes.com/2012–06–06/news/32078966_1_platinum-certification-leed-platinum-hotel>.

The Guardian (2010) 'The Savoy opens after pound 220 mn refurbishment' (online) (cited 8 June 2013) Available from<http://www.guardian.co.uk/travel/gallery/2010/oct/08/savoy-hotel-reopens-refurbishment-london>.

U.S. Department of Energy (2012) How Energy Efficient Bulbs Compare with Traditional Incandescents (online) (cited 25 July, 2013) Available from <http://energy.gov/energysaver/articles/how-energy-efficient-light-bulbs-comparetraditional-incandescents>.

UNCTAD (2010) 'The Contribution of Tourism to Trade and Development.'Note by the UNCTAD secretariat. TD/B/C.I/8 (online) (12 June 2013). Available from <http://unctad.org/en/Docs/cid8_en.pdf>.

UNEP (2013) 'Green Economy and Trade,Trends, Challenges and Opportunities.' (online) (cited 17 July 2013). Available from <http://www.unep.org/greeneconomy/Portals/88/GETReport/pdf/FullReport.pdf>.

Unruh, G., and Ettenson, R. (2010) 'Winning in the green frenzy.'*Harvard Business Review* *88*:11, pp. 110–14.

UNWTO (2013) 'Tourism Highlights 2013 Edition' (online) (cited 17 July 2013). Available from <http://mkt.unwto.org/en/publication/unwto-tourism-highlights-2013-edition>.

Warnken, J., Bradley, M., Guilding, C. (2004) 'Exploring methods and practicalities of conducting sector-wide energy consumption accounting in the tourist accommodation industry,' *Ecological Economics*, Vol. 48, 125–141.

Warnken, J., Bradley, M., Guilding, C. (2005) 'Ecoresorts vs. mainstream accommodation providers: an investigation of the viability of benchmarking environmental performance,' *Tourism Management*, Vol. 26, pp. 367–379.

Yildrim, K., Hidayetoglu, M.L., and Sen, A. (2012), 'Effects on sustainability of various skylight systems in buildings with an atrium,' *Smart and Sustainable Built*, 1:2, pp. 139–152.

Zhang, J. J., Joglekar, N.R., and Verma, R (2012) 'Exploring Resource Efficiency Benchmarks for Environmental Sustainability in Hotels' *Cornell Hospitality Quarterly*, 53:3, pp. 229–241.

Zientara, P., and Bohdanowicz, P. (2010) 'The Hospitality Sector: Corporate Social Responsibility and Climate Change' Tourism and the Implications of Climate Change: Issues and Actions,' *Bridging Tourism Theory and Practice*, 3, pp. 91–111.

CHAPTER 4

SUSTAINABLE TECHNOLOGY IN HOSPITALITY INDUSTRY: SOME FUTURE DIRECTIONS

PARUL WASAN

CONTENTS

ABSTRACT

Technology is the means with which Hospitality ensures better services for its customers and aids the growth of the industry. Growing number of tech savvy and environmentally aware customers and depleting profit margins have forced hospitality industry to look at sustainable technologies to bale itself out from these difficult situations.

Although, major technological trends have begun to play key roles in the hospitality industry from 'application environment and front office systems' to 'back-office and enterprise systems,' not much is visible in the academic literature. For the purpose of this chapter, technical literature from numerous technological vendors, working for installing new and/or upgrading the existing expertise, available in the public domain was used. This chapter proposes to identify sustainable technologies of the future in hotel operations and focuses on technological areas such as cloud based software systems, mobile/hand held computing devices, social media, analytics, etc.

The sustainable development strategy is that of the "triple bottom line," which combines economic viability with social responsibility and environmental protection (Elkington, 1997).

4.1 INTRODUCTION

There is a strong relationship between technology and hospitality industry. Technology is embedded in numerous ways in the operations in the hospitality industry. Technology is the means with which Hospitality ensures better services for its customers and aids the growth of the industry. *The strategic use of technology in marketing is one of the most significant opportunities the hospitality industry has at this moment* (Cline, 1999). Growing number of tech savvy and environmentally aware customers along with depleting numbers of hospitality personnel and profit margins are forcing hospitality industry to reconsider its processes and products. Hospitality industry is therefore looking at sustainable technologies to bale itself out from these difficult situations.

As the marketplace becomes more competitive, and building value becomes increasingly difficult, *hoteliers will need to work on many fronts at once. They will have to build analytical capabilities, keep up with advances in mobility and optimize existing touch point channels to apply technology strategically to create differentiated customer experiences* (Accenture, 2012).

As the focus on achieving more from less grows more intense, the question that consistently raises its head is 'how to do things faster, cheaper and differently; than how they were previously done.' The need of the hour is therefore to identify new ways and models of doings things that can add and create value in hotels of tomorrow. *Technology will likely be the most critical component of the value-creating model heading into the next millennium* (Olsen, 1996).

Additionally, growing environmental pressure from the governments and enforcement of extremely strict guidelines on environment protection have propelled the industry in revamping its systems both in the front office and in the back office operations, besides seriously considering green technologies.

Although, major technological trends have begun to play key roles in the hospitality industry from 'application environment and front office systems' to 'back-office and enterprise systems,' not much is visible in the academic literature. Save for isolated instances where academia has discussed the green applications, security and cloud computing in isolation, very little is available in a consolidated form for hoteliers to refer to. Although many hotel properties and chains have taken upon themselves to upgrade in the realm of technological advancements these have so far registered as isolated attempts on the firmament of hospitality industry as a whole.

Lack of appropriate and consolidated body of literature on galloping technological applications in hospitality industry has prompted this chapter.

For the purpose of this chapter, paucity of academic literature was offset by the availability of technical literature from numerous technological vendors in the public domain. These vendors are employed by the hospitality industry for the purpose of installing new and/or upgrading the existing technological expertise in the front office, back office, administration, operations, security (guests and data), services (F&B, laundry), etc.

Technology helps hospitality industry in reducing potential for services errors and its associated costs. In addition it enhances customer delight by increasing reliability, responsiveness, empathy perspectives and assurance. Hoteliers can manage the role of customers as 'coproducers' of services by incorporating IT and other technologies into production and delivery of services, thus raising or exceeding service standards. *This would allow firms to increase their operating profit through marginal price increases while being able to reduce the marginal costs (by reducing transaction costs) at the same time* (Chathoth, 2007).

'The digital era has transformed how consumers learn about a property and a brand, share information about it and book it. Technology helps define the experience that a guest has before, during and after a visit'(Loftus, et al., 2013).

For the first time in several years, insufficient IT budgets are no longer considered the biggest challenge facing hotel technology executives (Lodging Technology Study, 2013).

It is against this backdrop that this chapter proposes to identify sustainable technologies of the future in hotel operations of the hospitality industry. The chapter focuses on the following technological areas that are geared up to play a major role in creating future efficiencies streamlining processes in hotels and hospitality industry.

1. Cloud based software systems.
2. Mobile/hand held computing devices.
3. Social media.
4. Analytics.
5. Customized/personalized systems for the guests.
6. System and process integration in hotels.
7. Technology must account for a global perspective (Networks and scalability of global hotel chains).

In addition to the above through Green technology hoteliers can look at ways to improve sustainability in areas like energy efficiency, solid waste management, plastic and paper recycling, rainwater harvesting and water efficient technologies

4.2 CLOUD BASED SOLUTIONS OR CLOUD COMPUTING

The hospitality industry generates massive data and specialized information each day in numerous operational areas on its internal servers. Data and information management therefore becomes a top priority for the industry to increase operational efficiencies and profit margins. Therefore despite shrinking budgets, manpower shortage, highly dynamic markets and increasingly tech-savvy customers, globally, more and more hoteliers have begun to express interest in cloud-based hotel management solutions, with a hope of streamlining operations. *It has become critical* for the hotels *to stay ahead of the hospitality information technology curve. With cloud computing, organizations can extend the life of their existing systems with new innovations, improve time to market new systems through affordable pricing, and ultimately gain competitive advantages in the hospitality industry*(Hopkins, 2011).

Cloud Computing has been defined by The U.S. Commerce Department's National Institute of Standards and Technology (NIST) as *"a model for creating a convenient, ubiquitous, on-demand network, which is accessible to a shared pool of configurable computing resources and applications that can be swiftly provisioned and acted upon with a minimal amount of management effort or cloud provider interactions"*(Mell and Grance, 2010).

Depending upon the service requirement, different types of service models are used by the industry.

1. Infrastructure as a service (IaaS)—Examples of IaaS providers include: HP cloud, Google compute engine, Navisite, Rackspace, Amazon EC2, Ready Space Cloud Services and Joyent, Linode.

2. Platform as a service (PaaS)—Examples of PaaS include: Google App Engine, Windows Azure, Cloud Foundary, Force.com, Heroku, Engine Yard, Mendix, AppScale, OrangeScape, Jelastic, OpenShift, and AWS Elastic Beanstalk.

3. Software as a service (SaaS)—Examples of SaaS include: Microsoft Office 365, Petrosoft, Onlive, GT Nexus, Google Apps, CallidusCloud, TradeCard, Casengo, Marketo, and Salesforce.

4. Network as a service (NaaS)—This service includes bandwidth on demand, and a flexible and an extended VPN. Owners of the network infrastructure can provision a virtual network service to the third party through NaaS concept materialization (VNP–VNO).

On being asked "if they support moving their company's revenue management system to a cloud-based Software as a Service (SaaS) model, 46.3% of hoteliers agreed or strongly agreed that it's the right move" (Hotel Technology Study, 2013).

For the hospitality industry cloud computing ensures strategic advantage to the hotels.

4.2.1 BENEFITS OF CLOUD BASED TECHNOLOGY FOR HOTELS

1. An on-premise based IT system requires, constant maintenance, hardware update and purchase, while a cloud based system does away with all these activities. Its IT activities are managed by off-premises redundant servers. Hotels do not have to constantly scramble to update their systems because cloud software's ensure that there is an automatic upgrade implementation. The constant threat of compliance with the latest standards is thus taken care off. Therefore the implications on costs are tremendous and a saving of 45–65% are not uncommon (iTesso, 2013) for the hoteliers. They no longer have to earmark large sums of money for systems upgrade; instead they pay small fees for the cloud-based systems.

2. Unpredictable electrical outages upset the hospitality industry's efficient flow of operations, and although the guests may not feel it, the front office personnel are often left in limbo when his/her screen goes blank. Cloud based solutions do away with such an eventuality and ensure that there is continuous systems (service) availability.

3. Antivirus scanning can be an expensive computing resource operation. Also antivirus scanners typically require a lot of CPU and memory allocation. Computer resources of clients are spared the inconvenience of expensive process because (1) redundant and off-shore site backups of the data and critical information ensures that the data is safe from physical damage and that high levels of security are maintained at all times, and(2) The cloud automatically upgrades all the major web browsers for antivirus. It additionally scans the sites and warns the clients about possible harm that a malware may cause.

   For example, Google provides a cloud security service for Yahoo searches, and sites, which fail a Google antivirus check, receive a warning notice from the Yahoo search that the site may harm your computer. By using the benefits of scale, Google is able to provide and distribute an excellent and highly efficient form of cloud security. Google visits a huge number of sites regularly to index them for fast searches, and also analyzes the sites for malware using a variety of antivirus software (Walsh, 2009).

4. Most of the hotel staff needs to be trained only in the uses of the technology at the end level. This means that even non-tech savvy people at all levels can gain access to pertinent and mission critical data. Thus the cost of training them reduces considerably as the trained staff of the service provider does all the technical work.

An example of such a Technology would be Hotel Concepts' *The Enterprise Lodging system, iTesso*, the company calls it *"world's first cloud native hospitality technology solution, that will help reduce your total cost of* IT."

The company offers an integrated distribution property management system (IDPMS) with inbuilt functionality for controlling distribution channels besides other software on cloud for a small fee and requires only a Mac or PC with a browser facility.

Best Western International (Global), uses the cloud based hotel specific software of iTesso for total operations management including front desk, reservations, customer relationship management, reporting and invoicing, etc. Additionally, various other interfaces like the telephones, climate control, door locking system, room management, point of sale and central reservation systems are all managed through onsite terminals, workstations or simple windows servers at the hotel end.

4.2.2 APPLICATIONS OF CLOUD COMPUTING IN HOTEL INDUSTRY

The entire guest cycle in the hospitality industry can be taken over by a cloud based integrated property management system, distribution platform and central reservation system that can connect between a hotels CRS and GDSs, alternate distribution systems or act as a Property management system (PMS). Moving from an on-premise PMS system to an off-premise cloud based PMS system can accrue immense benefit to the hospitality industry in terms of costs, service availability, security, and latest software. Additionally, cloud computing ensures a flexible scale of computing power that can be distributed across different streams in a relatively short amount of time. It can also provide immediate access to hardware resources without needing any capital investments upfront, which greatly reduces the time requirements and cost of entry for hotels (Cruz, 2013).

'Interdependent feature' of tourism industry makes the companies in different sectors, that is, transportation, tour operators and hotel, heavily reliant on each other (Evans, et al., 2003). Hence, it requires various organizations in the tourism industry to work together as a value chain to add value and deliver product and services to the customer. The cloud opens up possibilities to partner with travel agencies, offbeat recreational companies, entertainment companies and others. This could facilitate guest attraction by coordinating the activities of various organizations in the hospitality industry and deliver exceptional product and service to the customer. This feature of cloud computing plays a great role in improving the overall service quality of the product that the consumers buy (Yilmaz and Bitici, 2006). It can help the hospitality industry to tie up with new eMediaries like the airlines, car rentals and hotels chains, etc., by allowing them to use their reservation systems, vertical industry portals (vortals)* and auction sites. Besides the Internet, GDSs can be further strengthened by the emergence of cloud based Platforms viz. Interactive Digital Television and mobile devices like tablets and phones, for example, recently displayed in a Hospitality Technology Exposition and Conference 2012, was a new mobile phone based check-in application, which allowed the guests to use their mobile phones and tablets as a room key.

Another **example** of a cloud based computing in the hospitality industry is Microsoft AZURE a cloud based development platform currently being used by the Intercontinental Hospitality Group (IHG). IHG uses this platform to integrate its IT services around the world for its data management and its 'GREEN ENGAGE' environmental initiative.

'GREEN ENGAGE' is an online sustainability system linked to IHG properties across the globe. Data about each site/property is fed into the system. The system then automatically generates reports and energy benchmarks. The hotel can then compare it with the best practices being followed by other hotels in the same climatic zones. Based on the issues raised in the energy report, 'GREEN ENGAGE' provides green solutions that cover every aspect of the hotel lifecycle ranging from picking up suitable sites (for new Hotels) to suggesting pro-environment cleaning materials for the hotels. It also trains the staff on sustainability. The return on investment, carbon reduction and potential impact on the guests is calculated for each action item suggested by GREEN ENGAGE. Finally, the system produces reports, which allow IHG to review an individual hotel's progress (IHG, 2013).

As of now, the in-house 'Enterprise Technology team' at IHG, has begun integrating two or more service models, to manage IHG data and contact centers, and other IT systems, to facilitate and maintain guest traffic across all its 4,600 branded hotels. This process further helps in simplifying access to all of IHG's global distribution systems, online booking platforms, reporting applications and other management tools. Additionally, by ensuring that its supply chain purchases energy-efficient equipment and implement Internet-based voice and data networks across the enterprise, IHG hopes to reduce the IT servers by 80%.

As cloud computing evolves many possibilities open up in future IT operations in the hospitality industry in *dynamic service pricing, system integration for quality inventory management issue control, and* controls for guaranteeing guest room availability (Official Blog of Hotel Ninjas, 2013).

4.3 MOBILE/HAND HELD COMPUTING DEVICES

A standard hotel guest is highly mobile and always connected. While customers use mobile devices/applications to interact with product and services in new ways, hoteliers look for mobile solutions to improve productivity and ability to collaborate. As the number of smart phones and tablet devices multiply so does the potential to harness the mobile technologies to streamline operations, and gather customer feedback. Mobile technologies can help hoteliers to develop an all-embracing mobile strategy which views the guest life cycle in totality. By evaluating how mobile applications and experiences can serve as a tool from booking to checkout, a hotelier can leverage technology to enhance the experience during the stay period. Additionally, by allocating more resources to mobile technology, a hotelier can accelerate revenue opportunities by the following methods.

(a) Reducing Service Response Time to Guest requests—Mobile devices equipped with hotel texting software enables staff to handle more guest requests in a short amount of time. Guests on the other hand can text staff members to make reservations or with a query without having to wait on hold. This can reflect in repeat visits to the hotel and improve their hotel experience.

(b) Improving Communications Between the Staff and With the Guests—Mobile hand held devices can be pre-programed with frequently asked questions among other things. With the help of this function the hotel staff can promptly answer guest queries. On the other hand any communication with the manager can remain confidential and may not cause embarrassment or disquiet in the public area.

(c) Increase Serenity in the Public Areas—Often employees talking on phones can be distracting to other people in a public area of the hotels and disastrous if the business calls turn to mundane topics. Mobile text messaging technology can contribute to the calmness of the public areas and restrict communications to relevant information only.

(d) Anywhere and Anytime Communication—This is an important function of hand held mobile device. With text-technology a hotel can improve its operational efficiency and response time by being able to reach an employee anywhere and anytime. This function plays a significant role in retaining the old customers, and less money is spend on acquiring new ones.

However, In mobile technology, efforts in mobile innovation have so far been focused on consumer-facing application development, with 42.7% of hotels currently offering a mobile application for consumer use, and another 22.5% planning to add one before mid-2013. As of now there's less impetus for employee-facing apps, although about 25% of hotel executives would prefer to access their company's revenue management software via a mobile app. As more and more GMs access real-time business intelligence to add transformative value to their decision-making process, the trend to develop employee-facing mobile apps on cloud based platforms, is likely to gain momentum as more vendors optimize their software for mobile dashboards. For example housekeeping and concierge perform an important function in a hotel. They are constantly on move and their services play a very significant role in providing a quality experience to the guest. A mobile device that connects them to the front desk can therefore be of tremendous help. Through this device they can instantly update the front desk about their location, send real time updates about the room readiness or respond to a customer request, problem or complaint without wasting too much time. Mobile platforms can be instrumental in increasing interactivity and building a stronger brand connection with the customer as data collected from them can be used for surveys or become part of the hotel's social media exercise.

Besides being sustainable mobile applications/hand held devices are also ecofriendly, for example by helping in keeping a track of different inventories in a hotel these devices can dramatically simplify daily operations and do away with endless amount of paper work. The hotel staff can also use their mobile devices to scan bar codes on various items of the inventory and can instantly account for its location, condition, and total numbers, thus making the inventory process more efficient and accurate.

An **example** of one such system of the future is InvoTech Systems, Inc.'s Advanced Management and Inventory Control System for commercial laundry, uniforms and linens, and security. This technology uses RFID chips that can be sewn onto the linen, uniforms and laundry. These then can be scanned by a hand held reader to expedite counting and tracking process. This means less time spent on manual handling.

Mandarin Oriental Miami is a 326 room 5 star property. It is a part of the Mandarin Oriental Hotel Group comprising of resorts, residences and hotels. It has recently scored 98.8 points out of 100 on an independent 'Safe and Sound' security audit, which the team credits to the SAMS Security System from InvoTech Systems, Inc. This hotel uses this security system for streamlining its security operations. This system is virtually paperless and saves the company money and resources, besides improving performance of the security organization. It systematically assures greater security for its employees and guests in the areas of keys and equipment tracking, managing patrols, security logs, lost and found, incidents logs and lockers and locks. In this way it prevents losses of valuables, reduces property liabilities as it documents incidents and security patrols, improves site security through visitor control, saves paper and provides guest satisfaction.

4.4 SOCIAL MEDIA

A study conducted by Peter O'Conner (2010) suggested that, presence of many hotel chains on the social media is not decisive which is to say that though they have a social media account they are not regular or active on it, nor do they respond to the criticism. He then goes on to say that traditional advertising approach on the Internet is no longer working for consumers, who are reacting in an unfavorable manner to these methods. Professionals, in the hospitality industry, aiming to improve contact with the customer, strengthen the brand image and enhance sales, are struggling to find a way through the constantly shifting maze of social media. O'Conner (2010) concludes by saying that given the way changes occur in social media, consumer statistics could already be changing and therefore it is critical for the hotel industry to: (a) seriously manage user generated content (b) change how it sells to consumers by taking into account consumers views reflected on user-generated content sites. With a systematic approach, a company can turn customer chatter into information—and information into strategy.

According to a new report by Globalwebindex, 82% of Facebook accounts are active users as compared to 62% for Twitter and 60% for Google Plus. At any given day there are more than 100 million users on Twitter alone posting messages from inane to insightful. This means a lot of comments and opinions in the ether. A report '2013 North America Hotel Guest Satisfaction Index Study' by J.D. Power, states that, *'among the most satisfied guests overall are those who seek out information through online hotel review sites and use it as the basis for their booking'* and *'although conventional word of mouth, friends and family remain the most significant factor in making travel decisions,*

- *1 in 5 have asked for an opinion online,*
- *1 in 5 are a fan of a company,*
- *1 in 5 are Twitter followers of a company,*
- *1 in 3 are posting pictures and reviews, and*
- *1 in 3 are somewhat influenced by social networks when making travel decisions*(Withiam, 2011).

Social media presents a golden opportunity for the hospitality industry to make greater contact with its customers, with an ultimate goal of developing a partnership for brand growth and development (Withiam, 2011).

Hotels all over the world and also a few restaurants have built their websites, to attract, engage and service present and future customers. A few have also optimized their sites for mobile apps. and search engines, with the aim of engaging the customers in a dialog about their likes and dislikes.

There are three ways in which hotels can target customers and enhance guest traffic.

1. Listen to the online conversations and proactively take the service to the next level.

2. By offering services online like those of Q and A, concierge, spa advice, travel desk, etc., a hotel can become a thought leader and add value to client engagement.

3. A constant vigil on the online trending on social media can help a hotelier identify unique business opportunities, brands and customer groups. By reaching out to them new business relationships, allies and channel partners can be developed.

The need of the hour is a comprehensive customer engagement strategy that will employ all social media, whether it's Facebook or Flickr, YouTube or Twitter, singly or together, and will also help a hotelier to keep an eye out for new applications and customer desires. By using all the social media channels or the 'Golden Triangle' a hotel property can saturate the search results page with its presence. Additionally by keeping a searcher's tendency in mind that they will not go beyond the first search page, a hotel can actually put itself on the top of the search list with hits for Twitter, Youtube, and Facebook or the 'Golden Triangle.'

This would further assist the hotelier to develop more targeted offers to attract customers to a specific property. And once on the property leverage this information to make the guest stay more memorable.

4.5 ANALYTICS

By developing analytics the hotels can fundamentally transform the way business discourses are conducted and decisions made in the industry. *Analytics drives insights, insights lead to greater understanding of customers and markets, and this understanding yields innovative brands, better customer targeting, improved pricing, and superior growth in both revenue and profits* (Accenture, 2012).

There is often a round the clock deluge of scattered data in the hospitality industry. Therefore, there is a need to collate and synthesize this information for meaningful purposes, to develop a deeper understanding of guest preferences, behaviors, expectations and requirements, and also to identify fresh opportunities to attract new guests and profitable segments. Hoteliers have to monitor performance of their property on all the social media channels in real time to respond to evolving consumer insights.

By using appropriate analytic methods, hoteliers can get a sense of what guests want generally and how they react to the hotel specifically. A survey conducted by Accenture in 2012, has short listed three areas from which data can be collected and analyzed.

- Often hotels attract a specific type of customer. It would therefore be profitable for the hotel if it could examine those factors that are instrumental in the customer decision making so as to develop better-targeted offers.
- Historical data about the purchasing behavior and preferences of the customer can be used to develop attractive offerings after the guest have checked-in on the property. This can be further facilitated by information harvested from third party external data points like 'Expedia.'
- A hotel's operational efficiency can be further enhanced and areas of improvement can be identified if the data from various functional and operational areas can be captured and evaluated.

Additionally, efficient analytics also enables the revenue management function to look at the revenue as an overall guest value rather than the room rates calculated in a traditional manner. Analytics helps hoteliers to use the captured data to develop new perspectives and insights about traditional loyalty programs, and understanding of the guests. Analytics also leverages information on the social media to understand (a) how their hotels and brands are faring in the real time, and(b) for comprehensive guest analysis. Additionally, data about the property operations can help the hotelier to identify improvements in both cost efficiency and effectiveness.

Although, there has been an increase in investment in business intelligence solutions; for improved decision making, more needs to be done. Leading analytic companies like the J.D Power and associates suggest aspects like consumer conversation analysis, market and trend analysis, brand and product analysis, and innovation analysis of the content on the social media by using web intelligence services.

Consumer comments on the social media and the Internet are unsolicited, unaided and unprompted. It is suggested that analysts consider chatter on the social media as unstructured commentaries of various social groups. Analysts would,however, find it challenging to establish a context of these comments. Therefore, for a detailed consumer conversation analysis, conceptually, analysts can develop a conversation segregation software to try an establish the context of different conversations taking place so that an analyst can go beyond the buzz with the help of monitoring software tools and identify the trends in consumer behavior pertaining to the industry.

Market and trend analysis of social media and Internet consumer comments often point out the service and technology gap between up-scale luxury hotel and regular hotels. Analysis of what is affecting the customer can help hotel properties to reconfigure their technology and service offerings. For example, leading luxury hotels often charge the guests on Internet usage, while a lot of regular hotels offer this service for free. Social media and the Internet comments reflect this dichotomy and so before this discontent becomes a customer uprising hotels need to take appropriate action.

Brand and product analysis on the other hand would sift through the Internet and social media chatter to identify those comments, which pertain to the value preposition being offered by the hotels. This would especially be true for the properties that place themselves in a particular niche' space.

An **example** of such a system is the Information Convergence and Analytics Services from Mphasis. It helps the hoteliers to control their information requirements and enables them to analyze, explore or discover disparate information. Services such as these; through data warehousing, enterprise search and data mashup engines, collate, correlate and analyze data through structured, contextual and exploratory analyzes. These services combine next-gen analytics with enterprise search to create user-friendly dynamic dashboards and applications for users to meaningfully analyze and correlate information from diverse sources. This result in a unified access to information, which contributes in driving revenues, building business insights, increasing competitiveness and cutting costs (Mphasis, 2012).

4.6   CUSTOMIZED/PERSONALIZED SYSTEMS FOR THE GUESTS

Customers and hotels are aware of the impact of personalized services on the guest satisfaction and revenue flow. A 2010 survey (Cunnane, 2010) indicated that 46% of the guests would welcome an alignment of customer and business requirements with IT for business optimization. This would imply commissioning customer interaction technologies that will pave way to cost control and provide differentiated customer experience. According to various sources (ResortSuit, 2013), *'Customization/personalization is the use of technologies that enable the dynamic insertion, customization or suggestion of content in any format that is relevant to the individual user, based on the user's implicit behavior and preferences, and explicitly given details.'*

A hotel achieves Guest-Centric Orientation (ResortSuit, 2013) when it operates keeping the guest's perspective in mind and delivers a compelling guest experience. A step in this direction would be to use fixed and variable guest information to create guest histories that help to define customer mix, categorize which benefits are important for different segments, increase efficiency and ensure that the hotel supply and capabilities match the guests' desires (Minghetti, 2003).

A guest-centric loop is established when both the organization culture and the information systems are aligned with a primary intention of maximizing guest experience throughout a guests interaction cycle. This can be further enhanced when personalization is overlaid on the guest-centric loop. When the guest-property information becomes bi-directional it increases ability of the guests to interact with the property in the manner they desire thereby increasing personalization of the services. Technologies that enable personalization provide three advantages to the spa, resort and hotel properties. First, it enables the guests to tailor their holiday experience. Second, it enables the property to analyze the pre and post stages of the guest-centric loop to encourage guest engagement and enhance guest experience. Third, the guests benefit during the stay because of increased access to information, services, and property amenities.

Personalization in hospitality is all about knowing your guests viz. their name, hobbies, allergies and other likes and dislikes. It is also about sending personal e-mails, confirming services and reservations, and serving their choice of drinks on arrival even before they are ordered. In tightly defined market segments personalization is also about developing special packages for the guest by mining information about them from databases.

In addition, when guest-centric technologies and personalization technologies come together they become a tool for hotels, spas and resorts with which to maximize Lifetime Guest Value (LGV) and drive business stability and revenue growth, besides developing long-term relationships with the guests and customers.

An **example** of one such technology is the Apple® based control automation. It integrates software solutions and media hardware for personalizing audio/video, communications, energy management and digital display in today's complex environments. Integrated solution providers like the Savant Systems LLC (Savant, 2013) were the first to offer native, IPhone, IPOD touch and iPad based applications to the hotel guests for complete in-room control and automation.

Another **example** of technology based applications is The Marlin Hotel Miami Beach Florida (The Marlin Hotel, 2011). This historic hotel was built in 1930s. It was upgraded to the 21st century in 2011, this time it updated its 15 guest suites and it's Bar to incorporate a fully controllable environment. Each guest upon check-in receives an Apple iPad, thus enabling him to customize room temperature, lighting, sound systems, window blinds. It also controls a preloaded film's library to be viewed on 60″ flat screen Apple Television sets hidden discretely behind mirrors in each room. The guests also have access to their very own media and data collections. The guests can also use an actual photograph of the room's interior on the iPad to gain precision control of the shades, light and media content in the room or the guest can use the 'home' button to activate various functions like art lighting, opening and closing of the window shades, etc. to create home away from home.

Once an Apple iOS device is docked, it seamlessly controls the customer user interfaces in the room by simplifying user control options by limiting or highlighting the visual functions.

Additionally this system guides the staff at the Bar to create a desired ambience for the guest by playing music from various sources and in different formats.

4.7   SYSTEM AND PROCESS INTEGRATION IN HOTELS

Despite tremendous advances in Internet technology, even today, a large number of people use traditional means like the telephone, word of mouth, fax, or online consultation and booking platforms to plan their travel itinerary. This implies that a potential traveler has to spend hours to register and re-register his/her personal information multiple times on various websites and then wait endlessly for the confirmation after making numerous payments to various service providers. Once across this error prone process, the traveler then faces similar situations even after checking into a hotel.

Hotels on the other hand face issues of managing guest experience by putting together the complete guest information; his/her travel itinerary, credit card details at various POS. In addition, hotels have to maintain an internal coordination in terms of technology and interpersonal interface to control the post visit fallout of the guest visit, that is, to say that hotels have to manage any negative publicity that may arise as a consequence of any negative guest experience. Both the tourists and hoteliers are therefore discouraged by disparate systems that have multiple touch points across the hotel. These make retrieving and linking guest profiles very difficult. This also matching on-property interactions with the information stored in CRM systems, call center logs and website visits an uphill task. A need for a seamless system that could integrate both their requirements and improve efficiencies across all the functional areas in the guest cycle and behind the scenes was therefore intensely felt.

The emergence of MAIS way back in 1996 tried to address the issues of collaboration of multiple intelligent software agents by providing a platform to enhance decision making through the use of different types of expertise. It integrated different agent type's viz. interface agents, task agents and information agents, which were considered necessary for supporting and seamlessly unifying information gathering from different Internet-based information sources and decision support systems.

Sycara and Zeng (1996) define these agents as*(1) Those which interact with the user receiving user speculations and delivering results (Interface agents) (2) Those which help users perform tasks by formulating problem solving plans and carrying out these plans through querying and exchanging information with other software agents (Task agents), and(3) Those which provide intelligent access to a heterogeneous collection of information sources (Information agents).*

Chiu, et al. (2009)have proposed a Collaborative Travel Agency System(CTAS) using MAIS framework. This system *adapts and coordinates collaborative agents with standardized mobile and Semantic Web technologies*. It also allows interoperability by combining varied data with web services technologies and the semantic web. *CTAS* (Chiu, et al., 2009)*offers layered framework that supports multiple platforms, especially wireless mobile platforms.* These technologies enable hotels to transition from function based to process-based systems of doing business and to respond immediately to time-critical information. Additionally, they assist disparate hotel systems to proactively push system data and important events directly to an intelligent messaging system to be shared by all the concerned persons or systems.

An **example** of such a system would be the eConnectivity middleware platform from Cendyn. It connects critical systems internally or across multiple hotels by interfacing with systems such as CRS, PMS, Sales and Catering, web booking engines, and back office and reporting. Systems such as these ensure seamless communication of reservations group and guest transactions. Additionally, platforms such as eConnectivity supports Enterprise Application Integration by: (1) checking for commonality between the new and old system (2) understanding the ways that could improve the legacy systems, and(3) formulating processes and procedures to prudently reuse the existing systems and at the same time add new data, applications, and processes. Further, when adding or migrating to new sets of applications becomes crucial in hotels, platforms of this nature often use the existing legacy system to improve communication between systems and to exploit e-commerce, extranet, internet and various other new technologies (Cendyne, 2013).

Among the few hotels and chains that have graduated to integrating systems and processes is an **example** of the CitizenM hotels, ever since its inauguration in 2008 at Schiphol airport in Amsterdam, it has incorporated technology in its every day operations. These hotels use technology integration both for creating a unique guest experience and also for lowering the operating cost. This seemingly impossible task is accomplished by unifying IP network environment where different applications interact with each other thus permitting a high level of guest personalization. Additionally, clustering of hotel and guest applications into a single network allows the hotel group to reduce its IT operations and maintenance costs.

These hotels have integrated wireless and wired infrastructure to accommodate applications and numerous hardware assets like the Check-in kiosks, LAN switches, CCTV cameras, room controllers, telephones, IPTV devices and streamers, etc. the data from the guests' on-line reservations is available at the time of check-in and in the guest rooms, any new information is also updated on the back room office systems of the hotel. Additionally, the staff freed from check-in paperwork, and cash processing now focuses on guest care especially in the Bar and Public areas, which invite them to feel at home. 'In terms of labor ratios, the hotel employs one full-time employee for every five rooms compared to the industry average of one full-time employee for every two rooms: a 60% savings on this important cost element.' The guests appreciate the novelty and anonymity of autonomous check-in at e-kiosk's, scanning RFID room cards for payment in the restaurant and in-room tablets to control room temperature, TV, ambience and wake-up time.

Further, with the help of cloud computing, the hotel chain has been able to move its PBX PMS and CRM systems to remotely hosted Data center to serve as a central resource to all the properties. The chain has thus saved future set-up costs. The Chain has streamlined its costs, benefited from economies of scale and developed a foundation for further business expansion throughout Europe, North America and Asia (Swisscom, 2013).

4.8 TECHNOLOGY MUST ACCOUNT FOR A GLOBAL PERSPECTIVE (NETWORKS AND SCALABILITY IN GLOBAL HOTEL CHAINS)

The better an organization can become at data integration, the better positioned decision makers—from marketing and sales to the C-suite—will be to appropriately synthesize and act on all disparate data sources. By leveraging internal and external data, a hotel can build a contextual understanding of the target guests. This entails linking data that is present with multiple service providers and in 'independent functional silos,' which could be both technology vendors and media agencies. Achieving relevance is at the heart of every hotel's operation, which essentially implies developing abilities to act in a precise and nuanced manner on the information gathered in the context of the target guest. Real-time segmentation of the guests provides an insight into guests'decision making and changes in intent at every stage. And, by using the economy and the flexibility that scalable global networks provide, a hotel can make this dynamic data more relevant, effective and affordable.

Technologies of future using Agile Service Networks on cloud hope to resolve the issue of scalability and integration in hotel technologies thereby ensuring a global perspective in the operations.

Through these types of technological networks, a hotel essentially deals with many different entities, including Software as Service platforms (SaaS), and Off and On premise service oriented applications in real time. Efficient working of such integrated systems depends upon appropriate and 'just-in-time' interaction between nodes. And depending upon the requirement, suitability and merits, different techniques for cloud-to-cloud, cloud to on-premise, and on-premise to on-premise integration can be used, either all at once or one at a time in a hotel.

The combination of these two technologies viz. agile service networks and cloud computing would ideally resolve the issues of vertical and horizontal scalability, and issues in business orientation through streamlined interactions between different organizations in the tourism and travel. Additionally, adding 'Infrastructure as a Service Platform'(IaaS) providers to the networks would enhance the total business value of the networks. Together, these technologies improve collaboration between users, and issues like storage or computing can be done away with. Besides decentralization of data storage and seamless sharing of cloud infrastructure, this web service technology efficiently facilitates the addition of new nodes to the network, which in turn decreases response time by reducing the marketing time for the organization (Zahedi, 2011).

A step in the direction would be to initiate such a process by analyzing the service networks through appropriate value networks tools and to further extend these networks to allow users (guests, hotels, associated service providers, vendors, etc.) to be a part of the value creation process in the supply chain. A futuristic service possibility would be to integrate the agile systems network of a hotel or hotel chain with numerous other systems networks' of hotels or hotel chains in its vicinity, across the country and internationally with the help of cloud technologies. Such an increased accessibility to customer information, through social media and various other online sources would benefit the adaption and design of agile services networks in the hotels and in the hospitality industry as a whole. These technologies allow business processes to spontaneously self-organize to enhance user satisfaction accurately; right at the first time of use. Additionally, the agile systems respond with the same alacrity during the course of service consumption and before the episodes of failures and breakdowns breakdown. Post, service consumption these systems speed up the incorporation of complaints and suggestions into business processes. Dynamic service design and flexible real time personalization provided by agile systems on cloud would thus enable hotels and the hospitality industry to move to a reputation-guided market system based on shared knowledge.

4.9   ECO-INNOVATION IN HOSPITALITY INDUSTRY

European Commission (2008) defines Eco-innovation as "the production, assimilation or exploitation of a novelty in products, production processes, services or in management and business methods, which aims, throughout its lifecycle, to prevent or substantially reduce environmental risk, pollution and other negative impacts of resource use (including energy)" (European Commission, 2008). Later, Oltra and Saint Jean (2009) defined eco-innovation as new or modified processes, practices, systems and products, which benefit the environment and so contribute to environmental sustainability (Oltra, Saint Jean, 2009).

The hospitality industry is characterized by high energy consumption be it in water, or energy. In the long run, the impact on the environment is usually considerable. There are numerous points of energy consumption in the hotel right from the front-office to kitchens, guest rooms, landscaping and more. Various studies have revealed that the most common practices of pro-environmental measures are undertaken in the areas of water conservation, waste reduction, and energy conservation.

'*Internationally, the most common formal environmental instruments applied by the hotel industry are codes of conduct, best environmental practices, ecolabels, environmental management systems (EMSs) and environmental performance indicators*'(Ayuso, 2006), however, futuristic step towards sustainable eco-innovation in the hospitality are in the direction of incremental changes and radical changes. It is a two pronged approach that is both cost and energy efficient and takes on a holistic view of ecofriendly transformation of hotels.

4.9.1 INCREMENTAL CHANGES

This approach taken by all the existing properties refers to gradual and continuous competence-enhancing modifications that preserve existing production systems and sustain the existing networks. Additionally it creates added value in the existing system in which innovations are rooted. An example of such exercise would be to gradually upgrade the hotel systems to cloud, wherein the existing hardware and software are aligned to storage and operational systems based in the cloud.

Another **example** of an incremental change would be the retrofitting of the 61-acre parking garage, of MGM Grand; Detroit, a four-diamond resort, with the 3,117 light-emitting diode (LED) lamps. According to Steve Zanella, President and COO of MGM Grand Detroit, this would reduce the annual energy use of the garage by 80%. It is one of the many energy conservation exercises initiated by the resort, as a part of the MGM Resorts *Green Advantage* sustainability platform.

Additionally, MGM Grand has also replaced energy consuming fixtures and technology with those that conserve the environment on its 160 acres of open lot parking area by installing 1,600 induction technology lighting fixtures, at its resorts in Las Vegas. *'With operating life up to 20 years these lamps are ideal for the hot Las Vegas climate. An estimated 2.7 million kWh will be saved annually following the project's completion'*(Hospitality Technology, 2013).

4.9.2 RADICAL CHANGES

This approach taken by new properties and refers to the replacement of existing components or the entire systems and the creation of new networks by adding value.

An **example** of this would be the new IHG Head Office at Broadwater Park, Denhams, UK. IHG, completely refurbished the new building by replacing the preexisting fitments, interiors and infrastructure with environment friendly material and technology. During the construction phase of the building, excessive use of electricity was curtailed by zoning the areas, and electricity was supplied to only those areas where work was going on. Besides reusing, and recycling on-site wastes, chipped timber was recovered for the fiber fuel as part of the recovery of non-recyclable materials. Around 91% of the total waste was reused or recycled at the end of the project. Low emission water based paints have been used on the walls of the new ecofriendly building. This building has solar perforated blinds attached to solar sensors, which automatically control the sunlight into the south, and west part of the building, this reduces glare by 62% and heat gain by 44%. Additionally, all preexisting lights in the building were replaced with LG3 compliant state-of-the-art energy efficient lighting to create optimum working conditions.

The new lighting is controlled with intelligent control mechanism, which includes daylight and movement sensors, which dim the perimeter lights when there is ample daylight and switch off the lights when the office is empty. Latest LED Cold Cathode and Fluorescent (CCFL) technology has been incorporated in all the Feature lighting. These put out additional 25,000 hours and last nearly 4 times long, it means a longer life span and increased energy efficiency (IHG, 2008).

As such eco-innovations are a mixture of elements of *dimensions of design, product/service business model, user and governance* (Carrillo-Hermosilla, et al., 2010). These dimensions have a significant role to play in recognizing the intricate features and the range of eco-innovations. According to Carrillo-Hermosilla, et al. (2010), eco-innovations scoring highly in the design of component addition but low in the design of system change can be expected to optimize existing process, leading to efficiency improvements and costs reductions while simultaneously reducing harmful impacts on the environment.

Example of such a '*design component addition*' is the customized NH key cards for guests, at the NH Hoteles in Spain. This way each guest as soon as he checks into his room would find the room lit and warmed according to his preferences. The project was developed by NH Hoteles in partnership with Siemens in 2008 to rationalize energy use. In addition to saving energy, NH managers believe that this system was a step in the direction of customized service that they provided to their clients. They felt this differentiated NH from their competitors. In addition The Hotel uses Green energy produced by 100% renewable sources like Bio-Mass, Geothermal, Sun and Wind and has installed a revolutionary system of producing energy from the up-down movements of the EcoEfficient elevators/lifts (NH Hoteles, 2013).

4.10 CONSTRAINTS EXPERIENCED BY THE HOTELS IN ADOPTING AND ADAPTING NEW TECHNOLOGIES

Ability to change in the hospitality industry depends upon many factors, viz. sophistication, competence and most importantly its history of action with technology adoption/adaption. Change often requires a reinterpretation of basic operational rules. Additionally, the hotel also requires time to publicize, carry out and adjust to new criterions, procedures and recommendations. Assimilation of new technologies often requires redefinition of roles and processes. This may act as a threat to (a) current business practices, and(b) individual roles and positions. It may also require (a) additional financial expenditure, and(b) prompt political maneuvering. Additionally, to function efficiently, clean technologies need large spaces, long gestation periods and knowledge of the subject, besides training and investors. Investors on the other hand find absence of innovative ideas a big constraint in the renewable energy and energy efficient sectors of clean technology (Ghosh, 2013).

A study conducted by National Research Council (US) Committee on Enhancing the Internet for Health Applications in 2000, identified two barriers viz. internal barriers and external barriers, that are responsible for an organization accepting or rejecting new technologies. Later authors likeKuruppuarachchi, et al. (2002) and Chan (2008) have found them to be true in the case of hospitality industry also. According to them both internal and external barriers may affect the technology adoption and adaption in the industry.

4.10.1 INTERNAL BARRIERS

According to NSCC (2004), internal barriers often impede efforts to carry out required change in an organization. Referred to as organizational inertia, this phenomenon is characterized by lack of responsiveness to internal and external environment, lack to competency and self-awareness and is marked by a reluctance to change. Especially in hotels with a long historical lineage, this inertia is due to (a) maintaining their heritage (b) large size, and(c) complicated internal hierarchies.

4.10.2 BARRIERS TO IT/EMS ADOPTION AND ADAPTION

In the case of IT adoption, *although many hotel managers admitted that IT offered many direct and indirect benefits, they preferred to maintain control rather than increase efficiency*(Leung and Law, 2012). Additionally, in case of IT as well as EMS adoption/adaption, because of limited exposure, internal politics, cost of implementation within the company, perceived difficulty in managing data and security threat, and lack of knowledge and adequate training mechanism and low support by senior management, most employees are reluctant to endure major changes in terms of adapting and learning that may accrue once processes relating to information technology or EMS are implemented. This stands true in the event where technology or EMS adoption is dependent on consensus building within the organization. Consensus building can take more time than it is required. This can become a barrier given the rapid pace at which technology changes. Constraints also develop because of genuine concerns about the new technology, as well as due to organizational apathy. Secondly, conflict often arises when management wavers between adoption of technology at local level or throughout the hotel chain.

4.10.3   OPERATIONAL BARRIERS

Majority of hotel buildings have been built during the periods when neither IT nor being Green were a priority. Converting these structures into IT enabled and Green buildings, therefore takes immense effort in terms of manpower, resources and cost layouts. Availability of (a) ecofriendly innovative materials, which are high-priced and difficult to source, and(b) vendors and experts who could translate the existing infrastructure into IT enabled and or ecofriendly building without shutting down the hotel are expensive and rare. Most hoteliers are therefore not comfortable in earmarking resources and efforts on IT and Green enabled practices, which except in few areas, have long gestation periods and therefore show no immediate results. Assuming that the desired changes are made, paucity of competent engineers, housekeepers, IT experts, vendors, contractors, landscape maintenance staff and managers that understand environmental systems, procedures and products hinder the smooth running of the operations.

4.10.4   FINANCIAL BARRIERS

Hospitality industry and hotels in particular often have to face stiff financial barriers while upgrading their existing infrastructure. Lack or readily available finance affects a hotel's innovation capacity (Gorodnichenko and Schnitzer, 2010). It further limits the capacity of large and small hotels to invest in technology. This aspect is especially true for domestic hotel groups and companies, who, as compared to the international hotel companies, face difficulties in their innovation activities because of costly and problematic access to external finance. Numerous reasons are cited for this anomaly, main being, careless financial records, unclear titles of the property, confusing data about future projections and unclear understanding of the firms capacity vis-à-vis the external environment

4.10.5   HUMAN RESOURCES BARRIERS

Advent of Web 2.0, technologies have increased the travelers' access to multiple data sources (Buhalis, 1998). This has further complicated the already complex situation for the hospitality industry, who is struggling to adopt and adapt the new technologies on various fronts. Web 2.0 brings with it a complex web of social media interactions, which if efficiently managed can enhance the image of the property and at the same time make it the chosen destination of travelers. Harnessing the social media expertise, and also further enhancing the capabilities, of the employees, especially those falling into the category of Gen X, can improve efficiency and bottom lines of the hotel.

Additionally, the challenges HRM faces in this flux can only be described as mammoth. The industry is striving to develop articulate and adaptable employees who can deliver the brand promise and at the same time be technologically literate and in-sync with the expectations of the tech-savvy customers. Law and Jogaratnam(2005) in the context of Destination Marketing Organizations have said that until *tourism-related managers fully understand innovative technologies and have the ability to use them...can these communication tools be effective for destination promotion.*

Although nearly all of the top managements in the industry are aware of the possibilities of the new technological advancements and what it can do to improve the efficiency and the hotel bottom line, this information seldom percolates down to the frontline workers at all the levels of the organizations, resulting in zero awareness about the need to know and understand new technologies (Lee and Wicks, 2010). Scant attention is paid to upgrade technological skill set of the employees at the work place. Additionally, no opportunities/encouragement is given to the employees to upgrade their skill levels, relating to emergent technologies at their own initiative (Lee and Wicks, 2010). Strassmann(1990) and Sigala, et al. (2001) have tried to identify possible reasons for 'low familiarity of technology' by the employees and the 'reluctance of the management in adopting new technologies.' Employees perceive that all forms of technology are difficult to use/learn and, therefore work-involving technology should be left to the experts in the area. Management, especially those of small and medium enterprises, on the other hand, perceive new technologies as an additional cost, besides lack of qualified instructors and paucity of funds inhibit small and medium hotels to develop their own off-the-job training programs.

4.11   EXTERNAL BARRIERS

External conditions are those in which the hospitality industry and the hotels in particular operate and define their expertise to capitalize on Information Technologies, Internet, and Social media. These conditions can be identified as market forces, laws policies and standards, technology and finance. In an ideal condition these work in synchronized manner resulting in a profitable enterprise. However, these also act as barriers.

> *Owners will continue to assess deferred maintenance spending at the property level, while changes in governmental regulations will present hotel companies with new restructuring and tax considerations (Ernst and Young, 2013).*

4.11.1   MARKET FORCES

The market place of the hospitality and tourism industry is undergoing a systematic segmentation. Terms like health tourism/health spa, sports tourism/sports spas, adventure tourism/hotels for adventure minded, eco tourism/eco-friendly hotels, game resorts in game reserves, Disney resorts within Disneyland, etc. are no longer a novelty in the hospitality industry. Any fluctuation in the costs or changes in the consumer preference in these areas can put immense pressure on the hospitality industry of the region, hosting these niche hotels. A positive change could boost demand (act as a stimuli for transformation), while a negative change can affect the viability of the technological (green/IT) upgrade (act as a barrier). In both the cases the industry would face interface considerations. Additionally, shrinking operating margins due to economic down turn, increased regulatory requirements, absence of coherent business model pertaining to technology inception and demonstrably low financial returns on investment, have been the reason for poor technology adoption in the hospitality industry.

4.11.2   LAW, POLICIES AND STANDARDS

Multiplicity of laws, central oversights, regulations, technical standards and professional guidelines are largely outside the purview of the hospitality industry. They are among the policy barriers that the industry faces on day-to-day basis. These constraints impede the business opportunities that could have been created through information technology applications. For example policy relating to broadband use for civilian purposes could restrict Internet technology interface at the existing and future hotel properties, and thereby impact the bottom line of the hotel. Additionally, regulations on data security can create barriers for information transfer across public communication networks acting as disincentive for the industry. Despite a visible push to introduce green technologies in the policies, specifics and standards of green technology have not kept pace with the latest development. This has created immense gap between the law/standards and the implementation.

4.11.3 FINANCIAL FACTORS

Although hotels continue to attract considerable investor interest, the economic uncertainty has shaped how investors target their investments, as they focus on cities with strong leisure and corporate demand drivers (Ernst and Young, 2013).

Financial aspects play a significant role in hospitality industry, especially if they pertain to tax and transactions, even in its most simple form namely the outright sale purchase of assets. Hospitality industry sometimes faces perverse mechanism for funding its projects. Viewed as 'rich man's indulgence,' financial institutions often put across difficult to follow terms and conditions. Hoteliers, owing to capital constraints, find creative ways to fund their projects. For example hotel developers are using the EB-5 program in USA. It is an immigrant investor visa category, which has been created for foreigners in USA, willing to invest in a business that can create minimum 10 permanent local jobs per investor (USCIS, 2012)

Various direct and indirect taxes and levis imposed on the industry under various heads like property tax, transfer tax, etc. further complicate the situation. For example in India the Hospitality sector falls under the State Government purview, and the Central Government offices only have an advisory role to play. This adds on to the existing financial woes of the industry. Additionally, a lot of electronic equipment namely computers, processors, routers, sever and networking fiber-optic equipment, and energy saving devices like lifts (elevators), etc. in few other countries, come under the luxury head and hence are taxed accordingly. For Small and Medium Hotels, this further acts as a dis-incentive to modernize beyond the basic level, thereby limiting their ability to fully use the capability of the information technology.

4.11.4 CUSTOMER BARRIER

Hospitality industry is usually driven by customer demand and although the customer clamor for more efficient data processing and security system, has driven the industry to improve its IT applications, the lack of awareness among the customers regarding the green technology has resulted in the hotels lagging in implementing EMS systems in a big way. A study carried out by Barsky, 2008, indicated that green issues, and eco-initiatives were important for the luxury hotel guests but they were of very low priority for guests on small budgets, looking for value for money. These guests, unlike the luxury hotel guests, were not willing to pay extra for the support of the green cause. Additionally, studies indicate that many hotels perceive that guests associated green practices are cost cutting exercises that result in fall in hotel standards, and that having a green credential negatively impacts their hotel (Silano, et al., 1997; Tzschentke et al., 2008)

4.11.5 TECHNOLOGY

Rapidly changing technology has itself become a barrier to change in the hospitality industry, which finds it hard to keep pace with the innovation and to juggle costs of constant change. As mentioned earlier in the chapter, significant changes in technology can create major upheavals in the organization, as this process is both expensive and time consuming. In terms of HRM constant orientation and training takes its toll on the HR performance. While in terms of finances it makes the existing investments obsolete and undermines the organization's performance. Bilgihan, et al.(2011) have quoted Yeh, Leong, Blecher, and Lai, 2005 in saying 'It is known that IT implementation, changes and updates can be costly,' and may have major implications on hotel operations (Sigala, 2005), and customer service.

4.11.6 CONSTRUCTION CHALLENGES AND BARRIERS

Numerous hotel groups and stand-alone hotels are now in the process of converting their existing properties or/are building new properties according to ecofriendly and IT enabling guidelines. Accordingly, they face numerous challenges and barriers in this endeavor.

Ad-hoc Industrial Advisory Group of the Energy-efficient Buildings PPP (2013) in its draft proposal has identified the following challenges and barriers that come in the way of constructing an energy efficient building. The major challenge that has been listed by the advisory group is to reduce carbon emissions by 90% and energy consumption by 50% by the year 2050 through sustainable business growth powered by affordable and durable services and new or refurbished buildings. It also calls for amplifying and accelerating the *collaborative research and innovation efforts to comply with energy demand reduction in buildings. It further reinforces the value chain optimization approach* (ECTP, 2012) in the following areas: (a) gaps that exist between *performance by design* and *performance when built* (b) innovations in material processing to reduce CO_2 footprint during the life cycle of new buildings (c) building envelops for efficient use of renewable energies (d) resizing energy equipment for optimizing real time supply and demand (e) increasing quality and productivity of construction workers by combining prefabrication of important components and automation/self-inspection of construction tasks (f) customizing building energy management system to synchronize with the customer use and (g) optimizing the reuse and recycle of the demolition waste

The draft report also highlightsvarious constraints faced by the building and construction industry owing to the ongoing economic and financial crisis in the world viz. *less purchasing power, and increasing building costs due to more stringent requirements to meet building energy performances, productivity of the workers, and interface costs.*

4.12   ROLE OF GOVERNMENT IN TECHNOLOGY ASSIMILATION

The role of Government in promoting technology relating to hospitality can be envisioned on the following fronts:

1. Technologically upgrading the existing feeder institutions/colleges of hospitality, either through grants or industry-academic partnerships. This would result in technologically savvy human resources development.

2. Government can also encourage the technology industry to develop newer hospitality related technologies through innovation or R&D. A

key issue here would be to develop a separate policy relating to hospitality and technology in hospitality.

3. Additionally, create a separate section in the technology ministry that deals exclusively with the technological developments in the hospitality. The main focus of this section would be to influence and guide companies in the hospitality sector to steer their policies, both at a national or international level, towards developing and manufacturing products and processes that improve environmental sustainability and industrial competitiveness.

4. Supporting the existing hospitality industry in its quest for technological upgraded by offering sops for adopting new and better technologies. Additionally, the government can (a) do away with multiplicity of laws and bylaws that cause hindrance to the growth of the industry, and(b) enforce stricter compliance and control over ISO 14001 environmental norms through regular environmental audits in a manner that is not detrimental to environment or the industry.

5. Rationalization of taxation laws and surcharges pertaining to service and luxury tax.

6. Rationalization of import duties on items that are comprehensively used in the hospitality industry.

7. Rationalization of labor laws, especially those deal with the hiring and firing of the employees. Additionally, give a tax breaks for employee training and development programs.

4.13 CONCLUSION

The key to building and maintaining customer loyalty in hospitality is to create a friendly and safe environment through superior services. Technologies that help to deliver such services not only help make way for new revenue opportunities but also enable the industry to gain a competitive edge, and enhance the guest experience. Galloping advances in information technologies coupled with a rapid progression towards service oriented engineering and agile and lean software development have greatly challenged the IT professionals in this industry. Already at the receiving end of limited resources, they are also required to meet the challenges of the unpredictable markets, and changing customer requirements, with feature rich and lasting dynamic technological solutions that do more for less.

Market forces in the consumer space drive new expectations from guests about how they want to interact with hoteliers. The continuing wave of change in business and technology represents an opportunity for hoteliers to focus their strategic technology investments for extending the reach of their brand and deliver more personal and relevant experiences to guests. Technology will play a key role, whether that involves using analytics to know and satisfy guests' expectations better than a competitor, pushing the possibilities of mobility or orchestrating all guest interaction channels to create more relevant experiences. Hoteliers must tightly manage and integrate consumer experiences by consistently creating relevant experiences across all channels (digital, social, mobile, traditional and in-person) and geographies, through a seamless array of digital channels and personal interaction points.

The trade-off that managers need to consider at this juncture is the insignificant increase in price and the operating costs of new technology versus the add-ons in the transaction costs and a loss in profit margins caused by not integrating new technology in the production process. Targeting investments in digital capabilities with analytics, mobility and relevance in mind can help the hospitality industry prepare for an increasingly competitive and buyer-driven market.

Although the hospitality industry has begun to accept the need for technological and green innovations, it is constrained by various internal and external factors that limit the pace of EMS and technology adoption/adaption. It is here that the government can intercede by streamlining and rationalizing numerous laws, regulations and technical standards pertaining to design, land acquisition, environment and labor.

Lastly it would be beneficial for the hoteliers to be critically aware of evolving transactional, operational and developmental environment in which the industry is steadily being maneuvered by the dynamic technologies around the world. Not only is it ensuring a standardization across different segments within the industry, it is also becoming a tool for wealth and knowledge creations, which if effectively harnessed and synchronized with the ever changing technological, HRM, and operational landscape, can auger tremendous growth for the industry.

*Vertical Industry Portal (vortal) is a portal website that provides information and resources for a particular industry. Vortals are the Internet's way of catering to consumers' focused-environment preferences. Vortals typically provide news, research and statistics, discussions, newsletters, online tools, and many other services that educate users about a specific industry.

KEYWORDS

- analytics
- cloud computing
- customization
- mobile technology
- process integration
- scalability
- social media

REFERENCES

Accenture (2012)'Getting personal with digital: Mastering the digital revolution in the lodging industry'(online)(cited 14th July 2013). Available from<http://www.accenture.com/us-en/Documents/PDF/AccentureGetting-Personal-Lodging-Master-Digital.pdf>.

Ayuso, S. (2006)'Adoption of voluntary environmental tools for sustainable tourism: Analyzing the experience of Spanish hotels,'*Corporate Social Responsibility and Environmental Management*, 13:4, pp. 207–220.

Barnes, F. (2007)'A sustainable future starts in the present,'*Caterer and Hotelkeeper*, October, 197:4495, p. 37.

Barsky, J. (2008)'Understand importance of green to guests,'*Hotel and Motel Management*, October, pp. 1–3.

Bilgihan, A., Okumus, F., Nusair, K., andCobanoglu, C. (2011) Barriers to Information Technology Change Project in Hotels (online)(cited 25 November 2013). Available from <http://scholarworks.umass.edu/cgi/viewcontent.cgi?article= 1276&context=gradconf_hospitality>

Buhalis, D. (1998)'Strategic use of information technologies in the tourism industry,'*Tourism Management*, 19, pp. 409–421.

Carrillo-Hermosilla, J., Del Río, P., andKönnölä, T. (2010)'Diversity of eco-innovations: Reflections from selected case studies,'*Journal of Cleaner Production*, 18:10, pp. 1073–1083.

Cendyn(2013)'eConnectivity: Connect critical interfacing systems'(online)(cited 15 August 2013). Available from <http://www.cendyn.com/econnectivity/>

Chan, E. S. W. (2008)'Barriers to EMS in the hotel industry,'*International Journal of Hospitality Management*, 27:2, pp. 187–196.

Chiu, D. K., Yueh, Y. T., Leung, H. F., and Hung, P. C. (2009)'Towards ubiquitous tourist service coordination and process integration: A collaborative travel agent system architecture with semantic web services,'*Information Systems Frontiers*, 11:3, pp. 241–256.

Cline, R. S. (1999)'Hospitality 2000—the technology: Building customer relationships,'*Journal of Vacation Marketing*, 5:4, pp. 376–386.

Cruz, Xath (2013)'Opportunities for the Hospitality Industry in Cloud Computing'(online)(cited 19 July 2013). Available from <http://cloudtimes.org/2013/04/17/opportunities-for-the-hospitality-industry-in-cloud-computing/>

Cunnane, Chris (2010)'Property Management integration: Redefining the role of PMS in hospitality'(online)(cited 4 August 2013). Available from<http://www.tblat.com/facebook/pdf/aberdeenpms.pdf>

Dev, C. S., and Olsen, M. D. (2000)'Marketing challenges for the next decade,'*Cornell Hotel and Restaurant Administration Quarterly*, 41, pp. 41–47.

ECTP (2012)'Energy-efficient Buildings PPP beyond 2013: Research and Innovation Roadmap'(online)(cited 25 November 2012). Available from <http://www.ectp.org/cws/params/ectp/download_files/36D2263v2_E2B_Roadmap_Infodays_V.pdf>

Elkington, John (1997)*Cannibals with Forks: Economic Prosperity, Social Equity and Environmental Protection*, London, Capstone.

Ernst and Young (2013)'Global hospitality insights: top thoughts for 2013' (online)(cited 25 November 2013). Available from<www.ey.com/Publication/vwLUAssets/.../Top_thoughts_for_2013.pdf>

European Commission (2008)'Call for proposals under the Eco-innovation 2008 program,'*DG Environment*(online)(cited 26 July 2013). Available from <http://ec.europa.eu/environment/etap/eco-innovation/library_en.htm>

Evans, N., Campbell, D. and Stonehouse, G. (2003)*Strategic Management for Travel and Tourism*, Oxford, Butterworth-Heinemann.

Ghosh, Aparna(2013)'Alternate Energy-Clean Tech Markets: Green Shoots and Headwinds, *Enterprise, Mint*, Thursday, November 28, 2013, Delhi, pp. 18.

Gorodnichenko, Y., andSchnitzer, M. (2010) *Financial constraints and innovation: Why poor countries don't catch up* (No. w15792). National Bureau of Economic Research,

Hopkins, Gregg (2011)'Why the Cloud is Right for Hospitality'(online)(cited 19 July 2013). Available from <http://www.hospitalitynet.org/news/4051622.html>

Hospitality technology (2013)'MGM Grand Detroit Completes One of Nation's Largest LED Parking Garage Retrofits'(online)(cited 26 August 2013). Available from <http://hospitalitytechnology.edgl.com/news/mgm-grand-detroit-completes-one-of-nation-s-largest-led-parking-garage-retrofits87955?referaltype=newsletter>http://www.hospitalitynet.org/news/4051622.html>

Intercontinental Hotel Group(2008)'Our Office: A step towards sustainability'(online)(cited 25 July 2013). Available from, URL: http://www.ihgplc.com/files/pdf/cr2008_denham_report.pdf>

iTesso, Enterprise lodging system (2013)'Products, iTesso Benefits'(online)(cited 18 July 2013). Available from <http://www.itesso.com/itesso.html>

Law. R., andJogaratnam, G. (2005)'A study of hotel information technology applications,'*International Journal of Contemporary Hospitality Management*, 17, pp. 170–180.

Lee, B. C., and Wicks, B. (2010)' Tourism technology training for destination marketing organizations (DMOs): Need-based content development,'*Journal of Hospitality, Leisure, Sport and Tourism Education*, 9:1, pp. 39–52.

Lodging Technology Study: Hotel Technology in 2013, Supplement to Hospitality Technology magazine (online)(cited 22 July 2013). Available from <http://hospitalitytechnology.edgl.com/reports/2013-Lodging-Technology-Study-83590>.

Loftus, Paul, Boushka, Mike, andPruvot, Anne (2013)'Transportation and Travel: Mastering the digital revolution in the lodging industry'(online)(cited 22 July 2013). Available from<http://www.accenture.com/SiteCollectionDocuments/PDF/AccentureOutlook-Mastering-digital-revolution-in-lodging-industry-Travel.pdf>

Mell, P., andGrance, T. (2010)'The NIST Definition of Cloud Computing,'*Communications of the ACM*, 53:6, p. 50.

Minghetti, V. (2003)'Building customer value in the hospitality industry: towards the definition of a customer-centric information system,'*Information Technology and Tourism*, 6:2, pp. 141–152.

Mphasis an Hp Company (2012)'Hospitality and Travel services'(online)(cited 25 August 2013). Available from<http://www.mphasis.com/pdfs/Hospitality%20and%20Travel%20Services.pdf>

National Research Council Committee (NSCC, US) on Enhancing the Internet for Health Applications: Technical Requirements and Implementation Strategies (2004)'Networking Health: Prescriptions for the Internet; 4, Organizational Challenges to the Adoption of the Internet,' Washington (DC): National Academies Press (US.) Available from <http://www.ncbi.nlm.nih.gov/books/NBK44715/>

NH Hoteles'(2013)'Learn about NH Hoteles' environmental action plans'(online)(cited 26 July 2013). <http://medioambiente.nh-hoteles.es/en/start>

O'Connor, P. (2010)'Managing a hotel's image on TriPadvisor,'*Journal of Hospitality Marketing and Management*, 19:7, pp. 754–772.

Official Blog of Hotel Ninjas (2013)'How Cloud Computing Has Changed and Continues to Transform the Hospitality Industry'(online)(cited 19 July 2013). Available from <http://blog.hotelninjas.com/2013/06/07/how-cloud-computing-has-changed-and-continues-to-transform-the-hospitality-industry/>.

Olsen, Michael D. (1996)*Into the new millennium: A white paper on the global hospitality industry*. Paris: International Hotel Association.

Oltra, V., Saint Jean, M. (2009)'Sectoral systems of environmental innovation: an application to the French automotive industry,' *Technological forecasting and Social Change* 76, pp. 567–583.

ResortSuite(2013)'Personalization—The new expectation in hospitality customer service, A ResortSuite White Paper February 2013'(online)(cited 4 August 2013). Available from <http://www.resortsuite.com/pdf/Personalization.pdf>.

Savant (2013)'About Savant'(online)(cited 4 August 2013). Available from <http://www.savantsystems.com/>.

Swisscom (2013) System Integration: Case studies—Citizen hotels (online)(cited 15 August 2013). Available from <http://www.swisscom.ch/en/business/hospitality/system-integration/case-studies/citizenm-hotels.html>.

Sycara, K., and Zeng, D. (1996)'Coordination of Multiple Intelligent Software Agents,' International Journal of Cooperative Information Systems, 5, pp. 2–3.

The Marlin Hotel (2011)'The Marlin Hotel, Miami Beach FL'(online)(cited 4 August 2013). Available from <http://www.savantsystems.com/mydocuments/0050010_marlin_hotel__view.pdf>.

US Citizenship and Immigration Services (2012)'EB-5 Immigrant Investor'(online)(cited 25 November 2013). Available from <http//www.uscis.gov>

Walsh, P. J. (2009)'The brightening future of cloud security,'Network Security, 10, pp. 7–10.

Withiam, G. (2011)'Social networking websites and the hospitality industry: holding the tiger by the tail,'Cornell Hospitality Research Summit Proceedings, 3, pp. 6–15.

Yilmaz, Y., andBititci, U. S. (2006)'Performance measurement in tourism: a value chain model,'International Journal of Contemporary Hospitality Management, 18:4, 341–349.

Zahedi, M. (2011)'Agile Service Networks for Cloud Computing. A thesis in partial fulfillment of the requirements for the degree Master of Science in Software Engineering,' Amsterdam, The Netherlands.

CHAPTER 5

MARKETING SUSTAINABILITY IN THE HOSPITALITY AND TOURISM INDUSTRY

MEGHNA RISHI

CONTENTS

ABSTRACT

In 1955, Peter Drucker discussed that sustainability is an important concept for the discipline of marketing and these thoughts found cognizance with that of the World Trade Organization, which noted that marketers in the hospitality and tourism industry must concentrate on sustainable tourism product as well as practices, since sustainability protects as well as creates opportunities for the future. Contemporary literature from the past decade (year 2000 onwards) indicates that marketers, not from a philanthropic perspective, must approach sustainable tourism, but from a strategic vision, since hospitality and tourism industry leads to substantial damage of the overall ecosystem. In this light, this chapter establishes sustainability as an imperative in the hospitality and tourism industry and discusses layers of issues, around establishing sustainability, which need to be addressed by the marketers. This chapter makes significant contribution for the academic literature as well as for the practitioners, by elaborating on the 'Sustainable Tourism Marketing Mix (STMM), which was initially propagated by Pomering et al. (2011). The STMM discusses the application and relevance of ten marketing elements, which could strengthen the sustainability focus for marketers. Examples of players within the hospitality and tourism industry, who have been successfully implementing various elements of the STMM, thereby setting a precedent with industry best practices, have also been discussed, from across the globe. This chapter hence establishes the criticality of the adaption of sustainability in the hospitality and tourism industry and also offers an insight into the consumer behavior and preferences towards Sustainability in this vibrant industry.

5.1 OPENING VIGNETTE[1]

"On July 19, 2009, then Environment Minister of India, Jairam Ramesh, greeted Hilary Clinton at ITC Green Center (Delhi, India) where the main agenda for both Dr. Manmohan Singh (Prime Minister, India) and Barack Obama's (President, USA) administration was to devise proactive strategies for thoughtful application of green technology, a subject that has shown its presence in the global discussion on climate change. ITC Green Center has been the building of the future due to its early adoption of sustainable

[1]This vignette is an excerpt from the case study titled 'Green Management and Environmental Sustainability: A case of ITC Green Centre' which has been published in the Emerald Emerging Markets Case Studies, Vol. 1, No 2, pp. 1–20. The case was co- authored by Meghna Rishi. The full reference of the case study is cited in the references list of this chapter.

construction and one of the members, who were involved to make this vision of ITC possible is Mr. Niranjan Khatri, GM WelcomEnviron initiative. It is one of the largest buildings built in an area of 1,70,000 square feet. It has platinum rating from US Green Building Council in the year 2005.

Ms. Clinton gave huge complements and support to the path that ITC, as a company, consciously chose, to make the future more sustainable for generations to come. She highlighted the commitment that Indian Private Companies along with government of India is making towards sustainable future:

Thanks to all of you for making us feel so welcome, once again, here in this historic capital, and particularly in this remarkable building. As you notice, other than the lights that are up there for the television cameras, there are no lights on. And there are so many features of this building that really demonstrate the viability of the kind of low-carbon but very attractive and efficient approach to saving energy and doing it in a way that, as we heard, saves water and solid waste, and certainly lower the carbon footprint. The tour that we have, the information that we were given, certainly underscores the importance of the ITC commitment and the partners who work with ITC. The ITC Green Center may not be a regular stop on the tourist map, and no one would confuse it with the Taj Mahal. But it is a monument in its own right. This Green Center not only represents the promise of a green economy, it demonstrates the importance of partnership between India and the United States in the 21st century. And today the Green Center is one of 11 buildings in India that has earned the elite platinum designation, the highest you can get. Now, certainly the business leaders with whom I have spoken are talking about how the private sector can play a role, along with the Government. Just consider the potential here. If all new buildings were designed to the same standards as the ITC Green Center is, we could eventually cut global energy use and greenhouse pollution by more than 20%, and save money at the same time. We need to scale up our efforts. We need to move from the smart design of individual green buildings to the smart design of whole communities to the retrofitting of buildings and communities, which will then lead to cities and countries. While improving energy efficiency is critical, it is only half the battle. We also need to accelerate efforts to bring clean power to the people of India by expanding the use of renewable energy, particularly for rural electrification, so that hundreds of millions of men, women, and children will have real energy options.

I will find inspiration from the ITC Green Center, this monument for the future. It uses half as much energy as conventional buildings, and energy saving means that it will pay back its additional up-front costs in only six years. So, this building is a model of environmental stewardship and economic develop-

ment, all wrapped up in one. And it is an inspiration. And it will keep us going through the long days and nights of actually hammering out an agreement, one that is fair and understanding, and doesn't sacrifice economic progress, one that we will be proud of, and one that we will then be able to tell our children in generations to come, When the crisis was upon us, we took action, and we took it together." (Singh et al., 2011)

5.2 SUSTAINABLE HOSPITALITY AND TOURISM MARKETING

Hilary Clinton's speech reaffirms the relevance of Sustainability and Environmental Value, in the global context. "Sustainable tourism marketing aims to create awareness about pro-sustainability products, and to increase their purchasing" (Wherli et al., 2013). As a concept, it emerged in 1980 s when literature started drawing the world's attention towards sustainable development and when it was realized that tourism as an industry, contributes potentially towards the "negative impact on environment and social fabric of destination." In 1987, the World Commission declared sustainable development on Environment and Development (WCED, 1987) as a mission that has implications for "environmental health, economic viability and social equity." In 1955 World Trade Organization defined sustainable tourism as the activity, which equips marketers in meeting the needs of the tourists as well as the host regions in the present time, such that enhancement and protection of opportunities could be done for the future (World Trade Organization, 1995). WTO suggests that Sustainable Tourism leads to the *"management of all resources in such a way that economic, social and esthetic needs can be fulfilled while maintaining cultural integrity, essential ecological processes, biological diversity and life support systems."*

Ogilvy PR and Totem Tourism (2011) highlight the comprehensive nature of sustainable tourism by defining it as a *"global approach to tourism that covers planning, development and the operations of tourism; that recognizes the wider negative impacts generated and attempts to increase positive impact along each of the four pillars of sustainable development (environment, social, cultural and economic)."*

Sustainable tourism, hence, is not just a concept, it is a complex process, that considers the impacts of tourism on the present as well as the future, and simultaneously works on making places better for people to visit as well as to live.

Peter Drucker, in 1955 emphasized that sustainability should get a place in the discipline of marketing by noting that the management of an organization must judge the value of their actions based on the capability of the action to promote public good and simultaneously on its capacity to make contributions to the society's stability and strength (Druker, 1955).

Almost two decades ago researchers like Pettie (1992); Coddington (1993) and Shrivastava (1994) also emphasized on the marketing of sustainable establishments by suggesting that organizations eventually lead to the systematic destruction of environmental value and no longer could they be treated merely as a "system of production." McDonagh (1998) took this perspective forward and suggested the importance of "developing a communicative process to facilitate ecological change."

From the perspective of the Tourism Industry, Hetzer (1965) proposed the term "Ecological tourism" and identified four strengths of "Eco Tourism," namely, reducing environmental impact, respecting local culture and minimizing harm to the same, maximizing benefits of economic nature for local communities and increasing tourist satisfaction. In 1983 Ceballos-Lascurain offered solution for the conservation of Northern Yucantan Wetland and used the ideas of "ecotourism" for the same. Research in coming years also focused on heritage tourism and issues of conservation and capacity management (vis-à-vis visitor numbers) (Cossons, 1989) were discussed. In the 1990 s researchers understood the implications of sustainable tourism and literature evolved in this area. May (1991) noted that hospitality and tourism developers need to become aware about the concerns around protection of environment and 'sustainability.' Ruschmann (1992) considered conservation and sustainability as a resultant of "ecological tourism infrastructures" and Klemm (1992) noted that sustainable development needed collaborative efforts. Carter (1993) cited in Eccles (1995) wrote, "If third world countries are to continue using tourism as a money-earner then a sustainable approach is needed."

Contemporary literature has made these views more pointed by enumerating the harmful effect, on the planet, of some specific industries. Gossiling, 2009 cited in Pomering et al. (2011) suggests that especially the tourism industry must take serious action towards Green Concerns as it is responsible for 5% of the emissions that accentuate changes in the climate. Polonsky et al. (2003) conceived this as the "Harm Chain" meaning that if tourism industry does not take cognizance of the harm implicated by each partner in the tourism chain, including the organizations, suppliers as well as the tourists, it would lead to a compounded effect converting the value chain to harm chain., Pomering et al. (2011), note that the solution to the envisioned environmental "Harm Chain" lies in the adoption of Sustainability Tourism Marketing Mix (STMM).

To evade this negative impact, it is important that all tourism-related activity partners coordinate their activities such that "Sustainable tourism marketing management" enables "social, economic and environmental well-being" (Gilmore and Simmons, 2007). This requires an organization's focus on making not just the micro environment sustainable but essentially addressing the "macro environment factors in marketing" which are designed to propel sustainable consumption (Kotler et al., 2006). Kaul and Gupta (2009), second this proposition and suggest that efficient planning and management are the cornerstones in controlling and monitoring the development of the growing tourism industry. Such controls constitute the elements of Sustainable Tourism and are critical "to conserve the biodiversity of tourist destinations." Belz and Peattie (2009), Mitchell et al. (2010) and Choi and Ng (2011) have elaborated that sustainable marketing is beyond the much discussed "Green Marketing" because of its broader orientation, which looks at not just the environmental dimension but synergies the same with the economic and social concerns as well.

Globally as well strategic planning for sustainable tourism is promoted at the level of Trade Blocs. Hospitality Marketers are encouraged to develop an all-encompassing approach to ensure that sustainability is viewed from a turn-key perspective. An example can be found from the ASEAN-Association of South East Asian Nations (The Regional Trade Bloc). For the Trade Bloc the ASEAN Green Hotel Award is granted half yearly, to tourism organizations, which exhibit the following:

Environment Friendly policies
- ✓ Green product usage
- ✓ "Air quality management"
- ✓ "Solid waste management"
- ✓ Water and Energy efficiency
- ✓ Local community collaborations

In the year 2012, 71 hotels in the ASEAN countries received the award and were encouraged to continue sustainability practices.

5.2.1 SUSTAINABLE TOURISM MARKETING: ITS RELEVANCE

Tourism as an industry contributes around 10% to the world income and it offers employment to about "one tenth of the world's workforce." In the third world countries, tourism is used as an economic development tool due to its capacity of employment generation and its influence on improvement of local infrastructure (Eccles, 1995). Alongside the numerous benefits of tourism, including its capacity to generate profits for the region and create memories for consumers, it also impacts the environment and has the capacity to disrupt the ecosystem. Sometimes, when the development in tandem with tourism is rushed, product life cycles as well as the environment are ignored (Eccles, 1995). Hence, it is imperative to weave sustainability in tourism to offer it the capability of conserving landscapes and protecting regions, which might otherwise be spoilt by industrial development (Ogilvy and Totem, 2011). The sustainability initiative has to be evolved because it offers a balance between local circumstances and local expectations and advances in environment and technology management (UNEP, 2005). Zinkeviciute (2009) suggest that sustainable tourism marketing is essential as it aims at minimizing further damage to the macro environment by addressing travel and tourism industry's impact on rising pollution levels, climate change, biodiversity decline, consumption of natural resources and waste accumulation.

Marketing of tourism traditionally has focused on creating smooth and efficient flows and exchanges between the tourists and the tourism industry players. It has in the process, avoided the negative impact that the industry implicates on "externalities" such as environment, society and culture. Therefore sustainable tourism marketing is considered an advanced approach which integrates these externalities into a "living system analysis" (Jamrozy, 2007); "a whole of destination approach" (Russel and Faulkner, 2004) and creates "sustainable economic development" (Van Dam and Apeldoorn,1996) and "sustainable communities and living systems." Mackenzie (2012) and Sheth et al. (2011), have even addressed sustainability as a "marketing paradox" but have highlighted that it is the only sensible way towards organizational growth. Jamrozy (2007) offers an elaboration to this and notes,

"Although redefined and addressing multiple stakeholders, the standard marketing definition still focuses on micromarketing activities, while a more sustainable approach to marketing first explores the role of marketing in the larger (macro) living system, where a simple exchange process between the company and customer is replaced with interdependent interactions and functions of a larger tourism system. Then role of marketing is connecting stakeholders in a complex system rather than merely creating advertising strategies."

Sustainability as an agenda in tourism marketing has to be viewed at a 360-degree initiative since it aims at organizational growth through an ethical path. It entails undertaking not just good practices but making appropriate investments "and challenging the premise that growth at any cost is a viable model" (Mackenzie, 2012). Usurped.

5.3 DIMENSIONS OF SUSTAINABLE TOURISM

Researchers exploring the area of sustainability, over the years have suggested that it has multiple dimensions. These dimensions are all expandable to business strategy level (Dyllick and Hockerts, 2002), have relevance from the economic perspective as well (Kranjc and Glavic, 2005) and have also been dovetailed in to a "corporate responsibility model" by Ketola, 2008. Choi and Ng (2011) also suggest that dimensions of sustainability (especially environmental and economic dimension) play a strong role in consumer preferences during the purchase decision. Sheth et al. (2011) refer to the concept of sustainability as a comprehensive one, indicating "triple bottom line" formulated by the popular 3Ps-"Planet, People and Profits." Before this Andriate and Fink (2008) also articulated the Triple Bottom Line and said that it helps in capturing competitive advantage through "social equity, ecological integrity and financial profitability." These dimensions of sustainable tourism marketing, are described below:

5.3.1 ENVIRONMENTAL SUSTAINABILITY

Environmental concerns and issues have emerged across the globe, in the form of acid rain (Eastern Europe), destruction of habitat, rising of sea levels and increase in droughts as well as floods. Literature focuses on "green marketing" and highlights under it the role of environment friendly products as well as environment friendly consumer behavior. Jamrozy (2007) suggests that promoting sustainability through environmental marketing is possible when "hospitality and attraction industries favor recycling, energy savings and other environmentally conscious activities. Environmental Marketing can go a step further when creating a new environmental consciousness that promotes preservation and conservation in the future."

5.3.2 SOCIO-CULTURAL SUSTAINABILITY

Socio-cultural dimension of sustainability, which does not get addressed by simple "green marketing" relates to concerns about the well-being of communities, society and people, which are viewed as "noneconomic form of wealth." It intends to find an equilibrium between society's needs and personal needs. It also finds solutions to strike a balance between human needs and the capacity of nature to support human activity without harming the ecosystem. Dinan and Sargeant (2000) suggest that marketing initiatives, like promotional campaigns, can drive socio-cultural sustainability by offering behavioral cues to tourists, thereby encouraging behavior that "benefits the society at large."

5.3.3   ECONOMIC SUSTAINABILITY

Sheth et al. (2011) describe the economic dimension of sustainability as the "impact of consumption on economic well-being of consumers associated with financial aspects such as debt-burden, earning pressures and work-life balance." This explanation takes into consideration not just the financial bottom lines/profits but also "the economic interests of external stakeholders, such as broad-based improvement in economic well-being and standard of living." Though all explanations on sustainable marketing suffer from the paradox that marketing as a discipline, typically promotes consumption and cannot hence bring about sustainability but researchers now look at the "macro-marketing challenge" (Kilbourne et al., 1997) which is about developing "sustainable consumption and quality of life." Practitioners and marketers however, do not usually look at dimensions of sustainability, not from a strategic, long-term perspective (Sheth et al., 2011). Barring a few exceptions, for most organizations, environmental sustainability is more compliance driven and initiatives towards social and economic dimensions of sustainability are "reactive and opportunistic" which get executed through programs falling under the larger umbrella of Corporate Social responsibility—CSR.

5.4   MARKETING MIX FOR SUSTAINABLE TOURISM

Marketing Mix for sustainable tourism requires elements that promote sustainability through inclusiveness (Pomering et al., 2011). Marketing sustainability in the tourism industry requires circumspect selection of the elements in the Marketing Mix. This helps hospitality marketers in "responding to the demands of environmentally conscious stakeholders, a planet in ecological crisis and the risks of litigation and regulation" such that market growth and profitability are also maintained. The marketing mix for sustainable tourism helps marketers in achieving "long-term economic sustainability and growth" which is a resultant of their environmental policies (Smerecnik and Andersen, 2011).

The next section elaborates such elements of a marketing mix, which promote sustainability by enumerating 10 marketing Ps. Application of each of these Ps, has been illustrated through industry examples from across the globe, in the next section. Each illustrative case offers an insight on how players from the global hospitality and tourism industry are weaving sustainability in their marketing mix. Elements of the STMM have also been elaborated within each illustrative case.

5.5 ELEMENTS OF SUSTAINABLE TOURISM MARKETING MIX: IDEAS IN PRACTICE

5.5.1 PRODUCT

Tourism Product must be envisioned, not just as the private product but also the Public product. The Public Product entails the social and physical environment, like streets, parks, weather, etc., whose negative effects, the tourism managers must reduce through relevant collaborations with the Government. When sustainability is weaved within the Tourism Product, the marketing manager focuses on the Internal aspects as well as the external aspects of the product. These include for example, internal initiatives as rating/certification processes, setting up audit processes and external aspects setting up paper-free reservations, creating a website which promotes sustainability among the consumers, etc. The element of Product receives more clarity through Illustrative Case 1.

Illustrative Case 1: *Matahari Resort and Spa, Indonesia: Eco-Product, Sustainable Communication.*

Matahari Resort and Spa, Bali, Indonesia is a luxury resort. It has been the recipient of ASEAN Green Hotel Award, thrice in a row from 2008 and is believed to be setting the highest standards for the future. Through the following initiatives, the hotel ensures the delivery of a sustainable product (Matahari Beach Resort and Spa, 2013):

- The hotel owns a "closed water cycle" which is capable of extracting as well as recycling water. The hotel also operates a "biological water treatment plant" which purifies the waste/recycled water and uses it for the gardens and parks in the resort. These initiatives are truly futuristic since global water consumption is estimated to double after every 20 years. Also, it is essential to conserve water since global water demand is 17% higher than the actual supply (Walker and Walker, 2012). Another reason for the hotel industry to essentially innovate environment-friendly water consumption practices, lies in the fact that consumers tend to use water with greater ease, when they stay at hotels (Darmame and Potter, 2011). Also daily washing of bed and table linen adds to the consumption levels (Billings and Jones, 2008).

- The hotel uses water-softening system that leads to lower water consumption. Research documents that when detergent is premixed with water, before water is pumped into the washers, it leads to almost 30% savings in water usage (Walker and Walker, 2012). Matahari Resort and Spa, have been quick to adapt these findings since all the hotel's laundry gets automatically dosed.
- Solar energy is used to heat water thereby conserving electricity consumption.
- Sustainability is also dovetailed in the menu offering as unprocessed and natural products are promoted in the cuisine. Here the hotel serves as a fine example of collaborating with local communities (*Partnership of STMM*) since it sources its herbs from partner plantations and local farmers, in turn, educating them as well, about producing through eco-friendly measures.
- The hotel team communicates this with its stakeholders through Social Media Platforms, visibly as a positioning strategy as well as an initiative to induce bookings. The hotel team quotes on Facebook:
  "We are proud that our efforts with the environmental principles and our harmonious relationship between communities of surrounding residents have been so highly recognized. We shall contribute to work hard to provide the best possible benefits to our guests together with excellent environmental performance and upgrading the green image of the hotel"

5.5.2 PRICE

The price which the tourism managers garner from consumers, must take into account the negative implications (to sustainability) of the tourism product. Batra (2006) suggests that for sustainable tourism development, the price must be "high enough to cover costs involved in putting right any damage caused by the tourist to the environment" and "to pay for the resources consumed by the tourist." It is essential hence to educate consumers such that they are brought to the level of willingness to pay for the external damage, caused by tourism. Billings and Jones (2008), also suggest that when consumers are charged for excessive use of resources (like water), it acts as an automatic deterrent to un-sustainable practices.

Illustrative Case 2: *The Tourism Industry: Sustainability and Pricing.*

Airlines induce voluntary payments from consumers, as a part of the ticket cost, for the carbon emissions resulting from the travel. Tourism managers can easily propel this practice forward by sensitizing consumers. Elaborative and explicit communication is essential to achieve this as consumers typically find it challenging to identify sustainable products mainly because many such sustainable elements might not be experienced directly by the tourists.

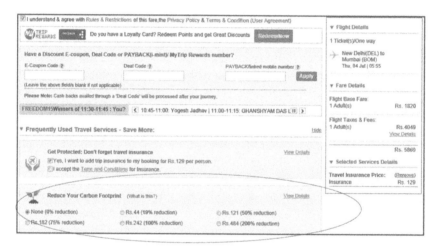

[2]**FIGURE 1**   Snapshot from a travel portal, inducing voluntary payment for carbon footprint reduction.

Figure 1 is a snapshot from an Online Travel Booking website—www. makemytrip.com.

It can be seen in Figure 1 that when consumers book a ticket (as visible on the right side of the figure), the airlines ask for a voluntary monetary contribution that could help in the reduction of the carbon footprint by up to 200%. These initiatives are in congruence with consumer preferences, which have been surfacing since the past 6 years. In the year 2007, a study conducted in Britain revealed that 34% holiday makers were willing to spend more money to facilitate reduction in their carbon footprint (Aitken, 2007). In the year 2011, a research conducted among 219 North Americans revealed that their purchase intentions are not significantly affected when firms with "poor environmental sustainability" reduce their prices (Choi and Ng, 2011). This is in contradiction to the findings of Beeton and Benefield (2002), who suggest that "price is inversely related to demand," indicating that aware consumers do not get swayed by the combination—lower prices and compromised sustainability.

Clearly hence, consumers are getting sensitized towards sustainability and pricing as an element of the STMM, can be determined accordingly. Conversely, however, it is also true that there is little literature suggesting similar consumer intentions from other parts of the world. It is necessary, therefore, to educate consumers about matters relating to travel and sustainability.

5.5.3 PLACE

In the parlance of tourism, place represents the tourism value chain, including travel agents (online and others), tour operators, transport providers, accommodation providers, etc. All partners of the Place element can contribute in reducing the carbon footprint on the tourists' travel by promoting transportation options like walking, cycling, sailing and public buses/trains. Tour operators can also play a role in directing tourist decision towards destinations and organizations with a sustainability product and focus. Findings in Mintel (2009), offer motivation for sustainable Place strategies by proving empirical evidence of tourists' desire for "slow travel" (Dickinson et al., 2011), through lesser environmentally damaging," lower carbon alternatives" like "land travel instead of air travel."

Illustrative Case 3: *Atlas Voyages, Morocco: Marketing Sustainability through the Place element.*

The Place element in tourism helps in formulating the "Total Experience" for consumers. Rishi and Gaur (2012) explain that "before deciding to stay in a luxury hotel, customers today explore the total experience that the property offers, in terms of, accessibility to popular markets, parking spaces available at the hotel and even the ease of hailing a cab from the hotel. Further a repeat purchase, by a hotel guest, is not just dependent on the stay experience at the hotel, but also on the experience that the customer has with the auxiliary services (transportation available to reach the hotel, the availability of tickets to the destination, hotel booking available on the Internet, etc.)."

It is therefore essential that sustainability is woven through the entire tourism value chain. An example of the same is offered by the Morocco based "inbound tour operator"—Atlas Voyages.

Atlas Voyages was established in 1964 and has over 12 branches across UK (Atlas Voyages, 2013). The tour operator has contributed significantly towards "developing regulations for food safety and hygiene" in Morocco, which in turn has supported Morocco's overall objective of attracting more tourists, by highlighting the place as environment friendly and with regulations that meet international standards (Tour Operators Initiative, 2003)[A].

Atlas Voyages developed a "suppliers' hygiene control campaign" for 17 hotels and restaurants which the company identified as its key suppliers (based on the frequency and volume of the business). The campaign focused on quality control for food as well as hygiene. Atlas Voyages requested Cristal Society, specialists in HACCP (Hazard Analysis and Critical Control Point), to conduct four visits at each supplier, to increase the awareness among the suppliers about hygiene issues. The following steps were taken during the campaign:

    i.   An audit of the suppliers' facilities and procedures was conducted by Cristal Society.

    ii. Cristal Society created a provision for a policy document on procedures and standards

    iii. Cristal Society also offered specific recommendations to each vendor, about improving hygiene, performance and quality.

    iv. Follow-up visits were conducted to ascertain whether all suppliers adhere to the recommendations and guidelines.

    v.   Annual visits are conducted regularly to these suppliers' facilities to ensure adherence to quality.

    vi. Atlas Voyages focuses its next phase of the campaign towards "energy saving and waste-recycling."

The customers of Atlas Voyages are also engaged in the process and the initiatives of Atlas Voyager as well as the suppliers, are highlighted, thereby maximizing the efficacy of the campaign.

The entire initiative has helped Morocco at the legal level, as well as at the official level by helping the country in building generalized rules, which abide by the international standards. The country updated the existing regulations and the entire program also helped Morocco in understanding the international tourists' expectations. The campaign executed by Atlas Voyager sensitized other suppliers as well, and *"OFPPT, a national training and certification institution, confirms that there is now a long waiting list of Moroccan hotels that have applied for HACCP audit and certification."* The country's objective of attracting more tourists through the unique selling proposition of "a strategy for protecting the environment," is getting largely fulfilled by the wheel of change, that Atlas Voyager has churned.

5.5.4 PROMOTIONS

Besides using Promotions as a means to communicate the brand message to the Publics, tourism marketers could further use these in four ways.

- To position their organization on the sustainable solutions it offers.
- To motivate consumers to include sustainable tourism product in their choice set and as their final purchase decision.
- To promote "environment-friendly practices" among tourists like insisting on lower water consumption by especially in the washrooms (Billings and Jones, 2008)

"Ecological Footprints" can be reduced when tourism managers use new media vehicles extensively in their media mix. Reducing the use of collateral like brochures and pamphlets and inducing consumers to download a soft version of the collateral, against some sales promotions like discounts, also go a long way in reducing the ecological damage.

Illustrative Case 4: *TUI, Nederland: Promoting Sustainable Tourism in Netherlands Antilles (Caribbean), through its 'Environmentally Aware Tourism' Project.*

TUI AG or the 'World of TUI' is the leading travel group of Europe, which operates in three sectors-"TUI Travel (tour operating, online sales, airlines and incoming agencies); TUI Hotels and Resorts and TUI Cruises"(TUI AG, 2013). TUI Nederland is the leading operator in the Dutch market and is a part of the World of TUI (TUI AG). In the year 1999, TUI Nederland began the ,'Environmentally Aware Tourism' Project, which was solely aimed at improving and promoting sustainable tourism in Curacao and Bonaire (Islands of Netherlands Antilles)(Tour Operators' Initiative, 2013)[B].

TUI Nederlands devised an integrated marketing communication plan to promote responsible travel. The project (campaign) included the following elements:

- **Voucher Booklet:** Customers, who chose a holiday to Curacao or Bonaire, are provided their air tickets in a Voucher Booklet, which offers details on how "environmentally sound practices," could be adopted, throughout the travel.
- **Engagement Through Videos:** KLM, the Dutch Airlines, is one of the partners of TUI Nederlands, for this project and during the flight lasting nine hours, travelers are shown a video that promotes the sustainable activities as well as sustainable excursions.

- **Resource Book in Hotel Lobbies**: All hotel lobbies are supplied with the "TUI Nederland Resource Book." This book motivates the travelers to choose sustainable excursions and attractions, and directs them towards the same.
- **Flyers and Brochures:** Flyers and brochures are available at all tourist destinations in the area, in all 'Green Hotels' and Dive Shops as well. This collateral material provides information about the best practices, which the tourists could adopt, and also encourages them to engage with "attractions and dive partners" who work towards sustainability.
- **Social Media:** "TUI AG sees the social media as an opportunity for open, respectful dialog with all company stakeholders." The tour operator group believes that knowingly or unknowingly, their employees and other internal/external customers, use the social media to promote the practice of sustainable tourism, since they breathe the concept daily, during their engagement with any of the entity from the 'World of TUI.' Further the company also uses Social media to promote sustainable tourism practices within the traveler community.
- **TUI Tour Representatives**: All tour guides as well as representatives inform the guests, during the welcome event, about conservation of resources, endangered species, souvenirs which are environmentally friendly or represent the cause, and ways through which local economies could be promoted (Dannenbaum, 2012).
- **Positioning the Project Through a Unique Logo:** A project logo has been created which features a blue cactus and an Iguana. All partners of the " Environmentally aware tourism project" use the logo in their communication and the promotional tools mentioned above, convey to the consumers that would be a wise and poised decision to choose travel partners who carry the Project Logo. This positions the proposition of sustainability as a hedonic need, among the minds of the consumers, thereby propelling them further to make a environmentally friendly choice.
- **Garnering Sponsorships from the Government:** TUI Nederlands is not only supported by all major stakeholders in the private sector, but a sponsorship of USD 61, 457 is given collectively by Neterlands ministry of Agriculture, Nature Management and Fisheries, Netherlands Center for Sustainable Development and Antillean Department of Environment.
- **Experiental Marketing Through a Climate Calculator:** TUI AG's partner in the project, Hapang Lloyd Cruises (which was earlier a fully

owned subsidy of TUI) sensitizes the customers and employees on the cruise, by using excellent "on-board technologies" to deal with the urgent challenge of "," soot, sulfur and nitrogen oxide emissions" of cruise ships. It further offers its customers a 'Climate Calculator.' This device has been created with the aid of "German organization Atmosfair." This climate calculator helps in dealing with unavoidable emissions by providing the customers an, "opportunity to offset carbon emissions from the cruise." The Climate Calculator checks for various parameters, which include "the cabin category and the length of the onboard stay." In tandem, it calculates the "climate footprint of the cruise" and the customers can offset the same by adopting other environmental friendly practices.

- **Online Communication**: Largely the communication with customers, employees as well as partners happens at TUI AG, online. This reduces the use of paper and is a small initiative to promote the cause of environmental sustainability.

- **Closing the Loop Through Feedback:** Customers of any of the TUI operators, can offer feedback through e-mails, after they have been exposed to the promotional material on environmental issues, through TUI or its project partners. Data from such e-mails, reveals that customers have become sensitive towards sustainability practices and their demands, with respect to sustainable tourism, are encouraging marketers to develop "environmentally friendly products"(Tour Operators' Initiative, 2013)[c].

5.5.5 PARTICIPANTS

Tourism participants include the customers, employees and partners, who have to be educated, managed and sensitized by the tourism managers about sustainable practices. Regular reviews about various practices, need to be formally communicated among all participants in the Tourism Value Chain, so that all can critically analyze the existing measures and suggest improvements. This would also involve regular trainings and workshops for the participants, around sustainability project related initiatives. Hilton Hotels in Continental Europe serve as an example for the use of partnerships in fostering sustainable tourism marketing.

Illustrative Case 5: *Hilton Hotels in Continental Europe: We Care Program (2006–2008)*

Bohdanowicz et al. (2011) suggest that a shift of an organization towards environmental management is closely connected with the people who actually carry out this change (and sometimes even resist the change)—the employees. For environment-friendly initiatives to be included in the organizational activities, it is imperative that the ,"human factor" remains supportive since they are at the helm of operational activities and have better insight into wasteful and damaging practices than the senior management (Rothenberg, 2003). Post and Altman (1994) highlighted that 'participants,' of the envisioned Sustainable Tourism Marketing Mix, can act barriers towards ecological change. This happens due to disengaged attitude of personnel; detached management which does not understand, or does not care, about the relationship between environment and economic costs, gap between the commitment of the top management and its execution within the organization and the "administrative heritage" meaning the past practices (Standard Operating practices) which are not environmentally sustainable.

The Hilton Hotels (part of the Hilton Worldwide which comprises of 10 brands) in Continental Europe took cognizance of the importance between sustainable tourism and the role of participants (especially employees) and launched their region-wide environmental program called ' We Care!' (Bohdanowicz et al., 2011). The We Care Program was launched in 2006 and it was based on five principles. On 1st January 2006, all Hilton Hotels in Europe received a "Green Box" which officially marked the beginning of the program. The contents of the Green Box were designed to motivate the Participants, encourage them to extend cooperation and all contents resonated with basic five principles of the program. Table 1 elaborates on the principles of the We Care Program and its interconnectedness with the Green Box.

TABLE 1   We Care program and the Green Box.

Five Principles of the We Care Program	Green Box and its Contents
Top Management endorsed and elaborated on an environmental policy	A video featuring an interview with Wolfgang Neumann (then, Area President), discussing the relevance of Environmental Sustainability initiatives for hotels.
ITP ("International Tourism Partnership") guidelines were created for ensuring that sustainability prevails in the choice of hotel site, design as well as construction	A Power Point presentation explaining, not just the ITP but all other aspects of the We Care Program.

TABLE 1   *(Continued)*

Five Principles of the We Care Program	Green Box and its Contents
Online courses on sustainable tourism—'eco-Learning'	For conducting training/environmental workshops, instructions were provided, on how these workshops should be run. These were regularly supported by the 'eco-Learning' courses.
LightStay—a global sustainability-monitoring tool devised and used by the brands of Hilton WorldWide (This monitoring program was earlier called the Hilton Environmental Reporting). LightStay reported, on a monthly basis, energy consumption per hotel and could make inter-hotel comparison of performance, comparison with country average and comparison with the Hilton Worldwide average as well.	Material to be used during workshops was provided. Training also included familiarization with the Computerized monitoring system (LightStay). Training material on comparing hotel's performance with the ITP benchmarks-the ITP EnvironmentBench.
Company's website dedicated to the program—www.hiltonwecare.com.	Linen and Towel "change on demand cards" were provided. This induced the involvement of guests in energy and water conservation.

To ensure that participants from varied processing areas (that are widely different), collectively identify and solve problems, the composition of the We Care Program team, called the Green Team, at each hotel was cosmopolitan. Figure 2 shows the Green Team's Composition. To maximize the Participants' buy-in, Hilton offered free mountain bikes to all employees of the best performing hotel.

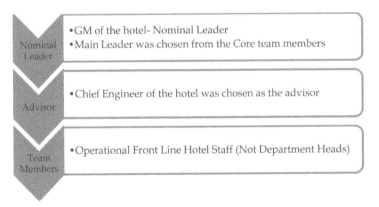

FIGURE 2   Green Team's composition at Hilton.

Figure 2 reflects Hilton's belief that the environment performance of a firm could only be improved when all initiatives are employee driven. This approach has also been recommended by Post and Altman (1994). It clearly reiterates that the success of Sustainable Marketing Management required strong support from the Participants in the Value Chain.

Andrew Forte, Director-Energy Management and Sustainability at the Hilton, shared with the media that (Bohdanowicz et. Al, 2011).

> *"In a nutshell, we care! delegates responsibility to team members who can really identify improvements and then implement them. Our aim was to create a culture in which all our team members feel empowered to propose improvements and then have the opportunity to actually change their actions. The results show that we are beginning to make a difference but this is just the start."*

Positive change augmented by the We Care! program in the first three years.

- Hilton Europe reduced the consumption of energy in its hotels by 6.7%, in the first year of the program. This exceeded the target of 5%, which the hotel had set for itself.
- The hotel saved more than USD 3 million as energy costs.
- Hilton hotels in Europe, reduced the water consumption by 8% per guest night.
- Energy consumption was reduced by 15%.
- CO_2 emissions were reduced by 8% per guest night, which translated into 28,600 tons CO_2 which was prevented from being released.
- Hotel group saved USD 16 million in its water and energy bills.
- Employees were self-driven in organizing green activities such as "Clean up the world" or "Earth Hour."
- The Hotel attributes savings of USD 9.6 million, to the changed human behavior.

5.6 PHYSICAL EVIDENCE

From the sustainable tourism perspective, physical evidence would entail the sustainability values, and policies which the employees (internal customers), along with the organization, are desired to follow. The physical evidence also includes what the customers are expected to do to promote sustainability. This offers internal as well as external customers a framework which puts the attempt to induce sustainable tourism, in perspective.

Illustrative Case 6: *Exodus and Its Responsible Tourism Policy*

Due to the intangible and unapparent (in the short run) benefits of sustainability in tourism, it is imperative that hospitality marketers work on creating physical evidences. Cues that act as evidences remind the consumer about the value proposition, remind as well as motivate the other stakeholders about the objectives of the organization or project and these might also help the consumers in assessing the quality of the product/service, while engaging in the purchase decision (Blythe, 2006).

As discussed in Figure 1, physical evidence as a part of the STMM, includes the incorporation of a policy or framework, which consistently reiterates the sustainability values. Hilton (Illustrative Case 5) is an example of the way organizations create evidences like the Hilton's Green Box or the ITP Guidelines, to emphasize on sustainable tourism practices.

Exodus, an adventure tour operator from UK developed physical evidence in the form of a 'Responsible Tourism Policy.' The policy consists of a Mission Statement, describing company's commitment towards sustainable tourism and a " Code of Practices," which details the management practices that would help in the policy's implementation.

5.6.1 THE MISSION STATEMENT OF THE POLICY

"Exodus operates tourism that fosters understanding, appreciation and conservation of the culture and environments we visit. We operate in a socially and environmentally responsible manner. We are committed to working with our clients and the people of our host destinations to ensure direct economic benefits at a community level, and to contribute to cultural and environmental conservation. With the continual monitoring of our operations, we aim to operate beyond best practice guidelines, endeavoring to set world-wide industry benchmarks for responsible tourism operations" (Tour Operators' Initiative, 2003)[D.]

The policy is aimed at the employees, travel partners, local communities as well as the customers. Exodus took varied measures, described in Table 2, to ensure that the practices and principles of responsible tourism are promoted among the mentioned stakeholder communities.

TABLE 2 Exodus' tourism policy and physical evidences.

Physical Evidence	Description
Code of Practice	Various management practices are described. The aim is to emphasize the importance of operations, which are economically, culturally and environmentally friendly.
Responsible Tourism Manager	A manager who is an expert in tourism as well as conservation. The aim of the position is to signal to all stakeholders of Exodus that sustainability is integral to the company's business.
Responsible Tourism Seminars	Exodus organizes multiple two-day seminars for its staff in entire UK. Employees from marketing, operations, sales and finance functions identify areas of improvement for the policy and also brainstorm over excelling in the implementation of sustainable practices. Feedback from the seminars is used to improve the "Code of Practice."
Training in the policy	New staff members are trained on the "Responsible Tourism Policy"
Intranet Updates	Regular Intranet updates about the policy and code of practices, acts as a motivational tool for everyone to move towards the fulfillment of a common goal (of ensuring sustainability).
Weekly Reporting	All departments organize weekly reporting meetings, which are attended by the Responsible Tourism Manager. Meetings monitor and update all about the implementation of the policy; new initiatives undertaken and feedback to improve the existing program.
Benefits for Local Communities	Exodus hires local guides, thereby supporting local communities. Largely purchases are made of local services and products and local operators are also roped in to implement the policy.
Limiting Group Sizes	Group size, for all tours, is limited to a maximum of 22 people. This ensures that local destinations are not over burdened by tourist footfall and their ecological balance remains maintained.
Tour Leaders	Tour leaders receive training on the policy and they highlight to the customers (tourists), local issues and ensure the adaptation sustainable practices by the customers.
Company Literature	Reference to the policy is included in all of the company's literature like trip notes, "pre-departure information packets," brochures, website and feedback forms. This promotes the policy among consumers and motivates them towards prudent behavior.

Besides the mentioned physical evidences, Exodus also undertook "recycling and energy management programs" at its Head-Office, thereby ensuring that no employee or customer touch-point remains oblivious of the Responsible Tourism Policy.

5.7 PROCESS

The activity flow of the tourism services has to be made sustainable through simple sustainable processes like:

- Online bookings and digital booking, avoiding paper use;
- Working through and producing wind or solar energy;
- Green supply chain management;
- Reducing the carbon emissions through efficient transport means;
- Recycling systems;
- Lesser energy consumption through key based and sensor based lighting systems.

Such processes intertwine sustainability with the mission of organizational growth, through the creation of customized blueprints and the commitment of hospitality marketers to target standards and achieve the same. An example from the emerging economy, India, serves as an explanation to the depth with which processes are used as an essential element in the sustainable tourism marketing mix.

Illustrative Case 7: *The Leela Gurgaon Hotels and Residence in Haryana, India: Processes promote sustainability*

Jauhari and Dutta (2010) suggest that service processes are critical in establishing a moment-of-truth for the customers and processes typically include the front as well as back end operations which are designed after understanding the service context. Processes also give the services a degree of tangibility along with aiding in stronger customer relationships.

From sustainable tourism marketing perspective, processes must be aligned with the cause of sustainability and must convey the importance of sustainable practices to the internal (employees) as well as the external customers (end consumer).

The Leela Gurgaon Hotels and Residences, in National Capital Region (India), has gained excellence in making its processes sustainability-friendly by engaging a 360 degree approach in its process transformation.

Hotel Leelaventure Limited owns and manages The Leela Palaces, Hotels and Resorts and The Leela Gurgaon Hotels and Residences is a part of the same group. Hotel Leelaventure Limited belongs to The Leela Group whose product portfolio includes luxury hotel as well as resort properties (Currently at 8 different locations in India), real estate development and IT and business parks. The Leela Gurgaon Hotels and Residences offers 322 five-star deluxe hotel rooms and 90 one, two, and three bedroom fully services luxury Residences (The Leela, 2013).

The Leela Group's focus towards sustainability comes from the vision of the group's Chairman, Captain C.P. Krishnan Nair, who has been the recipient of numerous awards, for his initiatives towards conservation of the environment. The Leela Gurgaon Hotel and Residences has dovetailed its processes with the sustainability by looking at environment saving as a well-thought collection of initiatives towards energy saving, electricity saving, water saving as well as HSD (High Speed Diesel) saving.

5.7.1 PROCESSES ENCOURAGE SUSTAINABILITY AT THE LEELA GURGAON HOTEL AND RESIDENCES

- **Energy effective lighting system**: Traditional lighting systems create lot of heat, which is not good for the air conditioning system. Leela Gurgaon Hotels and Residences hence, hires consultants to suggest alternate, higher quality lighting systems that are energy efficient and disseminate light but lesser heat. This in turn also saves energy, which would otherwise have been consumed by the air conditioning system to counter the extra heat from the lighting system.
- **Sustainability Practice with respect to the Air conditioning system**: The Guest rooms have been installed with the Card–Key mechanism. Typically in major hotels, even though electricity appliances switch off when the card is removed, the Air Conditioning system remains on. But at Leela, the AC system too switches off once the card is taken out. Guests return to rooms which might have high temperature and the rooms remain uncomfortable for at least 10–15 minutes. However, guests understand the relevance of such practices and do not complaint about the same. This is an inference of the fact that consumers (both International as well as Domestic Travelers) too, aim at extending their support towards resource conservation.
- **Minimizing the use of High Speed Diesel (HSD)**: At Leela Gurgaon, diesel gets consumed for two purposes—for the diesel generators and for the steam boilers and hot water generators. The hotel tries to maximize the boilers' efficiency, to avoid any diesel wastage, by conducting

frequent quality and machine checks. Since various machines and the laundry process require steam from these boilers regularly, minimizing the use of HSD is difficult, hence optimizing it is a process which helps the hotel in maintaining sustainability. Alternatively this is also important from the cost saving perspective. Since the unit cost of diesel in India has almost doubled in the past three years, the hotel is stringent about units used and it aims at reducing the consumption of HSD by making a year-on-year comparison of the consumption figures.

- **Use of Natural Gas**: The hotel has initiated the process of using Natural Gas for the generators and boilers. Since Natural Gas is Clean fuel, this results in release of lesser carbon dioxide as compared to petroleum or coal. In National Capital Region the supply of Natural gas is limited but Leela remained rooted to its commitment towards sustainability by arranging for Natural gas by associating with specific vendors.

- **Water Recycling and STP (Sewage Treatment plant) at the Leela**: The hotel has a centralized STP where all the sewage gets treated. The clean water from the STP gets recycled and is being used for cleaning, gardening and to some extent for the flushes in the washrooms as well.

- **Rain Water Harvesting mechanism**: The hotel boasts of a strong Rain water harvesting system which further enhances its capabilities towards water saving.

- **Solar Panels on the roof**: The hotel does not have a large roof area to accommodate an elaborate solar system. However, the hotel is devising a mechanism to install some solar panels so that contribution towards energy saving is maximized.

- **Substitution of refrigerant**: Hotels commonly use (or used) Refrigerant for Air Conditioning systems as well as the Refrigerators, even though the substance is harmful for the ozone layer. But Leela Kempinksi Gurgaon has started to use substances, which are more environmentally friendly now. Even the Indian Government has phased out the use of substances like the refrigerant, and is compelling organizations to substitute them with more sustainability friendly products.

- **Sustainability across the value chain**: Leela Gurgaon Hotel and Residences train their suppliers as well as vendors. Representatives from the hotel make regular visits to the suppliers' workshops, factories and observe the production processes, simultaneously making relevant corrective suggestions. This is also in compliance with the ISO 140001, which mandates the hotel properties to train suppliers in production, procurement as well as disposal processes.

- Garbage as well as other waste from the hotel is sent to Government certified vendors who are trained and equipped to treat the waste and dispose it in the most environment friendly manner.

5.7.2 THE MOTIVATION BEHIND DESIGNING SUCH PROCESSES

The hotel believes that sustainability friendly processes are necessary because they save on operating costs, they help the hotel remain in tandem with the consistent upgrades in Government policies and largely they also help the hotel in designing a better guest experience. Evolved hospitality marketers understand that such initiatives help in higher brand positioning because guests appreciate a hotel's concern for environmental and cultural causes.

To this the Chief Engineer of the Hotel, Mr. Anil Kumar, says:

"The hospitality experience which we offer to the guests gets further accentuated through environment friendly processes. Further if a hotel does not progress towards the sustainability path, it will eventually stagnate in terms of sales."

5.7.3 INVESTMENTS: WHO PAYS FOR THEM?

The government policies are being upgraded on a regular basis. All processes at the Leela Gurgaon Hotels and Residences, are in compliance with the latest Government regulations, which mandate the hospitality organizations to make investments towards such processes. Hence any progressive hospitality organization will make heavy investments towards processes, equipment and machinery to remain competitive in the industry.

Also such initial investments offer high returns in terms of cost savings hence it is wise to consider them.

The newer properties, internationally as well as in India, are being designed to remain technologically advanced and they have in-built sustainability friendly processes. Investments to the tune of INR 7,000 million are required to build a hotel property from the scratch and hence marketers consider it wise to incorporate systems, which will support the environment in this investment itself. However, even the properties that have been in existence since long, invest heavily in up-gradation of their infrastructure every 5 years. Hotels typically allocate budgets ranging from INR 30–40 million for renovation of infrastructure. This amount may exceed depending on the size of the hotel, its stature, the business, which the hotel is doing, and the profits, which it is making. Renovations are carried out for the restaurants, the lobby, the guest rooms and the machinery is also upgraded regularly. During such renovations, hoteliers incorporate pro-sustainability processes and appreciate investing towards the same, because of the long-term benefits, which get accrued, along with the elevation in the guest experience.

The owners of the hotel group typically pay for such investments. Technicians, consultants as well as experienced engineers are hired for this purpose and they design the infrastructure in such a way that returns on such investments start to garner from the first day of implementation itself.

5.7.4 ENVIRONMENTAL SUSTAINABILITY AND CONSUMER BEHAVIOR

Leela Gurgaon communicates to its customers that they are ISO 140001 certified and ISO 22000 (from the Food Safety perspective). Communication to this effect acts as a promotional tool as well. International as well as domestic consumers recognizes such certifications. Hence they prefer to stay in hotels that have relevant quality certifications and which can offer a physical evidence that they are 'Green Hotels' (Kumar, 2013). Guests, especially International travelers, today understand the importance of environment friendly practices and prefer such hotels. Though not all guests use 'Sustainable Processes' as strong selection criteria, while choosing a hotel, but when they are informed about the same they support the hotel in the aforesaid practices.

Sustainability processes and efforts clearly drive sales and positively affect the bottom line as well. Kumar, from Leela Gurgaon, expressed that:

"A hotel cannot survive in the long run, if it does not adapt processes that promote sustainability. For us as hospitality marketers, it is not just the bottom lines, which motivate us to take this route, but it is also a part of the social duty that we must execute. Environment-friendly practices improve our efficiency, reduce wastage and must be looked at as the only way of functioning."

5.8 PACKAGING

Packaging of tourism services can be strongly leveraged by bundling sustainable services. This means that tourism organizations and destination managers can engage sustainability oriented partners to offer services like transportation, food, etc., and offer a total tourism package which is environment friendly.

Illustrative Case 8: *Global Exchange Reality Tours: Packaging the Total Tourism Experience to Avoid "Greenwashing"*

Global Exchange is a Human Rights Organization and a licensed Travel Service Provider, in San Francisco, USA. It was incorporated 25 years back, in 1988, as a nonprofit organization and has been working ever since to promote "social, economic and environmental justice" (Globalexchange, 2013). The organization arranges Reality Tours with a vision that "meaningfully, *socially responsible travel can and does, change the world.*"

Global Exchange's reality tours are a perfect example of marketing sustainability through the packaging element, because the organization employs sustainable practices in the internal processes and in the external environment by involving only those partners who work on sustainability as well. They promote sustainability through the entire program by evaluating every element and aspect of the experience offered by the tour. Global exchange Reality Tours works on the ethos of social responsibility and exhibits the same by supporting local businesses, treating other countries and their people as equals, and educating the tourists/travelers about sustainability as well as local communities (thereby bringing people closer to each other). The following are some of the key initiatives by Global exchange Reality Tours in their attempt to avoid green washing (Hendricks et al., n.a.):

TABLE 3   Sustainable internal and external practices.

Sustainable Internal Practices	Sustainable External Practices
Use of products, which are sustainable, like cleaning supplies and garbage bags.	Sourcing organic food from suppliers who engage in sustainable practices.
Remaining paperless by making 95% of tool-kits and packages electronic.	Analyzing the social ramification of each tour.
Marketing through social media, word-of-mouth, testimonials from past travelers and press-releases.	Utilizing the services of local businesses in each of the tour location.

5.9   PROGRAMMING

Programming in the tourism industry relates to special events or activities, which are organized to induce higher consumer spending. Bringing the sustainability element is essential to avoid waste management or destination overload. Hence through the "carrying capacity concept" marketers can offer certainty of demand to suppliers and partners, reducing opportunities for wastage.

Programming has emerged as a critical element of sustainable marketing mix in the light of increasing natural disasters across the world. Social activists feel that unplanned, unsustainable path towards development, leads to such disasters. Disaster in India's state-Uttarakhand in mid-2013, created awareness among local authorities and travelers about the criticality of Programming. Massive floods and landslides leading to the death of more than 5,700 people and absolute mayhem in the lives of the region's dwellers hit the north Indian state of Uttarakhand. Further the state's dams and roads connected pilgrims to various religious destinations. The natural disaster left more than 100,000 pilgrims stranded (or dead) in the valley, since all these dams, bridges and roads were broken. The paramilitary forces as well as Indian defense personnel were engaged in the rescue mission.

Media across the nation labeled this as a "Man-made disaster" and it was published that " *The problem with bribing your way through the next infrastructure project is that nature does not accept bribes*" (Live Mint and the Wall Street Journal, 2013). This was indicative of the unauthorized building activities in the region along with excessive tourism (more than the region's carrying capacity). It was highlighted how hotel managers in the region consumed all the available water to cater to the tourists' need thereby depleting the much needed water-input, for local farmers. Activists suggested that building of tunnels and bridges in the "eco sensitive area" impacted the natural flow of rivers leading to colossal calamity (Forbes India, 2013; The Hindu, 2013).

Illustrative Case 9: *Sustainability Initiatives During the Australian Formula I ING Grand Prix*

The Australian Formula I ING Grand Prix Corporation (AGPC) understands the magnitude of this large event it organizes each year, and takes steps towards reducing the event's environmental impact.

In the year 2009, the four-day event, Formula I ING Grand Prix was attended by 280,000 supporters and AGPC understood that the race will have an impact of Victoria's (state in Australia) environment. The AGPC took the following steps to promote sustainability by programming various elements towards environmental as well as societal protection. These steps are enumerated below:

- The AGPC engaged in water recycling practices and the recycled water was used for the track surrounds.
- Waste management practices were adopted where sorted waste was collected and was processed to make reusable raw-material (Tourism Victoria, 2012).

- The AGPC has an "environmental packaging and waste recycling part-ner" in Cleanevent. To reduce the carbon dioxide, which got generated during the event, native trees in Victoria, were planted.
- FOTA-Formula One Team's Association, too exhibits commitment towards the cause of sustainability by boasting of "a 7% reduction in carbon emissions in the period 2009–2011" Top teams including Cater-ham, Lotus, Marussia, Mercedes, Force India, Sauber, McLaren and Williams, and follows an externally audited exercise to set a target to re-duce emissions from a baseline of 2009 (Crash, 2013). FOTA involved Trucost—an environment research analysis organization-to audit the teams against the set target and it was found that 24% emissions have been reduced with the racing cars of the teams. To counter environmen-tal challenges technologies like "*Turbocharging, fuel injection, variable valve timing and kinetic energy recovery systems (KERS)*" have all been developed by teams.

5.10 PARTNERSHIP

Cooperative marketing and communication efforts can foster sustainability through the entire tourism value chain. Enthusiasm and commitment for all partners is essential so that none performs activities for unsustainable eco-nomic gains. Partnership hence goes beyond, just the "Participants" and looks at coordinated action " from the Government; the corporate entity as well as the individual level" (Bohdanowicz et al., 2011).

Hall (2000) suggests that public participation is vital to tourism planning process and at all stages, "sustainability has to be treated seriously." Literature also highlights the criticality of partnering and it is believed that "Inter-depen-dence and interrelationship among stakeholders" makes the tourism planning process complex however "it is this change, complexity and uncertainty that form the backdrop against which planning for tourism is developed, tested and implemented" (McCool, 2009).

5.10.1   ILLUSTRATIVE CASE 10: DAYLESFORD AND HEPBURN SPRINGS

Daylesford and Hepburn Springs is located in Victoria, an hour's drive from Melbourne. This region has been defined as a "Level-one destination" mean-ing that it attracts a varied mixes of national (intrastate and interstate tourists) as well as international tourists and also has a strong appeal internationally.

The natural beauty of the region along with its "historic architecture, innovative and quality tourism enterprises, dynamic creative industries and diverse communities," make it a coveted tourism destination (Wary, 2011).

To promote sustainable tourism in the region various steps were executed in a phased manner and these were made possible by partnering with eminent entities. A description of each stage, along with the description of the partners in presented in Table 4.

TABLE 4   Partners and their role at the daylesford and hepburn springs.

Stage	Partners and Their Role
"Destination Steering Committee (SC)" was appointed	**PARTNERS**: *12 members in the committee—From Local Tourism and Business operators and Local Community Association.*
	Executive Team of the SC: President of local tourism association, General manager of Hepburn Shrine Council and similar experienced people.
	Independent Chairperson: Led the Team. Had a background in community leadership and exhibited high management skills.
	ROLE: With representation from various stakeholder groups, including Government; Business and Community, the committee aimed at discussing the progress of the strategic planning process and also providing advice to the tourism planners.
Developing and Communicating a strategic planning approach	**PARTNERS**: *Consultants, researchers were engaged*
	Bureaucrats and politicians were engaged
	ROLE: Conducting situation analysis to examine statistics of visitation, accommodation auditing, examining attraction and support facilities. This was documented as a report and was presented to the SC and Government officials by the consultants.
Regional expert panel	**PARTNERS** *Members with expertise in the regional tourism planning and execution process.*
	Chair, Australian Regional Tourism Marketing; Tourism Victoria's Regional Tourism Development Manager, Tourism Noosa's Marketing manager, Tourism New South Wales' Strategic Planner, Professional from Cultural tourism and a Professor of Repute.
	ROLE: Advised on the planning process and also offered feedback to the initial plan.

TABLE 4   *(Continued)*

Stage	Partners and Their Role
Stakeholder engagement	**PARTNERS:** *Eight Stakeholder Groups-Tourism Organizations and Tour Operators; Council; Environmental Groups; Business Groups; Cultural groups; Event/Festival Organizers; Community groups and Departments from the Government.* *Consultants and the SC were the change initiators. Local Citizens were also Involved* **ROLE:** Consultants conducted workshops with all partners to emphasize ways of "adopting a collaborative and sustainable approach to tourism planning." All partners created a vision statement after identifying values related to sustainable tourism management. All Partners engaged in intense discussions on key challenges and issues being faced by Daylesford and Hepburn Springs. Engagement of residents was planned through "Dedicated Planning Websites," along with media articles, publicity and PR initiatives. Citizen jury was created through a scientific and rigorous selection process. All jury members were informed in detail, about sustainable tourism, Government role in the same, and issues around regional tourism planning. The jury then deliberated on the offered information, offered recommendations and highlighted relevant issues from the community perspective as well. All the meetings and workshops led to the identification of 20 principal issues for Daylesford and Hepburn Springs, under the themes of destination management, destination development as well as marketing. To foster a collaborative relationship with all stakeholder groups, the report on principal issues was shared, for deliberation, with all stakeholders and feedback was again, requested. The Final action plan—"Destination Daylesford Strategic Tourism Plan" was released for public consumption and scrutiny, by the Council and was eventually accepted, even though it was radical and affirmed that authentic stakeholder engagement process can lead to the development of positive changes.

Globally, following sustainable processes is becoming desirable. While screening and recruiting employees, ITC Group of Hotels, puts an emphasis on the sensitivity the candidate has, towards green issues. Once hired, the management takes an initiative to consistently involve the employees in environment-friendly practices.

With the above arguments and illustrations, it can be established that it is critical to explore elements of marketing tourism sustainability to consumers. This concept entails not just an exhaustive description of the Marketing Mix for Sustainable tourism but would also elaborate on means to garner customer as well as value chain partners' buy-in.

5.11   SUSTAINABILITY AND CONSUMER BEHAVIOR

Consumers have a pivotal role in strengthening the process of sustainable tourism and hence alongside the emergence of knowledge around sustainable tourism, emerged the idea of "Green Consumerism." In 1992, Ottman identified that Green Consumerism is propelled by individuals who use the "power of their purchase decision" to look for ways of protecting the world and their own selves. Choi and Ng (2011) suggest that information about sustainability, when offered by a firm positively influences a consumer's evaluation of the organization as well as purchase intention. They note "Consumers indeed respond strongly to information about firms' sustainability orientations and strategies; they are more sensitive to statements of a company's sustainability virtues, and they react negatively to low sustainability" and they (consumers) "are influenced by multiple dimensions of sustainability." Research also indicates that consumers, irrespective of their geographic setting, are motivated to exhibit choices, which support sustainability. McDonald and Oates (2006) identified that 92% of the consumers understand that any effort towards sustainability makes a significant contribution. In the previous decade itself, 61% consumers from UK considered it important that tourism organizations take into account environmental issues (Market Opinion and Research International, 1997). In the year 2003 around 87% consumers from UK suggested that they look for "environmental information" of their travel destination before the booking or at least immediately after the booking (Miller 2003). In the US too, companies exhibit social reporting to strengthen consumer confidence and in the year 1997 itself, 43% US Companies "produced a separate environmental report" (Miller, 2011). The Advertising Age Poll cited in Solomon (2013) discusses the attributes, which are given importance by the consumers while making purchases. The poll notes that "energy-saving," "recyclable," and "socially responsible" are among the Top 5 brand attributes influencing consumers' purchases, across all age groups from ages 18 to 69. Sheth et al. (2011) note that "American consumers in increasing numbers are turning to frugality, and a majority of them are unlikely to turn back to overconsumption." They also cite Egol et al. (2010) and Booz and Company (2009), who suggest that consumer behavior is experiencing a fundamental shift towards "new frugality"—which is titled "Mindful Consumption" by Sheth et al. (2011).

These facts appear promising yet travelers who make sustainable choices are not evenly spread across the globe nor are they in substantial numbers globally. Prakash (2002) pointed that in the 1980s and 1990s, a surge in "green consumer behavior" was expected, but it never happened. This was in tandem with the findings of Davis (1993), that efforts towards green marketing have been unable to generate consumer enthusiasm in accordance with the marketers' expectations. In the report by Tourism Victoria (2012), it has been pointed that though the number of consumers, who are willing to bring a behavioral change with respect to their tourism habits, are growing, they are less in number presently. Also the study notes that even the consumers who are aware about the importance of sustainable tourism, are unwilling "to pay significantly higher rates or environmentally sustainable surcharges." Understanding consumers' motivation towards making sustainable tourism choices, therefore, holds importance.

Though it is believed that one motivator remains a consumer's "self-altruism" or his innate human need to exhibit selfish philanthropy, some researchers also suggest that tourism marketers must offer explicit information to consumers about the environmental impact of their businesses' functions, so that Green Consumers make a rational choice (US Travel data Centre, 1992; Swarbrooke 1996; Middleton and Hawkins, 1998; Miller 2011). The rationale for this, according to extant literature, is that consumers measure the "perceived effort or compromise" or the "degree of compromise" (Peattie, 1998, cited in McDonald and Oates, 2006) when making decisions around aspects of sustainability and they must be motivated to think about the "environmental information of their intended destination."

However, Ellen (1994), Schlegelmilch et al. (1996) and Ogilvy and Totem (2011) argue that in facilitating sustainable tourism's consumer decision-making process, marketers have to first decipher consumer attitude and consumer beliefs towards buying "sustainable holidays." This view is in resonance with Straughan and Roberts (1999) who assert that "ecologically conscious consumer behavior" results largely from "perceived consumer effectives" meaning, a consumer's belief that environmental pro-activeness (with respect to purchase decisions) is important because each individual has the capacity to induce change. Petty et al. (1983) developed the Elaboration Likelihood Model (ELM) and suggested that marketers can either take a central route *(when consumers "generate cognitive responses "to marketing content)* or a peripheral route *(when consumers are not motivated by marketing content's arguments but use cues-like style, aspirational elements, stimuli attractiveness-to react to the product/service)* to persuade consumers. The theory propagated by ELM has been taken forward in thought by Ogilvy and Totem (2011) as they suggest that tourism consumers make rational as well as emotional arguments while buying holidays. Hence marketers' efforts to initiate a behavioral change in consumers through the central route, that is through "supplying technically correct, logical information" is not always successful because majority of consumers are egoists, meaning "in real world everyday decision making, sustainability has no value (for them) beyond its ability to serve individuals' interests, even those of the self-proclaimed eco-conscious traveler." Hence sustainable tourism marketing must aim at developing tourism messages that are realistic, pragmatic and inspiring, not just for the already informed (engaged) consumer but for a wider range of tourists. Wherli et al. (2013) affirm this idea and suggest that sustainable tourism marketing has be to done through "emotional or rational message design and visual elements" since they influence the booking choices of consumers. These messages must be widely promoted to ensure higher reach because formation of appropriate consumer beliefs is also dependent on the credibility of the sources from where consumers gather information (McDonald and Oates, 2006).

5.12 ENGAGING CUSTOMERS ON SUSTAINABILITY: WHAT CAN MARKETERS DO?

Hotels (2007) cited in Bohdanowicz et al. (2011), highlighted the following:

> *"It is clear that current debate about climate change has highlighted the need for action from all of us. As more and more people look to book according to their conscience and beliefs, it is inevitable that hoteliers will need to demonstrate and communicate their commitment to saving the environment."*

This is indeed factual yet engaging consumers towards sustainable tourism remains a challenge for hospitality marketers.

Marketers can use various elements singularly or in combination from the Sustainable Tourism Marketing Mix to educate and motivate stakeholders.

McDonald and Oates (2006) suggest that marketers can also identify patterns in consumers' sustainable behavior and use such patterns in the marketing strategies. Through their research McDonald and Oates discovered that activities like 'using public transport rather than driving'; 'turning down electric heating and using warmer clothes instead'; 'switching off lights and not leaving them on standby' and 'not refilling the kettle each time it is used for boiling' are some of the sustainable activities which, according to consumers, require similar/equal efforts (compromise) to be practiced and have the capacity to make a big difference to the ecosystem. For promotional strategies marketers can use this learning to develop communication messages that motivate consumers for such similar activities, in a single message, thereby increasing the efficacy of the campaign.

In devising any sustainable tourism marketing strategy, hospitality marketers have to keep in mind that typically consumers use sustainability as a criteria only when other attributes like price, accommodation choice and the range of activities available, have been satisfied. Hence sustainability has to be developed as a positioning statement and as an aspirational cue which, with its association, elevates a consumer in his status perception (for the self). This can be achieved by using "Sustainability as Unique Selling proposition" (UNEP, 2005) and delivering highest quality standards in "sustainable products in tourism." The sustainability concept has to be positioned by marketers as 'fashionable' and a 'lifestyle value' with the engagement of media, consumer opinion leaders as well as distribution channels. In doing so, destination marketers can create communication campaigns for responsible visitors, which would not only educate and inform travelers about ways of reducing their travel's impact on the planet and people, but would also assist tourism business partners in better communicating their "green credentials."

Partnerships, as discussed in STMM, have an important role to play in offering sustainable tourism solutions. When tourism partners collaborate with an aim of educating 'first time travelers' to a place, it has a long-lasting effect on the sustainable tourism behavior of the consumer, during repeat visits to the same destination or even other places. UNEP (2005) notes that "first time tourists on a package such as trekking, diving or homestays have specific awareness raising and education needs before and during their experience, that will mark their behavior for future trips." Therefore, all partners in the tourism value chain must communicate to the consumers the need to develop cultural and environmental sensitivity as well as respect for the local communities and their needs. This can be done by designing credible sources like travel guides and sustainable tourism manuals which could be made available at multiple touch-points to the travelers.

Partnership would entail that the tourist receives sustainable tourism marketing communication from all sources, enlisted in Table 5. Also the suppliers in the tourism value chain have to be convinced about the merits (for them) of sustainable tourism's development so that sustainable tourism remains as an on-going initiative.

TABLE 5   Sources for sustainable tourism marketing communication.

Distribution Channels	Service Suppliers (*Direct Marketing to the Tourist*)	Promotion Media
Travel Agency	Accommodation Providers	Tourist Boards/Destination Management Organizations
Tour Operator	Transport providers	Guidebooks
Internet Retailers	Catering Vendors	Media
	Ground Service Agents	Travel Fairs
	Social/Cultural Event Organizers	Consumer Associations

Adapted from UNEP (2005).

Sultanate of Oman serves as an excellent example to highlight the collective role of suppliers in sustainable tourism development. Oman is working towards encouraging supplier practices, which are sustainable because of its firm belief that sustainable tourism is in 'national self-interest.' Training programs and awareness raising initiatives are being conducted for suppliers. Also suppliers who adopt sustainable practices, are given preferential terms. This can be taken as a precedent by other hospitality marketers in motivating internal as well as external stakeholders.

Marketers in the tourism industry can draw learning from the emerging idea about 'Mindful Consumption,' since it is believed to be "highly desirable for personal and social well-being and fits well with new frugality embraced by consumers." It also "aids long-term firm profitability" (Sheth et al., 2011). The implication for tourism marketers is to refrain from "over-marketing." Based on the concept of 'carrying capacity,' discussed earlier in this chapter, tourism and hospitality marketers could avoid indulging in over-advertising, aggressive pricing and promotional strategies and other hard selling techniques. Mindful consumption (MC) can be used to design sustainable tourism marketing mix. With the concept of MC the product, for instance, can be designed for multi-sharing (as done by the Branded budget hotel segment globally), the pricing should not promote the tourism organization/destination on the basis of being 'cheap' (to avoid acquisitive consumption), but on the basis of quality and value, promotions and marketing communication can be designed to educate consumers to reduce wasteful, acquisitive consumption and adapt sustainable tourist behaviors (as well as lifestyles) and place has to be created such that it is promotes the "shared use of products," facilitates sustainable behavior and does not consider mere financial bottom lines through over-consumption.

Designing the promotional message plays a critical role in sustainable tourism marketing. Wherli et al. (2013) note that for sustainable tourism marketing to be motivational for the tourists, the promotional messages have to be a blend of cognitive as well as emotional appeals. Wherli et al. elaborate this,

> *"People prefer more emotional communications about product related sustainability. This means people prefer texts like "we serve you only the highest quality regional products" to "regional products are served." The perceived emotionality of a text can be increased by telling a story, directly addressing the audience, using active sentence structure, adjectives, highly valued words and absolute formulations. The study also showed that emotionality is achieved differently in different countered and that instruments to increase the emotionality are only successful in certain markets."*

Hospitality marketers must hence create promotional messages such that they include authentic and culturally accentuated information about the destination. Authentic information will foster tourists' trust and respect thereby reducing their perceived risk with respect to the travel decision. Cultural tone of the promotional message, that highlights the pro-sustainability attributes of the destination, holiday or hotel, would lead the consumer to get emotionally engaged with the marketing message. The promotional message must also be simple since Smerencnik and Andersen (2011), note that "perceived simplicity plays a vital role on the process of adopting sustainability innovations." Hospitality marketers could use the text in their marketing communication to their advantage because consumers, when addressed through personalized, non-threating texts, respond positively towards sustainable tourism (Ye and Tussydiah, 2011). Also the visuals used in communication of the sustainable tourism mix, should have a positive sensory influence on the consumers. Visuals, for example of undisturbed landscape, beautiful surroundings, calm scenic area and blue skies, work as cues for sensory marketing and engage the consumers in a positive perceptual experience. Experiential marketing, either through statements or visuals, also have a strong role to play in influencing tourist behavior towards sustainable practices. Statements like, 'This sustainable tourism destination offers fascinating cultural and natural landscape or 'The fresh air and fragrance of this place (hotel/resort/destination) is comforting and refreshing,' create a positive imagery in the minds of the consumers and would play a role in influencing travelers' buying intentions.

Pomering et al. (2011) offer a glimpse of the future direction for marketing sustainable tourism as they point that,

> " If sustainability is to be the goal of all forms of tourism, including mass tourism, tourism management cannot simply be "business as usual." To meet this need, a managerial framework is needed that is sufficiently comprehensive and flexible to span differences in tourism scale and tourism's various components, such as destinations, tour operators, hospitality and transport providers, and attractions. Such a framework must also promote the collaborative partnership between tourism's interrelated components, the tourism "industry," to ensure that sustainability efforts are in concert rather than piecemeal, to transform activities on the supply side and tourists' demand-side behaviors."

Moeller et al. (2011), define sustainable tourism marketing radically and suggest that,

> "Destination managers and tourism business managers are no longer limited to measures of increasing environmental sustainability which are implemented at the destination, such as trying to educate tourists how to behave or imposing capacity restrictions for natural attractions. Managers can take more proactive measures, which do not require any action to be taken at the destination, namely inviting people who are intrinsically environmentally friendly. Therefore, instead of marketing a destination to all tourists (which will contain some inherently environmentally friendly ones and some who are not) and then trying to educate those who are not to behave in an environmentally friendly way at the destination, targeting the segment of environmentally friendly tourists in the first place, avoids the problem of having to "re-educate" them (with questionable success). As a consequence, the environmental footprint of tourism will "automatically" decrease because people who are inherently environmentally friendly will treat the natural resources at the destination with more respect. Also, if destinations wish to maintain educational activities, tourists who are inherently environmentally friendly are likely to pay more attention to those messages and demonstrate the desired behavioral change."

Hospitality and tourism marketers hence, have an interesting path to tread in deciphering the appropriate marketing mix for sustainable tourism. Initiatives like identification of 'green consumers' who could be economically attractive, developing a pro-sustainability positioning and creating sustainable tourism marketing mix elements remain some common start-points into the complex sustainability journey.

KEYWORDS

- **consumer behavior**
- **hospitality**
- **India**
- **marketing sustainability**
- **sustainability**
- **tourism**

REFERENCES

Aitken, S. (2007), 'The future's green,' *Precision Marketing*, Issue June 15, pp. 21–22.

Andriate, G. S., and Fink, A. A. (2008), 'managing the change to a sustainable enterprise,' in Wirtenberg J, Russell WG and Lipsky D (eds.), '*The sustainable enterprise field book: When it all comes together*,' Greenleaf, UK, p. 118.

Atlas Voyages (2013), '*About Atlas Travels.*' Online. Available at http://www.atlasvoyages.com/article.cfm?idarticle=8070. Cited on 18th June 2013.

Batra A (2006), 'Tourism Marketing for Sustainable Development,' *ABAC Journal*, Vol. 26, No. 1, pp. 59–65.

Beeton S and Benefield R (2002), 'Demand Control: The case for demarketing as a visitor and environmental management tool,' *Journal of Sustainable Tourism*, Vol. 10, Issue 6, pp. 497–513.

Belz F and Peattie K (2009), 'Sustainability marketing: A global perspective,' Wiley, West-Sussex.

Billings RB and Jones CV (2008), '*Forecasting urban Water Demand,*' 2nd Edition, American Water Works Association, p. 205.

Blythe J (2006), 'People, process and physical evidence,' *Principles and Practice of Marketing*, Thomson Learning, UK, p. 718.

Bohdanowicz P, Zientara P and Novotna E (2011), 'International Hotel chains and environmental protection: an analysis of Hilton's we care! Program, '*Journal of Sustainable Tourism*,' Vol. 19, No. 7, pp. 791–816.

Ceballos-Lascurain H (1983), 'Tourism, ecotourism and Protected Area,' in Kusler JA (ed.),' Ecotourism and Resource Conservation,' Vol. 1, Ecotourism Conservation project.

Choi S and Ng A (2011), ' Environmental and Economic Dimensions of Sustainability and Price Effects on Consumer Response,' *Journal of Business Ethics*, 104, pp. 269–282.

Coddington W (1993), *'Environmental Marketing: Positive Strategies for reaching the green consumers,'* McGraw Hill, New York.

Cossons N (1989), 'Heritage Tourism-trends and tribulations,' *Tourism Management*, Vol. 10, No 3, pp. 192–194.

Crash (2013), *'F1 teams achieve carbon emissions reduction.'* Online. Available at http://www.crash.net/f1/news/187328/1/f1_teams_cut_carbon_emissions.html. Cited on 1st September 2013.

Dannenbaum M (2012), 'Destination Sustainability: Sustainability Development Report 2011/2012,' TUI AG, Germany, p. 62.

Davis JL (1993), 'Strategies for environmental advertising,' *Journal of Marketing Management*, Vol. 20, pp. 273–319.

Darmame K and Potter R (2011), 'Political discourses and public narratives on water supply issues in Amman, Jordan,' in Mithen S and Black E (2011), *'Water, Life and Civilization: Climate, Environment and Society in the Jordan Valley,'* Cambridge Press, UK, p. 463.

Dickinson JE, Lumsdon LM and Robbins D (2011), 'Slow Travel: Issues for tourism and climate change,' *Journal of Sustainable Tourism*, Vol. 19, No. 3, pp. 281–300.

Dinan C and Sargeant A (2000), 'Social marketing and sustainable tourism-is there a match?,' International Journal of Tourism Research, Vol. 2, No. 1, pp. 1–14.

Dyllick T and Hockerts K (2002), 'Beyond the business case for corporate sustainability, Business Strategy and Environment, Vol. 11, pp. 130–141.

Druker P (1955), *'The Practice of Management,'* Heinemann, London, p. 382.

Eccles G (1995), 'Marketing, Sustainability development and International Tourism,' International Journal of Contemporary Hospitality Management, Vol. 7, Issue 7, pp. 20–26.

Ellen PS (1994), 'Do we know what we need to know? Objective and subjective knowledge effects on proecological behaviors,' *Journal of Business Research*, Vol. 30, pp. 43–52.

Forbes India (2013), 'Uttarakhand disaster is a wakeup call,.' Online. Available at http://forbesindia.com/article/close-range/uttarakhand-disaster-is-a-wakeup-call-rk-pachauri/35719/1. Cited on 1st September 2013.

Gilmore A and Simmons G (2007), 'Integrating Sustainable Tourism and Marketing Management: Can National Parks provide the framework for Strategic Change," *'Strategic Change,'* Vol. 16, pp. 191–200.

Globalexchange (2013), 'About Global Exchange.' Online. Available at http://globalexchange.org/about. Cited on 19th August 2013.

Hall CM (2000), *'Tourism Planning, policies, processes and relationships,'* Pearson Hall.

Hendricks WW, Stockton T and Correll D (n.a.), ' *California Sustainable tourism marketing handbook,'* California Travel and Tourism Commission, p. 18.

Hetzer ND (1965), 'Environment, Tourism, CultureLinks,' *Reprint in Ecosphere*, Vol. 1, Issue 2, pp. 1–3.

Hotels (2007), 'Green Convergence,' *Hotels Magazine*, June, pp. 10–11.

Jamrozy U (2007), 'Marketing of tourism: a paradigm shift towards sustainability,' International Journal of Culture, Tourism and Hospitality research,' Vol. 1, No 2, pp. 117–130.

Jauhari V and Dutta K (2010), 'Managing Service Operations and Processes,' 'Services,' Oxford University press, p. 240.

Kaul H and Gupta S (2009), 'Sustainable Tourism in India,' Worldwide Hospitality and Tourism Themes,' Vol. 1, Issue 1, p. 12–18.

Ketola T (2008), 'A holistic corporate responsibility model: Integrating values, discourses and actions,' Journal of Business Ethics,' No 80, 419–435.

Kilbourne WE, McDonagh P and Prothero A (1997), 'Sustainable consumption and the quality of life: a macromarketing challenge to the dominant social paradign,' Journal of Macromarketing, Vol. 17, No. 1, pp. 4–24.

Klemm M (1992), ' Sustainable Tourism development-Languedoc-Roussillon 30 years on,' *Tourism Management*, Vol. 13, No 2, pp. 169–180.

Krajnc D and Glavic P (2005), 'How to compare companies on relevant dimensions of sustainability, Ecological Economics, 55, Issue 4, pp. 551–563.

Kotler P, Bowen J and Makens J (2006), '*Marketing for Hospitality and Tourism*, Prentice Hall, USA.

Kumar A (2013), 'Personal Interview on Sustainability at Leela Gurgaon Hotel and Residences,.' Conducted on 30th July 2013.

Live Mint and the Wall Street Journal (2013), '*Don't blame nature for the Uttarakhand Flood Disaster.*' Online. Available at http://www.livemint.com/Opinion/hzKmWekwYOOtYKv8N-6dZIN/Dont-blame-naturefor-the-Uttarakhand-flood-disaster.html. Cited on 1st September 2013.

Mackenzie A (2012), 'The marketing paradox: sustainability needs to become responsible growth,' Market Leader, Quarter 4, pp. 14–15.

May V, 'Tourism, Environment and Development: Values, sustainability and stewardship,' Tourism Management, Vol. 12, No 2, pp. 112–18.

Matahari Beach Resort and Spa (2013), '*In 2008 Matahari Beach Resort and Spa received the "Green Hotel Standard.*' Online. Available at http://www.matahari-beach-resort.com/en/9/. Cited 17th June 2013.

McCool S(2009), 'Constructing partnerships for protected area tourism planning in an era of change and messiness,' Journal of Sustainable Tourism, Vol. 17, Issue 2, pp. 133–148.

McDonagh P (1998), 'Towards a theory of sustainable communication in Risk Society: Relating issues of sustainability to marketing communications,' *Journal of Marketing Management*, Vol. 14, pp. 591–622.

McDonald S and Oates CJ (2006), 'Sustainability: Consumer perceptions and Marketing Strategies,' *Business Strategy and Environment,* 'Vol. 15, pp. 157–170.

Middleton VTC and Hawkins R (1998), '*Sustainable Tourism: A Marketing Perspective,*' Heinemann-Butterworth Publishing, Oxford, UK.

Miller GA (2011), 'Consumerism in Sustainable Tourism: A Survey of UK Consumers, *Journal of Sustainable Tourism*, Vol. 11, No 1, pp. 17–39.

Mintel (2009), 'Slow Travel: Special report', January 2009, Mintel International Group Limited, London.

Mitchell RW, Wooliscroft B and Higham J (2010), 'Sustainable market orientation: A new approach to managing marketing strategy, Journal of Macromarketing, Vol. 20, Issue 2, pp. 160–170

Moeller T, Dolnicar S and Leisch F (2011), 'The sustainability-Profitability tradeoff in tourism: can it be overcome?,' *Journal of Sustainable Tourism*, Vol. 19, No 2, pp. 155–169.

Ogilvy PR and TotemTourism (2011), '*Sustainable Tourism Marketing Guide 2011,*' United Kingdom, p. 4.

Pettie K (1992), '*Green Marketing,*' Pitman Publishing, London.

Polonksy M; Carlson L and Fry M (2003), 'The harm chain: A Public Policy Development and stakeholder perspective, *Marketing Theory*, Vol. 3, No 3, pp. 345–364.

Pomering A, Noble G and Johnson l (2011), 'Conceptualizing a contemporary Marketing mix for sustainable tourism,' *Journal of Sustainable Tourism*, Vol. 19, No 8, pp. 953–969.

Prakash A (2002), 'Green Marketing, public policy and managerial strategies,' *Business Strategy and the Environment,*' Vol. 2 p. 285–297.

Rishi M and Gaur SS (2012), 'Emerging sales and marketing challenges in the global hospitality industry: A thematic analysis of customer reviews from the world's top two tourist destinations,' *Worldwide Hospitality and Tourism Themes*, Vol. 4, Issue 2, pp. 131–149.

Rothenberg S (2003), 'Knowledge content and worker participation in environmental management at NUMMI, *Journal of Management Studies*, Vol. 40, Issue 7, pp. 1783–1802.

Ruschmann D (1992), 'Ecological tourism in Brazil,' Tourism Management, Vol. 14, No 1, pp. 125–128.

Russel R and Faulkner B (2004), 'Entrepreneurship, chaos and the tourism area lifecycle,' Annals of Tourism research, Vol. 31, No. 3, pp. 556–79.

Singh A, Rishi M and Shukla R (2011), 'Green Management and Environmental Sustainability: a case of ITC Green Centre,' *Emerald Emerging Markets Case Study Collection*, Vol. 1, No 2, pp. 1–20.

Schlegelmilch BB; Bohlen GM and Diamantopoilos A (1996), 'The link between green purchasing decisions and measures of environmental consciousness,' *European Journal of Marketing*, Vol. 30, Issue 5, pp. 35–55.

Sheth JN, Sethia NK and Srinivas S (2011), 'Mindful Consumption: A customer centric approach to sustainability,' *Journal of Academy of Marketing Science*, Vol. 39, pp. 21–39.

Shrivastava P (1994), 'Castrated Environment: Greening organizational studies,' *Organization Studies*, Vol. 15, No 5, pp. 705–726.

Smerecnik KR and Andersen PA (2011), 'The diffusion of environmentally sustainable innovations in North American hotels and ski resorts,' Journal of Sustainable tourism, Vol. 19, No 2, pp. 171–196.

Swarbrooke j (1996), 'Understanding the tourist-some thoughts on consumer behavior research in tourism,' *Insight*s (November), pp. 67–76.

The Leela (2013), 'The Leela Gurgaon Hotel and Residencies,' Online. Available at *http://www. theleela.com/locations/gurgaon/hotel-information*. Cited on 13th August 2013.

The Hindu (2013), 'Uttarakhand disaster caused due to unplanned development.' Online. Available at http://www.thehindu.com/news/national/uttarakhand-disaster-caused-due-to-unplanned-development-medha/article4904428.ece. Cited on 1st September 2013.

Tour Operator's Initiative (2003a), 'Sustainable Tourism: The Tour Operators' Contribution,' *United Nations Environment Program, Division of Technology, Industry and Economics*, France, pp. 26–27.

Tour Operator's Initiative (2003b), 'Sustainable Tourism: The Tour Operators' Contribution,' *United Nations Environment Program, Division of Technology, Industry and Economics*, France, pp. 77–78.

Tour Operators' Initiative (2003c), Sustainable Tourism: The Tour Operators' Contribution,' *United Nations Environment Program, Division of Technology, Industry and Economics*, France, p. 76.

*Tour Operators' Initiative (*2003) [D] Sustainable Tourism: The Tour Operators' Contribution,' *United Nations Environment Program, Division of Technology, Industry and Economics*, France, pp. 16–17.

Tourism Victora (2012), '*Environmentally Sustainable Tourism Strategic Plan 2009–2012,'* pg 12.

TUI AG (2013), 'TUI AG in Profile.' Online. *Available at http://www.tui-group.com/de/unternehmen/profil.* Cited on 10th August 2013.

UNEP (2005), 'Marketing Sustainable Tourism Products,' United Nations Environment Program and Regione Toscana.

US Travel data Center (1992), '*Discover America: Tourism and the Environment-A guide to challenges and opportunities for travel industry businesses,*' Travel Association of America, Washington DC.

Van Dam YK and Apeldoorn AC (1996), 'Sustainable marketing,' Journal of Macro-Marketing,' pp. 45–56

Wary M (2011), 'Adopting and implementing a trans active approach to sustainable tourism planning: translating theory into practice, '*Journal of Sustainable Tourism,'* Vol. 19, No. 4–5, pp. 605–627.

Walker JR and Walker JT (2012), 'Exploring the Hospitality Industry,' 2nd Edition, Pearson, p. 119.

WCED (1987), 'United Nations World Commission on Environment and Development. Available at http://www.un-documents.net/wced-ocf.htm.

Wherli R, Priskin J, Demarmels S, Kolberg S, Schaffner D, Schwarz J, Truniger F and Steller J, 'How to communicate sustainable tourism products effectively to consumers,' *Presented at the World Tourism Forum*, Lucerne, 2013.

World trade Organization (1955), '*What Tourism Managers need to know: A practical guide to the development and use of indicators of sustainable tourism.* Madrid.

Ye H and Tussydiah IP (2011), 'Destination Visual Image and Expectation of Experiences,' Journal of Travel and Tourism Marketing, Vol. 18, No 8, pp. 997–1014.

Zinkeviciute V (2009), 'Strategic decisions of tourism companies in the context of sustainable development,' *Issues of Business and Law*, Vol. 1, pp. 54–62.

CHAPTER 6

DESTINATION MANAGEMENT AND SUSTAINABILITY

KIRTI DUTTA, SWATI SINGH, H. G. PARSA, and VINNIE JAUHARI

CONTENTS

ABSTRACT

The paper provides a perspective on how tourism can be made more sustainable keeping in mind the ecological principals. It explores the 4 M's—Management of Resources, Monetary Aspect, Manpower and Marketing model by taking a holistic view of the ecosystem and draws the constructs from the UNEP and WTO's (2005) guide to policy makers that provide a framework for the various stakeholders. Management of resources include 'resource efficiency' and 'environment purity' while monetary aspect includes 'economic viability' leading to 'community wellbeing.' The manpower aspect looks at both the employees and the visitors. For employees tourism would be a means of poverty alleviation for visitors tourism would be looked into from the aspect of cultural richness, biological diversity and physical resources. Keeping in mind this framework the paper explores the consumer's feelings and draws their attitude towards participation in and evaluation of tourist destinations employing these practices

6.1   INTRODUCTION

The global economic scenario in the last few years has been a matter of concern for all economies. One industry that continues to show positive growth in spite of the recessionary trends worldwide is tourism industry. It contributed ('direct, indirect and induced impact') USD 6.6 trillion to the world GDP (i.e., 9% of 'total economy GDP'), provided 260 million jobs (i.e., 1 in 11 jobs) and USD 1.2 trillion in exports (i.e., 5% of world exports)(World Travel and Tourism Council (WTTC), 2013). 'According to the latest *UNWTO World Tourism Barometer*, international tourism receipts hit a new record in 2012, reaching an estimated US$ 1075 billion (euro 837 billion) worldwide, up 4% in real terms, from US$ 1042 billion (euro 749 billion) in 2011.' The export earnings stood at 'US$ 219 billion in 2012, bringing total receipts generated by international tourism to US$ 1.3 trillion.' Thailand and India were the top two 'emerging economy destinations' that reported the 'highest receipts growth' at 25% and 22% respectively (UNWTO, 2013b). This robust growth in tourism was sustained in the first four months of the year 2013 when an extra 12 million tourists traveled worldwide (total tourists traveling were 298 million) in comparison to the same period during 2012 when the total tourists traveling were 286 million (UNWTO, 2013c). According to 'UNWTO Secretary-General, Taleb Rifai "…Tourism is thus one of the pillars that should be supported by governments around the world as part of the solution to stimulating economic growth,"' (UNWTO, 2013a). This is further corroborated by the fact that the 'direct contribution to world GDP is set to grow by 4.4% on an average per year over the next ten years' from 2013–2023. By 2023 'Travel and Tourism's total contribution will account for 10% GDP and 1 in 10 jobs' (WTTC, 2013).

Growth of tourism in Asia and the Pacific region shows the highest average annual growth rate in the period 2005–2012 and is growing at 6.2% followed by Africa at 6%. In Asia, South East Asia and South Asia showed the highest average growth rate at 8.3% and 8.2% respectively in the same period (UNWTO, 2013d). Globally tourism ranks fourth in the export category after 'fuels, chemicals and automotive products' (McIntire, 2011a).

Travel and Tourism industry is therefore a force to reckon with and countries can gain significantly by pursuing this sector vigorously (Ramgulam et al., 2012). It has been studied that tourism has a major impact (both positive and negative) on the environment (both natural and built) and the 'wellbeing and culture of the host populations.' Efforts therefore need to be made so as to maximize the positive effects and minimize the negative ones through 'sustainable tourism development' (UNEP—WTO, 2005). The issue of sustainability has been discussed in the context of tourism since the 'first World Conference on Sustainable Tourism (WTO, UNEP, UNESCO, EU, 1995).' Literature since then shows that the tourist activities are considered extremely "pollutant" (Holden 2008 cited in Battaglia et al., 2012) and at the local level there is a strong correlation between 'profitability of tourist businesses and preservation of the "environmental" carrying capacity of the territory where the activities take place' (Battaglia et al., 2012). The 'environment' stands for 'the broad set of natural, anthropological, economic and social factors characterizing a specific region' (Calabro and Iraldo (2002) cited in Battaglia et al., 2012). The current paper therefore focuses on the natural and anthropological elements in the management of resources, economic factors in the monetary aspect, social factors in the manpower section (where both the visitors and manpower of the host destination aspects are considered) and ties this with the marketing aspect to communicate the same to the tourists.

6.2 SUSTAINABLE DESTINATION MANAGEMENT

Compared to most of the other industries tourism is multi-resource based (like climate, topography, habitats, ecosystems, etc.) and not single resource based (Burton, 1995 cited in Amiryan and Silva, 2013). The diverse topography and rich heritage of India enables it to demonstrate all the three core forms of tourism highlighted in the context of developing countries (Lumsdon and Swift, 1998) like ecotourism, beach tourism and heritage/cultural tourism. This is a strong incentive in itself and requires conservation of tourism destinations (Amiryan and Silva, 2013). There are a number of players involved in the management of tourism destination—be it government or private players. Sustainable measures require to be adopted across all the players to ensure its successful implementation as no single stakeholder fully controls the planning and development of sustainable tourism (Jamal, Hartl and Lohmer, 2010). Marketing a place requires all the stakeholders to work strategically towards the planning, development of place competitiveness and marketing and promotion of the same to the target market (Metaxas, 2009). All the stakeholders need to be involved in the sustainable management of the destination and work as environmental protectors while accommodating the welfare and interest of the other stakeholders and the environment (Walker and Hanson, 1998).

Countries need to challenge the GDP (Gross Domestic Product) model to measure the 'wealth of a country' and include 'environmental happiness framework' in their measurement metrics to ensure happiness for its citizens—a case in point discussed is Bhutan which includes in its 'four pillars of happiness' the protection of the environment and considers it more important than GDP (Ramgulam et al., 2013). Thus Bhutan's Gross National Happiness Index enables it to maintain a balance between modernization and economic development while preserving its unique culture and pristine environment. Their model of 'high-value, low-volume' tourism has led to high-end tourists visiting the country and the revenue so generated is second only to hydropower in the country (McIntire, 2011b). Bhutan as a global best practice case is discussed in global best practices section.

Learning can also be drawn from the Japanese model where regulations are imposed on areas/landscapes that need to be preserved. The Ministry of Environment ensures that agreements are established with landowners of the area to be preserved. The area management responsibility is delegated to the nonprofit organizations and makes it possible to include the local people in management of the conserved areas. Central government needs to encourage the local governments for involvement of the 'local community' so that the management is bottom up and not top down (Hiwasaki, 2003). It has been studied that participating in sustainable development allows local community to live better according to their own values; instills confidence in their own ability to deal with local issues and also ensures a regular livelihood (Halme and Fadeeva, 2000). Let us now look at the role of the various stakeholders in sustainable destination management.

6.3   ROLE OF VARIOUS STAKEHOLDERS

Sustainable destination management implies the appropriate utilization of resources in a manner that the future resource requirements are not impaired (WTO, 1997). The aim being to create a win–win situation for all the tourism stakeholders (Jurowski, 2002) as the natural environment is an important variable impacting the 'demand' and 'supply' of tourism services (Ayuso, 2006). The national, regional and local governments and the tourism enterprises, local community and NGOs need to work in a harmonious and unanimous manner to ensure the smooth running of the tourism system (Shen, 2008). Literature shows a high correlation between profitability generated in tourism business and preservation of the environment of the region where tourism activities occur (Borzino, 1999 cited in Battaglia et al., 2012). A look at the 'contemporary tourists' shows that the 'tourists are ecologically aware and especially interested in experiencing the atmosphere and becoming familiar with the identity of the destination.' Selection of the tourist destination is primarily influenced by resources like landscape, ecology, traditional architecture, cultural tradition and climate (Gracan, Zadel and Rudancic-Lugaric, 2011). Thus the atmosphere is responsible for attracting the tourists to the destination and harming it would be similar to killing the goose that lays the golden eggs. Tourism businesses is therefore a part of the 'coherent regional offering' (Roberts and Hall, 2003) and needs to function in and sustain the regional offering.

The small and medium enterprises (SME) play an important role in ensuring the supply of tourist facilities. In the process they maintain the cultural integrity of the area where they are located by offering local cuisines and showcasing tradition and culture of the place. Participation in sustainable tourism practices helps such SMEs to gain competitive advantage, helps them in image improvement, ensures resource optimization and saving of costs and last but not the least enables them to influence the decisions taken by government (local, regional), larger corporations, etc. which would otherwise not have been possible for them (Halme and Fadeeva, 2000). Sustainable development of tourism can be explored through multi-stakeholder partnerships (Hiwasaki, 2003) and it is important for all the stakeholders to share the fundamental regard for the environment for successful achievement of sustainability (Walker and Hanson, 1998). This is easier said than done as the different partners may have conflicting goals, false expectations and/or short-term thinking (Halme and Fadeeva, 2000). The various stakeholders are the tourism enterprises that provide the tourism experience to the customers. Their aim should be long-term sustainability of the destination so that they can 'milk' the destination for longer period of time. The local community is the next most important stakeholder as they are a part of both the experience of the tourists and the service that is to be provided to them. The government through sustainable tourism can provide more jobs to them without discriminating on the basis of gender, race, disability, etc. This will lead to poverty alleviation and add to the prosperity of the local community. The role of environmentalists as stakeholders cannot be overlooked as they are responsible for ensuring sustainable practices are being enforced. Last but not the least the tourists are also important stakeholders (UNEP WTO, 2005) as they make the wheel go round by patronizing such destinations for a quality experience.

These various stakeholders can be seen in the bigger picture as the different players of a game where the goal is sustainability and the destination that manages to be sustainable and also draws the maximum number of tourists is seen as the winner.

6.4   CONSUMER INSIGHTS INTO CHOICE OF DESTINATIONS

The most commonly cited definition for tourist destination image is 'the sum of beliefs, ideas and impressions that a person has of a destination' (Crompton, 1979, p. 18). The image that the consumers have of a destination influences both the purchase behavior (Crompton, 1979) and post-purchase evaluation (Musa et al., 2010). However, studies also show that the positive attitude of the tourists towards sustainable destinations does not translate into purchases. Only one out of 20 tourists that have positive attitude actually purchase sustainable tourism packages or purchase local produce or purchase 'environmentally friendly transportation' (Chafe, 2005). It has been studied that a majority of such tourists do not want to change their purchase behavior to support sustainable tourism and the low demand for such destinations is 'one of the main barriers for or progress towards sustainable tourism.' So as to receive a favorable response from customers the correct beliefs need to be addressed and the quality of information plays an important intervening variable. Thus what motivates the tourists (tourism related) along with their sustainability values need to be addressed to influence the tourist's purchase behavior (Budeanu, 2007). The 'environmental information disclosure quality' is found to positively impact the corporate reputation, builds credibility among stakeholders and leads to sustainable growth of the company following such practices due to the competitive advantage provided (Rattanaphaphtham and Kunsrison, 2011). Thus following sustainable practices and communicating the same to the customers will lead to enhanced corporate performance.

Marketing of the sustainable tourism destination if used strategically can encourage more tourists to visit the destination and at the same time persuade them to perform sustainability practices at the destination. This marketing needs to be done not only on-site but off-site as well (Gilmore et al., 2007) in the form of information about the practices being followed so that it leads to image building and making the customers aware about what is expected of them when they visit such destinations. Literature shows that sustainable information source for travel and tourism are the travel guides, Internet and personal networks (McDonald et al., 2009). Thus information can be provided through the Internet on the company website in different languages for the global audience, travel guides, blogs and by providing memorable experience to the customers so that they spread positive word of mouth.

6.5 FROM SUSTAINABLE DESTINATION MANAGEMENT TO CONSUMERS CHOICE OF HOLIDAY DESTINATION

The sustainable management, role of stakeholders and consumer insights can be linked together for sustainable tourism development (see Figure 1). The government (both central and local) are responsible for sustainable destination development through their various policies and practices. The double arrow shows that as a result of this the government would itself follow sustainable practices and become environmentally responsible in its day-to-day activities as well. The local community also imbibes sustainable practices in its day-to-day life and ensures sustainability of the destination. Various service providers to the destination (airlines, travel agents, etc.) are the receivers, perpetrators and transmitters of sustainable destination information. Once they inform the tourists of the sustainable practices at the destination, they can imbibe and integrate this information into their activities also. The SMEs are the souvenir manufacturers, entertainment providers, etc., and they are responsible for the development and performance of sustainable practices at tourism destination. Hospitality firms are dealt with separately as they are the main actors and have maximum access to the tourists as far as delivery of services is concerned during their stay at the destination. They can highlight the various sustainable practices being practiced at their property and guide and influence the tourists to a 'sustainable' behavior while at the destination.

These firms can through their website inform the global audience about the sustainable practices being adopted and how it has impacted the planet. The transport service providers at the tourism destination, guides, etc., can all educate, influence, and ensure that the tourists behave responsibly. The development of sustainable destination needs to be communicated to the global audience for awareness and influence on their choice of holiday destination. Once at the destination the visible performance of sustainable practices and the education of the same to the tourists are bound to influence the tourists to behave responsibly. After their return from the destination it is suggested that a feedback be provided by the hospitality firms about how their sustainable behavior impacted the planet. This will enhance the holiday satisfaction, increase loyalty towards choice of sustainable holiday destination and lead to positive word of mouth.

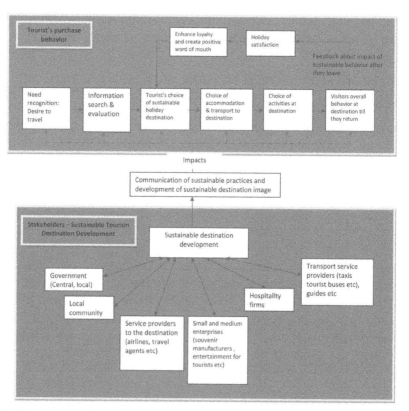

FIGURE 1   Integrated sustainable development (*derived from:* Budeanu, 2007; Gilmore et al., 2007; Holjevac, 2008).

6.6.1   RESEARCH FROM INDIA

The abovefigure shows a crucial link between Stakeholders sustainable tourism destination development and tourist's purchase behavior—communication of sustainable practices. The communication has to be affective for it to not only develop sustainable destination image but also influence the customers to purchase the tourism destination as well. The current research will focus on what is it that influences the customers the most as far as sustainable practices are concerned and which practices influence them to purchase the tourism destination.

6.6.2   CONSTRUCTS STUDIED

A concept associated with 'the many definitions of sustainable tourism is the 'Triple Bottom Line' and the term was first attributed to Elkington (1997).' The three distinct 'lines' are the economic bottom line, the people bottom line and the planet bottom line (La Lopa and Day, 2011) that is the economic, social and environmental. This concept of the Triple Bottom Line has been carried forward by UN WTO according to which the suitable balance needs to be established between the three for long-term sustainability (UN WTO, 2009). These three pillars can be represented in the 12 aims of the sustainable development agenda set by UNEP-WTO, 2005 where each aim impacts each pillar to varying extent. For example the cultural richness aim is primarily impacting the social aspect but also impacts the environmental aspect 'in terms of built environment' and how the society interacts with nature culturally. For the study we have also drawn from these 12 aims have been clubbed into the first three of the following four broad aspects for sustainability:

(1) Management of Resources: Keeping in mind the sustainability of the environment the resources need to be managed effectively and efficiently. This includes
- 'resource efficiency' that is the minimum use of natural resources in operation of tourism services
- 'environment purity' that includes minimum release of pollutants and minimum generation of waste while consumption of tourism facilities by visitors

(2) Monetary Aspect: The money generated from tourism needs to be directed towards further conservation of the area (Hiwasaki, 2003). The monetary aspect therefore includes

- 'economic viability': A tourism destination is viable when the local environment is well maintained. The money generated in the tourism activity should be partly retained in maintaining the environment. This also includes the money spent on brand building of the tourist destination, media management and ensuring that the delivery of services is as per the band promise is all covered. This not only attracts more tourists leading to enhanced business for the service providers but also enhances the earnings of the local community. The earnings can be used to develop support systems, amenities, etc. ultimately leading to community wellbeing.

(3) Manpower: Local people can be trained to provide services related to tourism—for example guide services, hospitality services, sightseeing services, etc.However, the impact of tourism is not limited to the people in the destination region but should also take into consideration the sociocultural and social impact on the individual tourist (Jamal et al., 2010) as well. The manpower aspect looks at both the employees and the visitors as follows:

- For employees tourism would be a poverty alleviation tool and also for social equity (as the employment generation would lead to earnings being fairly distributed throughout the community).
- Visitor fulfillment would be looked into from the aspect of cultural richness, biological diversity and physical resources to generate unique experiences.

(4) Marketing model: The 'tourism system' involves a number of players present at both regional and global level like the tourists, destination regions, generating regions, transit routes, etc.(Leiper, 2000 cited in Jamal et al., 2010). These players at different levels need to be made aware of the sustainable tourism practices of the destination areas to increase the awareness of the different partners leading to a positive influence on the choice of the tourist destination. The money spent on advertising and brand though marketing includes a host of activities the following paper would focus on the following:

- What needs to be communicated during the promotion of tourism destinations and how to market the destination as 'sustainable' according to the consumers?

Accordingly a study was conducted in Delhi and National Capital Region (in India) through a structured questionnaire. The constructs of the questionnaire were drawn from the four points discussed above and were sent to four experts from the hospitality industry and two experts from the academia for review. The final questionnaire was then administered personally to 178 respondents out of which 138 were valid as the rest were not aware of the concept of sustainable tourism. These respondents were educated about the same but their questionnaires were not considered for the study. The questionnaire had broadly three parts. The first dealt with the respondents' level of agreement with regard to whether the tourism industry should engage in the stated sustainable practice. The second part then tried to capture which of these practices if highlighted in the communication process would influence their willingness to patronize the destination following such practices. The third section dealt with the respondents' demographic information and their perception about the sustainable tourism destination and the kind of tourists that visit such destinations.

It was found that 20% of the respondents don't look for information related to the sustainable practices of the tourist destination; 45% pay attention to such information when presented but don't think about it otherwise and 34% of the respondents seek such information and use it in making their tourism destination decisions.

6.6.3   SUSTAINABLE PRACTICES TO BE ENGAGED IN BY TOURISM DESTINATION

Out of the different sustainable practices 28 were delineated for the respondents. Respondents were then asked to rate these on a 5-point Likert scale according to their belief of which sustainable practice should be enforced at the tourist destination. Principal Component Analysis along with Varimax Rotation and Kaiser Normalization was then applied with the help of SPSS and these 28 practices were reduced to 24 in the six factors that were derived from the factor analysis where the rotation was converged in nine iterations. These factors accounted for 67.763% of the variance (Table 1).

TABLE 1   Total variance explained for sustainable practice to be engaged in by tourism destination.

Component	Initial Eigenvalues			Extraction Sums of Squared Loadings			Rotation Sums of Squared Loadings		
	Total	% of Variance	Cumulative %	Total	% of Variance	Cumulative %	Total	% of Variance	Cumulative %
1	11.650	41.607	41.607	11.650	41.607	41.607	11.650	41.607	41.607
2	2.195	7.840	49.447	2.195	7.840	49.447	2.195	7.840	49.447
3	1.832	6.544	55.991	1.832	6.544	55.991	1.832	6.544	55.991

TABLE 1   *(Continued)*

Component	Initial Eigenvalues			Extraction Sums of Squared Loadings			Rotation Sums of Squared Loadings		
	Total	% of Variance	Cumula-tive %	Total	% of Variance	Cumula-tive %	Total	% of Vari-ance	Cumu-lative %
4	1.309	4.674	60.665	1.309	4.674	60.665	1.309	4.674	60.665
5	1.155	4.126	64.790	1.155	4.126	64.790	1.155	4.126	64.790
6	1.010	3.608	68.398	1.010	3.608	68.398	1.010	3.608	68.398
7	0.954	3.407	71.805						
8	0.867	3.095	74.900						
9	0.777	2.777	77.677						
10	0.707	2.525	80.201						
11	0.589	2.104	82.305						
12	0.565	2.019	84.325						
13	0.515	1.841	86.166						
14	0.509	1.816	87.982						
15	0.450	1.607	89.589						
16	0.376	1.343	90.932						
17	0.356	1.270	92.203						
18	0.341	1.218	93.421						
19	0.271	.967	94.388						
20	0.256	.913	95.301						
21	0.239	.852	96.153						
22	0.226	.807	96.961						
23	0.203	.727	97.687						
24	0.173	.619	98.306						
25	0.144	.515	98.822						
26	0.130	.466	99.287						
27	0.117	.419	99.707						
28	0.082	.293	100.000						

Extraction Method: Principal Component Analysis.

The sustainable practices at the tourism destination that should be imple-mented are captured in the six factors that have been delineated (see Table 2). The first factor that has been delineated is conservation of energy, cultural heritage, natural resources and job equality. This includes training people to be environment friendly and ensuring optimum utilization of resources. The government should ensure job equality and plow back monetary resources generated in the conservation and development of the destination. The richness of natural resources and cultural richness should be maintained to provide a distinctive experience to the tourists. The second factor has been captured is the stakeholders responsibility that includes all the service providers at the tourism destination like airlines, hotels, taxi service providers guides, etc. along with the government should not only practice conservation of resources but should also encourage visitors to adopt sustainable practices. The number and quality of local jobs should increase and there should be job security as well. Service providers should ensure that organization infrastructure has been built using local material. For a unique experience there should be biological diversity in the tourism destination and it is important for the destination to be visible and spread awareness about the same.

TABLE 2 Sustainable practice factors to be engaged in by tourism destination.

Factor	Construct	Aspect	Cronbach Alpha
	Train people at tourism destination to be environment friendly	Management of resources	
	Government and tourism destination service providers should create sensibility among visitors to respect environment and community	Management of resources	
	Service providers should minimize the use of scarce and nonrenewable resources in the development and operation of tourism facilities and services.	Management of resources	
1: Conservation of energy, cultural heritage, natural resources and job equality	Income generated by tourism (e.g., entry fees to monuments, museums, etc.) should be used for conservation of the destination	Monetary aspect	0.89
	Income generated should be used for development of destination	Monetary aspect	

TABLE 2 *(Continued)*

Factor	Construct	Aspect	Cronbach Alpha
	Government and company should ensure the level of pay, conditions of service and availability of job equally to all without discrimination by gender, race, disability, etc.	Manpower—local community	
	Destination should be culturally rich and should have historic heritage, authentic culture, traditions and distinctiveness of host communities	Manpower—Tourists	
	Destination should be rich in natural resources, landscapes, etc. to provide a unique experience to tourists	Manpower—Tourists	
	Tourism destination service providers (airlines, hotels, taxi drivers, tour guides, etc.) should encourage visitors to adopt sustainable methods	Management of resources	
	Government and service providers should support the conservation of environment and avoid the physical and visual degradation of the environment	Management of resources	
	Organization infrastructure has been built using local material	Monetary aspect	
2: Stakeholders Responsibility	Government/company of tourism destination should provide secure job to people of the local community	Manpower—local community	0.889
	Government/organization should increase the number and quality of local jobs	Manpower—local community	

TABLE 2 *(Continued)*

Factor	Construct	Aspect	Cronbach Alpha
3: Management of resources	Destination should have biological diversity—sea, mountains, etc. for unique experience to tourists	Manpower—Tourist	0.867
	Destination should have visibility as far as communications about the same is concerned	Economic viability	
	Train people at tourism destination for optimum use of natural resources (water)	Management of resources	
	Train people to use technology to save electricity (like solar heaters, energy saving light bulb, etc.)	Management of resources	
	Encourage business with environmentally friendly service providers	Management of resources	
	Train people for recycling products to reduce waste	Management of resources	
	Train people to use environmentally responsible cleaners	Management of resources	
4: Empowering Local community	Service providers should be encouraged to purchase local products (consumables like amenities, food items, etc.)	Monetary aspect	0.752
	Government should engage and empower local communities in planning and decision-making about the management and future development of tourism in their area, in consultation with other stakeholders.	Manpower—local community	
	Destination should provide informative material about sustainable practices	Economic viability	

TABLE 2 *(Continued)*

Factor	Construct	Aspect	Cronbach Alpha
5: Developing support systems	Income should be used for developing amenities like hospitals, hotels, etc., of the place	Monetary aspect	0.585
	Income should be used for developing support systems like schools, etc.	Monetary aspect	
6: Using environmentally friendly products	Train people to use organic products/environmentally friendly products	Management of resources	—

The third factor includes management of resources like water, electricity. It encourages business with environmentally friendly service providers, train people for recycling products to reduce waste, and to use environmentally responsible cleaners. Empowering local community is the fourth factor that includes purchasing local products, engaging them in planning and decision making for development of tourism in that area and provides informative material about sustainable practices. Developing support systems like schools and amenities like hotels, hospitals, etc., for the destination constitute the fifth factor that has been delineated. The sixth factor includes training people to use organic products or environmentally friendly products. A measure of construct reliability (Cronbach's Alpha) was computed for each dimension to assess the reliability of the set of items forming that dimension (see Table2). These α coefficients range from 0.89 to 0.585. As a rule α of 0.50 or more represent satisfactory reliability of the items measured. Thus the items measuring the dimensions appear to be sufficiently reliable.

6.6.4   SUSTAINABLE PRACTICES INFLUENCING WILLINGNESS TO PATRONIZE SUSTAINABLE DESTINATION

Failure to change attitude during communications is attributed to the fact that it does not address the right beliefs (Fishbein and Manfredo, 1992). Thus a study of the practices that the consumer feels should be adopted at sustainable tourism sites has to be followed with which such factor would influence them to make a purchase. Thus to explore if the sustainable practices information influences the respondent's willingness to patronize the destination; the respondents were asked to rank (on a 5 point Likert scale) their willingness to visit the destination knowing that the destination enforces sustainable practices. Principal Component Analysis along with Varimax Rotation and Kaiser Normalization was then applied with the help of SPSS and these 28 practices were reduced to 26 in the six factors that were derived from the factor analysis where the rotation was converged in eight iterations. These factors accounted for 69.382 % of the variance (Table 3).

TABLE 3 Total variance explained for sustainable practices influence on willingness to patronize the destination.

Com-ponent	Initial Eigenvalues			Extraction Sums of Squared Loadings			Rotation Sums of Squared Loadings		
	Total	% of Vari-ance	Cumu-lative %	Total	% of Vari-ance	Cumula-tive %	Total	% of Vari-ance	Cumu-lative %
1	9.182	32.794	32.794	9.182	32.794	32.794	9.182	32.794	32.794
2	4.220	15.073	47.867	4.220	15.073	47.867	4.220	15.073	47.867
3	1.898	6.778	54.645	1.898	6.778	54.645	1.898	6.778	54.645
4	1.669	5.959	60.604	1.669	5.959	60.604	1.669	5.959	60.604
5	1.357	4.847	65.452	1.357	4.847	65.452	1.357	4.847	65.452
6	1.100	3.930	69.382	1.100	3.930	69.382	1.100	3.930	69.382
7	0.927	3.312	72.694						
8	0.893	3.189	75.883						
9	0.765	2.732	78.615						
10	0.671	2.398	81.013						
11	0.611	2.182	83.195						
12	0.559	1.998	85.193						
13	0.466	1.663	86.856						
14	0.443	1.581	88.438						
15	0.419	1.497	89.934						
16	0.392	1.399	91.333						

TABLE 3   *(Continued)*

Component	Initial Eigenvalues			Extraction Sums of Squared Loadings			Rotation Sums of Squared Loadings		
	Total	% of Variance	Cumulative %	Total	% of Variance	Cumulative %	Total	% of Variance	Cumulative %
17	0.317	1.133	92.466						
18	0.295	1.053	93.520						
19	0.285	1.017	94.537						
20	0.261	.931	95.468						
21	0.250	.894	96.362						
22	0.219	.782	97.144						
23	0.179	.638	97.782						
24	0.177	.633	98.416						
25	0.128	.456	98.871						
26	0.118	.422	99.294						
27	0.109	.390	99.683						
28	0.089	.317	100.000						

Extraction method: principal component analysis.

It was found that there is a difference between the factors that customers feel should be enforced at the tourism destination and the factors that influence them to patronize such destinations (Table 4). The foremost factor that influences the purchase is that development of destination and empowerment of local communities. If the money generated from tourism is plowed back for development of infrastructure, amenities and support systems. Empowerment of local communities can be done by providing more number of secure and quality jobs and by involving them in decision making for future development of the area.

TABLE 4 Sustainable practices influence on willingness to patronize.

Factor	Construct	Aspect	Cronbach Alpha
1: Development of destination and empowerment of local communities	Income generated should be used for development of destination	Monetary	0.901
	Income should be used for developing infrastructure of the destination	Monetary	
	Income should be used for developing amenities like hospitals, hotels, etc. of the place	Monetary	
	Income should be used for developing support systems like schools, etc.	Monetary	
	Service providers should be encouraged to purchase local products (consumables like amenities, food items, etc.)	Monetary	
	Government/company of tourism destination should provide secure job to people of the local community	Manpower—local community	
	Government/organization should increase the number and quality of local jobs	Manpower—local community	
	Government should engage and empower local communities in planning and decision making about the management and future development of tourism in their area, in consultation with other stakeholders.	Manpower—local community	

TABLE 4   *(Continued)*

Factor	Construct	Aspect	Cronbach Alpha
	Train people at tourism destination to be environment friendly	Management of resources	
	Government and service providers should support the conservation of environment and avoid the physical and visual degradation of the environment	Management of resources	
2: Conservation of destination	Government and service providers should support the conservation of natural areas, habitats and wildlife, and minimize damage to them	Management of resources	0.824
	Income generated by tourism (e.g., entry fees to monuments, museums, etc.) should be used for conservation of the destination	Monetary	
	Organization infrastructure has been built using local materials	Monetary	
	Destination should be culturally rich and should have historic heritage, authentic culture, traditions and distinctiveness of host communities	Manpower—Tourists	
	Destination should be rich in natural resources, landscapes, etc. to provide a unique experience to tourists	Manpower—Tourists	

TABLE 4 *(Continued)*

Factor	Construct	Aspect	Cronbach Alpha
3: Destination diversity and communication	Destination should have biological diversity—sea, mountains, etc. for unique experience to tourists	Manpower—Tourists	0.81
	Destination should have visibility as far as communications about the same is concerned	Economic viability	
	Destination should provide informative material about sustainable practices	Economic viability	
4: Training for service providers	Train people at tourism destination for optimum use of natural resources (water)	Management of resources	
	Train people to use technology to save electricity (like solar heaters, energy saving light bulb, etc.)	Management of resources	0.737
	Encourage business with environmentally friendly service providers	Management of resources	
	Tourism destination service providers (airlines, hotels, taxi drivers, tour guides, etc.) should encourage visitors to adopt sustainable methods	Management of resources	
	Government and tourism destination service providers should create sensibility among visitors to respect environment and community	Management of resources	

TABLE 4 *(Continued)*

Factor	Construct	Aspect	Cronbach Alpha
5: Sensitizing visitors and application by service providers	Service providers should minimize the use of scarce and nonrenewable resources in the development and operation of tourism facilities and services.	Management of resources	0.805
	Train people to use environmentally responsible cleaners	Management of resources	
	Train people to use organic products/environmentally friendly products	Management of resources	
6: Social equality	Government and company should ensure the level of pay, conditions of service and availability of job equally to all without discrimination by gender, race, disability, etc.	Manpower—local community	—

The second factor that influences purchase is conservation of the destination. Government and service providers should support the environment friendly practices and conserve the natural and physical environment. The third factor highlights the importance of the diversity (cultural, natural, biological) of the destination for the tourists along with the marketing and brand building of the destination. The fourth factor emphasize the need to train the people at the destination for optimum use of resources and to conduct business with partners that are also enforcing environment friendly practices. The fifth factor appreciates the efforts by service providers in encouraging tourists to adopt sustainable practices and the visible use of such practices themselves. The sixth factor highlights social equity through equal job opportunities and level of pay without discrimination by gender, race, disability, etc. A measure of construct reliability (Cronbach's Alpha) was computed for each dimension to assess the reliability of the set of items forming that dimension (see Table4). These α coefficients range from 0.901 to 0.737 and are sufficiently reliable.

To further study the factors that deter the respondents from patronizing such destination the respondents were asked to rate (on a five point Likert scale) their perception about such destinations. Principal Component Analysis along with Varimax Rotation and Kaiser Normalization was then applied with the help of SPSS and these 11 practices were reduced to four factors that were derived from the factor analysis where the rotation was converged in six iterations. These factors accounted for 71.506 % of the variance (Table 5).

TABLE 5   Factor analysis for customer perception of sustainable destinations.

Compo-nent	Initial Eigenvalues			Extraction Sums of Squared Loadings			Rotation Sums of Squared Loadings		
	Total	% of Vari-ance	Cumu-lative %	Total	% of Vari-ance	Cumu-lative %	Total	% of Vari-ance	Cumu-lative %
1	3.035	27.590	27.590	3.035	27.590	27.590	3.035	27.590	27.590
2	1.990	18.094	45.684	1.990	18.094	45.684	1.990	18.094	45.684
3	1.633	14.845	60.529	1.633	14.845	60.529	1.633	14.845	60.529
4	1.207	10.976	71.506	1.207	10.976	71.506	1.207	10.976	71.506
5	0.619	5.626	77.132						
6	0.608	5.524	82.656						
7	0.544	4.944	87.600						
8	0.475	4.321	91.921						
9	0.376	3.423	95.344						
10	0.307	2.790	98.134						
11	0.205	1.866	100.000						

Extraction method: principal component analysis.

The perception of the respondents towards sustainable destination is not very encouraging. The relevance of the same increases in the light of the fact that 61% of the respondents have visited a sustainable tourism destination and so cannot be brushed aside as a myth. The first factor that has been highlighted is of skepticism as respondents feel that the sustainable places do not provide much leisure activities, there are many restrictions and the social circle does not attach much value to holidaying in such destinations (Table 6). Respondents also generally feel that these locations do not practice what they preach. The second factor highlighted is the issue of connectivity for Internet, mobile phones, TV, etc. The consumers are used to being connected 24 ′ 7 and so this can be a major deterrent for them. The safety of such destinations is another area of concern.

TABLE 6   Customer perception of sustainable destinations.

Factor	Construct	Cronbach Alpha
1: Skepticism	Holiday is a leisure time and these places appear to be inadequate to provide leisure	0.800
	There are too many restrictions	
	My social circle does not attach much value to a holiday in such locations	
	My family is not interested in visiting such locations	
	These locations actually do not practice what they are saying	
2: Connectivity and safety issues	These places are not well connected and Internet, TV, mobile phones will not work	0.664
	Safety issues	
3: Upscale	These places are expensive	0.718
	These places are for the elite and not common people	
4: Awareness	I don't think there are sufficient choices for such destinations	0.607
	I am not aware of many options for these kind of destinations	

The third factor highlighted is that these destinations have an image of being expensive and hence for the elite and not the masses. This is further corroborated by the fact that when asked to rank their views on which is the most appropriate target market for sustainable tourism the respondents felt that it was primarily for foreign tourists, elite, corporate, educational tours, educated city youth and common masses in that order (see Table 7). The last factor shows that the respondents are not aware and also think that there are no sufficient choices for such destinations. A measure of construct reliability (Cronbach's Alpha) was computed for each dimension to assess the reliability of the set of items forming that dimension (see Table6). These α coefficients range from 0.800 to 0.607 and are sufficiently reliable.

TABLE 7 Customer perception of target market for sustainable tourism.

Tourist Segment	Rank
Foreign tourists	1
Elite (rich people)	2
Corporate—annual meets, team building exercises, motivational leadership summits, incentives, etc.	3
Educational Tours for children	4
Educated city youth	5
Common masses	6

The majority of the respondents became aware of sustainable tourism practices and destinations through the Internet followed by TV, friends, newspaper and radio in the same order (see Table 8).

TABLE 8 Source of information.

Media	% of respondents
Newspaper	16
Internet	43
TV	18
Radio	6
Friends/Colleagues	17

6.7 GLOBAL BEST PRACTICES

In this section some global best practices have been drawn. The following case studies serve to provide some insight on how various stakeholders like the government, tour operators even airlines and other logistics companies have taken responsibility for contributing towards environmental sustainability of their operations and won accolades for their work internationally. The first example studied is that of tourism in Antarctica. That is primarily spearheaded by IAATO, which is an organization of tour operators who have taken responsibility of ensuring sustainability in the region. The second case deals with tourism in Bhutan which is a unique example of how tourism can be controlled and yet be profitable. The third example deals with Air New Zealand, which has won recognition world wide for its environmentally sustainable operations.

6.7.1 SUSTAINABLE TOURISM IN ANTARCTICA

6.7.1.1 INTRODUCTION

Tourism in Antarctica began in the 1950s when commercial tour operators began operating passenger ships for daring travelers on the look out for novel experiences. The first ship designed specially for this purpose was the ice strengthened cruise ship the Lindblad Explorer that traveled to the continent in 1969. Since then the industry has shown tremendous growth with passenger numbers surging from under 9000 in 1992–93 to as high as 46000 in 2007–08. (British Antarctica Survey 2013). Antarctica tourism in the 80s right through the 90s comprised of middle aged or older tourists traveling on cruises or small ships going ashore to limited locations to catch a glimpse of wild life, historic sites or even a visit to a specific country's research station. Over the years,however, the continent has begun to attract a younger crowd and logically the attractions now being offered include paragliding, waterskiing, diving or a variety of other adventure activities. (McGuirk, R., 2013) The primary residents of the remote, pristine environment of Antarctica happen to be local flora and fauna and human residents from various countries engaged in research. Majority of the tour operators that provide visits to Antarctica are members of the International Association of Antarctica Tour Operators (IAATO), which attempts to ensure that tourism to the continent safeguards its delicate ecosystem. Member companies of IAATO are spread across continents from Europe USA, Australia, etc.(British Antarctica Survey 2013).

6.7.1.2 TOURISM IN ANTARCTICA

Tourists arrive in Antarctic primarily through Argentina, Chile or through the Ross Sea at the opposite end of the continent, which is a 10-day journey by ship from New Zealand or Australia. Tourism season in Antarctica is limited to the summer from late October to early April, with little activity in the remaining part of the year. The season offers wide ranging and stunning land-scapes, unique flora and abundance of fauna.

TABLE 9 Antarctica tourism highlights.

Time of Year	Key Highlights
Late October and November	Adélie, chinstrap and gentoo adult penguins as well as Antarctic-breeding seabirds begin to come ashore for their court ship rituals, nest building and egg laying.
	Emperor penguins are also seen on the frozen Weddell Sea.
	Spring flowers blooming in Falkland Islands.
	South Georgia's female king penguins can be seen carrying their eggs on their feet.
	Oakum Boys—king penguin chicks can also be seen in the rookeries.
	Once clearing of the blue ice landing strips is complete flights and mountain climbers get access for inland expeditions.
	Increased daylight hours bring photo opportunities for photographers.
December and January	Research activity at the scientific bases in the Peninsula are at their peak.
	Penguin chicks begin to hatch, and can be found in "crèches" while parents begin to refill on food supply.
	"Feeding chase" where the chicks chase the feeding parent or any food yielding adult is an interesting activity.
	Whales are sighted in the Peninsula area.
	Seal pups are seen on beaches of South Georgia.
	The breaking ice allows access to rarely visited sites of the East Antarctic and the historic huts of Shackleton and Scott.
February and March:	Sightings of whales in the Peninsula peak.
	Fur seals are found along Peninsula and South Georgia.
	Penguin chicks begin to loose their fuzzy down develop their adult plumage.
	Parents abandon chicks and go out to sea to feed and fatten for their own molting season.
	By the end of February and early March most colonies are nearly vacant.
	Receding ice allows greater access for explorers.

Source: British Antarctica Survey (2013) available from http://www.antarctica.ac.uk/about_antarctica/tourism/. Accessed on 1st August 2013.

The landscapes during the tourism months are extremely bright and silent with a wide variety of flora and fauna in the peninsula. The Ross Sea harbors the Royal Society Range towering 4200 meters above the ice-covered waters of McMurdo Sound. This happens to be the beginning point of British expeditions to the South Pole during the heroic era of "Antarctica Exploration" from 1895 to 1015. The wooden huts of the early explorers can still be seen lining the coast. The Ross Ice Shelf another tourist destination is the world's largest block of floating ice covering an area equivalent of Spain with steep shinning cliffs rising as high as 200 feet above sea level. Tourists also visit the largest human settlement in Antarctica, which is the U.S. McMurdo Station with capacity to accommodate over 1200 people. Other than this another station frequented by tourists is New Zealand's Scott Base with a capacity to house 90 people. Tourists also visit a hut (once an expedition base) built by British explorer Capt. Robert Falcon Scott in 1902 near McMurdo Station. (McGuirk, R. 2013)

6.7.1.3 THREAT POSED BY TOURISTS

The financial crisis of 2008 impacted the tourists arrivals at Antarctica however the last few years have seen it rebounding into the list of desired destinations. Certain categories of tourism have seen a decline over the last few years. The decline was seen primarily in the cruise—only category in which large vessels carrying over 500 passengers sail across Antarctica waters but the passengers do not disembark for the shore. There numbers dropped from 14373 in 2011 to 4872 in the year 2012. This decline can also be linked to the ban on the use as well as carriage of heavy oil fuel in the Antarctica waters imposed by the International Maritime Organization (IMO), which came into effect on August 1, 2011. (McGuirk, R.2013) The major cause of worry for most environmentalists has been that the number of tourists now going for onshore visits has seen a year-by-year increase. Small and medium size expedition ships and yachts with a capability of carrying 500 or less passengers and conducting shore visits contributed 20271 tourists a surge of 9.4% over the previous year (2011). While other categories like Antarctic travel—air/cruise combine and land tourism reported 860 and 516 tourists respectively amounting to 2% of the total passengers carried by IAATO operators (MercoPress, 2012).

The tourists pose a threat to the delicate environment as well as to themselves. Boats/ships are a cause of air and water pollution and incase things do go wrong help is a long distance away. The downturn in tourist's arrival triggered by the economic meltdown gave an opportunity to the 50 odd nations that are a part of the Antarctica Treaty to set rules to mange tourism. Although the 28 nations that are a part of the Antarctic Treaty Consultative Committee made some 27 non-binding recommendations on tourism since the year 1966 only two have been made mandatory and neither of which has been imposed. (McGuirk, R., 2013) Every additional tourist on the continent poses a significant threat to the already vulnerable Antarctica Peninsula, which is among the most rapidly warming parts of the world. The delicate flora and fauna is also in constant threat from the possibility of introduction of exotic species and microbes from tourists that the continent is not accustomed to. Another disaster waiting to happen is that of oil spills caused by the cruise ships that travel across ice covered, storm prone, difficult to navigate waters. Although the IMO had in 2011 banned the use of heavy oil (below 60 degrees latitude south), the cruise ships were able to tide over this obstacle by the use of lighter fuels. (USA Today, 2013) Likewise the agreement that requires tour operators to be insured so as to cover the cost of rescue or medical operations was ratified by only 11 out of the 28 member countries. On similar lines another agreement in 2009 that barred ships carrying over 500 passengers from landing has the backing of only Japan and Uruguay, while United States that contributes the maximum tourists has not taken any stand (McGuirk, R., 2013).

6.7.1.4 GUIDELINES FOR ACTIVITIES IN ANTARCTICA

The Antarctica Treaty of 1959 governs all activities in the area. In 1991 a further protocol on environmental protection to the Antarctica Treaty was adopted by, the Antarctic Treaty Consultative Parties. The protocol establishes environmental principles, procedures and obligations for the complete protection of Antarctica's environment along with its associated ecosystems. It is applicable to tourist and government activity in the concerned area. The guidelines cover areas like protecting the wildlife, respecting protected areas, respecting scientific research, keeping the self-safe and Antarctica pristine.

Some of the major guidelines include:

TABLE 10 Guidelines for activities in Antarctica.

S. No.	Protect Antarctic Wildlife
1.	No touching, feeding or handling birds.
	Taking photographs should not affect their behavior and special sensitivity towards animals is required during their breeding and molting season.

| 2. | Not to damage plants by driving, or walking or landing over moss beds or lichen covered slopes. |
| 3. | No non-native plants or animals allowed into Antarctic. |

Keep Antarctica Pristine

1.	No disposal of garbage allowed on land, open burning is also prohibited.
2.	Collection or taking away of biological or geological specimens, rocks, bones, eggs, and fossils is prohibited.
3.	No painting or graffiti on rocks, buildings.

Source: http://iaato.org/visitor-guidelines Accessed 12th August 2013

6.7.1.5   SUSTAINABILITY MEASURES BY IAATO

More than the various countries responsible for safeguarding the interests of the continent it is IAATO (International Association of Antarctica Tour Operators) that has been attempting to protect the precious environment. IAATO is an organization that came into existence in the year 1991 to support, promote and practice environmentally safe travel to Antarctic. Over 100 tour operators from across various countries are members of IAATO. The members have established extremely clear cut guidelines and framed rules in accordance with the Antarctic treaty to ensure that tourism to Antarctica remains sustainable. (IAATO, 2013). Some of the measures taken by the body include:

1. Establishment of an impartial and timely process to determine the violation of bylaws, directives or standard operating procedures of IAATO.
2. In accordance with the IMO (International Maritime Organization) the new Polar Code is expected to limit the types of vessels allowed in the Antarctica waters by 2014.
3. As a part of its outreach program IAATO's members continue to educate staff, passengers about the impact of climate change on the environment of the continent through power point presentations during the voyages as well as in other venues. It also involves educating the passengers on the attempts made by IAATO operators in reducing their vessel's carbon footprint. (MercoPress, 2012)

IAATO advocates "self regulation" by staff and passengers to make Antarctica tourism sustainable. Members of IAATO along with the passengers donated US$470,000 during the year 2011–12 taking up the tally to US $

2.5 million over the last eight years. This money was donated to charitable organizations such as Save the Albatross, World Wildlife Fund, Oceanites, Antarctic Heritage Trust, etc. Other than this IAATO also transported numerous scientists, station and program personnel free or at a minimum expense to or from Antarctica during the 2012 season.(MercoPress, 2012)

6.7.1.6   CONCLUSION

Antarctica's pristine and less frequented environment offers excitement and freshness of experience as compared to other destinations. In the context of sustainability this region is perhaps the most vulnerable and makes it to the top of the list when we think of the concept of "environment protection or sustainability." It is quite evident that the impact of global warming on this area is having catastrophic repercussions on the rest of the world. The area is already beleaguered by the onslaught of global warming; matters are made worse by the recklessness of over zealous tourists that are endangering the delicate ecosystem. Unfortunately for the island, the 50 member countries that have been given the responsibility of safeguarding its interests are doing precious little. In the absence of an omnipresent control and discipline mechanism it is remarkable to see how the members of the IAATO have taken up the responsibility to safeguard the interests of the island by encouraging self regulation among the passengers they are bringing in as well as taking up the daunting task of implementing the guidelines set by the member countries.

6.7.2   BHUTAN: CONTROLLED TOURISM

6.7.2.1   INTRODUCTION

Bhutan opened up its tourism industry quite late in 1974. The tourism industry was opened up for the world with the primary objective of earning precious foreign exchange since the country due to its topography has limited revenue-generating sectors. The idea behind its tourism policy was to market the unique culture and traditions as well as the beautiful landscapes, exquisite flora and fauna to the outside world, which in turn would aid the country's socio economic development. The number of tourists coming into the country has seen a year on year increase. The tourist numbers have risen from a mere 287 in 1974 to over 7000 in 1999. The year 2012 saw as many as 105,414 tourist arrivals, of which 53,504 were international, and the 51,910 were regional tourists i.e., those coming in from India, Bangladesh and Maldives. (Dema,

K. 2013). The Department of Tourism is aiming to take this figure to 200,000 by launching various products to encourage tourism through out the year. The uniqueness of Bhutan's tourism lies in the fact that while other destinations as pristine and fragile as Bhutan's are facing erosion and destruction of natural resources its assets in terms of natural and cultural environment have been preserved well. So much so that the International community has applauded the efforts made by the authorities in according, the highest priority to conservation of culture and environment. This in turn has made Bhutan a prime destination for tourists. Bhutan has also attuned itself to the new opportunities that are constantly being created in the tourism industry and has readied itself to offer products that appeal to a wide array of tourists.

6.7.2.2 GOVERNMENT INTERVENTION

The Royal government of Bhutan has always been cautious of the impact both positive and negative that unrestrained tourism can have on the fragile environment of Bhutan. The government therefore adopted a policy of "high value-low volume" tourism from the very onset so as to control the nature of as well as quantity of tourists coming into the nation. This strategy of "high value and low volume" has created an image of high exclusivity, which in turn has resulted in high yields for the economy. Till the year 1991 the government's tourism policy was implemented by a quasi-autonomous as well as self-financing body the Bhutan Tourism Corporation (BTC). All the tourists visiting Bhutan came as guests of BTC, which held the responsibility of operating tour organizations, transport services and almost all the hotels and accommodation facilities. However, with the privatization of the tourism sector in 1991 by the government, private sector players were encouraged to actively participate in the sector. The country now has over 75 licensed tour operators in the country. Post privatization the government set up a regulatory body the Tourism Authority of Bhutan (TAB), later renamed as Department of Tourism (DOT) that operates under the Ministry of Trade and Industry. The primary function of the Department of Tourism is:

- To ensure compliance by travel agents with the tourism policy formulated by the royal government.
- Regulation of the number of and quality of foreign tourists coming into the country.
- Fixing rates for activities like trekking, expeditions as well as cultural tours.
- Receiving payments from tourists, processing tourist visas.

- Issuing as well as ensuring the compliance of guidelines and regulations that governs tourism activities.
- Ensuring the conservation and protection of culture and environment from pollution and exposure to activities of tourists.
- To develop and seek new opportunities in developing tourism for generating economic growth and foreign exchange(Trade Forum, 2011).

Currently there are no limits on the number of tourists allowed into the country, the volume of tourists are limited more by infrastructural constraints posed by the seasonality of the tourism in the country since tourists primarily visit the country in March-April and October–November. Every tourist visiting the country is required to pay a daily fee, which is used to ensure tourism in the country is made more sustainable. The minimum daily tariff imposed by the Department of Tourism is US$200 per tourist per day for the months of January, February, June, July, August, and December and US$ 250 for the months of March, April, May, September, October, and November (Tourism Council of Bhutan, 2013). Other than this it is also mandatory for the tourist to hire and be escorted by a local guide for their entire stay. This has been useful in preventing tourists from picking up pieces from protected destinations and taking them home as was observed in the case of the ruins of Machu Picchu. Sustainability of tourism is top priority for the nation and hence new development in tourism is looked at with great caution. Despite the low volume of tourists, tourism happens to be the largest revenue-generating sector in the country. (Tourism Council of Bhutan 2013)

6.7.2.3 CONTRIBUTION TOWARDS SOCIO-ECONOMIC GROWTH

The tourism industry in Bhutan has made considerable contributions towards the socio-economic development of the country particularly post the privatization of the sector in 1991. Tourism is a lucrative business with a large number of Bhutanese entrepreneurs investing in the sector. Other than tour operators a large number of Bhutanese have found employment as guides, cooks, transport operators as well as hotel and restaurant owners. Other than this tourism also contributes to rural incomes through transportation and portage. Tourism has also resulted in the development of the service sector particularly hotels, restaurants, transportation and communication. Another crucial impact of tourism has been the support that the local cottage industry has received as well as the setting up of handicraft shops in the frequently visited areas.

Bhutan's people have benefited greatly from its country's drive into sustainable tourism. The government has ensured that the happiness of its 7,500,000 odd citizens is at the core of all its strategic thinking it is no wonder that this country puts more stress on the gross national happiness (GNH) as opposed to gross domestic product (GDP). According to tourist industry estimates as many as 25.987 jobs were created in areas like guides, hotels, restaurants, airline, handicrafts, etc. compared to 23,095 in the year 2011. The tourism industry's contribution to GDP was US$152 million in 2012. Its listing as a top tourist destination for 2013 in major international magazines like Forbes, Traveler, National Geographic as well as the New York Times travel magazine have improved its prospects further.(Dema, k. 2013) Major attractions of Bhutan are its traditional culture, way of life, festivals, historic monuments, rich flora and fauna. Also known as Land of the Thunder Dragon," the wide variety of bio diversity in the country is an environmentalist's dream. Bhutan has received considerable praise from international agencies for the caution it has exercised in development of tourism while preserving the nation's natural and cultural heritage. The policy of high tariffs has been successful in keeping Bhutan tourism an exclusive and distinct experience.

6.7.2.4 CHALLENGES POSED BY TOURIST ACTIVITY

Growth in tourism in Bhutan has brought with it a host of challenges the adverse impact of tourists surge has begun to show on the environment. One of the major concerns in Bhutan's high alpine regions has been the destruction of vegetation and cutting down of small trees for firewood for creating trekking routes. While the locals in these areas require wood for fuel, tourism further adds pressure on the forests.

Another associated problem has been the erosion of delicate flora in the region, apparently tourist activities are not the only reason for this, the use of horses and yaks for trekking in high mountain areas has also had considerable impact. The creation of garbage trails from the inconsiderate disposal of non-biodegradable waste is another visible sign of concern associated with the tourism industry. Tourism has also promoted changes in livelihoods with locals shifting from the traditional and sustainable farming and cropping patterns to less sustainable yet more profitable livelihoods that serve the needs of high paying tourists. There is also reason to believe that excessive exposure to foreign tourists is eroding of Bhutanese culture and value systems. The government's policy of high value low volume has allowed tourism operators to receive high margins but increasing competition has begun to dilute the pricing integrity. Tour operators have begun to engage in discounting and giving rebates to foreign operators to grab business from competitors. This in turn has led to the deterioration of quality of service offered impacting the tourism industry in Bhutan as a whole(Dorji, T. nd).

6.7.2.5   CORRECTIVE MEASURES

Growth in any sector cannot occur without the associated perils. While the opening up of tourism and its subsequent growth has given windfall gains to the Bhutanese economy its evils have also taken a toll But fortunately the Government and the respective authorities have been quick on their feet so as to minimize the adverse impacts and have taken some corrective measures to curtail and minimize the loss.

1. Banning of use of firewood on treks, encouraging trekkers to use liquid petroleum gas or kerosene.
2. Levying a fine of Ngultrum 5,000 on tour operators that continue to use firewood on trekking routes or engage in littering the surroundings.
3. Even though the fine is a hefty amount the operators also run the risk of getting their trekking permits canceled upon being charged with two violations in a particular season.
4. The department has also constructed permanent camps, rest houses, toilets along the busier trek rotes.
5. The department of tourism also conducts training courses for guides and has also created a system for licensing cultural and trekking guides. The department has made it mandatory for all guides employed by the various tour operators to be licensed. This has ensured that all guides have been provided basic training in trekking and mountaineering techniques along with other nuances of critical for sustainable tourism (Dorji, T. nd).

6.7.2.6   THE WAY AHEAD

The royal government has begun to think more strategically in terms of long-term sustenance of tourism in Bhutan. The policy makers have realized that among the various new types of tourism that are emerging "eco tourism" serves the country's sustainable strategy well. The nation offers considerable scope in terms of eco tourism, which also has synergies with the government's vision of enhancing and preserving the cultural integrity of the Bhutanese people. Forests with a rich variety of flora and fauna cover over 72% of the land. About 43% of the country's land area has been declared protected area and has been opened up for tourism. The terrain also offers variety ranging from sub tropical to alpine. The country's rich biological resources comprise of over 165 species of animals and over 770 species of birds other than this Bhutan is home to over 60% of the endemic species found in the eastern Himalayas. Other than this Bhutan's rich flora includes over 50 different species of rhododendrons and over 300 species of medicinal plants used by the locals in traditional herbal medicine. (Tourism Council of Bhutan 2013) In September 2012, Time Magazine rightfully referred to Bhutan as "the last authentic place on earth." The richness of its natural environment has provided the royal government with more opportunities to earn from sustainable tourism and simultaneously conserve resources (Ghosh, B., 2012).

6.7.2.7 CONCLUSION

Bhutan has been to able to achieve sustainability goals in its tourism without any global aid, the single minded purpose of its government and people to adopt eco friendly measures have now become engrained in the very fabric of its tourism and hospitality industry. Very few counties in the world have been able to achieve with tourism what Bhutan has accomplished. It has displayed to the world that controlled tourism is possible and can be used to ensure sustainability of the tourism industry in the long run. The growth in the tourism has provided the much-needed foreign exchange to the government's revenues, to employment generation and to development of the region as a whole. Tourism has also provided the opportunity to the nation to showcase its rich heritage and culture to the rest of the world. Tourism has further raised the impetus to conserve the country's rich flora, fauna and culture. Bhutan has in a very short duration established very clear cut tourism policies that are sound in implementation it has also developed excellent tourism destinations and provided training to raise a qualified and responsible reservoir of personnel. Bhutan has provided the world with a shining example of the possibilities of sustainability in tourism. It has displayed that armed with the right intentions the government of a country along with the relevant stakeholders can achieve the impossible.

6.7.3 AIR NEW ZEALAND

6.7.3.1 INTRODUCTION

Airlines from the very beginning have provided convenience and comfort to the travelers. As competition in the industry increased airlines came up with economy brands to lure more price conscious consumers as a result air travel that was once the privilege of the premium classes is now within the reach of the commoners as well. The increase in the number of airlines operating across the world has increased manifold the number of jets owned and leased by each one of them. The convenience of airplanes has come with their share of problems. Airlines alone are a major contributor to the depletion of the ozone layer, as a result over the years a number of them have adopted environmentally sustainable practices. It also true that a large number of airlines have also been motivated by the rising cost of aviation fuel to switch to the lesser costly sustainable fuels. Airlines have also realized that consumers and environment watchdogs alike are closely monitoring their policies and practices and these green practices are likely to tilt the consumer's preference in their favor. Hence the rush to either reduce carbon footprint or initiate a carbon offset program. Amongst the various green measures adopted, airlines are modernizing fleet with more fuel efficient planes, installing winglets to reduce the drag effect and fuel consumption, reduce idle time for planes, offering carbon offset programs and researching alternative fuel sources to reduce reliance on fossil fuels. A forerunner in the cause for environment sustainability happens to be a relatively young and small airline Air New Zealand. The airlines began operations in the year.... but has displayed considerable initiative and foresight in the adoption of sustainable practices. The airline has continuously made efforts to reduce its carbon footprint and to become the world's most environmentally sustainable airline. Over a five-year period the airline has managed to bring down its carbon emissions by 15% to 142,000 tons

6.7.3.2 THE GREEN CALLING

The comprehension of Air New Zealand's environmentally sustainable practices is incomplete without an understanding of the country i.e., New Zealand's green orientation. The adoption of eco tourism or "clean and green," policy has been a deliberate and sustained effort by the New Zealand government as well as concerned stakeholders. Not very long ago the country was a poor performer in terms of industrial and agri waste management as well as recycling. As a result of the continued onslaught of pollution contributed by inhabitants and tourists over the years, many of its delicate eco systems along with the accompanying exotic birds and animal species have become endangered. However, things have changed for the better with farmers as well as industries employing better and sustainable methods for waste management, weed control and reforestation. Likewise tourism operators and organizations are also working in tandem with the government and local bodies to support sustainable tourism. Over the years New Zealand has managed to develop a reputation for sustainable tourism and its "100% Pure New Zealand," promotional campaigns reinforces its resolve. The approach to tourism in New Zealand has been developed encompassing two traditional Maori principles manaakitanga (hospitality) and kaitiakitanga (guardianship), that is, welcoming visitors but at the same time protecting the local culture and environment. Its Tourism Strategy 2015 already has in place a number of sustainability measures to be implemented in the coming years. Other noteworthy achievements have been the Qualmark Responsible Tourism Operations program partnered by Tourism New Zealand and the New Zealand Automobile Association that has also helped in adoption of green practices. New Zealand's Environmentally Sustainable Tourism Project run by Ministry for the Environment and the Ministry of Tourism has also laid down practices to be followed by participating tour operators for improving environment sustainability (Frommers nd).

Under such a backdrop it is of little wonder that the national airline, Air New Zealand is also following the path very clearly laid out by the country of its origin.

6.7.3.3   INITIATIVES BY AIR NEW ZEALAND

Air New Zealnd over the years has adopted a number of initiatives to make the airlines environmentally sustainable. Since fossil fuel is a major contributor to air pollution the airlines along with other partners like Rolls Royce and Boeing has attempted to encourage the usage of sustainable bi fuels in aviation. Air New Zealand is the only airline to have participated in the world's first commercial test flight using sustainable second-generation biofuel derived from the plant Jatropha curcas (Frommers nd.).The airline played a major role in the adoption and certification of sustainable aviation biofuels through the data provided by the test flights undertaken by the airline in 2008. It has been collaborating with a number of players in their research and development of aviation bio fuels. It entered into an MoU (Memorandum of Understanding) with New Zealand based company Licella to develop a technology for the conversion of woody materials and other bio mass into high quality bio-crude oil. These initiatives are particularly important in light of the aviation industry's target of carbon neutral growth from 2020. Air New Zealand is already a member of the 'Sustainable Aviation Fuel Users Group' (SAFUG)(Fuseworks media, 2011). Another feather in the airline's green cap was the founding of the Air New Zealand Environment Trust in the year 2008. The primary objective of the Trust was to restore the endangered ecosystems in New Zealand and make a positive difference in the world. The Trust helps communities support projects by giving grants as well as provides funding to research to develop ways to improve New Zealand's environment. The first project that was taken up by the Trust was the conservation of 100 acres of Mangarara Station in Hawke's Bay. The Trust contributed to the purchase and planting of 85,000 trees in the area. This enabled the creation of "carbon sinks" that will in the future also harbor many of the endangered species (Air New Zealand website, 2013). The airline has also collaborated with other like-minded companies that are dedicated to the cause of sustainability. Car rental companies Budget and Avis, provide financial support to the trust through its customers who avail its services in New Zealand. Hotel Grand Chancellor has its own green practices in place other than these it provides donations to the trust for Air New Zealnd Environment every reservation made online. It also gives its customers the option of making donations to the trust at the front desk. The airline also gives an opportunity to its passengers to make a contribution to the trust when they book their tickets online(Air New Zealand website, 2013). The airline also boasts of a 3000 strong internal Green Team that is dedicated to promoting sustainability both at home and work. Other than this the airline has also taken up some restoration projects in New Zealand two of which include:

1. Re-vegetation of Pilot's Beach:

Pilot's Beach located on Dunedin's Otago Peninsula is home to the breeding colony of Little Blue Penguin that has been a major tourist attraction. However, the pressure from visitors, lack of weed and pest control has compromised the vegetation putting at risk the colony. However, with the intervention of the Air New Zealand Environment Trust re vegetation of the area is successfully on its way and it is expected that the flora that once adorned this area will soon be back in its full potential.

2. Restoring the Ōkārito wetland complex:

The Ōkārito wetland complex located near Franz Josef Glacier on the West Coast is a wet land of national importance. Ever since the arrival of humans in New Zealand over 80% of the wetlands have been lost due to clearing of vegetation as well as drainage while the remaining wetlands are threatened by declining water quality and onslaught of pest animals. The wet land supports a number of endangered species like the white heron kotuku, royal spoonbill, Australasian bittern matuku and rowi, New Zealand's rarest kiwi. Air New Zealand Environment Trust (ANZET) provided the Department of Conservation (DOC) with a four year sponsorship to restore the wetland to its former glory (Air New Zealand website 2013). In a very short time this relatively small as well as young airline has made a considerable contribution towards the environmentally sustainable vision and mission of New Zealand. The efforts made by the airline have been recognized by the international fraternity. It was named the winner in the Global Tourism Business category at the World Travel and Tourism Council's (WTTC) annual Global Summit held in Abu Dhabi, United Arab Emirates in 2013. The awards received entries from 46 countries across seven continents (Tfsn, 2013).

6.7.3.4   CONCLUSION

As the cry for environmental sustainability turns from a whisper to a roar and consumers grow more conscientious most airlines have begun to put their houses in order and have voluntarily begun to check their carbon emissions as well as adopt sustainable practices. Organizations like Air Zealand are bringing home the thought the environment sustainability or concern for the environment is not the task and duty of the governments alone but an imperative for all stakeholders. The damage that the human race has done to the world can be undone only by the sustained and continuous efforts of all concerned.

6.7.4   RECOMMENDATIONS

Tourism has a huge potential to bring about positive changes through the adoption of sustainable measures that ensure the environmental, economic and sociocultural well-being. There is growing awareness among the consumers regarding sustainable practices and they are paying attention to such information, which also influences their purchase decision. All the activities need to in integrated and coordinated so as to gain 'social, economic and environmental well-being' (Gilmore et al., 2007). The idea is not to dilute the hedonistic experience that the tourists are seeking but to provide it in a manner that secondary satisfaction of having behaved responsibly (Burgin and Hardiman, 2010) is also gained.

Factor analysis shows that there is a difference in the order of what the consumers feel that the tourism destination should practice and what influences their purchase decision. The only construct common in the first factor of both is that the income generated from tourism destination (in the form of fees for monuments, museums, etc.) should be used for developing infrastructure of the destination. The two aspects common in the second factor of both is that government and service providers should support the conservation of natural areas, habitats and wildlife and minimize damage to them and that organization infrastructure has been built using local material. Thus these aspects should be highlighted by the destinations as these have a two pronged effect on the customers.

A tool suggested to influence the sustainable behavior in tourists is to give a feedback to the tourists about the implications of their behavior (Budeanu, 2007). Thus tourist destinations can follow-up with the tourists post their trip and inform them about the positive impact their purchase of a 'sustainable' holiday had on the planet vis-à-vis their purchase of a 'normal' holiday. This will also result in the achievement of the secondary satisfaction of having behaved responsibly.

The study highlighted that the respondents felt that sustainable tourism is for foreigners, elite, corporate, school children, youth and lastly for the masses. This perception requires to be changed particularly because over the years India has seen a surge in both domestic as well as international tourism. Moreover this rise in tourist numbers is not coming from the top SECs alone but the lower and middle SECs have become major contributors. Other than this the youth traveling with friends on vacations short and long as well as rural Indian consumers moving beyond the traditional "pilgrimage tourism" to other forms has also added to this sizeable number. The increasing number of tourists is exerting extreme pressure on the fragile eco systems of many of the Indian tourist sites that don't have the required infrastructure or practices to deal with the increased levels of pollution as well as degradation of the local community both in terms of flora fauna and value systems. With a growing number of tourists the awareness with respect to sustainability has to be widespread and it will only be achieved by participation of all concerned stakeholders. The research uncovered that a number of the respondents were displaying skepticismtowards sustainability, were worried about connectivity and security issues as well as had the misconception that "whatever is sustainable is going to be expensive." Again clarity in communication should be provided by stakeholders engaged in sustainable tourism with respect to pricing structure and the fact that a tourism destination need not be in the middle of nowhere to be sustainable even a hotel located in the middle of a bustling city can be sustainable environmentally likewise a cab service or an airline can be equally environmentally sustainable. Respondents are of the view that environmentally sustainable tourism should ensure conservation of energy and culture, responsibility of stakeholders, effective management of resources, empowerment of local community and development of support system, that is, a portion of the income generated should be spent for the welfare of the community. Hence while incorporating sustainable practices tourism operators or the government while formulating policies should ensure that these factors are carefully adhered to as they are perceived as being important by the target group. Moreover when questioned on which factors related to environmental sustainability would encourage them to visit a sustainable tourist destination the respondents were of the view that messages related to depiction of a tourist destination or operator indulging in the empowerment of the local community, development of the destination, adoption of methods for conservation of the destination, training of service providers, sensitization of the visitors towards sustainability of the destination as well as adoption of measures for social equality in the community would encourage them to patronize the service. Hence in designing the promotional messages for their respective destinations that are practicing methods of environmental sustainability the companies or governments in question should highlight the above-mentioned factors in their communication so as to be effective in attracting the "green" tourists. The youth in India have emerged as the initiators of change and since India boasts of primarily a youth population, companies dedicated to environmental sustainability should focus on attitude change of the youth as influencing them is likely to hasten the change. Moreover according to the study the Internet appeared to be the most important medium that the respondents used for searching for such information hence companies should focus on this medium to get their promotional messages across to the targeted group.

KEYWORDS

- **destination management**
- **economic viability**
- **management of resources**
- **manpower**
- **marketing**
- **sustainability**

REFERENCES

Air New Zealand website 2013: "Air New Zealand Trust Manifesto,"http://airnzenvironment-trust.org.nz/manifesto/ Accessed 3rd September 2013.

Air New Zealand website 2013: "Air New Zealand Trust Partners,"http://airnzenvironmenttrust.org.nz/supporters-and-partners/#Hotel Grand ChancellorAccessed 3rd September 2013.

Amiryan, H and Silva, G (2013), "Sustainable tourism development in Armenia," International Journal of Management Cases, Special Issue, Vol. 15, Issue 4, pp. 153–169.

Ayuso, S (2006), "Adoption of voluntary environmental tools for sustainable tourism: Analyzing the experience of Spanish hotels," Corporate Social Responsibility and Environmental Management Vol. 13, Issue 4, pp. 207–220.

Battaglia, M; Daddi, T and Rizzi, F (2012), "Sustainable tourism planning and consultation: evidence from the project Inter.Eco.Tur," European Planning Studies, Vol. 20, Issue 2, pp193–211.

British Antarctica Survey (2013): "Tourism in Antarctica,"http://www.antarctica.ac.uk/about_antarctica/tourism/. Accessed 1st August 2013.

Budeanu, A (2007), "Sustainable tourist behavior—a discussion of opportunities for change," International Journal of Consumer Studies, Vol. 31, pp. 499–508.

Burgin, S and Hardiman, N (2010), "Ecoaccreditation: win-win for the environment and small business?," International Journal of Business Studies—Special Edition, Vol. 18, Issue 1, pp. 23–38.

Chafe, Z (2005), "Consumer demand and operator support for socially and environmentally responsible tourism," available from http://www.rainforest-alliance.org/branding/documents/consumer_demand.pdf accessed on 31 August, 2013.

Crompton, J L (1979), "An assessment of the image of Mexico as a vacation destination and the influence geographical location upon that image," Journal of Travel Research, Vol. 17, pp. 18–23.

Dema, K. (2013): "Projected target surpassed,"http://www.kuenselonline.com/projected-target-surpassed/ Accessed 24TH August 2013.

Dorji, T. (ND): "SUSTAINABILITY OF TOURISM IN BHUTAN,"http://www.mtnforum.org/sites/default/files/publication/files/6471.pdfAccessed 23rd August 2013.

Fishbein, M., and Manfredo, M. J. (1992). A theory of behavior change. In M. J. Manfredo (Ed.), Influencing human behavior: Theory and applications in recreation, tourism, and natural resources management (pp. 29–50). Champaign: Sagamore Publishing.

Frommers nd.: "Sustainable Travel and Ecotourism,"http://www.frommers.com/destinations/newzealand/0313020277.html#ixzz2dP54N400. Accessed 3rd September 2013.

Fuse works Media (2011): "Air NZ signs MOU with biofuel company Licella"). http://www.voxy.co.nz/business/air-nz-signs-mou-biofuel-company-licella/5/110526. HYPERLINK "http://www.voxy.co.nz/business/air-nz-signs-mou-biofuel-company-licella/5/110526.%20%20Accessed%2011th%20September%202013"Accessed 11th September 2013.

Gracan, D; Zadel, Z and Rudancic-Lugaric, A (2011), "Management of sustainable tourism development: case study of Plitvice lakes National Park," International Journal of Management Cases, pp. 24–33.

Gilmore, A; Carson, D and Ascencao, M (2007), "Sustianale tourism marketing at a world heritage site," Journal of Strategic Marketing, Vol. 15, pp. 253–264.

Ghosh, B. (2012): "'This Is the Last Authentic Place on Earth'http://content.time.com/time/magazine/article/0,9171,2126071,00.html#ixzz2dO0YuVgm. Accessed 23rd August 2013.

Halme, M., Fadeeva, Z. (2000) "Small and Medium-Sized Tourism Enterprises in Sustainable Development Networks—Value-Added?" *Greener Management International*, Vol. 30 pp. 97–113.

Hiwasaki, L (2003), "Tourism in Japan's parks and protected areas: challenges and potential for sustainable development," International Review for Environmental Strategies, Vol. 4, issue 1, pp. 107–126.

Holjevac, I A (2008), "Business ethics in tourism—as a dimension of TQM" Total Quality Management, Vol. 19, Issue 10, pp. 1029–1041.

IAATO 2013: "What is IAATO?" http://iaato.org/what-is-iaato. Accessed 2nd August 2013.

Jamal, T; Hartl, C and Lohmer, R (2010), "Socio-cultural meanings of tourism in a local-global context: implications for planning and development," Pranjana: The Journal of Management Awareness, Vol. 13, Issue 1, pp. 1–15.

Jurowski, C (2002), "Best think tanks and the development of curriculum modules for teaching sustainability principles," Journal of Sustainable Tourism, Vol. 10, Issue 6, pp. 536–545.

Lumsdon, L M and Swift, J S (1998), "Ecotourism at a crossroads: the case of Costa Rica, Journal of Sustainable Tourism, Vol. 16, pp. 155–172.

McDonald, S; Oates, C; Thyne, M; Alevizou, P and McMorland, L-A (2009), "Comparing sustainable consumption patterns across product sectors," International Journal of Consumer Studies, Vol. 33, pp. 137–145.

McGuirk, R. (2013): "The Antarctic is left defenseless to tourism" http://www.independent.co.uk/environment/nature/the-antarctic-is-left-defenseless-to-tourism-8537546.html. HYPERLINK "http://www.independent.co.uk/environment/nature/the-antarctic-is-left-defenseless-to-tourism-8537546.html.%20Accessed%203rd%20August%202013"Accessed 3rd August 2013.

McGuirk, R. (2013): "Antarctica Tourism Damages Environment Of Pristine Land" http://www.huffingtonpost.com/2013/03/16/antarctica-tourism-environment_n_2888668.html Accessed 1st August 2013.

McIntire, K (2011a), "The big picture: Tourism and Sustainable Development," International Trade Forum, Vol. 2, Issue 2, pp. 6–8.

McIntire, K (2011b), "Bhutan: A model for sustainable tourism development," International Trade Forum, Issue 2, pp. 15–17.

MercoPress (2012): "Antarctica tourism rapidly adapting to new environment-friendly rules,"http://en.mercopress.com/2012/05/22/antarctica-tourism-rapidly adapting-to-new-environment-friendly rules. Accessed 1st August 2013.

Musa, R; Yusof, J M; Chui, C T B; Hassan, F H; Rahim, F A and Hashim, R H (2010)"Factorial Validation of Ecotourism Destination image and ecotourists' motivation: empirical analysis of Taman Negara National Park (TNNP), Malaysia," in edited Proceedings of the 9th European Conference on Research Methodology for Business and Management Studies, edited by Esteves.

Ramgulam, N; Raghunandan-Mohammed, K and Raghunandan, M (2012), "An examination of the economic viability of sustainable business tourism in Trinidad," Review of Business and Finance Studies, Vol. 3, Issue 2, pp. 69–80.

Ramgulam, N; Raghunandan-Mohammed, K and Raghunandan, M (2013)"Environmental sustainability in the 21st century: An assessment of Trinidad's Business Tourism Market," Review of business and Finance Studies, Vol. 4, Issue 1, pp. 51–61.

Tattanaphaphtham, K and Kunsrison, R (2011), "Environmental information disclosure quality, competitive advantage and sustainable growth of Thai listed firm: perspective of resource based view," Journal of International Business and Economics, Vol. 11, Issue 3, pp. 134–146.

Tfsn (2013): "Air New Zealand Wins Global Sustainable Tourism Award,"). http://www.theflyingsocialnetwork.com/archives/14523. Accessed 3rd September 2013.

Trade Forum Editorial (2011): "Bhutan: A model for sustainable tourism development"— http://www.intracen.org/Bhutan-A-model-for-sustainable-tourism-development/#sthash. WXHrxO0x.dpuf. Accessed 23rd August 2013.

Tourism Council of Bhutan (2013): "Minimum Daily Package,"http://www.tourism.gov.bt/plan/minimum-daily package Accessed 23rd August 2013.

Roberts, L and Hall, D (2003), "Consuming the countryside: marketing for 'rural tourism,'" Journal of Vacation Marketing, Vol. 10, Issue 3, pp. 253–263.

Shen, F (2008), "Connecting the sustainable livelihoods approach and tourism: A review of the literature," Journal of Hospitality and Tourism Management, Vol. 15, Issue 1, pp. 19–31.

UNEP WTO (2005), "Making Tourism more Sustainable: A guide to policy makers" available from http://www.unep.fr/shared/publications/pdf/DTIx0592xPA-TourismPolicyEN.pdf accessed on 28 April, 2013.

UNWTO (2013a), "International tourism to continue robust growth in 2013", available from http://media.unwto.org/en/press-release/2013–01–28/international-tourism-continue-robustgrowth-2013 accessed on 19 August, 2013.

UNWTO (2013b), "International tourism receipts grew by 4% in 2012", available from http://media.unwto.org/en/press-release/2013–05–15/international-tourism-receipts-grew-4–2012 accessed on 19 August, 2013.

UNWTO (2013c), "An extra 12 million international tourists in the first four months of 2013" available from http://media.unwto.org/en/press-release/2013–07–17/extra12-million-international-tourists-first-four-months-2013 accessed on 19 August, 2013

UNWTO (2013d)"UNWTO: Tourism Highlights," available from http://dtxtq4w60xqpw.cloudfront.net/sites/all/files/pdf/unwto_highlights13_en_lr.pdf accessed on 20 August, 2013.

USA Today 2013: "Antarctica concerns grow as tourism numbers rise,"http://www.usatoday.com/story/travel/destinations/2013/03/16/antarctica-tourism-rise/1993181/Accessed 1st August 2013.

Walker, R H and Hanson, D J (1998), "Green marketing and green places: a taxonomy for the destination marketer," Journal of Marketing Management, Vol. 14, pp. 623–639.

World Tourism Organization(1997), "Agenda 21 for the travel and tourism industry: towards environmentally sustainable development," World Tourism Organization, World Travel and Tourism Council and the Earth Council.

World Travel and Tourism Council (2013), "Economic Impact of Travel and Tourism 2013 Annual Update: Summary, 2013" available from http://www.wttc.org/site_media/uploads/ downloads/Economic_Impact_of_TT_2013_Annual_Update_–_Summary.pdf accessed on 31 August, 2013.

CHAPTER 7

SUSTAINABLE TOURIST DESTINATIONS: CREATION AND DEVELOPMENT

SANDEEP MUNJAL and PARUL G. MUNJAL

CONTENTS

ABSTRACT

A sustainable tourist destination is one that ensures the continuity of its natural and cultural resources, along with being socially and economically viable. While the market forces represent commercial viability concerns, it is imperative that long-term goals are set for destination development that enable sustaining of the very cultural and natural resources that make the destinations unique. Economic leakages and insensitive development dilute the positive environmental, cultural and socioeconomic impacts, resulting in an adverse effect on sustainability at large. There is a contrast between the developed and developing world in terms of role played by government versus private investments in providing or facilitating infrastructure, services and facilities that are critical for tourist destination creation and development. It is imperative that the challenges be understood and solutions found that focus on a long-term sustainable approach, rather than short-term gains. The case studies bring out the various issues and approaches that can help get an overview of the current scenario with respect to tourism destination development. The success achieved by certain destinations, though true to their own unique contexts, can guide and inspire others to emulate those practices that are relevant for them and be driven to seek their own unique solutions.

7.1 INTRODUCTION

A tourist destination may vary in scale from an individual self dependent resort, a natural location, a village, a city or town that offers a multifaceted, complex and dynamic experience, a regional landscape or a country as a whole. Depending on what kind of infrastructure or resources a location offers, it is coined as a leisure, fashion, retail, volunteer, medical, sex, slum, rural, cultural heritage, sacred, volunteer, community, adventure or eco tourism destination. With the strengthening of Meetings, Incentives, Conferences and Exhibitions (MICE) segment at various destinations, the line between leisure and business tourists is getting blurred. Hence, not only are there emergent trends in the kinds of tourism, there are also overlaps in the motivation of tourists, opening further avenues. Financial viability is an important factor that is giving rise to quite a few of these trends. For example, due to state-of-the-art medical facilities and supporting infrastructure being made available at the much lesser cost in a country like India, there is influx of visitors from various other countries, especially in Western Asia and Africa. A similar concern may also be seen in the MICE segment where events such as weddings and conventions may cost less along with offering a unique experience.

The motivation that drives tourists and what the destination has to offer are two ends that get connected in the process of tourist destination development. The process of development of a tourist destination over time depends on various factors such as types of visitors, tourist experience, impacts on destinations, involvement of locals and occurrence of new tourist cycles (Chistaller cited in Mason, 2008, p. 26). Researchers such as Cohen, Plog, Doxey and Butler categorize the psychology and types of tourists to understand their preferences in terms of destinations, along with charting the response of local communities from euphoria to antagonism with growth of tourism and the life cycle of a destination (Mason, 2008, pp. 27–33).

Giaoutzi and Nijkamp (2006) offer an interesting linkage between the issue of sustainability and the cycle of tourism growth at a destination. A tourist destination irrespective of the resource base that creates the attraction and visitor interest goes through a cyclic journey in which as the visitation numbers grow, the impacts, both positive as well as negative also chart a trend that mirrors its tourism related development. From initial discovery, to growing popularity and a state of saturation, the destination finds itself maximizing the economic potential and other benefits. Yet, if sustainable principles are not practiced, it also witnesses maximum pressure on its resources. Unless a destination rejuvenates itself and conserves its resources, it is bound to fade away or get into decline. It is Muller's 'Magic Pentagon'(1994) that can save the day (see Figure 1). The solution lies in ensuring that interests of all stakeholders are maintained in balance and the equilibrium is retained. Economic health, well being of locals, satisfaction of visitors, culture and protection of resources are the five constituents of the magic pentagon that can potentially ensure that a destination enjoys the fruits of tourism development in a sustainable manner.

The offering of a destination is typically unique, hence able to attract visitors, the destination itself being defined by its social, cultural, economic and environmental context. Tourism acts as a driving force that can have positive or negative impacts on each of these contributory dimensions, depending on the level of sensitivity and exploitation. Environmental degradation, cultural 'commodification'[1](Hill, 2011), 'acculturation'(Mason, 2008, p. 59), social disharmony and economic susceptibility due to dependence on tourists inflow are some of the commonly faced negative impacts. Sustaining the cultural resources of a destination that would otherwise be lost due to neglect and providing livelihoods to local population are among the positive impacts. The debate or conflict is inherent in the term 'sustainable tourist destination' as it outlines the externality of the process, with destination being dependent on 'tourism' and sustainability being defined over and over again, with a focus on the 'local.'

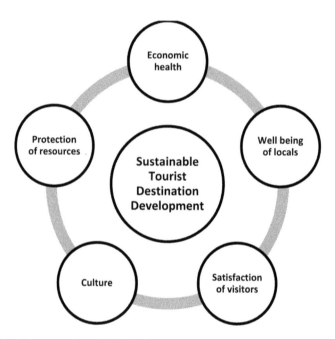

FIGURE 1   Representation of the 'Magic Pentagon'(Muller, 1994).

7.2 METHODOLOGY

The methodology involves literature review, along with aggregation and analysis of case studies from the international and Indian context, charting successful approaches to sustainable tourism destination development and management across the developed and developing world. Some case studies have been selected to emphasize on the issues and challenges related to sustainability of tourist destinations as well. The framework of study involves exploration of four types of destinations that show critical interface with various dimensions of sustainability. The derivations from these have been further emphasized by discussing the role of economics and stakeholders as two primary areas that guide sustainable development of tourist destinations, followed by the inferences.

7.3 TYPES OF DESTINATIONS AND THEIR VARIOUS CHALLENGES TOWARD SUSTAINABILITY

The principles of sustainability in tourism may be outlined as ecological or environmental, social, economic and cultural, along with the extent of educational, conservational and local participation level in the tourism activity. The challenge lies in the fact that the principles are subjective and so is the measurability of sustainability (Mowforth and Munt, 2009, p. 109).

The issues and opportunities of each tourism destination are unique, dependent on its resources, consumers and their motivations, policy frameworks and the stakeholders involved. According to Mowforth and Munt (2009, pp. 110–111), there are ten tools of sustainability in tourism, namely: area protection, industry regulation, visitor management techniques, environmental impact assessment, carrying capacity calculations, consultation and participation technique, codes of conduct, sustainability indicators, foot printing and carbon budget analysis and fair trade in tourism. But these tools too have limitations and can be subjected to manipulation for partisan purposes (Mowforth and Munt, 2009, p. 118). According to Dodds (2007), the process of moving towards a sustainable tourism destination requires the understanding the issues and potential in a holistic manner, where the quality of life of residents and visitors, managing and protecting social and environmental aspects and adopting a nonlinear approach are imperatives.

The various dimensions of sustainability namely social, economic, cultural and environmental all have a role to play in the development of a sustainable tourist destination. To discuss the same, the four typologies taken up for analysis are representative of leisure, religious, nature based and cultural heritage tourism destinations (Figure 2). Each of these typologies addresses the four dimensions of sustainability, while maintaining focus on a few if not all.

There is a strong overlap in the motivations that drive the tourists towards each type of destination. For leisure tourists, often the natural and cultural resources are the source of attraction. When the natural and cultural resources of a location are overlaid on each other, these represent distinctive cultural landscapes that define the destination. The complexity of multiple associational values over a site may give rise to sacred or pilgrimage sites and other forms of cultural heritage based tourism destinations.

The various scenarios of juxtaposing motivations and keys aspects of sustainability under consideration can be seen in the following discussion.

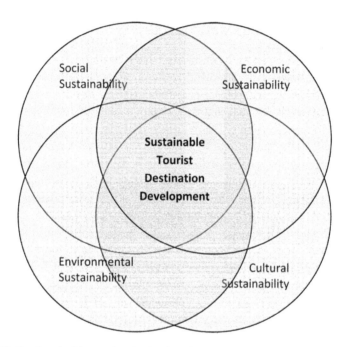

FIGURE 2 Sustainable tourist destination development through overlap of the four dimensions of sustainability.

7.3.1 THE RESORT: A LEISURE TOURIST DESTINATION

Wall and Mathieson[2] (2007, p. 199) define a 'resort' as 'the place where people go for vacations or recreation and may be described more specifically as health, inland, coastal, mountain or ski resorts or on the basis of their geographical characteristics,' also referring to a specific hotel or establishment that 'provides substantial entertainment and recreational facilities.' They also add another typology as the 'integrated resort' that has additional problems of its own. According to them, environmental impacts of resort developments include architectural pollution, ribbon development and sprawl along coastlines, valleys and scenic routes, overloading of infrastructure, segregation of local residents and traffic congestion (Wall and Mathieson, 2007, pp. 203–204).

Developing countries such as India are witnessing increasing urbanization, giving birth to urban agglomerations with their own issues. The National Capital Region was originally surrounded by agricultural lands that are also getting consumed by the urban sprawl. Weekend getaways established at a two to three hour driving distance from the urban territory offer breaks from the urban lifestyle, some examples being the Heritage Village Resort and Spa Manesar, Tarudhan Valley Golf Resort and The Westin Sohna Resort and Spa that have developed over the last decade and a half along with the 15th century Neemrana Fort-Palace and the 20th century Pataudi Palace that are heritage properties converted to 'non-hotel' hotels. In most of these weekend getaway resorts, the setting may be immaterial to the visitor, as the activities within serve as magnets. A break from the hustle bustle of the urban activity; these provide an escape to a relaxed, recreational experience, introverted in character, alienated from the environment around.

FIGURE 3   The Reception block of the Baagh Resort, Kanha National Park in Madhya Pradesh, built in the tribal tradition used by the local population around the resort. Local materials and labor were utilized in the process. It acts as a showcase of the traditional building crafts and the entire project has generated livelihood opportunities for the local population.

Resorts may also be may situated in wilderness, quiet natural landscapes or rural setting without much urban development around. These in turn have the potential to link up with rural and nature based tourism, depicting the multiple dimensions of a destination that come together to position it as a tourist destination (Figure 4). Examples of this typology in India includes resorts close to wildlife sanctuaries or national parks such as The Baagh Resort at Kanha National Park in Madhya Pradesh or historic hunting lodges, forts and summer palaces that have unique settings and have been converted to heritage hotels, such as the 14th century Hill Fort Kesroli, set in a rural landscape with an adjoining village visible from the ramparts and the INDeco Hotel cum Museum at Swamimalai Village in Tamil Nadu. An international example has been taken in the form of the Tufenkian Heritage hotel chain based out of Armenia.

FIGURE 4   Potential for sustainable development due to resorts.

In all cases, the resorts employ workers from the surrounding areas in construction or restoration activity and also daily operations, procure raw materials such as produce and dairy from the local people and interest the guests in the rural surroundings and the local community. There are direct as well as indirect benefits to the community around due to these resorts in the form of training, capacity building, livelihood opportunities and provision of a consumption avenue for what they produce. In case of the Baagh Resort and the Hill Fort Kesroli, the ownership is not local, hence the power does not lie with the local community. In case of the INDeco Leisure Hotel in Tamil Nadu, India and Tufenkian Heritage hotel though, the ownership has a sense of a mission towards the development of the rural hinterland and they have multiplied the effect by opening more outlets, affecting change at a regional level. The INDeco leisure Hotels and the Tufenkian Heritage hotel chain stand out as an example of private initiative to build a tourism destination, firmly entrenched in principles of sustainable development. **Refer Box 1.**

Box 1: Resorts and Regional Development in Rural Hinterlands

Tufenkian Heritage Hotel Chain, Armenia

Tufenkian's goal was to develop and market the rural countryside of Armenia as an undiscovered tourist destination. Today with hotels located in Yerevan, Sevan, Dilijan and Lori, Tufenkian has been able to create a sustainable tourist destination that has visitors flocking to experience the rural Armenia. The basic tenets of sustainable development, one that is sensitive towards environmental, sociocultural and ecological concerns find representation in all activities undertaken. The construction of the hotels was based on design that represented the local culture, architecture and history. Local building material and craftsmen were deployed all along, ensuring participation of the local communities at multiple levels. Once operational, the hotels employed local people to a large extent, and where required filled gaps in the skills and knowledge required through training programs.

Local produce is used by the hotels and the communities have been supported to augment their production capacities to meet most of the needs of the hotels. The other tourism related services too have been added over the years along similar approaches. The impact has been a strong local community engagement and participation. The economic leakages are minimal, and as a result positive socioeconomic impacts are quite visible. Tufenkian impact on the region has been largely positive. Support to local charities, use of solar energy, tree plantation drives, efforts to conserve natural resources have gone hand in hand with the business initiatives and growth. In fact the local government and other stakeholders have also been encouraged to support the development of the region as a major tourist destination. The strategic choice has clearly been that of achieving financial profitability over a long-term without compromising on the need to mitigate the negative impacts of tourism growth in the region. Rural Armenia has witnessed economic growth through increased private and public investment, that has reduced poverty, increased education levels and has a positive impact on the lives of local people without damaging the environment (Hergnyan, 2010).

Key impact on dimensions of sustainability:		
	Positive impacts	Negative impacts
Social	Training and capacity building of local community, provision of social infrastructure	—
Economic	Minimal economic leakages and private and public investment in the region	—
Environmental	Tree plantation drives and solar energy generation, conservation of natural resources	—
Cultural	Promotion of local culture and history, use of traditional construction technology	—

INDeco Leisure Hotels, Swamimalai, Tamil Nadu, India

The case of INDeco Leisure Hotels demonstrates 'responsible development,' driven by an individual and his mission for social, cultural and economic development in a rural hinterland. Initiated in 1996 with the setting up of a hotel cum museum in village Swamimalai, Kumbakonam, Tamil Nadu, the initiative became a phenomenon over the years with a multiplying effect. The focus has been on the promoting local art, culture, lifestyle, traditional practices, food and vernacular architecture, along with providing employment to the local population and offering the guests an authentic experience of the rural heritage. Training of staff is undertaken to promote the arts and crafts of the region, as also the operational skills related to hospitality. Locally produced materials are used in the construction and operational activities, reducing economic leakages and provided a steady market linkage. Lost menus and utensils are searched for and any object of the past is meaningfully linked to its history. The local people are participants as resources and means of outreach for the local heritage, while the museum serves as a center for learning and research (Borgia, 2012).

Key impact on dimensions of sustainability:		
	Positive impacts	Negative impacts
Social	Training and capacity building of local community, support to marginalized segments of community	—
Economic	Minimal economic leakages, livelihood generation for local community	—
Environmental	—	—
Cultural	Use of traditional construction materials and technology, training and promotion of local arts, crafts and culinary heritage, providing the guests an authentic experience	—

Typically in any resort development, the processes and activities within the resort are very different from the surroundings in which it sits, yet in each case, the resort has a social, cultural, economic and environmental impact on the surroundings and communities residing in these. The extent of sustainability of such a destination depends on whether the impacts are positive or negative, who the beneficiaries are and if the goals that are being set are oriented towards short-term gains or long-term impacts. If the entire process of development has a sensitive approach at the heart of it, the resorts can actually act as drivers of regional development in a sustainable manner, while if the concern is completely commercial and disjointed from the needs of the communities around, the same can act as disruptive forces that degrade the environment around.

7.3.2 NATURE BASED TOURISM DESTINATIONS

Beach towns and hill stations are two prime examples of tourism destinations that have developed as mass tourism destinations all over the world. The peaceful natural experiences these earlier offered have been replaced by noisy, congested and over commercialized ones, especially in peak tourist seasons. The reason for the visit was the natural landscape, but over the life cycle of these destinations, a number of artificial activities were also added, to rejuvenate the destination to attract more and more tourists. The environment itself has degraded as a result of exceeding carrying capacities and insensitivity (Figure 5).

FIGURE 5   View of marble rocks at Bedaghat along River Narmada in Madhya Pradesh, from the ropeway that provides access from one bank to the other. The visitor infrastructure at the location that is thronged by regional tourists is at a manageable scale as of now. Non degradable waste generated due to tourist activity and addition of large scale tourist infrastructure that can be detrimental to the environment are threats that need to be addressed at policy, regulatory and implementation levels.

One such example is that of the 'hill station' Shimla, located in the north Indian state of Himachal Pradesh. The quaint 19th century colonial summer capital of has subsequently turned into a mass tourism destination, serving as a major economic driver for the hill town and the region around it, but the overexploitation due to tourism has resulted in large-scale ecological degradation. Yet, the tourism policy of the State ignores the issue of environmental sustainability, community consultations and impact assessments of further growth of tourism at the city or regional level. **For details, refer to Box 2.**

> **Box 2: Nature based Tourism: Who's Prerogative?**
>
> **Shimla, a Hill Station in North India**
>
> The concept of setting up and shifting to a summer capital by the British in India, as in the case of Shimla and Nainital among others, resulted in

the setting up of hill resorts that served as administrative centers during the summers, starting in the second half of the 19th century. These naturally pristine environs were hence developed to form urban centers, with an increasing population growth, leaving a colonial imprint in the form of bungalows, administrative buildings, market avenues, clubs, recreational areas and boarding schools. The idea of 'hill stations' was given rise to, popularizing the trend of visiting climatically favorable locations for leisure among the domestic population. The improvement of transport facilities by road and rail enabled the process, as did the motivation to emulate the colonizers by the middle class generated due to the colonial rule over the country that directly or indirectly effected a social and cultural change. The attempt to emulate the western world hence begun continues till date, though the character of urban development was lost in post-colonial interventions. The tourism influx saw an explosive increase from the mid-1980s to mid-1990s with accompanying increase in hotels and hotel rooms by 500% developed in a chaotic, haphazard manner. At present Shimla, the capital of the state of Himachal Pradesh is a 0.17 million population city with over 3 million annual tourist population and peak visitations in the month of June (0.46 million), about 95% of which are domestic tourists over the year (Himachal Tourism, 2008).

The city is bursting at its seams in terms of urban expansion and is a nightmare in terms of infrastructure provision and overcrowding during the peak months. Over the last six years alone the tourist visitation has grown from 2.5 million to 3.5 million, with no real capacity building measures to speak of. The adverse impact of tourism related activity is visible all round, from damage to ecology in the form of deforestation, uncontrolled construction activity, pollution of air, water resources (Himachal Tourism, 2008).

The Tourism Policy 2005 for the State maintains a mission statement 'to make tourism the prime engine of economic growth in the state by positioning it as a leading global destination by the year 2020.' How does one address the question of sustainability in such a scenario? The policy emphasizes on the need to take pressure away from the saturated destinations to lesser known locations. The Policy intends to position the State as whole as a 'destination' and lend focus towards rural tourism, pilgrim tourism, eco tourism, and adventure tourism. The push towards building tourist interest in some of the lesser known destinations the state currently is also supported by a marketing strategy. There is at least on paper, mention of infrastructure related investment and also intent to seek private capital thrust, but the policy is quite unclear on the critical issue of sustainability. The action plan does not talk about managing the impact of mass tourism in cities like Shimla (Himachal Tourism, 2008).

Key impact on dimensions of sustainability:		
	Positive impacts	**Negative impacts**
Social		Power not in hands of local community
Economic	Generation of employment opportunities	Overdependence on tourism as source of livelihood
Environmental	Attempt to promote ecotourism at policy level	Ecological degradation, loss of character, over-crowding
Cultural	Projects for conservation of built heritage	Lack of authentic experi-ence due to uncontrolled development

Lugu Lake in South China

Lugu Lake is located on the border of Yunnan and Sichuan provinces in the South-West of China. Covering an area of 50.4 square kilometers, with an average depth of 45 meters, this lake is surrounded by mountains and lush green forests, and offers amazing experience of nature's bounty. Its elevation is 2,690 meters above sea level and the lake is probably one of the few of its kind that have not been contaminated by human activity and development in China. The destination is quite well known for the unique culture of Mosuo people, who are 'matriarchal.' The emergence of the area as a popular tourism destination is due to both the culture and the natural scenic beauty that it offers.

Early 1980s Beginning of initiatives from the local community at a very small scale, hence **bottom up approach** to tourism development planning and strategy formulation

2005: Over the two decades, development of 74 hotels with a bed capacity of 3,500 and many other services and facilities to ensure tourist needs were met. Issues of management started emerging and some negative impacts of development started surfacing: many hotels were constructed too close to the lake, sewage disposal became an issue and the lake started getting polluted, cultural impacts became obvious, social ills like prostitution found footing. The destination had become completely dependent on tourism as a means of economic sustenance and nearly the entire local population was engaged in one way or the other. The earlier means of livelihood, primarily agriculture, had taken a back seat. The stage was set for the government to come in to stabilize and control the development with a **top down approach**.

Post 2005 Two key differences in approach towards tourism development: the 'scale' and loss of local control in decision making. With big government involvement the region saw large scale infrastructure investments in the form of road links, airport, tourism town, bridges, refuse dump site, engineering project to manage pollution levels and many large capacity hotel projects. Nearly 80 million Yuan were invested in three years to get the destination on the global tourism map, ready with all the facilities and services that demanding tourists would come to expect. Equally in focus was the understanding that for this growth to be sustainable ecological conservation was a strategic imperative. Efforts were made both at policy and implementation level to ensure that any further expansion is planned and not at the cost of sustainability, agricultural land is protected and cannot be used for any other purpose. A code of conduct for industry and visitors was put in place and enforced to ensure that negative impacts of tourism related development are mitigated to the extent possible.

The socioeconomic benefits are clearly visible in the improvement in the living conditions of the local people through business and employment opportunities. The success story is a result of a committed government involvement, engagement between all stakeholders and participation of an empowered community. It is not that there are no trouble spots or adverse impacts of the growth path that the destination has charted, but it still stands out as an example for developing nations with such resources to emulate. The shift in approach in the second phase has rendered a dramatic change in the scope of the destination and unlocked its potential as an eco-cultural tourism destination. The destination has also been alert to not become a 'mass tourism' location; ensuring principles of sustainable development are factored in at policy levels and duly implemented. While role of big government has taken away most of the direct involvement in decisions in sharp contrast with the first phase, the same has given the control and balance that was required (Gang, 2011).

Key impact on dimensions of sustainability:		
	Positive impacts	Negative impacts
Social	Through government control, improved living conditions, involvement of all stakeholders	Power shift from local community to government
Economic	Large scale public investment generating livelihoods and economic growth, protection of agricultural land to diversify economy	-
Environmental	Government control led to ecological conservation, control on further expansion	-
Cultural	Consciousness about not making it a mass tourism destination, orientation towards alternate tourism approach	-

Central Coast Region of Western Australia

The Central Coast Region of Western Australia is one of the top 25 global biodiversity 'hot spots' in terms of marine and terrestrial environments. This clearly establishes the need for any tourism related activity to be sensitive to the ecological concerns ensuring long-term sustainability of the fragile nature based resources. Located in a developed nation that is identified as tourist friendly destination, which recognizes tourism as a core sector of the economy makes this region's experience with sustainable tourism development rather interesting.

Tourism planning and policy are embedded in multitudes of public institutions with political connect, supported by government funding. Due to the importance given to tourism sector, marketing, promotion and research find government support through many initiatives. The tourism infrastructure has been developed with both government support and private investment. It is quite evident that there are different organs operating from central to state to local levels with mandates for managing various aspects of tourism in the region.

Agencies involved in the process	Roles and Responsibilities
Commonwealth Government	Provides broad policy framework
Western Australian Tourism Commission (WATC)	For marketing and promotion
Department of Conservation and Land Management (DCLM)	Manages State-owned, protected areas that are clearly enlisted
Western Australia Planning Commission & Department for Planning and Infrastructure (DPI)	Undertakes long-term land use planning
Local government at town/city level	Ensures proper visitor facilities and infrastructure, protects the interests of the local communities

A workshop organized to weigh in the status of tourism development and its impacts generated the below listed recommendations to achieve long-term objective of sustainability:
1. setting and working towards realistic goals
2. proactive, transparent and flexible planning processes
3. formation of balanced partnerships between resource managers and commercial sectors
4. definition of and adherence to environmental standards
5. commitment to implementation of appropriate management plans
6. adequate funding from varied sources
7. coordination of the local and regional tourism industry
8. leadership shown by the tourism industry
9. increasing the professionalism of the tourism industry by adopting codes and guidelines
10. meeting criteria of various accreditation programs and community involvement

There is no debate that sustainable development and mitigation of any negative impacts is critical for the tourist destinations in the region. Despite available structure in the form of organizations and guidance from policy frameworks and environmental codes and regulations, the above stated recommendations face many issues on the ground. Given this structural support, is tourism in the region being managed and developed in a sustainable manner? A fragmented sector with overlapping regulatory or advisory arms with often divergent approaches and even differing objectives faces challenging times. On one hand the stakeholders want the visitation to the pristine nature based destinations to grow in numbers, more facilities and infrastructure to be put in place to support the same and also ensure this is achieved with principles of sustainability in tow. An uphill task by all means (Priskin 2003).

Key impact on dimensions of sustainability:		
	Positive impacts	**Negative impacts**
Social	Focus on community development at local govt. level	Conflict of interest due to multiple agencies with different focal areas
Economic	Government support and private investment into tourism development	Tourism based economy, dependent on external funding
Environmental	Policy and regulatory framework to guide ecologically sensitive development	Growth in tourism may conflict with fragile ecosystem
Cultural	-	

The case of China and Australia emphasize on the role of the government and legislation in controlling environmental degradation, along with promoting nature based tourism. **Refer to Box 2**. In case of China, the process showed a shift from local decision making to that by the government, while in Australia the challenge is managing the conflicting voices from various stakeholders, wanting increase in tourist activity on one end and the following of sustainability principles on another. The Central Coast Region is being marketed as a nature based destination of choice aggressively. As tourism activity grows with increasing visitation, the pressure on the ecologically sensitive region will be high. This will render making sustainable choices and imperative for protecting the region and its tourism resources.

The case of Shimla in India demonstrates how immature the handling of the issue of sustainability is as of now. There is a need to conduct a detailed impact assessment, to establish the adverse impacts from socioeconomic as well as ecological contexts and chart a policy direction that helps mitigate the same. Carrying capacities need to be determined to ensure towns like Shimla don't lose their character and charm as a tourist destination. The awareness level of the local communities and their participation in taking decision that impact their towns' potential as a tourist destination is a must. Learning from success stories from various parts of the world, including some from developing nations like India will go a long way in building sustainable tourist destinations that deliver the promise of social and economic well being without sacrificing the very resources that made them popular and attractive.

The solution may lie in establishing policy and legislative frameworks and investment from the government to ensure that the negative impacts caused by tourism are reversed if possible and prevented in future. But, can and should the local voice be done away with? The ecotourism initiatives in India at a small scale demonstrate how the community can contribute to sustainable tourism destination development. **Refer to Box 4**. If there is a way to expand this sense of ownership in the community, it may be through reduction of the external stake to an extent where it finds balance with the local needs.

7.3.3 RELIGIOUS TOURISM DESTINATIONS

The concept of religious tourism has been around for centuries, across all religions. With the UNWTO (2011) estimating 600 million national and international religious and spiritual voyages in the world, these is a clear suggestion to religious tourism being a serious segment of the tourism industry.

The location of these pilgrimage centers may be in urban centers such as the Vatican City, Jerusalem, Varanasi and Mecca or sacred locations in the Himalayas, such as Kedarnath. One of the most sacred and remote of the four most important pilgrimage destinations for Hindus, Kedarnath has suffered the wrath of nature through massive destruction and loss of life due to flash floods. The flash floods of June 2013 took the ugly form of a calamity at Kedarnath and the surrounding areas due to excessive human intervention on the sacred, fragile landscape in the Himalayas, leaving thousands dead. The meaning of pilgrimage has been altered to 'consumer tourism' for the masses that resulted in provision of ill planned roads, construction on river channels, use of non indigenous building material and technology along with sewage and garbage dumping into the river valley, as opposed to the pilgrimage, 'undertaken with a very small ecological footprint, and a heightened consciousness about the sacred earth on which the pilgrim walks, and the sacred site a pilgrim visits'(Shiva, 2013). A similar case in point is that of Vaishnodevi, located in the Trikuta mountain range in the northern most state of Jammu and Kashmir that is the second most visited religious site in India with more than 10 million visitors recorded in 2011, a major leap from the 1.4 million in 1986. The unprecedented increase in number of visitors is due to the provision of infrastructure facilities, including construction of roads, halting points, shops, overnight accommodation, hospital and even a helicopter service to take visitors up to the destination. While this is quoted as part of major achievements by the Shri Mata Vaishno Devi Shrine Board (2013), it may be another disaster waiting to happen, with the transformation of the hard to reach religious pilgrimage to an easily accessible and well-provided journey for the masses.

Another such case is the Govardhan Hill the Braj region in north India that is established as a cultural landscape with its *kund*s (water tanks), groves of trees, bowers and arbors in groves, boulders and rocks, dance performance areas and the entire ridge itself having multilayered sacred associations. Each of these has associated ritual enactments in the present time, with the ancient rite of circling the sacred hill, known as *parikrama* being a prime one. The dynamic cultural landscape sees an increasing number of pilgrims, accounting to 5–7 million annually, stressing the carrying capacity of the landscape. A road constructed along the route in recent years has reduced the journey by rickshaw or tonga by half, taking away the intended experience of the journey. There is a shift from the notion of pilgrimage to package tourism, taking a toll on the natural resources themselves, serving as detrimental to the environment and the sacred experience (Sinha, 2011) (Figure 6).

FIGURE 6   Brahm Sarovar at Pushkar, Rajasthan, set in the Aravalli Hills is established as a religious tourism destination for centuries. While the culture is being influenced by influx of international visitors, the physical environment is undergoing change with construction of hotels and guest houses (visible in foreground) as the historic fabric is being neglected or replaced.

Key impact on dimensions of sustainability:		
	Positive impacts	**Negative impacts**
Social	-	Initiatives such as distribution of food causes pollution due to use on non degradable disposable bottles, plates, glasses, etc. that are dumped around
Economic	Growing economy due to growing number of visitors	Dependence on visitor related employment, moving away from traditional livelihoods
Environmental	-	Degradation due to interventions to enable masses to travel, pollution
Cultural	-	Improved accessibility taking away the authentic experience, shift to consumer tourism

The sacred destinations in fragile environments were usually established by saints or monks who would use these as a place for quite meditation, reverence and abode, without disturbing the landscape around. The superimpositions of various associations over these landscapes and revival of religious fervor due to sects who rediscovered and revalidated these meanings have resulted in their being turned into mass tourism destinations. Even the tasks undertaken with religious intent such as distribution of free food and drinks are being carried out in such a way that they cause negative impact on the environment. The large scale use of plastic or foam disposable plates and glasses that are then dumped without a second thought, turn the whole idea of goodwill upside down. The irony is that the sacred landscapes or pilgrimage destinations in remote areas were established through embodiment of the unique natural resources with spiritual meaning and cultural associations and the manifestation of the religious fervor is in fact destroying the natural resources and ecological balance. This brings into question the cultural reference of what religious tourism stands for and how far it has come from the conception of pilgrimage.

7.3.4   CULTURAL HERITAGE TOURISM DESTINATIONS

The spectrum of cultural heritage tourism destinations is quite wide, ranging from those coined as world heritage sites, cities or cultural landscapes by UNESCO to a historic mansion of regional significance or even rural heritage that has a vernacular character. While the developed world has been able to tap the potential of its cultural heritage resource to a large extent, with focus on heritage management over decades, the challenge of applying principles of sustainable tourism at world heritage sites that are established as tourist destinations still looms large. A particular case example is of world heritage sites (WHSs) in UK, that highlight the lack of active planning and managing of the social and cultural dimensions of sustainability as opposed to the environmental sustainability dimension, 'lack of grass roots consultation' and 'limited assessment of local economic characteristics and tourism infrastructure capacity'(Landorf, 2009, p. 66) (Figure 7). According to Landorf, 'the implication of this is the isolation of WHSs from their local economy and an associated impact on the equitable distribution of the benefits of a sustainable approach to tourism development.'

Hence, it is no surprise that the developing world that struggles with explosive population growth, poverty, poor social and physical infrastructure, while being rich in cultural heritage resources, is unable to mobilize its resources to safeguard or manage these resources or tap their potential towards development. The question of sustainability becomes even more critical in these parts of the world. Cultural tourism sector if well managed has a strong pro-poor potential as it results in creation of jobs for communities living in and around heritage rich areas. The destinations gain from tourism driven infrastructure development, improving the living conditions of the local community as well (Abakerli, 2012). The case of Kachhpura in Agra, a city known to the world as a significant tourist destination due to the Taj Mahal, is such an example that offers a possible solution towards sustainability of tangible and intangible cultural resources and expansion of the destination from a singular landmark focus to a more holistic one. **Refer to Box 3.** The key to the process is appropriate partnerships and community participation (Bapat, Khosla and Kumar, 2010).

FIGURE 7   The prehistoric World Heritage Site of Bhimbetka near Bhopal, Madhya Pradesh, India, is set amidst agricultural land. There is no direct involvement with the local communities, a potential that is getting lost.

A new participant in the process of rural development, the Indian Trust for Rural heritage and Development has a focus on promoting 'rural heritage tourism,' with the realization that it can have an extraordinary impact on a rural community. The strategy has a clear directive to ensure that the 'local community members participate at all stages to ensure that tourism benefits the community and helps to enhance, rather than degrade, the very heritage on which it depends'(Misra, 2012, p. 92). If followed through, this approach could help guide the development of sustainable tourist destinations across the rural and urban heritage rich landscapes of the country, with inter-linkages forged in the form of tourism circuits and learnings shared, resulting in an overall holistic and sustainable development process.

Box 3: Cultural Heritage and Destinations
Kachhpura, Agra, India

Kachhpura is a traditional settlement along the River Yamuna, located across the Taj Mahal, with historical structures and ruins in around it. The settlement suffered from poor sanitary conditions, the population consisted of marginalized daily wage laborers or shoe makers and the heritage structures and remains of a Mughal garden revealed following flash floods in 1987 from the Mughal period, suffered from neglect. The cultural resources included the built heritage and also the living traditions in the form of arts and crafts of the local community. Through a partnership model between the community and local, national and international governmental and nongovernmental organizations, infrastructure upgradation and heritage walk development took place, using traditional knowledge systems with community participation. The result was urban renewal along with expanding the heritage tourism potential of Agra as a destination and all without uprooting or marginalizing the local community, but in fact centered around them, with a sense of ownership in the settlement and now also the built heritage resources (Bapat, Khosla and Kumar, 2010).

Key impact on dimensions of sustainability:

	Positive impacts	Negative impacts
Social	Social and physical infrastructure development for the settlement	-
Economic	Growing economy due to growing number of visitors, adding another source of income	-
Environmental		-
Cultural	Sense of pride inculcated in the local community, cultural heritage interpreted through walks	-

City Palace Udaipur, Rajasthan, India

The City Palace Complex is a major destination for domestic and overseas tourists. It is located in the heart of the 16th century lake city of Udaipur in the state of Rajasthan in India. The city's architectural and cultural heritage combined with its unique geographical setting of lakes and the Aravalli mountain range attracts close to 8 million tourists annually, including many international visitors. The complex spread over nearly 6.5 acres has parts that are under the custodianship of Maharana of Mewar Charitable Foundation (MMCF), a non-profit organization supported by the erstwhile royal family. In addition there are parts, which are privately held by the royal family and deployed as residences or as commercial hotels. The most historic core of the palace complex was converted to a museum that is essentially the most significant tourist attraction in the city. The foundation utilizes its resources towards maintenance of the Palace Complex, including the conservation of the built fabric of the heritage structures, as well as the sociocultural heritage that is more than 500 years old.

The approach of the custodians is reflected in the nomenclature that identifies them as 'Eternal Mewar,' which in itself brings sustainability at the center of every decision that impacts the destination. In 2004 MMCF secured a planning grant from the Getty Conservation Master Plan, to guide future development of the Complex. The objective was to pursue planned interventions aimed at maximizing the tourist potential of the destination, and also ensure conservation of the site, adhering to international norms and standards. Facilities were designed on the basis of a set of planning documents developed after conducting detailed research, surveys, documentation and analysis, to balance the concerns of preserving the cultural continuity on one hand and the need to mobilize revenue generation on the other. It was recognized that fiscal sustainability and conservation of heritage must not come at the cost of each other. Facilities and services enhancements and additions have been implemented at various levels such as world class interpretation in existing galleries, reuse of locked spaces for incorporating additional galleries and visitor facilities, enabling access for the differently abled, setting up of an interpretation center and developing heritage merchandise for dissemination of the organized outreach events. The Complex generates revenues from ticket sales and other services and facilities; the foundation deploys the same towards the day to day running aspects as well as making investments towards conservation projects and for service enhancements that would further improve the visitor experience. There is an ongoing effort to add value to the complex, ensuring it is available as a heritage resource for the future generations (Munjal and Munjal, 2011).

Key impact on dimensions of sustainability:		
	Positive impacts	**Negative impacts**
Social	Continuity of custodianship	-
Economic	Financially sustainable, generates employment for local residents,	-
Environmental	Focus on minimizing environmental impacts through planning framework	-
Cultural	Physical conservation ensuring continuity of cultural resources and their significance; adaptive reuse, new galleries and outreach activities, enabling continuity of cultural heritage significance	-

Elmina, Ghana

Elmina, the capital of Komenda-Edina-Eguafo-Abrem District, is a small city located approximately 160 kilometers south-west of Accra, the national capital of Ghana. Covering an area of about 64 square kilometers, it has a population of less than 50,000. Fishing, salt mining, canoe and boat building, trading and tourism are the principle economic activities for the local people. Fishing alone provides direct and indirect jobs to about 75% of the inhabitants of Elmina. Historically when in 1470 Portuguese explorers 'discovered' the rich gold lands on the West African coast, Elmina found itself strategically located and soon became the heart of the West African gold trade to start with and as the slave trade picked up, the city became a hub of related activity.

The city boasts of an impressive array of built cultural heritage. The impressive castle of St. George was constructed by the Portuguese as far back as 1482 and still holds the status of Africa's oldest European building. The forts and castles along the Ghanaian coast stand as monuments for the slave trade and these have emerged as destinations for cultural heritage tourism. The existence of Portuguese and Dutch influence in Elmina are still visible through the presence of the fort and castle, churches and cemeteries, old merchant houses, Dutch streets and family names and celebration of Dutch Christmas. These assets as well as the rich traditional culture of the indigenous people and the charm of the picturesque fishing harbor provide the uniqueness of Elmina as the nucleus of tourism development in the Central Region of Ghana.

With the support of the government at the center as well as district level, the city has taken steps to emerge as a tourist destination. Attracting about 100,000 tourists annually, of which over 70,000 are foreign tourists, Elmina plans to increase the visitor numbers from both the international as well domestic segments to realize economic gains in terms of valuable foreign exchange as well employment creation both direct and indirect. Recognizing the potential of Elmina as a tourist destination, private investment and participation in the tourist related services has become active. Star category resorts, good quality restaurants and retail locations catering to the needs of tourists have come up to meet the needs of the increasing number of tourists.

Notwithstanding the economic potential of the heritage evidenced through the large numbers of tourists who visit Elmina, tourism-related employment opportunities are still limited and the living standards in Elmina are low and this is also reflected in the environment. The fishing harbor is silted and polluted, the beaches are covered with waste, the city's drainage system is poor and basic road, telecommunication and electricity infrastructure are inadequate. Health care facilities and education opportunities for the vast majority are quite dismal. The government in recent years has taken steps to harness the tourism potential with a clear objective of supporting the socioeconomic needs of the local community, to improve their standard of living and to eventually deploy the success of Elmina a role model for other such destinations to emulate. The government initiated a strategic planning approach that involved participation of a host of stakeholders, these included politicians, local government staff, GMMB, Ghana Tourist Board, Environmental protection Agency, community-based organizations, formal and informal business community, professional organizations, consultants, religious bodies, fishermen, 'Asafo' groups, nongovernmental organizations, international agencies, diplomatic missions and the media. A task force was put in place and a rigorous planning process was launched, it resulted in awareness generation among stakeholders and also established a clear agenda. The policy framework that emerged was one based out of consensus and there was clarity on the forward path.

Focal areas under the plan:
• waste management and drainage;
• tourism and local economic development;

- fishing and fishing harbor;
- education and health.

To ensure momentum in terms of implementation on the ground the city has a monitoring process that reports on the status of projects and also helps establish forward timelines on their completion.

The approach has resulted in a planned development that has community support and is alive to sustainability concerns. The city has attracted investment, tourism revenues are growing and impact on socioeconomic parameters is becoming visible. Though the city has a long way to go still to establish itself as a successful tourist destination, the learning's are quite clear. Wide community participation, awareness generation, sense of ownership and a planned approach that factors in sustainability is the way to go (Arthur and Mensah, 2006).

Key impact on dimensions of sustainability:		
	Positive impacts	**Negative impacts**
Social	Initiatives for awareness generation, focus on health and education as part of policy framework, use of participatory approach involving all stakeholders	-
Economic	Active private investment in tourist infrastructure, growing tourism revenues, employment generation, focus on local economic development and fishing along with tourism development	-
Environmental	Planning framework stresses on conservation of the fishing harbor, waste management and drainage	If unchecked, growing tourist infrastructure can dilute the character of the place and lay stress on natural resources
Cultural	Cultural resources being tapped as magnets for tourists	Threat of cultural commoditization, erosion of the indigenous culture, taking away the authentic experience

The focus on environment, economics, social as well as cultural frameworks is an extremely significant part of developing cultural heritage tourism destinations. It is important to understand the interdependence of continuity of cultural significance and sustainability if such a focus is to be maintained. The national and international tourism, planning and conservation frameworks have evolved around the idea of sustaining the resources, but how these are implemented on the ground is the prime challenge.

The case of the 16th century City Palace Complex in Udaipur is an example of such an implementation framework that aims at positioning the complex as a sustainable tourist destination that serves as a local as well as tourist landmark in the lake city of Udaipur (Figure 8). **Refer to Box 3**. The complex is under ownership of a nongovernmental foundation that has patronage from the royal family of Udaipur and is committed to sustaining the resource economically and in terms of maintaining its cultural significance and minimizing negative impact on the sociocultural and environmental context (Munjal and Munjal, 2011).

FIGURE 8   The introduction of visitor facilities at Moti Chowk in City Palace Complex, Udaipur reflects the continued spirit of improving the visitor experience, as per a planning framework based on appropriate documentation, research and analysis. Addition of new galleries, interpretive signage and outreach activities demonstrate the implementation of sustainability driven objectives through a policy and planning framework specially developed for the complex.

It would be an ideal situation for developing countries if the resources of a cultural heritage destination are sustained through tourism along with sustaining the community around by providing sources of livelihood, within a framework that ensures that the negative impacts are minimized. A constant commitment towards the cause would be required in terms of developing the planning frameworks and ensuring their implementation if such a model is to be replicated. The same message is echoed in the case of Elmina. **Refer to Box 3.**

Another case is the Qutub Minar Complex in Delhi, a designated world heritage since 1993. A study of the satisfaction over services available at the Qutub Minar Complex revealed that the visitors are willing to pay more for better services. The improved revenues in turn should find way in to provision of state-of-the-art facilities and interpretation at the heritage sites (Munjal and Tripathi, 2012). This is a major challenge in case of nationally protected heritage sites in India, due to the centralized functioning of the Archaeological Survey of India (ASI). This points towards the difference in approach towards a private foundation managed heritage site versus a central government protected and managed heritage site. While the foundation has a specific focus and interest in the individual site, the central government has over 3,650 ancient monuments and archaeological sites and remains sites to manage (ASI, 2011), hence the lack of individual focus.

The destination could develop on the basis of its tangible heritage such as historic structures or intangible heritage such as arts and crafts and traditional knowledge systems and in a number of cases, both of these. A major challenge lies in heritage tourism being seen as a means to cultural commoditization, with the assumption that through the process, in the interest of the requirements of the tourist, those of the residents are marginalized or neglected (Arthur and Mensah, 2006).

The extreme conservationist approach may end up isolating or 'museumizing' the cultural resources, while the extreme market oriented approach may result in its 'commodification'(Hill, 2011). In both cases, the question of authenticity becomes important. Authenticity is an important issue when discussed in context of cultural resources, as it the most paramount factor that lends cultural significance to the resources. The continuity of the cultural significance for future generations in turn is an important requisite for their sustainability. As the resources become un-authentic or staged the visitor experience becomes poorer in qualitative experience, whether it is due to strict 'museumization' that pushes the local community involvement away or formalizes it to a large extent or over 'commodification' such that the resources lose social and cultural meaning for the local community, except serving as sources of income. Hence, 'authenticity' and 'sustainability' have a strong interdependence on each other and also contribute strongly in characterizing the cultural heritage tourism destination. The solution to the issue may lie in ensuring that the heritage conservationist, manager, entrepreneur and product 'serve multiple goals at one time without alienating any particular group of people'(Arthur and Mensah, 2006, p.301). The trick may lie in development for all and not just focused on the heritage tourism product, passing the benefit to the locals and empowering them to take decisions about the levels of acceptable change.

7.4 ALTERNATE TOURISM DESTINATIONS: A SOLUTION?

Before tourism gained importance as a trend across the world due to various factors such as financial robustness that made the mass consumers able to go beyond sustaining themselves in search of recreation around the middle of the 20th century or the technological and infrastructural advancements that made travel from one place to another feasible, the existing rural or urban areas had their own socioeconomic, cultural and environmental frameworks. In most cases, the influx of tourism brought cultural and environmental deterioration while having a positive impact on the economy.

As a response, new forms of tourism with prefixes such as 'alternative, appropriate, responsible, low impact and sustainable' are evolving, but these are relatively smaller in scale as opposed to mass tourism and are evolving with the presumption that mass tourism is a cause of negative impacts in the form of environmental, social and cultural degradation, unequal distribution of financial benefits, the promotion of paternalistic attitudes, and even the spread of disease. The new forms of tourism may also result in similar problems, though the evidence of their impact may be harder to collate (Mowforth and Munt, 2009).

The 'nature first' or 'conservation first' approach that was being driven towards the end of the 20th century has now been replaced with an understanding that the resources need to be conserved along with integrating benefit of local communities in the process, rather than their alienation (Butcher, 2003). This emphasis is reflected in the growth of community tourism, though whether the beneficiaries of such tourism, the poor, nature based communities have real options and choices to make is another issue that Butcher (2008) expresses.

'New moral tourism' as opposed to mass tourism can be a means of paving the path to development in the 'third world', combining goals of conservation and development and ensuring direct benefits to the local communities. At the same time, it is important that the free spirit of adventure and joy that is critical to the experience of a leisure tourist be maintained, without the moral burdens attached (Butcher, 2003). Hence, both alternate and popular forms of tourism have their own place in the sustainable tourism destination development process. One cannot completely replace the other, the solution may be in their balanced coexistence.

There is a lot of potential to explore in terms of alternate forms of tourism in developing countries such as India with their diversity in terms of cultural and natural assets. Two examples of ecotourism in rural areas reflect initiatives that have been undertaken by the local communities, essentially women of the two distinct locations, with the benefits going directly to these women themselves. **Refer to Box 4**. There is least economic leakage in these cases and the small scale of the ventures is an important characteristic. The threat is that this may be a transient stage and the models could be extended with external investors coming in to reap profits. The experiences remain authentic only if the impacts are small. If the economic benefits increase greatly, then the lifestyle of the local people is bound to change, in turn resulting in acculturation of the population and deterioration of the visitor experience.

Box 4: Community Based Ecotourism

Ganeshpura, Gujarat

In a small village named Ganeshpura, Gujarat, India, 41 women got together to form a cooperative to promote rural livelihoods in the area and are now working towards achieving self sustainability through ecotourism, positioning the village as a destination in the process. The women turned their unused un-irrigated land into an ecotourism destination. Starting with basics, they got training in hotel management strategies and planning methods, to run the establishment in an efficient manner, providing personalized hospitality to the guests. A number of groups from the urban areas have got associated as users and proliferators of the operation, new facilities are being added, a website has been initiated and the cooperative is moving towards complete self sustainability (Pandya and Senma, 2012).

Key impact on dimensions of sustainability:		
	Positive impacts	Negative impacts
Social	Capacity building, training, empowering of rural women	-
Economic	Additional income generation, moving towards self sufficiency	-
Environmental	Low ecological footprint	-
Cultural	Promotion of rural traditions and culture	Threat of cultural commodification

Himalayan Homestays

The fragile Himalayan valley is facing climate change, impacting the agricultural patterns that turn unpredictable. The setting up of homestays in villages of Korzok and Rumbak in Ladakh and Thembang in Arunachal Pradesh has empowered the women who run these, providing them an alternated source of income. The initial support for setting these up came either from international agencies like World Wide Fund for Nature India or local nongovernmental ones like Snow Leopard Conservancy India (SLC). In Korzok, a capacity building exercise was conducted, with women from Markha valley sharing their experiences with their peers in Korzok, while in Rumbak, the SLC, Department of Tourism and Department of Wildlife have provided training over the years. This kind of tourism has 'restored the pride of the community in its culture and traditional heritage' and provided the women with an alternate source of income. The community has become incentivized to conserve the biodiversity in the designated community conserved area in Thembang. The challenges of such establishments are ensuring that this does not become a mass tourism exercise, the stake remains in the hands of the local community, solutions for plastic waste management be found, the community continue to build its capacity to run the homestays efficiently, the guests are sensitive to the concerns of the fragile landscape and the individual character of the homestays is maintained. If the challenges are handled appropriately, it is a win–win situation for all, as long as the community is empowered, cautious, sensitive and responsible (Bhatt, 2012).

Key impact on dimension of sustainability:		
	Positive impacts	**Negative impacts**
Social	Empowering of local women through capacity building	-
Economic	Providing source of livelihood in view of changing environmental conditions	Increasing external participants running homestays can result in economic leakages
Environmental	Focus on inorganic waste management, limiting traffic, sensitizing the guests	Increase in visitor numbers can be a major threat to the fragile setting
Cultural	Promotion of the local culture and traditions	Threat of cultural commoditization and loss of authenticity

Although, it is relevant to look at success stories of alternate forms of tourism, the fact remains that these cannot replace mass tourism and that each needs to chart its own course towards sustainability.

7.5 THE PUSH AND PULL OF ECONOMICS

The question of sustainability in developing tourist destinations necessitates understanding the significance of the economic factors. Economic factors along with political ones have dominated as decisive elements in development across time. Be it the process of urbanization that was initiated with diversification of professions and initiation of trade in ancient civilizations or the real estate development especially in developing countries in the current context, economic considerations have driven the process and continue to do so. Hence, sustainability in the economic sense is the most important driver in any business or development. The traditional industries that have been able to repackage themselves for mainstream market are the ones that are still booming. Those that failed to do so are being sustained by support from the government in terms of production as well as retail. The more natural process definitely is the one driven by market forces. A similar assumption can be applied to the tourism industry. Whereas, the new forms of tourism may be evolving as fashionable statements for the few, the continuity and viability of these is dependent on the marketability of these. The mainstream tourist activity goes on as a robust economic contributor to the GDPs of a number of developing countries. Hence, it may be significant to map how social, cultural and environmental or ecological sustainability can feature in this mainstream industry. Globally, the tourism industry is experiencing a cyclic return to the idea of the niche experience for a few through the new forms of tourism, which in turn would probably again get translated into mass consumer products. The new trends in tourism certainly hold an important position as fashion statements that generally transcend into the mainstream, as in case of the garment industry. These may eventually be absorbed to some extent in tourism practices of mass tourism along with some push and pull from conservationists, activists, regulatory mechanisms and the academia.

An economy that is completely reliant on tourism for sustenance can never provide authentic experiences that the visitor hopes to avail. In such an economy that lacks real cultural, social and economic rigor, what remains is the inauthentic, staged, commoditized tourism experience that results in 'zooification'(Mowforth and Munt, 2009) or 'acculturation'(Mason, 2008) of the local communities. Hence, the key to development of sustainable tourist destinations lies in the social, cultural and economic empowerment of the local communities without their complete dependence on tourism as a source of employment.

Even today, as national and local tourism policies in the developing world reflect an emphatic focus on positioning 'tourism as the prime engine of economic growth,' the objective in itself is contrary to the development of sustainable tourist destinations. This points towards the need for a radical change in approach at the policy and planning level, along with at the community level.

7.6   ROLE OF THE VARIOUS STAKEHOLDERS

There is a diverse perception of tourism impacts by various stakeholders, observers or commentators on the basis of the value positions they hold (Mason, 2008, p. 37). The local community, visitors, private investors, philanthropists, non government organizations and government organizations at central, state and local level, all have a role to play when it comes to operationalizing the ideal of a sustainable tourism destination.

7.6.1   THE HOSTS AND THE VISITORS

The impacts that tourist destinations in the form of isolated resorts, heritage hotels, villages, towns or cities, regional landscapes or a country as a whole; remain at the center of discussion from the perspective of sustainability and development. Who controls and manages these impacts is the most important question. As the local communities are the original stakeholders who have an association with the natural or cultural resources of the location that develops into a tourist destination, it is being established that they are the ones who should be taking a call on the process. The communities may suffer from lack of decision-making ability and empowerment, which in turn calls for awareness generation and capacity building. The threat to such capacity building is that it may be motivated by the vested interests of external market, political or conservationist forces. Hence, the tourism industry may guide development to some extent, but it is the local awareness, empowerment and engagement that can truly make a difference.

In contrast to a manufactured product, the experience that a tourist destination offers is dynamic, depending on multiple factors that include the state and management of cultural or natural resources, condition of tourist infrastructure, available human resources, time of the day or year, seasonal factors and extent of commoditization of the resources and the preference and expectation of the visitor. The visitor or tourist experiences the environment as a whole that includes social, physical, cultural and economic factors. The experiences may be 'authentic' or 'staged' and this in turn brings in the debate of sustainability of the destination that is driven by tourist inflow. Whether the visitor accepts or rejects the staged, commodified tourism product is a variable, based on his level of awareness and education. In this sense, a clear difference may be mapped between domestic and international tourists in India, where the majority of domestic tourists, much larger in number compared to the international tourists, may find the more commercial and staged forms of tourism acceptable, as opposed to the international visitors who are typically in search of an authentic experience. The quality of tourism product in terms of interpretive services and tourist facilities need to cater to both and generate awareness towards sustainable tourism in all. The visitor is the consumer and his experience is the main takeaway on which the success of the destination depends. In case of alternate tourism destinations, fragile landscapes and social-economic and cultural scenarios, the sensitivity and awareness of the visitor is paramount if the negative impacts are to be minimized and the destination is to be developed as a sustainable one.

With rampant globalization, more often than not, international tourists end up participating in the process of 'economic leakage' as they purchase goods and services, the profits from which go to foreign owners as opposed to local beneficiaries (Mowforth and Munt, 2009). Hence, a tourist may have the best intention of contributing to the local economy, knowingly or unknowingly, the maximum expenditure that he would make, notably on air travel and accommodation may actually leak to economies in the developed world. Hence, the power does not really translate to the local community. The inclusion and empowerment of the local community or government certainly requires their participation as stakeholders and beneficiaries of the tourism product development and service provision. In this context, domestic tourism may hold a much better position with respect to empowering the local economy and transferring the stake to local communities and businesses.

Do the local communities have the ability to decide on the course of developing sustainable tourist destinations is another debatable issue, as illustrated by the following example. What is perceived as rural, semi urban or vernacular heritage by the conservationists and protagonists and consumers of cultural heritage tourism may be looked at as a vestige from poorer times by the locals. As a result of their economic empowerment, the traditional communities automatically begin to imitate the lifestyle and construction technologies of their global or neighboring 'modern' counterparts as introduced to them through media or personal visits due to employment opportunities in other areas.

The transformation from the characteristic traditional construction with locally made roof tiles, masonry walls with mud plaster and timber roof framework to generic reinforced cement concrete frame structures with brick walls and cement plaster in the villages of Central India is one such example. The changing character that results from these transformations are perceived as negative by the cultural heritage tourism promoting participants and positive by the local communities. It is worth mentioning here that the local communities are aware of a poor environmental performance of the new construction materials and technology, but it is a mistake that they all wish to make first and reflect on later.

Does the empowerment of the community in this context mean conducting research on the benefits of the traditional ways and disseminating the same? Will this be a justified approach of educating the local community? Is the research community open to their rejecting the ideas and continuing with the transformation? Can a middle ground be found? Will that be good enough for the consumers of cultural heritage tourism? This further highlights the issue of dynamism and authenticity of cultural heritage resources.

The consciousness of the local community that showcasing the traditional way can be a source of livelihood for them in terms of managing home stays and bed and breakfast operations in itself leads to a kind of commoditization of their life style that is critically looked upon in social and tourism studies. Hence, only in very remote areas can such traditional experiences be offered in an authentic manner, though tourism in such areas would eventually result in 'acculturation' of these communities and 'commoditization' of their culture, unless undertaken in small numbers. Hence, the process of tourist destination development in itself can be looked upon as an oxymoron. How does one develop a tourist destination in a sustainable manner? Probably by taking a less utopian approach and establishing a level of acceptable change in a social, cultural and environmental context.

Globalization features prominently in the debate of sustainable tourist destination development in the so-called'Third World' or developing countries. The 'international integration' allows learning from mistakes made elsewhere in the world along with providing models that are being replicated in an out of context scenario. The distinctiveness of the various cultures and environments of the developing world is certainly celebrated by the global voice while the same comes under threat due to global exposure, of which tourist influx is also a means. What the local communities draw from the global experience depends on the level of their awareness, education and empowerment, supported by various external frameworks.

7.6.2 PUBLIC-PRIVATE PARTNERSHIPS

Pursuit of sustainability is an objective that all tourism destinations would identify with, but the extent to which the ground reality matches the stated objective varies from destination to destination. How do we ensure that tourism related development at destinations adheres to principles of sustainability? La Lopa and Day (2011) in their pilot study on 'readiness' for change towards sustainable business practices in Wales, recognize that moving away from traditional tourism practices to more sustainable options is both complex as well as challenging. A transition to sustainable practices needs a change agent. Typically for most destinations, this responsibility falls in the lap of the 'national tourism authorities' or the 'destination management organizations.'Although, the nomenclature may vary across nations, these entities typically frame the tourism policy, advise governments, market tourism and guide businesses engaged with tourism. The study also recognized that the inability of these change agents to bring about the expected transition finds its roots in the fact that the businesses that constitute tourism infrastructure continue to act independent of the organizations or authorities with the mandate for change. In fact the tourism authorities and the destination management organizations usually have limited authority to enforce change and must rely on programs that include education, encouragement and persuasion to achieve system-wide change. This explains why successful practice of sustainable tourism at a destination is both challenging and complex to implement.

Although, it is quite easy to build the concerns for sustainable tourism development in policy documents at a national, state, regional or city level, the challenge is in actually operationalizing the concept through action. Private investment in the form of services and/or facilities those are required as a part of tourism infrastructure is recognized as a critical ingredient in the success of any tourism destination development. The private participation typically comes in when the public spending in basic infrastructure is made and the environment is favorable for further investment.

Across the world, private individual funds or corporates as a part of their corporate social responsibility have acted as contributors towards positioning cultural resources as tourism destinations. In case of Colonial Williamsburg, Virginia, USA the original historic area was re-created and developed as a 301 acre popular heritage tourism destination, through the initial support from John D Rockefeller Jr., now managed by the Colonial Williamsburg Foundation. A number of historic and cultural landmarks that also serve as sustainable tourist destinations have also been supported globally by corporations such as American Express, expanding through partnerships with organizations such as World Monuments Fund and National Trust for Historic Preservation (Munjal, 2013).

In India, Reliance Industries Limited worked on a 50–50 public private partnership model with the Government of Gujarat to provide interpretive displays and visitor facilities at Dwarka, an established destination for religious tourists whereas others have contributed towards conservation and promotion of cultural resources. The local, state and central governments have also initiates schemes and campaigns such as Clean India, Adopt a Monument, incentives for heritage homes, along with the establishment of the National Culture Fund to the channeling of private investments towards promotion and preservation of cultural heritage (Munjal, 2013). Such initiatives help in strengthening the visitor experience, in turn contributing to the cultural heritage tourism destination.

One major challenge in the local community claiming its rightful stake in the destination development process has been identified as the poor level of awareness and empowerment. In order to provide for the same, the government machineries have been devising schemes and processes within these, such as the Jawaharlal Nehru National Urban Renewal Mission launched by the Government of India in 2005 targeting the urban areas. Under the Mission, 63 mission cities were identified originally, for which City Development

Plans were to be formulated. Toolkits for the same were provided by the Ministry of Urban Development (MoUD), Central Government, to assist the local bodies in the process, wherein 'Tourism' features as an important cross cutting theme. The process outlined the significance of stakeholder consultations at various stages of the plan preparation, capacity building of the urban local bodies and encouragement to public-private partnerships (MoUD, 2011). The same model was taken up by the Madhya Pradesh state government to cover each of its small, medium or large town Urban Administration and Development Department, 2008), a model that may be taken up by other states as well in due course. The State is rich in cultural and natural resources and the plan preparation process and implementation model enables that these resources be addressed and the community, private local and large investors as well as government machinery participates in developing the destination around these. The important question being, how deep their understanding of sustainability is! Whereas, the ideal is rightly placed, the correct implementation assumes that the government machinery has the correct capacity, the community is aware and active in the process and the private investments are positively motivated, an assumption that has a long way before materializing.

Czernek and Niezgoda (2011) probe barriers to public and private cooperation in pursuit of sustainable tourism. Whereas, the success of any tourism destination depends on both public and private initiatives, for sustainable tourism practice both must work together. In their research in Poland, the authors documented that given the difference in goals, values and operating practices, the two systems seldom cooperate. The public sector is focused on the sociocultural and environmental aspects, and has a long-term view of realizing its objectives, while the private participants are focused on economic gains. Private sector finds it hard to ignore the call for quick return on investments, looking to achieve break-even and profitability in the shortest period of time. Putting this in perspective, for private stakeholders long-term gains emanating from sustainable practices come a distant second to the primary profit motive. Bridging this gap is the key to move forward with the agenda of sustainable tourism destinations.

7.7 CONCLUSION

There is ample evidence to recognize that tourism has emerged as a quintessential tool for economic growth and related sociocultural change in societies across the globe. Governments in developed and developing nations alike have harnessed the potential that tourism and related activities offer, to stimulate, develop and grow economies at national, regional and community (city/town/village) level. The political patronage has remained strong irrespective of certain negative impacts. In fact in many cases the impact assessment has been ignored or has remained superficial. The political pressure has often translated into a mindless rush to move ahead with public spending aimed at creating infrastructure that supports tourism activity. The policy framework has also supported momentum that enthuses private investment to spot the opportunity, and come in to do the rest in terms of offering facilities and services for the sought after visitors or tourists. There are examples of tourism destinations that have traced the cyclic path of discovery, growth, saturation and eventual decline. The decline here is really a representation of lack of implementation of principles of sustainability. In many cases the damage to the very resources that created the destination is such that no redemption is possible. The deterioration in the offering is mirrored by the transition in the visitor base from the initial explorers to the irresponsible mass tourist.

When a local community embraces tourism related activity as means of livelihood, it changes and eventually becomes dependent, if not hostage to the economic gains that tourism promises. Any decline thereafter has ramifications for these communities. These communities are critical stakeholders, along with the governments, visitors and private investors. Whereas, approaches and objectives may vary from one stakeholder to another, what is common is the fact that over a long-term horizon, they win or lose together.

The question that deserves an answer is, why do some destinations thrive and embrace sustainable tourism practices while others fail? There seems to be a basic agreement on the overall understanding of 'sustainable tourism' practices, what is harder to find is an agreement on the method to achieve the desired outcome. Given the inherent complexity around the nature of tourism activities and the range of actors involved in various capacities, achieving sustainability will require an unwavering commitment and understanding from all stakeholders. There are case studies of successful implementation that can be emulated by others and those that highlight the issues involved; these are not restricted to a particular national, cultural or geographical context, but come from diverse corners of our world. The best practices and methods must be documented and shared for the benefit of others. The mistakes made by some should warn others not to make the same mistakes with similar disastrous consequences. The change from traditional approaches to tourism development to those entrenched in principles of sustainability will need change agents that have both the desire as well as mandate to facilitate and if required enforce that change.

Irrespective of the nature of tourist destination or the format of tourism in practice—from mass tourism, to alternate tourism to eco tourism to any other emerging form, what is going to be critical is to assess both positive as well as negative impacts, so that they remain in balance **(Figure 9)**. Proper planning and enforcement of policies and protocols will go a long way in managing or mitigating the negative impacts at a sociocultural, economic or environmental level.

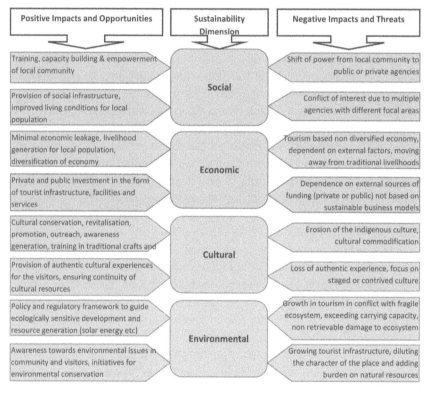

FIGURE 9   Summary of the positive and negative impacts with respect to the four dimensions of sustainability as drawn from the four types of tourist destinations taken up as case studies. These point towards opportunities and threats that must be addressed to ensure sustainable tourist destination development.

Sustainability has emerged as not just a desirable aspect of tourism destination development, but rather an imperative. It's a way of life, an orientation and a long distance approach towards decisions that will impact our future. As communities and people understand this, destinations will work towards making choices that will ensure they remain sustainable over a long-term, adding value without the negative sociocultural, economic or environmental impacts.

KEYWORDS

- environment
- impact assessment
- responsible tourism
- socio-cultural development
- stakeholder engagement
- sustainable destinations

REFERENCES

Abakerli, S. (2012) 'Crafting India's Economic Growth and Development,' *Context: Built, Living and Natural,* 9: 2, 4–11.

Arthur, S.N.A and Mensah, J.V. (2006) 'Urban management and heritage tourism for sustainable development: The case of Elmina Cultural Heritage and Management Program in Ghana,' *Management of Environmental Quality: An International Journal,*17:3, 299–312.

ASI (2011) 'Monuments'(online)(cited 14 August 2013). Available from <http://asi.nic.in/asi_monuments.asp>.

Bapat, J., Khosla, R. and Kumar, M. (2010) 'Community based Approach for Historic Settlements: Kachhpura, Agra,' *Context: Built, Living and Natural,* 7: 2, 119–126.

Bhatt, S. (2012) 'Community Based Homestays: Innovation in tourism,' *Context: Built, Living and Natural,* 9: 2, 77–83.

Borgia, S. (2012) 'Responsible Development,' *Context: Built, Living and Natural,* 9:2, 69–76.

Butcher, J. (2003)*The Moralization of Tourism: The Sun, Sand...and Saving the World?,* London and New York, Routledge, Taylor and Francis Group.

Czernek, K. and Niezgoda, A. (2011)'Barriers to Public-Private Cooperation Towards Sustainable Development of a Tourist Destination,' *Proceedings of International Conference: An Enterprise Odyssey.*

Dodds, R. (2007) 'Sustainable Tourism in Destinations: Sustainability or Just a Rejuvenation Effort?,' *in* Raj, A. (ed.), *Sustainability, Profitability and Successful Tourism,* New Delhi, Kanishka Publishers, Distributors, pp. 3–17.

Gang, C. (2011) 'Sustainable Development of EcoCultural Tourism in Remote Regions: Lessons Learned from South-west China,' *International Journal of Business Anthropology,* 2:1, 123–135.

Giaoutzi, M. and Nijkamp, P. (2006) 'Emerging Trends in Tourism Development in an Open World' *in* Giaoutzi, M. and Nijkamp, P. (eds.), *Tourism and Regional Development: New Pathways,* Hants, UK, Ashgate Publishing Ltd., pp. 1–12.

Gusain, R. (2013) 'Exclusive: NASA satellite images show new stream in Kedarnath after disaster,' *Mail Today,* Dehradun, June 29 (online)(cited 3 July 2013). Available from <http://indiatoday.intoday.in/story/exclusive-nasa-satellite-images-show-new-stream-in-kedarnath-after-disaster/1/286019.html>.

Hergnyan, M. (2010)*Tufenkian Heritage Hotels: Enhanced Employment Opportunities in Distressed Rural Areas,* Growing Inclusive Markets, UNDP.

Hill, L. L. (2011) 'Indigenous culture: both malleable and valuable,' *Journal of Cultural Heritage Management and Sustainable Development,* 1: 2, 122–134.

Himachal Tourism (2008)(online)(cited 4 July 2013). Available from <http://himachaltourism.gov.in>.

Jamieson, W. (1998) 'Cultural Heritage Tourism Planning and Development: Defining the Field and Its Challenges,' *APT Bulletin,* 29:3/4, 65–67.

La Lopa, J. M. and Day, J. (2011) 'Pilot Study to Assess the Readiness of the Tourism Industry in Wales to Change to Sustainable Tourism Business Practices,' *Journal of Hospitality and Tourism Management,* 18, 130–139.

Landorf, C (2009) 'Managing for sustainable tourism: a review of six cultural World Heritage Sites,' *Journal of Sustainable Tourism,* 17:1, 53–70.

Mason, P. (2008)*Tourism Impacts, Planning and Management,* Oxford, Elsevier Ltd.

Misra, S.K. (2012) 'Rural Heritage and Economic Development,' *Context: Built, Living and Natural,* 9: 2, 91–95.

MoUD (2011)*Jawaharlal Nehru National Urban Renewal Mission*(online)(cited 15 August 2013). Available from <http://jnnurm.nic.in/>.

Mowforth, M. and Munt, I. (2009)*Tourism and Sustainability: Development, globalization and new tourism in the Third World,* London and New York, Routledge, Taylor Francis Group.

Muller, H. (1994), 'The Thorny Path to Sustainable Tourism Development,' *Journal of sustainable Tourism,* 2: 3, 106–23.

Munjal, P. G. (2013) 'Corporate Social Responsibility in the Cultural Heritage Sector: An overview of the Indian scenario,' *in* Batra, S. and Vikas, S. (eds.), *Global Competitiveness and Corporate Governance Imperatives in Emerging Economies,* Gurgaon, School of Management Studies, Ansal University, pp. 403–413.

Munjal, S. and Munjal, P. G. (2011). 'City Palace Udaipur: A Case Study for Sustainable Heritage Tourism through Services Enhancement,' *Proceedings of the 5th International Conference on Services Management,* 23–30.

Munjal, S. and Tripathi, G. (2012) 'Heritage Tourism Management: Service enhancement and sustainability,' *Context: Built, Living and Natural,* 9: 2, 41–52.

Pandya, J. and Senma, N. (2012) 'Ganeshpura Village, Gujarat: An ecotourism destination,' *Context: Built, Living and Natural,* 9: 2, 65–68.

Priskin, J. (2003) 'Issues and Opportunities in Planning and Managing NatureBased Tourism in the Central Coast Region of Western Australia,' *Australian Geographical Studies,* 41:3, 270–286.

Sinha, A. (2011) 'Sacred Landscapes of Govardhan in Braj: Imagined, enacted and reclaimed,' *Context: Built, Living and Natural,* 8: 1, 41–50.

Shiva, V. (2013) 'Mountains into molehills,' *Hindustan Times,* New Delhi,5 July, p. 14.

Shri Mata Vaishno Devi Shrine Board (2013) 'Major Achievements'(online)(cited 3 July 2013). Available from <https://www.maavaishnodevi.org/major-achievements.aspx>.

UNWTO (2011)*Religious Tourism in Asia and the Pacific* (online)(cited 3 July 2013). Available from<http://asiapacific.unwto.org/en/publication/religious-tourism-asia-and-pacific>.

Urban Administration and Development Department (2008)(online)(cited 15 August 2013). Available from <http://www.mpurban.gov.in/>.

Wall, G. and Mathieson, A. (2006)*Tourism: Change, Impacts and Opportunities,* Harlow, England, Pearson Education Limited.

NOTES

1. Also referred to as 'commoditization' by authors such as Mason (2008, p. 59).
2. The authors cite Medlik (1994) and Wall (1996) in offering the definition.

CHAPTER 8

HERITAGE COMMUNICATION AND SUSTAINABLE TOURISM

GAURAV TRIPATHI and SANDEEP MUNJAL

CONTENTS

ABSTRACT

This chapter aims at discussing the importance of communicating the need for deploying sustainable measures at heritage sites. Since tourism is a service therefore, there is an enormous need to appreciate that the tourists are the co-producers of tourism services. Therefore, communications made to the tourists are ultimately aimed at achieving economic sustainability. Therefore, this chapter aims at promoting the sustainable heritage value of tourist sites for potential tourism usage. This chapter is based on review of literature bonded with a case study on City Palace Museum, Udaipur. The case discussion of the heritage site and recommendations made about the sustainable tourism practices are the results of the ongoing research project at the site. The chapter discusses a blend of theory and practice, which is aimed at the sustainable practices at heritage sites. Although sustainable practices exist across various tourist sites, a great deal of support from the tourists is required. This can be done by making them aware about the best practices aiming at sustainability. This chapter would find interest among the tourism practitioners on the practical side while the tourism researchers would find this useful in deriving new research directions. Government organization related to tourism would find it useful in making nationwide policy decisions.

8.1 INTRODUCTION

Marketing is about satisfying the consumer needs. The rise in customer satisfaction is due to the strong marketing efforts. With the advent of environmental concerns, the focus of marketing has not only changed but there is a shift in the customer's perception towards the offering they subscribe. This might be very suitable to many of the tangible offerings but holds true for services as well. One might be of the opinion that only the tangible offerings (manufactured goods) account for depletion of resources, which may be due the inherent nature of such offerings. However, it is not at all astonishing to believe that the services also account for the diminution of the resources. Although the services are intangible, their contribution towards the depletion of the resources can be well judged from the physical evidence that they exhibit. It is sometimes overlooked that the attempt to produce a memorable experience for the customers will result in greater reduction of the available resources. This in turn may affect the sustainability of their business, as many of these resources are non-renewable. Reduction in the non-renewable resources would shorten their supply and hence the cost would increase thereby leading towards reduced sustainability. This reduced sustainability is not just based on achieving profits but it is also about the availability of the resources without which the manufacturing of the service experience cannot take place.

Munjal and Tripathi (2012) discussed in the Indian context, which being a developing country, on achieving sustainability of the heritage resources in terms of economic, socio-cultural and environmental aspects. Since the economic sustainability, which includes financial sustainability, precedes all other types of sustainability will help in achieving other types of sustainability by way of investments. However, most organizations do not tend to move ahead further from the economic sustainability and look forward towards achieving sustainability in terms of the environmental aspects. However, still many research works have been conducted on the ecological sustainability apart from the economic sustainability as these two can be measured in absolute terms while the socio-cultural sustainability is more of a subjective aspect (Butler, 1999). Socio-cultural aspects govern the way human beings behave towards the environment they live in. It is the inheritance, which govern their attitude to think about the benefit of others through their personal actions. To address this heritage marketing and communications aspects viz., demarketing, promotion, developing brand awareness, co-operation between benefiting parties, pricing, marketing sustainability, visitor management are discussed in light of the sustainability issues.

Therefore, the key research question is how to communicate to the individuals and to the society at large towards the importance of sustainability to them. There needs to be a strong communication on how the human actions can make the environment more liveable and lasting which perhaps will have socio-cultural connotations. Consequently, the key objectives are:

- To discuss the theoretical background pertaining to the communication aspects and their linkage with sustainability at heritage sites.
- To discuss the communication related sustainability aspects that are carried out at the City Palace Museum, Udaipur.

8.2   STRUCTURE AND METHODOLOGY

This chapter aims at developing the conceptual framework for sustainability at heritage tourism sites and the role of marketing in general and communications in particular. This chapter is based on both review of literature and the case study analysis of a heritage site. The extant literature is reviewed for each of the keywords to achieve this. Further, marketing and communication theories are discussed in relation to heritage sites and museums. The case of

City Palace Museum, Udaipur is discussed with implications for sustainable management of the heritage assets at the site. The case study analysis is based on the recommendations made to the site management during the research project carried out by the authors at the heritage site under study. This is followed by the conclusions.

8.3   REVIEW OF LITERATURE

The review of literature is prepared by reviewing the extant literature pertaining to heritage communication and sustainable tourism. The discussion first encompasses how marketing and communication are related to sustainability and aspects of heritage tourism. Further, the discussion also looks into the role of communication and marketing in the context of tourism in general and heritage in particular. Further, the focus is laid on sustainable tourism at heritage sites, which is further narrowed on the communication aspects of sustainability, which is discussed as an integral part of marketing. Finally, the discussion arrives at communicating the sustainable heritage tourism practices, which encompasses the best practices in this area. This is elaborated further with a brief focus on museum marketing and sustainability. This discussion is further used to discuss the implications for the heritage site managers through the case of City Palace Museum, Udaipur.

8.4   HERITAGE TOURISM

Heritage Tourism is defined as travelling to sites, which are of historic or ethnic importance and includes places namely, parks, palaces, forts, and other historical sites. It also includes visiting heritage sites of different cultures crossing international boundaries (Hoffman et al., 2002). Heritage is often connected with 'national representation," "symbolic foundations" and "sense of belongingness" (Park, 2010). According to MacDonald (2006), heritage can be identified as the tangible indication of one's own cultural characteristics, which can be understood as activities connected with "continuity, persistence and substantiality of collective identity." Heritage tourism is often understood as a consumer driven phenomenon and hence its capitalist facets are quite evident in its marketing activities (Rowan and Baram, 2004). This is in fact a deterrent to its sustainability.

Heritage varies between two extremes—built heritage and natural. Built heritage sites like museums, forts, etc., are privileged due to maintenance activities by the managing organization. This is at times guided by its tourism demand and also due to the management philosophy of gaining profits for which the managing organization would focus on promoting the heritage value of the site. Natural heritage is connected with natural vegetation, mountains, beaches, forests, etc. Natural heritage is not considered within the scope of this chapter.

It is also important to consider the values inscribed at the heritage site, due to which its importance is proliferated through generations and also due to the surrounding developments. The latter may affect the heritage value of the site both positively and negatively, and hence its attraction and sustainability in future. This leads to the discussion on what is the significance of the heritage site, which might be evaluated based on the response from the visitors. Significance of a heritage site suggests its relevance to the culture. The conservation/restoration plans are highly dependent upon the significance of the heritage sites (Armitage and Irons, 2013).

Heritage value can be adjudged based on three broad parameters—societal, economic and environmental (Armitage and Irons, 2013). It is important to decipher these three parameters as the same might be used for the achieving sustainability (Munjal and Tripathi, 2012).

8.4.1 SOCIETY

It is very important to understand why the society values heritage. It is basically the inheritance, which has proliferated over the period of time and has become the value of the society over the generations. The various dimensions of the value include "aesthetic, spiritual, cultural, social and educational" (Armitage and Irons, 2013). Chen and Chen (2010) identified the influence of tourism on perception of the community towards associating with the site. This also leads towards balancing the negative outlook of the tourists with the affirmative. Although societal but the effect on community was economically motivated which came up from the tourism. The influence of society can be supportive towards better operations in site management (Sadiki, 2012). This is also advocated by Miller and Twining-Ward (2005) for different sites recognized as the World Heritage Sites.

8.4.2 ECONOMIC

Economic aspects of the heritage sites are linked with the financial angle. However, more importantly these have to be monitored from the point-of-view of conserving the heritage property in which the level of heritage tourism and its impact would have monetary appraisal on the surroundings and the heritage property itself (Brown, 2004).

From the economic angle, the investment in heritage conservation would attract more tourists, which in turn would lead to a spill over effect on the properties located in and around the vicinity of the heritage site, which would lead to further investment in tourism, perhaps by the local communities thereby gaining more economic prosperity. This would also create more employment emanating from the conservation and maintenance of the heritage site.

8.4.3 ENVIRONMENTAL

The global focus is now on understanding the duty of warding off any potential scope of irreparable change in the ecological system of the earth. There is a lot of spotlight on protocols viz., Kyoto aiming at conservation of the environment, reducing the rate of global warming, etc. Horrigan (2009) discovered the approaches towards policies by the community and government and discussed the "green rating metrics" for heritage properties. This research also pointed out the scope of conservation approaches, which can be applied to the heritage sites, which are currently being applied on commercial properties. Concisely, the amount of research focus on such approaches is very limited.

Sodangi et al. (2011) considered heritage buildings as an indispensable component of the environment. The key agents contributing to its deterioration are solar radiations, winds, moisture that result in the physical weathering of the site. Therefore, it is now well established that the heritage value quotient at the built sites is being reduced due to the environmental factors viz., societal (a.k.a. socio-cultural/community), economic (a.k.a. financial/monetary) and environmental (a.k.a. ecological).

8.5 MARKETING AND COMMUNICATION

"Marketing is the activity, set of institutions, and processes for creating, communicating, delivering, and exchanging offering that have for customers, clients, partners, and society at large" (AMA, 2013). Misiura (2006) considers marketing as the management function, which satisfies the customers while achieving the profit making objectives. The two definitions have one thing in common which is the focus on customers; however, the key difference is the focus on society which was not the case earlier as depicted in the later definition. Achrol and Kotler (2012) have discussed the three contemporary and emerging levels of Marketing viz., "sub-phenomena (consumer experiences and sensory systems), its phenomena (marketing networks), and its super-phenomena" (sustainability and development). The authors further discuss that focus of marketing has led to excess of everything including waste, which have destructive outcomes. Therefore, it is imperative to see that how much marketing is tolerable by the society. Hence, Marketing shall focus on creating a consumption environment, which leads towards healthier results

Marketing involves using the marketing mix strategies to provide value to the consumer. Communication is the process of sharing meaningful information between individuals and organizations. Marketing communication is a representative of the elements of marketing mix model, which aims at providing value to the consumer. It is the holistic way of promoting an offering. This suggests that marketing and communication cannot be put in isolation from each other (Barker et al., 2012).

8.5.1 TOURISM COMMUNICATION AND MARKETING

Tourism marketing mix is highly customized due to the varied typology namely, heritage, beach, medical, hill station, etc. Sadiki (2012) pondered on three key factors in the context of marketing at the sites recognized as the world heritage site by UNESCO viz., "brand equity, political contributions, and visitor management."

Tourism is highly dependent on marketing more strongly than other service offerings because the customers (tourists) have a greater variety of choices and varying stimulus for their travel plans (Raju, 2009). Since the competition is very high in the tourism context, an effective communication along with a creative/innovative tourism offering is essential (Thai, 2011). Lumsdon (1997) states that marketing in the context of tourism, is a managerial way of foreseeing and catering to the needs of likely tourists. The role of monetary transaction is not just limited to profit making but it also focuses on gains to the community. It is worth noting that the tourism dealing between the tourists and the service provider must be satisfactory. In addition, it is also inclined towards socio-cultural needs, visitor satisfaction and ecological balancing.

8.5.1.1 BRAND EQUITY

Misiura (2006) discussed that the trust and loyalty are induced through brand awareness. A recognition as the UNESCO world heritage site provides a branding support and influences the visitor's perceptions about the heritage site. Therefore, brand awareness can be considered as a tool for marketing at heritage sites, especially with the recognition from UNESCO as world heritage site (Portia et al., 2011).

8.5.1.2   POLITICAL CONTRIBUTIONS

Ryan and Silvanto (2010) discussed the effect of political factors of a particular country on tourism promotion. In case a heritage site or any other tourist site is listed among the world heritage sites the political support is automatically extended to those sites for its effective promotions. Ryan and Silvanto (2010) found that democracy and political instability are pivotal in relation to the promotion of a tourist site in any country. Political instability has negative connotations toward tourism and its promotion.

8.5.1.3   VISITOR MANAGEMENT

This is related to the management of tourists at the heritage site. How visitors impact the heritage site is quite subjective. The management of visitors depends upon their number, time taken for the visit, use of personal vehicles to reach the site including parking, photography, marching style (Shackley, 1998) and even writing graffiti on the walls of the site, which has been a huge concern for maintaining the erstwhile heritage of the site. It should be noted that a high number of tourist footfalls is not the ultimate criteria for determining the success of a heritage site, which in fact might adversely affect the heritage site in terms of reduced preservation. Therefore, visitor management should endeavour towards striking a balance between tourist satisfactions and conserving the authenticity of the site for sustained heritage tourism, which can be suggestively done by deploying demarketing tools (Fullerton et al., 2010). Demarketing can be of three types—general, selective and ostensible (Kotler and Levy, 1971). General demarketing focuses on reduction of total demand, selective demarketing attempts to persuade against certain segments towards visiting the site and lastly ostensible demarketing attempts to create scarceness in the demand which on the flip side creates a huge increase in demand. Demarketing can also be included in the marketing mix model, which would result into bringing in more environmentally cognizant visitors and hence the site management would be able focus on the specific market segments (Fullerton et al., 2010).

8.5.2   HERITAGE COMMUNICATION AND MARKETING

For effective promotion, the core product at the heritage site needs to be preserved which may limit the damage of due to any future deterioration. Regular maintenance would reduce scope for restoration, which would otherwise restrict public access temporarily or permanently. This would create malaise is the minds of visitors and would reduce profits for the managing organization. Therefore, decision about restoration is to be made with utmost case (Armitage and Irons, 2013). Misiura (2006) describes that heritage marketing is a subset of marketing in any other venture. The focus is mainly on the customers and the role of the marketer is to find out the customer (tourist) needs and satisfying them. However, there is a clause of protecting the heritage site in case of heritage marketing. This suggests that heritage marketing like marketing in general also aims at creating and satisfying demands without losing the heritage attractions in future. This can be done by managing the number of visitors and setting up quality guide service, which would help in improving the tourists' experience. Heritage marketing holds importance as it brings history to present with focused targeting of visitors and appropriate physical artefacts.

8.6   SUSTAINABLE TOURISM

Sustainable tourism involves putting together the natural environment, which is culturally empathetic and acceptable at the societal levels and also environmentally protecting at the destination/site (Meuser and Von Peinen, 2013). It is worth noting that the idea of sustainable tourism is strongly connected with ecological viewpoint, however, it is not limited only to this viewpoint (Giudici et al., 2013). In the words of McElroy and de Albuquerque (2002) sustainability aims to protect a stable income source by way of creating a competitive tourism destination through community participation without diminishing the socio-cultural and natural belongings.

8.6.1   CHALLENGES TO SUSTAINABILITY

Russo (2002) suggested that the sustainability at heritage sites could be very challenging due to the lack of resource to preserve it. Moreover, the phenomenon of oversaturation also leads to stained infrastructure such as roads, buildings, etc. Other challenges to sustainability includes scale and speed of urbanization, agglomerations, socioeconomic fragmentations, health issues due to unsafe drinking water, improper sewage facilities, waste disposal issues, lack of waste recycle policies, land development policies, etc. (Cohen, 2006).

8.6.2 SUSTAINABILITY AND SUSTAINABLE TOURISM AT HERITAGE SITES

For achieving sustainability at heritage sites, it is mandatory for every generation to pass on the heritage assets to the forthcoming generations with no or insignificant differences in terms of size and quality which was inherited from their ancestors (Fyall and Garrod, 1998). It must be noted that it is difficult to reproduce the past heritage assets and also the increase in visitor activities vis-a-vis the local residents seems unstoppable (Caserta and Russo, 2002). This suggests an inequitable growth of tourism in the heritage context. To manage such an erratic growth of heritage tourism a conscientious effort is required in using and managing the heritage site and other assets in its vicinity, which is simply termed as sustainability.

There is a growing need to for sustainable tourism, which is due to the rising threats on the heritage tourism. Caserta and Russo (2002) raised the warning that too much of cultural/heritage tourism demand would result into reduction of heritage value at the site. In addition, the authors found that the heritage resources are vulnerable to misuse and hence there exists a strong need to setup quality policy for the management of the heritage property. Sustainability issues have been seen with a myopic vision at the heritage sites wherein satisfying the visitors has taken precedence over issues like traffic and overcrowding thereby aiming at achieving revenues but not preserving the heritage property (Fyall and Garrod, 1998). The authors further suggest the need for re-examining the heritage management objectives especially the one pertaining to generating revenues, which should take cognizance of preservation of heritage assets.

Since the focus of this study is on the heritage sites, it is also important to understand what is meant by sustainability in the context of heritage sites. The tourism related to heritage sites requires a different way of sustainability. It is the sustainability of the legacy and tradition, which needs to be maintained in its original form such that the current and future generations are able to relive the ancient or past eras (Peterson, 1994). When the newer generations attempt to visit the heritage sites, the expectation of the facilities is not antiquated on the site. They require the facilities to be current and the heritage site management attempts to provide them in the best possible manner. Therefore, sustainable tourism poses challenges altogether while attempting to balance the dichotomous situation where on one side the priority is to maintain the ancient artefacts while providing modern support facilities to the visitors. The key challenge is to provide amenities with expected quality levels while maintaining the authentic cultural integrity of the site (UN 2001, cited in Dhiman and Dubey, 2011). Since at primarily sustainability is visualized from the financial point of view it is quite necessary that the sustainable tourism suggest at striking the right balance between revenue enhancement and heritage conservation.

Lu and Nepal (2009) suggested that all forms of tourism should focus on achieving sustainability. This will lead towards a change in the way tourism business operates. Sustainable tourism as interpreted by Butler (1999) should focus on achieving sustainability at the mass scale. In other words, the focus on sustainability has shifted from small scale to the mass level (Lu and Nepal, 2009). In addition, the focus of sustainable tourism shall contemplate the sustainability of the total ecological system and not just the tourist site Farrell and Twining-Ward (2004). Sustainable tourism aims largely at enriching the present tourism experience of the visitors without deteriorating the resources for potential future usage (Bramwell and Lane, 1993). Polonsky et al. (2003) pointed out that sustainable tourism should focus on reducing the resource destruction, which occurred consequently while creating and delivering tourism experience to the visitors.

In addition, Bansal (2005) deliberated that the sustainable tourism is contextualized by "economic prosperity, environmental integrity and social equity." In other words, these three considered together comprise the boundaries of the sustainable tourism. Moreover, these also account for tourism value chain in the context of sustainable tourism (Pomering et al., 2011).

World Tourism Organization (2007) has outlined 12 sustainability indicators for the capacity measurement of tourism sites. These are "economic viability, local prosperity, employment quality, social equity, visitor fulfilment, local control, community wellbeing, cultural richness, physical integrity, biological diversity, resources efficiency and environmental purity." There might be certain site-specific indicators but the aforementioned indicators can be understood as the general indicators for sustainability.

Taking into consideration the heritage sites in India it is obvious that much of the popular sites were constructed in the medieval period especially during the Mughal Empire. These include forts, mosques, palaces, minarets, etc. Interestingly, their caretaking royal families convert many of these into heritage hotels and museums. Several such examples can be found the state of Rajasthan in India. These sites are augmented with accommodation facilities, food service, cultural shows, handicrafts and souvenir shops, etc. However, many a times the original heritage is affected not only due to the augmented services but mostly due to large scale unorganized urbanization closer to the heritage sites. This is obvious in some market palaces wherein the modern style buildings are constructed closer to the older structures. An effective tourism development plan in place would minimize the adverse affects of commercialization and urbanization on the built heritage sites.

According to the guidebook on 'Indicators of Sustainable Development for Tourism Destinations,' published by World Tourism Organization (2004), the sustainability issues related to the heritage site includes the demolition and deterioration of old heritage sites, threatened historic districts (a.k.a. endangered heritage sites), loss of historic character of districts, protection of historic sites and districts, cost of protection reuse of heritage sites, new legislation, contribution (or revenues) generated from the tourism, tourism management at the site and the level of tourism usage which the heritage site provides.

There is an ever-increasing demand for heritage tourism. It involves more educated tourists from high-income groups who want to gain insights about the past cultures. Hence, economic growth and development are positively influenced by the heritage tourism (Jasparo, 2003). The steep rise in tourist footfalls at heritage sites affects the social and ecological aspects of the heritage site. It has been the case that the tourists' use of heritage site facilities cost more to the site then it earns (Russo and Van Der Borg, 2000). This suggests a strong need for researching on the sustainability issues at the heritage sites as the increase in heritage tourists suggests demands for sustainability at the heritage sites. For achieving sustainability in heritage tourism host-guest perspective should be considered wherein the positive tourist experience go hand in hand with positive perceptions from the local residents thereby creating mutual respect for each other.

It also important to look at the sustainability at the heritage sites based on the cultural intangibles. The cultural heritage management focuses on preserving the heritage property, which involves the relevant stakeholders, viz., tourists, the tourism industry and the heritage site management. These stakeholders provide a strong moral and social contribution while acting towards the heritage site conservation and hence its sustainability (McKercher and du Cros, 2006). Sustainability at the built heritage sites can be achieved by conservation and also by controlling tourist activities.

8.7   SUSTAINABILITY, COMMUNICATION AND MARKETING

Byers (2008) discussed the concept of sustainability in a simplified way in which the human beings affect and are affected by the earth owing to their individual and group behaviours. Therefore, human beings need to alter their contemporary way of living such that the earth is fit enough and so do the living beings. In this regard, it is worth noting that 'green' and 'sustainability' have become buzzwords and are also synonymous to each other (Brophy and Wylie, 2013).

There are various definitions related with sustainability, which would provide an insight into the theoretical underpinning on the topic. A key definition comes from the Brundtland Report by United Nations (2007), which says that the sustainable development supports the present without harming the scope for future. According to Mr. Desai who is a senior advisor on this commissioned report, it is now imperative to discuss the environmental and economic policy issues under the same roof. In addition, the report discusses the three guiding pillars pertaining to sustainability—"Environment, Economy, and Society." According to Fyall and Garrod (1998), sustainability is about how well the resources are managed in such a way that the future generations are able to make use of it.

8.7.1   SUSTAINABLE MARKETING

Achrol and Kotler (2012) provided the concept of sustainable marketing and the rising consumer prosperity, which are at opposite ends to each other. In other words, it is the carrying capacity, which is perhaps falling prey to the ever-expanding desire to consume more. The basic premise of sustainable marketing is the transition from the consumer focus to the focus on nature. As most of the big economies are close to their threshold capacities the resultant would be a crisis. The issue of resource stabilization is also a burning issue, which says that due to societal consumption at mass level, there are several ecological consequences, which are negative. These consequences are resource depletion, environmental degradation, excessive pollution, and waste production (due to consumption and after consumption). This will lead toward making the planet repulsive to live in.

According to Hawken (1993), the large sized firms are having a strong foothold across the globe and hence should take up direct responsibility of addressing the ecological and social problems encountered by our society. Hawken (1993) further states that every business experiences the three issues "what it takes, what it makes and what it wastes." What it takes is regarding the depletion of resources, what it makes is the production of goods and services and what it wastes is the consequence of resource extraction and industrial production of goods and services. Therefore, it is implied that the large size firms, customers and society at large, are responsible for these three activities which affects the sustainability of the our environment, resources and in-turn the business of the corporations. Hence, the concept of sustainable marketing ponders on satisfying the consumer needs by way of communicating the sense of responsibility among the consumers, producers and community with minimal harm to the resources and ecosystem.

It is worth noting that marketing has been usually seen as an opponent of the sustainability, however, it can also play a vital role in accomplishing sustainability. The AMA (2013) definition has considered societal issues under the purview of the marketing. Therefore, marketing can play an important role in deploying sustainable tourism, which is the key focus of this paper. This paper describes the special case of heritage tourism and delineates how the concept of sustainability is significant for heritage sites. In addition, the key focus is on how effective communication to the visitors can develop partnerships with them, which would lead toward realizing sustainable tourism. The brighter side of the marketing would then be invoked in the minds of the advocates of sustainability. Communication is one of the key elements of marketing mix, which helps in promoting not only a product or service but also concepts and ideas. It is the way of linking up with the consumers. Sustainable tourism is one such idea whose prospects can be broadened by way of effective marketing communications.

Emerging economies like India and China are moving fast on the track of economic prosperity but also have significant sections of the society, which are suffering. This also suggests the needs for marketing which focuses at the base of the pyramid. The management focus on marketing, which is evolving, is constituted by sustainable marketing efforts and growth expectations from the base of the pyramid. The mammoth task is to achieve both of them at the same time. Till date marketing has been holding a position, which is reactive and passive in comparison to the sustainable marketing efforts. This has been due to the myopic viewpoint, which says that these might be more costly and less valuable for the ultimate purpose. This approach might result into reduced sustainability and hence a proactive vision is suggested by Achrol and Kotler (2012), which requires change in the philosophy by firms and individuals. The first one aims at communicating about the ill effects of extravagant consumption. Second focuses on increasing the segments which includes consumers which are ecologically conscious by way of developing and marketing high quality products at the similar price levels e.g., LOHAS segment (Cortese, 2003). The third way is to demarket certain product/services, which either can be harmful or are scare. The latter issue of scarcity is well connected with heritage sites. Concisely, the focus on effective communication of these three proactive ways should be looked into.

It is worth noting that communication is an integral part of marketing. The adoption behaviour is influenced more by direct channels of communication rather than mass media especially when time is a constraint (Prins and Verhoef, 2007). Behavioural changes can be imposed by using persuasion techniques, which require direct and personal communication strategies (Iyer et al., 2013).

8.7.2 MARKETING AND SUSTAINABLE TOURISM

Although marketing focuses on enhancing the tourist experiences, the need for economic sustainability pushes towards increase in sales. The tourism marketers have long time been focusing on increasing sales which ultimately happens thereby treating tourism as a commodity and not any special offering (Buhalis, 2000). This suggests a strong strategic misfit by the tourism promoters wherein the role of marketing appears to be diminished. Therefore, there is a clear need for delineating the concept of marketing from sales particularly for the tourism companies. Marketing as described by (Pomering et al., 2011) is a "market-related activity" which reflects an organization's image in the minds of the consumers. The role of the marketer is to create and communicate the right blend of offering, which can provide value to the consumers or more specifically the tourists in the present study.

The role of marketing is to recognize the changes in the external environment of business and act accordingly to create customer value, which makes the role of marketing more pivotal for the organization. Various marketing concepts have been linked with sustainability in the context of tourism viz., social marketing (Dinan and Sargeant, 2000), de-marketing (Beeton and Benfield, 2002) and most importantly the advocacy on societal marketing (Buhalis, 2000), which was later included in the definition of marketing by AMA (2013).

Marketing is incomplete without discussing the concept of Marketing Mix, which provides the holistic approach towards marketing applications. Since tourism is a service, therefore services marketing mix by Booms and Bitner (1981) holds importance. However, looking at the uniqueness of the tourism industry vis-a-vis other services industries 3 more elements were added to this model viz., partnerships, programming and packaging (Morrison, 2009). Pomering et al. (2011) later on created "Sustainability Tourism Marketing Mix" using the aforementioned 10Ps by giving due consideration to the socio-cultural, economic and environmental factors.

Packaging, Programming and Partnership being the new elements are detailed further in light of the three bottom line uncontrollable factors. In addition, the Promotion mix is discussed for creating a link between the sustainable tourism and the potential visitors and repeat visitors.

8.7.2.1 PACKAGING

Packaging is derived from the concept of bundling wherein the associated services are used as complementary like transport, food, sightseeing packages, accommodation, etc. In addition, it is a way in which the core product is augmented and made more presentable to the visitors. The key challenge is to assess how the complete package will exhibit sustainability. Each element of the package needs to be assessed for its contribution to sustainability. Packaging can be altered at times to provide a more desirable offering and easy access to the masses especially in the context of heritage sites (Apostolakis, 2003). However, packaging may alter the core tourism product and hence may result into loss of expected authenticity of the heritage site. According to the study conducted by Apostolakis (2003), repackaging was well recognized by the visitors, which included barriers, disabled access, food and beverage outlets, live cultural performances, etc. Interestingly, most visitors found these modifications positive. It is suggested that packaging shall involve the demarketing element.

8.7.2.2 PROGRAMMING

It refers to the development of certain services or improvement of the existing ones, which might make the whole package more fascinating and hence would result into increased consumer spending. This would certainly bring in more revenues but perhaps not the economic sustainability. This might be due to the difficulties in the management of the increased waste. Therefore, a right balance needs to be crafted between the level of programming and the carrying capacity. A right mix of programming with packaging would help in overcoming the sustainability challenges.

8.7.2.3 PARTNERSHIPS

In the words of Morrison (2009) partnerships in the context of tourism is referred as "cooperative promotions and other cooperative marketing efforts by hospitality and travel organizations." Partnership should be analyzed together with Programming and Packaging. It is useful in managing the footprints, which can be due to ecological or socio-cultural factors. Partnership is essential because it helps in bringing together different entities of the value chain. All different entities working together will generate revenues for the all service providing entities involved and hence will account for economic sustainability. Otherwise, these entities may be sidelined on occasions when separate, and hence may not find the individual businesses flourishing. One of the key areas of co-operation among the partners is the promotions in the form of co-operative advertising (Chhabra, 2009) which otherwise would be very costly.

8.7.2.4 PROMOTION

According to Belz and Peattie (2009) marketing communication (or Promotion) would help in communicating the consumers and stakeholders about the sustainable offerings and also creating the organization's brand image. Choice of media is also a key antecedent to achieving sustainability, which must aim at reducing the use of paper and hence saving more trees (Pomering et al., 2011). Use of online tools and social media would help in tourism promotion and also achieving ecological sustainability. Buhalis (2000) has earlier pointed out that promotion is the mechanism by which consumers can be educated about sustainability and hence the tourist site management should aim at promoting ecological sustainability by deploying an appropriate communication mix. This will also affect the way consumers purchase the tourism products as against the traditional methods. Chhabra (2009) proposed the Strategic Sustainable Heritage Tourism Model (SSHTM) wherein the communication mix is kept at the centre and is understood as being planned based on various components viz., environment analysis, market segmentation, research, and mission.

8.8 COMMUNICATING AND MARKETING SUSTAINABLE HERITAGE TOURISM

In the previous section the basic understanding about the heritage, communication (including marketing), sustainability, and tourism is discussed first in isolation and then in association with each thereby understanding the need for sustainable measures to be deployed at heritage sites. The sustainable measures are being deployed at the heritage sites with substantial intensity, however, there is a need for understanding the role of tourists as well such that they are aware about the phenomenon and are ready to contribute towards achieving sustainability at the heritage sites. This needs a guided communication, which obviously will be a part of the marketing mix. The previous section did mention about this in general which is more specified and detailed further as part of the marketing recommendations.

8.8.1 MARKETING RECOMMENDATIONS

A common feature of all the museums across the globe is about storytelling wherein the artefacts are used for storytelling, which may be societal in nature (Beck, 2012). A good idea would be to setup the sustainability and conservation initiatives also in the storyline mode such that it creates a sense of responsibility in the minds of visitors and hence would support the cause.

The key marketing recommendations suggested by Sadiki (2012) in the context of world heritage sites are as follows:

8.8.1.1 DEMARKETING

This technique is useful for controlling the number of tourists and even restricts certain segments. It is a way for preventing certain visitor types from visiting the site. It might affect the revenues in the short run but guarantees the revenues in the long run. As discussed previously under the visitor management section of tourism communication demarketing have strong reasons to be used as a tool for visitor management. Leask and Fyall (2006) suggest that messages can be circulated using brochures to the tourists by discouraging them to visit during the peak hours. In Cyprus, selective demarketing was deployed to persuade against young tourists from visiting heritage sites (Beeton and Benfield, 2002). In addition, ostensible way of demarketing can be used to stimulate greater demand for alternate site (or other sections within the site). This will allow certain other sections a period of rest and hence sustainability could be easier to achieve. This also will not adversely affect the revenues in the short run. However, there needs to be a plan in place to choose such alternate sections, which needs to be rotated after some period. Fullerton et al. (2010) have mentioned five different strategies for making effective use of demarketing strategies viz., "educating potential visitors,' "marketing to desirable markets,' "publicize other sites as alternative destinations," "use a seasonal schedule for access," and 'making access to fragile areas difficult or restricted."

8.8.1.2 PROMOTION

Interestingly, this tool can be used in an alternative way to control the access to the site (Beeton and Benfield, 2002). Accessibility also relates to information around the sites using different media, which can also be used as a medium for persuasion in which the demarketing tactics can be coupled. Tourists can be stopped from entering certain areas or can be encouraged to visit during non-peak seasons.

8.8.1.3 DEVELOPING BRAND AWARENESS

A good way of creating brand awareness is using the UNESCO world heritage sites association. Sites not coming under UNESCO recognition can also create strong brand awareness by way of promoting their sustainability plans and green strategies. Creating awareness is one of the ways in which brand awareness can be created (Portia et al., 2011).

8.8.1.4 CO-OPERATION BETWEEN BENEFITING PARTIES

It is not only the heritage site management, which receives the revenues but other contributing parties are also benefited. Co-operation from benefiting parties can provide sustainability through various initiatives (Chen and Chen, 2010).

8.8.1.5 PRICING STRATEGY

Increase in price would increase revenues but would also bring down the demand and hence would reduce visits from careless visitor traffic, which may otherwise reduce any potential for warding off corrosion of the heritage property (Fyall and Garrod, 1998).

8.8.1.6 MARKETING SUSTAINABILITY

Heritage sites like museum can preserve the artefacts by preventive conservation (Caple, 2000). Proper storage of the historical artefacts can help in simultaneous conservation and visitation. In fact, the surrounding environment can also be preserved for the prevention of the artefacts. Apart from this, public awareness through various media like print, online, etc. would be useful within the site. Education can also lead to sustainability, which is again done by way of communication (Aplin, 2002; Sadiki, 2012), which in turn is a marketing activity.

8.8.2   MUSEUM MARKETING AND SUSTAINABILITY

Museum is a place, which is one of the constituents of the heritage and hence heritage tourism. According to Henderson (2005), museum is place for popular entertainment based on local culture and heritage. However, more recently museums have become an agent of social change, centre of cultural activities and storehouse for heritage and related wisdom. Although, museums have been predominantly focusing on heritage conservation they have also shown focus towards profit making. For this, museums have launched their marketing campaigns to have an access to masses, develop relationships with the tourist communities and compete vertically in the tourism value chain. The next section focuses on the sustainability marketing initiatives taken up by the City Palace Museum, Udaipur as a case study.

8.9   CASE STUDY: CITY PALACE MUSEUM UDAIPUR

City Palace Museum is under the custodianship of the Maharana of Mewar Charitable Foundation (MMCF) since 1969. It is a popular tourist site for the tourist visiting Udaipur, which include both domestic and foreign tourists. The whole complex is magnificently situated in the city of lakes—Udaipur alongside the Aravalli mountain range. The complex has received a grant from Getty Foundation, Los Angeles, USA and it has "Conservation Master Plan" in place for future sustainability (Munjal and Tripathi, 2012).

8.9.1   MANAGERIAL IMPLICATIONS FOR ACHIEVING SUSTAINABILITY

Implications are drawn from literature and UNESCO's sustainability indicators for the City Palace Museum Complex, Udaipur. First, we discuss the implications based on the UNESCO's sustainability indicators. This is followed by implications based on previous studies.

8.9.1.1   ECONOMIC VIABILITY

The City Palace Complex under the custodianship of MMCF is guided by the concept of 'Eternal Mewar,' which in essence is about ensuring the continuity of the house of Mewar, its customs, traditions and the built heritage that has defined its existence over the centuries. MMCF has a strong, well-capitalized balance sheet that ensures long-term financial well being. The operating financials over the decades have ensured that revenues and expenses have remained in balance, thereby ensuring no dilution of the asset base. Efforts to improve services and visitor experience have resulted in strong tourist numbers, and the volume growth has been largely driven by domestic traffic. The impact of seasonality has also become minimal. The nature of tourists shifts from budget to those with higher spending, but volume remains strong year round. Lack of dependence on the foreign tourists has insulated the destination from any adverse impact of the rather fickle international tourist segment.

Opening more parts of the complex for visitor experience and also improving services in general and sharper focus on interpretation of the site's history have yielded positive results. The city level infrastructure, access and transport continue to be a drag, and the government needs to do more.

8.9.1.2   LOCAL PROSPERITY, EMPLOYMENT AND SOCIAL IMPACT

The complex itself employs nearly 200 local people; the indirect impact would be even larger. Local artisans find support in the form retail opportunities and through participation in various cultural events, fairs and religious functions held round the year. MMCF supports many initiatives aimed at educating children and also offering vocational training. Lake Pichola, which is a landmark as well as a critical resource for the city has been revitalized through efforts of MMCF. The complex is the prime attraction that gets tourists to visit Udaipur. As tourism has thrived, it has allowed local people to invest and operate the services and facilities that tourists require, from hotels, guesthouses, retail shops, restaurants; local transport infrastructure to guide services, the local community remains the main beneficiary.

8.9.1.3   VISITOR SATISFACTION

The city complex has made investments to improve its services and facilities aimed at meeting the needs of the tourist visitors. The feedback from the visitors has been used in that respect, introducing multiple language audio guides, sound and light shows, interpretation centre, setting up of new art galleries are all initiatives aimed at ensuring a superior visitor experience. Hygienic restrooms and better food and beverage facilities are being put in place. The visitor cycle is being monitored from the ticketing to the exit to make changes as required. Despite challenges, handicap access has been facilitated, and security protocols put in place to ensure the safety and security of visitors to the complex.

8.9.1.4   PHYSICAL INTEGRITY AND CULTURAL RICHNESS

The planning process funded by the Getty Foundation has guided interventions aimed at ensuring that all conservation efforts to protect the built fabric of the complex are as per internationally accepted norms. In fact, nearly half of the revenue generated by the complex is deployed towards conservation projects managed by area experts. MMCF also funds annual events that have cultural implications to ensure that continuity of traditions; religious ceremonies and its connectivity with the community are retained. Investments in training of craftsmen, artists and folk musicians are also focused on ensuring their continuity. The city complex has retail areas that allow local craftsmen and artists to showcase talent, and earn livelihoods.

8.9.1.5   RESOURCE EFFICIENCY AND ENVIRONMENTAL PURITY

From use of solar power, to efforts to revitalize the once almost dry lake 'Pichola' and focus on reduced energy consumption, the complex has made efforts to reduce the ecological footprint. Rainwater harvesting, greening of the surrounding areas have had a positive impact. With the green belt restored and the lake being revitalized, the habitat of hundreds of Bats and Vultures that were endangered has been restored.

These efforts are ongoing. Other implications are discussed in the following sections.

8.9.1.6   TRAVEL DEMARKETING/OPTIMIZING

Many tourists arrive from the foreign countries, which contribute to varied fuel consumption via airways. Packaged planning can be done for regular visitors from foreign location by way of a travel intermediary. This might optimize the use of air fuel. In addition, this packaged tourism can be done planned for off-peak seasons such that the site load due to excess tourists in the peak season can be managed.

8.9.1.7   CULTURAL INHERITANCE

Adaption to the ecological challenges results in sustainability which is managed through cultural changes in "values, attitudes, and habits" towards treating the environment (Worts, 2006). Culture is inherited and it is transformed over the period of time. The conservation and ecological accountability needs to be built up as part of the socio-cultural learning at the domestic levels. Although, tourists at heritage sites are high in terms of intellectual capability and education and are responsible and mindful visitors, a significant section of the visitors still do not consider such issues as their priority and part of their societal responsibility. This needs to be culturally embedded. This is not only required at the tourist site but also at the surroundings. Though this looks tough, but can still be promoted using print or online media to the domestic visitors. In fact, the visitors and the surrounding stakeholders can be educated and encouraged for creating cultural change exhibiting more environmental responsibility. Hence, the museum can position itself as socially responsible by being active in creating sustainability (Byers, 2008). Culture can be crafted and communicated through the conservation of artefacts and their management (Gurian, 1999)

8.9.1.8   MUSEUM STORYTELLING

Museum can start educating about the sustainability by way of storytelling (Beck, 2012). Visiting museum can expose the tourists to various narrative spaces. These can be used to educate the visitors about the sustainability and green initiatives. This phenomenon is picking up and is known as edutainment, which means a combination of education and entertainment (Leboeuf, 2004).

8.9.1.9   SUSTAINABILITY DISPLAYS AT THE MUSEUM SITE

Sustainability at the museum site can be promoted by communicating through its content and design. The museum must put its green exhibits in line with its mission such that it is able to lucidly communicate and display the sustainability phenomenon. Sustainability can also be communicated using green design exhibits (Wylie and Brophy, 2008).

8.9.1.10   DEVELOPING LOHAS

Lifestyle of Health and Sustainability (LOHAS) (Cortese, 2003) is a special segment, which focuses on sustainable living and green initiatives. The site visitors must also be educated about adapting such lifestyle behaviours, which would help in educating the larger section of tourists. In addition, such educational initiatives would lead towards an ecologically positive change in the local culture.

8.10   DISCUSSIONS AND CONCLUSIONS

This chapter was aimed at discussing the extant literature pertaining to the heritage sites and their efforts towards sustainability and its communication. The case of City Palace Museum, Udaipur is discussed in this regard. Based on the review of literature and the managerial implications discussed pertaining to the case of City Palace Museum, Udaipur it is well taken that there exists a lot of scope for sustainable future for the heritage, which is being managed by MMCF. The suggestions for managing sustainability at the heritage site under study are discussed in conjunction with the sustainability indicators outlined by the UNESCO. There are key suggestions in this regard, which include travel demarketing/optimizing, cultural inheritance, museum storytelling, sustainability display at the museum site, and developing LOHAS.

In addition, it would be worth noting the role of digitization in today's world, which has host of applications. The visitors need to be communicated strongly and effectively about the sustainability initiatives taken up at the heritage sites. The communication should also be directed at the role of tourists in achieving sustainability at the heritage site. Navarette and Owen (2013) have suggested the option of digitization as a converging activity, which is based on the integration of heritage objects and its cultural information via the museum libraries. However, the same is not discussed in an integrative manner with the communication link. The digitization effort can show improved results if it is deployed via Internet and social media. It would enhance sustainability at the site with effective promotion of the cultural value of the heritage site. The site management can support virtual museum visits via Internet. This would reduce footfalls and but not really the net profits as the reduced footfalls can possibly reduce conservation costs in the long run. The virtual museum visits can bring in some revenue and this can be well promoted via the social media.

MMCF has endeavoured into digital promotion efforts through their official website http://www.eternalmewar.in/. The website maintains lot of information pertaining to the Eternal Mewar, Hotels, Collaborations, Research, Museum and more importantly its media activities. The website also allows the visitors to sign up for their newsletter and they can even follow the website updates using various social media links. As on 30th Nov 2013, the official Facebook page of the Eternal Mewar had more than 65000 'likes' since its inception in 2011. It also encapsulates photographs and videos and events through social media. The connections however are mostly Indian but gradually increasing on the international side. The page also invites the tourists for special events e.g., the forthcoming 'World Living Heritage Festival 2014,' which is scheduled in March 2014. In the past event like World Tourism Day and local festive events like Ashwa Pooja, Kartik Poornima, etc. are shared via social media. The social media deployment is in the nascent stage, however, efforts need to be made to direct the social media campaign on the sustainability side.

Although various tourist destinations and sites are using the social media for increasing their visitor footfalls the achievement of sustainability, it is closely linked with the visitor education and involvement whose aim is not necessarily an increase in the number of visitors. Internet has been a key medium for contact between the tourist sites and the potential tourists and open many doors for both marketing the site and sustainable tourism. It has also been able to provide what the tourists want be provide differentiated offerings. Different stakeholder groups work together at the heritage sites and aim at achieving goals, which include non-monetary aspects such as conservation and local development. This is different from any footfall generation campaign, which aims at promoting value to the visitors by way of thoughtful advertising. The campaigns aiming at sustainability should rather look at more creating more sensible tourists' expectations and hence would account for increased satisfaction (Ely, 2013). Ely (2013) also indicated that the consumers are aiming more at experiences that are meaningful instead of simply the tourism products and look towards more sustainable tourism experience, which considers a wider range of stakeholder groups. This strongly suggests that the tourists are looking forward for sustainable tourists. Heritage tourist sites can look more towards such tourists by way of database management of previous visitors. Social media can also be deployed, as it is a very economical and convenient way of searching for the right sustainable tourism offering. Social media campaigns might look at travel demarketing/optimizing, cultural inheritance, museum storytelling, sustainability display at the museum site, developing LOHAS as some of the general campaigns

MMCF can use a more specific campaign through their social media interface. This shall include linking with the online interpretation centre, which would help in disseminating layers of history about the place; dissemination of the promotional information of the site using the online media, a glimpse of the library, which documents and publishes using print media about the site and also the promotions to build brand equity. In addition, videos of events, which are organized to ensure cultural continuity to get media attention, can also aim at promoting sustainability via the social media. The focus needs to be enlarges on how the tourists are connected with sustainability and how they can be communicated more on sustainability practices at the City Palace Museum, Udaipur.

KEYWORDS

- communication
- heritage sites
- India
- museum
- sustainability
- tourism

REFERENCES

Achrol, R. S. and Kotler, P. (2012) 'Frontiers of the marketing paradigm in the third millennium,' *Journal of the Academy of Marketing Science*, 40:1, pp. 35–52.

AMA (American Marketing Association) (2013) *What are the definitions of marketing and marketing research*. (online) (cited 12 September 2013) Available from <http://www.marketing-power.com/content4620.php>

Aplin, G. (2002) *Heritage identification, conservation, and management*, New York, Oxford University Press.

Apostolakis, A. (2003) 'The convergence process in heritage tourism,' *Annals of tourism research*, 30:4, pp. 795–812.

Armitage, L. and Irons, J. (2013) 'The values of built heritage,' *Property Management*, 31:3, pp. 246–259.

Bansal, P. (2005) 'Evolving sustainability: A longitudinal study of corporate sustainable development,' *Strategic Management Journal*, 26:3, pp. 197–218.

Barker, N., Valos, M. and Shimp, T. (2012) *Integrated Marketing Communications*, Cengage-Brain.

Beck, S. C. (2012) 'The Intangible Museum: Common Threads' Master Thesis, Göteborgs University (online) (cited 12 September 2013) Available from <https://130.241.16.4/bitstream/2077/29467/1/gupea_2077_29467_1.pdf>

Beeton, S. and Benfield, R. (2002) 'Demand control: The case for demarketing as a visitor and environmental management tool' *Journal of Sustainable Tourism*, 10:6, pp. 497–513.

Belz, F.-M. and Peattie, K. (2009) Sustainability marketing: A global Perspective West Sussex, Wiley.

Booms, B.H. and Bitner, M.J. (1981) 'Marketing strategies and organizational structures for service firms' in Donnelly J.H. and George, W.R. (eds.), *Marketing of services*, Chicago, IL, American Marketing Association, pp. 47–51.

Bramwell, B. and Lane, B. (1993) 'Sustainable tourism: An evolving global approach,' *Journal of Sustainable Tourism*, 1:1, pp. 1–5.

Brophy, S. S. and Wylie, E. (2013) *The green museum: A primer on environmental practice* 2nd Ed, Maryland, Rowman and Littlefield.

Brown, S. (2004) 'How to extract cash from old bricks,' *The Estates Gazette*, 4:436, pp. 112–113.

Buhalis, D. (2000) 'Marketing the competitive destination of the future,' *Tourism Management*, 21:1, pp. 97–116.

Butler, R.W. (1999) 'Sustainable tourism: A state-of-the-art review,' *Tourism Geographies*, 1:1, pp. 7–25.

Byers, R. (2008) 'Green Museums + Green Exhibits: Communicating sustainability thorough content + design,' M.Sc. University of Oregon, Oregon (online) (cited 12 September 2013) Available from <https://scholarsbank.uoregon.edu/xmlui/bitstream/handle/1794/8260/Byers_fall2008_project.pdf>.

Caple, C. (2000) *Conservation skills judgment, methods and decision making*, London, Routledge.

Caserta, S. and Russo, A. (2002) 'More means worse: Asymmetric information, spatial displacement and sustainable heritage tourism,' *Journal of Cultural Economics*, 26:4, pp. 245–260.

Chhabra, D. (2009) 'Proposing a sustainable marketing framework for heritage tourism,' *Journal of Sustainable Tourism*, 17:3, pp. 303–320.

Chen, C. F. and Chen, P. C. (2010) 'Resident attitudes toward heritage tourism development,' *Tourism Geographies*, 12:4, pp. 525–545.

Cohen, B. (2006) 'Urbanization in developing countries: Current trends, future projections, and key challenges for sustainability,' *Technology in Society*, 28:1, pp. 63–80.

Cortese, A. (2003) 'They care about the world (and they shop, too) ' *The New York Times*, 20 July.

Dhiman, M. C. and Dubey, A. K. (2011) 'Sustainable tourism development in India: An empirical examination of stakeholders' perceptions,' *International Journal of Social Ecology and Sustainable Development*, 2:2, pp. 41–53.

Dinan, C. and Sargeant, A. (2000) 'Social marketing and sustainable tourism: Is there a match,' *International Journal of Tourism Research*, 2:1, pp. 1–14.

Ely, P. A. (2013) 'Selling Mexico: Marketing and tourism values,' *Tourism Management Perspectives*, 8, pp. 80–89.

Farrell, B. H. and Twining-Ward, L. (2004) 'Reconceptualizing tourism,' *Annals of Tourism Research*, 31:2, pp. 274–295.

Fullerton, L., McGettigan, K. and Stephen, S. (2010) 'Integrating management and marketing strategies at heritage sites,' *International Journal of Culture, Tourism and Hospitality Research*, 4:2, pp. 108–117.

Fyall, A. and Garrod, B. (1998) 'Heritage tourism: at what price?' *Managing Leisure*, 3:4, pp. 213–228.

Giudici, E., Melis, C., Dessi, S., and Ramos, B. F. P. G. (2013) 'Is intangible cultural heritage able to promote sustainability in tourism?' *International Journal of Quality and Service Sciences*, 5:1, pp. 101–114.

Gurian, E. H. (1999) 'What is the object of this exercise? A meandering exploration of the many meanings of objects in museums' in G. Anderson (eds) *Reinventing the museum: Historical and contemporary perspectives on the paradigm shift* Lanham, MD, AltaMira Press, pp. 269–283.

Hawken, P. (1993) *The Ecology of Commerce: A Declaration of Sustainability,* New York, Harper Collins.

Henderson, J. C. (2005) 'Exhibiting Cultures: Singapore's Asian Civilizations Museum,' *International Journal of Heritage Studies*, 11:3, pp. 183–195.

Hoffman, T. L., Kwas, M. L. and Silverman, H. (2002) 'Heritage tourism and public archaeology,' *SAA Archaeological Record*, 2:2, pp. 30–32.

Horrigan, K. (2009) 'A study of international approaches to the relationship between heritage conservation and sustainability,' final report of 2009, Churchill Fellowship, Winston Churchill Memorial Trust of Australia (online) (cited 31 August 2013). Available from <http://churchilltrust.com.au/site_media/fellows/Horrigan_Kenneth_2009.pdf>

Iyer, S., Velu, C. and Mumit, A. (2013 in Press) 'Communication and marketing of services by religious organizations in India,' *Journal of Business Research* (online) (cited 12 September 2013) Available from <http://dx.doi.org/10.1016/j.jbusres.2013.03.012>.

Jasparo, C. (2003) 'Culture and 'Human Security': A role for archaeology and the past?,' *Regional Development Dialogue* 24:2: pp. 11–21.

Kotler, P. and Levy, S.J. (1971) "Demarketing? Yes, Demarketing!,' *Harvard Business Review*, 49:6, pp. 74–80.

Leask, A. and Fyall, A. (2006) *Managing world heritage sites*, Burlington, Massachusetts, Butterworth-Heinemann, Elsevier

Leboeuf, D. (2004) 'Heritage communication through New Media in a Museum context' *CAA conference* (online) (cited 31 August 2013). Available from <http://proceedings.caaconference.org/files/2004/95_Leboeuf_CAA_2004.pdf>

Lu, J., and Nepal, S.K. (2009) 'Sustainable tourism research: An analysis of papers published in the Journal of Sustainable Tourism,' *Journal of Sustainable Tourism*, 17:1, pp. 5–16.

Lumsdon, L. (1997) *Tourism Marketing*, International Thomson Business Press

Macdonald, S. (2006) 'Undesirable heritage: Fascist material culture and historical consciousness in Nuremberg,' *International Journal of Heritage Studies*, 12:1, pp. 9–28.

Mathieson, A., and Wall, G. (1982) *Tourism, economic, physical and social impacts*, Longman.

McElroy, J.L. and de Albuquerque, K. (2002) 'Problems for managing sustainable tourism in small islands,' in Gayle, D.J. and Apostolopoulos, Y. (eds) *Island Tourism and Sustainable*

Development: Caribbean, Pacific, and Mediterranean Experiences, Westport, CT, Praeger pp. 15–31.

McKercher, B., and du Cros, H. (2006) 'Culture, heritage and visiting attractions,' in Buhalis, D. and Costa, C. (eds) *Tourism business frontiers: Consumers, products, and industry*, Amsterdam, Elsevier Butterworth Heinemann. pp. 211–219.

Meuser, T. and Von Peinen, C (2013) 'Sustainable tourism "Wish you weren't here"' in Jenkins, I., and Schröder, R. (eds) *Sustainability in Tourism: A Multidisciplinary Approach*, Germany, Springer Gabler, pp. 85–102.

Miller, G. A., and Twining-Ward, L. (Eds.). (2005). *Monitoring for a sustainable tourism transition: The challenge of developing and using indicators*, Oxfordshire, UK, CABI Publishing.

Misiura, S. (2006) *Heritage marketing*. Oxford, Elsevier Butterworth Heinemann.

Morrison, A. (2009). *Hospitality and travel marketing* (4th ed.). Albany, Delmar Cengage Learning.

Munjal, S. and Tripathi, G. (2012) 'Heritage Tourism Management: Service Enhancement and Sustainability,' *Context*, 9:2, pp. 41–52.

Navarrete, T. and Owen, J. M. (2011) 'Museum libraries: how digitization can enhance the value of the museum,' *Palabra Clave*, 1:1 (cited 28 November 2013). Available from <http://eprints.rclis.org/16747/1/PCLP%202011%20v1n1a3.pdf>

Park, H. Y. (2010) 'HERITAGE TOURISM: Emotional Journeys into Nationhood,' *Annals of Tourism Research*, 37:1, pp. 116–135.

Peterson, K. (1994) 'The heritage resource as seen by the tourist: The heritage connection' in Van Harssel, J. (ed.) *Tourism: an Exploration*, 3rd Edition, New Jersey Englewood Cliffs, Prentice Hall, pp. 242–249.

Polonsky, M.J., Carlson, L. and Fry, M. (2003) 'The harm chain: A public policy development and stakeholder perspective,' *Marketing Theory*, 3:3, pp. 345–364.

Pomering, A., Noble, G. and Johnson, L. W. (2011) 'Conceptualizing a contemporary marketing mix for sustainable tourism,' *Journal of Sustainable Tourism*, 19:8, pp. 953–969.

Portia, Y., Reichel, A. and Cohen, R. (2011) 'World heritage site- is it an effective brand name?:A case study of a religious heritage site' *Journal of Travel Research*, 50:5, *pp.* 482–495.

Prins, R. and Verhoef, P. C. (2007) 'Marketing Communication Drivers of Adoption Timing of a New E-Service among Existing Customers,' *Journal of Marketing*, 71:2, pp. 169–183.

Raju, G.P. (2009) *Tourism marketing and management*, Delhi, India, Manglam Publications.

Rowan, Y. and Baram, U. (2004) *Marketing heritage. Archaeology and the consumption of past*, Walnut Greek, CA, Altamira Press.

Russo, A. P. (2002) 'The "vicious circle" of tourism development in heritage cities,' *Annals of tourism research*, 29:1, pp. 165–182.

Russo, A.P. and Van Der Borg, J. (2000) 'The strategic importance of the cultural sector for sustainable urban tourism' in Fossati, A. and Panella, G. (eds) *Tourism and sustainable development*, London, Kluwer Academic Publishers, pp. 71–98.

Ryan, J. and Silvanto, S. (2010) 'World Heritage Sites: The purposes and politics of destination branding,' *Journal of Travel and Tourism Marketing*, 27:5, pp. 533–545.

Sadiki, F. A. (2012) 'Sustainable Tourism Marketing Strategies at UNESCO World Heritage Sites' University of Nevada, Las Vegas (online) (cited 31 August 2013). Available from

<http://digitalscholarship.unlv.edu/cgi/viewcontent.cgi?article=2478&context=thesesdissertations>

Sodangi, M., Idrus, A., Khamidi, F. and Adam, A. D. (2011) 'Environmental Factors Threatening the Survival of Heritage Buildings in Nigeria,' *South Asia Journal of Tourism and Heritage*, 4:2, pp. 38–53.

Shackley, M. (1998) *Visitor management: Case studies from world heritage sites*, Boston, MA, Butterworth.

Thai, T. N. (2011) 'Marketing aspects in tourism development: The marketing analysis of Vietnam tourism industry for long-term development' BBA Thesis, Seinäjoki University of Applied Sciences, Finland (online) (cited 31 August 2013). Available from <http://publications.theseus.fi/bitstream/handle/10024/33922/TOURISM.pdf?sequence=1>

United Nations (2007) 'Framing Sustainable Development: The Brundtland Report—20 Years On,' (online) (cited 31 August 2013) <http://www.un.org/esa/sustdev/csd/csd15/media/backgrounder_brundtland.pdf>

World Tourism Organization (2004) 'Indicators of Sustainable Development for Tourism Destinations: A Guidebook,' Madrid, Spain (online) (cited 31 August 2013). Available from <http://mekongtourism.org/website/wp-content/uploads/downloads/2011/02/Indicators-of-Sustainable-Development-for-Tourism-Destinations-A-Guide-Book-by-UNWTO.pdf>

World Tourism Organization (2007) 'Sustainable tourism indicators and Destination management,' *Regional Workshop*, 25–27 April, Kolašin, Montenegro.

Worts, D. (2006) 'Fostering a Culture of Sustainability,' *Museums and Social Issues*, 1:2, pp. 151–172.

Wylie, E., and Brophy, S. (2008) 'The Greener Good: The Enviro-Active Museum,' *Museum News, Washington*, 87:1, pp. 40–4.

CHAPTER 9

SUSTAINABLE CULINARY PRACTICES

SANJAY SHARMA

CONTENTS

ABSTRACT

The chapter explores the potential to transform culinary professionals to act more sustainably. It covers current practices from hotels and restaurants and suggests ways of making a kitchen "Green Kitchen." The study incorporates ideas from industry practitioners in leadership operational positions. This chapter illustrates the potential to transform culinary professionals through adopting ways discussed and examples cited in the chapter; it also highlights the challenges faced by the professionals while implementing them. Sustainability is a multidimensional aspect, which is perceived to be a reunion of environment, society and economy in varying proportion. These dimensions are coupled with Hospitality and Tourism businesses since ages. Food and Beverage being a core function of the hospitality business contributes significantly to the society and economy at large; however, it also consumes significant natural resources from the environment. In essence culinary sustainability is the use of culinary recourses responsibly which are discussed further in detail.

"What we are doing to the forests of the world is but a mirror reflection of what we are doing to ourselves and to one another."

— Mahatma Gandhi(Campbell et al., 2008)

9.1   INTRODUCTION

The concepts and ideas presented in this chapter narrate a practical link between the literature and practical implementation of sustainable culinary practices. The latest available and gathered theory is advocated by the perspectives of the leading practitioner chefs. A culinary roundtable conference was organized in 2013, which hosted the leading executive chefs, and culinary professionals to discuss the implementation of the culinary sustainability issues hence it incorporates varied views from industry practitioners.

The chapter primarily focuses on the gastronomy and sustainable culinary practices. It discusses various perspectives on sustainability; starting from what sustainability is, to diverse perceptions on culinary best practices. It also covers the likes of growing and harvesting, carbon footprints, buying local and organic farming. Based on the literature review, a Green Leaf "Farm to Farm" model is proposed which discusses the steps of food processing and the challenges faced. The chapter would help hoteliers to probe their operating procedures to make them more sustainable however it would also help the students to upgrade their knowledge and may raise a debate among the academic fraternity.

In Maslow's hierarchy of needs, Food being a basic necessity finds a place at the bottom of the pyramid (Mullins, 2010), irrespective of where we are positioned in the pyramid, we do interact with food in some form or the other. With the growing popularity of the convenience food and developing economies most of us do not get directly involved in procuring, processing and cooking of the food. While dining, we rarely discuss about the growing of the cereals or about the rearing of the meat, whether it was directly purchased from the farmers or there were any middlemen involved in the process? Is the food produced locally? Or the miles it has traveled before reaching the table? How significant is to discuss these questions has itself become an issue to be probed further. All the activities and the processes involved in procuring and processing of the food impacts the society, environment and economy, which in-turn affects the future availability of the natural resources and the quality of life for generations to come. In this light, we should together need to behave more responsibly to be able to sustain better quality of life for a longer period of time.

Fundamentally it is proven that "*Energy can neither be created nor can be destroyed but can be transformed from one form to another*" similarly all the resources used by us in domestic and commercial kitchens are converted from one form to another to enhance experience i.e., raw material into delicious meals, electric energy used for water heaters and air-conditioners, petroleum products in cosmetics and transportation, paper used is obtained from trees, in almost all the examples natural resources are used and are converted to meet or exceed our expectations, consequently it is vital for us to sustain our natural resources. This chapter in particular is looking forward to develop a clear understanding on the importance of retaining our natural culinary resources for the decades to come. It would discuss and suggest ways to make our kitchen more sustainable. The focus is not only on the product manufactured but also on ethical practices and developing environment friendly processes.

9.2 LITERATURE REVIEW

9.2.1 SUSTAINABILITY

"Sustainable" and "Sustainability" are interchangeably used terms,however, both are not defined consistently. For many, Sustainability is simply the protection of the environment,however, academicians see sustainability as a multidimensional discipline build on three important pillars of environment, economics and social justice or equality (Susan and Saunders, 2012). Sustainability is defined in indistinct ways by various researchers (Bluhdorn 2007; Bluhdorn and Welsh, 2007), however, the foundation of the argument revolves around the nucleus of ecosystem. It is the degree to which or whether or not the humans have used natural goods and services from the ecology (Costanza et al., 1997; Daily et al., 2000).

A range of best practices is emerging at local and national level. Government, Corporations and Nonprofit organizations are playing a pivotal role in initiating green practices. Individuals, groups, societies are seeking novel ways to live more ethically and sustainably (Lewis, 2013). The enduring progression of conceptualizing and implementation of sustainability among the individuals, groups and societies globally necessitates the development of a framework on sustainability for application to research scholars, corporations and in practice (Starik and Kanashiro, 2013).

The idea of sustainability has received a worldwide popularity in hospitality sector as a part of strategy to magnetize "green consumers,"(Sirakaya et al., 2013), arguably in practice actual consumers are scarce to get motivated and value sustainability to book a hotel room or purchase sustainable products from alternative hospitality businesses (Fishbein and Ajzen, 1972; Spash, 2002). However, values imparted are vital in determining the attitude and behavior of an individual. It significantly influences the purchase intentions of consumers (Stern, 2000; Stern and Dietz, 1994), this consequently augment sustainability revolution, a movement by individuals, societies and organizations to nurture the competence for environmental and socioeconomic long-term quality of life improvement (Edwards, 2005). It is no longer possible to flip a print media or turn on a telecast medium or look into Internet source and not come across an article, which talks about green movement. Conservation, renewable energy, climate change, community supported agriculture, organic and many more together forms green movement and are always linked with sustainability (Lopa, 2008).

9.2.2 FOOD SUSTAINABILITY

When we talk of food, we can talk of ecosystem, environment, economy and social sustainability. Our food habits have a large impact on our society and our community. The concept of culinary sustainability essentially incorporate aspects of sustainable or green kitchen, sustainable cuisine, food value system, sustainable product and process innovation, waste management, culinary trends, renewable energy and local food system. Our choice and those of the middlemen and suppliers we buy from affects the society and the environment. Therefore it is important to know about the growing and processing of our food.

To understand the relation of food with the ecosystem, we need to first understand the concept of *"Food Loss."* Food loss is the reduction of the food mass throughout the supply chain. This includes all the steps from harvesting to the disposal of the leftover,however, the food left at the end of the cycle is known as "food waste," though wasting food largely relates to the buying behavior and consumption pattern of the consumers (Parfitt et al., 2010).

Globally one third of the total food prepared for human consumption gets lost or wasted, which amounts to approximately 1.3 billion ton per year, however, food waste and loss also occurs in the early stages of food processing chain. In comparison to developed countries, a low-income country observes food loss mainly during early and middle stages of the cycle and very less is wasted at the consumer level (Figure 1), (Gustavsson et al., 2011).

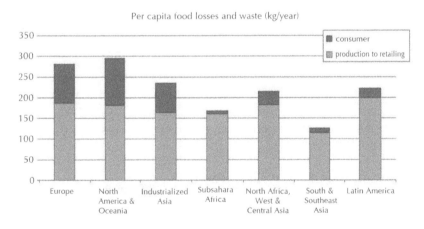

FIGURE 1 Per capita food losses and waste, at consumption and pre-consumptions stages, in different regions. *Adopted From: (Gustavsson et al., 2011).*

The effective waste management could be found in the management of three R's: *R*educe, *R*euse and *R*ecycle. These three "R" could be observed and implemented at various stages of food processing. It would help produce optimum quantity and reduce waste. The practical implementation of the processes at various steps (Gustavsson et al., 2011; Unilever Food Solutions, 2011) could be seen as:

- Farming: food waste due to spillage or mechanical damage during and post harvesting (e.g., sowing, fruit picking, threshing, etc.).
- Storage (Farmer/Retailers): food loss due to spillage during post harvest handling, storage and distribution from farm to stores and further to distributors.
- Processing: Processing by the farmers to make the crop usable.
- Purchasing: Loss due to extra ordering without physical stock inventory. Have real time control over inventory and stock.
- Storage: Storing the good in FIFO.
- Mise en place: Processing the raw material in best possible manner to reduce the processing loss and get maximum yield. Mechanically the yield is consistent and better than manually.
- Cooking: Using appropriate time and best suitable method to optimum utilization of the resources.
- Portioning and Plating of food: Standard portioning would prevent plate waste.
- Disposal: take notice of the plate waste and dispose organic waste sustainably. (Gustavsson et al., 2011; Unilever Food Solutions, 2011),

Futuristically, we need to cautiously integrate the environmental and social concerns. Hospitality been an integral part of the society consumes and disposes a significant amount of natural resources. It needs to understand the importance of ecosystem thus needs to act responsibly. One such initiative started in twin cities of Canada through local food initiative that strives to create a synthesis between social and environment objectives to attain structural change in the way food is produced, processed and consumed (Connelly et al., 2011).

9.2.3 CULINARY SUSTAINABILITY

While talking to culinary professionals one would realize that some of the aspects of sustainability are philosophical and are gastronomy aligned. When it come to sustainable, chefs largely tend to focus on the use of locally available fresh ingredients,however, when it comes to production and service, the food handlers need to emphasize on the aspects of thermal, electrical, mechanical and evidently operational issues. Many food service operators are struggling with the issue of how to make their food businesses more sustainable? For most operating a more environmental friendly operation means buying only non endangered fish and seafood, buying locally produce raw material whenever possible and devotionally following a recycling program (King, 2006).

Hoteliers need to understand that sustainability is also about understanding new technologies and new product specifications, senior managers need to educate themselves on these aspects before the knowledge is transferred to peer and subordinates, it is about the operational cost of small manufacturing unit or of the cooling of a walk-in or a deep refrigerator.

With depleting environment and increased awareness on sustainability, all the sectors are initiating steps in search of alternate energy sources. The latest energy policy has encouraged to alternate energy production from environment, and renewable resources. Amongst the renewable resources, biomass plays a key role and is largely adopted across industries (Cocco, 2007). ASDA (Now Wallmart), is known for using chicken trimmings and leftover cooking oil to run their trucks. Oil and other used fats could be used by converting into bio-diesel or e- diesel. Biodiesel fumes more efficiently that leaves no additional carbon in the environment therefore acting optimistically on global warming (Chomka, 2003).

Beyond a total of 6.5 billion people in the world, nearly 1.44 billion have no access to electric energy, almost 2.5 billion cook food with biomass using wood, sawdust, charcoal, dung and other unhealthy ways and half a billion use mineral coal. World Health Organization (WHO) estimates approximately 2 million die per year prematurely due to illness linked with pollution caused by indoor cooking, majority of these population survive on the remote areas of developing countries. It progressively makes more sense to use natural resources optimally. Past couple of decades has witnessed several initiatives in designing and implementing of appropriate and renewable energy technologies for household however only a few have been able to penetrate significantly and could hold on long-term sustainability (Sanchez et al., 2013).

9.3 UNDERSTANDING, IMPLEMENTATION AND IMPLICATION

9.3.1 BUYING LOCAL

One of the aspects of *"Culinary Sustainability"* is buying local. It has multiplier effects on the production cycle and environment. Like every end product depends on the raw materials used similarly cooking good food is about using freshest, finest, and swiftly available ingredients. Essentially no chef however imaginative, skillful or competent he or she is, would be able to produce a scrumptious meal unless excellent quality raw ingredients are made available. Which means we need to shorten the distance food travels between the farm and the fork.

Reducing the distance would help in numerous ways, it would not only help to produce a delicious meal retaining all the possible nutrients but would also reduce the carbon footprints left behind. Buying locally would reduce on the direct and hidden costs allied to environment. It involves the cost of the use of fossil fuel, increased air pollution, global warming, and reduction in the level of glaciers, damage to road and sea ways. Transportation of the long distance food that needs refrigeration increases ozone depletion by releasing unfriendly gases which negatively affects the global food chain. None of these factors are considered by the consumers while shopping, producing or processing of the goods, not even the producers pay attention to the cost of hidden or unhidden consequences.

Realizing the importance of growing and procuring local food, Taj group of hotels initiated sourcing local food for "The Taj," Ooty. Located on the western ghats of India, Ooty is India's one of the most sought after tourist destination, moreover varied climate has helped Ooty in cultivating exotic herbs like oregano, parsley and basil (Taj Hotels, 2013). Other food outlets too are viewing on parallel theme, for instance Rajesh Wadhwa, Executive Chef, Taj Palace, New Delhi, envision Masala Art, Indian restaurant to use local ingredients if neighboring farmers able to sustain, eventually shifting the same concept to main kitchen as well (Madan, 2011).

Likewise Te Hotel, New Delhi, India invites its customers to delightfully savor its freshly prepared food especially made to order. The hotel believes in catering sumptuous food ethnically served and is prepared from the ingredients procured locally. Every dish conveys a fresh story of its origin prepared by organic raw material purchased locally, even the meat, some fruits and dairy is procured from the nearby farmers giving food a distinct quality and taste (Te Hotel New Delhi, 2013).

The concept is traveling across India with groups like "*Locavers*" taking initiative to consume food that is grown within 100 miles. Inspired by such initiatives and in passion to serve back society, Siddharth Dominic, Owner CGH Group of hotels, planned to incorporate "*50 Miles Menu*" in his restaurant, Spice Village, Kerala. For the restaurant it's a win-win situation as it would help reduce the carbon foot prints and would also protect livelihood of local farmers giving guests a different experience. The food is fresh and nutritious which otherwise gets depreciated in the journey from soil to supermarket.

While discussing the consequences of buying local, Anderson (2008) has expressed his views on the concept of going local; he explains "*the major advantage of localizing food system, underlying all other advantages is that the process reworks power and knowledge relationship in food supply system which have become distorted by increasing the physical, social and metaphorical distance between the producers and consumers,"* both the authors have argued to give priority to local and environment integrity before corporate profit centers.

Buying local is increasingly becoming a global trend with more and more companies looking for freshly available local ingredients, Bon appétit a subsidiary of compass group, USA pioneered in implementing the concept and already purchases 30% of its food from with 150 miles, however, Sub Way was the leading green company even before sustainability was in trend, to be the world's "greenest quick service restaurant," Sub Way started formal sustainability efforts (Doherty, 2010).

Encouraging hoteliers and restaurateurs to buy local would help build a local food supply system with a closely knit consumer and producer relationship within a small radius of the local area. This local food supply system would have multiplier effects ranging from creating local employment to improving the neighboring infrastructure, from becoming more economically sustainable society to fulfilling health and environmental needs. It would restrict financial leakage to multinationals and would help build local business competitive advantage (Sharples, 2003). However, (Buck et al., 1997) analysis these advantages more deeply and assemble them as:

- The system would help to strengthen local economy as less money is transmitted to corporations based outside the local community. This will gradually help the local business to build on their production capacity resulting in creating more jobs, paying more taxes to the local government, providing more healthy options to buyers and most importantly reinvesting the money back into the local farms and businesses.
- Farmers and buyers are more closely tied which can potentially create healthy competition among the local farmers, helping the retailers, distributors and ultimately consumers. With the decrease of the number of middlemen, farmers are bound to get better compensation for their produce.
- It positively impacts the society development and revitalization. It helps in creating a unique relationship between the producer and the end customer.
- Helps in making small and medium families financial stable, it helps to protect the local history, culture and ecology.
- Helps to protect environment by reducing the carbon footprints from traveling long distances (Buck et al.1997).

9.4   CARBON FOOTPRINTS AND GREEN HOUSE EFFECT

In 2008, the food retailers at Guardian climate change summit, UK debated on the prospects and consequences of labeling and comparing the labeled food. Surprisingly there was no consensus on the way products are labeled. Katherine Symonds, sustainability manager, Tesco proposed on calculating the category average of the carbon footprints rather than comparing individual packets and products. The head of corporate social responsibility at Pepsico, UK, Andrew Smith said some of our products are labeled as *"you have made a commitment to reducing your carbon footprints,"* however, once more products are labeled, it would be easier to compare. As per Erika Coghlan, Public affair chief, the biggest challenge for Coca Cola enterprises is to adopt a strategy that would work across several markets (Watson, 2008).

(Coca-cola.co.uk)

(Tesco.co.uk)

Reducing carbon footprints essentially means burning less gas, fuels, oils and other petroleum products not only in transporting but also in preparing the meals to reduce the emission of green house gases. The company also labels the packed food products indicating the dishes prepared with low carbon footprint ingredients (Food Management, 2007).

While debating the efforts to control carbon footprints, the food-marketing institute (McSwane et al., 2010) has recommended five steps to measure carbon footprints.

- *Establish an organizational boundary*
- *Define an operational boundary*
- *Collect necessary data*

- *Convert the data into carbon footprint*
- *Establish a baseline year and set an emission reduction goal*

Step1. Depending on the model of operation the organizational boundary defines where to measure emissions. If there is complete operational control then 100% of the emissions are recorded by single management. This includes operational and financial control and would also reap 100% benefit from the consequences however in equity share approach, the percentage of the emissions is shared equivalent to the share owned, this includes joint ventures, franchises and management contract run organizations.

Step2. Operational boundary keeps an inventory on specific emissions of an organization. The emissions are categorizes into three categories depending on the organizations capacity to control each of them.

- Direct emissions: emissions by the processes that are directly controlled by an organization. E.g. emissions from cooking fuels, refrigerators, company owned vehicles, etc.
- Indirect emissions: emissions by the processes that are not controlled directly by the organizations. E.g. emissions by electricity generating plants that supply electricity to the organizations.
- Optional emissions: emissions caused by the middle men, suppliers and the consumers where the company has very little or no control.

Step3. The organization then needs to collect data depending on the usage and production capacity the data would differ from company to company. The FMI has to gather following data by every food handler, manufacturer and retailers.

- Cubic feet of natural gas combusted
- Calculated and actual pounds of refrigerant lost
- Amount of fuel consumed by the company vehicles and types of vehicles used
- Actual kilowatt hour of energy consumption for all units
- Electricity grid (e-Grid) factors for each unit
- Type of green power purchased and its emission factor

Step4. This involves converting the data into carbon footprints. After gathering the emission levels, the collected data is converted into CO_2e-value. Although there are norms to convert the raw data however software calculations are more accurate, it saves time and helps to keep a consistent record of all the data.

Step5. Baseline year is the first year of collecting data efficiently and confidently and thereafter emissions reduction goals can be set for each succeeding year.

9.5   FOOD DISPOSAL

Hoteliers are increasingly realizing the importance of protecting the environment and captivating appropriate steps, Restaurants across the globe are finding composting to be a healthy way to "*go green*" however an average person still finds composting tedious. The biggest challenge however is still to teach staff about what is compostable and what is not. The basic guide for the operators is; if the waste was once alive, it can be used to compost, which includes all the types of vegetable, meat, poultry seafood and even animal bones.

9.6   COMPOSTING

Composting is an essential part of recycling and an ultimate way of giving back to the environment sustainably. The process is easy with exceptional rewards. Compost encourages earthworms in soil; it nourishes solid with useful nutrients and helps in water retention (Tull, 2010). Chef Gary Coltek has environmentally upgraded dining services at Kennesaw State University, Georgia by emphasizing on triple bottom line of 3P's,that is, *People, Profit and Planet*. His focus is to minimize environment impacts by various initiatives like departments closed loop waste management system which composts about 60,000 pounds of food waste every month. The composted waste is processed into a nutrient dense water source, which is used for irrigation at campus farms thus closing the loop. Their initiative also prevents 44,000 pounds of non-compostable waste from dumping in the landfills and nearly 220 gallons of used oil is recycled yearly to be used as a biodiesel (Ramsey, 2013).

Similarly Chef Srinivisan, Executive Chef, Radisson Blu Plaza hotel New Delhi, India, uses a mechanical compost grinder to compost the food waste of the hotel. The food waste is converted into manure, which is further used in horticulture. Inspired by the concept of sustainability, the promoters of IIMT Oxford Brookes University, Gurgaon, India which is known to create global hospitality leaders has decided to nurture new campus a "*Green Campus*"; they plan to have in-house compost plant and use the compost in fresh organic herb garden within the campus. Likewise Joe Ducati, general manager of CulinArt at George school, Philadelphia, has created a 400 square foot garden, cultivating the soil, watering the fields and harvesting the crop to be used by the organization for various conferences and events within the campus (King, 2006).

Burgerville, a Vancouver, Washington based fast-food chain claims to even compost glasses, straws and other utensils however these wares are prepared of vegetable based plastic and is considered 10% costlier than otherwise used. The management encourages the customers to segregate the leftover, which is guided by posting pictures and procedures over the trash bins. The trash bins are double checked by the staff members. This practice not only helps the restaurant but also educates the general public about the green practice (Brookes, 2009).

In 2008 an organic food company, Hain Celestial UK, the main sandwich supplier of Marks and Spencer was awarded the recycling performance of the year. The award was well received for the company's encouraging concern towards environment in an organic way. The producer disposes animal waste sustainably in the environment by an anaerobic digestion unit which essentially converts the recyclable waste into biogas and manure which is easily used in the farm land (Pendrous, 2008). On similar lines, Mark Sandridge, CEO of Sandridge food, US took the initiative to participate in fresh sustainable approach by becoming an energy star participant to help improve energy efficiency. Expressing concern, Mark says "as *a company we have the responsibility to act responsibly to help preserve the environment and natural resources for future generations.*" The company has collaborated with a Waste-to-Energy Company to convert its food waste to compost; this could be further used for fertilizers consequently resulting in reducing 1.5 million tons of waste from landfills.

The biodegradable kitchen solid waste has mainly three routes to get disposed off; disposal directly in the local surroundings (Mostly for domestic kitchens), disposing at landfills and using as animal fodder. Conventionally two ways of disposing are more popular i.e., directly in soil or indirectly as animal fodder however the water waste is traditionally discharged in soaking pits or municipal sewage or into open drain (Schouw et al., 2002).

Alternatively a biological method of composting *"Vermicomposting"* could be adapted to compost culinary leftover more sustainably. Vermicomposting uses earthworms to convert the organic residue into biological compost. Essentially *"Eisenia fetida"* earthworm is used for the entire process where the leftover is passed through the digestive track of the worm making it organically compostable(Epstein, 1997). The process is a combination of ingestion, digestion, and assimilation of the organic matter by the microorganisms. The process is a bio-oxidative process in which the worms act together with microorganisms and food particles that acts as a catalyst in accelerating the entire process. The conversion process is principally accomplished by microorganisms however the earthworms are the vital source to speed up the conversion (Dominguez, 2004).

9.7   ORGANIC FARMING

The contemporary approach of agriculture is drifting to traditional way of farming. The *"Organic Farming"* is back in trend accompanied with all the positive societal and health benefits. Organic farming is an integral part of culinary sustainability and is the first step in nurturing ethical practices. Numerous private food certifications have being cropped up in the recent past however the United States Department of Agriculture (USDA, 2008) have formulated a collection of standards for selling organic food products. Similarly for all the European markets, Soil association based in the United Kingdom is liable to certify organic products. The main role of these organizations is to check the authenticity of the produce, to see if the food is processed as per the laid norms by the company (USDA, 2008).

Some of the basic and common norms to get the organic products are:
- Crop cultivation should be done with suitable rotation including nitrogen-fixing plants which includes broad beans and peas.
- Plants and animals need special care by feeding balanced diet.
- Antibiotics are not acceptable in organic farming.
- Animals should be kept is open space with sufficient are to make them roam and act naturally.
- Packed and canned food should contain 100% organic food.

Organic farming is essentially without the use of fertilizers and pesticides; it works on conservational farming system, takes the advantage of nitrogen fixing plants and produce maximum possible animal fodder on the farm, further the endangered spices finds their place in farms to help increase biodiversity (Sloan et al., 2013).

9.8   WATER SUSTAINABILITY

Water being an integral part of human evolution, approximately 3% of the total water available on the planet is suitable for drinking and agriculture purpose but with the increase in world population the consumption of water by humans has almost tripled in the past couple of decades. Out of all the activities, agriculture contributes to almost 90% of the total water consumption however on an average it is estimated that we drink 1600–5000 liters of water globally depending on individual diet (Hall and Gossling, 2013).

Consequently agriculture is most vulnerable in depletion of the availability of natural water. It is anticipated that the depletion of available water table along with increasing pollution has lead to decreasing precipitation level causing draft in many places (Hall and Gossling, 2013). Hospitality domain of the industry consumes significant amount of water. On an average globally commercial kitchens use 500 to 4000 liters of water to produce 1 kg of wheat, around 10,000 liters of water for 1 kg of beef, 1 kg of fruit may require 700 to 880 liters of water, production of 1 kg of chocolates may require 24,000 liters of water, Hence the food production operation would get affected with the depletion of the availability of usable water.

Ironically most of the drinking water available in the global market is sold in non biodegradable plastic bottles having said that even while purchasing water bottle we can be more environment conscious by buying labeled spring water, distilled water or even purified water. It is hard to judge the quality of water sold as packaged drinking water as the boundaries for labeling only drinking water is not defined clearly which encourages the customers to buy alternative natural water which is packed with few carbon footprints. The kitchen leftover water, which is drained, can be used for horticulture purpose provided the detergent and soap used in kitchen and hotel is a biological soap and would not create harm to surrounding flora and fauna.

To make the kitchen environment friendly and water conscious, hotel chefs and managers need to install in-house water purification system, a water recycling plant, star rated energy efficient gadgets and appliances, depending on the availability one can try to use compressed natural gases, develop green eco friendly kitchen, self growing of exotic herbs making them fresh and lo-cally available. A green environment friendly cafeteria and pantry, a sustain-able food packaging station, water wise dish washing system and a separate space to gather environment sustainability information (Tull, 2010). With de-veloping economies increasing urbanization, industrialization and waning ef-fective use of water in agriculture together grounds future availability of water conversely to achieve sustainable water development, number of intrusion are mandatory in the form of technological, social and institutional. Some examples that could be implemented are rainwater harvesting, drip irrigation and institutional arrangements (Alagh, 2010).

9.9 FINDINGS AND IMPLEMENTATION

9.9.1 TOOLS, TECHNIQUES AND TRADITIONS(HOTELS, RESTAURANTS, CATERING SERVICES AND HOUSEHOLDS)

In 2011, the national restaurant association of United States surveyed leading chefs and culinary professionals to probe the upcoming trends in culinary domain. The best trending culinary theme was *"Sustainability"* very closely followed by *"Hyper Local"* chased by Children's Nutrition, Gluten free food, Back to Basics (Miller, 2011). Reading the trends closely indicates a clear inclination of the culinary professionals towards optimally using and protecting the natural resources. Sustainability, Using of locally available ingredients, organic food, and allergy free food were some of the common trending themes across all categories of food and beverage outlets ranging from quick service to fine dining restaurants.

In the era of information technology with the rise of community website we are fortunate enough to easily access, assemble, assimilate and implement the required data. The industry needs contemporary tools and techniques to combat ongoing challenges effectively and efficiently fortunately more tools and techniques are being created every day. The biggest challenge however is to maintain a harmony between the use of the modern tools and sustainable environment. As more and more professionals know about new techniques, more and healthy ideas are generated resulting in the betterment of the culinary domain. The floating of idea and experiences in online debates is joined by number of people making it more interactive, knowledge sharing and exciting. This results in making the ideas widely accepted and successful.

9.9.2 ENERGY EFFICIENT APPLIANCES

Majority of the energy is consumed by the electric appliances used in kitchens. Mainly refrigerators, salamanders, heavy-duty grinders, and provision for fresh air consume more of the energy. Out of all the equipment, refrigerators contribute a maximum carbon footprint, which makes it significant to maintain them. Refrigerators door seal should be checked consistently to see if we are losing on the cold air if needed; it should be fixed at the earliest. Avoid frequent opening of the refrigerator doors as it take extra energy to cool the air, which just entered in. Never overburden the refrigerators as it hinders the flow of air resulting in more time to regain the desired temperature. No hot equipment and cooking ranges should be installed near any kind of refrigeration. Ensure the thermostat is working properly and desired temperature is automatically attained. Do not put hot food items in the fridge, let them cool and the place them in the refrigerators. Try to install branded star rated refrigerator, which consumes least electricity yet, very efficient (Tull, 2010).

Dishwasher is big equipment, which needs attention. It consumes high electricity resulting in increased carbon footprints. In dishwashing, try to avoid washing utensils in running water instead it should be scrapped in dustbin directly. Run the machine when it is completely full, this saves energy and is also very efficient. Slow down the temperature of the water as per the requirement, washed plates can be air dried by opening the door on the last cycle, empty the food trap more frequently. Sustainable kitchen developments would also avoid using toxic cleansers. Environment friendly and green cleaning agents are available in the market, which can be used to replace harmful cleaning agents. For instance some of the naturally available cleansers in the kitchen are baking soda, table salt, lemon juice, white vinegar, flour. Using these substances would not make drained water toxic hence could be used by horticulture department.

The commercial kitchen could have separate section for the research and development of more sustainable techniques. This section would keep all the records of the best practices followed. It would also track the savings done by implementing green practices. This will help motivate staff to act more responsibly; it also indicates the intentions of the management towards their commitment in preserving sustainable resources. A list of information could be displayed for the staff to refer to. For instance information on seasonal availability of fruits and vegetables, exact time for cooking of meats, grains and vegetables to save energy, money saved from green practices, composting details, standard recipes and suggested menu items for daily buffet of coffee shop and fine dining restaurant. Even the food home delivered could be packed here more eco friendly way, which means this stations also needs to have environment friendly packaging materials including packaging boxes, carry bags and disposable plates if required.

9.9.3 EATING RESPONSIBLY

Sustainable kitchen is also about creating awareness among the customers for healthy and unhealthy options available in the market. For instance according to Jesse Cool (2008) some of the food items are treated with more pesticides than others hence they retain more pesticides. Consequently the consumers could either neglect the ill effects or alternative they could buy the substitutes available in the market with similar vitamins and minerals.

TABLE 1   High pesticide foods with available alternatives.

High Pesticide Food	Main Nutrient	Healthy Alternatives
Apple	Vitamin C	Water melon, Banana, Oranges
Bell pepper	Vitamin C	Green peas, Broccoli, Romaine Lettuce
Celery	Potassium	Apricot, Avocado, Raw Mushroom
Cherries	Vitamin A and C	Orange, Blueberry, Raspberry,
Grapes	Flavonoids	Peanut, Peanut Butter
Lettuce	Vitamin A and K	Chard, Kale, Collard, Mustard green
Nectarines	Vitamin A and C	Orange, Watermelon, Grapefruit
Peaches	Vitamin A and C	Orange, Watermelon, Grapefruit
Pear	Vitamin C	Water melon, Banana, Oranges
Potato	Vitamin C and B	Broccoli, Cauliflower, Banana
Spinach	Vitamin A and K	Chard, Kale, Collard, Mustard green
Strawberry	Vitamin C	Water melon, Banana, Oranges

Adopted from Jesse Cool, 2010.

It is wise for us and for the generations to follow that we start to implement the concept of sustainability. It should not just be a philosophical concept however the philosophy needs to be converted into action. In the following section we would look at some more practical recommendations that can be followed to make kitchen more sustainable. IIMT, Oxford Brookes University, Gurgaon, India organized a roundtable conference in 2013 for the corporate and executives chefs and leading culinary professional. The summary of the conference for culinary sustainable challenges and suggestions are compiled here to make it more productive.

- Try and cook seasonally available vegetable, avoid using fruits not in season
- As far as possible, Plant a garden in-house for the exotic herbs which otherwise are expensive to import
- Adhere to ethical practices by implementing recycling and composting
- Ask the vendors for the ways their meats are reared, try and educate them to nurture more sustainably
- Check for the sea food endangered species and avoid using them
- Verify the way your seafood is caught, ensure they adopt sustainable practice
- Search for local farmers who can supply directly to the hotel as per the need

- Avoid buying too glazy fruits, it could be polished similarly look for unpolished lentils
- Try to use whole grains in bakery rather than refines, for instance whole wheat, Whole rye, Whole Oats, Wild rice, Brown rice, Bulgur wheat
- Vegetable to be cooked crunchy, semi cooked and steamed
- Cook food from fresh ingredients to lower the sodium, mostly sodium is consumed through packed food
- Buy canned food with no salt labeled, it helps to preserve nutrients
- Try and serve meat dish with a vegetable preparation especially in Indian cooking where usually meat is eaten with carbohydrate and no accompanying veggies
- Try making salad dressings with yogurt instead of oil
- As far as possible use lemon juice in marinades and food preparations instead of synthetic vinegar
- Garnish the dishes with fresh herbs and vegetables

Similarly Drummond and Brefere (2009) have suggested ways for menu planning that would help to make it healthier and more sustainable. Menu planning is an opportunity to add foods which are rich in nutrients and could be served as accompaniments to the main dish. It also provides an opportunity to balance fat and sodium to sustain healthier life. Following questions could be asked while planning a meal.

- Does the everyday meal provide required number of servings of each food group to be able to receive an average 2000 kilocalorie?
- Do most of the menu servings have balanced nutrients without additional sugar and fats?
- Is the menu well balanced to have whole grains in the day's meal?
- Check if the meat items used and tender and lean
- Are meat alternatives available with similar nutritional values
- Does the menu have vegetables from across varieties ranging from leafy vegetables to dark vegetable from starchy to iron rich vegetables

The authors also emphasized on indicating food items causing allergies. Although there are more than 160 food items causing allergy to people however the law identifies eight most common food items that may cause allergy, these food items contribute to almost 90% of the food allergy caused to consumers.

- Fish
- Nuts (Like almonds, chestnuts, walnuts)
- Eggs
- Peanuts

- Crustaceans (like Lobsters, oysters, crams, mussels)
- Milk and Milk products
- Soybean
- Wheat

Apart from the indicated list, it is advised to look at other allergens like mushrooms, spices, condiments, colorings, flavorings and additives in the labeling.

While discussing sustainable kitchen; the importance of eating healthy becomes an integral part of the discussion however eating healthy has various definitions; predominantly it covers seven basic themes (Falk et al., 2001) which are: Eating healthy is eating *low food*, *healthy/unprocessed foods*, and *balanced food* to *prevent disease*, to *maintain nutrient balance*, to manage an *existing disease* and to *control weight*. Incorporating healthy ingredients in food have always been known to be a key component that leads to good health nevertheless people has different opinions to foresee healthy food. These opinions have developed from their experiences in life however the culinary practitioners could help the community to understand healthy eating better.

There are multiplier benefits of eating healthy and balanced diet is an important part of maintaining good health. Depending on the lifestyle, the key to healthy diet is eating right number of calories; the calorie requirement for an average men and women is 2,500 and 2,000 calories respectively. This requirement could be fulfilled by eating a wide range of foods so that the body is receiving all the nutrients it needs. In a basic meal the starch content should not be more than 1/3 of the total food that we eat, which means we need to keep a check on the starchy food intake that includes potatoes, pasta, rice, breads and some cereals. Likewise too much of saturated fat can increase the amount of cholesterol in blood which may cause heart diseases, this encourage us to avoid food items which are high in cholesterol and saturated fat. Hard cheese, cream, cakes, butter, rich cookies, sausages, pies, ghee, lard and bard are rich in unhealthy fatty acids. Similarly the intake of sugar and sugary beverages should be avoided as far as possible (NHS, 2013).

Drawing from the literature and the culinary roundtable conference, the practitioners could adopt the following steps to plan healthy menus and serve a better tomorrow:

- Scrub the vegetables rather than peeling; to help prevent water soluble vitamins;
- Promote and serve puree and thin soups instead of cream soups;
- Use fresh herbs instead of dried; to help retain medicinal values and its flavor;

- Cook the food in healthy cooking oils such as coconut oil, olive oil, mustard oil or rice bran oil;
- Serve pineapple with meats especially red meats as it helps to break-down the proteins present in meat making it easy to digest;
- Choose lean meat, cut off the extra trimmings and cook and serve the birds without skin;
- Aloe Vera helps in digestion; chefs can plan desserts based on Aloe Vera syrup, this would help in the assimilation of the food;
- Use grain breads for sandwiches rather than white loaf bread;
- Use healthy cooking alternatives which includes steaming, baking, grilling, braising and boiling;
- Marinade the meats with lemon juice or vinegar to aid digestion;
- Healthy eating is also about how do you eat; take your time to chew food and avoid eating alone;
- Never skip breakfast, try to have whole meal cereals with some fruits and a serving of skimmed milk;
- Last but not the least; Increase the numbers of meal in a day to smaller meals and avoid eating heavy meals at night.

9.10 CONCLUSION

In a sustainable kitchen it is important for us to keep a pace with the latest technological advancements of the microenvironment. As a starting point the culinary managers could develop a list of sustainable ideas and see their contribution in each of the area identified. The areas could be on the sustainability aspects discussed so far in this chapter however within the hotel or catering premise, the contributions could be in various ways.

To make the complex process of sustainability simpler, a *Green Leaf "Farm to Farm" Model*(Figure 2) is derived from the literature review. The *Green Leaf "Farm to Farm" Model* illustrates all the steps from growing of the raw materials to disposing them back to the farm. The entire cycle is primarily dominated by producers (Farmers) and consumers. It is estimated that 30–50% (1.2–2 billion tones) of all the food produced on the planet is lost before reaching a human stomach (Fox, 2013). Furthermore the *potential wastage zone* equally lies between the producers and the consumers. The controllable potential wastage factors on the producer's zone are relatively difficult to manage, as most of the factors are dependent on uncontrollable aspects, for e.g. government policies, natural calamities, yield of the crop, approval of subsidies, etc. There is very little that a buyer or a consumer can do to control wastage in farmer's zone however the potential wastage zone that lies on the consumer side is termed as *critical wastage zone*, most of the wastage during these steps could be controlled by consumers hence are internally controllable.

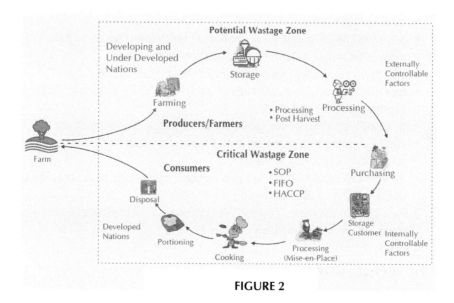

FIGURE 2

Looking at the food wastage record collected by WRAP, UK (2008), it becomes even more important to take preventive steps to control wastage. The data shows the wastage on the controllable zone is very significant in number. According to WRAP (2008) report, one third of the total food we buy, we throw away. The main reasons for throwing away of the food which could have been used otherwise are:

• Left on the plate after a meal (1,225,700 tons worth £3.3 billion)
• Passed its date (808,000 tons worth £2.2 billion)
• Looked, smelt or tasted bad (750,500 tons worth £1.8 billion)
• Went moldy (465,700tons worth £960 million) and
• Left over from cooking (360,600tons worth £830 million)

The internally controllable consumer zone could implement following steps to control on the pilferage:

Purchasing—The process that relates to buying activities which includes determining of the required quantities, placing of the order, receiving the ordered items and making of the payment to the supplier. Within the step of purchasing, there are smaller steps, which can be vital in saving the eventual wastage.

- The easiest way is to purchase the optimum quantity and do not dump inventories in the stores however a par stock is advisable to maintain.
- Economies of scale comes handy for the non perishable and long shelf life food items.
- Cook seasonal and locally available ingredients; this would not only enhance the taste of the food but would also reduce on the carbon footprints.
- Set standard purchase specifications and adhere to them while ordering and purchasing goods.
- Market price fluctuations requires enduring attention, suppliers need to be constantly monitored and if required, revive the purchasing policies however annual contracts with the suppliers on the agreed rate are more useful in budgeting and forecasting.
- An Enterprise resource planning software could be installed to maintain the records, It also alerts the supplier automatically howeverinstallation charge could be a constraint.

Storage—Stocks in hand are significant in numbers, as high-end hotels do operate with high stock inventories. High-level inventories not only engage space but also cost money howeverthe available stock needs to meet the demand. Considering the cost of spoilage and storing, some preventive steps could be put in-place to prevent ill effects.

- Store the food items as per the HACCP standards to prevent cross contamination.
- Try to replace and use smaller refrigerators against walk-in chillers, this saves the electricity and also reduce carbon footprints left behind.
- Vacuum packing of the goods increases the shelf life and also prevents from absorbing strong odors. E.g. Eggs, Onion, Garlic, Mushroom, Cheese, etc.
- Dry store to be kept clean at all times and should be free from rodents.
- All the food items should be circulated and used in first in first out order (FIFO).

Processing (Mise en place; Peeling, Cutting, Chopping)—This step is the base for a memorable culinary journey. Controlling at this stage depends on various factors however use of technology, adopting latest trends and skilled staff is the key to success. The integration of technology with cooking styles has helped chefs in multiple ways. Availability and use of trendy gadgets increases yield and maintain consistent quality, hence the staff should be trained and motivated to use modern equipment. Some of the leading hotels have opted for convenience food; which means using readily available basic food for e.g. most of the hotels have stopped preparing fresh mayonnaise instead they purchase readily available. Similarly some leading hotels have either out-sourced their bakery or use frozen desserts from the market. This indeed saves direct and indirect cost however their health benefits are at debate.

Cooking—It could be deciding factor between a chef and a good chef. Sometimes we tend to ignore this step to analyze for critical food wastage however we can save significant amount of direct and hidden cost at his stage of the cycle. Some of the tips that could come handy at this stage that lead to culinary delights are:

- Use of the right utensil for the right quantity of food.
- Cooking temperature needs to be as accurate as possible; this saves energy and also prevents food loss during cooking.
- Cooking time needs to be adhered to; for instance hardboiled egg takes 8 min, pasta takes 8–12 min(depending on the variety).
- Right cooking method should be used to retain the quality of food and to save cost. Boiling, blanching and steaming could interchangeably be used very effectively.

Portioning—The literature review shows that1, 225,700 tons worth £3.3 billion of food is left on the plate after a meal; this implies either we are not able to control and serve the right portion of food to the customers or the customers are not ordering and eating responsibly. As an entrepreneur serving right portions help to save money, customers feel value for money and most importantly we help the environment to be more sustainable. Likewise customers need to act more responsibly to help prevent food wastage.

Disposal—The leftover food needs to be discarded more ethically. The serving staff of the hotels and the consumers should use right bin for right disposal. Use clearly demarcated biodegradable and non-biodegradable waste bins. Try to adhere to the thumb rule of *"anything which was once alive is biodegradable."* Depending on the usage, financial ability and the availability of space, commercial sectors could use various methods for disposal that could range from automated composting plant to vermicomposting.

It is being observed from the literature review (Gustavsson et al., 2011), that in developing and under developed countries; the food loss is more at the farming, harvesting, post harvesting and processing stages however ironically the developed countries waste more of the food at consumer level. The developing countries may lack basic infrastructure, tools and modern techniques to control wastage at farmer's zone but the developed countries need to pay more attention on educating and training on the importance of controlling wastage through acting more responsibly.

The initial effort for all of us should aim to control wastage at every step of the proposed model depending on which part of the cycle we fall. The internal controllable zone is critical wastage zones and need significant supervision in every step. The key to control wastage and using ingredients more sustainably lies in adhering to the critical principles of:

- *FIFO* (First in First out).
- *SOP*(Standard Operating Procedures).
- *HACCP*(Hazard Analysis and Critical Control points).

These three core pillars to make kitchen more sustainable should be implemented in every step of the critical wastage zone. Apart from enforcing core pillars, culinary managers' could also improvise on:

- Implement conscious menu engineering.
- Ordering sensibly.
- Consistently updating the inventory level.
- Regular training of the staff on being sustainable.

The consumer zone could also plan to implement *"waste audit"* on every step. Based on the usage the managers can plan a waste audit program, which could have following steps:

- Keep a record of the current and past wastage of all the food and beverage outlets.
- Breakdown the total food wastage level and identify potential wastage steps. The identification should involve all the steps from purchasing to disposal.
- Take preventive steps on specific areas and guide the staff members on preventing wastage.
- Train the staff on how to prevent or minimize the wastage and also train them on the importance of controlling pilferage.
- Check again on all the steps for the levels of the food wasted.
- Prepare a comparative chart against the previous wastage record.
- Share the numbers with the staff members irrespective of increasing or decreasing.
- Retrain the staff; as most of the times the staff members become complacent with the new efforts hence it is vital to remind and retrain the employees.
- The weekly record should be extended to monthly and the figures should be shared with all the employees on monthly basis to gain on the confidence of the employee.

- This would encourage employees to follow and retain best practices implemented.

The key element to achieve zero wastage in a kitchen could be attained by:

- Cooking whole ingredients to best possible especially fruits and vegetables.
- Using tools and improvised techniques to get maximum yield.
- Storing the purchased goods responsibly.
- Portioning as per the standard operating procedures.
- Turning all the food waste to use (Stock from peels, trimmings and compost from leftover).
- Unused peels and stems could be used to make essence and stock rather than composting.
- Vegetable and fruit peelings and pulps could be used in the beauty spa and health centers of the hotels.
- Roots of the vegetables could be used in bathtub to create natural cleanser.

Additionally chefs and culinary professionals could practice *"No Bin Day"* once a week; wherein all the staff members are motivated not to waste anything and observe the day as zero wastage days; alternatively on remaining days the chefs can take away the garbage bins and can only be allowed to discard after registering the wastage. This would keep a record on the wastage and would also give a record of the employees wasting the food. Looking at the trend of food wastage, chefs can modify the staff menus and the employees can be mentored on the need of saving the food for long-term food and environment sustainability.

Fresh herbs are crucial part of a sustainable kitchen. All the consumers essentially hoteliers could try to grow fresh herbs within the hotel premise where ever possible. Growing fresh herbs in-house could be projected as a USP (Unique selling proposition) of the hotel however herbs like parsley, thyme, rosemary, basil and cilantro could last fresh up to two weeks if stored refrigerated in water with the water being changed every alternative day.

What role if any should government play in encouraging sustainability? Although, the private sectors are contributing in sustainable development, it is imperative for the government to equally participate, having said that, globally governments have acknowledged and discussed the issue of sustainability and are progressively taking initiatives in support with private partnership. According to KPMG (2009) report, the government has four roles to spur sustainability:

- Policy development

- Facilitation
- Regulation
- Sustainability management within government

However, government needs to be more industry focus to obtain better results, they need to have more specific plans and incentives to promote best practices. To encourage customers buy green products and follow green practices, a rebate on sales tax on the purchase of green products could be implemented, for example Italy has incorporated a rebate (1%) on the purchase of green products. Likewise a tax rebate on entrepreneurs would encourage retailers to promote and sell more of green products. With new legislation, India would be the first of the Nations to have corporate social responsibility bill which mandates the profit making organizations to spend on corporate social activities, France on the other side has introduces mandatory corporate sustainability reporting (Bell, 2002). On similar lines government could mandate the hospitality operators to keep a record of annual food wastage and their preventive steps. An annual track record could be built and based on the performance; incentives could be offered to the operators. An annual hospitality conference organized by the government where the best performers from the industry are rewarded and are invited to share their annual performance and preventive steps implemented in place would help.

9.10.1   FOOD FOR THOUGHT

Most of us do want to eat healthy and also want delicious food to be low in fat, cholesterol and full of healthy nutrients. Some of us are bothered about the calorie intake but most of us only regret when mentored by the medical supervisors or by our family and friends. We walk into the hyper mart and want to buy without hesitation yet feel like to shop more cautiously and sustainably. We do look for healthy alternatives on the organic section of the super market but sometime step back for various reasons. Organic foods are relatively expensive but have multiplier positive effects in the long run. What, How and When do we eat have various consequences on our body and simultaneously on the natural environment. It is imperative to shop and eat keeping in mind the four dimensions of sustainable lifestyle namely society, economy, health and environment. Sustainable practices would help to reduce global warming, reduction of the greenhouse gases, limiting air and water pollution. It shrinks deforestation resulting in erasing soil erosion and preventing drying of the forests. Overall it helps to reduce the depletion of the ozone layer, which eventually would affect the life style of all the living creatures.

On similar principles, Sodexo have formulated 14 guiding principles for a better tomorrow (Figure 3), (Sodexo.com). The figure covers most of the aspects to act sustainably and preserve our environment from getting depleted. Likewise other organizations, hotels, restaurants and catering companies could form their own guiding principles and train their staff to contribute positively to save environment.

FIGURE 3

However, cooking and consuming sustainably, we could have a huge impact on environment. It is vital for us to create awareness among all the class of the society. We need to set goals to preserve natural resources; this can be achieved by formulating guiding principles based on the two pillars of *"Ethics"* and *"Responsibility."* Consequently, we need to consciously use the naturally available resources, educate youngsters and try not to waste food or dispose the leftovers ethically, increase awareness on responsible energy use and carbon footprints, promise ourselves to make the planet toxin free. It is time for us to act together responsibly to sustainable food security locally as well as globally, try to connect with local culture and tradition through community food, be more efficient and generous by giving back to the society.

KEYWORDS

- alternate energy resources
- food disposal management
- food ethics
- green kitchen
- responsible eating
- sustainable development
- sustainable gastronomy

REFERENCES

Alagh, Y. (2010). The food water Interlinkage for sustainable development of India. *South Asian Survey*. 17 (1), 159–178.

Anderson, M. (2008). Rights-based food systems and the goals of food systems reform. *Agriculture and Human Values*. 25 (4), 593–608.

Bell. J. David. (2002). The Role of Government in Advancing Corporate Sustainability. Environmental Futures Forum. 1 (1), 1.

Bhatia, M, S. (2011). International Journal of Cyber welfare and Terrorism. Weapons to be used in cyber war. 1 (3), 11.

Bluhdorn, I. (2007). Sustaining the unsustainable: Symbolic politics and the politics of simulation. Environmental Politics, 16, 251–275.

Bluhdorn, I., and Welsh, I. (2007). Ecopolitics beyond the paradigm of sustainability: A conceptual framework and research agenda. Environmental Politics, 16, 185–205.

Brookes, S. (2009). *Green compost rising.* Available on: www.monkeydish.com/go/oct09. Last accessed 29 September 2013.

Buck, D. Getz, C. Guthman, J. (1997). From Farm to Table: The organic vegetable commodity chain of North Carolina. European society for rural sociology. 37 (1), 1.

Campbell, A., Kapos, V., Lysenko, I., Scharlemann, J., Dickson, B., Gibbs, H.K., Hansen, M. and Miles, L. (2008) Carbon emissions from forest loss in protected areas: Cambridge, UK, UN Environment Program World Conservation Monitoring Center (UNEP-WCMC). Available from: http://www.unep-mc.org/climate/pdf/Carbon_loss_from_PAs_summary.pdf(Accessed 27 August 2013).

Chomka. (2003). Waste oil disposal faces a crysis. *EBSCO Copyright*. 1.

Cocco, D. (2007). Comparative study on energy sustainability of biofuel production chains. *Journal of Power and Energy*. 221 (637).

Cocacola.co.uk. Available from: http://www.coca-cola.co.uk/press-center/2009/september/coca _cola_urges_uk_to_recyle_more_and_cut_their_carbon_footprints.html(Accessed 23 October 2013).

Connley, S. Markey, S. Roseland, M.(2011). Bridging sustainability and the social economy: Achieving community transformation through local food initiatives. *Critical Social Policy.* 31 (2), 308–324.

Cool, J (2008). *Simply Organic A Cookbook for Sustainable, Seasonal, and Local Ingredients.* California: Chronicle Books LLC. 248.

Costanza, R., dArge, R., deGroot, R., Farber, S., Grasso, M., Hannon, B., and van den Belt, M. (1997). The value of the world's ecosystem services and natural capital. Nature, 387, 253–260.

Daily, G. C., Soderqvist, T., Aniyar, S., Arrow, K., Dasgupta, P., Ehrlich, P. R., Walker, B. (2000). Ecology: The value of nature and the nature of value. Science, 289, 395–396.

Doherty, K. (2010). *Carbon Calculation.* Available on: www.foodlogistics.com. Last accessed 15August 2013.

Dominguez, J. (2004) State-of-the-art and new perspectives on vermicomposting research. In: Edwards, C.A. (ed.): CRC Press, Boca Raton, Florida. Earthworm Ecology, pp. 401–424.

Drummond, K. Brefere, L (2009). *Nutrition for Food Service and Culinary Professionals.* 5th ed. California: John Wiley and Sons Inc. 656.

Edwards, A. R. (2005). The sustainability revolution: Portrait of a paradigm shift. Gabriola Island, British Columbia, Canada: New Society.

Epstein, E. (1997). The Science of Composting. Boca Raton, FL: CRC Press.

Falk, Laura Winter, Jeffery Sobal, Carole A. Bisogni, Margaret Connors, C, M. Devine. (2001). Managing Healthy Eating: Definitions, Classifications, and Strategies. Health Education and Behavior. 28 (4), 425–439.

Fishbein, M., and Icek Ajzen. (1972). Attitudes and opinions. Annual Review of Psychology 23:487–544.

Food management (2007), available from: www.food-management.com(Accessed 15th September 2013).

Fox. T. (2013). Global food, Waste not, want not. Available from: http://www.imeche.org/docs/default-source/reports/Global_Food_Report.pdf(Accessed 05th December 2013).

Gustavsson, J. Cederberg, C. Sonesson, U. Oterdijk, R. Meybeck, A. (2011). *Global Food Losses.* Available from: http://www.fao.org/publications/en/. (Accessed 24th Ausust 2013).

Hall, C. Gossling, S (2013). *Sustainable Culinary System.* USA: Routledge.

King, P. (2006). Growing Sustainably: Seeding Sustainably. *Foodservice director.* 19 (8), 20.

KPMG. (2009). Available from: http://www.kpmg.com/GR/en/IssuesAndInsights/Articles Publications/Sustainability/Documents/Sustainable-insight-April-2009.pdf. (Accessed 4 October 2013).

Lewis, T. (2013). There grows the neighborhood': Green citizenship, creativity and life politics on ecoTV. *International Journal of Cultural Studies.* 15 (3), 315–326.

Lopa, J. (2008). Going green in the food service industry and culinary classroom. *CHEF EDUCATOR TODAY.* Spring (spring).

McSwane, D. Richard, H. Rue, R. Graf, A. (2010). *Essentials of Food Safety and Sanitation—Food Safety Fundamentals—*Available from: http://www.fmi.org/forms/store/ProductFormPublic/　　search?action=1&Product_categories_Checkboxes=D#sthash.HIW00BkC.dpuf.

Available: http://www.fmi.org/forms/store/ProductFormPublic/search?action=1&Product_categories_Checkboxes=D. (Accessed 15 September 2013).

Madan, R. (2011). *Locavores drive the 50-mile food fetish.* Available from: http://articles.timesofindia.indiatimes.com/2011-08-28/special-report/29937908_1_carbon-footprint-locavoreguests. (Accessed 4 October 2013).

Miller, R. (2011). *Culinary Trends.* Available from: http://www.restaurant.org/News-Research. (Accessed 15 September 2013).

Mullins, L. J. (2010). *Management in Organizational Behaviour.* Essex: Pearson.

NHS, UK. (2013). Available from: http://www.nhs.uk/Livewell/Goodfood/Pages/eight-tips-healthy-eating.aspx(Accessed 15 September 2013).

Parfitt, J. Barthe, M. Macnaughton, S.(2010). Food waste within food supply chains: quantification and potential for change to 2050. *Philosophical Transactions Biological Changes.* 365 (1554).

Pendrous, R. (2008). *Insight: Manufacturing.* Available from: www.foodmanufacturer.co.uk. (Accessed 29 September 2013).

Ramsey, L. (2013). Seeking what is next. *Foodservice director.* 26 (7), 28.

Sanchez, T, Dennis R.Pullen, K. (2013). Cooking and lighting habits in rural Nepal and Uganda. *Journal of Power and Energy.* 0 (0), 1–13.

Schouw, N. Tjell, J. (2003). Social and institutional feasibility of recycling nutrients in waste in Southern Thailand. *Waste Management and Research.* 21 (1), 393–404.

Sharples, L. (2003). Food tourism in the Peak District National Park, England. In Food tourism around the world: development, management and markets Oxford: Butterworth Heinemann.

Sirakaya, T, Baloglu, S and Mercado, H. (2013). The Efficacy of Sustainability Values in Predicting Travelers' Choices for Sustainable Hospitality Businesses. Cornell Hospitality Quarterly. XX (X), 1–12.

Sloan, Philip, Willy Legrand, and Joseph S. Chen. (2013). Sustainability in the hospitality industry: Principles of sustainable operations. Oxon, UK: Routledge.

Sodexo: http://www.ccr.sodexo.com/

Spash, Clive L. (2002). Informing and forming preferences in environmental valuation: Coral reef biodiversity. Journal of Economic Psychology 23 (5): 665–89.

Starik, M and Kanashiro P. (2013). Toward a Theory of Sustainability Management: Uncovering and Integrating the Nearly Obvious. *Organization and Environment.* 26 (1), 7–30.

Stern, Paul C. (2000). Psychology and the science of human-environment interactions. American Psychologist 55 (5): 523–30.

Stern, Paul C., and Thomas Dietz. 1994. The value basis of environmental concern. Journal of Social Issues 50 (3): 65–84.

Susan, M.and Saunder, K. (2012). Pillar Talk: Local Sustainability Initiatives and Policies in the United States—Finding Evidence of the "Three E's": Economic Development, Environmental Protection, and Social Equity. *Urban Affairs Review.* 49 (5), 678–717.

Taj Hotel. (2013). *food and culture.* Available from: http://www.tajhotels.com/cities/Ooty/foodandculture.html. (Accessed 26 September 2013).

Te Hotel. (2013). *Local food.* Available from: http://tenewdelhi.com/media.php. (Accessed 26 September 2013).

Tesco.co.uk, Available from: http://www.designcouncil.org.uk/about-design/Types-ofdesign/Packaging-design/Sustainability/ (Accessed 25th October 2013).

Tull, D. (2010). *The Natural Kitchen Your Guide to the Sustainable Food Revolution.* Unites States: Process Media. 284.

Watson, E.(2008). *Carbon labeling has not put its best foot prints forward.* Available from: www.foodmanufacturer.co.uk. (Accessed 15 September 2013).

WRAP. (2008). The food we waste (V2). Available from: http://www.wrap.org.uk/category/materials-and-products/food(Accessed 05th December 2013).

USDA.(2008). Available from: http://www.agcensus.usda.gov/Publications/2007/Online_Highlights/Organics/index.php(Accessed 15 September 2013).

Unilever Foods. (2011). *Work Smart wise up on waste.* Available from: http://www.unileverfoodsolutions.co.uk/our-services/your-kitchen/wise-waste-app. (Accessed 24th August 2013).

CHAPTER 10

SUSTAINABLE EMPLOYEE PRACTICES

MONI MISHRA

CONTENTS

ABSTRACT

This chapter highlights the significance of understanding and implementing issues of sustainability in organizations today. It documents an empirical study of the process of developing sustainable employee practices in Williamson Magor and Company Limited which is a multi-local, multi-business unit organization doing business globally. It throws light on what are some of the organizational and managerial changes that have occurred in response to environmental changes in India. It is concluded that the field of research dealing with the focus on sustainable employee practices and role of HRM is in its infancy. Some insights into different integrative mechanisms and subsequent HRM practices are underlined that both Indian and foreign companies are undertaking to compete through a sustainable advantage in this emerging market. The study conducted has been exploratory in nature, and issues of implementation and the involvement of the stakeholders remain a serious concern.

10.1 INTRODUCTION

This chapter highlights the significance of understanding and implementing issues of sustainability in organizations in various sectors of business, today. It documents an empirical study of the process of developing sustainable employee practices in organizations during changing environments brought about by globalization and a world-wide emphasis on sustainable development, and the challenges organizations face in responding to those changing environments. Findings have implications for organizations in the hospitality and tourism sectors.

Few empirical studies have looked into the process of integrative mechanisms to bind changes related to sustainable employee practices in organizations. The role of human resource management during such changing times is one such process. This chapter examines this process with an emphasis on sustainable employee practices via in-depth study of two large firms—one, Williamson Magor, which is the market leader in its respective industry across the globe and the second, Hindustan Unilever Limited, India's largest fast moving company. These two cases have been chosen for this study as they lead us to support the belief that a proactive role of human resource management (HRM), especially focusing on employee practices in organizations which are both sustainable and profitable, is a key factor for an organization functioning effectively in these changing times. Both WM and HUL are producers of products which have a large deployment in the hospitality industry and hence these organizations give insights from the supply side. In the current discourse on Corporate Social Responsibility (CSR) and issues of sustainability, there is an increasing focus on strategic CSR that blends the perspective of profits with the perspective of social goals. The base of the pyramid model (Prahalad, 2005) which exemplifies this approach has used Hindustan Unilever Limited (HUL) as a prime example to illustrate this approach, and adds significantly to current research (Poonamallee, 2011).

Williamson Magor and Company Limited is a multi-local, multi-business unit organization doing business globally. It reflects issues of social integration within the workforce and the wider community as well as the future that migrant workers see for themselves, which are discussed from a human resource perspective. These issues also form a common theme between WM and the hospitality sector (Devine, et al., 2007), and hence insights drawn would be useful. Since deregulation and the opening of the Indian economy in the decade starting 1990, this Indian firm has proactively geared itself with strategies to adapt to foreign competition. The strategy of the firm is to succeed in the vibrant, emerging Indian market.

The chapter looks into the specifics of the Indian market and its characteristics and underlines some of the key concerns of managing organizations in India to promote and integrate sustainable employee practices. Specifically, the chapter focuses on the following issues: what are some of the organizational and managerial changes that have been occurring in response to environmental changes in India; what strategies have managers developed, when faced with competition by both Indian and foreign firms, towards developing and promoting sustainable employee practices; and, what are some of the challenges and difficulties they have encountered in the process.

The potential contribution of the chapter is two-fold. First, for HR managers, researchers, and consultants across various sectors such as hospitality and tourism, as also others, the study provides crucial information regarding context specific HRM variables defining sustainable practices. Second, the chapter throws light on the general notion of sustainable employee practices and the role of HRM in an emerging economy like India and how professionalized HRM practices, with an array of integrative mechanisms emphasizing sustainable employee practices can be aligned to meet the unique challenges that international management offers.

The chapter concludes on the note that the field of research dealing with the focus on sustainable employee practices and role of HRM is in its infancy. The chapter attempts to underline insights into different integrative mechanisms and subsequent HRM practices that both Indian and foreign companies are undertaking to compete through a sustainable advantage in this emerging market. The study conducted has been exploratory in nature, and issues of implementation and the involvement of the stakeholders remain a serious concern, which need to be addressed.

10.2 SUSTAINABILITY: THE EMERGING DISCOURSES AND CONCERNS

Most organizations world over have been forced to take a relook at their strategic initiatives, and weave them into integrative mechanisms that consolidate the changes within the organizations. Towards this end, organizations across the globe are slowly but surely shifting their focus to broader and deeper issues surrounding concerns like sustainability. Organizations have begun to realize the significance of a wide spectrum of activities under the umbrella of sustainability such as green initiatives, education support and empowerment of the underprivileged, responsible environment management, providing on-site laborers humane working conditions, enriching local communities through social and skill building interventions and so on. Organizations are gradually beginning to understand that the sustainability perspective needs to be interwoven in the business model since any form of redevelopment impacts society at large and stakeholders specifically. Sustainability as an integrative mechanism is slowly spreading its wings in various sectors of Indian and international business. Even investors are slowly taking note of a sustainability mindset. The perception is that sustainable business practices are becoming a necessity, and over a period of time this is becoming apparent as well. Organizations are working towards long-term sustainability, and translating sustainability into basic values apart from the vision and mission of the organization. These organizations practice it in a way to sustain in the future—not only at the entrepreneurial level, but at each and every level and tier of the organization. Employees in the organizations seek to align themselves to these values, provided they have the willingness and the integrity, and they are in pursuit of excellence, and look forward to long-term sustainability of every member, including stakeholders and suppliers. In the process, these organizations focus on creation of wealth, and not just generation of profits, whereby the philosophy, which spurs them, is working with people as part of the organization for the overall well being of the nation and the world at large. In the process, in these organizations, the employees get enriched as well. Hence sustainable employee practices become one of the primary areas of focus for today's organizations world over.

10.2.1 REFLECTIONS IN CURRENT RESEARCH

Reviewing significant movements forward in existing literature, one finds that in a world of scarce resources, organizations will increasingly need to focus on "green" performance indicators. Especially while considering the returns on assets, companies will have to essentially take into consideration return on resources (Haanaes, Michael, Jurgens and Rangan, 2013). Studies conducted in this area also indicate that the focus needs to be oriented towards processes evolving naturally, focusing on the local environment and resource, since their objective is continual adaptation keeping pace with the fast changing external environment (Gouillart and Billings, 2013). Hence, co-creation or finding solutions to problems collectively and exploiting opportunities would be an effective strategy. This strategy would enable organizations to connect with external partners and stakeholders, and strive to increase the number of members and segments. Expanding the network will create a very vibrant web of human interactions and firms, which build on these, will be in a win-win situation throughout the ecosystem.

Organizational culture continues to strongly influence performance of employees in organizations (Sinha, 1990). Results of a case study which indicate that a culture that rewards the commitment and hard work of its employees will deliver sustained growth and higher productivity, and a richer pool of talent to draw on (Beyersdorfer, Dessain and Ton, 2012) are in synchronization with findings of Van Maanen and Barley (1984) and Chatman and Jehn (1994), who suggest that almost every organization has certain core values that are shared across the entire organization. Thus what senior managers believe—for example that it is important to reward and foster individual and team efforts—gradually becomes embedded as the core value which finds its spread across the whole organization. At Coca-Cola, while trying to rejuvenate an "inward-looking" "arrogant" corporate culture, the CEO emphasized the significance of creating and embedding sustainable communities in all markets where they operated, to have a sustainable business (Ignatius, 2012).

Another significant thought in this direction is drawn from research conducted in Brazil (Jones, 2012) which indicates that although organizations negotiate in a world where commitment to environmental and ethical issues is rising, organizations need to be clear about their goals—to not necessarily find a niche in the west like the US or Europe, but to have a global portfolio which can be adjusted with regularity to reflect the knowledge acquired in different markets, setting their own standards in developing sustainable employee practices. It implies that organizations need to move beyond the stereotypes of globalization and recognize that growth opportunities lie even in countries like Chile, Argentina and Mexico. Such a perspective will allow new insights to emerge regarding employee practices in organizations.

When excellence is made part of the internal logic of organizations, it lays the foundation for creating a commercial success, and is evidence that following responsible business practices is not in conflict with the bottom-line imperatives of the organizations (Beard and Hornik, 2011). This would create a climate where organizations would be willing to take on a higher burden of developing and maintaining sustainable employee practices.

A common business phenomenon is discussed, which is—when successful organizations face big changes, they often do not succeed in responding effectively. Sull (2002) calls it active inertia, i.e., an organization's tendency to persist in established patterns of behavior. Drawing from examples from industry leaders, four dimensions are focused upon—strategic frames (become blinders), processes (harden into routines), relationships (become shackles) and values (turn into dogmas). Caution is evoked as these dimensions can subvert action if channeled in the wrong direction.

Relevant research is reflected in a study of the concept of psychological contract as a mechanism for exploring mutual expectations of employers and employees in the hospitality, tourism and leisure sector (Kelley-Patterson and Goerge, 2002). An attempt was made to understand the elements that may define the initial psychological contract of the graduate employees as they enter the sector and the types of organizational HR (human resource) practices that are observed to be meeting the needs of the employees. The findings indicate that while graduate recruits had contractual expectations that can be described as transactional (contracts based on economic exchange of short duration), employers had expectations that were both transactional and relational (enduring contracts based on trust). There is evidence that indicates (Morishima, 1996) that contract varies with time, culture and organization; that it can be a powerful influencer on employee satisfaction, productivity and organizational commitment (Shore and Tetrick, 1994).

A study by the Department of Tourism and Hotel Management, Kurukshetra University, India (Chand, 2010) indicates that formal manpower planning, flexible job description, formal system of induction, production/service staff responsible for their service, social appreciation and recognition may constitute the most important HRM practices in the Indian hospitality enterprises. The usage of HRM practices is critical in the context of hospitality enterprises because of people centricity and the services nature of the work involved. Hospitality industry is a people-centric industry where human capabilities are argued to determine the level of service quality and organization performance. Given the rapid growth of the Indian hospitality sector, this study takes forward published empirical investigation related to this research theme and is very insightful.

Another study seeking to investigate the turnover phenomenon in the Jordanian hotel sector and to examine the impact of human resource practices on employees' turnover intentions (Altarawneh and Al-Kilani, 2010) found that job analysis had a significant effect on employees' turnover intentions. Useful strategies suggested included incentive plans based on rewards, bonuses, salaries enhancement and performance appraisal reports which could be reconsidered in the surveyed hotels.

An online debate on training and retaining the best talent in the hospitality industry (Goddard, 2013) reflects employee empowerment and employee participation as significant dimensions, which determine employee retention. It indicates that clear cultural values and strong personal links between teams and leadership help in greater retention of key personnel. Other ideas, which reverberate through the debate, highlight that the best way to retain staff is to give them more responsibility and empower them to make decisions.

A study of restaurant workers in India, in which the effects of empowerment and transformational leadership were examined on employee intention to quit (Gill, Mathur, Sharma and Bhutani, 2011) highlights the importance of retaining staff in the hospitality sector. Through a survey of a sample of restaurant services employees from India, employee perceptions and judgments were examined and it was found that the degree of reduction in employment intention to quit is associated with the improvement in the degree of empowerment and transformational leadership in the Indian hospitality industry. These findings are synchronous with the findings of Avey et al. (2008) and Moynihan and Landyut (2008) wherein they indicate that empowerment reduces employee intention to quit, and also with the findings of Russell (1996) and Oluokun (2003) which highlight that transformational leadership reduces employee intention to quit. The authors emphasize that customer contact service employees (CCSEs) play a boundary-spanning role in the hospitality services industry where they interact with many individuals from inside (fellow employees and managers) and outside (guests) their organization. This large role set requires them to satisfy frequently variegated need and expectations of multiple parties, and only one of their parties is their manager/supervisor (Gill and Mathur, 2007). Since employees are required to perform pro-social behavior and demonstrate dedication to the hospitality organization, it becomes imperative that the Indian hospitality managers and supervisors empower employees and use transformational leadership since empowerment and transformational leadership reduce employee intention to quit.

In a review of the study of Green HR practices and its effective implementation in the organization (Cherian and Jacob, 2012), it has been recommended that organizations essentially need to balance the industrial growth and ensure that the environment where one lives is well preserved and promoted (Daily and Huang, 2001). Researchers have presented the adoption of these practices with a number of different advantages which would ultimately benefit the firm. This has led to the emergence of the ideas of "green and competitive" HR practices in organizations (Wagner, 2007; Molina-Azorin et al., 2009). Benefits such as improvements related to firm's operational performance (Jackson et al., 2011), promotion of teamwork (Jabbour et al., 2010), improvements in organizational culture (Jabbour et al., 2012) and reduction on overall cost (Hart, 1997) were associated with the adoption of such green and competitive HR practices. The study also identifies that the management systems will enable improvements in synchronization with other management strategies of the firm (Wagner, 2007). Researchers in these studies are giving importance to the adoption of environmental practices as a key objective of organizational functioning making it important to identify with the support of human resource management practices (Jackson et al., 2011; Daily and Huang, 2011; Sarkis et al., 2010). Current debate around the issue reflects uncertainty associated with how green management principles can be implemented effectively in organizations thereby arriving at improved sustainability for the organization.

10.3 SUSTAINABILITY AT WILLIAMSON MAGOR

The forces of globalization and the changing business environments have triggered policy changes in the strategic initiatives taken by McLeod Russel India Limited (Tea Division), a Williamson Magor (WM) Group Enterprise for superior performance—by focusing on people as its sustainable drivers. A study of the organization highlights the challenges that the organization faced during the shifting of alignments and also shows how they responded by re-designing their internal processes (Mishra, 2013). A vital component in this process that has helped the organization to leverage itself in the current times is a culture of sustainability.

10.3.1   WILLIAMSON MAGOR: A HISTORICAL ROADMAP

Williamson Magor is among the largest tea plantation groups in India, owning tea estates, which are more than 130 years old. It represents about one-fifth of the total tea produced in Assam. The company which was earlier 'Williamson Magor' is now owned by the Magor family of Kolkata, and functions as McLeod Russel India Ltd. They have tea estates in Assam, West Bengal, Vietnam and Uganda. The enterprise started in 1869, when two Englishmen formed a firm to take care of the Assam tea estates, and based themselves in Kolkata. Earlier their office was at 7, new China Bazaar Street from where they moved to 4, Mangoe Lane in 1894. The Williamson Magor office continues at this location in Kolkata. As the partnership grew stronger, in 1954 its status changed to that of a limited company, and was renamed Williamson Magor and Company Limited. In 1964, Brij Mohan Khaitan became its Managing Director. Soon thereafter, Williamson Magor merged with another company, Macneill and Barry Limited, which had interests in other businesses as well as in tea. The new company, which was now called Mcneill and Magor Limited, became the single largest producer of Assam tea, when the Guthrie family of UK sold their shareholdings, including the Makum and Namdang Tea Companies in the McLeod Russel Group to Khaitans. The company was once again renamed Williamson Magor and Co. Ltd in 1992.

Some years later, McLeod Russel India Limited was merged with Eveready Industries India Limited after which the new Company had two divisions to look after—the bulk tea division which managed the tea estates of Mcleod Russel and the battery division. In 2004, the two divisions demerged into two separate companies, and from now onwards, McLeod Russel could focus on its core business of tea production. Gradually, Mcleod Russel acquired Borelli Tea holdings (2005), Doom Dooma Tea Company (2006) and the Moran Tea Company India Limited (2007), all of which have been merged making McLeod Russel India Limited the largest tea producing company on the globe.

Some international collaborations have also added a feather to its cap. In 2009, Borelli acquired Phu Ben Tea Company Limited from Vietnam and in 2010, the Rwenzori Tea Investments Limited from James Finlay International Tea Holdings Limited was acquired and added to its basket. Also, the Uganda

Wing of Mcleod Russel runs six estates producing over 15 million kilograms of tea annually.

10.3.2 THE METHOD

I drew upon the experiences of a large number of managers from the Tea Division of the Williamson Magor Group Enterprise shared in terms of narratives obtained through in-depth interviews. At the start of the research project, after their consent was taken, confidentiality of data to protect identities was assured. Qualitative research, that is, case study, gave a thorough grounding and a feel for real-life situations especially when research was in its early stages. To develop a clear understanding of the innovative usage of sustainable employee practices and strategies that were adopted during promotion of employee growth and development in organizations for superior performance, there was a need to look at varied data from multiple sources and study the phenomenon in its own context. The case study method permitted a holistic analysis of a wide range of dimensions, open ended and descriptive data, and multiple data sources and data collection techniques within the research setting.

This study focuses on in-depth narratives of managers in the organization through which the processes that this organization followed via the role of innovative sustainable employee practices during promotion of employee growth and development were explored and understood. Yin's (1984) model follows a holistic analysis of a wide range of dimensions while Eisenhardt (1989) uses multiple case design as it provides more scope for attempting generalization to a single-case setting. A deliberate choice has been made to focus on depth rather than breadth, keeping in mind that it is unrealistic to try to attempt both detailed, in-depth analyzes of organizations and also look at a large sample of firms at the same time (Mintzberg 1979; Ulrich 1997).

The choice of the organization was done taking into consideration the following factors: willingness of the organization to help in the study by providing data and an organization that was proactively promoting employee growth and development in its organization as drawn from pilot interviews and as reported in business journals/books (Piramal, 1997). McLeod Russel India Limited (Tea Division), a Williamson Magor Group Enterprise was chosen as the site for the study.

In order to understand the contingent effects of the turbulent environment, both archival and primary data were collected through interviews. To start with, an in-depth analysis of archival data was undertaken, analyzing articles and documents concerning each organization, including consultant reports, annual reports, and industry reports.

The data required in this study called for top management involvement. That was because the information involved strategic decisions, which were to be taken by the organization, and only the top management was able to take the necessary steps to process the information sought. The data required were mostly post-hoc. The interviewees needed to have knowledge of events and also be either participants in the change process or have observed it closely, so that they could reconstruct an accurate account of the strategies. This research also necessitated interaction from a wide array of informants from both the HR as well as other functional departments. Interviewing a range of informants enabled crosschecking of the data collected, identifying multiple perspectives and the different interpretations of the issue within the organizations.

Continuous effort was made to increase the reliability and validity of the study through multiple engagements with the managers at their work settings. Multiple respondents across functions and hierarchy together with HRM heads, professionals and executives provided the required reliability and validity. They provided insights into the growth of the organization during the economic liberalization process and verified the details in the subsequent interviews. The study undertook several measures in getting accurate and actual information. Trust was built with the organization and executives with multiple visits and by keeping contact during the course of the research project.

Before the fieldwork was undertaken, an interview protocol was prepared which was improved and revised after discussions with experienced academicians and HR professionals. There were various questions in the interview protocol which were related to different dimensions which were considered to be playing a significant role in the study, such as the changing nature of the environment, processes and strategies adopted to keep pace with these changes and promote sustainability in the organizations through employee practices, and so on. The respondents were also asked to describe their roles and contributions to the change process, the climate and culture of the organization, formal and informal relationships, and the implementation issues during adoption of the change processes.

Results were compared and contrasted across multiple correspondents and functions and themes, which emerged were further pursued to extract leads to understand in-depth the sustainability process. Table 1.1 provides some of the important questions that were asked during the interview process.

TABLE 1.1   Interview Questionnaire.

- What are the recent changes in your organization?
- What are the business challenges? What strategies did you adopt to fight these challenges?
- Can you share a brief history of the tea gardens?
- Describe the structure and composition of the workforce in the tea estates.
- Was the HR strategy related to the overall business strategy? If yes, why and how, if not, why do you think it is not? How would you think you would achieve your strategy without people being involved?
- Do you think sustainability needs to be prioritized in the agenda of organizations?
- Is sustainability understood as an idea by workers at the operative level?
- Tell me some milestones, current/recent activities and new strategies and practices. How were these activities operationalized and implemented?
- Tell me the practices of sustainability that you follow in your organization.
- Did the introduction of these new activities impact commitment of workers to the organization; opportunities to develop new skills and innovate; vision and values; working and living conditions;

The conversations revolved around the need to examine the role of sustainable employee practices contributing towards employee growth and development in the organization in the context of a turbulent environment. Detailed field notes and transcripts of the conversations were maintained and many of the conversations were recorded with the consent of the managers.

10.3.3 REPRESENTATIONS OF SUSTAINABILITY IN THE NARRATIVES OF MANAGERS AT WILLIAMSON MAGOR GROUP (TEA DIVISION)

Given the backdrop of the organization, clearly Williamson Magor (WM) has a very large employee base. WM is by far the largest as far as tea is concerned. It has companies in Uganda and Vietnam, which are all part of the McLeod Russel Group. WM has more than 53 estates in North East India out of which 48 are in Assam and the rest are in North Bengal. It manufactures approximately 1.15 million kilograms of bulk tea, which by a long shot, is the largest. WM has three levels at which the employees operate—one is the corporate office at Kolkata; one really large employee base is in the estates—WM would have nothing less than 1 lakh plus employees worldwide—this is the picture at the grassroots level and the upper echelons. WM also has people at the supervisory level. In all these three levels, because of the very nature of the job, it is a very niche industry, and it is a very conservative industry in the sense that this is an industry, which is 175 years old. The company itself is more than 130 years old; it is also mainly a rural based industry where the corporate strength would not be more than 100.

The base-level workforce at WM is essentially migratory population, especially in India. This population came in many years ago, when the British started tea estates. They cleared forests in Assam and North Bengal and then they brought in the intelligentsia to look after the account books. The British drew these people from the local ethnic population—there were Bengalis from erstwhile Bengal, which is East Pakistan, and there were local ethnic Assamese with a certain level of education, who managed account books and other sundry records. With the management in place and the scribes in place, one required the grassroot level workers. It was, however, difficult to find locals who would be willing partners in this endeavor, as they were very peaceful and a contented lot, not wanting much—they were happy with their land which used to give them one crop, and were not really interested in menial work or hard work. Hence at the grassroots level, it was difficult to get people in sufficient numbers for the tea gardens. So tribals were brought in from Chotanagpur, and from Jharkhand. At that time, they had the system of coolie-sardars, or 'coolies' as they were called. Coolie sardars were employed on a commission basis. They were brought in from different places like Andhra Pradesh and Telangana, in the beginning of the 19th century, somewhere around 1836–1837. In this way, people were constantly being brought in, throughout the 19th century and even towards the early part of the 20th century. These people settled down in these tea gardens, and generation after generation, multiplied and stayed on. So, essentially, these people belong to various tribal groups—the Mundas, the Kharias and also the Telengana tribals.

10.3.4 SUSTAINABILITY INITIATIVES

10.3.4.1 SHARING OF REVENUES: THE SYNERGY OF THE 'TEA TRIBES'

Even today, in the state of Assam, if one looks closely, these tribals are possibly more in number than the ethnic Assamese. They are the largest vote bank in the state. One would wonder that they would probably have merged with the local population. The fact is, they have merged very well but they have formed a very different, a very clear-cut identity of their own. They call themselves the 'tea tribes' and they still follow the various social customs, which their brethren follow in their own home states. They follow all the social, religious and ethnically specific festivals. They are very clear about their roots. They are still deeply connected with their roots and, for instance, they still speak their native language. They speak Assamese and also Bengali, but among themselves they speak their own language. So they have maintained a very close connect with their roots despite having merged into the mainstream population. This is an India -specific characteristic and as there are tea estates primarily in Assam, this would be the story of Assam.

In Vietnam it is slightly different. The Communist Government there has basically given holdings to each person. Each individual has a plot of land. The plot of land belongs to the government—the State. The bush that is grown belongs to the individual and his family and McLeod Russel Group have factories, which buy the leaves from them. And when they buy the leaves from them, they also advise them and guide them on the best agricultural practices. That essentially is the story in Vietnam. Hence, as a private company, WM is buying the material, continuing to treat it and sell it in the commercial market and in the process, they also engaging with them. It is sustaining very well this way. This is the current scenario in Vietnam.

Even in India today, there is a new element that has come in, that is, there are a lot of small tea growers in Assam and Bengal. People have converted their smallholdings into primarily tea growing areas and they are also selling their tea to WM and to various other companies. Based on the market trends, payments are made to them, which are, hence, very profitable. In this way it is sustainable for them as well for the company. It is also important to understand that tea in India is a seasonal crop. It starts cropping in the month of March and continues till November, after which, in December it tapers off. So during the peak flushing/cropping period WM engages even the temporary workers. It is to be noted that all the workers are housed in the estate and these temporary workers come from the families of the permanent workers. There are a few who come from outside and also a few who come from the immediate vicinity. Everyone is provided housing facilities or given a house rent allowance instead.

In Africa WM has an estate or a large holding which is the field as well as the factory, and everything is owned by the Company. Also, the work-force there is an ethnic work-force drawn from the local regions. In all the estates under the ambit of WM, practically 90% of the work-force is resident within the estate. It is important to note here that the estate holdings of WM are large, i.e., almost 800 hectares, or 3000 acres. So roughly in about 2500 to 3000 acres one would have a work-force/population of about 5000 people, out of which 1200 would be roughly permanent workers and another 1000 workers would be temporary.

10.3.4.2 SUSTAINABILITY: THE ENVIRONMENT AS AN ENABLER WITH A FOCUS ON MEDICAL AND HEALTH-CARE ASSISTANCE

Proactive efforts are made to ensure that workers are leading comfortable and healthy lives. Consistent development programs are being rolled out to ensure the well being of all the workers. Most of the workers who are working with WM are residents of the estate. They are being provided facilities and care over and above the wages that they get. They are all part of the provident fund system, the gratuity system and all other mandatory the laws of the land. Two very important acts—the Plantation Labor Act and the Factories Act—are implemented with precision for the workforce. These two acts are all encompassing and cover a very wide range of benefits for the workers. They are provided health care—every estate has a hospital where small cases are attended. In the hospital, WM have a full time doctor and complete paramedical staff; they also have an outpatient and an in-patient department, as well as advanced facilities for surgical interventions. Also, for any medical care that cannot be provided in the estate, the cases are referred to hospitals in the nearest town. So, for WM, health of the workers is a priority, as also family welfare.

Gender issues are recognized and attended to with requisite care. Women's empowerment is also focused upon while implementing these programs. WM encourages every mother to deliver her child at the hospital, and gives incentives to people to make sure that would-be mothers are brought to the hospital for delivery. Post-delivery mother and childcare is a primary concern. WM has one central hospital in the Dooars in North Bengal and two on each bank of the river Bramhaputra. In these hospitals managed by WM, there is a much larger compliment of specialists as well as instrumentation, and cases, if need be, are referred to these hospitals. And in case even these hospitals cannot handle the matter WM sends them to government hospitals in Dibrugarh, Guwahati or Siliguri.

10.3.4.3   SUSTAINABILITY REFLECTED THROUGH ETHICAL WORK PRACTICES

WM has won accolades for the futuristic steps forward that they have taken towards applying sustainability practices to their organization. All levels and hierarchies at WM have been closely involved in the entire process as ideas of sustainability, which have emanated from the top management, have cascaded down to the very last tier of workers at the grassroots level in the organization.

WM has undertaken to acquire certain certifications, which are ethically compliant—international certificates such as ISO 22000 and similar others. Apart from these, the special ethically compliant certifications which WM have gone ahead to acquire include Fair Trade Certification since 2008, and Rain Forest Alliance Certification, more recently. A closer look at these certifications will help understand their flavor. A number of estates of WM are fair trade certified. They have about eight estates on fair trade, i.e., these estates are subjected to a certain set of standards which are worldwide standards created in Europe. Also, there are a number of principles, which they need to follow to maintain standards—of ethics, health and environment. They are also subjected to audits by independent bodies annually, which provide them cluster certifications. With such a certification, once it comes through, the organization is accorded the status of a fair trade purchaser or a fair trade supplier. WM is a fair trade supplier, which means that as an estate it has the certificate to operate as a fair trade supplier. WM would supply to another party, say X, who is, similarly, a certified fair trade buyer. The buyer would buy WM's tea at a price which is market friendly, but because he supporting these ethical standards, he is also willing to pay a certain margin over and above the agreed price, which in today's context is half a Euro for every quantity of tea which is purchased. This practice actually indicates an appreciation of the fact that both parties are meeting the quality standards. What it means is, since party X finds a partner in WM, it therefore offers WM certain benefits.

It is important to note here that when the buyer is paying WM half a euro extra, the extra money is not coming to the management at WM. At the grassroots level, the estate forms what is known as the 'Fair Trade Body,' which is a registered body. This body constitutes only elected members of the workforce and does not include the members of the management board. The management acts as a guide, but does not have the exercise to vote. Hence the extra money goes to workers at the grass-root level—there is a bank account opened in which it is deposited and they decide how to use that money for their welfare. WM has Fair Trade Bodies in Africa, and in India and has other certifications in Vietnam.

The management at WM acts as a guide for them at this juncture, advising them on the kinds of projects in which they can invest, ranging from new ventures like, for example, bio-gas treatment plants which would help generate energy, or compost manufacture plants, or a dairy among the non-employed people, to maintaining and promoting the already existing projects like 'night schools,' for which support is also provided by the management. Advice is given on how to fence off their houses in the estates, how to build 'pucca' drainage so that there is no accumulation of water, making a library, or making a small 'pathshala,' and other similar activities, which will benefit in their day to day living. These activities are outside the mandatory requirements established by the government, which organizations have to essentially adhere to. WM engages in these activities on a continuous and on-going basis, to improve the living conditions of, and infuse a sense of well being in its large workforce. It enables them to decide how best to use the extra money that is coming their way as a result of the company adhering to certain high ethical standards. These changes have not happened overnight; they have been very gradual. Tremendous appreciation has been received for such endeavors from the grass root level workers. Many estates of WM, which are non-Fair Trade, are showing a keen desire to get similar benefits as their Fair Trade estate counterparts. WM is trying to roll out a program whereby the Fair Trade estates adopt some of the nearby estates of WM of the non-Fair Trade category, so that the benefits percolate to a larger number of the workforce. So WM is charting out a novel path towards sustainability for the future, for the growth and development of the organization as well as for its workforce.

The latest is a certification called the Rainforest Alliance Certification, which focuses on environment standards, and which many of the estates of WM have earned. Again, as per this certification, a large body of international buyers would be buying tea from companies which are ethically compliant and rated accordingly, like WM. The difference between Trade Fair Certification and Rainforest Alliance Certification is that in the latter, no extra money is being shared with the workforce, but the organization is pending that money and ensuring that it is able to maintain and protect the environment. There are a series of principles and approximately 900 criteria which the estates have to meet; out of these, certain criteria are mandatory, which the organizations 'must' comply with, while marks are assigned for compliance with other criteria, after which the rainforest certification is given to the estate. The estate/

organization then gets a priority as far as selling its products to the outside world is concerned. So the organization stands to gain in the long-term.

10.3.5 IMPLICATIONS

The benefits of such sustainability initiatives being implemented by the organization are clearly reflected in outcomes such as retention of employees, a high level of loyalty to the firm, and deeper commitment. Implications point towards the fact that as already indicated, organizations in the hospitality sector will have to undertake similar efforts to attract and retain talent. Current literature indicates that employee empowerment and employee participation are significant dimensions, which determine employee retention. If a psychological contract gets established among the employers and employees based on such dimensions through sustainability initiatives similar to those described above, firms will have a larger number of employees who are loyal, deeply committed and would work beyond the call of duty to take the firm forward. Hence, the hospitality and tourism community will need to weave in their understanding and implementation a variety of views concerning sustainability and also address the economic, social and environmental issues facing the industry and the planet. They will also need to understand how to blend the different strands of sustainability in their business operations in varied economic and political contexts and times.

Sustainability: The Experience of Hindustan Unilever Limited

Sustainability has been a priority with Hindustan Lever across all its products, processes and plants, especially in the recent years. The company's focus on sustainability has been reiterated, as conveyed in the ideas of William Hesketh Lever, the founder of Lever Brothers. HUL primarily empathizes on the maxim of 'doing well while doing good.' Hence it becomes a much larger purpose, for which commitment is manifested in terms of global sustainability activities by HUL.

HUL, through its Unilever Sustainable Living Plan (USLP) which was launched in 2010, gave a massive push to its sustainability drive as well as defined the future course of action for the company: It aimed to 'double the size of the business while halving the carbon footprints of its products, increase the company's positive social impact and source 100% of agricultural raw materials sustainably' (Economic Times, August 15, 2013). As a result, in almost 190 countries across the globe, HUL brought about significant changes in the way it manages it diverse businesses. A discerning shift was seen in the policy of the company to 'delink growth from environmental impact and recouple growth with societal good' (Economic Times, August 15, 2013).

Challenges in Attaining Leadership in Sustainability Initiatives

(a) Delegation of Responsibility in Implementing Sustainability

It has not been an easy route to success as far as rolling out sustainability at HUL is concerned. India has been one of the first countries where USLP was launched along with the parent company, Unilever Global. The company has set as one of its agenda cutting back its carbon footprint for the entire value chain from vendor up to the customer, as consumers play a vital role in impacting the goods produces by HUL.

Competition from other players in the field like Proctor &Gamble and ITC is tough in the marketplace every day. However, the program of sustainability has been implemented by HUL with great success. An innovative strategy has been to delegate the responsibility of injecting sustainability into brands with the brand managers and the category heads, and sustainability is not being tackled through a separate division. Monitoring is done by a cross-functional governing council. Every business unit has had targets tied to sustainability since inception of the USLP. Impact of business for the end user is what HUL is primarily interested in. Innovation continues to be the focus, and at least 25–30% of the HUL portfolio gets innovated on, at any point of time. Innovations which the brand teams have since developed include a new packaging for Pond's talcum that uses less plastic. This idea, once it was floated by the brand and category team, went through a rigorous Innovative Process Management (IPM) process, which included questions related to environmental impact. The savings in plastic could be used to add attributes or offer a better price to the consumer. They are now reflecting a mindset wherein brands are being crafted in the spirit of sustainability, that is, sustainability has to be woven in the brand promise itself. It is only such brands, which are investing in this, which will be the ones that are 'future ready.' HUL is using flexible packing, in some cases pouches that have caps and can be reused, across products like Lifebuoy hand wash Liquid, Shower Gels, Domex, Kisan, even tea.

(b) Focus on Use of Environment-Friendly Products

The research question to which HUL is trying to find an answer is whether using less plastic in the packaging will be reason enough for a customer to opt for the Ponds brand. A conclusion is still to be reached but preliminary research shows that although consumers may say that they care about environment-friendly products, when the time comes to act, they go back to their regular brands—this phenomenon is called the 3:30 paradox: only 3% of the 30% of consumers, who call themselves ethical shoppers, are such. However, what will definitely matter in future is the way a company does business: There is a certain proportion of customers for each product in the market, who will have respect for and even admire companies that have sustainable objectives. This, in due course, will translate into positive choices favoring the brand. In the long run, it will develop among the consumers a positive attitude, loyalty and a basis for a relationship with the company and its products. This may be a very small percentage of the total consumers, but even then it would make a real difference to the brand and finally the company in question.

(c) Creating Sustainable Eco-Systems

While implementing strategies to promote sustainability at HUL, supply chain team at the organization has had to take a major responsibility. HUL is engaged in the process of creating ecosystems where sourcing of agri-materials is sustainable. This is also a requirement as per ULSP at HUL. Secondary sources indicate, for example, that for the ketchup business of HUL, for which it needs a lot of tomato paste, HUL joined hands with the Government of Maharashtra involving around 1,500 farmers in Nasik to grow tomatoes using less water and fertilizer, and the results are encouraging with nearly 70% of paste requirements now being fulfilled with sustainably sourced tomatoes (Economic Times, August 2, 2013). It is also indicated that though the percentage varies in different products, the company is getting its sourcing policy in place. While in tea, 15% is being sourced from sustainable sources, in palm oil, 100% sourcing is covered by 'Green Palm' certificates. Also an innovative practice is that HUL has started is that there is a team of agriculture experts within HUL's sourcing department who help farmers with sustainable agricultural practices. All these innovations are linked to improving the effective and successful functioning of the organization, and in developing a more satisfied and loyal workforce committed to the organization with a long-term orientation.

When sustainability at HUL focuses on manufacturing and logistics, the main areas to be dealt with are waste, water and energy. HUL uses the 2008 carbon footprint as baseline for comparison with current findings. Its serious intent in implementing these plans is visible in actions like, for example, factories at some locations being shut down completely for a day to measure the water and energy consumption and check for leakages. Waste that was shipped to landfill from factories was eliminated, and of the 38 factories, today 33 are zero landfill; also, reduction in total waste from HUL's manufacturing sites stands at 77% as against the 2008 baseline (Economic Times, August 2, 2013). These measures are commendable in the light of the fact that very few organizations have in the current years shown this king of commitment, translated into actual action.

(d) Innovative Business Practices

Evidence also points to the fact that sustainability brings tremendous benefits when the constraints force innovation. In HUL's factory in Mysore, for example, the waste that was left after processing coffee was used in a biomass boiler as fuel. HUL is now systematically shifting to fuel that uses factory waste or waste from other industries like coconut shells or cashew nuts. While only 8% of energy consumed was from renewable sources two years back, today it is touching 20% (Economic Times, August 2, 2013). At HUL, the logistics team is also closely involved in promoting sustainability. It works on four pronged principles—'travel less, load more, use alliances and buy smart.' At HUL, therefore, through smart planning, information technology and some native intelligence, the warehouse and logistics operation is designed in a way to minimize travel and cut carbon footprint. HUL moves 30 lakh tons of product every year, and hence, even minor savings accumulate into substantial gains. The company also takes care that service levels do not get affected at distributor level in this aggressive search for best possible sustainable solution. HUL's service levels have increased to around 95%in terms of case fills, from 88% 3 years ago.

Indeed, the approach of HUL for doing business is different. This is clearly reflected in the way the company is running its water business, which it took off in 2008–09, scaling up subsequently. HUL has redefined the category with innovative products that include an industry first tabletop purifier and the first electric purifier that allows storage. Despite the price of the purifier, the effectiveness of the machine in terms of germ kill is the same across all of their products. Innovations are also led by the philosophy with which the organization moves—in its electric purifier, if the battery drains out, the product shuts off completely. This is because, in line with its safety promise, the company chose to opt for safe water or no water. More than 9 million people gained access to safe drinking water from Pureit in India by the end of 2012.

(e) Eliciting Local Support

HUL has businesses across seven countries, including Brazil, Sri Lanka, China, Indonesia and Bangladesh. Water business is getting special attention at HUL, because water is a very important business for Unilever corporate. Apart from the business concerns, and emphasizing their responsibility towards society and environment, Unilever has set up a Unilever Foundation that works along with NGOs, state governments and governmental agencies to engage local communities in conserving water. Partnerships have resulted in water conservation potential to the extent of 25 billion liters for HUL. In line with the same philosophy of giving back to society, as part of its ULSP promise of helping more than a billion people by 2020 in protecting lives and providing hygiene, brands like Lifebuoy are spearheading behavioral change programs with an aim to reduce incidence of diseases, and promote healthy living. In 2012 Lifebuoy hand-washing programs reached over 17 million people and since 2010, it has touched more than 50 million people. In the last few years the scale, seriousness and resources given to HUL's programs have changed immensely in magnitude. The company now visualizes it as an investment to the future of the brand. HUL has managed to build a solid track record in terms of adopting sustainable practices after two years of devoted attention to it. The innovations teams are working in a planned and systematic manner to bring out products that use less water, whether it is Magic, a product that uses significantly less water in rinsing laundry and is currently being test marketed in Andhra Pradesh or TRESSemme, a dry shampoo. As concerns about planet earth mingle with concerns of corporations in doing business, sustainability is being voiced as a primary concern by more and more people, as also more and more employees in more and more ways. Some companies which have a vision understand that it is not just about goodwill, but about genuinely caring for the world and its people, and they are taking proactive steps to develop and synergize sustainable practices with organizational business needs. Large internal change programs at HUL have had some positive results—when the USLP program was implemented, it inculcated a sense of meaning and purpose in the HUL workforce. This has inspired them to work and innovate for a brighter future. Other organizations are also emulating HUL for similar reasons and moving in similar directions.

Some of HUL's sustainability accomplishments include the following: 45 million people globally gained access to safe drinking water from Pureit in-home water purifier till 2012; by the end of 2012, 66% of HUL's food portfolio (by volume) is compliant with the 5 gram salt target; the company has more than 30,000 freezers with Hydrocarbon (HC) technology deployed in India; over 60% of tomatoes used in Kissan ketchup in India are from sustainable sources; a total of 77 tea estates in Assam, West Bengal and Tamil Nadu have been certified 'Sustainable Estates' by the Rainforest Alliance till the end of 2012; Kwality Wall's mobile vending operations provide entrepreneurship opportunities to over 6,500 migrant laborers across India; by 2015, HUL expects 70 billion liters of water to be harvested, 1 million people to benefit and 15% rise in crop production expected in villages across India; carbon-dioxide emissions per ton of production in India reduced by 22% water use by 29 % waste by 77% compared to 2008; 30 sites became zero-discharge site out of 38 sites; rainwater harvesting implemented in 22 sites.

(Source: Economic Times, August 2, 2013).

10.4   DIRECTIONS FOR FUTURE RESEARCH ON SUSTAINABLE EMPLOYEE PRACTICES: SOME REFLECTIONS

Primarily as researcher, I have tried to understand what is the level at which organizations are seriously considering providing and creating best practices—industry specific, organization specific and business specific, which would sustain overall good human living. Organizations also need to contribute in giving back to society, which may be understood in terms of Corporate Social Responsibility and other such things. But what one is looking for are changes at a much deeper level, since organizations are operating in the context of a society—in fact, organizations are a very intrinsic part of society. What is being examined as a thesis is that unless and until there is an attitude to take care of these people who are employees in the organizations and would be primarily dependent on these organizations, given the fact that there is a power equation that operates in all societies, and given the fact that the organizations are the providers and determiners of the quality of life of these people to a large extent, people will not be benefitted in the real sense. So, what needs to be understood as research endeavor is (i) what is the level of maturity of organizations vis-à-vis such ideas, and (ii) are organizations actually making attempts to translate these kinds of ideas in terms of do-able action, in a way such that it is actually making a difference to the lives of people?

The discourse above reflects the idea that sustainable management and related aspects are becoming agenda points for the business community in India, although they have not been translated very effectively in concrete business practices across various business sectors. The following concerns have emerged as significant and in need of immediate attention:

- What are sustainable employee practices? Primarily, sustainable employee practices focus upon developing a sustainable strategy, which must address the interests of all the stakeholders, especially those on the fringe of society who are primary beneficiaries of the profits of the organizations. Also, these sustainable strategies need to be closely linked with sustainable employee practices that are 'do-able' actions to sustain the environment and to sustain life.
- Why are they important for current day organizations? How do these 'people practices' link with sustainable business practices?
- A sustainability mindset needs to be developed along with tangible successes in organizations, which is a big challenge. For example, a company (name withheld to maintain confidentiality) has saved 300 million pounds in costs through eco-efficiency programs in manufacturing

operations, which is part of a plan to halve its environmental footprint by 2020. Initiatives ranged from small actions like ensuring lights are turned off to larger investments such as biomass boilers. However, along with tangible successes, there are challenges in terms of how to change consumption habits of its consumers. Towards this end, the company is stepping up efforts to find new business models to drive product innovation and research. A related challenge before the company is to ensure continuity in good practices among vendors and suppliers.

- Are organizations exhibiting a sustainability mindset? Is it being reflected in employee practices?
- Are investors also taking note of a sustainability mindset, and the need for employee practices to promote the same in organizations of the future?

10.5 CONCLUSION: THE ROAD AHEAD

The exposition has underlined some insights into the different mechanisms and subsequent sustainable employee practices being undertaken by the Williamson Magor Group to compete in a globally competitive market. It takes initial steps towards exploring the complex process of employee growth and development through sustainable employee practices at WM. HUL's case also highlights similar issues. And there are some answers provided to questions like: Can sustainable employee practices be designed to facilitate employee growth and development? Can managers and practitioners be trained to effectively implement such practices in organizations across various sectors in India and abroad? Can evaluations and rewards be tied to successful implementation of such sustainable employee practices?

In India, which is the largest black tea producing nation in the world with a production of 1,100 million kilograms, in 2013, employee practices are finding a translation in the development of a sustainable code to promote responsible and ethical sourcing of teas. It is these practices, which promote growth and development of the employees as well as organizations. These measures have been taken up to safeguard against poor quality of tea produced, and also because there is a stress on quality as purchasing power in the country is increasing together with the awareness for food safety standards, which is spreading fast. The sustainability code is being developed in partnership with the Sustainable Trade Initiative, Solidaridad of Netherlands, Rainforest Alliance with the support of Hindustan Unilever (HUL). The code, which will be marked on teas and packets by producers and packeteers through a logo, encompasses all aspects of tea production and seeks to embrace sustainability principles to boost productivity and maintain safety standards to include quality compliance. It is important to note that a very significant part of this whole exercise is the inclusion of small tea growers, who contribute 33% of India's total tea production, in the mainstream. Initially, 600 factories, 500,000 farm workers and 40,000 small growers will be included under the India Sustainable Tea Program (Economic Times, July 4, 2013).

B schools in India are planning to start a course on sustainable management so as to make future managers adept at tackling environmental problems, social and human rights issues, developmental economics and corporate social responsibility, and to weave these in a workable business model (Economic Times, 24 September, 2013). Such a vision for the future indicates that sustainability is being understood as something 'fundamental' to organizational existence and excellence.

KEYWORDS

- environment
- integrative mechanism
- management
- narrative
- organizations
- sustainability

REFERENCES

Altarawneh, I. and Al-Kilani, M.H. (2010). Human Resource Management and Turnover Intentions in the Jordanian Sector. In Research and Practice in Human Resource Management, Vol. 18 (1), June 2010, pp. 46–59.

Avey, J.B., Hughes, L.W., Norman, S.M., and Luthans, K.W. (2008). Using positivity, transformational leadership and empowerment to combat employee negativity. Leadership and Organizational Development Journal, 29 (2), pp. 110–118.

Bayersdorfer, D., Dessain, V. and Ton, Z. (2012). Bonuses in Bad Times. Harvard Business Review, July August 2012, pp. 153–157.

Beard, A. and Hornik, R. (2011). 'It's Hard to Be Good.' Harvard Business Review, November 2011, pp. 88–96.

Chand, M. (2010). Human Resource Management Practices in Indian Hospitality Enterprises: An Empirical Analysis. In Managing Leisure, Vol. 15, pp. 4–16, Routledge.

Chatman, J. A., and Jehn, K. A. (1994). Assessing the relationship between industry characteristics and organizational culture: How different can you be? Academy of Management Journal, Vol. 37 (3), pp. 522–553.

Cherian, J. and Jacob, J. (2011). A Study of Green HR Practices and its Effective Implementation in the Organization: A Review. In International Journal of Business and Management, Vol. 7 (21), pp. 25–33.

Daily, B. and Huang, S. (2001). Attaining sustainability through attention to human resource factors in environmental management. In International Journal of Operations and Production Management, Vol. 21 (12), 1539–1552.

Economic Times, July 4, 2013. Sustenance Comes at a Price for Tea Lovers.

Economic Times, August 2, 2013. HUL's 'Sustainability' Battle: How CEO Nitin Paranjpe is trying to Attain a Leadership Position.

Economic Times, September 24, 2013. New B-School Buzz: Sustainability Management.

Eisenhardt, K. (1989). Building Theories from Case Study Research. Academy of Management Review, Oct 1989, Vol. 14 (4), pp. 532–550.

Gill, A. and Mathur, N. (2007). Improving employee dedication and prosocial behavior. International Journal of Contemporary Hospitality Management, Vol. 19 (4), pp. 328–334.

Gill, A. Mathur, N., Sharma, S.P. and Bhutani, S. (2011). The Effects of Empowerment and Transformational Leadership on Employee Intentions to Quit: A Study of Restaurant Workers in India. In International Journal of Management, Vol. 28 (1), pp. 217–229.

Goddard, D. (2013). Training and Retaining the Best Talent: The Online Debate. Caterer and Hotelkeeper, Vol. 203, 4763, pp. 36–38.

Gouillart, F. and Billings, D. (2013). Community Powered Problem Solving. Harvard Business Review, April 2013, pp. 71–77.

Haanaes, K., Michael, D., Jurgens, J. and Rangan, S. (2013). Making Sustainability Profitable. Harvard Business Review, March 2013, pp. 110–114.

Hart, S. (1997). Beyond greening: Strategies for a sustainable world. Harvard Business Review, Vol. 75(1), pp. 66–76.

Ignatius, A. (2011). Shaking Things Up at Coca Cola. Harvard Business Review, October 2011, pp. 94–99.

Jabbour, C.J.C., Santos, F.C.A., Nagano, M.S. (2010). Contributions of HRM throughout the stages of environmental management: Methodological triangulation applied to companies in Brazil. In International Journal of Human Resource Management, Vol. 21 (7), pp. 1049–1089.

Jabbour, C.J.C., Jabbou, Lopes de Sousa, A.B., Govindan, K., Teixeira, A.A., and Freitas, Ricardo de Souza, W. (2012). Environmental management and operational performance in automotive companies in Brazil: The role of human resource management and lean manufacturing. In Journal of Cleaner Production.

Jackson, S., Renwick, D., Jabbour, C. J. C., Muller-Camen, M. (2011). State-of-the-Art and Future Directions for Green Human Resource Management Zeitschrift fur Personal for schung. German Journal of Research in Human Resource Management, Vol. 25, pp. 99–116.

Jones, G. (2012). The Growth opportunity That Lies Next Door. Harvard Business Review, July–August 2012. pp. 141–145.

Kelley-Patterson, D. and George, C. (2002). Mapping the Contract: An exploration of the comparative expectations of Graduate Employees and Human Resource Managers within the Hospitality, Tourism and Leisure Industries in the United Kingdom. In Journal of Services Research, Vol. 2., No. 1.

Mintzberg, H. (1979). The Structuring of Organizations. Englewood Cliffs, NJ: Prentice-Hall.

Mishra, M. (2013). Case: Tea Division at Williamson Magor: Surging Ahead with a Focus on Sustainability. Under publication.

Molina-Azorin, J.F., Claver-Cortes, E., Lopez-Gamero, M.D., and Tari, J.J. (2009). Green management and financial performance: A literature review. In Management Decisions, Vol. 47 (7), pp. 1080–1100.

Morishima, M. (1996). Renegotiating psychological contracts: Japanese style. In C.L. Cooper and D.M. Rousseau (Eds.), Trends in Organizational Behaviour, Vol. 3, John Wiley and Sons.

Moynihan, D.P., and Landyut, N. (2008). Explaining turnover intention in state government: Examining the roles of gender, life cycle and loyalty. In Review of Public Personnel Administration, Vol. 28 (2), pp. 120–130.

Oluokun, M.O. (2003). The relationship between transactional and transformational leadership behaviors and employee turnover intentions in municipal sector organizations. D.B.A. Nova South-eastern University.

Piramal, G. (1997). Business Maharajas. New Delhi: Penguin.

Poonamallee, L. (2011). Corporate Citizenship: Panacea or Problem? The Complicated Case of Hindustan Lever. Journal of Corporate Citizenship, Greenleaf Publishing.

Prahlad, C.K. (2005). The Fortune at the Base of the Pyramid: Eradicating Poverty through Profits. Upper Saddle River, NJ: Wharton School Publishing.

Russell, R. G. (1996). The relationship between transactional and transformational leadership styles and employee turnover intentions. D.B.A. Nova South-eastern University.

Sarkis, J., Gonzalez-Torre, P., and Adenso-Diaz, B. (2010). Stakeholder pressure and the adoption of environmental practices, and the mediating effects of training. In Journal of Operations Management, Vol. 28 (2), pp. 163–176.

Shore, L.M. and Tetrick, L.E. (1994). The psychological contract as an explanatory framework in the employment relationship. In C.L. Cooper and D.M. Rousseau (Eds.), Trends in Organizational Behaviour, Vol. 1, John Wiley and Sons.

Sinha, J.B.P. (1990). Work culture in the Indian context. New Delhi: Sage.

Som, A. (2008). Organization Redesign and Innovation HRM. New Delhi: Oxford.

Sull, D. N. (2002). Why Good Companies Go Bad. In Harvard Business Review on Culture and Change, pp. 83–106.

Ulrich, D. (1997). Human Resource Champions—The Next Agenda for Adding Value and Delivering. Harvard Business School Press.

Van Maanen, J. and Barley, S. (1984). Occupational Communities: Culture and Control in Organizations. In B. Straw and L. Cummings (Eds.), Research in Organizational Behaviour. London: JAI Press.

Wagner, M. (2007). Integration of environmental management with other managerial functions of the firm: Empirical effects on drivers of economic performance. In Long Range Planning, 40(6), 611-628. http://dx.doi.org/10.1016/j.lrp.2007.08.001

Yin, R. K. (1984). Case Study Research—Design and Methods. New York: Sage.

CHAPTER 11

EFFICIENT EQUIPMENT: SOURCES FOR SUSTAINABILITY IN THE HOTEL INDUSTRY

SUBRATA KUMAR NANDI

CONTENTS

11.1   INTRODUCTION

"The concept of the ecofriendly hotel and resort is almost a contradiction in terms in an industry that bases the rankings of its members on perceived opulence, luxury and grandeur."

– Iwanowski and Rushmore (1994: 34)

The above observation highlights the apparent dichotomy which exists within the hotel industry, where providing greater comforts to the guests and adopting sustainable practices appear to be two mutually exclusive objectives. Yet, there are examples of some of the top luxury hotels in the world, who have successfully embraced sustainable practices without sacrificing the elements of luxury in their service offerings. The increasing focus on sustainability by the hotel industry may have resulted from the global concern for environmental degradation; the changes in attitudes of consumers towards sustainable practices by hotels have also been of help. In addition to that, stringent legal enforcements by government in many parts of the world have necessitated the move towards sustainable practices. Traditionally, this industry has not been considered as a major polluter, and therefore was never subjected to scrutiny about its negative environmental impact. However, in recent times the industry has come under scrutiny (Jackson, 2010), forcing organizations in the industry to adopt processes and procedures that reflect their concern for the environment. By being sensitive to environmental issues, the hospitality industry as a whole can not only contribute to environmental conservation, but is also likely to gain through reduced operating expenses (Iwanowski and Rushmore, 1994). Therefore, players in the industry may be encouraged to adopt sustainable systems and processes, as such efforts can also contribute to their bottom-line.

One of the important areas of focus for the hotel industry can be efficient use of energy. Specific actions aimed at better use of energy can lead to reduction in operating costs of hotels. This does not however, mean that hotels have to bring down their service standards to achieve their environmental goals. Research indicates that even while maintaining the same levels of service, the industry may still be able to reduce the environmental impact of operations. However, both researchers and practitioners have emphasized the need to achieve a balance between the adoption of sustainable practices and maintaining competitiveness (Zhang et al., 2012).

Equipment and machinery, that include power generators, air-conditioning equipment; laundry systems; lighting equipment; and restaurant appliances, account for considerable energy consumption in hotels. Thus, using energy efficient equipment can considerably reduce the environmental impact of hotel operations and also result in cost savings for the hotel.

Using a review of existing literature on sustainability, this paper attempts to highlight the importance of energy efficient equipment to the operations of a hotel. The structure of this paper is as follows:

Section 11.2 discusses about the environmental impact of the hotel industry. This section also traces the sustainability efforts by the hotel industry. Section 11.3 deliberates on the green lodging practices, which are prevalent in the industry. In section 11.4 we discuss how equipment are important targets for achieving the sustainability goals for the industry. Worldwide there are several agencies, which are involved in defining standards for sustainability. Section 11.5 discusses about these standards. Section 11.6 discusses the use and implementation of sustainable equipment by some organizations across the globe. Based on the industry best practices highlighted in the previous section, Section 11.7 discusses the possible implications for the industry and suggests a roadmap for the industry to achieve sustainability through energy conservation. Finally, Section 11.8 presents the conclusion of the findings from this study.

11.2 ENVIRONMENTAL IMPACT OF THE HOTEL INDUSTRY

A hotel consumes different resources for its operations, aimed at providing good quality products and services to customers. The inputs to the business processes in a hotel gets converted into revenue generating products and services as well as cost generating wastes. These wastes can be in the form of energy wastes, solid/liquid wastes and time and manpower wastes. Adoption of sustainable practices requires minimizing or eliminating these cost generating wastes.

Specifying the operational requirements of hotels, Hsieh (2012) observes that hotel operations require water, heating, cooling, lighting, a laundry system, and appliances; and all of these have significant impacts on the environment. The sustainability efforts of hotels require reduction of the inputs like water and energy, and reduction or elimination of wastes related to other operations. By expending such efforts, hotels would be considered as environmentally sensitive.

According to a report by Hotel Energy Solutions (2011), hotel facilities are among the top five in the tertiary building sector to be significant consumers of energy. Today, the hotel industry is characterized by higher than average consumption of water and energy and generation of large volumes of waste, as compared to other types of buildings (Erdogan and Baris, 2007), and hence have a significant impact on the environment. The contributors to hotel energy consumption are heating and cooling rooms, lighting, use of hot water by guests, meal preparation, swimming pool, etc. HVAC accounts for the single largest energy consumption in hotels, accounting for nearly 50 percent of the total energy consumption; followed by domestic hot water, accounting for 15 percent of energy use; and lighting, which can account for 12 percent to 40 percent of the energy use. The other energy consuming services include catering and laundry, and sports and health facilities (Hotel Energy Solutions, 2011).

Kasim and Scarlet (2006) identify the key environmental impacts of hotels as energy and water consumption; waste production; atmospheric contamination and chemical use. Similarly, other researchers identify the hotel industry's environment impact as water and air pollution, energy induced emission and waste generation (Kasimu et al., 2012). The extent of the impact of hotels on the environment can be gauged from the fact reported by US Energy Protection Agency (Energy Star, 2013), that nearly 50,000 hotels in America, on an average, spend more than $2000 per available room on energy, which constitutes about 6 percent of the total operating cost of the hotels. Sloan et al. (2009, as referred in Liu and Sanhaji, 2010) present some startling facts about the environmental impact of the hotel industry, which perhaps highlights the need for demonstrating greater environmental concern. According to the authors, a hotel generates 1 kg of waste per guest per night, and 170–200 kg of carbon dioxide per square meter of room floor area per year. In addition to this, a luxury hotel also uses 170–440 liters of water per guest per night.

Jackson (2010) offers a framework, which shows how a lodging property interacts with the environment and the negative environmental externalities that are generated, as shown in Figure 1. It is evident from the figure, that there are various types of resources that a lodging facility requires to serve its customers well. The resource used can have significant negative environmental externalities like consumption of energy, and water; and generation of wastes and air pollution. The sustainability efforts of hotel organizations should be aimed at addressing each of these issues identified in the above framework viz. reduced use of water and recycle where possible; reduce air pollution by using green fuel for running equipment; reduce energy through greater efficiency and judicious use of equipment; reduce and recycle solid and liquid wastes by appropriate procedures and policies

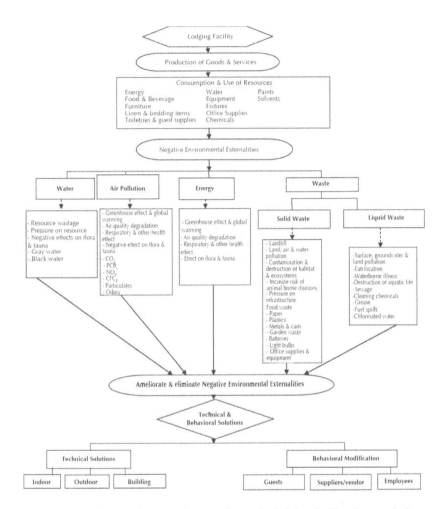

FIGURE 1 Negative environmental externalities of a lodging facility. *Source*: Jackson, L.A. (2010: p. 220).

11.3   GREEN LODGING PRACTICES

Jackson (2010) defines green lodging as "concerted and deliberate efforts and practices by lodging operations and their agents, to mitigate, ameliorate and eliminate the negative impacts of lodging activities on the environment." To achieve the above objectives, it is important to understand how lodging facilities, during their operations, may impact the environment. Since the objective of a lodging property is to offer comfort to its guests, all the physical elements including equipment, which are installed are meant for safety and comfort, and are esthetically pleasing. Many of these equipment, in the process of their operation, can lead to negative impacts on the environment.

Green practices are associated with the focus on reducing the negative impacts of energy and water use; waste generation and indoor air quality (Jackson, 2010). The consumption and use of energy in hotels differ from other commercial establishment because of the diverse nature of facilities which hotels have, viz. lodging rooms, kitchens, restaurants, in-house laundry, facilities for recreation, service and business centers, etc.(Jackson, 2010). The use of energy is primarily in the form of electricity, though for heating purposes diesel is a commonly used fuel. In addition to energy, the other most important negative environmental externality of a lodging facility is the consumption of water. Water is used for various purposes like cooking, drinking, cleaning, laundry, sanitation, recreation, and HVAC systems. The other negative environmental externalities are indoor air quality and waste generation. The sources of air pollution include particulates, inorganic gaseous compounds, bioaerosols, and combustion sources like gas, oil, wood, furnishing, wet or damp carpets, cleaning products, central heating and cooling systems, etc. (Jackson, 2010). Finally, the lodging industry generates a lot of solid and liquid wastes, which not only add to the cost to the environment but also for handling them. To address these problems, recycling of wastes; and waste conservation can make significant economic sense.

The green practices adopted by the hotel industry are also guided by various initiatives by government or independent agencies that lay down policies and procedures for developing sustainable practices. For example, in Singapore the Singapore Hotel Association and the National Environment Agency have come together to lay down a set of guidelines called the "3R Guidebook for Hotels," meant for waste reduction. This initiative was launched in 2011 and expects the participating hotels to voluntary commit towards solid waste reduction in the Singapore hotel industry (Singapore Hotel Association, 2011). The objectives of the program include implementation of waste minimization and waste recycling programs; impart training for effective execution of the programs; and sharing of knowledge and expertise to reduce the learning curve of hotels.

Sustainability certainly has its benefits for the hotel industry. The various benefits that may accrue to a hotel by adopting sustainable practices include cost savings; additional revenues; greater financial stability; lower long-term risks; longer staying power, etc.(Bader, 2005). Goodman (2000) highlights how Scandic Hotels turned around their business by focusing on sustainability as one of the two areas of improvement. Apart from working towards achieving water and energy efficiency, Scandic developed an Internet based environmental index, which helped it evaluate environmental performance across categories like waste disposal, equipment, adoption of temperature monitoring system, percent of low energy consuming bulbs, and food and beverages (Goodman, 2000).

Therefore, there are opportunities for promoting environmental sustainability in the hotel industry, through efforts like adoption of systems for tracking and reduction of resources and wastes; use resource efficient appliances; transition to renewable energy sources; recycling of material; educating guests and employees to display environment friendly behavior; local sourcing to reduce transport related environmental impact; co-operation with other firms with high environmental standards and compliance with legislation (Bohdanowicz et al., 2011). And the cost of adopting such efforts may not be high. For example, it has been found that the cost of energy can be reduced to the extent of 20 percent without significant investment in energy saving initiatives (O' Hanlon, 2005, as referred in Jackson, 2010).

Although there are increasing evidences of the hotel industry being sensitive to the need for environmental sustainability, the origin of the sustainability movement can be traced to the Report of the United Nations' World Commission on Environment and Development published in 1987 titled "Our Common Future," better known as the Brundtland Report (United Nations, 1987). The report was perhaps a call to humanity to be concerned about the future generations. The rapid environmental deterioration caused by continuous exploitation of natural resources and generation of byproducts which are detrimental to the environment, has suddenly forced everyone to think of finding ways to retard if not reverse the negative environmental impact. Like other industries, the lodging industry has also woken up to this reality, and there are evidences of the adoption of green practices across various areas of the lodging segment (Jackson, 2010).

For the hotel industry, adoption of sustainable practices is not a 21st century phenomenon. There are evidences of these efforts even earlier, as the findings presented by Enz and Siguaw (1999) indicate. The authors, while examining the four best practice champions named in a best practices study by the Cornell University School of Hotel Administration, highlight some of the practices adopted by these four hotels. All these hotels had adopted systems for waste recycling and incorporated organizational changes to manage their environmental efforts. One of these hotels (The Colony Hotel in Kennebunkport, Maine) also had an education and guest involvement program in place. These examples emphasize that the hotel industry had been concerned about the environment for many years, though their motivations for adoption of sustainable practices may have been different. Although, some may be motivated by the "rightness" of these actions; others may be motivated by the demands of their guests for "greener operations"; and yet others be forced by the government regulations (Enz and Siguaw, 1999). Some of the agencies facilitating the green efforts outline specific procedures and guidelines to achieve the objectives. Table 1 lists the 14 guidelines of the American Hotel and Lodging Association.

TABLE 1   Fourteen minimum guidelines for going green.

1. Monitor your hotel's electric, gas, and water usage
2. Implement a towel reuse program
3. Implement a linen reuse program
4. Implement a recycling program
5. Staff training on implementing green practices
6. Providing information for guests on green practices
7. Install energy efficient interior light bulbs
8. Form an environmental committee to develop a green plan for energy/water/solid waste use
9. Install digital thermostats in guestrooms and throughout the hotel
10. Install 2.5-gallons per minute showerheads or less in all guestroom baths and any employee shower areas.
11. Install 1.6-gallon toilets in all guestrooms
12. Implement a recycling program for hazardous materials found in fluorescent bulbs, batteries, and lighting ballasts through licensed service providers
13. Purchase Energy Star labeled appliances and equipment
14. All office paper products should have 20% or more post-consumer recycled content

Source: AH&LA (2013).

There are several changes in the external economic and environmental conditions, which have contributed to the increased environmental sensitivity in the hospitality industry as a whole. Goldstein and Primlani (2012) observe that the hospitality sector woke up to the needs for environmental considerations in their service offerings, by integrating elements of nature into resort experience, more than five decades ago. During the 1960s and 1970s, several events like the 1969 Santa Barbara oil spill; and the 1973–74 oil crisis made people aware of the potential impact of environmental degradation and the uncertainties of energy supplies. These events forced the hospitality industry to focus on energy conservation strategy mostly to keep the energy cost in check. The 1980s and 1990s ushered in a new era in the sustainability movement with the United Nations Conference on Environment and Development (UNCED) at Rio de Janerio in 1992 encouraging several environmental initiatives pertaining to environmental certification and green building programs. The seriousness about sustainability in the hospitality industry was evident from the establishment of the Green Hotels Association (GHA) in America during the 1990s (Meng, 2011). The Earth Summit at Rio in 1992 identified the tourism industry as one of the priority areas for sustainable development. Since 2000, sustainability efforts by hotel organizations have been formalized with firms incorporating environmental objectives into their corporate social responsibility (CSR) initiatives. However, Bohdanowicz et al. (2011) argue that corporate social responsibility and environmental sustainability may not necessarily be linked, although the latter may in many cases be central to the CSR efforts of a firm. This period also witnessed the wide acceptance of the LEED green building program (Goldstein and Primlani, 2012).

11.4   EQUIPMENT AND THEIR ROLE IN SUSTAINABILITY

Iwanoski and Rushmore (1994) observe that "An environmentally sensitive hotel is one that has altered its equipment, policies, and practices to minimize the strain on the environment" (p. 35). In the above definition, one of the key contributors towards minimizing environmental strain has been identified as alteration (modification) of equipment. Whereas, most of the conservation efforts are explained by the 3Rs (Reduce, Reuse, and Recycle), where the first "R" possibly subsumes the energy consumption by equipment, this industry may possibly do well to clearly consider using the terms "remodel" (redesign) or "replace," particularly in the case of equipment and machinery. Because of their potential for saving on energy consumption, equipment can become an important target for improvement for achieving sustainability in the hotel industry.

As discussed earlier, energy conservation is one of the ways used by hotels in reducing their environmental impact. And this can be achieved by focusing on the equipment used and studying their use and mode of running. The importance of equipment in energy consumption is evident from the list of equipment identified by Green Seal, as objects of energy saving (Table 2).

TABLE 2 List of equipment identified by Green Seal.

Room Equipment: televisions, video cassette players/recorders, DVD players, alarm clocks, hair dryers, irons, coffee/tea makers.
Office: fax machines, copiers, printers, computers, monitors.
HVAC Equipment: chillers, packaged terminal air conditioners, central air conditioners, central heat pumps, split ductless heat pumps, geothermal heat pumps, water heaters.
Where Applicable:
Kitchen Equipment: freezers, refrigerators, cooktops, ovens, dishwashers.
Laundry Equipment: boilers, washers, dryers, extractors.

Source:Greenseal (2011).

Similarly a set of criteria has been identified by the European Commission in 2009 and illustrated in Table 3.

TABLE 3 Energy-related criteria of the EU flower (ELTAS) by European Commission.

Criteria #	Mandatory / Optional	Specific aspect addressed by the criteria
Type of energy used		
1	M	• Electricity from renewable sources (at least 22%)
2	M	• Use of Coal and heavy oils
30	O	• Generation of electricity through renewable energy sources (at least 20%)
31	O	• Energy from renewable energy sources
34	O	• District Heating
35	O	• Combined heat and power
36	O	• Use of heat pump
48	O	• Swimming pool heating with renewable energy sources
Equipment efficiency / Equipment regulations		
3	M	• Efficiency and heat generation
4	M	• Air conditioning (class A)
7	M	• Switching off heating or air conditioning
8	M	• Switching off lights
9	M	• Energy efficient light bulbs
10	M	• Outside heating appliances
32	O	• Boiler energy efficiency
33	O	• Boiler NOx emissions
37	O	• Heat recovery
38	O	• Thermoregulation
40	O	• Air conditioning (15% more efficient than class A)
41	O	• Automatic switch-off air conditioning and heating systems
43	O	• Energy efficient refrigerators, ovens, dishwashers, washing machines, dryers/tumblers and office equipment
45	O	• Refrigerator positioning
46	O	• Automatic switching off lights in guest rooms
47	O	• Sauna timer control
49	O	• Automatic switching off outside lights

Source: Hotel energy solutions (2011).

It is evident from the two criteria mentioned above that equipment and fixtures can be the sources for energy conservation in hotels. Chan et al. (2013), in their study of hotels in Hong Kong, found that that the choice of water heating system can have a significant impact on the energy consumption and cost for hotels. There are three different energy sources used by boilers in hotels for heating water, including diesel oil, gas, and electricity. Because of their combustive nature, diesel oil and gas generate significant air pollutants in the form of smoke, carbon dioxide, oxides of sulfur and nitrogen, and particulate matter (Chan and Mak, 2004). Also, the low combustion efficiency of traditional diesel and gas powered boilers result in more consumption of diesel and gases. An alternate to using diesel of gas for energy generation for water heating in conventional boilers, it may be prudent to use heat pumps, which work on the compression principle used in refrigerators, and transfer the heat that can be used for pre-heating. The use of heat pumps cannot only reduce the energy consumption, it also contributes to saving and reduces emission of harmful gases in the atmosphere.

There are several studies, which report about the opportunities facing the food service industry in achieving energy efficiency, with respect to the equipment, which are used in restaurants. Since a restaurant is an integral part of a hotel, a discussion about the developments taking place in restaurant equipment can be indicative of the possibilities for the hotel industry as a whole. Also there are opportunities that hotels can exploit by reducing energy usage by equipment in the restaurants. As mentioned earlier, there are formal certifications, which are available for equipment, one of the most popular being the Energy Star certification.

11.5 ENVIRONMENTAL CERTIFICATION AND LABELING

There are many reasons which govern the adoption of sustainable practices by organizations, some of them being legal/regulatory compliance requirements; stakeholder pressure; ethical concerns; basis of competitive advantage; and efforts by senior management (Jackson, 2010). These sustainability initiatives are influenced by the benefits to be exploited viz. profitability through reduced costs, improved customer satisfaction; high employee loyalty, competitive advantage, compliance of regulations, and minimizing operational risks (Graci and Dodds, 2008).

The various efforts at sustainability are driven by factors like cost savings, incentives and regulatory requirements. Reducing costs through better management of energy and wastes, can add to the profitability of firms, even if there is no increase in its revenues. The economic logic of energy saving can be understood from the fact that, considering a return rate of 10 percent, a saving of 10 units in monetary terms would be equivalent to generating an additional sale of 100 units. Since energy savings require active participation from people, there has to be a comprehensive management policy to conserve energy. Such a policy may entail a clear understanding and recording of energy usage by various equipment, which are being used so that appropriate actions can be taken to reduce the energy usage. In addition to direct cost savings, there are several incentives, which are available for adopting green practices by the industry, in the form of grants, tax rebates, and expeditious regulatory clearance (Goldstein and Primlani, 2012).

As shown in Figure 1, Jackson (2010) based on his study identifies two sets of solutions for reducing the adverse environmental impacts viz. technical and behavioral. Technical solution means the use of equipment and fixtures that reduce or eliminate the negative externalities that would require existing equipment to achieve higher levels of efficiency standards. One of the ways of achieving this is to understand the levels of performance by using equipment, which have been certified for being more "environment friendly" than others, which are used to perform the same function. In recent years there has been emergence of agencies, which formally assess certify the green initiatives of organizations. Two such agencies, which are widely recognized around the world, are the US Green Building Council (USGBC) and Energy Star. USGBC is better known for its Leadership in Energy and Environmental Design (LEED) program, which authenticates green buildings based on their compliance with existing environmental standards across five categories viz. Material and Resources, Energy and Atmosphere, Water Efficiency, Sustainable Sites and Environmental Quality (Liu and Sanhaji, 2010). On the other hand Energy Star, where the US Department of Energy is a participant, offers energy management programs to reduce the environmentally harmful use of energy, using a system of rating based on benchmarking with comparable facilities. Table 4 gives a list of agencies in different parts of the world, and the nature of their certifications.

TABLE 4 Major environmental certification and labeling agencies.

Certification	Description
EcoLogo http://www.ecologo.org/en/	EcoLogo was founded by the Canadian Government in the year 1988, and has become a respected certification standard in North America. EcoLogo certification covers a large variety of categories. As per the definition by ISO, EcoLogo is a Type I ecolabel, which sets its scientifically derived criteria to capture the entire lifecycle of the product, based on comparison of a product with others in the same category.
EU Ecolabel http://ec.europa.eu/environment/ecolabel/index_en.htm	The EU Ecolabel is a voluntary label program, which helps in identifying products and services which have a reduced environmental impact throughout their life cycle.
Eco Mark Program, Japan http://www.ecomark.jp/english/syoukai.html	The Eco Mark program, an initiative of the Japan Environment Association is a Type-I label, based on ISO 14024.
Eco Mark Program, India http://envfor.nic.in/legis/others/ecomark.html	The government of India instituted a labeling scheme for Environmental products in the year 1991. Any product which is made, used or disposed in ways that reduces the environmental impact can be eligible for the "Ecomark" label if they meet certain environmental criteria
Blue Angel. Germany http://www.blauer-engel.de/en/blauer_engel/	The Blue Angel, created in 1978 by the German government, is the oldest environment-related labeling sheme for products and services in the world. Over 11,000 products across more than 125 categories carry the Blue Angel ecolabel.
Energy Star http://www.energystar.gov/	ENERGY STAR was established by the U.S. Environmental Protection Agency (EPA) in 1992, for conducting research in engineering and technology to "develop, evaluate, and demonstrate non–regulatory strategies and technologies for reducing air pollution." It is a voluntary program to identify and promote energy–efficient products and buildings to reduce energy consumption, improve energy security, and reduce pollution through voluntary labeling of or other forms of communication about products and buildings that meet the highest energy efficiency standards.
Green Seal http://www.greenseal.org/AboutGreenSeal.aspx	Started in 1989, Green Seal develops product and service standards based on life cycles, and offer third-party certification for those that meet the criteria in the standard.

Source: Compiled by the author

The rise in the demand for these certifications has been driven by the savings in costs and the goodwill that a firm earns through this (Liu and Sanhaji, 2010). Yet, the hospitality industry woke up to the reality of sustainability much later than other industries, perhaps because of the invisible nature of their impact on the environment and their inability to visualize how guest comfort and sustainability can be achieved simultaneously.

Corporations today are not only expected to adopt environmentally friendly operations, they are also expected to report their environmental and social performance in addition to the financial results. Some countries have stipulated the disclosure of information relating to environmental efforts by companies (Jose and Lee, 2007).

Goldstein and Primlani (2012) observe that the current trends in facility management in the hotel industry are focused largely on achieving optimal efficiency of operations in the areas of energy, water, and waste. The authors report that, energy consumption is related to operation of HVAC equipment, cooking, lighting, and miscellaneous power. Efforts at energy savings are measured in both for front of the house and back of the house efficiencies. The former include minimizing plug loads and lighting retrofits; while the latter includes proper scheduling of equipment, proper calibration, maintaining proper ventilation and avoiding simultaneous heating and cooling. With respect to water conservation, hotels are found to adopt fixture retrofits; linen and towel reuse programs, plumbing system improvement for HVAC and recycle of water or rain water harvesting. Wastes in hotels can result from durables, consumables, food wastes, hazardous material and oil. There are several strategies by hoteliers to reduce, recycle and reuse these wastes.

11.6   SUSTAINABLE EQUIPMENT: SOME CASE STUDIES

A report published by the World Wildlife Fund in association with Hotel Investment Conference Asia Pacific and Horwath HTL (WWF, 2010) presents nine case studies of sustainable practices adopted by some of the hotels in Asia, which among other things highlight how choice of energy efficient equipment can add to valuable savings in energy. The summary of the findings of some of the hotels showcased in the study is presented below:

11.6.1   CROWNE PLAZA, MELBOURNE

Since 2005, the hotel has been able to reduce its energy consumption more than 25% per month from a level of 365,000 kWh to 260,000 kWh, despite

registering higher levels of occupancy. This has been brought about by a series of actions as below:
- Replacement of incandescent bulbs with compact fluorescent bulb in 2010.
- Installation of variable speed drives in 2008 to regulate motor and pump speeds based on the demand levels, with an expected energy savings of 30 percent.
- Installation of sensors in guestrooms, with automatic temperature adjustments.
- Installation of airblade dryers in public bathrooms in place of warm air dryers, which resulted in savings on paper towels and maintenance (2010).
- Phased installation of LED lights (2010).

In addition to energy conservation, the hotel also made some changes in its equipment and fixtures for water conservation. Its equipment related water conservation initiatives include:
- Installation of special shower heads with restricted water flow (2006).
- Use of flow restrictors to reduce guestroom water pressure resulting in water saving to the tune of USD 26,785 per year.
- Installation of dual flush toilets of lower volume of water per flush (2004).
- Installation of waterless urinals in public places, saving 6 to 12 liters of water per flush.

11.6.2 EVASON, PHUKET

The Evason, Phuket also adopted several changes with relation to its equipment and fixtures. Some of its initiatives, which resulted in considerable energy and resource savings are:
- Replacement of split type air-conditioning with a centralized mini chiller system, resulting in a 510,000 kWh per year improvement in energy consumption resulting in a saving of USD 44,000 per year.
- Using the force of gravity to distribute water instead of using water pumps, by locating water tanks at the highest point of the property.
- Using solar energy for water heating in main guestrooms and heat recovery pumps for heating water in pool villas.
- Reduction in carbon emission by replacing diesel hot water boiler with LPG boiler.
- Use of bio-diesel from used cooking oil.

- Installation of a biomass absorption chiller, leading to a saving of USD 41,000 per year fuel cost.

11.6.3 INTERCONTINENTAL BORA BORA RESORT AND THALASSO SPA

This resort property has adopted a unique system for air-conditioning called Sea Water Air Conditioning (SWAC), in addition to other initiatives, by which they were able to reduce energy consumption. The other initiatives include:
- Use of 8 to 10 watt LED lights in place of 60 watt incandescent bulbs.
- Automatic sensors which turn off air conditioning when sliding doors are left open for extended periods.
- Use of solar energy for water heating in staff residences.
- Dual flush toilets.
- A garden shredder for shredding garden waste, cardboard and paper into mulch, thereby reducing the volume of wastes to be removed.

11.6.4 OBEROI, UDAIVILAS

The resort has adopted several initiatives with respect to equipment and fixtures like:
- Chillers with temperature control, based on occupancy and load demand.
- Installation of solar panels for heating of pools.
- Use of screw compressors instead of reciprocating compressors in chillers.
- Heat recovery systems from chillers and use for domestic water heating.
- Replacement of CFL garden lights with LED bulbs.

11.7 IMPLICATIONS FOR THE INDUSTRY

The findings of this paper suggest that there are considerable opportunities for the hotel industry to reduce their environmental impact. A hotel can look at energy savings by optimizing the operations of various equipment used within its various sub-functions, which can cumulatively contribute to its energy saving goals. Among the various sub-functions, which a hotel can consider are the food service operations, laundry, air-conditioning and lighting. Some of the specific aspects of each are discussed below.

A significant 30% of the energy consumption in a restaurant results from food preparation. Refrigeration accounts for 13% to 18% (Sustainablefoodservice.com (2013a). The other elements, which consume energy include HVAC systems, exhaust hoods, and water heater. Proper maintenance and judicious use of these equipment can help food service industry to achieve their sustainability goals. Today there are several options, which food service organizations have in terms of choosing Energy Star rated/labeled equipment. In addition there are organizations like Food Service Technology Center (FSTC) and Consortium for Energy Efficiency (CEE), which encourage energy efficient equipment. For example, the California based FSTC extends rebates to California based businesses when they use energy efficient equipment. The incentives available in California are as high as $1000 per unit. The FSTC provides a list of cooking equipment that have been tested by them. These include ovens (convection, rack, combination); fryers; steam cookers; griddles; and insulated holding cabinets. Steam cookers can bring about significant savings of water and energy. In recently tested equipment, FSTC found that use of heat sink fins allowed quicker transfer of energy and reduced the time to boil water by almost half, as compared to normal equipment (Sustainablefoodservice.com, 2013a).

Today there is large variety of choices available for refrigeration equipment. New commercial ice machines which are both energy and water efficient to the extent of 15 and 10%, respectively, are available in the market today. Changes are not only taking place on the technology for reducing energy consumption, there are changes, which are also been witnessed in the nature of refrigerants used. The harmful effect of CFC (chlorofluorocarbons) saw it being replaced by hydro chlorofluorocarbons (HCFC) and hydro fluorocarbons (HFCs).

Heat recovery systems, which captures heat from hot waste water and air discharged from refrigerated units and used for preheating of inlet water in a water heater can result in significant energy saving. While electric heaters can be more efficient, they tend to be more expensive than gas operated heaters. One may also consider solar heaters, for at least preheating.

There are equipment, which claim to save $11,000 annually of water and energy costs for foodservice operations. The equipment is capable of cleaning and sanitizing more than 6,000 dishes an hour. The savings in energy is achieved by preheating cold water by capturing the exhaust heat of the equipment and therefore reduce the energy required to achieve the required temperature for rinsing (Hobart, 2013).

Ventilation in commercial kitchens consumes significant levels of energy while removing smoke, vapor and other compounds, which result from cooking. About 28 percent of the energy consumption in an average commercial kitchen results from the exhaust hoods and HVAC systems (Sustainablefood-service.com, 2010). There are ventilation systems available today which leads to energy savings by reducing exhaust airflows, with design innovations, which include natural capture of effluent and force-feeding the effluent into the hood of the exhaust (Gaylord, 2013).

Water-saving equipment and strategies are the basis of effective water-conservation program, and in fact, have been widely implemented within the hospitality industry—perhaps because of the fast payback. Many devices are available that reduces the amount of water that comes out of a faucet or showerhead or that is used to flush a toilet.

The above discussion of a few opportunities about energy saving in commercial kitchens can also be extrapolated for an entire hotel premise. The promise of sustainable equipment is quite encouraging considering the potential savings. There are several examples of hotel organizations looking at energy saving through greater equipment efficiencies. The next section discusses a few case studies of hotel/resorts from across the world, which highlights the important role of equipment in addressing their sustainable efforts.

While the benefits of energy efficient equipment cannot be ignored, the only challenge is the cost of installation, which may deter organizations from adopting initiatives towards environmental conservations, as they may be concerned with the payback period and the upfront investment. As one can intuitively appreciate that replacing existing equipment can result in significant costs. However, it is important to understand that the benefits of the new systems can only be reaped over a longer time horizon. Some of the green alternatives with significant long-term benefit potential are use of solar power for lighting and water heating; use of variable lighting; and use of energy efficient lighting (IDS, 2011).

Technology has facilitated the remodeling of equipment for making them more energy efficient. IDS Softwares Pvt. Ltd. (IDS, 2011) highlights some of the initiatives that have been undertaken by hotels to this effect. For example, by using wireless controllers for key card, lighting and air-conditioning; which automates these operations based on the presence or absence of the guest in the room. Thus, when the guest leaves the room the lighting and air-conditioning is turned off automatically. In some of the hotels in the USA, the heating system is also powered by technology.

Zhang et al. (2012) offer a framework for categorizing the environmental initiatives based on two dimensions of investment and period of payback. The options having a short payback period are easily implementable and are low in terms of initial investments. The ones, which require minimum investments include energy audit, system for evaluation of process, international training and educating customers about the green efforts. However, most of the efforts at environmental sustainability require significant upfront investment, and have a long payback period. Energy efficient equipments fall under this category.

Today there are online tools, which are available for benchmarking operations with industry standard. For example, the Environmental Protection Agency in the US has created such a tool called "Energy Star Portfolio Manager" which helps in measuring and tracking energy and water consumption and emission of greenhouse gases (Energy Star, 2013b). Already 40 percent of the US commercial building space has been benchmarked in this tool. Alternately, one can devise as system of data collection on energy consumption at preset intervals and study the pattern of energy usage to understand why fluctuations happen. This may possibly provide guidance about what do to address any adverse changes in the energy consumption recorded. Developing a schedule for starting and shutting down of equipment and lights can also be used as a means of energy conservation.

While keeping an eye on the energy consumption during running of equipment can give one the opportunity to evaluate the functioning of equipment, an important aspect that cannot be ignored is the need for preventive maintenance. Often by shutting down operations for preventive maintenance for a short duration can result in significant improvement in performance of machines, which is often ignored. One has to overcome the mentality of "why fix until it's broke?" A regular maintenance schedule will improve the performance of equipment.

A practical way of reducing energy consumption in HVAC systems, which is often ignored, is to adjust the thermostat. Installation of a programmable thermostat allows maintaining various levels of temperature depending on the time of the day or the need. For example, hotels can consider maintaining higher levels of temperature during the night. Proper sealing and insulation can increase the efficiency of heating and ventilation systems and at the same time save energy. Use of energy efficiency motors like variable frequency drives and NEMA (National Electrical Manufacturers Association) Premium motors can be considered.

As discussed earlier, lighting can account for significant energy consumption. Perhaps the simplest way to reduce energy consumption is to turn them off when not required. In recent times, the development of technology allows hotels to make use of lights which are less energy consuming, as compared to the traditional lighting. Incandescent bulbs, which have traditionally been used for lighting, consume a lot of energy. At the same time they release energy in the form of heat thereby increasing the load on the air-conditioning systems (Sustainablefoodservice.com, 2013b). While the cost of the incandescent lights is relatively low as compared to other options available today, they have low life, which can add to the increased maintenance cost. A better alternative available for hotels is fluorescents. Technology for fluorescents is improving rapidly, with new technology (T-8) fluorescents consuming 50 percent of the energy consumed by the earlier technology (T-12)(Sustainablefoodservice.com, 2013b). The other forms of lamps which are gaining acceptance because of their low energy consumption, while maintaining the same level of lighting are compact fluorescent lamps (CFLs); Cold Cathode Compact Fluorescent Lamps (CCCFLs): High Wattage Compact Fluorescent (HW-CFLs); Light Emitting Diodes (LEDs), etc.

By reducing, reusing and recycling wastes a considerable savings can be achieved by saving on the cost of transportation of wastes to landfills which are located far away. Similarly, there are considerable opportunities for energy savings from using energy efficient lighting, heating, ventilation and air-conditioning equipment, as is evident from the case studies discussed in the previous sections.

The Florida Green Lodging Program (2013) guidelines offer specific suggestions for best management practices in green lodging. Many of these suggestions, which are discussed below pertain to equipment, either for improving energy efficiency or for waste reduction. Some of the key elements of this program are highlighted below:

11.7.1   WATER CONSERVATION BEST MANAGEMENT PRACTICES (BMP)

It is appropriate to have a preventive maintenance schedule for equipment, which consume water; so that any problem can be identified before it causes major disruptions and wastages. Using low-flow fixtures like faucets, shower-heads and toilet flushes can conserve water. Other conservation method may include waterless urinals, low-flow, pre-rinse nozzles in beverage and kitchen areas.

11.7.2   GENERAL ENERGY EFFICIENCY BMPS

Similar to preventive maintenance in case of water consuming equipment, for energy consumption it is important to conduct energy audits and keep monthly records of energy usage. This would allow for tracking the energy usage. Further energy savings can be achieved by installing energy efficient doors and windows that can considerably reduce HVAC energy costs. Other simple, yet practical method for energy conservation is to use ceiling fan for creating air circulation in low ventilation areas; and use of exhaust fan only where it is necessary. Adoption of an Energy Management System (EMS) program would allow monitoring of energy load.

11.7.3   LIGHTING ENERGY EFFICIENCY BMPS

Some of the best management practices related to lighting energy efficiency include use of CFLs instead of incandescent lamps; use of LED light; replace-ment of old ballasts with electronic ballasts; installation of occupancy sensors for automatic turning on or off of lights; and use of sensors and timers for outdoor lighting control.

11.7.4   EQUIPMENT ENERGY EFFICIENCY BMPS

Use of Energy Star rated equipment can result in considerable energy effi-ciency. Since the HVAC systems are major consumers of electricity, adoption of measures like correct thermostat settings, scheduled maintenance; regu-lar filter change, use of programmable thermostats, prevent leakage through doors/windows; capture heat and recycle it in the system, etc.

11.8   CONCLUSION

The fact that the need for sustainable processes are being recognized by the hotel industry, has resulted in many hotels actively adopting processes and systems which are meant to conserve energy and other resources to offer the same level of services while at the same time reducing then negative environmental impacts. The various ways in which the hotel industry may negatively impact the environment has been discussed. The exiting best practices adopted by the hotel industry and the guidelines offered by various governmental and non-governmental agencies indicate that implementation of sustainable practices would require both technical and behavioral efforts. In addition to addressing the technical aspects of adopting green practices, the behavioral component can be equally important for implementation. This would require changes in the behaviors of guests, employees as well as vendors. It has been found that the decision regarding equipment is governed by the payback period and the initial investment required. Most of the hotels discussed here have consciously invested in technology with long payback period. However, if one also considers the rise in energy prices, the payback period may actually be less than what it is normally thought to be. The benefits of adopting sustainable equipment are much larger than what pure financial figures may reflect. Many of the hotels, which have adopted sustainability highlight this aspect and try to gain competitive advantage out of their efforts. This chapter focused on the role of equipment in pushing through the sustainable agenda in hotels.

KEYWORDS

- energy efficiency
- green lodging
- hospitality
- hotels
- sustainability
- sustainable equipment

REFERENCES

AH&LA (2013), "14 Minimum Guidelines for Going Green," American Hotel and Lodging Association, available athttp://www.ahla.com/Green.aspx?id=24562.

Bader, E.E. (2005), "Sustainable hotel business practices,"*Journal of Retail and Leisure Property*, 5 (1), pp. 70–77.

Bohdanowicz, P. (2005), "European Hoteliers' Environmental Attitudes: Greening the Business,"*Cornell Hotel and Restaurant Administration Quarterly*, 46(2), pp. 188–204.

Bohdanowicz, P., Zientara, P. and Novotna, E. (2011), "International hotel chains and environmental protection: an analysis of Hilton's *we care!* program(Europe, 2006–2008),"*Journal of Sustainable Tourism,* 19(7), pp. 797–816.

Chan, W.W. and Mak, B.L. (2004), "An estimation of the environmental impact of diesel oil usage in Hong Kong hotels," Journal of Sustainable Tourism, Vol. 12 No. 4, pp. 346–55.

Chan, W.W., Yueng, S., Chan, E. and Li, D. (2013), "Hotel heat pump hot water systems: impact assessment and analytic hierarchy process,"*International Journal of Contemporary Hospitality Management*, 25(3), pp. 428–446.

Energy Star (2013), "Hotels: An Overview of Energy Use and Energy Efficiency Opportunities," available at http://www.energystar.gov/ia/business/challenge/learn_more/Hotel.pdf[accessed September 29, 2013].

Energy Star (2013b), "Energy strategies for buildings and plants" available at http://www.energystar.gov/buildings/facility-owners-and-managers/existing-buildings/use-portfolio-manager?*c*=evaluate_performance.bus_portfoliomanager.

Enz, C.A. and Siquaw, J.A (1999), "Best hotel environmental practices,"*Cornell Hotel and Restaurant Administration Quarterly;* 40(5), pp. 72–77.

Erdogan, N., and Baris, E. (2007), "Environmental protection programs and conservation practices of hotels in Ankara, Turkey,"*Tourism Management,* 28, pp. 604–614.

Florida Green Lodging Program (2013), "Best Management Practices,"http://www.dep.state.fl.us/greenlodging/files/BMPs.pdf.

Gaylord (2013), http://www.gaylordventilation.com/Products/ELX/.

Goldstein, K.A., andPrimlani, R.V. (2012), "Current Trends and Opportunities in Hotel sustainability," HVS Sustainability Services, http://www.4hoteliers.com/features/article/6618.

Goodman, A. (2000), "Implementing Sustainability in Service Operations at Scandic Hotels,"*Interfaces,* 30(3), pp. 202–214.

Graci, S. and Dodds, R. (2008), "Why go green? The business case for environmental commitment in the Canadian hotel industry,"*Anatolia: An International Journal of Tourism and Hospitality Research,* 19(2), pp. 251–270.

Green Seal (2011), *A certification guidebook for GS-33—Green Seal's Environmental Standard for Hotels and Lodging Properties,* http://www.greenseal.org/Portals/0/Documents/Standards/gs-33%20 stnd%20dev/GS-33%20Guidebook%202.19.2013.pdf.

Hobart (2013), "Commercial Dishwashers," available at http://www.hobartcorp.com/products/commercial-dishwashers/advansys/advansys-cler-conveyor-type/.

Hoff, C. (2012), "Water Conservation Starts in the Dishroom,"http://www.sustainablefoodequipment.com/Water-Savings/Learn-Best-Practices/Articles/Water-Conservation-Starts-in-the-Dishroom/.

Hotel Energy Solutions (2011), Analysis on Energy Use by European Hotels: Online Survey and Desk Research, Hotel Energy Solutions project publications - First edition: 2010 Revised version, July 2011.

Hsieh, Y-C. (2012), "Hotel companies' environmental policies and practices: a content analysis of their web pages," International Journal of Contemporary Hospitality Management, 24(1), pp. 97–121.

IDS (2011), "Hotels Going the 'Green' Way with Technology," IDS Softwares Pvt. Ltd., http://www.4hoteliers.com/features/article/6500.

Iwanowski, K. and Rushmore, C. (1994), "Introducing the Eco-Friendly Hotel,"*Cornell Hotel and Restaurant Administration Quarterly*, 35(1), pp. 34–38.

Jackson, L.A. (2010), "Toward a framework for the components of green lodging,"*Journal of Retail and Leisure Property*, 9(3), pp. 211–230.

Jose, A. and Lee, S. (2007), "Environmental reporting of global corporations: a content analysis based on website disclosures,"*Journal of Business Ethics*, 72(4), pp. 307–321.

Kasim, A. and Scarlet, C. (2007), "Business Environmental Responsibility in the Hospitality Industry," Management, 2(1), pp. 5–23, www.fm-kp.si/zalozba/ISSN/1854–4231/2_005–023.pdf.

Kasimu, A.B., Zaiton, S., and Hassan, H. (2012), "Hotels Involvement in Sustainable Tourism Practices in Klang Valley, Malaysia,"*International Journal of Economics and Management*, 6(1), pp. 21–34.

Liu, P. and Sanhaji, Z. (2010), "Green Initiatives in the U. S. Lodging Industry,"*Cornell Real Estate Review*, 8(1), pp. 64–77.

Meng, N.K. (2011), "The potential of hotel's green products in Penang: an empirical study,"*Journal of Global Business and Economics*, 3(1), pp. 196–213.

Singapore Hotel Association (2011), *3R Guidebook for Hotels*, http://app2.nea.gov.sg/docs/default-source/energy-waste/3r-guidebook-for-hotels.pdf?sfvrsn=2.

Sustainablefoodservice.com (2010), "Sustainable Kitchen—Achieving lower volumes, not just blowing smoke," available at http://sustainablefoodequipment.gyrohsrclients.com/Energy-Savings/Learn-Best-Practices/Articles/Achieving-Low-Air-Volumes-Not-Just-Blowing-Smoke/.

Sustainablefoodservice.com (2013a), "Efficient Commercial Kitchen Equipment," available athttp://www.sustainablefoodservice.com/cat/equipment.htm[accessed September 28, 2013].

Sustainablefoodservice.com (2013b), "Energy Efficient Lighting," available at http://www.sustainablefoodservice.com/cat/lighting.htm.

United Nations (1987), "Report of the World Commission on Environment and Development: Our Common Future," available at http://conspect.nl/pdf/Our_Common_FutureBrundtland_Report_1987.pdf.

WWF (2010), "Towards the business case for sustainable hotels in Asia," Hotel Investment Conference Asia Pacific with Horwath HTL, and World Wildlife Fund, available at http://www.hicapconference.com/files/towardsthebusinesscaseforsustainablehotelsinasia.pdf.

Zhang, J.J., Joglekar, N. and Verma, R. (2012), "Pushing the frontier of sustainable service operations management—Evidence from US hospitality industry,"*Journal of Service Management*, 23(3), pp. 377–399.

CHAPTER 12

SUSTAINABLE RESTAURANTS: CURRENT PERSPECTIVES AND WAY FORWARD

RUMKI BANDYOPADHYAY and SANDEEP MUNJAL

CONTENTS

ABSTRACT

Business environment today plays a significant role in creating sustainable wealth in the society. The purpose of this chapter is to identify and build a set of sustainable indicators that will help the restaurant sector for its sustainability, derived extensively from a blend of review of past studies conducted in this area worldwide and practitioner's insights to develop a pathway of embedding green in restaurant operations. The extensive review of studies made the authors to comprehend the green management practices at restaurants The study aimed to develop a framework for progressive improvement on sustainable practices considering the variables viz., people management, employees, vendors, customers, raw materials, chemicals, facilities, utilities and energy. The model has made an attempt for value addition of sustainable management and practices at restaurants. The study deliberated to focus on a typical case of Hauz Khas village, Delhi, India; its adverse impact on environment in restaurant operations. The study was able to make an attempt to identify the deliverables of the sustainable approaches of 5 star deluxe hotels, mid scale 3–4 star hotels representing international and domestic chains, four stand alone restaurants were part of this study in Delhi-NCR, India. The findings from the study suggests a fabulous prospect for restaurant operators to pursue and implement sustainable policies and practices that leads to cost savings, branding and a constructive mark on the environment. However, this is only possible with a combined effort from all the key stakeholders viz., Restaurant owners, management and employees, Government and Customers.

12.1 FOOD SERVICE INDUSTRY: IS THE GROWTH STORY GREEN?

Food service industry is growing at 18% annually for the last five years and is anticipated to attain a turnover of approximately US$992 billion by the end of the year 2014. Café's and restaurants have a market share of 50%, while Asia-Pacific region accounts for 43%. With the growing demand in this sector, it is pertinent to reflect on the preferences of guest's or customers while they choose a restaurant. Primarily customers choose a restaurant based on quality of the food, cleanliness, behavior of employees. (Deveau, 2009; Dutta et al., 2008; Hu, Parsa, and Self, 2010; Restaurant and Food Services Industry, 2013).

Globally, the environment is put under terrific strain by human activity resulting in disturbing the biological equilibrium, depletion of natural resources, environmental pollution, warming of the earth, raise in sea levels, etc. Climate change is the result of past actions.

Various studies conducted in the Unites States concluded that cities consume 2/3rd of the global energy produced, 76% of carbon dioxide (CO_2) emissions are from cities on account of transport, industry and construction related activities. Studies have shown those buildings and construction activities use 40% energy resources, 30% mineral resources and 20% water resources of the world. These activities also account for 40% of CO_2 emissions, 30% solid wastes and 20% water pollution in the world. (Green Building Platinum Series).

An intense global competition has led the human life more opportune and contented; hence there has been an overuse of natural resources, which in turn leads to ecological disbalance. (Hirsh, 2010). Global warming has further impacted the depletion of the stratospheric ozone layer, water, air, noise, light pollution, and the damage caused by acid rain and desertification (Chen and Chai, 2010; Ramlogan, 1997). Thus, due to these impacts, the protection of environment has become crucial and pertinent.

Green economy in today's world is a billion dollar sector that includes not only ecofriendly and green lifestyle products, but also organic agriculture, renewable energy, clean tech, water and waste management, natural resources and land management. The effects and challenges of global warming have made people more aware and conscious about going green. This has indeed spearheaded the concept of green practices or the green attitude. In order to sustain in the competitive world green business strategy is very essential and is a must while it may not be wrong to state that the future is dependent on this initiative of going green. Ample of studies conducted on the international context, found that the emerging concepts such as green marketing, green labeling, greening industries promotes the green practitioners from imitators in the long run and also boosts up with confidence of generating cash flows. Research conducted in this context found that customer is willing to pay more while the same adds to the credibility of such kind of business. Evidences are available particularly with the developed countries while it is controversial in the developing countries with particular reference to Asia.

Consumer's consciousness has led to a budding demand for ecofriendly products. In fact, this rising demand has compelled all the socially responsible companies of all the sectors to develop and practice environment friendly products. (Schubert, 2008). This trend is also visible particularly in the area of hospitality since there is indeed a greater consumption of water, energy, raw materials, increased emission of greenhouse and the generation of waste. (Bazoche, Deola and Soler, 2008; Han and Kim, 2010; Lee et al., 2010; Loureiro, 2003). Restaurant industry will not be able to escape from this trend as well for its survival since the continued perceptive of growth in healthy products and healthy food consumption created in the society has resulted the emergent of green restaurants. (Hu, Parsa and John, 2010; Schubert, 2008).

Studies conducted in this area concluded a significant correlation between environmental insights and consumers and their ecofriendly deeds. (Ellen, Wiener and Cobb-Walgren, 1991; Hu et al., 2010; Laroche et al., 2001). There are few studies which focused on just environmental concerns within the hospitality industry. (Han et al., 2011; Rodriguez and Cruz, 2007; Scanlon, 2007; Tzschentke, Kirk and Lynch, 2008; Wu and Teng, 2011), and very few have in particular with restaurant industry have made an attempt to examine the environmental issues and challenges. (Hu et al., 2010). However, consumers' awareness, attitudes, and environmental concerns toward green restaurants and their intentions to dine are not been examined in totality. At this juncture, industry practitioner's perspectives are very vital to make the authors to understand the implications of consumer's knowledge of green practices at the restaurant to make it sustainable.

12.2   SUSTAINABILITY: THE RISING HOPE

Sustainability as a concept has made an impact a decade back with the world commission of on environment and development (WECD) introduced the movement of sustainability. A decade later, sustainability has become the key success factor and a conception pertinent to both government and the industry as well. (Kuosmanen and Kuosmanen, 2009). Conversely, since the last ten years, this concept has gained a momentum worldwide with particular reference to the sensible thoughts and an alarm prevailing about sustainability in the society in contrast to the traditional behaviors, which focused only on theoretical issues and framework. (Sheth et al., 2011). The inclination towards sustainability emerged with a viewpoint of corporate social responsibility, green initiatives, fair trade practices, environment protection, social responsibility, green economy, green marketing, etc. Globally, government and the industry, is moving towards the concern with regard to the application of sustainability in reality for its long-term feasibility. This step has been made keeping the interests of social and environmental responsibility. Principles such as economic viability, proactive and voluntary collaboration among stakeholders, a generalized and application model development and practically workable model development. (Frontier Arch Biosphere Reserve

(FABR), 2012) is being used International hotel chains. Subsequently in due course of time, due to green practices, an increased brand image and corporate reputation is being build which indeed is a precious assets of an organization. Green practices will stimulate a segment of the population who value these practices which will in turn will gain a competitive advantage among other players within the industry.

To create energy efficient buildings and meet the criteria of an environment LEED certification needs to be in existence. The purpose of LEED certification is to monitor and control the aspects such as water efficiency, energy saving, prevention of carbon dioxide emissions. LEED rating systems promotes not only commercial buildings but is also geared towards residential constructions as well. There are a growing number of evidences that are influenced with these practices and are using LEED guidelines at the time of designing their restaurants. Prominent example in this regard McDonald's, Yum Brands, Chipotle, Starbucks and Denny's which are LEED certified Restaurants. In fact, McDonald's have started using fryers which are more energy efficient with less consumption of cooking oil. It is notable that Mc-Donald's was awarded as Platinum LEED certification, which is the United States Green Building Council's highest award. McDonald's have also initiated more natural lighting, recycling programs, rainwater harvesting in some of their locations. (Going Green, 2008; Green Building Council, 2009; Elan, 2010; Darden Restaurants, 2013). Franchisees such as Subway have also adopted greener practices by opening up LEED certified facilities and thus save money in turn by reduction of energy and usage of water through LEED designing process. On similar lines, quick service hamburger chain in the region has also adopted green practices with healthy menu choices. (Elan, 2009; Evos Signs South Florida, 2009). There are other restaurant chains locally who have implemented environment friendly practices by purchasing equipment that reduces waste and uses less energy, adopting local foods, ban of disposable cups, selling biodynamic and sustainable wines, train employees on green practices. (Going Green, 2008)

To spearhead the green movement at the restaurants, Green Table Network guidelines are valuable to this industry (Green Table Network, 2013). The set guidelines dictates elimination of Styrofoam and non-recyclable plastics, implementation of paper recyclable's, installation of low flow fixtures on all dish-washing sinks, post "turn it off" light and faucet reminders, retrofit current incandescent lighting to energy efficient technologies, purchase 30%–100% processed chlorine-free paper products, have a sustainable purchasing policy, and choose one protein on their menu from an organic/sustainable/

ethical source (Young, 2009). These efforts can help restaurants to increase their bottom line with an improved guest satisfaction and intangible benefits to society as well.

Studies conducted in the area of quick service restaurants in Switzerland found that the majority of respondents supported the use of local foods compared to the branded. The National Restaurant Association (NRA) is in partnership with Energy Star, Turner Foundations, and Food Service Technology Centre to create an environmental program at the restaurants. (NRA, 2009). Study conducted by NRA found that the initial investment required to set up a green restaurants is high, however the restaurants will experience returns on their investment as well. Study conducted in Boston; found that restaurants save money by replacement of trash service, recycling and compositing, replacing standard toilets with low flow toilets, reducing consumption of energy by installing energy efficient equipment, implementing smoking bans, participation of activities for reduction of carbon footprint. (First, 2008; Gise, 2009; Dutta et al., 2008). On a similar lines, Green Restaurant Association (GRA), a non-profit organization is the USA also provides cost-effective and convenient guidelines so that the restaurants could operate and be more environmental responsible. (www.dinegreen.com). Primarily, there are three types of certification that is provided to the restaurant and listed the following as an environmental guideline:

(a) Energy efficiency and conservation
(b) Water conservation and efficiency
(c) Recycling and compositing
(d) Purchasing sustainable, local, and organic foods
(e) Pollution prevention
(f) Use of non-toxic and chemical products
(g) Sustainable furnishings and building materials (only apply to new builds)

Sustainability with in hospitality industry is set as a approach for setting up of operations, for example, building brand image, corporate reputation, increase trust, reduction in cost and thus earning earnings. (Boerner, 2010; United National Global Compact, 2010). These activities further induce hospitality services or product led services, which is solely operated and controlled by the private sectors. However, it is highly recommended by the practitioners that it is imperative that both government and private players together progress as a model to appraise sustainability for the sustainable growth of an economy and not just for one single operation. (Kiewiet and Vos, 2007; United Nations Global Compact, 2010; Crittenden et al., 2011; Herremans

et al., 2011). Measurement models have been used by the international players in the industry (Dingwerth, 2007), for example, Delta hotels, one of the
largest independent hotel chain has initiated ecofriendly policies and adopted
sustainable practices that can assess the progress of the key areas of concern
in sustainability: energy and atmosphere, energy, water, waste, procurement
of food and materials, facilities, carbon footprint, community involvement,
engagement of guests. (Delta Hotels, 2012). Intercontinental, Hilton, Wynd-
ham are some of the hotel chains which also developed and initiated sustainable practices. (Tepelus, 2008; Hsieh, 2012).

Although, there is a rising interest in the consumption level and perception towards more environmental friendly products (Sheth et al., 2011; Robin,
1999), yet consumers also give priority to varied factors such as accessibility, affordability and convenience of these ecofriendly products and services. (World Business Council for Sustainable Development, 2012; Iannuzzi,
2012). Here, consumers need to be educated to care about self, community
and nature for a broader change in the uneven spending and consumption
pattern. Linking to this, industry needs to think about financial viability and
economic benefits to a broader society. (Dahlsrud, 2008; Jackson, 2009; Sheth
et al., 2011).

12.3   GREEN: THE NEED OF THE HOUR

"Green and Go-Green" are being used interchangeably at a macro level in
majority of the industries globally. The business practices include ecofriendly,
green, organic, locally produced, environmentally sound, sustainable, biodynamic and energy efficient, reduction in carbon footprint. (Deveau, 2009;
Dutta et al., 2008; First, 2008; Gise, 2009). Ecofriendly practices are also
gaining momentum in the world of travel, tourism and hospitality leading
to a significant contribution to environment, cost-effectively. (Tzschentke
et al., 2008). Green practices include renewable resources, conserving water, implementing a recycling program such as recycling glass, cardboard,
cooking oil; composting, low pollution, energy conservation throughout the
production process, usage and disposal cycle, packaging, transportation, furnishings, building material, waste management. (Elan, 2009; Hu et al., 2010;
Tzschentke et al., 2008).

"Green" has become the buzz word for today's business, while the customers are more aligned towards choices of products that are more ecologically conscious by paying a premium amount. (Manaktola and Jauhari, 2007;
Han, Hsu, and Sheu, 2010; Robinot and Giannelloni, 2010; Susskind and

Verma, 2011; Schubert et al., 2010). A study was conducted comparing the green practices of restaurants of India and United States and their willingness to pay 10% more towards environment friendly practices. (Dutta et al., 2008).

"Green" is not simply a color; the concept of "green" represents: eco-friendly, social justice and economic development, and healthy. While "environmental protection" stresses reduced waste and pollution, the concept of "green" is broader." Green practices are predominantly vital in the restaurant industry, where building and managing strong brands has become one of the critical tasks of restaurant owners and brand managers (Jeong and Jang, 2010; Schubert et al., 2010). A few authors among others perceive that with engagement of green practices at restaurants, there has been a positive impact on the brand recognition and financial deliverables. (Schubert et. al. 2010).

12.4 GREEN: IS IT CUSTOMER'S FIRST CHOICE?

Several studies concluded that consumers who have an inclination towards green behaviors pay for the services a more than what is originally being demanded for. Studies conducted in the context of India found that the hotels should offer similar products and services as any other non-green practicing hotel so that the guests choose the hotel to stay just because it is practicing green. The study found that 85% of the respondents in the survey that was conducted believed that they should pay a premium for the parts associated with green practices. While 52% of the respondents believed that should pay a premium for all the costs that is associated or related to green. The guests who believed that a premium should be paid felt that 4–6% can be paid more for the green initiatives. (Manaktola and Jauhari, 2007). On a similar lines, study conducted by Dutta et al. (2008) comparing the guest perceptions in restaurants in India and the United States for green practices, found that the respondents in India were more health conscious and about the green products and services, while were not willing to pay a premium for the green services. In contrast to the same, respondents from the United States were willing to pay 10% more for the restaurant services which have implemented green practices. Although hotel chains are taking initiatives for ecofriendly products however are skeptical unless majority of the guests demand for green practices. (Kasim, 2004). Another study conducted by Kasim (2004) in the context of Malaysia to understand the perception of domestic and international tourists to choose a hotel to stay and a restaurant to dine out found that the respondents who are conscious about green and healthy practices at home yet they are not much concerned about the same practices while they out from their home while in travel. The study also found that the guests are willing to use local products and local food instead of branded ones, yet they were not willing to pay more for the green hotels. (Choi and Parsa, 2006; Choi et. al. 2009; Dutta et al., 2008).

12.5 THE RESTAURANTS: EMBRACING SUSTAINABILITY

Restaurants engaging themselves in green practices, will achieve less environment and social problems that might arise at their operational level of the restaurants. An approach towards ecofriendly it reduced solid waste, water consumption, energy consumption, air pollution. (Johnson, 2009; Butler, 2008; Carbonara, 2007). Purchase of green products such as foodstuffs, nontoxic cleaning and chemical corporate and biomass agricultural waste products not just create brand image but also builds in green practices in the supply chain as well. For instance the manufacturer or the farmers will be compelled to produce or deliver only green products to such restaurants. These activities will in turn not only promote to the economic growth but also invite job opportunities to the economy as well (Ismail et al., 2010).

Regardless, the budding importance in green initiatives, yet there is a paucity of studies conducted in this area of hospitality especially in restaurants (Hu et al., 2010; Jang et al., 2011). However, there have been some studies that have been conducted by the authors with regard to sustainable environmental tourism (e.g., Moeller et al., 2011; Tsaur et al., 2006; Weaver and Lawton 2007; Williams and Ponsford, 2009), while some studies with particular reference to the reduction of solid waste, water consumption, energy consumption and air pollution (Johnson 2009; Butler 2008; Carbonara 2007). The concern to the environmental and social orientation has led to creation of value and image to the hotels (Chan, 2008; Lee et al., 2010). Infact, Claver-Cortes et al., 2007; Tari et al., 2010; Molina-Azorin et al., 2009; Kim and Han 2010, Cornell pointed out that there is a connect between tourism sector and environmental orientation and economic performance in the hotel industry (Garcia and Armas, 2007).

Studies in the context of sustainability have been mentioned as an "emerging megatrend" (Lubin and Esty, 2010). Hotels and restaurants promotes locally sourced organic ingredients, reduction in usage of carbon footprints, ski areas installing wind powered chairlifts, and so forth (Caterer and Hotelkeeper, 2010). Research carried on in this area concludes a greater job satisfaction of employees in organizations committed to sustainability (Parish et al., 2008; Walsh and Sulkowski, 2010).

In the process of enhancing sustainability and ecotourism, the managers of restaurants are bound to respond to the green trends such as local foods, organic foods, low –carbon foods, etc., since for a restaurant, natural resources and physical environment are the most essential assets in the tourism industry.

Figure 1 demonstrates green management practices for restaurants at Taiwan based on the studies conducted by Green Restaurant Association in US (2009), Green Table in Canada (2007), the Worcestershire Green Party in the UK (2009), the Environment Association in Japan (2007), Restaurant and Catering in Australia (2010), and studies on green restaurants in Taiwan (e.g., Lai and Hu, 2008; Hsu, 2008).

Green Practices at Restaurants

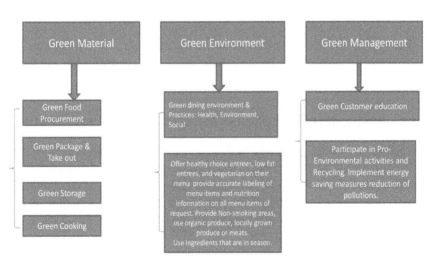

FIGURE 1   Green practices at restaurants: a conceptual framework (Adapted from: Wang et al., 2013; Choi and Parsa, 2008).

Environmental concerns were initially related only to the industries, which had an impact on the environment directly. However, during 1980s through 1990s ecological pressures affected at a macro level. Unlike the immense polluters such as the metallurgical or chemical industry yet the hospitality industry also exposes to the conflicts arising through implementing environmental policies. Customers seeking hospitality services demands extra pampering with lashings of hot water, high-pressure showers, freshly laundered linen, an ample supply of towels, abundant supplies of food and drink, the availability of swimming pools.

12.6   GREEN MANAGEMENT PROCESS: PROCUREMENT

Procurement of green food would engage in developing supply chains that will deliver goods in a way that suffice the standards of green practices minimizing the impact on the environment, thus leading to sustainability. A series of strategic questions arises because the customer's preferences and perceptions are changing with the first issue with the food itself while the concern is does the food has an impact on the environment? While the second concern is with the production system that is being imposed and does this have an impact? The third component is inclined towards at which location the food is produced and the distance taken from the producer to the processor, and finally to the consumer. The foods that the customers eat viz., fish, beef or vegetables, do these have an impact on the environment?, does it have an impact on the cost with green practices? Research in this context has primarily concentrated on the making of greenhouse gases (GHGs).

12.7   RESTAURANTS: ADVERSE ENVIRONMENTAL FOOTPRINT

The introduction to sustainable practices, intense internal competition, changes in climate and the consistent growth in the travel and tourism industry constrained the restaurant industry at multiple levels of challenges and therefore is more cautious to use clean water, energy and farmland (Gössling et al., 2011; Kasim and Ismail, 2012; Department for Environment, Food and Rural Affairs, 2007).

There are three principal levels of global warming agent's viz., carbon dioxide, nitrous oxide and methane. Research suggests that methane is 72 times as powerful as carbon dioxide in terms of its global warming potential and nitrous oxide is 289 times as powerful, based on their effect over a 20-year period (IPCC, 2007). Although there is a large body of literature available in this context, however confirming the link between GHGs and global warming is stills a pertinent question (BBC, 2013; Guardian, 2010; Kasim and Ismail, 2012). Different foodstuffs have considerable variations in the amount of GHGs that are produced for instance animal products have to a large extent GHG than plant products.

Green restaurants may be defined as "new or renovated structures designed, constructed, operated, and demolished in an environmentally friendly and energy-efficient manner" (Lorenzini, 1994, pg.119). The prime focus of a green restaurant as compared to a traditional restaurant is on three R's viz., reduce, reuse and recycle and two E's viz., efficiency and energy. LEED (Leadership in Energy and Environmental Design) standards, an internationally recognized green building certification, stated that any structure must be "premeditated and built aiming at improving performance energy savings, water efficiency, CO_2 emissions reduction, improved indoor environmental quality, and stewardship of resources and sensitivity to their impacts" (USGBC). Restaurant chains, such as Arby's, Carl's Jr., Chipotle Mexican Grill, and Subway, fall into the category of green restaurants. Arby's and Chipotle each have at least one LEED-certified restaurant (Elan, 2009). Chipotle Mexican Grill has even incorporated a wind turbine into one of its restaurants that should generate more than 7% of its power needs.

The following are a few of the recommendations listed by the Green Restaurant Association.

1. *Energy efficiency and conservation*: A better energy efficiency of lighting, refrigeration, air-conditioning, and gas appliances.

2. *Water efficiency and conservation*: A better water efficiency of toilets, faucets, laundry, and sprinkler systems.

3. *Recycling and composting*: Transition to recycled products with the highest post consumer content available and non-tree-fiber paper products: napkins, paper towels, toilet paper, office paper, take-out containers, coffee jackets, plates, and bowls.

4. *Sustainable food*: Sustainable food products support the long-term maintenance of ecosystems and agriculture for future generations. Organic agriculture prohibits the use of toxic synthetic pesticides and fertilizers, irradiation, sewage sludge, and genetic engineering. Locally grown foods reduce the amount of pollution associated with transportation primarily by fossil fuels. Plant-based foods require fewer natural resources and create less pollution per calorie consumed.

5. *Pollution prevention*: Achieved through reduction at source, reuse, or improving operational practices.

6. *Recycle*: Recycled, tree-free, biodegradable, and organic products. Recycled products are made from materials that are collected from postconsumer or postindustrial waste sources. Tree-free products are made from alternative plant sources such as hemp or kenaf. Biodegradable products are capable of being decomposed by biological agents, especially bacteria. Organic products are grown without the

use of toxic synthetic pesticides and fertilizers, irradiation, sewage sludge, and genetic engineering.

7. *Chlorine-free paper products*: Chlorine-free paper products are unbleached or whitened with alternatives such as hydrogen peroxide, oxygen, and ozone.

8. *Nontoxic cleaning and chemical products*: Replace hazardous chemical products with biodegradable and nontoxic alternatives; dish detergent, germicides, disinfectants, toilet bowl cleaners, drain cleaner, floor wash, floor polish, glass cleaners, degreasers, and laundry detergent.

9. *Renewable power*: Electricity and power are available from renewable resources such as wind, solar, geothermal, small hydro, and biomass. These energy sources cause dramatically less air pollution and environmental damage compared to fossil fuel, nuclear, and large-scale hydroelectric energy source.

10. *Green building and construction*: Green design and construction practices significantly reduce or eliminate the negative impact of buildings on the environment, occupants, and the local community.

11. *Employee education*: There is a definite need to train all employees, managers, and owners about green practices. Topics covered include an environmental profile of the restaurant industry, a history of environmental issues relevant to food service: landfills, water pollution, air pollution, clear-cutting, and global warming, and data describing the restaurant impacts on the environment

There is indeed a dearth in the studies on the effects of green practices on the industry, thus it is important to note the customer's variations with regard to different attributes.

12.8　THE RESTAURANTS: GREEN PRACTICE TRENDS

The mounting volume and significance of the restaurant industry dictates that its direct environmental effects (e.g., energy use, solid waste generation, air and water use, carbon emissions, food safety concerns and refrigerant use) need to be documented and addressed. Recognition of reduction of solid waste, water consumption, energy consumption, air pollution is relatively a new phenomenon. Hotels and restaurants generate hefty quantities of solid waste, including packaging, food scraps and cleaning and maintenance materials, of which some are toxic. This waste is often composed carelessly in waste dumps, causing serious environmental pollution (Carbonara, 2007; Cummings, 1997; Erdogan and Tosun, 2009).

Prior studies that were conducted to identify the green practices at the restaurants primarily include; recycling and compositing products such as glass, plastic, metal, cardboard aluminum which are mainly recyclable in restaurants. While the quality of the soil is improved by the composite of the food waste. Energy and water efficient equipment in certain areas in the restaurants such as Kitchen, dining area, restroom can be applied. Ecofriendly packaging, organic food with menu sustainability, which can be thought and made from Non-toxic materials (Hasnelly, 2011). A number of the studies in the area of green restaurants had been conducted in the western countries such as the Green Restaurant Association, 2008; 2009; Green Seal, 2009; Green Table Network, 2007 and Weinstein, 1994). Few studies have also been conducted in the context of Asia (e.g., Japan Environment Association, 2007; Lai and Hu, 2008; Hsu, 2008; Hu et al., 2010; Teng et al., 2012).

National Restaurant Associations stated that 62% of consumers said they are more likely to spend their money at a restaurant if they know it is green (NRA, 2011). A positive effect on corporate brand image and financial benefits has also been observed through engagement in green restaurant practices, as well as positive contribution to the economic sustainability of the local community (Schubert et al., 2010).

Natural groceries with no chemical pollutants or any synthetic blend that is bent through local agriculture suffice the meaning of green food and beverage (F&B) industry (LaVecchia, 2008; Gold, 2007). A study conducted in the context of U.S concludes that 69% of the respondents look forward for the use of organic food on their menu (Poulston and Yiu, 2011). Thus leading to the sustainable growth of natural balance and well being to the flora and fauna as well (Sloan, Legrand, and Chen, 2009). Taking the case of Mc Donald's as a prominent example, changed their casing approach from Styrofoam to cardboard so as to generate waste that is recyclable and lessen burning of oil (Szuchnicki, 2009). Starbucks ranked first in this category of restaurant chains to be socially and environmentally responsible. This is executed with the use of recyclable take-out containers, use of energy efficient lighting in seating areas, use of water efficiency equipment throughout in all the locations (Brookes, 2009). Other brands, which adopted green practices are Wendy's, Burger King and Yum (Dutta et al., 2008).

Studies conducted in this context conclude that engagement with green practices might have a significant impact on the cost management of a restaurant as well. Implementing an energy-management strategy that improves energy efficiency saves money and improves the bottom line while reducing the environmental impact of the property. Lower energy use means less energy produced at the source, which in turn means a reduction in greenhouse gas emissions and a lower energy bill for the restaurant. Other benefits include reduced financial risk, strengthened customers relations, increased harmony with the community, improved image and enhanced loyalty with the key stakeholders (Choi and Parsa, 2006; Manaktola and Jauhari, 2007; Szuchnicki, 2009) Use of compact fluorescent lights, reuse of linens—saves water, detergent, Installation of green roofs, etc., are also some of the measures wherein operation cost can be minimized for a restaurant industry (Green Hotels and Responsive Tourism Initiative, 2012) (Green hotels). "Green" businesses have proven to be competitive and are currently open to greater opportunities (Dolnicar, 2010).

12.9   RESTAURANTS AND SUSTAINABILITY: AN INDIAN PERSPECTIVE

India is rapidly becoming a preferred destination for tourism, both International as well as Domestic, with an annual growth of about 15%. The hospitality sector is a major consumer of energy in different forms for various end-uses. There is significant scope for direct energy saving as well as energy generation through the installation of Solar Water Heating and other Renewable Energy Technologies (RETs). For instance, appropriate solar thermal systems can be installed for heating water for various requirements in the rooms, and kitchen, etc., or for providing steam at higher temperatures for various applications. Solar photovoltaic systems and devices—such as streetlights, garden lights, corridor lights, billboards, or rooftop systems meeting captive power requirements can be installed in hotels. On the other hand, through use of bio-methanation or biogas plants not only food leftovers and kitchen wastes, including fruit and vegetable wastes are disposed off in an environmentally sound fashion but the biogas produced from these plants can be used as an energy resource. Besides these, green/energy efficient building designs can be introduced based on solar passive concepts and techniques, resulting in considerable savings in energy consumption in buildings, particularly from the large air-conditioning loads in hotels. Thus, such interventions can not only bring about savings but also substitute conventional electricity or fossil fuels resulting in a cleaner environment, making the hotels and restaurants 'green' in true sense (Teri, 2011).

Some of the prominent cases implementing solar water heating systems in the context of Indian hotels include; Spice Village, Idukki, Kerla, Trident, Jaipur, Rajasthan, Udai Vilas, Udaipur, Rajasthan, Radisson Hotel, Agra, Uttarpradesh, Gateway Hotel, Bengaluru, The Leela, New Delhi, Country Inn and Suit, Gurgaon, Haryana, Radisson, Ranchi, Jharkhand, while ITC Mauya, New Delhi and Clarks, Ajmer, Jaipur have Solar Steam Generation Systems as a practice. The Emerald Hotel and Executive Apartments, Santacruz, Mumbai have Solar Photovoltaic System (Ministry of New and Renewable Energy, 2012).

12.10   ENERGY

"According to Pacific Gas and Electric's Food Service Technology Center (FSTC), "restaurants are the retail world's largest energy user. They use almost five times more energy per square foot than any other type of commercial building… using the latest EPA carbon equivalents, that amounts to 490 tons of carbon dioxide produced per year per restaurant" (Horovitz, 2008).

Energy includes electricity, fossil fuels, water and sewage, certain vehicle fuel, hot water and chilled water. However, primarily, energy use is consumed by cooking and food preparation, ventilation and cooking (Legrand, et al., 2010; Sustainable Food Services, 2013). Energy management includes switching off the lights and heaters and not in use or when floors are not occupied. Studies conducted in early 20th century proposes a series of energy saving measures such as insulating the roof, posing closing devices on doors, fitting all radiators with individual thermostats and implementing an on-going staff training plan, installation of a computer-controlled air conditioning system, the installation of double glazing, the installation of an energy-efficient kitchen, the purchase of fuel-efficient refrigeration, and the purchase of fuel-efficient transport are the typical measures of energy management at restaurants.

Water is also one of the central elements at the restaurant and hospitality industry. Water is scarce resource and its role is in numerous activities such a laundry, food production, washrooms, dishwashing. The same can be managed for lower water usage through water flow controllers, faucet aerators, push button activated showers in public areas (Greenhotelier, 2005; Baker, 2005; Stipanuk, 2002; Webster, 2000). Conservation of water is the key cause to premises of a restaurant, influential to usage of energy. Pumping, boiling, delivering clean water to restaurant premises indeed consume ample amount of energy consecutively results in carbon emissions.

12.11   THE GREEN MANAGEMENT PROCESS: CORPORATE SOCIAL RESPONSIBILITY AT WORK

Corporate social responsibility, a relatively new concept have been added in the literature of the world of business. The concept derives not just economic benefits such as reduced financial risk but also concentrates on social desirable goods and services, which is the yardstick of the ethical standards of the business. However, this is also to note that in the past social dimensions were neglected and business focused on environmental strategies only. To be precise, waste generated from furniture and fittings could be reused by local charities, food leftover could also be distributed to local charities thus these little steps will lead to being sensitive to the local community (Green Hotelier, 2007). Some measurement such as sorting and collecting from waste with separate bin, reduction of usage of plastic, aluminum and polystyrene foam, employing local community. Clean environmental working conditions for employees and paying fair wages. Guests being informed about environmental practices at restaurants. Restaurant being engaged with any other restaurants or any organizations and promoting sustainable practices.

Following are some of the indicators of corporate social responsibility:

1. Organically certified food ingredients used in the process of food preparation.
2. Locally sourced food ingredients from a close proximity as possible thus leading to support the local community.
3. Seasonal food ingredients.
4. Balance between vegetarian/fish/meat/chicken/egg/and other animal products offered in the menu.
5. Organic wines being served.
6. Kitchen staff properly trained on environmental standards.
7. The food safety control tool Hazard Analysis and Critical Points (HACCP) to be fully implemented.
8. Adherence of socially inclusive, affordable and reflective local communities, culture and seasonality.
9. Involvement of high environmental standards and reduction of energy consumption.
10. Promoting animal welfare and valuing nature and bio-diversity that comply with national regulatory standards and the international standards being developed by the World Organization for Animal Health (OIE).

11. Providing suitable menu information and food offerings to guests so that choices can be made based on food provenance and sustainability.

12. Ensuring the transportation systems facilitate fuel/energy efficient sourcing and distribution of food from the point of production/processing to the point of consumption.

13. Ensuring that the food being offered to guests are prepared with minimum amount of addictive's, and no usage of color or preservatives and the same is being informed to the guests as well.

14. Ensuring corporate code of practice to address the issues raised by the International Labor Organization's Declaration on the fundamental principles of Human Rights at work (Rimmington and Hawkins, 2006; Legrand, et al., 2010).

12.12   THE GREEN MANAGEMENT PROCESS: DINING ENVIRONMENT AND PRACTICES

Innovative services are the key to survival for the restaurants keeping in view the competitive scenario. Any restaurant must be inclined towards critical attributes with respect to designing the physical environment providing an exclusive and a novel experience to the guests such as the facility's esthetics, ambience, spatial layout, seating comfort, electronic equipment/displays, cleanliness and social factors of a facility affect the psychology of customers (Chen, 2011; Jones, 1996; Ottenbacher, 2007). Horng and Hu, 2008 and Hu, Horng, and Sun, 2009). A study conducted by Liu and Jang, 2009 concluded that outdoor dining have become imperative in today's changing lifestyle. Studies concluded by Addis and Sala (2007), Wall and Berry (2007) and Han and Ryu (2009) established that the restaurant environment is influential to the pay-in price, contentment and trustworthiness. Several authors are of view that interior variables are important attributes compelling a customer to pay a premium price for the service at the restaurant (Ryu and Jang, 2008). Thus leading to an extent that restaurant managers are struggling to create an innovative environment to create a center of attraction for the guests and through word of mouth and positive feedback restaurants will lead to increased patrons (Ryu and Han, 2010; Heung and Gu, 2012). In addition to the several authors research in this context, intense temperature alteration has enforced restaurants to disburse more thought towards communal responsibility (Chau, Tse, and Chung, 2010; Baraban and Durocher, 2010). Facing the budding recognition of creating an exemplary ambience, leading to intensifying operating costs, as the owners of the restaurants have to invest more in designing the physical environment (Gössling et al., 2011; Hu, Parsa, and Self, 2010; Johnson, 2009). Therefore, several authors have suggested that the restaurant managers should be inclined more towards practices of green and sustainability which leads not only reduction to operating costs through the design of more efficient spaces, the conservation of energy and water, the renewal of equipment, and the implementation of energy consumption changes (Baraban and Durocher, 2010; Lorraine and Saffron, 2010). The reason being the restaurant and food service industries consume large amounts of water and energy and produce large amounts of waste and air pollution and therefore this sector should be more inclined towards preventive measures so as to reduce the impact of the pollutant variables on the environment. A study conducted by Hu et al., 2010) recommended that any restaurant should move towards economizing energy, reducing waste, and preventing chemical contamination and maximizing other indicators of eco-friendliness, comply with government policy help to reflect on communal responsibility as well.

There is indeed an abundance of the literature in the context of environmentalism in the area of hospitality due to the mounting needs of the society. However, majority of the studies have been conducted in the lodging sector (Bohdanowicz, et al., 2011; Kasim, 2007, 2009), Typically, food service is the third biggest revenue stream after transport and lodging.(World Trade Organization, 1998). Researchers in this context have explored a series of findings food related areas. Studies conducted in this area found that there is direct correlation between local food, authenticity and the tourism experience (Sims, 2009; Gössling et al. (2011). Rogerson (yr) in the context of South Africa examined those policies with regard to food purchasing behavior by the customers. Although, an ample of studies have been conducted in the area of food services yet, research in the context of restaurant is an unexplored area and therefore very limited studies in the context of U.S, Taiwan Malaysia in particular have been conducted in this area.

Studies explored in the context of U.S found that there is a dire need for engagement in green practices since there a majority of the consumers who are habitual of dining out. In Asian countries, especially in Taiwan and Malaysia a similar findings have been concluded and therefore there is a large number of street food, coffee shops and restaurants are available in plenty. This is due to fact of the people being mobile throughout the day (Schubert et al., 2010).

Studies explored in the restaurant industry theoretically are divided into three different perspectives—Health, Environment and Social. Further researchers in this area have explored ten dimensions:

(1) Support of healthy lifestyles;
(2) Sustainable agriculture;
(3) Safe food practices;
(4) Macro environmental factors;
(5) Environmentally friendly practices;
(6) Green activism;
(7) Community involvement;
(8) Socially responsible design;
(9) Fair human-resource practices; and
(10) Socially responsible marketing.
(Krol, 1996; Carroll, 1989; Carroll, 1989; Mohr, 1996; Meriläinen, et al., 2001; Mohr, 1996; Carroll, 1986, Drumwright and Murphy, 2001).

12.13   HEALTH CONCERNS

Considering the growing need of ecofriendly products, services, healthy and safe food and due to the fact of the conclusions of varied research carried in different countries especially in the context of U.S, Taiwan and Malaysia, where dining out of consumers are in the lifestyle. To sustain this, restaurant should inculcate a culture of serving nutritionally and balanced food (Allison, 2004). Food habits such as organic, low fat foods, elimination of antibiotics in livestock, food preservatives will indeed develop and enhance the sales of a restaurant and also sustain many other employment opportunities as well (Cavanaugh, 2004; King, 2003; David, 2003; Watson, 2002). This is also pertinent that in spite of all these efforts, if there in so effective communication in terms of labeling and nutritional information to the consumers is indeed essential (Nayga, 2000). As a mandate food safety standards, disclosure of precise information with regard to the preparation of the food (Lynch, 2000). It is also noticeable of the fact that policy of non-smoking is strictly enforced at the restaurants which is valuable for both employees and clientele (Cumming and Sciandra, 2003).

12.14   ENVIRONMENTAL CONCERNS

Green Practices are in increasing phenomenon in the macro environment, while restaurant services is an integral part of an economy being the third largest contributor to an economy as noted earlier. Operationally routine revision needs to be implemented for a larger benefit to the economy, such a recycling of paper such as napkins and paper cups, reducing the use of fluorocarbons, plastic materials used at restaurants. Here, the role of both government and the private players needs to be enforced for a better green environment practices at a macro level as well. McDonald's, Starbucks are prominent examples to be cited who themselves are into Green Activism.

12.15   SOCIAL CONCERNS

Socially responsible restaurants have launched many programs for the senior citizens by not only spending time and energy but also money as well (Paul, 1998). Starbucks is a very prominent example who have provided coffee for CARE (a worldwide relief and development foundation) (Parkard, 2001).

McDonalds has also promoted its employees' participation in community service such as tutoring children and painting classrooms (PR Newswire com, 2000). In 2004, Outback Steakhouse received the Restaurant Neighborhood Award for its outstanding community involvement practices. Research conducted in this area concluded that consumers have a positive outlook and intent towards organizations that are socially responsible. Research also found that there is also a secondary level of being responsible to the society by recruiting senior citizens and disable persons within the organizations, employee benefits, work life balance, healthy environment, equal employment opportunity guidelines, etc. (Bhattacharya and Sen, 2004; Murray and Vogel, 1997; Creyer and Ross, 1997; Lord, Parsa, and Putrevu, 2004). Starbucks as a prominent example again, since it treats its employees like a family (Schultz, 1997).

12.16   MANAGERS' ATTITUDES TOWARD GREEN PRACTICES AND WILLINGNESS TO CHARGE

Attitude towards green practices is influenced by four-dimensional structure, which is perceived as the key factor for the responsibility towards the environmental concerns (Laroche et al., 2001; McCarty and Shrum, 1994; Roberts, 1996). A study by Han et al. (2009) while examining the guests of the hotel decision making towards choosing a hotel concluded that the attitude towards green behavior is the key factor for overall green hotels. Customers more conscious towards green environment and green practices also pay more at the restaurant. Subsequently, through word of mouth more customers flow in and also there is a revisit of the customer at the restaurant. Han et al., 2010; Han and Kim, 2010). Evidences from researchers concluded that a positive attitude and intention will result in revisiting a green hotel (Lam and Hsu, 2004). A study conducted by Hu et al. (2010) examined the effects of knowledge gained for ecofriendly products and practices by the consumers of a restaurant's also patronize a green restaurant. Results of the study showed significant positive correlation between knowledge and green patronize of restaurants (Schubert, 2008; Szuchnicki, 2009). The study had been carried in the context of Malaysia.

12.17 THE GREEN MANAGEMENT PROCESS: CONSUMER PERSPECTIVES

A study on green restaurants conducted in China, found that although the perception of guests who rated that fresh air and ventilation is what they demand for the key factor for green practices while the hotel employees rate Safe and clean food as a better green practice. While these were the perceived factors by hotel employees and the guests, the restaurants did not discontinue to usage of disposable ware, doggy bags, serving wild/banned animals as a part of their items in the menu. To conclude there is dire necessary to educate customers and also the hotel employees regarding the green environment and practices at the restaurant. Heung, Fei, and Hu (2006; Heung et al., 2006). While a study conducted in Taiwan, found that customer knowledge of green practices were an important determinant to patronize a restaurant. The study concluded that consumers with higher income levels, higher education level are a key factor to patronize a restaurant. An observation was made by the author that those who have attained the age of 41 showed more inclination towards green restaurants. (Hu et al., 2010).

Evidences from various researchers examined a significant impact on the decision-making process and knowledge on green practices (Kaplan, 1991). Blackwell, Miniard and Engel (2006), Laroche et al. (2001) and Loureiro (2003) have recommended that the consumers' knowledge is positively correlated with consumer behavior. Further, Nabsiah, Elham, and Tan (2011) also established that all segment in exchange decision processes is influential by patrons knowledge. Bradley, Waliczek and Zajicek (1999) examined on the correlation between environmental knowledge and attitude towards environment by the consumers and found that both the variables were significantly correlated. A different study conducted by Samantha Smith (2009) concluded that with an increase of consumer's knowledge on environmentally friendly products, there is also an enhancement of attitude towards environmental friendly products. While Nabsiah et al. (2011) found that the concern towards environment, knowledge of green product, knowledge on environment is significant to green purchase behavior of green volunteers. Thus to conclude from these studies consumers knowledge would definitely and indeed affect the attitude, concern towards the environment and intent towards green restaurants. There are also studies that have been conducted by Loureiro (2003); Bazoche et al. (2008); Yang (2007) found purchase behavior is allied with a consumer's knowledge of green issues. Hu et al. (2010) argued that two variables, that is, consumers' knowledge of sustainable restaurant practices and environmental concerns are key determinants of consumers' intentions to patronize green restaurants. The study also found that consumers' knowledge of green restaurants is influential on their intent to stand by for a green restaurant ultimately by their ecological concerns and biological behaviors.

Restaurant Operations Impacting Environment Adversely: The Case of Hauz Khas Village

The Hauz Khas Village is located in the heart of south Delhi (India) and represents culture and heritage that dates back to the Khalji and Tughlaq era. The area was inhabited by artisans, artists and local village inhabitants for decades in a landscape marked by a lake-side area of ancient tombs. Given the proximity to 'south Delhi' the area soon became one of Delhi's trendiest night spots, visited by the social elite with ample spending power. In no time this destination was swarming with new restaurants and boutique shops that came up to take advantage of the emerging trends and the social setting that the Village offered. Many of these Restaurants opened without required permits or approvals, and made no efforts to minimize their environmental footprint.

The adverse impacts of the development without any concern for the environmental and even sociocultural aspects were soon visible. The lake was polluted in no time with uncontrolled discharge from the restaurants and other businesses. Issues of garbage disposal were also becoming apparent. The groundwater level fell drastically and at a social level the local community was facing onslaught of people visiting the night spots and restaurants over the weekends, creating havoc with the peace and quiet of the place.

Reacting to a petition filed by Mr. Pankaj Sharma the National Green Tribunal ordered 34 restaurants to be closed effective 20th September 2013. None of these restaurants had relevant clearances and their owners maintained they had no idea about what licenses or environmental clearances were required before opening these businesses. None of them had undertaken any measures to install effluent treatment units and had been polluting the local water body. The role of enforcement agencies like the Delhi Pollution Control Committee (DPCC) too came under the scanner. With more than 50,000 restaurants mushrooming all over the city, this case is really the tip of the ice berg. The DPCC is visibly dysfunctional and clearly not doing its job. With restaurants drawing underground water, causing water pollution and other environmental hazards, it's about time the civic agencies got their act together.

As the case moves forward, the livelihood of nearly 2000 families is at stake, as also is the sustainability of the Hauz Khas Village, its ancient monuments, the cultural heritage and environment. While the court has given some reprieve to those who are willing to comply with all environmental directives, the restaurant owners must understand that it is their responsibility to ensure they adhere to all environmental regulations and conduct their business ethically, minimizing their ecological footprint on the communities where they run their operations. The case also highlights the need for the government agencies to play a positive role in terms of communicating the environmental requirements and ensuring the restaurant businesses are clear about the same. All the stakeholders need to work together to push the city restaurants to embrace green practices (NDTV, 2013).

12.18 PRACTICING SUSTAINABLE APPROACHES: THE GROUND REALITY AND ISSUES IN THE INDIAN CONTEXT

The recommendations of the 'Green Restaurant Association' provide a guide map for restaurant operations to emulate to minimize their environmental footprint and practice sustainable approaches to managing their businesses.

A survey was conducted in the National capital Region, involving participation of restaurant operation managers, general managers and chef managers. In all 11 respondents were interviewed to solicit information on the approach of their restaurant operations on the issue of embracing sustainability and implementing environment friendly measures on the ground. They represented a range of food service establishments from those situated in hotels classified as 5 star deluxe (Radisson Blu Plaza, NH8, The Grand, Vasant Kunj,

The Crowne Plaza, Gurgaon, Taj Palace Hotel, Delhi and Double Tree by Hilton, Gurgaon), to those situated in mid scale 3–4 star hotels (Sarovar Portico, Gurgaon and The Lemon Tree, Gurgaon) representing both international as well as domestic chains, Four stand alone restaurants (Bercos, Gurgaon, Down Town Café, Gurgaon, The Pind Baluchi, Gurgaon and The Indian Grill, Gurgaon) were part of the survey conducted. The budget and the unbranded, un-organized segment was not part of this study.

The survey findings were segregated into the below listed focal elements:

12.18.1 ENERGY EFFICIENCY, USING RENEWABLE POWER AND CONSERVATION

All respondents identified this as an area where they were actively pursuing options to minimize consumption. From using energy efficient equipment, switching over to more energy efficient lighting, using motion sensors, to designing spaces for maximum day light utilization, these restaurant operations were making an effort to be energy efficient. Innovative practices like opening restaurant 'section by section' are being deployed at the Taj Palace. Their large conference facilities were renovated to replace old energy guzzling HVAC systems with more efficient latest technology. The stand-alone restaurants were limited by their investment ability to use technology for energy savings, but were nonetheless concerned to save on their energy costs by all possible means. Use of renewable power was restricted to use of solar power by large hotels. None of the freestanding restaurants reported any measures to harness renewable power. In fact most reported running on expensive generator back up provided by their facility managers. Air conditioning was mentioned as the biggest energy use component, and the restaurants were trying to find balance between maintaining a comfortable environment and minimizing energy costs. The high cost of energy and its impact on already struggling bottom line emerged as a unanimous motivator for business to work on the aspect of energy efficiency and conservation.

12.18.2 WATER EFFICIENCY AND CONSERVATION

All the surveyed hotel based operations reported that interventions like rain water harvesting, effluent treatment systems other legally mandatory norms were being followed. Restaurants operating out of planned commercial retail complexes too stated the same. When asked about monitoring their consumption levels, and whether they were drawing ground water most either had no information or declined to comment. General Manager at Crowne Plaza, Gurgaon mentioned that their parent company was committed to best environmental practices, and effort were being made not only to educate employees but also guest to prevent misuse of water. Using faucets in kitchens that reduce water flow and hence consumption, as well as exhaust systems that minimize need to consume water in cleaning hood systems was becoming popular with new restaurant kitchens that are coming up. As it is becoming costly to procure water, managements are reacting to the need to use the same more efficiently.

12.18.3   RECYCLING AND COMPOSTING

While all respondents reported their operations were segregating waste, they were not sure if this was resulting in actual recycling of waste. The standalone restaurants were disposing 'grease' based waste appropriately, and also adhering to legal requirements as mandated by the pollution control board and the green tribunal guidelines. The stand alone restaurants operating out of commercial retail spaces were not composting. The hotel based restaurants however reported having sewage treatment, composting and related processes. The Radisson Blu Plaza, has a mechanized composting facility on site.

12.18.4   SUSTAINABLE FOOD

The restaurant operations were found struggling on this front. Some had made efforts to start herb gardens, and others were making efforts to build a supply chain that was more sensitive to environmental concerns. Most stated using organic food (raw products) was not finding favor as the price impact was substantial. Being located in urban centers these operations did not have any substantial green spaces wherein they could grow their own vegetables, etc. Bercos was the only restaurant operation that was buying produce directly from local producers; all others had long-term contracts with established large scale vendors.

When asked about changes in terms of menu offerings in view of sustainability concerns, the over whelming response was that while menus today reflect a 'vegetarian' focus, the analysis of sales trend do not indicate any move away from 'non vegetarian' or rich vegetarian diet. In fact the general manager at India Grill was quite categorical in stating that 75% of their customers are non vegetarians, and the segment is clearly driving the eat out business in NCR.

12.18.5 POLLUTION PREVENTION

When asked about the issue, none of the interviewed respondents had any well-informed response. No one had clarity on the forms and quantum of pollution. The undertone of the respondents was that they have a business to run, so some adverse impacts were to be expected. The Gurgaon based business blamed lack of proper electricity, water supply as a reason for over dependence on use of generators (diesel based), and drawing ground water. The stated that lack of a master sewer system is a huge problem, most have deployed septic tank systems or other forms of decentralized sewage management systems.

12.18.6 CHLORINE-FREE PAPER PRODUCTS, NONTOXIC CLEANING AND CHEMICAL PRODUCTS

Managers were aware that they were using recycled paper based packing material, but use of plastic was also prevalent and they were not clear if what they were using was environment friendly grade or not. While restaurant operators based out of large hotels were confident that their purchase department would be sensitive towards using non-toxic cleaning chemicals, they were not clear on the expectations. Restaurant managers at free standing restaurants shared that they used popular brands and assumed they were compliant to regulatory requirements if any.

12.18.7 GREEN BUILDING AND CONSTRUCTION

None of the respondents had any inputs on this aspect.

12.18.8 EMPLOYEE EDUCATION

The respondents shared that the focus of employee education was directed towards those aspects where cost savings could be realized. Some operations like those at The Grand mentioned marking 'environment awareness' week, restaurant managers at the Bercos and the India Grill mentioned using daily briefings towards reminding employees to save electricity, follow best practices in kitchens towards creating and managing waste. Focus on managing production to minimize waste was mentioned by a majority of operators. At Pind Balluch the employees record the weight of waste every day to generate awareness and to minimize the same.

12.18.9   PRACTICAL IMPLICATIONS: AN INSIGHT FOR THE INDIAN RESTAURANT SECTOR

- Restaurant operations are focusing on aspects like energy consumption due to significant cost savings that are possible.
- The higher end restaurant establishments operating out of established hotels are adhering to the environmental regulations.
- There are gaps in understanding of what environmental regulations stand-alone restaurants are required to follow. The green tribunal or appropriate local pollution boards needs to do more to clarify the requirements and their mandate to seek compliance.
- Employee education in this aspect needs to move beyond only those aspects that bring in cost savings.
- CSR initiatives towards sustainable environmental practices would be welcome
- Restaurant operations are not engaging with the customers and that will be critical to implement practices that may require them to change in terms of their service and product expectations.
- There is hardly any documented impact assessment; as a result no restaurant business has clarity on the environmental footprint that they are creating. Restaurant managers have no data to analyze how per person consumption levels commercially compare against typical domestic household standards.
- Design, construction and architectural interventions sensitive to environmental must be encouraged in both new setups as well as old operations undergoing renovations.
- While the survey ignored non-branded and budget segment of restaurant operations, the unorganized restaurant segment, the challenges towards adhering to legal requirements as well as lack of focus on environmental concerns is likely to be more severe.

12.19   THE WAY FORWARD AND CHALLENGES

There is a tremendous opportunity for restaurant operators to pursue environment friendly policies and implement changes that result in cost savings, positive branding and a positive environmental footprint. This however will require an integrated approach that brings all stakeholders together, ensuring each delivers on their end. The key stakeholders are:

- Restaurant owners, management and employees.

- Government at various levels and its associated functions.
- Customers.

What must they do to imbibe and enforce green practices?

12.19.1   RESTAURANT OWNERS

1. Invest in green initiatives: this may include technology, energy efficient equipment, facility design and guidance on operating practices.
2. Keep abreast of the 'law' and ensure compliance of all environmental rules and regulations.
3. Conduct periodic impact assessment to map progress on all business aspects that impact environment.
4. Recognize that sustainable environmental practices will have positive long-term implications for their business, the society in which they operate.

12.19.2   RESTAURANT MANAGEMENT AND EMPLOYEES

1. Implement environment policy through appropriate decisions related to standard operating procedures.
2. Support innovative approaches towards the reduce, recycle and re-use aspects of energy, water and material consumption.
3. Communicate best practices, train teams and motivate employees to be change agents.
4. Reward implementation and positive results, recognize individual and team achievements.

12.19.3   CUSTOMERS

1. Recognize they are central to the ability of restaurant operations to pursue green practices.
2. Show support by patronizing businesses that may efforts to reduce adverse environmental impacts.
3. Ask questions, seek clarifications from restaurant operators to send a strong message that you care about environmental issues and consider that as an aspect in your choice of restaurants that you patronize.
4. Adapt service and product expectations to accommodate restaurants to pursue a green agenda.

12.19.4 GOVERNMENT

1. Deconstruct the law with respect to environmental aspects impacting the food service establishments of various types for the businesses to understand and implement.
2. Clarify the role, authority and punitive power of key governmental bodies so that there are no ambiguity on functions and jurisdiction.
3. Create public awareness, communicate, inform the stakeholders about specific requirements and offer support to enable compliance. Achievers can be rewarded.
4. Vigilance to identify defaulters, penalize as per law, ensure that businesses new or old are aligned with green practices.

The biggest challenge for any change process is to get the stakeholders committed to the cause. Given the nature of restaurant business in India, and a general apathy to environmental concerns there are many challenges:

- Restaurant sector is largely constituted by unorganized, unbranded operations, small in scope and size.
- Education level of owners, managers and employees is varied; a large part of the work force has no formal education.
- Government agencies involved and entrusted with enforcement of environmental regulations are neither equipped nor driven to do the job.
- Customers remain disconnected with the environmental issues; awareness levels are low in general.
- The approaches that are common in the developed world may not be relevant to the realities of developing economies; there will be need to bring in the local context.
- Weak supply chain, cold chain aspects in developing countries are critical drain points.
- Turning sustainable practices into elements of competitive advantage remains a challenge for the restaurant sector at large.

Figures 2 and 3 will provide the readers a snap of green restaurant operations consolidating the findings of the survey and the literature in this context.

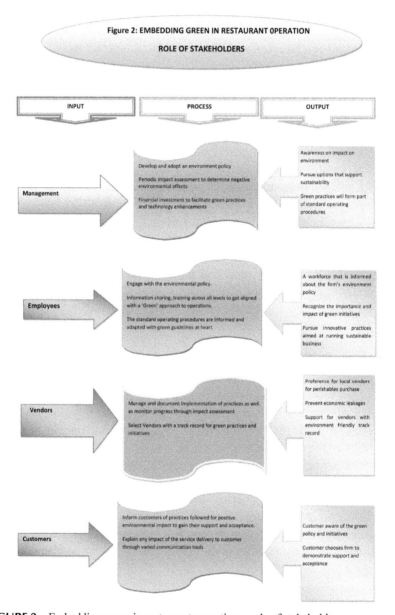

FIGURE 2   Embedding green in restaurant operation—role of stakeholders.

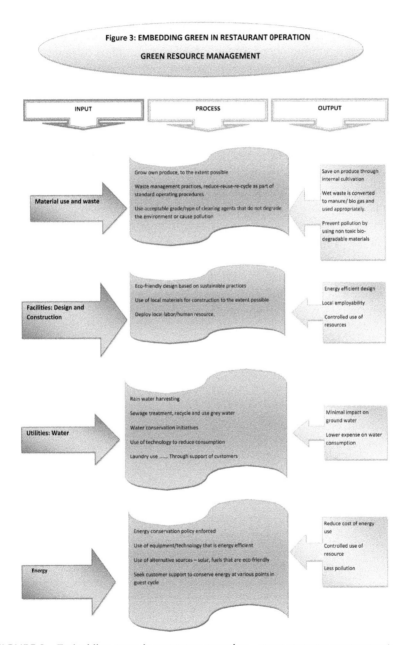

FIGURE 3 Embedding green in restaurant operation—green resource management.

The response of the commercial restaurant sector in the different developmental context demonstrates a sharp variance. As is evident from the study, the business operating out of developed economic context have responded to the need for sustainable practices in tandem with the regulatory frameworks that have emerged. In developing countries like India, while the branded top tier segment especially restaurants based out of five star deluxe hotels have demonstrated progress in implementing green practices as mandated by law and also cost reduction compulsions. They need to continue to build sustainable practices and also encourage and inform both employees and the customers as critical stakeholders for continued progress. The large unorganized and unbranded part of the commercial restaurant seen in developed economies remains the challenge. It is here that the government has a role to play. Appropriate government organs must work to build momentum in facilitating the process of involving this segment and ensuring that green practices are absorbed in a phased manner. Impact assessment must be done to ensure that the negative environmental impacts are monitored and steps taken to mitigate them to the extent possible. Success will depend on how effectively the various stakeholders will work together in years to come.

KEYWORDS

- customers
- global warming
- green environment
- recycling
- restaurants
- sustainability

REFERENCES

Addis, M., and Sala, G. (2007), "Buying a book as a Christmas gift: two routes to customer immersion," The Service Industries Journal, Vol. 27, Issue 8, pp. 991–1006.

Allison, P. (2004), "Here's to Your Health," Restaurants and Institutions, Vol. 114, Issue 4, pp. 48–55.

Baraban, R. S., and Durocher, J. F. (2010), Successful restaurant design. Hoboken, New Jersey: John Wiley and Sons Inc.

Bazoche P., Deola C., and Soler L. (2008), An Experimental study of wine consumers' willingness to pay for environmental characteristics. 12th Congress of the European Association of

Agriculture Economists (online) Cited on 20th September, 2013, Available from: http://www.legrenelle-environment.fr/grenelle-environment.

BBC (2013), "Some arguments made by climate change skeptics," (Online) Cited on 20th September, 2013, Available from: www.news.bbc.co.uk/1/hi/sci/tech/8376286.stm.

Bhattacharya, B.C. and Sen, S. (2004), "Doing Better at Doing Good: When, Why and How Consumers Respond to Corporate Social Initiatives" California Management Review, Vol. 47, Issue 1, pp. 9.

Blackwell R, Miniard P, Engel J (2006), Consumer Behavior (10th ed.). Thomson South-western: Mason, OH.

Boerner, H. (2010), "Sustainability rises to top of strategy setting for growing number of corporate leaders," Corporate Finance Review, Vol. 15 No. 1, pp. 32–4.

Bohdanowicz, P. (2005) "European hotelier's environmental attitudes: Greening the business," Cornell Hotel and Restaurant Administration Quarterly, Vol. 46, pp. 188–204.

Bradley JC, Waliczek ™, Zajicek JM (1999), "Relationship between environmental knowledge and environmental attitude of high school students," Journal of Environmental Education, Vol. 30, Issue 3, pp. 17–21.

Butler, J. (2008), "The compelling "hard case" for "green" hotel development," Cornell Hospitality Quarterly, Vol. 49, pp. 234–44.

Carbonara, J. (2007), "Foodservice goes green," Foodservice Equipment and Supplies, Vol. 60, Issue 9, pp. 48–54.

Carbonara, J. (2007), Restaurant goes green, Restaurant Equipment and Supplies, Vol. 60, pp. 48–54.

Carroll, A. (1989), Business and Society. Cincinnati, OH: South-Western.

Cavanaugh, B. (2004). Organic. Nation's Restaurant News, Vol. 38, Issue 25, pp. 42.

Chau, C.K., Tse, M.S., and Chung, K.Y. (2010), "A choice experiment to estimate the effect of green experience on preferences and willingness-to-pay for green building attributes," Building and Environment, Vol. 45, pp. 2553–2561.

Chen, W.J. (2011), "Innovation in hotel services: culture and personality," International Journal of Hospitality Management, Vol. 30, pp. 64–72.

Choi, G., and Parsa, H.G. (2006), "Green practices II: Measuring restaurant managers' psychological attributes and their willingness to charge for the green practices," Journal of Foodservice Business Research, Vol. 9, Issue 4, pp. 41–63.

Choi, G., Parsa, H.G., Sigala, M., and Putrevu, S. (2009), "Consumers' environmental concerns and behaviors in the lodging industry: A comparison between Greece and the United States," Journal of Quality Assurance in Hospitality and Tourism, Vol. 10, Issue 2, pp. 93–112.

Claudia, S.K and Sarah, F. (2010), "A Review of Restaurant Sustainable Indicators," Advances in Hospitality and Leisure, Volume.6, pp. 167–183.

Creyer, E. and Ross, W.T. (1997), "The Influence of Firm Behavior on Purchase Intention: Do Customers Really Care About Business Ethics?," Journal of ConsumersMarketing, Vol. 14, Issue 6, pp. 421–432.

Crittenden, V.L., Crittenden, W.F., Ferrell, L.K., Ferrell, O.C. and Pinney, C.C. (2011), "Market-oriented sustainability's conceptual framework," Journal of the Academic Marketing Science, Vol. 39, pp. 71–85.

Cumming, P. and Sciandra, R. (2003), "New York's Smoke-Free Regulations: Effects on Employment and Sales in the Hospitality Industry," Cornell Hotel and Restaurant Administration Quarterly, Vol. 44, Issue 3, pp. 9–16.

Cummings, L.E. (1997), "Waste minimization supporting urban tourism sustainability: A mega-resort case study," Journal of Sustainable Tourism, Vol. 5, pp. 93–108.

Dahlsrud, A. (2008), "How corporate social responsibility is defined: an analysis of 37 definitions," Corporate Social Responsibility and Environmental Management, Vol. 15, pp. 1–13.

Darden Restaurants. (2012), Darden sustainability. (Online) Cited on 20th September, 2013, Available from http://www.darden.com.

David, B. (2003), McDonald's Seeking Cut in Antibiotics in Its Meat. New York Times.

Delta Hotels (2012), Delta Green Watch (online) Cited on 20th September, 2013, Available from:www.deltahotels.com/en/greens/thedelta- green-watch.

Department for Environment, Food and Rural Affairs. (2007), Food service and eating out: An economic survey. Surveys, Statistics and Food Economics Division, Department for Environment, Food and Rural Affairs (DEFRA) (Online) Cited on 20th September, 2013, Available from: http://archive.defra.gov.uk/evidence/economics/foodfarm/reports/documents/Food%20 service%20paper%20Jan%202007.pdf

Deveau, D. (2009), "Fight the power," Foodservice and Hospitality, Vol. 41, Issue 11, pp. 47–52.

Dingwerth, K. (2007), The Global Reporting Initiative Then New Transnationalism: Transnational Governance and Democratic Legitimacy, Palgrave Macmillan, New York, NY.

Dolnicar, S. (2010),"Identifying tourists with smaller environmental footprints," Journal of Sustainable Tourism, Vol. 18, pp. 717–734.

Drumwright, M. and Murphy, P. (2001). Corporate Societal Marketing. In P.N. Bloom and G.T. Gundlach (Eds.), Handbook of Marketing and Society. Thousand Oaks, CA: Sage Publications, pp. 162–171.

Dutta, K., Umashankar, V., Choi, G., and Parsa, H. G. (2008), "A comparative study of consumers' green practice orientation in India and the United States: A study from the restaurant industry," Journal of Foodservice Business Research, Vol. 11, Issue 3, pp. 269–285.

Elan, E. (2009), Subway franchisee scores a hit with green store design, Nation's Restaurant News, Vol. 43, Issue 26, pp. 14.

Elan, E. (2010), LEED-ing the way. Nation's Restaurant News, Vol. 44, Issue 6, pp. 16.

Ellen PS, Wiener JL, Cobb-Walgren C. (1991), "The role of perceived consumer effectiveness in motivating environmentally conscious behaviors," Journal of Public Policy and Marketing, Vol. 10, pp. 102–117.

Erdogan, N., and Tosun, C. (2009), "Environmental performance of tourism accommodations in the protected areas: Case of Goreme Historical National Park," International Journal of Hospitality Management, Vol. 28, pp. 406–414.

Evos Signs South Florida Franchise Agreement. (2009) Nation's Restaurant News, from the restaurant industry, Journal of Foodservice Business Research, Vol. 11, Issue 3, pp. 269–285.

First, D. (2013) (Online), Cited on 20th September, 2013, Available from: http://www.boston.com/ae/restaurants/first.

Frontier Arch Biosphere Reserve (FABR) (2012), "Building a national model for sustainable tourism," (Online) Cited on 21st September, 2013, Available from: www.fabr.ca.

Gössling, S., Garrod, B., Aall, C., Hille, J., and Peeters, P. (2011), "Food management in tourism: Reducing tourism's carbon foodprint," Tourism Management, Vol. 32, pp. 534–543.

Gise, M. (2009), "Ecofriendly baby steps can grow green initiatives," Nation's Restaurant News, Vol. 43, Issue 21, pp. 44.

Going Green. (2008) Nation's Restaurant News, Vol. 42. Issue 49, pp. 55

Gold, M.V. (2007), Organic production/organic food: What is organic production? (online) Cited on 20th September, 2013, Available from: http://www.nal.usda.gov/afsic/pubs/ofp/ofp.shtml.

Gössling, S., Garrod, B., Aall, C., Hille, J., and Peeters, P. (2011), "Food management in tourism: reducing tourism's carbon 'foodprint,'" Tourism Management, Vol. 32, Issue 3, pp. 534–543.

Graci, S., and Dodds, R. (2008), "Why go green? The business case for environmental commitment in the Canadian Hotel Industry?," Anatolia: An International Journal of Tourism and Hospitality Research, Vol. 19, Issue 2, pp. 251–270.

Green Building Council Honors McDonald's, Gives HQ LEED Certification. (2009).

Green Building Platinum Series, Building Planning and Massing (online) cited on 20th September, 2013, Available from: http://www.bca.gov.sg/GreenMark/others/bldgplanningmassing.pdf

Green Hotelier (2005), Saving energy in kitchens. Green Hotelier, Issue 34, pp. 1–4.

Green Hotelier (2007), "What does it mean to be a sustainable hotel?" Green Hotelier, Issue 44, pp. 24–26.

Green Restaurant Association (2008), Serving up a green menu, Business and the Environment Vol. 14, Issue 11, pp. 1–4.

Green Restaurant Association (2013), Green Restaurant ™ 4.0 Standards: New Certification Standards (Online), Cited on 20th September, 2013, Available from:http://www.dinegreen.com

Green Restaurant Association, 2009. Green Restaurant ™ 4.0 Standards: New Certification Standards (Online) Cited on 20th September, 2013, Available from: http://www.dinegreen.com

Green Restaurant Associations (2011) (Online) cited on 20th September, 2013, Available from: http://www.greenrestaurant.com.

Green Seal (2009), GS-46 Green Seal ™ Environmental Standard for Restaurants and Food Services (Online) Cited on 21st September, 2013, Available from:http://greenseal.org/certification/standards/gs46 restaurantfoodsvcs.cfm

Green Table Network (2013) Green table sustainable foodservice (Online) Cited on 20th September, 2013, Available from: http://www.greentable.net.

Green Table Network (2013). What Defines a Green Table Network Restaurant or Foodservice Outlet? (Online) Cited on 20th September, 2013, Available from: http://greentable.net/Diners.

Guardian (2010), "Climate change skepticism," (Online) cited on 20th September, 2013, Available from www.guardian.co.uk/environment/climate-change-skepticism.

Han H., Hsu Li-T., Lee Jin-Soo (2009), Empirical investigation of the roles of attitudes toward green behaviors, overall image, gender, and age in hotel customers' ecofriendly decision-making process, International Journal of Hospitality Management, Vol. 28, pp. 519–528.

Han Heesup, Hsu Li-Tzang, Lee Jin-Soo, Sheu Chwen (2011), "Are lodging customers ready to go green? An examination of attitudes, demographics, and ecofriendly intentions," International Journal of Hospitality Management, Vol. 30, pp. 345–355.

Han Heesup, Hsu Li-Tzang, Lee Jin-Soo, Sheu Chwen (2011), "Are lodging customers ready to go green? An examination of attitudes, demographics, and ecofriendly intentions," International Journal of Hospitality Management, Vol. 30, pp. 345–355.

Han Heesup, Kim Yunhi (2010), "An investigation of green hotel customers' decision formation: Developing an extended model of the theory of planned behavior," International Journal of, Hospitality Management, Vol. 29, pp. 659–688.

Han Heesup, Kim Yunhi (2010), "An investigation of green hotel customers' decision formation: Developing an extended model of the theory of planned behavior," International Journal of Hospitality Management, Vol. 29, pp. 659–688.

Han, H., and Ryu, K. (2009), "The roles of the physical environment, price perception, and customer satisfaction in determining customer loyalty in the restaurant industry," Journal of Hospitality and Tourism Research, Vol. 33, Issue 4, pp. 487–510.

Hasnelly (2011), "Winning Strategies Value Creation of Customer Loyalty of Green Food Product," Journal of Asia Pacific Business Innovation and Technology Management, Vol. 1, Issue 1, pp. 47–59

Herremans, R., Pyasi, N. and Lu, J. (2011), "The journey toward sustainability reporting: How accountable are the tourism industries?" Tourism Recreation Research, Vol. 36 No. 3, pp. 247–57.

Heung, C. S., and Gu, T. (2012), "Influence of restaurant atmospherics on patron satisfaction and behavioral intentions," International Journal of Hospitality Management, Vol. 31, pp. 1167–1177.

Heung, V., Fei, C., and Hu, C. (2006), "Customer and Employee perception of a green hotel: The case of five-star hotels in China," China Tourism Research, Vol. 2, Issue 3, pp. 270–297.

Horng, J. S., Hu, M. L., Hong, J. C., and Lin, Y. C. (2011), "Innovation strategies for organizational change in a tea restaurant culture: a social behavior perspective," Social Behavior and Personality, Vol. 39, Issue 2, pp. 265–273.

Horovitz, B. (2008), Can restaurants go green, earn green? Cited on 20th September, 2013, Available from: http://www.usatoday.com/money/industries/environment/2008–05–15-green-restaurants-ecofriendly n.htm.

Hsieh, Y.C. (2012), "Hotel companies' environmental policies and practices: a content analysis of their web pages," International Journal of Contemporary Hospitality Management, Vol. 24 No. 1, pp. 97–121.

Hsu, L.H. (2008), An initiative investigation of establishing the index of environmental management system for green restaurant in Taiwan, Thesis of Graduate Institution of Hospitality Management, National Kaohsiung Hospitality College.

Hsu, L.H. (2008), An initiative investigation of establishing the index of environmental management system for green restaurant in Taiwan, Thesis of Graduate Institution of Hospitality Management, National Kaohsiung Hospitality College.

Hu Hsin-Hui, Parsa HG, John Self (2010) "The Dynamics of green restaurant patronage," Cornell Hospitality Quarterly, Vol. 51, Issue 3, pp. 344–362.

Hu Hsin-Hui, Parsa HG, John Self (2010), "The Dynamics of green restaurant patronage," Cornell Hospitality Quarterly, Vol. 51, Issue 3, pp. 344–362.

Hu, H. H., Parsa, H. G., and Self, J. (2010), "The dynamics of green restaurant patronage," Cornell Hospitality Quarterly, Vol. 51, Issue 3, pp. 344–362.

Hu, H.H., Parsa, H.G., Self, J. (2010), "The dynamics of green restaurant patronage," Cornell Hospitality Quarterly, Vol. 51, Issue 3, pp. 344–362.

Hu, H-H., Parsa, H.G., Self, J. (2010), "The dynamics of green restaurant patronage," Cornell Hospitality Quarterly, Vol. 5, Issue 3, pp. 344–362.

Hu, M. L., Horng, J. S., and Sun, Y. H. C. (2009), "Hospitality teams: knowledge sharing and service innovation performance," Tourism Management, Vol. 30, pp. 41–50.

Iannuzzi, A. (2012), Greener Products: The Making and Marketing of Sustainable Brands, Taylor and Francis Group, Boca Raton, FL.

IPCC (2007), Working Group I. Climate Change 2007: The Physical Science Base, Intergovernmental Panel on Climate Change, Geneva, Cited on 20th September, 2013, Available from: www.ipcc.ch/ipccreports/ar4-wg1.htm.

Jackson, T. (2009), Prosperity Without Growth: Economics for a Finite Planet, Earthscan, London.

Jang, Y.J., Kim, W.G., Bonn, M.A. (2011), "Generation Y consumers' selection attributes and behavioral intentions concerning green restaurants," International Journal of Hospitality Management, Vol. 30, Issue 4, pp. 803–811.

Japan Environment Association (2007), The Green Purchasing Network (Online) Cited on 20th September, 2013, Available from:http://www.gpn.jp/basic/green life/index.html

Japan Environment Association (2007), The Green Purchasing Network, Cited on 21st September, 2013, Available from: http://www.gpn.jp/basic/green life/index.html

Jeong, E.H., Jang, S.C. (2010), "Effects of restaurant green practices: which practices are important and effective?" "Caesars Hospitality Research Summit," Cited on 20th September, 2013, Available from: http://digitalcommons.library.unlv.edu/hhrc.

Johnson, R. (2009), "Organizational motivations for going green or profitability versus sustainability" Business Review, Vol. 13, Issue 1, pp. 22–28.

Jones, P. (1996), "Managing hospitality innovation," Cornell Hospitality Quarterly, Vol. 37, Issue 5, pp. 86–95.

Kaplan S. (1991) Beyond rationality: Clarity-based decision making. In Environment, cognition and action, ed. T. Garling and G. Evans, pp. 171–190. New York: Oxford University Press.

Kasim, A. (2004), "Socio-environmentally responsible hotel business: Do tourists to Penang Island, Malaysia care?," Journal of Hospitality and Leisure Marketing, Vol. 11, Issue 4, pp. 5–28.

Kasim, A. (2007) "Towards a wider adoption of environmental responsibility in the hotel sector," International Journal of hospitality and Tourism Administration, Vol. 8, Issue 2, pp. 25–49.

Kasim, A. (2009) Managerial attitudes towards environmental management among small and medium hotels in Kuala Lumpur, Journal of Sustainable Tourism, Vol. 17, Issue 6, pp. 709–725.

Kasim, A., and Ismail, A. (2012), "Environmentally friendly practices among restaurants: Drivers and barriers to change," Journal of Sustainable Tourism, Vol. 20, Issue 551–570.

Kasim, A. (2009), Managerial attitudes towards environmental management among small and medium hotels in Kuala Lumpur," Journal of Sustainable Tourism, Vol. 17, Issue 6, pp. 709–725.

King, P. (2003) Going Green: Social Consciousness Turns into Responsibility as Operators Focus on Foods, Fish, and Environment. Nation's Restaurant News, Vol. 37, Issue 42, pp. 23.

Krol, G. (1996) Consumer Note Marketer's Good Causes: Roper. Adverting Age, Vol. 67, Issue 46, pp. 51.

Kuosmanen, T. and Kuosmanen, N. (2009), "How not to measure sustainable value (and how one might)," Ecological Economics, Vol. 69 No. 2, pp. 235–43.

Lai, H.S., Hu, H.H. (2008), The trend of green industry: a study of green restaurant in the food service industry, Research report for National Science Council, Taiwan. Grant number: NSC 96–2415-H-130-010.

Lai, H.S., Hu, H.H. (2008), The trend of green industry: a study of green restaurant in the food service industry, Research report for National Science Council, Taiwan. Grant number: NSC 96–2415-H-130-010.

Laroche M, Bergero J, Barbarot-Forleo G (2001), "Targeting consumers who are willing to pay more for environmentally friendly products," Journal of Consumer Marketing, Vol. 18, pp. 503–520.

LaVecchia, G. (2008), "Green: The new gold," Restaurant Hospitality, Vol. 92, Issue 4, pp. 39–44.

Lee Jin-Soo, Hsu Li-Tzang, Han Heesup, Kim Yunhi (2010), "Understanding how consumers view green hotels: how a hotel's green image can influence behavioral intentions," Journal of Sustainable Tourism, Vol. 18, Issue 7, pp. 901–914.

Liu, Y., and Jang, S. C. S. (2009), "Perceptions of Chinese restaurants in the U.S.: what affects customer satisfaction and behavioral intentions?," International Journal of Hospitality Management, Vol. 28, Issue 3, pp. 338–348.

Lord, K.R., Parsa, H.G., and Putrevu, S. (2004), "Environmental and Social Practices:Consumer Attitude, Awareness and Willingness to Pay," In D. Scammon, M. Mason, and R. Mayer (Eds.), Marketing and Public Policy: Research Reaching New Heights, Salt Lake City, UT: American Marketing Association, pp. 25–28.

Lorenzini, B. (1994), "The green restaurant, part II: Systems and service," Restaurant and Institution, Vol. 104, Issue 1, pp. 119–36.

Lorraine, W., and Saffron, O. (2010), "Green identity, green living? The role of proenvironmental self-identity in determining consistency across diverse proenvironmental behaviors," Journal of Environmental Psychology, Vol. 30, Issue 3, pp. 305–314.

Loureiro M (2003) Rethinking new wines: implications of local and environmentally friendly labels. Food Policy, Vol. 28, pp. 547–560.

Loureiro M. (2003), "Rethinking new wines: implications of local and environmentally friendly labels," Food Policy, Vol. 28, pp. 547–560.

Lynch, A. (2002) WAPT"Restaurant Report" Keeps Consumers Informed of Healthy, Unhealthy Restaurants. Mississippi Link, Vol. 10, Issue 24, p. 4.

Management and Green Marketing. Business Strategy and Environment, Vol. 9, Issue 3, pp. 151–162.

Manaktola, K., and Jauhari, V. (2007), "Exploring consumer attitude and behavior towards green practices in the lodging industry in India," International Journal of Contemporary Hospitality Management, Vol. 19, Issue 5, pp. 364–377.

Meriläinen, S., Moisander, J., and Pesonen, S. (2001). The Masculine Mindset of Environmental

Ministry of New and Renewable Energy (2012) (Online), Cited on 20th September, 2013, Available   from:http://www.mnre.gov.in/schemes/support-programs/special-area-demonstration-project-program/.

Mohr, L.A. (1996). Corporate Social Responsibility: Competitive Disadvantage or Advantage? In Proceedings of the 1996 Marketing and Public Policy Conference. American Marketing Association, pp. 48–49.

Murray, K.B. and Vogal, C.M. (1997), "Using a Hierarchy of Effects Approach to Gauge the Effectiveness of Corporate Social Responsibility to Generate Goodwill Toward the Firm: Financial versus Non-Financial Impacts," Journal of Business Research, Vol. 38, Issue 2, pp. 141–159.

Nabsiah AW, Elham R, Tan SS (2011), "Factors influencing the green purchase behavior of Penang environmental Volunteers," International Business Management, Vol. 5, Issue, pp. 38–49.

Nayga, J.R. (2000) "Nutritional Knowledge, Gender, and Food Label Use," The Journal of Consumer Affairs, Vol. 34, Issue 1, pp. 97–103.

NDTV (2013), Decision on closed Harz Khas Village, Restaurant today (Online) Cited on 8th October, 2013, Available from:http://www.ndtv.com/article/cities/decision-on-closed-hauz-khas-village-restaurants-today-423322

Ottenbacher, M. C. (2007), "Innovation management in the hospitality industry: different strategies for achieving success" Journal of Hospitality and Tourism Research, Vol. 31, Issue 4, pp. 431–454.

Packard, B. (2001) Sustainability Practices Presentation. National Recycling Coalition Conference.

Paul, K. (1998) "Govt. Promises ASFSA that School Nutrition is a Top Priority," Nation's Restaurant News, Vol. 32, Issue 8, p. 16.

Poulston, J., and Yiu, A.Y.K. (2011), "Profit or principles: Why do restaurants serve organic food?," International Journal of Hospitality Management, Vol. 30, Issue 1, pp. 184–191.

Remmington, M. and Hawkins, R. (2006), Corporate social responsibility and sustainable food Procurement, British Food Journal, Vol. 108, Issue 10, pp. 824–837.

Restaurant and Catering Australia (2010), Green Table Australia, Cited on 20th September, 2013, Available from:http://www.restaurantcater.asn.au.

Restaurant and Food Services Industry: Market Research Reports, Statistics and Analysis (Online) Cited on 28th September, 2013. Available from: http://www.reportlinker.com/ci02054/Restaurant-and-Food-Services.html,

Roberts JA, Bacon DR (1997), "Exploring the subtle relationships between environmental concern and ecologically conscious consumer behavior," Journal of Business Research, Vol. 40, pp. 79–89.

Roberts, J.A. (1996), "Green consumers in the 1990 s: Profile and implications for advertising.," Journal of Business Research, Vol. 36, Issue 3, pp. 217–231.

Robin, N. (1999), "Making sustainability bite: transforming global consumption patterns," The Journal of Sustainable Product Design, pp. 7–16.

Robinot, E. and Giannelloni, J.L. (2010), "Do hotels' 'green' attributes contribute to customer satisfaction?," Journal of Services Marketing, Vol. 24 No. 4, pp. 157–69.

Rodriguez FJG, Cruz Y del Mar Armas (2007), "Relation between social-environmental responsibility and performance in hotel firms," International Journal of Hospitality Management Vol. 26, Issue 4, pp. 824–839.

Rogerson, C. Tourism-agriculture linkages in rural South Africa: Evidence from the accommodation sector. Journal of Sustainable Tourism, Vol. 20, Issue 3.

Ryu, K., and Han, H. (2010), "Influence of the quality of food, service, and physical environment on customer satisfaction and behavioral intention in quick-casual restaurant: moderating role of perceived price," Journal of Hospitality and Tourism Research, Vol. 34, Issue 3, pp. 310–329.

Ryu, K., and Jang, S. C. (2008), "Influence of restaurant's physical environments on emotion and behavioral intention," The Service Industries Journal, Vol. 28, Issue 8, pp. 1151–1165.

Ryu, K., and Jang, S. C. (2008), "DINESCAPE: a scale for customers' perception of dining environments," Journal of Foodservice Business Research, Vol. 11, Issue 1, pp. 2–22.

Samantha S. (2009), Eating clean and green? Investigating consumer motivations towards the purchase of organic food, ANZMAC, pp. 1–8.

Scanlon N. (2007), "An analysis and assessment of environmental operating practices in hotel and resort properties," International Journal of Hospitality Management, Vol. 26, pp. 711–723.

Schubert F (2008). Exploring and predicting consumers' attitudes and behaviors towards green restaurants. Unpublished master thesis, College of Education and Human Ecology, Graduate School of The Ohio State University.

Schubert Franziska (2008), Exploring and predicting consumers' attitudes and behaviors towards green restaurants, Master thesis, College of Education and Human Ecology, Graduate School of The Ohio State University.

Schubert, F., Kandampully, J., Solnet, D. and Kralj, A. (2010), "Exploring consumer perceptions of green restaurants in the US," Tourism and Hospitality Research, Vol. 10 No. 10, pp. 286–300.

Schubert, F., Kandampully, J., Solnet, D., Kralj, A. (2010), "Exploring consumer perceptions of green restaurants in the US," Tourism and Hospitality Research, Vol. 10, Issue 4, pp. 286–300.

Schubert, F., Kandampully, J., Solnet, D., Kralj, A. (2010), "Exploring consumer perceptions of Green restaurants in the US," Tourism and Hospitality Research, Vol. 10, Issue 4, pp. 286–300.

Schultz, H. (1997). Pour Your Heart into It. New York, NY: Hyperion, pp. 131–139.

Sheth, J.N., Sethia, N.K. and Srinivas, S. (2011), "Mindful consumption: a customer-centric approach to Sustainability," Journal of the Academy of Marketing Science, Vol. 39, No. 1, pp. 21–39.

Sheth, J.N., Sethia, N.K. and Srinivas, S. (2011), "Mindful consumption: a customer-centric approach to Sustainability," Journal of the Academy of Marketing Science, Vol. 39, No. 1, pp. 21–39.

Sims, R. (2009), "Food, place and authenticity: Local food and the sustainable tourism experience," Journal of Sustainable Tourism, Vol. 17, Issue 3, pp. 321–336.

Sloan, P., Legrand, W., and Chen, J.S. (2009), Sustainability in the hospitality industry: Principles of sustainable operations. Amsterdam: Butterworth-Heinemann.

Stipanuk, D.M. (2002), Hospitality facilities management and design, Lansing, USA: Educational Institute of the American Hotel and Lodging Association.

Susskind, A.M. and Verma, R. (2011), "Hotel guests' reactions to guest room sustainability initiatives," Cornell Hospitality Reports, Vol. 11, No. 6, pp. 4–13.

Sustainable Food Services (2013) (Online), Cited on 20th September, 2013, Available from: http://www.sustainablefoodservice.com/cat/energy-efficiency.htm.

Szuchnicki, A. L (2009), Examining the Influence of Restaurant Green Practices on Customer Return Intention, UNLV Theses/Dissertations/Professional Papers/Capstones, University of Nevada Las Vegas (Online) Cited on 20th September, 2013, Available from: http://digitalscholarship.unlv.edu/cgi/viewcontent.cgi?article=1161andcontext=thesesdissertations

Tepelus, C.M. (2008), "Social responsibility and innovation on trafficking and child sex tourism: morphing of practice into sustainable tourism policies?," Tourism and Hospitality Research, Vol. 8 No. 2, pp. 98–115.

Teri (2011), Campaign on Solar Water Heating and other Renewal Energy Technology in Hospitality Sector (Online), Cited on 20th September, 2013, Available from: http://www.teriin.org/index.php?option=com_ongoingandtask=about_projectandpcode=2010RT13ti

Tzschentke NA, Kirk D, Lynch PA. (2008), "Going green: Decisional factors in small hospitality," Intentional Journal of Hospitality Management, Vol. 27, Issue 1, pp. 126–133.

Tzschentkea, N.A., Kirka, D., Lynchb, P.A. (2008), Going green: decisional factors in small hospitality operations," International Journal of Hospitality Management, Vol. 27, Issue 1, pp. 126–133.

United Nations Global Compact (2010), A New Era Of Sustainability: UN Global Compact – Accenture CEO Survey 2010, UNGC, New York, NY.

Wall, E. A., and Berry, L. L. (2007) "The combined effects of the physical environment and employee behavior on customer perception of restaurant service quality," Cornell Hotel and Restaurant Administration Quarterly, Vol. 48, Issue 1, pp. 59–69.

Wang, Y.F; Chen, S.P; Tsang, C. (2013), "Developing Green Management Standards for Restaurants: An Application of Green Supply Chain Management," International Journal of Hospitality Management, Vol. 3, pp. 263–273.

Watson, A. (2002), "Organic Label Frustrates Small Farmers" Knight Ridder Tribune Business News, p. 1.

Worcestershire Green Party (2009), Worcester Green Party Policies, Cited on 20th September, 2013, Available from:http://www.worcestergreenparty.org.uk/localsites/worcester/policies8.html

World Business Council for Sustainable Development (2012), Sustainable Facts and Trends: From a Business Perspective, WBCSD, Geneva, Cited on 20th September, Available from: www.wbcsd.org/about/ contact.aspx.

World Trade Organization. (1998) Tourism services: Background note by the Secretaria,. Cited on September 20, 2013, Available from http://www.wto.org/english/tratop_e/serv_e/w51.doc

Wu, KS, Teng, YM. (2011), "Applying the extended theory of planned behavior to predict the intention of visiting a green hotel," African Journal of Business Management, Vol. 5, Issue 17, pp. 7579–7587.

Yang, YC (2007), Identifying key factors that influence consumers' purchase intentions toward green restaurant, Master of Graduate School of Tourism, Ming Chuan University.

Young, L. (2009), " Making the grade," Foodservice and Hospitality, Vol. 22, Issue 3, pp. 50–52.

CHAPTER 13

CONCEPTION OF SUSTAINABLE ACCOMMODATION PRACTICES IN HOTELS FOR TOMORROW

ANJANA SINGH and BANDANA RAI

CONTENTS

ABSTRACT

The purpose of this chapter is to outline and congregate the sustainable accommodation practices through extensive in-depth literature review and critical content analysis of best sustainable accommodation practices in Hospitality sector in Domestic, International and Independent units. Important and common elements were grouped together and framework was developed for continuous and successful implementation of green practices in lodging establishments. To congregate the information from literature and industry and to understand the gaps and challenges, the framework was further verified and tested on selected hotels. Findings from this research highlighted the level of awareness and initiatives among hotels with respect to sustainability of accommodation practices in the Hospitality industry and further recommended the 3I's Framework of Accommodation Sustainability (FASM). Though some of the industry reports did not support and share the practical challenges at different stages of sustainable practices. This article will allow many operators and important stakeholders of hospitality sector to initiate and execute sustainable accommodation strategies.

13.1   INTRODUCTION

Travel and Tourism contributed to 9% of GDP crossed over 1 billion tourists from 995 million in 2011 where Asia Pacific recorded the strongest growth with 7% increase in arrivals (UNWTO, 2013). This sector has also been responsible in creating 260 million jobs directly or indirectly, hence acting as a catalyst for economic and social transformation of especially developing and less developed countries. However, due to its close relationship with the environment and natural resources, it has also negative impacts like air and water pollution, loss of biodiversity, encroachment, labor issues, extensive use of chemicals in laundry, improper waste disposal generated from rooms and other parts of the hotel and many more. (Bohdanowicz, 2006). The rising religious tourism industry in Uttarakhand, hill station in India attracted multi story lodging properties, in eco sensitive zones breaking all the norms and inviting landslides and rainfall. Heavy rainfall made 60 people died and more than 60,000 pilgrims were stranded (Down to Earth, 2013).

In large cities of U.S., existing buildings contributes to almost 80% of the carbon emissions through their energy costs and an average hotel spends around US$2,196 per available room in energy costs, representing 6% of all operating costs (Deloitte, 2011). The five star hotels in the Capital of India, that is, New Delhi consumes 14 million liters of water and produce around 10 million liters of sewage everyday (NDTV, 2013). Another survey reveals that in India, there has been an overall increase of approximately 9% in energy costs on the basis of per available room (FHRAI, 2012). These figures alarm the urgent need for more sincere, honest and innovative green sustainable practices in accommodation sector. It's time to dispute all those practices, processes and luxury requirements that bears the risk to damage the environment.

Due to continuous rise of conscious levels of consumers and other organizational bodies, it is now imperative for hotels to embrace green sustainable practices for the benefit of local environment and future generations. About 62% of the hotels, retail and restaurant in United States will be tagged as "green" by 2015. About 67% of green hotels reported lower energy usage in their buildings with higher occupancies (McGraw Hills construction, 2013). In another news, 32 five star hotels of New Delhi have signed a memorandum with the government expressing their commitment to comply with environment guidelines and take steps in the area of energy and water by September 2015 (Economic Times, 2013). Many companies across globe are acknowledging the impact of its operations on green house emissions but very few companies have included sustainable strategies into their business models (Travel and Tourism, 2011). Ethical and social responsibility of Hospitality Industry has put pressure on managers to invest and drive the sustainable practices to diminish the burden of environment. One can realize from above data that the consumers and government have been playing an important role in pressurizing hotels to adopt sustainable practices. McGraw Hill constructions report (2013) also confirms that top three influencers in driving green buildings are consumer demand, market demand and regulations. According to the survey by Deloitte (2011) of Business Travellers, 95% of the respondents agreed that hotel should be taking green initiative but this interest does not necessarily translate in buying or paying premium price for greener rooms. Consumer purchasing decisions and readiness to pay extra has been very unclear but these issues cannot undermine the need to communicate and implement the sustainable practices and influence the consumers to buy them.

According to the survey, a typical occupied guest room generates 28 pounds per day depending on the kind of the hotel and number of occupants (NCDNER, 2013). Compendiums, promotional leaflets, note pads, shampoo bottles, bulbs, Hallway and corridor lighting, all correspond to small items but indicate the opportunity to improve on the processes related to accommodation provided to consumers. There are many hotels that have understood the sustainability concept and applied it in their respective properties but we still have many hotels especially the yesteryears who find it confusing and difficult to implement.

There is a lack of explicit and dedicated literature related to sustainable green practices in rooms and allied areas. The available information from the literature and the industry is quite isolated in nature, which leads to confusion. Thus the objective of this chapter is to classify and document the sustainable accommodation practices of green hotels. To overcome the inadequacies, the authors have conducted a detailed literature review on sustainable development in hospitality and green accommodation practices in hotel. Based on the literature review, authors have subsequently conceptualized 3I's framework indicating successful management of green accommodation practices in hotel. Finally, the chosen ten hotels on different relevant criteria's mentioned in methodology were critically studied on 3I's framework to identify and highlight the challenges and gaps in hotel's green sustainable practices. The framework can also be used as a guide by lodging institutions to understand the key deliverables, which are critical for success. In the end, this chapter has also some recommendations and implications for managers which can be further explored in their lodging properties.

13.2 METHODOLOGY

Research has combined the academic literature and industry reports in conceptualizing the futuristic sustainable accommodation practices and its overall successful implementation. The aim is to cite best practices from global and Indian hospitality industry through semi-structured interviews from Indian managers, company websites, industry reports and trade journals.

Through comprehensive literature review, this chapter draws from several sources of theory which are internationally published materials and literatures related to sustainability business, lodging and hospitality chains. Post reviewing the available literature, few very essential dimension of sustainability implementation came out quite explicitly, which helped in shaping our 3I's framework. The framework known as "3I's Framework of Accommodation Sustainability Management (FASM)" derived from the findings of the literature underline the flow, process and elements applicable to any lodging industry. The chapter highlights the sustainability practices, challenges and gaps in green hotels and has analytically framed the 3I's Framework. It aims to develop a framework and core principles under which accommodation or lodging properties can build their sustainability management. The dimensions mentioned in the framework was further tested and verified with industry practices before developing it as acceptable sustainability model. The chapter has used content analysis of websites, trade journals and annual reports to identify the processes and activities performed by the lodging properties According to Neuman (2003, p. 219)"content analysis is a technique for gathering and analyzing the content of text. The content refers to words, meanings, pictures, symbols, ideas, themes or nay message that can be communicated." To broaden the sample, we have selected ten hotels based on inventory, travelers' preference and sustainable practices as it is important to balance sustainable practices with guest delight at strategic as well as operational level. The hotels ranked on inventory have been selected from Hospitalitynet to determine the commitment at strategic level. The travelers' preference of hotels 2013 was taken from the most preferred travel sight Trip Advisor to interface the guest concern towards sustainability management. The hotels ranked on sustainable criteria have been selected from Independent Traveler.com. It is published by The Independent Traveler, Inc., a subsidiary of TriPadvisor LLC. To substantiate the information shared on company' website, further Indepth interviews with identified Senior Managers of the selected Indian hotel units (IHG, Hilton, Accor) was taken to discuss the sustainable accommodation practices in the hotel.

13.3 SUSTAINABLE DEVELOPMENT IN HOSPITALITY

The concept of sustainability still not widely understood and applied from the time it was framed and adopted by World Commission of Environment and Development as "a kind of development that meets the needs of the present population without compromising the ability of future generations to meet their own needs" (WCED, 1987). The broad scope of definition limits the opportunity for an individual to understand his role in macroeconomic and social environment (Stead and Stead, 1996). Though over the years, organizations have identified sustainability as a significant part of their strategic objectives and few of them have included in their mission and plans (Siegel, 2009). The sustainability plan can range from marketing and advertising green products, changes in operational process, communication and accountability of different stakeholders throughout the process. The hospitality industry has also been with the trend and has been offering green products and services (Peattie and Crane, 2005). Many studies have witnessed the fact that a lot of tourism destinations have been developed through serious sustainable environmental measures and hospitality Industry has also been a beneficiary through these above policies and practices (Mihalic, 2000; Huybers, 2003).

13.4   ROLE OF STAKEHOLDERS IN DRIVING SUSTAINABLE PRACTICES

Researchers have identified inter-related viewpoints in explaining that how both internal and external forces pressurize the organizations to adopt environmental practices (Clemens and Douglas, 2006, Aragon and Sharma 2003). The forces do affect the organization but the effect may not be uniform and consistent as the numbers, pressure and influence of these active external forces may vary. There are studies confirming that external forces like regulatory bodies industry barriers, competition, pressure from other stakeholders influence and assist in the adoption of green sustainable practices. Also, managers who are responsible can significantly bring change through their decisions, commitment and can influence the environment too (Bohdanowicz, 2005; Bansal and Roth, 2000). According to AHLA (2008) there are three sets of stakeholders who can contribute in the growth of green hotels. The first being the internal that is developers, owners and managers, second set of group members who are large corporations, travel management companies and government and third group comprises of travelers. One of the perceived barriers in green hotel design, construction and operation found in the AHLA (2008) report on High performance Hospitality was aligned thinking and perceptions of developer, owner and manager due to their distinct financial drivers which clearly indicates the need for collaboration among internal stakeholders to achieve success in green projects.

Developing value for shareholders has always been a concern. Stakeholders and customers now increasingly consider the environmental and social impact of the products and services they are consuming. Customers have conveyed green concern in many forums but are apprehensive on paying extra price for similar products and services (Manaktola and Jauhari, 2007; Kasim, 2004). One of the reasons is that customers are usually doubtful about declaration of environmental sensitive products and services and fear as "green wash" (Hartman and Ibanez, 2006). Further customers perceive more value in those organizations who display their concern through their practices (Hu and Wall, 2005). Customers who pay for environmentally product or service should perceive the quality as higher as promised by the team and compared to other non-green hotels. This is important as customers have paid extra price only for green services and it might lead to trust deficit for future (D'souza et al., 2006). Miller and Baloglu (2011) confirmed in their study that majority of the population from their sample has shown unwilling behavior to pay extra for green services and were quite confused with different eco labels and its constituents. There is a need to share the details of the green hotels and its eco-label so as to avoid any gaps and skepticism among the guests. The study also mentioned that there was hardly any variation in the sustainability preferences of business and leisure guests.

Graci and Dods (2008) confirmed in their research that hotel will take up green program only when it is business driven and profitable in terms of cost savings, competitive edge, employee and customer loyalty and minimum operational risks. Customer inputs, perception and initiatives do play an important role especially in service processes. Metters and Vargas (2000) suggests that service design processes with high customer contact should be more effective and service processes with low customer contact should be more efficient; though as a researcher we can argue that customer can play an integral role in resource efficiency if communicated properly.

13.5   GREEN ACCOMMODATION AND ITS PRACTICES

As discussed above, green hotel has not been defined uniformly across industry though few relate it to building efficiencies like reflective roofs and other relate it to operational sustainable services like towel reuse program, different bins, etc. Jackson (2010) has identified green practices are the ones where you nullify the negative effects related to energy use, water consumption, waste generation and indoor air quality. The AHLA (2008) report on High performance Hospitality research's team identified hotel's level of commitment to environment friendly practices based on design and construction and operational effectiveness. Under design and construction, the process related to site development, energy and water consumption, waste generation, materials and resources, indoor air quality where as operations include customer processes, marketing, community outreach, guest amenities and back of the house administration. Ricaurte (2011) include elements like Organizational Governance, environment, Society, Product Responsibility, Labor Practices and Human Rights related to Sustainable Development. Based on above researches, it reflects that Sustainable hotels will not only have to improve the operational process, design but also make positive contributions towards employees and society.

Lodging Industry in California with over 4 million rooms generates waste of 6 million tones every year (Calrecycle, 2013). Lodging facilities are usually one of the few top buildings among commercial buildings, which produce higher usage of electricity, water and generation of waste (Balaras, 2003). The UNWTO Report in year 2008 reported that accommodations are the second largest contributor of CO_2 emissions in Tourism sector. Green practices can not only make profits but also ensure the safety and luxury to guest. Energy usage might differ from hotels to hotels depending on number of facilities offered like guest rooms, kitchens, restaurants, health club, spa laundry, business centers, etc. Hotels usually consume energy for Heating, ventilation, and air conditioner (HVAC) operations, fuel, lighting and other extra requirements (HVS, 2012). Water usage in hotels includes the use for sanitary purposes, gardening, cleaning, drinking, cooking, laundry, etc. Water has accounted for 15% of the utility bills in many hotels. However, solutions in form of green housekeeping measures can reduce water use by 50% (Ecozys, 2013) Indoor air quality is also of significant importance for lodging properties. Clean air directly relates to sustainable green practices and as well as reduce health hazards for guest and employees. Indoor pollutants in lodging properties include gaseous compounds like fumes, smoke, dust, oil, gas, kerosene, etc. Waste management is one of the challenges in urban and metro cities leading to serious pollution (Kumar et al., 2009). Bohdanowicz (2005) estimated that typical hotel generates in excess of 1 kg of biodegradable and non-biodegradable waste from guest room leading to tons of waste per month. Waste prevention not only protects the environment but also make economic sense derived out from common sense.

Discussion of sustainability does involve its scope and performance measurement within the business. Bohdanowicz et al. (2007) mentioned that to measure sustainability in hospitality, we need to monitor energy, waste, air quality, water and recently added GHG emissions. Chan (2009) in his study mentioned that evaluations of hotel performance are also based on ISO 14001 which examine energy, water, and waste consumption in an occupied room. Though there have been many social impacts, which have been overlooked and difficult to measure. Ricaurte (2011) has offered the framework, which identifies and standardizes the sustainability indicators in the area of Sustainable Development and Quality of Life. Interestingly he has encompassed the GRI and ISO 26000 guidelines, which include Organizational Governance, communities, product Responsibility, labor practices, human rights and Environment. It also includes measurements related to Satisfaction, well-being and happiness quotient of society, which indicates the future range of the measurement. Though these non-financial instruments are not very specific for measurement but it is being included and U.S. Green building council has studied green practices with the context of human experience (Pyke et al., 2010).

Awards are token of appreciation given for achievement whereas Rewards are usually given to be an encouragement to an individual (BBC, 2013). There have been many awards and rewards from the Government as well as various institutions from the fraternity to acknowledge the teams who have made exemplary achievements in environment responsibility. Department of Energy distinguishes commendable performances in sustainable areas of energy, water and vehicle fleet management (EERE, 2013). There is much such Industry specific awards organized in Global context like Global Business Travel Association Award for Sustainability, Hotel Visionary award from Hospitality technology magazine, National Business Travel Association for Responsible travel management, etc. Government programs and rewards are usually to motivate people to amend their behavior and developments, which the industry has been slow to respond. There has been variety of incentives by government like tax benefits, technical assistance, exemption from certain taxs, etc.(Deloitte, 2009). Goetz (2010) explained in his research that incentives have been successful in promotion of sustainability practices rather than forced and control measures.

Organizations are continuously changing and innovating their ways of sustainable green business. Companies do need to look, assess and monitor the level of risk associated with sustainability planning and practices at each level of operation and strategic processes in collaboration with all stakeholders (Barratt, 2008). According to the report of Deloitte (2009) on Risk and Rewards for building Sustainable Hotels, Risk management framework should focus on accountability, transparency in initiation and implementation stage where all the stakeholders are involved. Training, communication and monitoring becomes a vital part of the risk management framework. The heavy investments require the practical analysis and evaluation of business decisions so to minimize risk and optimize return of Investment (HVS,2012).

The literature suggests there has been an increase in the sustainable efforts in accommodation sector but there is more to happen in the areas of giving value to stakeholders through genuine green practices. Accommodation sector also need to identify the correct and standardized measurement techniques so to understand the performance and benchmark its practices at global level. The literature suggested the core areas, which are conducive to sustainable accommodation. These core areas are energy, water, waste, indoor air quality, customer deliverables.

13.6   3I'S FRAMEWORK OF ACCOMMODATION SUSTAINABILITY MANAGEMENT (FASM)

The literature suggests that successful implementation of sustainability practices in the accommodation sector lies in the core principles under 3I's which is Institution, Implementation and Implication (see Figure 1). We need to maintain visibility and high level of communication with all the stakeholders during these three stages

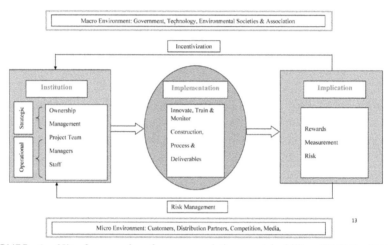

FIGURE 1   3I's framework of accommodation sustainability (FASM) (FASM) management.

The first stage Institution indicates the harmony between different internal stakeholders who are responsible for making decisions decisions at strategic level and implementation at operational level. The two important levels under this stage are strategic and operational. It has been witnessed that employees loose all the zeal and motivation to implement sustainability measures when it was not aligned with corporate strategy. The owners and promoters need to be equally passionate about sustainable measures and should hire a project team early in the process who could be innovative in their ideas and can help in achieving the triple bottom line, which is environment performance, Social Performance and Economic performance (Elkington, 1998). Hotels should also educate their employees regarding green design and how to operate efficiently. A green luxury experience can be designed that communicates the green experience without compromising on the luxury. Architects and Designers need to work closely with engineers to create such products and services, which are pleasing and yet have low environmental impact. An aim and clear understanding of the green certification process can help in using certified products and services. The Internal stakeholders have the pressure from microenvironment where customers, travel management companies have indicated their preference for green accommodation. The macro environment as well as stakeholders like Government, NGO's and Green Associations have also played an important role in regulating necessary practices and institute benefits to those who are following the green practices.

The second stage is Implementation, which indicates the major areas as construction, process and deliverables. It is important for green hoteliers to understand the need and comfort of the guest right at the institution level and implement them effectively. If contractors, designers and Engineers are hired right early in the process, it may cost little more but it saves money and increases the existence of the building. Green practices are focused on energy and water conservation, Reducing and recycling waste and indoor air quality. There has been a lot of data indicating the higher wastage generating from an occupied room. Customers are willing to stay in green hotels but not at the cost of comfort and luxury. Thus the implementation also focuses on influencing the customer behavior towards laundry, linen and supplies. These behavioral changes require specific training to Front desk staff and knowledge sharing with customers regarding hotels' efforts to reduce environmental footprints (Jackson, 2010). Through proper training, it will be easier for hotels to communicate their green efforts to customers at different stages of guest cycle like in reservation confirmations, at time of check in, signage in rooms, etc. Hotels can have similar system like in airlines where they can inform customers on carbon credits that they have contributed during their stay and reward them accordingly. The Implementation stage also gets influenced from external stakeholders related to practices and policies that are being implemented in the hotel. Once the green accommodation has been designed and constructed it's important for employees from all core departments especially housekeeping, maintenance to remain fully engaged. We also need to keep reflecting and innovate green practices in the organization so to be more efficient and profitable. These innovations need not necessarily cost more than its returns.

The third principle is Implication,which highlights the importance of sustainability measurement, Rewards and Risk. The sustainability measurement index should have a holistic approach encompassing financial and non-financial benefits. Literature has discussed the various elements like governance, sustainable practices, labor, community outreach as well as quality of life. It's very important to understand and measure the impact of sustainable investment decisions and operations on both environmental and economic performance. The benchmark and bar needs to be meaningful and achievable. One can also measure its success through guest response and feedback on organization's green processes and operations. After measurement it's important to highlight the best practices and share awards and rewards with stakeholders. We can also incentivize our employees, suppliers and other stakeholders who have participated in green drive accordingly. It is also imperative to analyze the risks and barriers if any in achieving sustainable goals and objectives. Risk can be understood as divergence from the anticipated outcome. It needs to be examined at all levels i.e., at Institute level and at Implementation level. The Implication level emphasizes to analyze the divergent outcome and possible barriers in achieving the desired results. One can have risk committee to analyze various risks associated at different levels and contingency plan to overcome them.

13.6 FINDINGS AND DISCUSSION (INDUSTRY PRACTICES)

Post reviewing the available literature, few very essential dimension of sustainability implementation comes out quite explicitly which needs to be checked and enquired with industry practitioners before developing an acceptable sustainability model. To broaden the sample mix, ten units and chain hotels were randomly selected. The three lists considered consist of inventory, guest preference and sustainability orientation respectively as it is important to balance sustainable practices with guest delight at strategic as well as operational level (Table 1).

TABLE 1 Mix of sample hotels to study sustainable accommodation practices.

S. No.	Name of the Hotel Company	Context	Criteria
1.	Intercontinental Hotel Group	UK	Top 10 brand hotels with regard to inventory (Hospitalitynet, 2013)
2	Hilton	USA	
3	Accor	France	
4	Home Inns	China	
5	Four Seasons Resort Hualalai	Hawaii	Amongst Top 25 in Traveler's Choice 2013 Award (CNN Travel, 2013)
6	Cape Grace	Cape Town Central, South Africa	
7	Onyria Marinha Edition Hotel and Thalasso	Cascais, Portugal	
8	Orchard Garden Hotel	San Francisco, California	Top 10 Green Hotels of World by (Independent Traveler, 2013)
9	Old Chapel Forge Bed and Breakfast	Chichester, England	
10	Graycote Inn	Bar Harbor, Maine	

13.6.1   INTERCONTINENTAL HOTEL GROUP

IHG being the largest hotel chain in the world with nine brands, 4,600 hotels and another 1,000 hotels in pipeline spread across almost 1,000 countries and territories also has achieved numerous milestones in the area of sustainable practices (IHG Hotels, 2013).

Their Sustainable initiative known as "Green Engage" is already rolled out in more than 50% hotels across the chain. The key findings from various documents related to this initiative are further studied under three main headings as Institution, Implementation and Implication(Green engage,2013).

13.6.1.1   INSTITUTION

As on date, 2,270 hotels of IHG have already partnered on their Sustainability program popularly known as "Green Engage." The group is looking forward to roll out this sustainability drive towards Environmental issues and operating cost to rest of the group units as well through continuous communication with IHG Owner's Association in year 2013 (Green engage, 2013).

They continued to engage with their stakeholders through a number of channels including videos, forums, meetings, individual interviews, surveys and through websites such as our CR Report, IHG Planet CR face book page and CR Resource Centre located on the hotel intranet, Merlin.

13.6.1.2   IMPLEMENTATION

- Launched a carbon calculator within Green Engage using the industry approved carbon measurement methodology to enable partner hotels apply it immediately.
- Launched a Green Meeting checklist for hotels, which guides hotels through the kind of issues that could arise in conversations with meetings planners.
- Developed further new features within Green Engage such as multi-unit reporting and a water benchmark.
- Exceeded their three-year target (2010–2012) to reduce energy per available room by between 6 and 10% in our managed and owned estate with a reduction of 11.7%.
- Reduced carbon footprint in all the owned and managed hotels by 19% per occupied room in a year.
- Made it convenient for more of guests to locate and book Green Engage hotels.

- Launched revised Green Solutions, which are the activities in Green Engage that partner hotels can implement to manage their environmental impacts.

13.6.1.3 IMPLICATION

- Awarded the Global Business Travel Association (GBTA) Gold Medal for Sustainability.
- Awarded the Hotel Owners' and Franchisees' Transatlantic and European League (HOFTEL) Owner Friendly Innovation Award for Green Engage.
- Shortlisted for the World Environment Centre Award for Sustainability.
- IHG named in Canada's 'Green 30' list 2011.
- IHG has been recognized as the most environmentally and socially responsible hotelier in Australasia, after being awarded the inaugural Responsible Travel Management award (RTM) by the National Business Travel Association (NBTA) 2010.
- 2009 Hotel Visionary Award fromHospitality Technology Magazine for Green Engage.
- Eco-lodging Award at the China Hotel Investment Summit (CHIS).
- Worldwide Hospitality Award for best initiative in sustainable development.
- Condé Nast Traveller 2009 World Savers Award for Willard InterContinental Washington DC.

As highlighted by one of the General Manager of Crowne Plaza (a brand under IHG Flag), the initiatives at unit level are quite focused and result oriented when it comes to the application of "Green Engage" guidelines. To mention a few: using heat from air conditioners in hot water system, ample lighting options at the construction stage, heat resistant walls, Grey water uses, transition from bulb—tube lights—CFL and LED, etc. He admitted that both management and ownership of the unit are quite aware of the fact that these sustainability practices are the only solace considering the expensive scarce resources. He also appreciated government's support and motivation to promote these drives in Indian context.

13.6.2 HILTON

As a global company operating more than 3,900 hotels in 90 countries, Hilton focuses on vibrant and sustainable communities. The mission of their strategic giving is "To harness our passion and expertise to address the social, economic, and sustainability issues that impact our business and are important to the communities where we live and work." (Hilton Hotels, 2013).

13.6.2.1   INSTITUTION

The Hilton group has a sustainability drive as The LightStay™ system to analyze performance across 200 operational practices, such as housekeeping, paper product usage, food waste, chemical storage, air quality, and transportation. It also provides a "meeting impact calculator" feature that calculates the environmental impact of any meeting or conference held at a property. More than 3,800 properties across the group are already following and benefitting from this sustainability drive. Best practices are shared across the chain from Corporate to unit level and vice versa(Living Sustainability, 2013).

13.6.2.2   IMPLEMENTATION

Learning and communication plays the most important role in rolling out the initiatives at different strategic and management level. They believe in continuous improvement in practices as per the change in business environment and internal challenges.

In 2010, Hilton Worldwide properties reduced 6.6% Energy use, 3.8% Water use, 7.8% Carbon output and 19% Waste output by engaging into innovative processes and deliverables. The step by step process starts with embracing a mission and strategy which then is communicated in form of key commitments as energy efficiency, CO_2 reduction, water efficiency, waste reduction, renewable energy, and sustainable buildings and operations which includes building design and construction, hotel and corporate operations, and purchasing. Engage team members through effective communication and training to ensure its integration into the guest experience. Goal focused performance is measured, analyzed, improved and shared across the group. Local, National and International legislations are also considered and adhered to in this drive of sustainability. Communities, both internally and externally is engaged and communicated with the achieved and targeted performance (Living Sustainability, 2013).

13.6.2.3   IMPLICATION

They use a third party to verify their system, processes, and results. Just like a financial statement, current performance can be validated while establishing benchmarks for continuous future improvement.

Hilton Worldwide and all properties within their global portfolio of brands have already achieved ISO 9001:2008 certification (Quality Management) and ISO 14001:2004 certification (Environment Management). They are one of the largest-ever volume certifications of commercial buildings across any industry (Living sustainability, 2013).

The core benefits of actively managing their business through the lens of sustainability helps to protect world globally, construct advanced design buildings, improve operational efficiency, serve communities, engage team members and above all, an enhanced guest experience.

Hilton hotels have also partnered with other stakeholders with similar objective on various projects as Global soap Project to reduce waste and saving lives, one bar of soap at a time; Good 360 to Reduce, reuse and repurpose; Sundane Institute for Awarding and supporting sustainability awareness.

13.6.3   ACCOR HOTELS

Accor, the world's leading hotel operator and market leader in Europe, is present in 92 countries nearly 3,500 hotels and 500,000 rooms serving different market segments. The hotels group has set benchmark for many operational initiatives in different hospitality areas.

13.6.3.1   INSTITUTION

In April, 2012 "Planet 21"—Sustainability module was launched that runs in all the member hotels at different strategic and operational levels. Accor was one of the first hotels to actually conduct a research by name of "Earth Guest Research" within the group by PWC to understand and validate their gut feel about different critical areas of sustainability in hotels in year 2011 (Planet 21, 2013).

Few of the results of this survey were quite alarming and an eye opener for practitioners. The very fact of sharing the result and analysis of this internal report with community explains the level of commitment and responsibility this hotel company possesses towards the cause. It also invites other hotel companies to share similar kind of work as they believe that growth can be achieved only by working together. In this report Mr. Denis Hennequin, CEO-Accor Group admits that the more you take from environment (human resource or water or energy), more is your responsibility to care for it as your business largely depends on timely availability of these inputs. It also insists on the fact that is not discussed explicitly by many organizations to share the challenges created to environment by indirect business operations as logistics or vendors (Earth Guest Research, 2011).

This hotel company has been working for this cause since last 19 years with a program by name of "Earth Guest" which focuses on energy, water, waste and biodiversity. The group has a dedicated "Sustainable Development" department responsible for social and ethical cause.

13.6.3.2   IMPLEMENTATION

The Group's policies have allowed Accor hotels to come a long way. For example, water consumption per rented room dropped 12% from 2006 to 2010, and energy consumption per available room dropped 5.5% over that period. Today, 85% of hotels have water flow regulators and 82% have compact fluorescent lamps. In 2009, Accor also embraced Plant for the Planet, a bold reforestation project—and group-wide efforts to optimize laundry costs have allowed it to finance 1.7 million trees since then (Table 2).

TABLE 2   Planet 21 initiatives by Accor hotels (Planet 21 Program, 2013).

Health	1	Ensure healthy interiors
	2	Promote responsible eating
	3	Prevent diseases
Nature	4	Reduce our water use
	5	Expand waste recycling
	6	Protect biodiversity
Carbon	7	Reduce our energy use
	8	Reduce our CO_2 emisions
	9	Increase the use of renewable energy
Innovation	10	Encourage eco-design
	11	Promote sustainable building
	12	Introduce sustainable offers and technologie
Local	13	Protect children from abuse
	14	Support responsible purchasing practices
	15	Protect ecosystems
Employment	16	Support employee growth and skills
	17	Make diversity an asset
	18	Improve quality of worklife
Dialogue	19	Conduct our business openly and transparently
	20	Engage our franchised and managed hotels
	21	Share our commitment with suppliers

Some of the initiatives by Accor group towards sustainable accommodation practices:

- In year 2012 the group went online on e bay and put second hand furniture on sale.
- Novotel brand initiated e learning on sustainable development for employees.
- Plant for the Planet project, aimed to plant 3 million trees by using the savings generated by towel reuse by guests.
- The "100 solar hotels" project, designed to promote solar technology in the hotel industry.
- Intranet by name of OPEN to record and communicate unit wise water and energy consumption and compare the same with benchmark set by management.

13.6.3.3   IMPLICATIONS

- Received Condé Nast Traveler's World Savers Awards, 2011.
- Tourism for Tomorrow Award 2010 given to Accor by the World Travel and Tourism Council (WTTC) to award the Group's best practices in sustainable tourism around the world.
- LEED ("Leadership in Energy and Environmental Design") certification for the Motel 6 Northlake-Speedway, which rewards construction of the establishment's high-performance, sustainable buildings.
- Certification of the future Suite Novotel Issy-les-Moulineaux, one of the first hotels to be certified to France's High Environmental Quality (HQE®) standards for service sector buildings.

13.6.4   HOME INNS

Home Inns Group was founded in 2002 in china with a vision of a comfortable lodging experience to travelers. They operate with professional and courteous service, comfortable rooms, convenient locations and economic pricing principles. They supply all the basic amenities and services to the guest and ensure that every traveler has a productive stay across china.

They operate in 243 cities in china with a total of 1,682 hotels. They wish to optimize on the growing number of travelers to China. Home Inns has got the record of opening highest number of hotels in 2010–12 (Homeinns, 2013).

Even if the Group has been experiencing the flavor of growth and success over last few years and also claims to sustain operational profitability which has gradually increased every year, the website broadly misses it's focus on best practices. Their belief in standardization and quality control over different franchised, managed and owned brands is not supported by the communication and publication of the same. The financial reports and analysis available for investors and media lacks the achievements and benchmark set for energy and related cost. They do use modular fixtures and pre-designed areas but their impact on sustainability is not measured. The market they operate in, has been in news for many sustainability related issues, which makes it quite obvious for this hotel company to be proactive and cautious on the same.

There is an opportunity and need for the management to respond in this direction and communicate internally as well as externally with different stake holders about the initiatives taken and proposed. This would add to their financial figures and increased customer loyalty.

13.6.5   FOUR SEASONS RESORT HUALALAI (HISTORIC KA'UPULEHU, HAWAII)

Located on the North Kona Coast of Hawaii Island, Four Seasons Resort Hualālai at Historic Ka'ūpūlehu has 243 guest rooms and suites A peerless collection of native Hawaiian art complements expansive, open-air living spaces and Island-inspired décor.

Under umbrella of a sustainability cautious of management group, the first drive this hotel has undergone is plantation project of 5,00,000 Koa trees on the island as a reforestation partnership with a Hawaii-based company. They have also established an information kiosk meant to look like a traditional Hawaiian hale at the resort to promote the Koa tree project as a new guest experience. That means guests can sponsor a "legacy" Koa tree in their name for $40 eac. The money goes to the planting and upkeep of the tree, which will never be harvested. This effort aims to create a strong sense of place, which has actually contributed largely in getting the 1st place in Traveler's Choice Awards 2013 on Trip Advisor. The hotel participates in employee and guest education on this legacy program. (Pacific Business News, 2011)

At Hualalai, the latest initiative is the development of the EcoCrescent at King's Pond. Here, guests enjoy carafes of filtered water, rather than plastic water bottles, and find that great care is taken to green each detail throughout the room. In the bath area, for example, ceramic shampoo, conditioner and lotion containers replace disposable plastic bottles, rubber spa sandals replace disposable slippers, and the environmentally friendly linen program is automatically in place. The Operations are improved and evaluated on various green practices such as a resort wide recycling program, the placement of recycle baskets in all guest rooms, the use of bamboo plates for banquet and special functions, the purchase of biodegradable plastic bags for deliveries, the use of remanufactured toners in office equipment, the purchase of a non-toxic dry cleaning machine, the installation of a salt water sanitation system in the Palm Grove pool area, and the recycling and reuse of boxes, milk crates and packing material (Supporting Sustainability, 2013).

Hawaiian Legacy Hardwoods CEO Jeff Dunster said "securing a philan-thropic and tough hotel company Four Seasons as a partner on the Hawaiian Legacy Reforestation Initiative is significant because it taps into the lucra-tive visitor industry by promoting ecotourism, while fostering reforestation." (Four Seasons Hotels, 2013).

13.6.6   CAPE GRACE

The Cape Grace with almost 200 rooms is surrounded by water from three sides on the Victoria and Alfred Waterfront. Positioned asthe city's power hotel, each of the guest rooms has a distinct decor featuring antiques, hand-painted fabrics, and thoughtfully chosen African artifacts; all provide the convenience of iPod docking stations, flat-panel HD televisions and compli-mentary Wi-Fi which makes it a nice combo of technology and basics (LHW, 2013).

The Green Grace Committee was founded to address environmental im-pact of employees, guests, visitors, contractors and suppliers, in addition to ensuring adherence to local legislation and statutory requirements.The com-mittee's vision is"to look beyond the obvious and drive environmental aware-ness through responsible tourism practices, while simultaneously maintaining exceptional service and guest satisfaction." The three major areas that the hotel identified for the sustainable practices were Energy, Water and Waste (Green Grace, 2013).

Energy: Considering the limited energy resources and cost involved few major processes followed are as:

- Lights and air conditioning units are only switched on for arrival and occupied rooms and natural light is encouraged.
- Weight sensitive elevators are installed.
- Insulation on pipes and boilers to avoid any kind of energy lose.
- Water: Many initiatives are introduced in the system to manage wastage of this resource and also minimize the cost component as:
- Indigenous water-wise plants are considered to create a feel of original-ity and also half empty water bottles are used for plant irrigation.

- Jacuzzi filtration to minimize wastage of water.
- Low-flow shower heads in all the bathrooms and flush mechanism adjusted at 7 liters from 11 liters earlier.
- Guests choose how often they would like their bed linen and towels laundered.
- During drainage, instead of disposing of the existing swimming pool water (100–000 liters) it is stored in several pods until the pool needs to be refilled.

Waste: Managing and reusing waste from different operational areas is a big challenge and hence needs a special attention as:

- The hotel either donate or dispose outdated or broken computers via an E-waste company
- Used kitchen cooking oil is recycled into bio-diesel to be reused.
- Flower refuse is used for compost in the garden area.
- Used batteries, CFL's and fluorescent tubes are correctly disposed of
- Printer, photocopier cartridges, cardboard, paper, leather, plastic, glass and aluminum cans are recycled in all the concerned operational areas.

13.6.7 ONYRIA MARINHA EDITION HOTEL AND THALASSO

An unit inaugurated on 1st April, 2011 under Onyria Resorts chain based out of Portugal this hotel group is one of the most preferred by travelers across the worlds. Awarded as the 3rd from top as per the Traveler's Choice 2013 on Trip Advisor, this hotel is known for its style and luxury standards. Offering best of the services and facilities, it meets up with a combination of business and leisure market's expectation (Onyria Marinha, 2013).

But, surprisingly, the hotel website does not mention anything on the "Environmental Policy" page. There is lack of communication with regards to Operational commitment and initiative with regard to such a burning issue of sustainability in present environment. There is a mention of uses of stone and wood as an essential part of decoration but the objective is to create a natural fluidity that intentionally highlights the "spirit of the place."

Even on the website of Onyria resorts, the mention of Environmental policy is very generic and explains the broader commitment "to make a ecoefficient management to minimize the environmental impacts of its activities and services, prevent pollution and make a rational use of natural resources" (Onyria Golf Resorts, 2013).

This case is a live example of interrelation between strategic and operational concern about given issue. The group on the whole needs to communicate and express their sustainable practices to all the stakeholders and consciously improve on training and monitoring the initiatives at all the levels in various operational areas.

13.6.8 ORCHARD GARDEN

Under management of Portfolio Hotels and Resorts, this hotel was inaugurated in November 2006 this smoke-free 86 rooms in downtown San Francisco was the only hotel in the city to be certified by the U.S. Green Building Council for environmentally friendly design (Orchard Garden Hotel, 2013).

13.6.8.1 INSTITUTION

The hotel was constructed with an objective of sustainable practices/processes at all the stages. To mention a few is; site was chosen with transportation and urbanization issues in mind, car pool and drop off points were design, provision for bicycle storage, environment friendly green materials uses in construction was planned. Also, documentation and training was encouraged at different stages of planning the hotel.

13.6.8.2 IMPLEMENTATION

Process established for construction waste management as this category of waste contains almost 60 to 70% of total waste.

Hotels uses a mix of 21% regionally manufactured product and 55% regionally extracted materials in daily operations.

No permanent irrigation to avoid wastage of water. Planter liners were equipped with built-in irrigation. Also, low-flow plumbing fixtures were used in rooms and public areas.

Rooms have a key card controlled energy supply with a target to reduce 20% energy consumption.

The building is well insulated resulting in less energy use for heating and air-conditioning and making the guest rooms very quiet.

In-room recycling bins separate glass and paper to promote thorough recycling and specially designed carpets are used which include recycled content and have low chemical emissions. Menus/collateral/toilet papers are 100% recycled and inks used on all collateral and stationery are soy-based.

Organic, citrus-based cleaning products are used throughout the hotel, which are effective like other traditional chemicals but better for the staff and the environment (Orchard Garden Hotel, 2009).

13.6.8.3   IMPLICATION

The Orchard Garden Hotel has been awarded LEED® (Leadership in Energy and Environmental Design) certification by the U.S. Green Building Council (USGBC). San Francisco's first hotel to earn this honor in June, 2007, the Orchard Garden was only the third hotel in the U.S. and fourth hotel in the world with this certification.

By following LEED guidelines, the hotel was able to reduce operating cost and also create a more healthy environment for visitors and guest.

13.6.9   OLD CHAPEL FORGE BED AND BREAKFAST (CHICHESTER, ENGLAND: OLD CHAPEL FORGE BED AND BREAKFAST)

This 17th-century house and chapel of Old Chapel Forge stay in the heart of England's Sussex countryside is an eco friendly lodging option for nature lovers. It has been awarded the highest award from the Green Tourism Business scheme for its Environmental programs (Old Chapel Forge, 2013).

13.6.9.1   INSTITUTION

The aim of this hotel's management is to offer a Green Tourism Experience to its guests. Tourism South East Managing Director Bob Collier said: "Not only have the owners of Old Chapel Forge demonstrated a real commitment to sustainability, which runs throughout the business, but they have been true pioneers and champions in increasing awareness of environmental issues within the tourism industry." This hotel has been leader in introducing environmental initiatives and its progressive, proactive activity across so many areas of its operation has been recognized time and again (Old Chapel Forge, 2013).

The management also has been actively involved in organizing lectures and seminars on this concern by partnering with other stakeholders.

13.6.9.2   IMPLEMENTATION

The hotel has many eco processes at place including the use of solar panels to heat water, and partnerships with local farmers and merchants to provide locally grown organic meals. Other green efforts include composting, gray water recycling and guest education.

Through every aspect of operations they strive to use environmentally friendly alternatives whether including uses of only organic and locally produced food.

The management also has links with local bike hire companies and happily promote scenic walks to the guest to help a less polluted environment.

13.6.9.3   IMPLICATION

Being a member of the Green Business Scheme (the world's most credible tourism program on sustainability from United kingdom) the efforts have been rewarded by being winners of the Tourism South East green tourism award 2006, an International Green Apple Award 2006 and a West Sussex Design and Build Award 2006. Also, members of Hospitable Climates; the green tourism arm of the Hotel Catering Managers Association (HCIMA) and work within the hospitality industry as a consultant, continuously trying to make green tourism a reality.

13.6.10   GRAYCOTE INN

Bar Harbor's first Green Certified lodging has many initiatives in different departments, which contribute in making this hotel an unique product.

The inn is located very close from Acadia National Park and within walking distance of Bar Harbor's shops and restaurants supports a low-gas getaway. The Graycote Inn offers all the comfort and charm of a traditional English B 'n B with an ecofriendly twist. The inn has managed its resource use with low energy consuming lighting, high-efficiency furnaces and air-conditioning units, and water conservation fixtures on all toilets, showers and sinks(Bed and Breakfast, 2013).

To reduce waste, all styrofoam food packaging has been discontinued, and the inn has established comprehensive composting and recycling programs.

In 2006, the Graycote Inn received the Environmental Leader Certificationfrom the Maine Department of Environmental Protection, which was renewed in 2008 and 2011 for improved processes (Graycote Inn, 2013).

In 2012, the Bar Harbor Chamber of Commerce designated the Graycote Inn an Environmental Business Leader.

TABLE 3 Sustainability grid of selected hotels (as per the data available on the concerned resources).

S No	Name of the Hotel Company/Unit	Institution		Construction	Implementation			Implication	
		Strategic	Operational		Process	Deliverables	Measurement	Reward	Risk
1	Intercontinental Hotel Group	☺	☺	☺	☺	☺	☺	☺	X
2	Hilton	☺	☺	☺	☺	☺	☺	☺	X
3	Accor	☺	☺	☺	☺	☺	☺	☺	☺
4	Home Inns	X	X	☺	X	X	X	X	X
5	Four Seasons Resort Hualalai	☺	☺	X	☺	☺	☺	☺	X
6	Cape Grace	☺	☺	☺	☺	☺	X	☺	X
7	Onyria Marinha Edition Hotel and Thalasso	☺	X	X	X	X	X	X	X
8	Orchard Garden Hotel	☺	☺	☺	☺	☺	☺	☺	X
9	Old Chapel Forge Bed and Breakfast	☺	☺	☺	☺	☺	☺	☺	X
10	Graycote Inn	☺	☺	☺	☺	☺	☺	☺	X

13.7 CONCLUSION

The 3I's Framework of Accommodation Sustainability Management (FASM), which was developed as a result of Literature review and was established with the study and evaluation of best Industry practices of leading hotels with regards to inventory, traveler's choice and sustainability (Table 1).

Organized sector of hotel industry shows a respectful degree of awareness about the relevance, challenges and initiatives under sustainable accommodation management. Many of the leading hotels have taken up the issue very seriously and many innovative techniques are explored and practiced globally. Common platforms are also created to address these issues, which include different stakeholders, both internally as well as externally. Government is also supporting the cause by introducing policies and subsidies for practitioners.

The most alarming finding was lack of commitment and communication to identify the risk involved in practicing sustainability. Only Accor group of Hotels has mentioned briefly about the challenges faced during this drive at different level of management. But lacks in sharing the ways to manage these risks (Table 3).

The other revealer is prioritizing the Environmental goal during initial years of survival. Hotels in initial years travel miles together to win the guest by crossing boundaries of highest luxury but fail to think about the sustainable issues, which is need of the hour.

Strategic commitment and clarity plays the most important role in driving such practices in largest of the chain. Operational success is quite dependent on the seriousness of communication of standards from the management.

Environment and Sustainability is definitely an area of concern for hoteliers but expects a greater attention and commitment from different stakeholders. An industry specific guideline needs to be developed and practiced by the partners across the globe to get maximum returns on the investment, both in terms of financial statements and guest experience.

13.8 RECOMMENDATION

There are some very interesting and revolutionary options to escalate these drives by benefitting different stakeholders and there is a need for further research in these options.

At Institution stage: it is recommended that all the stakeholders should be in sync with regard to understanding of the objective and commitment towards the drive. There is a need for clear and seamless communication among the internal team members, which should further be shared with external stakeholders and society on the whole. There is a need for inclusion of environmental priorities at strategic as well as operational level to achieve overall objective of the drive at all the levels.

At implementation stage: There is a need for innovation and creativity in different operational activities to reach a revolutionary sustainable platform. Some suggestive ideas are mentioned as below.

Hotel industry needs to work out a flexi tariff model, where guest pays a fix component for basic services and a variable component as per the energy uses. This tariff may be implemented in new hotels as it needs room specific energy consumption meters to be installed for each room. Prior to installation, we need to identify the return on initial investment to develop the infrastructure and technological aids to support the flexi tariff model. This model may initiate a revolution to engage all the stakeholders within and outside the industry as it will benefit both consumers and service providers.

The other area of further study is technological application and challenges related to sustainability. A very useful and least optimized area is QR code uses to replace menu card and other service center materials in the room. It will add a considerable amount of value to financial and non-financial aspect of hospitality business.

At implication level: It's important to understand the challenges and effectiveness of the innovative green practices implemented in operations of the lodging properties. There is need for Research scholars, academicians and industry practitioners to arrive on the platform to share the data on return of investment towards sustainable drives and further draw conclusions post critical evaluation of the same. This study will open a venue for many sustainable initiatives. It will clear the unsaid doubt and inhibition of stakeholders to practice innovative ways to retain hospitality business in a progressive environment, both internally and externally.

KEYWORDS

- **accommodation**
- **framework**
- **implementation**
- **inception**
- **institution**
- **sustainable**

REFERENCES

Aragon-Correa, J. A., and S. Sharma. 2003. A contingent resource based view of proactive corporate environmental strategy. Academy of Management Review 28: 71–88.

BBC (2013) reward/Award (online) Cited from 10/09/13. Available from http://www.bbc.co.uk/worldservice/learningenglish/language/askaboutenglish/2010/03/100309_aae_reward_page.shtml.

Balaras, C.A. (2003) Editorial.The Xenios project. (online) cited from 10/09/13. Available from http://www.meteo.noa.gr/xenios/newsletter01.pdf.

Bansal, P. and Roth, K. (2000) Why companies go green: A model for ecological responsiveness. Academy of management Journal 43 (4): 717–736.

Barratt RS (2008)Corporate Sustainability: Some Challenges for Implementing and Teaching Organizational Risk Management in a Performability Context, Handbook of Performability Engineering, pp. 857–874.

Bed and Breakfast (2013) Overview (online) cited on 12/09/13. Available from http://www.bedandbreakfast.com/maine-bar-harbor-graycote-inn.html.

Bohdanowicz, P. (2005) European Hoteliers' environmental attitudes: Greening the business. Cornell Hotel and Restaurant Administration Quarterly 46 (2): 188–204.

Bohdanowicz, P. 2006, 'Environmental Awareness and Initiatives in the Swedish and Polish Hotel Industries—Survey Results' International Journal of Hospitality Management, Vol. 25, no. 4, pp. 662–668.

Bohdanowicz, P. and Martinac, I. (2007) Determinants and benchmarking of resource consumption in hotels—case study of Hilton International and Scandic in Europe. Energy and Buildings 39: 82–95.

Calrecycle (2013)Business Waste Reduction, Don't Throw Your Profits Out With the Trash, Fourth Edition. (online) cited on 10/09/13. Available from http://www.calrecycle.ca.gov/reducewaste/business/FactSheets/Throw4.htm.

Clemens, B., and T. J. Douglas. 2006. Does coercion drive firms to adopt "voluntary" green initiatives? Relationships among coercion, superior firm resources, and voluntary green initiatives.Journal of Business Research 59: 483–91.

Chan, W.W. (2009). Environmental measures for hotels' environmental management systems. International Journal of Contemporary Hospitality Management, 21(5), 542–560.

CNN Travel (2013) World's top 25 hotels named by Trip Advisor. (online). Cited on 12/09/13. Available from)http://travel.cnn.com/worlds-top-25-hotels-according-triPadvisor-659436.

Deloitte (2009) Risk and Rewards for building sustainable hotels (online). Cited on 12/09/13. Available from http://www.deloitte.com/assets/dcom-greece/local%20assets/documents/attachments/real%20estate/riskandrewards_hotels.pdf.

Deloitte (2011) Hospitality 2015, Game changers or spectators. (online) cited on 15/07/13. Available from http://www.deloitte.com/assets/Dcom-Tanzania/Local%20Assets/Documents/Deloitte%20Reports% 20-%20Hospitality%202015.pdf.

D'Souza, C. Taghian, M., Lamb, P. and Peretiakos, R. (200 Green products and corporate strategy: An empirical investigation. Society and Business Review,1(2):144–157.

Economic Times (2013)5-star hotels in Delhi to take environment-friendly steps by September. (online) Cited on 15/07/13. Available from http://articles.economictimes.indiatimes.com/2013–06–03/news/39714736_1_five-star-hotels-waste-water-green-hotels

Ecozys (2013). Hospitality H_2O, water efficiency guide. (online) cited on 13/09/13. Available from http://www.ecozys.org.uk/docs/water_efficiency07.pdf

Earth Guest Research (2011) The Accor's group Environmental Footprint (online) cited on 15/09/13. Available from http://www.accor.com/fileadmin/user_upload/Contenus_Accor/Developpement_Durable/img/earth_guest_research/2011_12_08_accor_empreinte_environnementale_dp_bd_en.pdf.

EERE (2013) Federal Energy Management Program(online) cited on 10/09/13. Available from http://www1.eere.energy.gov/femp/program/waterefficiency_bmp14.html.

Elkington, J. (1998), Cannibals with Forks: The Triple Bottom Line of the 21st century, New Society Publishers, Stoney Creek, CT.

Four seasons hotel(2013) Four Seasons Resort Hualalai. (online) cited on 5/09/13. Available from http://waimeaoceanfilm.org/2013/wp-content/uploads/2013/04/Four_Seasons_Hualalai.pdf.

FHRAI (2012) Indian Hotel Industry survey in consultation with HVS and Ecotel (online). Cited on 15/07/13. Available from http://www.hvs.com/Content/3216.pdf.

Graci, S. and Dodds, R. (2008) Why go green? The business case for environmental commitment in the Canadian hotel industry. Anatolia: An International Journal of Tourism and Hospitality Research 19 (2): 251–270.

Green Engage (2013) Introducing Green Engage® Hotels by IHG (online) Cited on 12/09/13 http://www.ihg.com/hotels/us/en/global/support/greenengagehotels.

Green Grace (2013) Green Grace. (online). Cited on 14/09/13. Available from http://www.cape-grace.com/#/en/AboutUs/SocialResponsibility/GreenGrace.

Goetz, K.S. (2010) "Encouraging sustainable business practices using incentives: a practitioner's view," Management Research Review, Vol. 33 Issue 11, pp. 1042–1053.

Gray Cote Inn (2013) Recognitions Received (online) cited on 12/09/13. Available from http://www.graycoteinn.com/.

Hartmann, P. and Ibanez, V. A. (2006) Green value added. Marketing Intelligence and Planning 24 (7): 673–680.

Hilton worldwide (2013) Travel with Purpose. (online) cited on 10/09/13. Available from www.hiltonworldwide.com/corporate-responsibility/

HomeInn (2013) Overview. (online) cited on 12/09/13. Available from http://english.homeinns.com/phoenix.zhtml?c=203641&p=irol-homeProfile.

Hospitalitynet (2013) World Ranking 2013 Of Hotel Groups and Brands. (online). Cited on 3/9/13. Available from http://www.hospitalitynet.org/news/4060119.html.

Hu, W. and Wall, G. (2005) Environmental management, environmental image and the competitive tourist attraction. Journal of Sustainable Tourism 13 (6): 617–635.

Huybers, T. (2003) Environmental management and the competitiveness of nature-based tourism destinations. Environmental and Resource Economics 24 (3): 213–233.

HVS (2012) Current Trends and Opportunities in Hotel Sustainability (Online). Cited on 10/09/2013. Available from http://www.hvs.com/article/5655/current-trends-and-opportunities-in-hotel-sustainability/

Independent Traveller (2013) Top 10 Ecolodges and Green Hotels (online) Cited on 12/09/13. Available from http://www.independenttraveler.com/travel-tips/hotel-and-b-and-b/top-10-ecolodges-and-green-hotels/2.

Jackson, L.A. (2010) Toward a framework for the components of green lodging. Journal of retail and Leisure Property, 9(3):211–30.

Kasim, A. (2004) Socio-environmentally responsible hotel business: Do tourists to Penang Island, Malaysia care? Journal of Hospitality and Leisure Marketing 11 (4): 5–28.

Kumar, S., Bhattacharyya, J., Vaidya, A., Chakrabarti, T., Devotta, S. and Akolkar, A. (2009) Assessment of the status of municipal solid waste management in metro cities, state capitals, class 1 cities, and class ii towns in India: An insight. Waste Management 29:883895.

Living sustainability (2013) Positively Influencing tomorrow. (online) Cited on 12/09/13. Available from http://www.hiltonworldwide.com/corporate-responsibility/sustainably/.

LHW (2013) The leading hotels of the world. Cape Grace. (online) cited on 15/09/13. Available from http://www.lhw.com/hotel/Cape-Grace-Cape-Town-South-Africa

McGraw hill constructions (2013) World green Building trends-Smart market report (online) Cited on 15/07/13. Available from http://www.worldgbc.org/files/8613/6295/6420/World_Green_Building_Trends_SmartMarket_Report_2013.pdf.

Manaktola, K. and Jauhari, V. (2007) Exploring consumer attitude and behavior towards green practices in the lodging industry in India. International Journal of Contemporary Hospitality Management 19 (5): 364–377.

Metters, Richard and Vargas, V. (2000) A typology of de coupling strategies in mixed services. Journal of operations management 18(6):663–682.

Mihalic, T. 2000. Environmental management of a tourist destination. A factor of tourism competitiveness. Tourism Management 21: 65–78.

Millar, M. and Baloglu, S. (2011) Hotel guests' Preferences for Green guest room attributes. Cornell Hospitality quarterly, 52:302.

NCDNER (2013) Hotel/Motel waste reduction, N.C. Division of Pollution Prevention and Environmental Assistance (DPPEA) (online0, Cited at 15/07/13. Available at http://portal.ncdenr.org/c/document_library/get_file?uuid=d0345ad5–0c2b-4363-bd5c-e8d9bb58d583&groupId=38322.

NDTV (2013)Delhi's five-star hotels asked to cut down water consumption (Online). Cited on 15/07/13. Available from http://www.ndtv.com/article/cities/delhi-s-five-star-hotels-asked-to-cut-down-water-consumption-353910

Neumann, W. (2003), Social Research Methods: Qualitative and Quantitative Approaches, Allyn and Bacon, Boston, MA.

Old Chapel Forge (2013) Welcome to the old chapel forge. (online) cited on 12/09/13. Available from http://www.oldchapelforge.co.uk/aims.htm.

Onyria Marinha (2013) Presentation. (online) Cited from 13/09/13. Available from http://www.onyriamarinha.com/en/Hotel/Apresentacao.aspx.

Onyria Golf Resorts (2013) Environmental Policy. (online) Cited on 5/09/13. Available from http://www.onyriaresorts.com/en/Environmental-Policy-Grupo-Onyria.aspx.

Orchard Garden Hotel (2013) Welcome to the orchard Green Hotel. (online). Cited on 12/09/13. Available from http://www.theorchardgardenhotel.com/.

Orchard Garden Hotel (2009) Sustainable Hospitality Presentation (online). Cited on 12/09/13 Available from http://www.theorchardgardenhotel.com/images/pdfs/sustainable-hospitality-presentation-feb-2008.pdf.

Pacific Business News (2011) Four Seasons Hualalai plan will expand koa forests. (online) cited on 15/08/13. Available from http://www.bizjournals.com/pacific/print-edition/2011/09/16/four-seasons-hualalai-plan-will-expand.html?page=all.

Peattie, K. and Crane, A. (2005) Green marketing: Legends, myth, farce or prophesy? Q ualitative Market Research 8 (4): 357–370.

Planet 21 (2013) Planet 21 (online) cited on 13/09/13. Available from http://www.accorhotels.com/gb/sustainable-development/index.shtml.

Planet 21 programe (2013), The Planet 21 programe (online) cited on 13/09/2013 Available at http://www.accor.com/en/sustainable-development/the-planet-21-program.html.

Pyke, C. McMahon, S., Dietsche, T. (2010). Green building and Human experience: Testing green Building strategies with volunteered Geographic Information. Washington, DC: Us Green Buiding Council.

Ricaurte, E. (2011) Developing a Sustainability Measurement Framework for hotels: Toward an Industry-wide reporting structure, Cornell Hospitality Report, 11, 13, 4–38.

Stead, W.E., Stead, J.G., 1994. Can humankind change the economic myth? Paradigm shifts necessary for ecologically sustainable business. Journal of Organizational Change Management 7 (4), 15–31.

Supporting Sustainability (2013) Four seasons of preservation. (online) cited on 9/9/13. Available from http://livingvalues.fourseasons.com/?cat=12#sthash.mICqWEkl.dpuf.

Travel and Tourism (2011) World Travel and Tourism Council-The authority on world Travel and Tourism (online) cited on 11/07/13. Available from http://www.wttc.org/site_media/uploads/downloads/traveltourism2011.pdf.

UNWTO (2013) UNWTO Tourism Highlights (online), Cited on 7/7/13. Available from http://mkt.unwto.org/en/publication/unwto-tourism-highlights-2013-edition.

WCED, 1987. Our Common Future. World Commission on Environment and Development, Oxford University Press, Oxford.

CHAPTER 14

TOURISM POLICY: A COMPARATIVE STUDY OF MALAYSIA AND TURKEY

NASTARAN LALEH and BANAFSHEH M. FARAHANI

CONTENTS

ABSTRACT

Today, tourism is one of the primary factors in the sustainable development of communities and on this basis, different countries' attention is needed to be successful in the field. Since, one of the main pillars of the development of the tourism industry is designing a proper tourism policy for countries; the idea of studying flourishing countries in tourism absorbs the attention of different researchers. Accordingly, in the present article, the tourism policy in two successful countries including Malaysia and Turkey is taken into consideration. The reason behind this selection is because these two Asian countries have similar situations toward the sustainable development of tourism and the tourism industry has made significant progress in those aforementioned countries in recent years. Content analysis of each tourism policy by considering the number of attributes has been done to determine the strength and weak points about each policy separately. It should be noted that on the basis of the results obtained from this article, it can be acknowledged that the performance of Turkey in the absorption of international tourists has been more favorable in comparison with Malaysia.

14.1 INTRODUCTION

Nowadays, tourism as an income generating industry has been paid attention in various communities and many countries with investments in this area and adopt favorable policies have been able to take advantage of the benefits of tourism. Because they have found that the development of tourism in the country could lead to sustainable economic development. On this basis, these countries have many efforts for tourism development with the use of the existing potentials in the country and with the aim of attracting tourists and have done proper measures with policy making in the field of tourism and with the use of management strategies.

Malaysia and Turkey have been very successful in tourism in recent years and their name could be seen between popular tourism destinations in the national and regional levels. Looking at the statistics of tourist arrivals and according to the increasing number of tourists and growing tourism development in these countries can be sought. In fact, these countries with their rich natural and cultural attractions have been able to perform positive actions in the direction of tourism development and they are trying to make better situations for the sustainable development of this industry and to benefit from its positive advantages from developing tourism infrastructure. Tourism is an important source of income in these countries that its development has led to economic development. Hence, paying attention to the positive benefits resulting from tourism in these countries has led to the development of the policy in this field. The adoption of these policies can be a platform for the growth and development of tourism, and provides the situation that both tourists and the host community can benefit from tourism opportunities in the country.

Tourism policies can include all rules, regulations and goals for different countries to be noticed designed for sustainable tourism development. Consequently checking tourism policies of Malaysia and Turkey can help to identify the items of sustainable development or non-development of tourism in these countries as well as the aspiration that Malaysia and Turkey are trying to reach through tourism. Furthermore by checking out these policies, it can be concluded which country has been more successful in attracting tourists.

14.2   TOURISM CONTEXT IN MALAYSIA

Malaysia's effort to attract tourists began in 1960, and in 1972 under the Ministry of Industry and Commerce, Tourism Development Company was established. Association of tourist agencies was formed in 1974, and finally the Ministry of Culture and Tourism Malaysia was established in 1987. In 1990 the Ministry of Culture and Tourism Malaysia organized the first program of the year 'to visit Malaysia.' The aims of this event were to raise awareness of Malaysia's world media. It caused 6 million tourists visit Malaysia that year. In 1992, a study of planning, developing and promoting tourism took place in the state emphasis on the development of foreign relations, promoting local attractions and rural development related jobs in rural tourism, cultural exchanges between people and improve tourism Malaysia's image in the world. Moreover, nature tourism, agricultural tourism, river tourism and tourism-oriented culture and heritage, were emphasized. Tourists with specific interest were also considered in he mentioned study.

Statistics show that the rate of tourist arrivals was 24/7 million in 2011 and 25/03 million in 2012. This can be a reason, which shows the increasing development of tourism in Malaysia comparing to previous years. Most of the tourist arrivals in 2012 are allocated to Singapore (13 million), Indonesia (2/3 million people) and China (1/5 million). This factor has led to consider tourism in Malaysia in 2011 as the third most important foreign income (after production and palm oil).

Malaysia's Federal Government is committed to the development of tourism and according to the recognition of government; the important role of tourism in sustainable development, job creating and social development is reflected in the national economy. This issue is reflected in the national economic recovery plan in 1998. WTTC estimates that, by considering the average annual GDP growth and forecasting South-east Asia's tourism, the prospects of development in Malaysia's tourism will be good. Nevertheless, if the policy framework could lead to tourism development and if Malaysia could make the situation for the sustainability of its market, so its effects will be more than forecasts. While the private sector can and must play the important role in the development of quality products and services to respond to the domestic and international demands the federal government needs to show leadership by encouraging investment, making infrastructure, coordinating tourism policies and activities with local and state governments. This could be lead to make an integrated approach to the management and development of tourism. Business confidence in rapid growth of demand has led to the considerable investment of the private sector. So, more efforts should be done to encourage the sustainable demand and extend related infrastructure and accordingly, opening the areas of the country that haven't use tourism benefits. Also, consumer interest should be maintained in a condition in which the security of tourists is guaranteed. However, there will be barriers for non-availability to tourism potentials in the future:

1. Employment: Tourism has an important role in the employment of people in Malaysia. It is estimated that there is a relatively little growth in employment over the next nine years—2.9% annually for jobs directly in tourism and 2.5% for jobs related to tourism economy—the available workforce is unlikely to keep up with tourism demand.

2. Economy: Malaysia like other developed or developing countries is experiencing an economic slowdown. Malaysia is considered as a low—cost destination but the strength of the US dollar will reduce its marketing advantages.

3. Industry measurement: Tourism research in Malaysia needs quality and quantity improvement. It could be true about economic data in this industry such as tourism expenditure patterns. The lack of proper data makes it difficult to measure trends in tourism demand and reduce the ability of tourism industry for estimating future trends.

4. Investment: The foreign and domestic sector of investment has suffered from the result of the Asian economic crisis.

5. Government expenditure: the found being allocated for tourism from the government is very low. The government has estimated that the

cost of providing services for tourism in Malaysia is 2.1 percent of whole expenditure.

6. Safety and security: It seems that safety and security in Malaysia are reduced. The government of tourists' home countries warns them to be careful in regards to safety, health, and well-being while traveling to Malaysia.

7. Sustainability: Although, Malaysia is known as an unspoiled destination, there are some examples of exploitation of natural resources.

8. Marketing and promotion: According to the experiences, demand for Malaysia as a tourism destination grows if the funding for marketing and promotion is increased.

14.3 MALAYSIA'S TOURISM POLICY

1. Plan for the future
   - Establish a National Tourism Development Plan in consultation with state and local governments and the private sector.
   - Monitor trends in travel and tourism demand so as to anticipate and adapt products to changing demand.
   - Focus on market and product diversification to reduce the heavy dependence on traditional markets and to increase yield.
   - Market and promote more effectively to spread the benefits of tourism to all parts of the country and to all stakeholders.
   - Work more closely with the private sector to address existing concerns and develop public-private sector partnerships in areas such as marketing and promotions, product development, as well as education and training.
   - Anticipate future investment needs by introducing new incentive schemes for private sector capital investment and small business development, especially to encourage heritage and nature-based tourism enterprises.

2. Highlight the strategic importance of travel and tourism
   - Recognize travel and the tourism's impact across the wider economy and its ability to diversify the Malaysia's economy, and ensure to be measured on an annual basis by a national tourism satellite account.
   - Reflect travel and tourism in mainstream policies for employment, trade, investment and education, ensuring that the underlying policy framework is conducive to dynamic growth.

- Communicate the strategic importance of travel and tourism at all levels of government and industry, as well as to local communities.

3. Develop the human capital required for growth
   - Promote a positive image of the travel and tourism industry as a provider of jobs and career opportunities for all Malaysians.
   - Take advantage of travel and tourism's potential to provide jobs for young people, first-time job seekers, minority groups and women looking for part-time employment.
   - Recognize that travel and tourism employment is concentrated in small businesses and local communities throughout the country and across the whole employment spectrum.
   - Continue to place education and training at the forefront of travel and tourism development, introducing it in the high school curricula and adopting measures to improve skills.

4. Encourage open markets and skies and remove barriers to growth
   - Progressively liberalize trade, transport and communications, both through regional trading regimes such as ASEAN and the World Trade Organization's General Agreement on Trade in Services.
   - Open up air transport markets by providing increased incentives to attract more long-haul services, and improve regional networks by expanding liberal aviation accords.
   - Upgrade marketing and promotions to match prevailing competitive approaches and restructure the MTPB as a public—private sector partnership, coordinating national, state and local efforts.
   - Build safety and security provisions into national, state and local strategies, and place special emphasis on travel and tourism in overall policing strategies.
   - Develop fiscal regimes that encourage tourism growth, exports, investment, infrastructure, business innovation and job creation.

5. Match public and private infrastructure to customer demand
   - Develop an agreed process for forecasting travel and tourism infrastructure demand—especially in the accommodation sector, which will have high credibility in the industry and with the investment and financial community.
   - Develop new conference/convention facilities to meet the growing demand from this high-yield sector.
   - Continue to expand infrastructure, including airports and air traffic control, and streamline immigration and border clearance facilities.

- Co-ordinate with state governments to improve road networks across the country, opening up new areas for tourism development.
- Encourage state governments to improve land-use planning and protection to ensure that the patterns of flow do not adversely affect the natural or built heritage.
- Introduce increasing incentives for the rapid modernization and up-grading of Malaysia's rural infrastructure to spread the benefits of travel and tourism across the country.
- Highlight the dangers of excessive, unplanned development, which can result in unhealthy competition, declining operating performances and profits.
- Develop access to capital resources and encourage capital investment in Malaysia's travel and tourism industry from domestic and foreign sources.

6. Favor technological advancement
   - Provide support for local Malaysian companies so that they can develop access to technological advances and compete more effectively with foreign-owned companies.
   - Take the lead in the development of a national tourism portal, together with partners from the private sector, so as to improve distribution of Malaysia's tourism products and develop e-marketing skills.

7. Promote responsibility in natural, social and cultural environments
   - Ensure that the procedures and guidelines for planned and sustainable tourism expansion incorporated in the National Ecotourism Plan are communicated to all stakeholders and implemented as widely as possible.
   - Adopt the principles of Agenda 21 for the travel and tourism industry developed by WTTC, the World Tourism Organization and the Earth Council.
   - Ensure that the socioeconomic, cultural and environmental benefits of travel and tourism are spread equitably across the population in all parts of the country, and actively encourage local community engagement and empowerment.
   - Introduce new financial programs to provide incentives for local community-based sustainable tourism enterprises.
   - Seek branding for Malaysia's key natural and cultural resources through international designations and create new national designations (World Travel and Tourism Council, 2002).

14.4 TOURISM CONTEXT IN TURKEY

Tourism in Turkey is based on archaeological and historical attractions as well as beautiful beaches in the Aegean and Mediterranean sides. In addition, in recent years, religious tourism and health tourism are considered as important factors in attracting tourists to Turkey. Tourism in this country has grown since the late 80th century with the rise of Turgut Ozal, as Prime Minister and his laissez-faire policies and valuing private sector. Many laws were passed in 1983 in Turkey, which were the founder of the new measures to attract foreign investors. In the first years, changes and promotion policies of Ozal government were effective and statistics of tourist arrivals from 1/3 million in 1983 were reached to 2/1 million in 1984. In the same year, neighboring countries, Greece hosted 6 million and Spain 40 million tourists. However, there was good growth in Turkey, so that in 1992 this figure rose to 7 million people. Turkey's tourism revenue increased from $ 770 million in 1985 to 3/6 billion in 1992. Although many crisis over the years—including terrorist attacks and the economic crisis—were as an obstacle to the progress, but Turkey managed to pass all of them. Statistics show that tourist arrivals have been over 30 million people in 2012 and the number of foreign tourists has increased 0/59 percent (30/4 million) in the first 11 months of 2012 compared to the same period last year. The highest number of tourist arrivals to Turkey is allocated to Germany (4/8 million), United Kingdom (3/5 million) and Russia (2/4 million) (Ministry of Culture and Tourism, 2012). This has led Turkey to become the sixth popular tourist destination in the world in 2012, according to the World Tourism Organization.

By accepting sustainable tourism approach, the tourism industry will achieve a significant position that could be lead to employment and regional development and it will be ensured that Turkey will become international brand tourism and one of the top five tourism destinations receiving the highest number of tourists and tourist revenue by 2023. So, following actions could be done to achieve the prospects:

- Trying to eliminate the interregional differences with the aim of achieving sustainable development.
- Trying to increase competitiveness in the tourism industry by creating regional tourism brands instead of relying on cheaper products.
- Planning tourism sites with the aim of sustainable development and creating viable and high quality environments.

- Trying to support the economic and social objectives of government with tourism development.
- Using sustainable environmental policies to support tourism development.
- Improving and developing the international cooperation.
- Matching development policies subdivision in the same track with the national development plan.
- Following global trends and demands and trying to make proper plans accordingly.
- Developing tourism through a multifunctional approach and by focusing on destinations.
- Developing tourism in all seasons by diversifying tourism products.
- Trying to promote tourism and raise awareness in public, private companies and NGOs about ecotourism and agri-tourism.
- Increasing the effectiveness in marketing for domestic and international tourism and marketing efforts.
- Having a variety of diverse tourism types in different areas, consequently establishing tourism site with alternative tourism by providing tourism facilities and utilities.
- Creating tourism products according to tourists' character.
- Using tourism as an effective tool to promote economic and social development of backward regions and disadvantaged groups.
- Encouraging private sector for active involvement in making tourism infrastructure and transportation projects to alleviate the burden on the public.
- Using suitable governance mechanisms with collaboration and cooperation of central and local government as well as civil actors in tourism decision-making processes.
- Holding instructional courses on tourism and enforcing the effective operation of specific systems to enhance labor quality.
- Trying to develop infrastructure related to tourism and solve the environmental problems in areas in which tourism activities can be done.
- Supporting from extraordinary accommodation facilities by conserving the regional architectural assets.

14.5   TURKEY'S TOURISM POLICY

1. Planning: To exhibit a planning approach that supports economic growth, is physically applicable and socially oriented and fairly reflects the principle of sustainable tourism.

2. Investment: To boost tourism investments by designing incentive schemes that would make tourism investment projects economically feasible and viable.

3. Organization: To achieve institutionalization through councils to be established at national, regional, provincial and local levels within the context of 'Good Governance,' to ensure full and active participation of the tourism sector as well as all related public and private entities and NGOs in relevant decision-making processes.

4. Domestic tourism: To provide alternative tourism products based on acceptable quality and affordable prices to various groups in the society.

5. Research and development: To ensure top priorities of R&D efforts in the tourism industry among public and private sector and tourism organizations.

6. Transportation and infrastructure strategies: To eliminate the transportation and infrastructure problems of densely populated and fastest growing tourism centers.

7. Marketing and promotion strategies: To commence with marketing and promotion activities at each destination, in addition to the national marketing and promotion campaigns with the ultimate objective of branding of a national, regional and local scale.

8. Educational strategies: To set up and introduce an education program in tourism, which would yield measurable outcomes.

9. Strategy of service quality: To activate total quality management in every constituent of the travel industry.

10. Strategy of city branding: Manage branding of cities rich of cultural and natural heritage and thereby convert them into a point of attraction for travelers.

11. Strategy of tourism diversification: To develop means for alternative tourism types led particularly by health, thermal, winter, golf, sea tourism, ecotourism and plateau tourism, conference and expo tourism activities.

12. Regions to host rehabilitation efforts for tourism areas: To make arrangements for handling in the first place and strengthening the infrastructure of areas where mass tourism activities grow intense and for extending the tourism season throughout the entire year in these regions.

13. Tourism development zones: To use tourism as a key tool for local and regional development in tourism development areas encompassing more than one city to be transformed into destinations.
14. Tourism development corridors: To develop a certain route for tourism on definite themes, by rehabilitating historical and natural texture.
15. Tourism sites: To plan tourism settlements capable of competing the world examples by becoming a global brand.
16. Ecotourism zones: To develop nature tourism with reference to development plans (Ministry of Culture and Tourism, 2007)

14.6 A COMPARISON OF MALAYSIA AND TURKEY'S TOURISM POLICY

1. Development planning: Development planning of tourism is the first tourism policy of these countries that seeks to achieve sustainable tourism development and more effective cooperation between public and private sector. Because these countries by considering the economic advantages of tourism seeks to develop tourism in all the national and local levels so that it can benefit the whole community.
2. The international market: Although both countries have relatively adopted the same policies in this area, but considering the statistics seems that Turkey has taken the lead from Malaysia. According to this statistic most tourist arrivals to Turkey were from European countries in 2012 while at the same time the most tourist arrivals to Malaysia were from Asian and neighboring countries. This can happen for several reasons. First, Turkey is a European—Asian country and includes both eastern and western cultures while Malaysia is an Islamic country and because of the conflicts between Muslims and other religious groups, reduce the attention of European communities is likely to this country. Second, due to the low number of flights from Malaysia to Europe comparing to Turkey, European tourist arrivals is faced with more restrictions. Third, by considering distance as an important factor in choosing a tourism destination, it can be said that one of the reasons for European tourists to choose Turkey is a shorter distance. Since Malaysia and Turkey's attractions are fairly similar, so tourists prefer to travel to a destination that has a shorter distance with their country and they are more affordable. In conclusion, we can say that comparing to Malaysia, Turkey has been less successful in attracting international markets.

3. Economy: As regards, one of the important roles of tourism is the economic development of communities so; Malaysia and Turkey have noticed this important issue and have used tourism development as an important tool in the direction of career development and more incomes. In these countries, tourism is an important source of foreign revenue that needs the support of government, effective cooperation between the private sector and government and more investment for the development.

4. Training: Tourism education at different levels and even the general public can be positive and beneficial to the development of tourism. As these countries try to develop their tourism infrastructures so much more so, skilled workforce trained in the field of tourism can be an important factor. Hence, these countries have considered training of manpower in their tourism policies.

5. Transportation and infrastructure: Country's transportation system serves as a bridge between tourists and the host community. Therefore, transportation system has an important role in increasing of tourist entering into the country. Malaysia and Turkey have paid attention to this important issue and have adopted policies aimed at improving and developing infrastructure. Malaysia should always consider the fact that the development of transportation, in particular the development of the country's airlines has a significant impact on the development of international tourism.

6. Ecotourism: Considering that these countries have the potentials for development of different types of tourism and have been successful in these fields for example in health tourism, but they continue their efforts for more development of ecotourism and introducing new and unknown natural attractions. In particular, Turkey has adopted policies that could be used to develop different forms of tourism in different seasons.

7. Marketing and advertising: Marketing and advertising activities require public funding and the continuing efforts of the Government and the Ministry of Culture and Tourism. It seems that marketing policies of these countries have been relatively successful but it is necessary for these countries especially Malaysia, in addition to keeping present markets, concentrate on attracting new markets for more growth and development in tourism. Malaysia's promotional efforts with the slogan "Malaysia truly Asia" to develop tourism markets and trying

to become a tourism brand has been successful in Asia but Malaysia should strive to develop their marketing strategies.

8. Security: One of the obstacles that may hinder the progress of Malaysia's tourism is a security Issue It seems that some tourists avoid visiting the country due to lack of security. While there is no reason to say Turkey is safer than Malaysia and making a negative image of Malaysia for tourists could be because of the negative advertisement in western media and using some problems to make this view. It is also possible that tourism in Turkey will be changed due to the recent crises in the country (in the popular protests against the construction in the Gezi park).

9. Sustainable development: The concept of sustainable development means when the governments try to use available environmental resources to satisfy the needs of the present, without having the ability to ignore the needs of the future. On this basis the use of a sustainable development approach in tourism means to emphasize the conservation of resources and reduction of the environmental and cultural impacts of tourism and enhance the positive economic, social and cultural effects. Countries with the adoption of policies and strategies for the development of tourism are seeking to achieve sustainable tourism development and it can be seen in Malaysia and Turkey's tourism policy. Marketing strategies, the development of partnerships between the public and private sector, paying attention to the development of infrastructures, paying attention to the training of human resources are all the issues that can be seen in tourism policies of these countries and shows the attention of these countries to the concept of sustainable development especially sustainable tourism development.

14.7 CONCLUSION

Today, all countries use tourism as a way to the comprehensive development of their country. Because they have found that, the development of tourism has the positive benefits particularly economic development for communities. Therefore, they are trying to take advantage of existing capacity in the country to achieve development. Nevertheless, each country should adopt policies according to its potentials and natural and cultural resources that include the aims of tourism sustainable development in the country and the aims that governments try to reach them through tourism. Malaysia and Turkey also have noticed to this issue and have used different policies in various sectors.

Given that, these countries have relatively, similar conditions and potentials in tourism development and have adopted relatively similar policies in the field of tourism. Considering the statistic of tourism arrivals to these countries in 2012 it can be said that they have been successful in operating their policies but there are also weak points that they are trying to resolve them and want to reach the highest rank in the world attracting tourists through these policies. However, a careful review of these policies can be concluded that Turkey has been more successful than Malaysia in the absorption of tourist arrivals, while tourism in Malaysia is more ancient. Of course, according to the reviews in this article it can be said that many factors have been effective in this and some factors like transportation, distance and culture have had an important role in this development.

KEYWORDS

- Malaysia
- tourism development
- tourism policy
- Turkey

REFERENCES

Ministry of Culture and Tourism (2007). Tourism strategy of Turkey 2023.

Moghadam, F. (2011). Amazing promotions, Tehran, Siteh.

Tharsis, C. (2011). Policies, Guidelines and Potential Tourism Opportunities in Sabah.

World Travel and Tourism Council, MALAYSIA (2002). The impact of travel and tourism on jobs and the economy.

INDEX

H

For Product Safety Concerns and Information please contact our EU
representative GPSR@taylorandfrancis.com
Taylor & Francis Verlag GmbH, Kaufingerstraße 24, 80331 München, Germany